timed to coincide with centenary
of his birth p. viii

selected part 1, p. 4
p. 96 "great value" to
his services

T. E. LAWRENCE

The Selected Letters

T. E. LAWRENCE

The Selected Letters

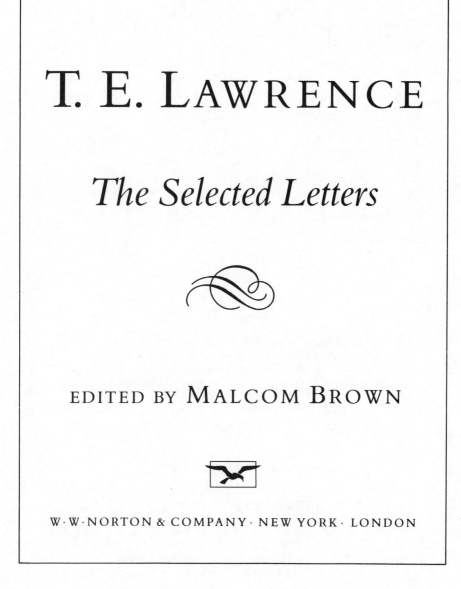

EDITED BY MALCOM BROWN

W·W·NORTON & COMPANY · NEW YORK · LONDON

Selection and text of letters, other than text of
Public Record Office correspondence, © Trustees of the
Seven Pillars of Wisdom Trust
Public Record Office letters by T. E. Lawrence, Crown Copyright
Introductions and notes © Malcolm Brown 1988
First American edition, 1989.

Printed in the United States of America.

ISBN 0-393-02684-1

W. W. Norton & Company, Inc., 500 Fifth Avenue,
New York, N. Y. 10110
W. W. Norton & Company Ltd., 37 Great Russell Street,
London WC1B 3NU

1 2 3 4 5 6 7 8 9 0

Contents

Preface

T. E. Lawrence — scholar, archaeologist, soldier, diplomat, author, international celebrity (known for ever as 'Lawrence of Arabia'), and, under the aliases Ross or Shaw, most extraordinary of ordinary servicemen — wrote to Flight Sergeant H. A. Ford of the Royal Air Force on 18 April 1929: 'I am trying to accustom myself to the truth that probably I'll be talked over for the rest of my life: and after my life, too. There will be a volume of "letters" after I die.'

Shortly after his premature death in 1935, his friend the novelist E. M. Forster undertook the task of preparing such a volume, but ill-health and the fear that publication of Lawrence's often outspoken correspondence might result in a spate of libel actions (Forster was caught up in one himself even as the project was being launched) caused him to withdraw. The editorship passed to the critic and novelist David Garnett, whose *The Letters of T. E. Lawrence* and abridged *Selected Letters* were published in 1938.

However, that was half a century ago, and the Trustees of the *Seven Pillars of Wisdom* Trust, of whom the leading member is Lawrence's younger brother A. W. Lawrence, have decided that it is time that a new volume should be produced, to include some of the best material already in print, but also, and more importantly, to make available many of the great number of letters not in Garnett or which have come to light or been released into the public domain since Garnett made his selection. The Trustees themselves have been accumulating material over the years which they have added to the already substantial collection held on reserve in the Bodleian Library, Oxford; this collection, largely of typed, checked transcripts in a score or more of bound volumes, has provided the central core of the present book. There are also many valuable collections available elsewhere. The Bodleian Library has numerous letters not in the reserve collection, including some to Geoffrey Dawson of *The Times* and an excellent series to Sergeant Pugh of the R.A.F. The three hundred or so letters to George Bernard Shaw's wife, Charlotte Shaw, access to which Garnett was firmly refused despite his best attempts to persuade, are now deposited in the British Library, London, which also holds the small but interesting collection of letters to C. F. Bell of the Ashmolean Museum, Oxford. Lawrence's letters to Lady Astor are preserved in the archives of the University Library at Reading. There are large, well-documented general collections in the United States, notably at the Harry Ransom Humanities Research Center at Austin, Texas, and the Houghton Library, Harvard. Among other smaller collections are those at Jesus College, All Souls College, St Antony's College, Worcester College and the Ashmolean Museum in Oxford, and at King's College, Churchill College, the Fitzwilliam Museum and the University Library in Cambridge. The Imperial War Museum at Lambeth and the Royal Air Force Museum at Hendon also have some letters. In addition, there are many important letters and reports by Lawrence preserved in the Public Record Office at Kew, London, not catalogued or collected but scattered through the mass of files relating to the Arab Revolt and the activities of the Arab Bureau and the Egyptian Expeditionary Force during the First World War. These were embargoed until 1968 or in some cases even later, so that they were unavailable not only to Garnett but also to those biographers, of whom the most important was Richard Aldington, who sought to reassess, or more strictly to reduce, Lawrence's reputation in the 1950s and after — in Aldington's case, attempting a task of almost total denigration.[1] The publication of a substantial selection of material from the war period is long overdue, both because it might, and I believe should, lead to a fairer and more balanced assessment of Lawrence's role in the Arabian campaign than has pertained in recent years and also because of the interesting light it casts on numerous aspects of the campaign itself and on some of the other personalities involved in it. The Public Record Office also holds some valuable documents relating to Lawrence's post-war political activities at the Paris Peace Conference and subsequently in the Middle East during the period when he was attached to the Colonial Office.

In addition to the letters from these sources now in the public domain, there are many not available or untraceable because they are in private hands, for his letters are collectors' items and regularly appear in sale rooms with reserve prices which bracket him with other such famous names as Winston Churchill, Oscar Wilde or Robert Burns. But even with this disadvantage (which would make the publication of a collected edition an almost impossible venture) there is more than enough material to hand to produce a substantial new volume to coincide with the centenary of his birth.

The letters themselves are arranged in seven parts chronologically, each part having its own introduction which gives the necessary biographical

1 Lawrence of Arabia: *A Biographical Enquiry* by Richard Aldington, (Collins, 1955).

background and comments on the main trends and content of Lawrence's letter-writing during the period in question. In general the letters have been left, with some assistance from footnotes, to tell their own story, but occasionally I have intervened with brief explanatory paragraphs to indicate a major development or landmark in Lawrence's career. Many letters are printed in full but numerous others have been shortened and in some cases it seemed worth including only key paragraphs. All my omissions are marked with the following unambiguous typographical device [...]; where a series of dots occurs in the letters without such brackets they are Lawrence's own — it was his lifelong habit to indicate in this way a pause for thought or a change of direction. I should add that I have also used square brackets to indicate such editorial interjections as an assumed date or address (and for one other important purpose given below). Dates are given on the left and are usually printed as Lawrence wrote them; addresses are on the right and have frequently been shortened, particularly when, as often happened in his service years, he included his number, rank and name.

As already implied, there are many letters in this volume which are published (or, I should add with due caution, believed to be published) for the first time. On the whole — apart from some exceptions referred to below — the reader can assume letters to be such unless they are followed in the note of source by the initials *DG* or *HL*. *DG* indicates that the letter was in David Garnett's 1938 volume. *HL* indicates that the letter is in the volume of *Home Letters of T. E. Lawrence and His Brothers* edited by his elder brother M. R. Lawrence and published in 1954;[1] but for reasons given in the General Introduction this will almost always be followed by the reference *Bodleian Reserve*, meaning that the text has been checked against the originals (still retained in the reserve collection) and is printed here as written and not as M. R. Lawrence published it. Where *HL* occurs on its own the letter or extract is precisely as printed in *Home Letters*, but this occurs rarely because where M. R. Lawrence did not alter his brother's text he regularly changed his paragraphing, thus, in my view, interrupting the letters' natural flow. I have restored Lawrence's paragraphs and I believe the letters read much better because of this. Where I have reinstated passages deleted by M. R. Lawrence I have indicated this by enclosing them within square brackets.

The exceptions mentioned above are firstly, a small number of letters already published in the 1963 volume (originally issued as two separate books) entitled *T. E. Lawrence to His Biographers: Robert Graves and Liddell Hart* — these are indicated in the source note by the letters *RGB* or *LHB*;

---

1 The book also contains letters by T. E.'s brothers Will and Frank, both of whom lost their lives on the Western Front in 1915.

and secondly, some letters to Sir Hugh, later Lord Trenchard, for whom my usual source was either the Bodleian Reserve Collection or the R. A. F. Museum at Hendon, but to which I have added the initials *HMH* as an indication that they also appear in H. Montgomery Hyde's *Solitary in the Ranks*. These books have been singled out because they make much use of complete letters.

I must emphasise that certain other letters have appeared — usually in the form of extracts, though some have been printed in full — in Lawrence biographies or articles about him or in other similar works. I have included such information only when it seemed important or relevant to do so, or (since publications about Lawrence are international, multi-lingual and legion) when it was known to me.

Introducing an edition of *The Intimate Journals of Charles Baudelaire* Christopher Isherwood wrote: 'After some thought, I have decided not to attempt annotations. . . . [W]hat does it matter to the average reader who Moun was, or Castagnary, or Rabbe? Read this book as you might read an old diary found in the drawer of a desk in a deserted house.' I have resisted such a brilliantly simple solution to the problem of footnotes, but at the same time I have tried to avoid the opposite trend of including a full *Who's Who* biography of everyone mentioned, whatever their role in the letter writer's life. My aim has been to enrich the reader's understanding and enjoyment of the letters without cluttering the pages with too much detail. I have not managed or indeed tried to explain everything — to know all the answers one would have to have a mind as well stocked as that of the writer himself, and his range of knowledge, reading and experience was formidable.

I must end with a personal word. Before becoming a full-time author I was for many years a producer of historical documentary programmes for BBC Television. Twice in my career I collaborated in the making of major programmes about Lawrence: *T. E. Lawrence 1888–1935* in 1962, and *Lawrence and Arabia* in 1986. In the course of working on those programmes I came to know A. W. Lawrence — and also met a number of others from T. E. Lawrence's wide circle of contemporaries, including Sir Basil Liddell Hart, Sir Alec Kirkbride, Canon E. F. Hall, C. F. C. Beeson, A. H. G. Kerry, H. F. Matthews, Mrs Celandine Kennington, Air Commodore and Mrs Sydney Smith, Jock Chambers, Arthur Russell, Tom Beaumont, Pat Knowles, even Lowell Thomas, and, very briefly, David Garnett. When working on the later programme I was commissioned, together with its producer Julia Cave, to write an illustrated biography of Lawrence, which has now been published under the title (after a phrase of Aubrey Herbert's) *A Touch of Genius*. In early 1986 there came a second offer, this time from A. W. Lawrence himself, to undertake the task which has resulted in this present volume. I am responsible for its plan and style, but the balance of

old and new material is much as he foresaw it, and I share with him the
feeling that it is important to give substantial space to the war years, without
which there would have been no 'Lawrence of Arabia'. He also encouraged
me to include only the essential parts of letters where it seemed appropriate,
thereby excluding much material that was routine or repetitious. The choice
of letters has throughout been mine, however, and he has not attempted to
influence or censor me. He has been a most benign patron. I should like to
take this opportunity to express my gratitude to him, and also, if I might,
to pay tribute to a remarkable man who has not only been, indeed still is,
a scholar and writer of distinction in his own field, but has also for over
fifty years borne with both patience and pride the burden of being, as it
were, his brother's keeper.

    To my gratitude to him I must add the same to his fellow trustees of the
Seven Pillars of Wisdom Trust, Mr Michael Carey and the Hon. H. A. A.
Hankey C.M.G. C.V.O.; and to my publishers, to whom I am greatly
indebted for their constant encouragement and support.

Malcolm Brown
20 July 1988

Acknowledgements

In addition to those mentioned in the Preface I should like to express my thanks to the following:

at the Bodleian Library, Oxford, D. S. Porter (until recently Senior Assistant Librarian), Colin Harris, Serena Surman and the rest of the staff of Room 132; at the Houghton Library of the University of Harvard, Vicki Denby; at the Harry Ransom Humanities Research Center of the University of Texas at Austin, Cathy Henderson; at the Imperial War Museum, Roderick Suddaby, Keeper of the Department of Documents; at the Ashmolean Museum, Dr Roger Moorey and his secretary Ruth Flanagan; at Jesus College, Oxford, Dr D. A. Rees; at All Souls College, Oxford, Peter S. Lewis and Norma Aubertin-Potter; at Worcester College, Oxford, Lesley Le Claire; at St Antony's College, Oxford, Gillian Grant; at King's College, Cambridge, Dr Michael Halls; at Churchill College, Cambridge, Elizabeth Bennett and Lesley James; at the Department of Archives and Manuscripts, Reading University Library, Michael Bott; at the R.A.F. Museum Hendon, Peter Murton; at Eton College, Michael Meredith; at the BBC Written Archives, Caversham, Geoffrey Walden;

also the staffs of the Public Record Office; the British Library; the British Library Newspaper Library, Colindale; the Cambridge University Library; the Fitzwilliam Museum, Cambridge; Kettle's Yard, Cambridge; the Liddell Hart Centre for Military Archives, King's College, London; the Tate Gallery Archives; the Royal Commission on Historical Manuscripts, Quality Court, Chancery Lane, London.

Others whom I should like to thank include Dr John E. Mack of Harvard University (author of the Lawrence biography *A Prince of Our Disorder*); Dr D. C. Sutton, of Reading University, whose *Location Register of Twentieth Century English Literary Manuscripts and Letters* (published 1988) was particularly useful; Christopher Matheson; Ingrid Keith of the T. E. Lawrence Society; and Arthur Russell, fellow soldier with Lawrence in the Royal Tank Corps and later one of his bearers.

I should also like to thank those who helped me in the matter of footnotes, including Doreen Harris, Shirley Seaton, Peter Murton, and, especially, my wife Betty, who also typed many letters and subsequently read and checked the text at all stages from first assembly to completion and finally helped with the indexes.

Very specially I must express my gratitude to A.J. Flavell, Assistant Librarian of the Bodleian Library and organiser of the Bodleian's Lawrence Centenary Exhibition, 1988, who read through much of the text and the footnotes and elucidated a number of obscure but important references; and to St John Armitage C.B.E. who subjected my editorial matter, my choice of material and my footnotes to rigorous and helpful examination, and contributed some valuable footnotes as well. I took most but not all the advice I was given and must accept responsibility for any errors or shortcomings the book may contain.

Finally the Trustees of the *Seven Pillars of Wisdom* Trust and I should like to thank the original recipients of the letters printed in this book and also, where applicable, their present owners, without whose placing of Lawrence's letters in known and secure sources this centennial collection would not have been possible.

A Note on the Text

Many letters have been transcribed from the originals or from photocopies of originals, but use has also been made of typed or previously printed transcriptions. Almost all Garnett letters and the majority of 'home letters' have been reproduced as previously published. In the case of letters from the Bodleian Reserve, most have been taken from collections checked against the originals by E. M. Forster, A. W. Lawrence or David Garnett. I have not thought it necessary to identify the small number which do not come within this category. Like Garnett's, this book contains a mixed economy in the matter of 'and' versus '&'. In his selection, for example, letters to him, his father Edward Garnett and Lionel Curtis are printed with 'and' throughout, whereas the ampersand occurs in letters to D. G. Hogarth, John Buchan and E. M. Forster. Some editors prefer to standardise with 'and' but in my own 'new' letters I have retained the '&', (thus following the practice of such recent collections as the letters of Evelyn Waugh, E. M. Forster and Dylan Thomas). The letters to Mrs Charlotte Shaw are a major exception to this rule, as the typed transcriptions in the possession of the Trustees of the *Seven Pillars of Wisdom* Trust contained 'and' throughout and I have not attempted to re-ampersand them. It should be added that Lawrence seems to have used both forms interchangeably.

Obvious mistakes have been corrected and names of literary works, periodicals, ships, etc. have been italicised. Postscripts have been uniformly put at the end of letters. All the numbered footnotes in small type are mine; those indicated by asterisks are Lawrence's own.

With regard to the spelling of Arabic names, there being no accepted transliterations from the Arabic, Lawrence and his contemporaries spelt as they wished; I have retained the original spelling in all the letters and reports here reproduced. In my own editorial matter and footnotes I have generally used the forms preferred in the two indexes (the Index of Place Names and the Personal Index) printed in *Seven Pillars of Wisdom*); thus Abdulla not Abdullah; Feisal not Feisul; Jidda not Jeddah; Wejh not Wedj; Akaba not Aqaba.

For Lawrence's own approach to this problem the reader is recommended to turn to the Preface to *Seven Pillars of Wisdom* contributed by A. W. Lawrence.

T. E. Lawrence: Biographical Summary

Born 1888, 16 August, Tremadoc, North Wales
Oxford City High School, September 1896 to July 1907
   In northern France studying castles, summers of 1906 and 1907
Jesus College, Oxford, October 1907 to June 1910 (1st Class Honours in
   Modern History, 1910)
   In France, studying castles, summer of 1908
   In Syria, studying castles, summer of 1909
   Wrote his thesis, *Crusader Castles*, winter of 1909–10
At Jebail in Syria, studying Arabic, winter of 1910–11
Excavating at Carchemish (Jerablus) under D. G. Hogarth and R. Campbell
   Thompson, April to July 1911
   Walk through northern Mesopotamia, summer of 1911
Excavating in Egypt under Flinders Petrie, beginning of 1912
Excavating at Carchemish under C. L. Woolley, spring 1912 to spring 1914
   At home in Oxford, summer of 1913
   Survey of Sinai, January to February 1914
At Oxford and London, summer of 1914, completing *The Wilderness of
   Zin* (archaeological report on Sinai co-written with Woolley), eventually
   at War Office; commissioned October 1914
In Egypt as Intelligence Officer, December 1914 to October 1916
   On special duty in Mesopotamia, March to May 1916
   Journey to Jidda with Ronald Storrs, October 1916
   First meeting with Feisal, October 1916
   Joined Arab Bureau, November 1916
Attached to Arab forces, December 1916 to October 1918
   Akaba expedition, May to July
   Akaba falls, first meeting with General Sir Edmund Allenby, July 1917
   Promoted Major, summer 1917
   Deraa episode, November 1917
   Present at official entry into Jerusalem, December 1917
   Battle of Tafileh, January 1918

Promoted Lieutenant-Colonel, March 1918
Enters Damascus, 1 October, leaves Damascus 4 October 1918
Present at meetings of Eastern Committee of War Cabinet, October to
    November 1918
    With Feisal in France and Britain, November to December 1918
In Paris for Peace Conference, January to October 1919
    Journey by air to Egypt, May to June 1919
    At All Souls College, Oxford (as Fellow), and in London, 1919 to 1921
Adviser to Winston Churchill, Colonial Office, 1921 to 1922
    On missions to Aden, Jidda and Transjordan, August to December 1921
    Resigns from Colonial Office, July 1922
Joins Royal Air Force as John Hume Ross, August 1922 to January 1923
    Discharged following press disclosure of his identity
Private T. E. Shaw, Royal Tank Corps, March 1923 to August 1925
    Acquires cottage at Clouds Hill, near Bovington Camp, Dorset
Aircraftman Shaw, Royal Air Force, from August 1925 to March 1935
    Subscribers' edition of *Seven Pillars of Wisdom* completed 1926
In India, January 1927 to January 1929: *Revolt in the Desert* (popular
    abridgement of *Seven Pillars*) published and later withdrawn; *The Mint*
    completed; brought back to England following press stories claiming he
    was involved in a rebellion in Afghanistan
At various air stations in England, March 1929 to March 1935, working
    principally on high-speed marine craft
Retires to Clouds Hill, spring 1935
Has accident on motor-cycle near Clouds Hill, 13 May 1935
Dies in Bovington Military Hospital, 19 May 1935
Funeral at Moreton, Dorset, 21 May 1935

Based on chronological table in *T. E. Lawrence by His Friends,*
edited by A. W. Lawrence, 1937

General Introduction

Lawrence wrote and received innumerable letters, but relatively few of those he received have survived. His standard practice was to destroy them. He did this not out of malice or contempt but because he felt that once a letter had been read and understood its purpose had been fulfilled. For him a letter was a private communication that should not be hoarded for later scrutiny by strangers. Moreover, throughout his Army and Air Force years — the peak period for his correspondence — he had little more than his own bed space in which to keep his possessions and other people's letters held a very low priority.

Writing from his R.A.F. base in India on 29 March 1927 to Mrs Charlotte Shaw, his most constant correspondent in the last decade or so of his life, he admitted to her that of late he had 'regretfully destroyed many letters of yours' in spite of their being 'first class, as pictures of today, and historically valuable'. He expanded on the subject — evidently in response to a comment from her — in his letter of 12 May: 'I do not want you to feel that in burning your letters I'm doing anything wanton. It's not that. They are personal documents, and I feel that they belong utterly to me, when they reach me: as though you wrote them only for me, and kept no share in them, after you had posted them. They could not be shown to anybody else, without breach of intimacy between us. [...] Nor can I keep them safely: what place have I where to keep anything? Service men have the privacy of gold-fish in their bowls. The other fellows read my books, and see my pictures, and use my mug and plates, and borrow my clothes, and spend my money, and overhear and oversee every act and word and expressed thought of mine from sunrise to sunset. So what room have I for a private life? [...] So after I have read them I burn them.'

That letters might be seen by other than their intended recipients was bad enough; that they might be published for consumption by the general reader he found even more offensive. One of his very last letters, to his American friend Ralph Isham, written on 10 May 1935, was a cry of protest on hearing that an American university had published a letter of his 'without even attempting to ask my permission first'. He continued: 'As you know, I greatly dislike the publication of private letters (except after very full consideration).' Yet, as is clear from his letter to Flight Sergeant Ford quoted at the head of the Preface, he foresaw the possibility of such treatment and, to his annoyance, that knowledge could sometimes affect his style. He wrote to his publisher friend K. W. Marshall on 6 September 1932: 'My letters ceased being personal seven years ago, when an American magazine advertised a batch as "characteristic products of a remarkable adventurer". That cured me of writing sense.' He even wrote once to Mrs Shaw (19 January 1930), 'Perhaps I am not writing to you, but for my some-day "Life and Letters".' He was aware that she preserved his letters to her as regularly as he destroyed her letters to him.

The existence of not only this new volume but also its predecessors is, of course, a tribute to the fact that fortunately most of Lawrence's recipients followed Mrs Shaw's practice of preserving letters rather than his of destroying them. Doubtless many correspondents kept his letters because they were written by one of the most famous men of the day, but this was surely not the sole reason. His letters had a quality which made them unlikely candidates for the fire or the waste paper basket. Even when brief, routine or apparently casual, they were consciously and carefully crafted and carried a distinctive hallmark. They were usually very legible (his handwriting generally presents no problem to the transcriber) and though they were not always comfortable reading, being sometimes written in depression and often in self-disparagement, they almost always had pace, vigour and a sense of style.

Though he took pains over his letters he did not believe in re-writing. 'Nobody ever wrote a good letter in a fair copy,' he stated to Charlotte Shaw on 14 April 1927. 'It's the first draft, or none.' But if he was to write a serious letter, the task must be worthily accomplished. He described his letter-writing philosophy to his artist friend Eric Kennington in a letter of 6 August 1934: 'It is very difficult to write a good letter. Mine don't pretend to be good ... but they do actually try very hard to be good. I write them in great batches, on the days when at length (after months, often) the impulse towards them eventually comes. Each tries to direct itself as directly as it can towards my picture of the person I am writing to: and if it does not seem to me (as I write it) that it makes contact — why then I write no more that night.' 'In great batches': one thing that has been interesting to me as an editor assembling material from many sources has been to note how much his mood could vary in letters written on the same day. Determining a possible order of writing has been a considerable problem and I make no claims always to have found a satisfactory solution. I am well aware that the pack might be shuffled in a number of different ways.

Consciously crafted they might be, but their author was not attempting to achieve through letters the literary success which he came to feel eluded him in the writing of *Seven Pillars of Wisdom* or *The Mint*. He wrote to G. W. M. Dunn, fellow airman and published poet, on 19 July 1934: 'I don't think much of letters as an art form. Not even Fitzgerald, or Keats; or D. H. Lawrence or Gertrude Bell's. They always have something ragged, domestic, undressed about them.' Yet his letters have attracted many admirers and much has been claimed for them. In the *Dictionary of National Biography* Sir Ronald Storrs wrote: 'It has indeed been said that he would have survived (as would Edward Fitzgerald without *Omar Khayyam*) if only as a letter writer.' Similarly Basil Liddell Hart, a great admirer of Lawrence and one of his early biographers, has commented: 'For my own part, I wonder if he may not live longest in literature through his letters.'

Lawrence would certainly have rejected such praise, and not merely because of his veneration for the 'real thing' in literature and art. He also felt that letter-writing was distinctly second best to a good face-to-face conversation. 'What a whale of a letter,' he commented after writing the quasi-obituary on himself which Robert Graves drew out of him in February 1935: 'Five minutes' talk would have been so much more fun!' He wrote to his friend in Aleppo, E. H. R. Altounyan, doctor and poet, on 7 April 1934: 'I have 1800 other letters to answer, and have spent all this time, and wasted all this ink, on addressing a being 2000 miles away from me in space, and three weeks in time. Long before you get this note you will be a different creature, and out of reach of all my thoughts. That is the murrain upon correspondence. Five minutes of a meeting, once a blue moon, was worth all the letters that Lord Chesterfield addressed to his son.'

'1800 letters': he was doubtless exaggerating, but certainly from the moment he became famous until his death he was pursued by hordes of correspondents who would never leave him alone. They included admirers, well-wishers, sycophants, cranks, enquirers, would-be suitors, former serving-men who claimed acquaintance on the strength of, say, having trod the deck of the same ship in the Red Sea during 1917 or 1918, or people simply prompted to converse with him because he was a celebrity in the public domain. This was yet another reason why as ordinary serviceman Ross or Shaw he had no compunction in destroying his correspondence. He had little chance of storing it and even less chance of answering it. His 'justifiable percentage' — all he could cope with — was, as he told the Labour M. P. Ernest Thurtle in April 1929, 20%. For the rest? He wrote to Sergeant Pugh, with whom he had worked at the R.A.F. Cadet College, Cranwell, from India on 30 June 1927: 'Do you remember how that tray on the table used to get blocked solid: and how then I'd stuff the new-coming letters into those pigeon holes on my left, till they too were tight: and then we'd light the stove, & I'd chuck the time-expired ones by armfulls into the fire, and groan over answering the rest?' Also from India, on 23

March 1928, he wrote to his mother: 'If everybody ceased writing to me from today I could be free of back-correspondence in ten weeks at 16 letters a week. Letters take on the average $\frac{3}{4}$ of an hour each, if you add in the getting pens & ink out of my box, & the job of getting them to the post office. [. . .] The letters bore the people who get them as much as their letters bore me, I suppose. Who invented this curse?'

In the same letter he mentioned an idea which he was ultimately to take up seriously in the last weeks of his life. 'I think I shall print a small card "to announce cessation of correspondence" and send it to the 300 or 400 of my regular addresses. After that I shall write not more than one letter per week, & take a holiday once a quarter.' Early in 1935 he had a card specially made bearing the message: 'To tell you that in future I shall write very few letters.' 'I'm sending out dozens of the enclosed', he wrote to a Tank Corps friend on 6 March. 'Good idea?'

There were many people, of course, with whom he was happy to correspond, but he never got the relief he sought from the endless obligation to write letters. He was writing them — often on the backs of his specially printed card — almost to the day of his fatal accident. Yet with all his doubts, disclaimers and apparent contempt for the form, he is nevertheless, I believe, one of the most articulate, consistently interesting and rewarding letter writers of this century. One reason for this, of course, was the urge born in him to write well, whether he was composing a signal from the desert or a letter to the great and famous. Another reason was that with the challenge of the war years and the political years over, his energy and talent needed to find some kind of outlet at a time when he had deliberately lowered his ambitions — so that although he sometimes raged against letter-writing it was arguably necessary, indeed vital, to him that he was forced to do so. To quote from a recent letter to me from St John Armitage, a Middle East specialist with long experience of the area and people and an impressive knowledge and understanding of Lawrence: 'Once Lawrence left the Middle East and government, he had a comparatively empty life or, rather, he had to create his own challenge to make life worthwhile. People, authorities, did not turn to him, he had to turn to them to keep "in the swim". Thus *Seven Pillars* and regular exchanges, such as those with Charlotte Shaw, in particular, were lifelines, and letter-writing in general was his salvation. Without the latter his years in the ranks would have been a total drop-out. Lawrence was a genius who denied himself full expression, and I believe that letters allowed him to unleash his intelligence and intellect both of which were constrained by the narrowness of his chosen position.'

Yet Lawrence could have his doldrums. He is perhaps especially tedious in his self-disparagement, and in particular his disparagement of *Seven Pillars of Wisdom*, his highly idiosyncratic account of the Arab Revolt, in writing which he consciously attempted to create a major work that would have more value than a mere war memoir. In the now famous Lyttelton/Hart-Davis correspondence there is a forthright comment on this tendency by George Lyttelton, dated 4 June 1958. 'I took up last week the letters of T. E. Lawrence — which', he tells Rupert Hart-Davis, 'clearly should have been edited by you.[1] You would have eliminated much of the endless jaw about the *Seven Pillars* and his ultimately repellent utterances about its entire worthlessness, which never strike me, at least, as quite sincere. I don't wonder that many of far less venomous spirit than Aldington have been allergic to him, but I expect you have noticed that, like G. B. S., everyone loved him who knew him in person and not only on paper.' Lawrence faced and resisted equally persuasive arguments against his condemnatory attacks on his book from his admirers and friends. The Cambridge writer and critic F. L. Lucas wrote to him in 1928: 'You are ridiculous about *Seven Pillars.* . . . You admit you're not qualified to criticise (it's not true; but that's *your* hypothesis); the hardest thing in the world is to judge one's own work; ergo, your opinion that it's bad, is worthless; and when I say it's superb, I'm right.' Such arguments were unlikely to shift his view. When his former Oxford friend Vyvyan Richards took him up in 1923 on the same subject, his terse reply was: 'Self-depreciation is a necessity with me.'

While understanding the exasperation of both Lucas and Lyttelton, I believe his letters show that his condemnation of what almost everybody else thought was a most distinguished work was not a pose or a ruse to win greater praise but was the result of a genuine conviction that however hard he might try, he was an imitative artist and not a real one. The completion of *Seven Pillars* left him convinced that his hopes of creating a book to stand beside such works as *Moby Dick* or *The Brothers Karamazov* were vain. He felt that there was an uncrossable barrier between himself and the genuine writer. As he wrote to E. M. Forster on 29 November 1925: 'You can rule a line, as hard as this pen-stroke, between the people who are artists & the rest of the world.' Similarly he wrote to John Brophy on 19 November 1929: 'I think I did write better than the average retired military man: but between that and "writing" there is a gulf. I have talked to many whom I think great writers. All of them have a likeness, in that they get some pleasure out of the phrases as they are born. Not the finished work, perhaps. Few look back with pleasure: but there is joy in the creation, and I have never had anything but weariness and dissatisfaction. This I put down to my works being an imitation, made with great care and pains and judgement, of the real thing.' He concluded that he was not quite the professional writer just as he had been not quite the professional soldier or

---

1 Rupert (now Sir Rupert) Hart-Davis had been at Jonathan Cape when Garnett was compiling his 1938 collection and had been responsible for preparing the text for the printers, a contribution which Garnett acknowledged in his Preface.

the professional diplomat. Nor was he; what is remarkable, however, is not that he performed so inadequately, as he would have it, but that he did so well in all these fields. I have taken note of Lyttelton's strictures, but I have not excised Lawrence's self-disparagement entirely, for his assaults on himself are part of him, and they are also likely to be eloquently and even wittily expressed.

Most of the quotations used so far in this Introduction are from letters believed to be in print here for the first time. But, the question will be asked, what *significant* revelations or insights can be found in this selection of letters that are not available in previous published editions?

A basic difference between this selection and its predecessors, is that it is unexpurgated. Garnett felt obliged to omit materal that was too frank for the 1930s but which we in the 1980s have no qualms about reading. He also did not have to hand some of the most enduringly interesting and revealing of Lawrence's letters. In the case of M. R. Lawrence, his tactic was to remove anything in his brother's letters that was remotely outspoken or contentious. The passages he excised — almost always without indicating that any deletion had taken place — are often precisely the passages that catch the eye when reading the originals. Bob Lawrence, as M. R. Lawrence was generally known, was the one Lawrence son who fulfilled his mother's ambition by devoting his life to Christianity; he became a medical missionary with the China Inland Mission. When he edited his brother's letters his mother was still alive. These two factors affected him to the extent that he felt obliged to censor his more brilliant brother. The original text shows, for example, that T. E. Lawrence had forthright, indeed advanced, views about the relation of Britain and other such powers to the emergent nations — views sharpened by thinking about China, where not only his brother but also his mother went to propagate their evangelical Christian beliefs. 'We used to think foreigners were black beetles, and coloured races were heathen,' he wrote to his mother on 16 June 1927, 'whereas now we respect and admire and study their beliefs and manners. It's a revenge of the world upon the civilisation of Europe.' This (and there are other variations on this theme) is an important statement in the light of the fact that he is still thought of in some circles as an almost archetypal imperialist. On the level of family relations, the original text confirms how correct he was in his often quoted statement to Mrs Charlotte Shaw (8 May 1928) that his mother was always 'hammering and sapping' to break into 'the circle of [his] integrity'. Writing to his mother in China on 28 December 1925 he rebelled against this pressure: 'You talk of "sharing my life" in letters: but that I won't allow. It is only my own business. Nor can anybody turn on or off the tap of "love" so called. I haven't any in me for anything. Once I used to like <u>things</u> (not people) and <u>ideas</u>. Now I don't care for anything at all.' Five years later, writing on 27 September 1933, he felt impelled to defend his younger brother Arnold (A. W. Lawrence), now a married man, from similar maternal encroachments. 'You are inclined to persecute him, you know. People brought up together, when full grown, rather resent their relatives. I think Arnie does not want to see too much of us, and the best treatment for that is to see too little. When he feels safe — sure that we are not trying to "get at" him — he will lose that nervousness. If any of us really needed anything, we would help each other. Till then, do let each manage his own affairs.' M. R. Lawrence had, of course, every right to remove such passages, but there can be no offence in printing them now.

As already indicated in the Preface, I have also included a great deal of previously unpublished material relating to the war period. I have written at some length on this subject in the Introduction to Part 2: The War Years, and will therefore simply state here my belief that his letters and reports give little support to the view that he was a military charlatan who later rode to celebrity on the back of Lowell Thomas's publicity machine. That his role was a most important one, and seen as such at the time, is also substantiated by the reports and letters of others involved in the campaign, including such men as Colonel Newcombe, Colonel Wilson, Colonel Joyce, Brigadier-General Clayton, Major Buxton, D. G. Hogarth, Lord Lloyd, Field Marshal Lord Wavell and Field Marshal Lord Allenby, and the Arab leader Sherif Feisal, later King Feisal I of Iraq. Lawrence was too unconventional a soldier to win everybody's approval but the overall opinion was that he was the best man for an extremely difficult and important task and that he performed it supremely well.[1]

Some evidence relating to his family background has also emerged (see the Introduction to Part 1: The Early Years). There are various references in the new material to his illegitimacy — some jocular, some more poignant — but perhaps the most important letter, which I am pleased to be allowed to publish, is that to his solicitor, the Hon. Edward Eliot, dated 16 June 1927, in which he reported his decision to change his name by deed poll to Thomas Edward Shaw and asked Eliot to attend to the necessary legal processes. The letter reveals that he had never seen his birth certificate and was in doubt as to his original name — in fact he *was* registered as Lawrence, not as he thought possible under his father's family name of Chapman — and implies that he thought Shaw might possibly be an intermediate name only, 'for eventually, I suppose, Chapman it will have to be'. He added: 'There is a lot of land in that name knocking about: and I don't want to chuck it away, as Walter Raleigh, for whom I have a certain

---

1 For an account of the war years using much new material of the kind referred to above see *A Touch of Genius: The Life of T. E. Lawrence*, already mentioned in the Preface.

regard, gave it to my father's first Irish ancestor. I have a feeling that it should be kept in the line. My father's death [his father had died in 1919] wound up the baronetcy (a union title, of all the rubbish!) and one of my brothers is breeding heirs. So the family looks like continuing, in the illegitimate branch!' The implication is surely that he hoped he might somehow be able in due time to graft the 'Lawrence' branch of the family back into the family tree. His joke to David Garnett that his translation of the *Odyssey* ought to be called Chapman's Homer might have had an underlying seriousness.[1] To Sir Ronald Storrs he wrote in January 1935, just before leaving the R.A.F., 'I venture to hope we shall see each other, but I don't know where I shall live, or what do, or how call myself.' There is surely in all this a hint of weariness with his various assumed identities, and an understandable longing, half-romantic, half-realistic, to secure himself to firm and long-established roots.

The book also contains material with a bearing on the much discussed subject of Lawrence's sexuality. The truth, I believe (in line with almost everyone who knew him personally), is that he was neither heterosexual nor homosexual in practice. Replying on 26 March 1929 to F. L. Lucas, who had been tackling him about the chapter in *The Mint* in which he had quoted the Oxford preacher who had implored his young friends 'not to imperil [their] immortal souls upon a pleasure which, *so I am credibly informed*, lasts less than one and three-quarter minutes', Lawrence wrote: 'The period of enjoyment in sex, seems to me a very doubtful one. I've asked the fellows in this hut (three or four go with women regularly). They are not sure: but they say it's all over in ten minutes: and the preliminaries — which I discounted — take up most of the ten minutes. For myself, I haven't tried it, & hope not to.' Similarly he replied to Robert Graves on 6 November 1928 when discussing the same chapter: 'As I wrote (with some courage, I think: few people admit the damaging ignorance) I haven't ever: and don't much want to.' On the matter of homosexuality, in a letter of 21 December 1927 to E. M. Forster, after commenting admiringly on Forster's curious homosexual ghost story *Dr. Woolacott*, and adding that it had helped him to come to terms with his own enforced homosexual experience at the hands of the Turks, he stated: 'I couldn't ever do it, I believe: the impulse strong enough to make me touch another creature has not yet been born in me.' As if that were not clear enough, when enthusing in September 1929 to Robert Graves about the latter's autobiographical *Goodbye to All That*, Lawrence wrote of Siegfried Sassoon, fellow officer with Graves in the trenches: 'S. S. comes out very well. I'm glad of that, for I like him; homosex and all.' Not, surely, the remark of someone who thought himself to be homosexual; and it should be added that neither

---

1 *The Familiar Faces* by David Garnett, p. 104.

Forster (of whose homosexuality he was well aware) nor Graves nor Lucas was the sort of man to whom he would write with other than complete frankness.

There remains his strong and affectionate relationship with his Arab friend at Carchemish, Dahoum, who has been generally accepted as being, at least in part, the 'S. A.' to whom he dedicated *Seven Pillars*, and later with R. A. M. Guy, a young aircraftman, a number of letters to whom are printed in this book. There is no evidence in either case to suggest any physical relationship. The letter to C. F. Bell in Part 1, dated 10 December 1913, shows that both Leonard Woolley (in charge of the Carchemish dig) and Lawrence liked and admired Dahoum, but there is no hint of improper behaviour, rather the tone is that of the standard *badinage* of a scholarly, all-male world. Dahoum was a youth whose potential both men recognised and encouraged; and A. W. Lawrence has told me that the impression he left when he visited Oxford was that 'he was a very nice chap' whom all the family liked. As for Lawrence's letters to Guy, they are basically caring ones calculated to reassure a young man who plainly much admired Lawrence and was grieved to find their friendship interrupted by the senior man's abrupt departure from the R.A.F.; Guy was in any case shortly to be married. Perhaps the one thing which has angered his closest R.A.F. and Tank Corps friends more than anything else as Lawrence's reputation has come under the scrutiny of some of his modern interpreters has been the speculation that he was a homosexual. The discussion had no meaning for them. The idea had never crossed their minds. And these were men living in the same hut and aware of his friendship with such men as Forster and Sassoon — who were, indeed, thanks to the classless conviviality of Lawrence's Dorset cottage, Clouds Hill, friends of theirs too.

But he was not sexless. 'I'm so funnily made up, sexually,' he wrote to E. M. Forster on 8 September 1927, refusing to read the latter's overtly homosexual unpublished novel *Maurice*.[1] ('Sexually' is correct; not 'sensually', as the letter is transcribed in Garnett.) It has now been acknowledged that he submitted himself to beatings in the last decade or so of his life, which his brother A. W. Lawrence believes were in the tradition of the mediaeval flagellants (Lawrence was well versed in mediaeval history and knew of them) but which have also been interpreted in more modern terms as having a sexual as well as a punitive element; and it is undeniable that there was, as is made clear in *Seven Pillars*, a sexual element in his response to the beating he suffered in 1917 at Deraa. (There is a thorough and sympathetic analysis of this subject in the Pulitzer Prize biography of Lawrence *A Prince of Our Disorder*, by Dr John E. Mack.) By contrast, it was also quite possible for women to feel that he had heterosexual potential.

1 Published in 1971, the year after Forster's death.

Indeed, Lady Astor plainly thought him capable of even having an affair and virtually (and, so it seems, almost jealously) accused him of such — see his letter to her of 11 December 1933, wittily denying the charge. He later wrote confidentially to her (26 November 1934), that there was a particular R. A. F. officer's wife who wrote regularly to him while he rarely wrote back: 'Am I a beast? But she wants something which I want to keep, and she ought to understand it.' There seems never to have been any actual likelihood of his getting married, but more than a few people close to him thought that he might have done so if circumstances had been appropriate. Precisely what he *was*, in these highly personal terms, is difficult to define and, in the end, is not our business, but there seems to me some value in attempting to use the evidence of his own letters to clarify what he was not.

There is an important statement on this whole subject in a letter by A. W. Lawrence to a Miss Early, an American lady, dated 17 December 1963, of which a copy is held in the Bodleian Reserve collection. 'No one who knew him or worked with him ever believed him to be a homosexual. He wasn't, though homosexuality disgusted him far less than the abuse of normal sex and attitude of some of the men in the huts in the R. A. F. or Tank Corps. He had more respect for women as *people* than many men. The circumstances of his life, not his birth, account for much of his ill-ease. We were a family of five boys with little or no contact with girls of our own age or mental interests. He chose to study Near Eastern archaeology and conditions in countries where it was then impossible that young women should travel or work. I, on the other hand, took up Classical archaeology, a subject which many women could take up, and while still a student at the British School of Archaeology in Rome met and married a fellow-student. T. E. had no such opportunities to meet women of his own age and with similar mental interests. After the war it was too late. Dr. Ernest Altounyan, I think and so does my wife, was correct in writing: "Women were to him persons as such to be appraised on their merits (not their sex).... He never married because he never happened to meet the right person; and nothing short of that would do; a bald statement of fact which cannot hope to convince the perverse intricacy of the public mind." Nearly all his friends were married, certainly his most cherished friends, and their wives found no difficulty with him.'

From other letters it is clear that some of the claims made about Lawrence for which he has been much derided are in fact true. When researching their biography *The Secret Lives of Lawrence of Arabia* Phillip Knightley and Colin Simpson decided to check whether Lawrence had been offered, in 1934, the Secretaryship of the Bank of England. They wrote to the Bank and were informed that no record could be found of his having been offered the Secretaryship but that he had once been considered for the post of night porter (as indeed he had, see pp. 379–382). They used this reply to support the statement in the opening pages of their book that 'any attempt to take a cool look at the Lawrence legend dissolves into a quicksand of hearsay, rumour and fantasy'. However, in December 1986 clear evidence that such an offer was actually made was put up for sale at Sotheby's in the form of (i) a letter by Lawrence to the Hon. Francis Rodd — Rodd had sounded him out on the Bank's behalf — refusing the offer, (ii) an explanatory note by Rodd describing how the offer came to be made, and (iii) a letter by Sir Leslie O'Brien, former Chief Cashier of the Bank of England, promising to 'stop saying that the only job he [Lawrence] was ever offered was that of nightwatchman'. (The reader is referred to Lawrence's letter to Rodd dated 23 November 1934, on p. 500; it was printed by Garnett, but with the precise nature of the offer made to Lawrence unfortunately concealed by omissions.)

Similarly Lawrence has been accused of having had the fanciful idea that he might be called by the nation to the task of reorganising home defence. Lady Astor's last letter to him, fortunately not destroyed but preserved in typed copy form in the Bodleian Reserve collection and here quoted as a footnote to his reply, dated 8 May 1935, shows that such an offer was indeed under serious consideration at that time. He was invited by her to come to Cliveden to meet, among other people, Stanley Baldwin, who later that month as Lord President of the Council made a major statement on Britain's air policy producing such headlines as 'R. A. F. at home to be trebled'. A few weeks later Baldwin was Prime Minister. That Lawrence, with his reputation still high in the British establishment, should have been thought capable of contributing in this area makes very good sense: see for example his letter to Lionel Curtis of 19 March 1934 (p. 482). His refusal of the invitation to Cliveden, dated 8 May 1935, is the last letter in Garnett's collection. Unfortunately, the context of the letter was not given nor the nature of the job on possible offer. Five days later Lawrence had his motor-cycle accident and six days after that he was dead, leaving much grief among his friends and many unanswerable questions as to how the course of his life, both public and personal, might have developed.

Unanswerable questions certainly, but I believe I have been able to assemble some interesting new material which throws light on Lawrence's state of mind in the last few weeks of his life. Although brief, this seemed an important enough period to be given a separate section of the book. What emerges from these last letters is that he had found no equilibrium in his new situation, in that he wrote at times with vigour and energy and at other times in deep depression and unease. Which mood prevailed when he went on his last motor-cycle ride on 13 May 1935 it is impossible to know.

Apart from such specific contributions to what I believe to be a more accurate interpretation of the man, I am also pleased to be able to print letters hitherto unpublished to, among others, Lady Astor, Lord Trenchard, Lord Lloyd, Major-General Alan Dawnay, Sir Ronald Storrs, Peake Pasha, Colonel Newcombe, H. St J. B. Philby, Wilfred Scawen Blunt, Mrs Thomas Hardy, E. M. Forster, Robert Graves, Liddell Hart, Edward and David Garnett, Henry Williamson, Ezra Pound, Noël Coward, Eric Kennington, Augustus John, Ernest Rhys, R. D. Blumenfeld (Editor of the *Daily Express*); and to members of 'the rank and file' who served with him, such as H. W. Bailey, T. W. Beaumont and S. C. Rolls from the war period, 'Jock' Chambers, R. A. M. Guy, Dick Knowles and Sergeant Pugh of the R. A. F. and Alec Dixon, 'Posh' Palmer and Arthur Russell of the Tank Corps. If there is a jewel in the crown it is perhaps the extensive usage for the first time of many eloquent, revealing, and at times confessional letters to Charlotte Shaw, overall his most intimate correspondent. As I have said, she denied any use of them to David Garnett, but a year after Garnett published she relented. On 6 March 1939 she wrote to her friend Dorothy Walker (I quote verbatim from Janet Dunbar's biography of Charlotte Shaw, *Mrs G. B. S.*): 'I think T. E. meant his letters to be published. He was an inexpressibly complicated person. In a sense he was tragically sincere. But, also, he always had one eye on the limelight. You say you are thankful I do not allow any of my letters to be published. Now I feel this book shows they ought to be published just to show how much better he could be than anything in that [word crossed out].'

Plainly the book referred to is Garnett. Perhaps one can conclude that Charlotte Shaw would have been pleased that at last there was to be a substantial publication of Lawrence's letters to her — 'my letters' as she calls them in her comment to Dorothy Walker — and that their author would not in the end have objected too angrily to the decision, first made shortly after his death and repeated now, that some of his many hundreds of letters should be made available to the general reader.

Abbreviations

Bodleian Reserve The reserve collection of T. E. Lawrence papers placed
in the Bodleian Library, Oxford, by the Trustees of the *Seven Pillars of
Wisdom* Trust

Bodleian Library Letters held in the Bodleian Library, Oxford, which are
not part of the reserve collection

DG *The Letters of T. E. Lawrence* edited by David Garnett (1938)

HL *The Home Letters of T. E. Lawrence and His Brothers* edited by M. R.
Lawrence (1954)

RGB *T. E. Lawrence to His Biographers: Robert Graves* (1963)

LHB *T. E. Lawrence to His Biographers: Liddell Hart* (1963)

HMH *Solitary in the Ranks* by H. Montgomery Hyde (1977)

University of Harvard Houghton Library, University of Harvard

University of Texas Harry Ransom Humanities Research Center, the
University of Texas at Austin

University of Reading Department of Archives and Manuscripts, Reading
University Library

PRO (plus File No.) Public Record Office, Kew, Richmond, Surrey

All other sources are named in full.

Note: As stated in the Preface the device [. . .] indicates an editorial omission,
while dots within a letter are Lawrence's own. Matter previously omitted
from the *Home Letters* is enclosed within square brackets.

*'Ware letter-writing.
It's a bad habit.*

T. E. LAWRENCE TO EDWARD GARNETT
7 SEPTEMBER 1922

I · THE EARLY YEARS

to

1914

1 *Introduction*

In the mid-1880s an Anglo-Irish landowner called Thomas Chapman, master of South Hill, a country house not far from Dublin, fell in love with the governess whom he had appointed to look after his four daughters. He was approaching forty and the governess, born illegitimate in County Durham and brought up in Scotland, was fifteen years his junior, but for her he gave up his home and his inheritance (he was heir to a baronetcy) and then proceeded over the next decade and a half to found a second family of five sons. Edith, the abandoned wife, was a severe, sourly religious person with a reputation which won her the nickname of 'the Vinegar Queen'; but Sarah, her successor, though attractive, energetic and lively, was far from being a free-thinking modern woman — indeed in religious commitment she was Edith's equal. The circumstances of her union with her former employer were always to leave her, and him also to a lesser extent, with a sense of guilt and, since Edith outlived her husband and had no thought of conceding a divorce, the name they assumed in their new life, Lawrence, would never be other than a convenient alias. Nevertheless, after some years of wandering they successfully set themselves up as what was to all intents and purposes a normal, middle-class family (with just a hint of gentility) in a large semi-detached house at 2 Polstead Road in north Oxford.

They brought up their sons — of whom T. E. Lawrence, born in Tremadoc, North Wales, in 1888, was the second — to be regular attenders at St Aldate's Church, which was presided over by a veteran and much-loved evangelical divine Canon A. M. W. Christopher. Meanwhile one by one the Lawrence brothers enrolled at the recently established Oxford City High School, which gave them a sound, classically based education and prepared them for acceptance into Oxford University. Montague Robert (Bob) and the third son William George (Will) went to St John's College; Thomas Edward (known throughout his boyhood as Ned) and the fourth son, Frank Helier (so named because he was born when the family was residing briefly in St Helier, Jersey), went to Jesus College; Arnold Walter

(Arnie, not born until 1900, the youngest by some years), went to New College.

The mother, in addition to looking after the religious upbringing of the boys, provided stern discipline and a well-run household. The father, who adopted no profession but lived, by his own description, as a gentleman of 'independent means', provided his sons with interests: bicycling, photography, and an awareness of mediaeval history. It was these interests that combined to make the young T. E. Lawrence into a dedicated and enthusiastic traveller, first in England and Wales and then further afield in France, where he visited churches and castles, sketching, photographing, and writing full and regular accounts of his experiences and discoveries in his letters home. In his school and undergraduate years he covered thousands of miles, sometimes with his father or one or other of his brothers, sometimes with school-friends, but more often alone, on his specially built three-speed bicycle. Reading Modern History at Jesus College, he decided to offer a thesis which involved the making of detailed comparisons between the castles of western Europe and those of the Middle East built during the Crusades. To research the latter he spent eleven weeks of the summer vacation of 1909 journeying on foot through Syria and Palestine, visiting numerous castles and bringing back many photographs, plans and drawings. The prevailing belief among mediaeval historians was that the castle-builders of the East had been the principal innovators, and that those of the West had been their timid imitators. Lawrence took a diametrically opposed view, arguing his case with much vigour and weighty evidence in a thesis which contributed crucially to his gaining a first-class honours degree.

His examination success and the friendship and patronage of D. G. Hogarth, Keeper of the Ashmolean Museum, Oxford, led to the next step forward. He was elected to a four-year Senior Demyship (post-graduate scholarship) at Hogarth's college, Magdalen, and appointed by the British Museum to an important archaeological dig, of which Hogarth was in charge, at Carchemish on the upper Euphrates: the money accruing from the Demyship to help finance him as an archaeologist. An earlier plan to produce a thesis on mediaeval pottery for a B.Litt (Bachelor of Letters) degree was abandoned. By Christmas that year he had fulfilled a long-held ambition to visit Greece, had also tasted and enjoyed Constantinople and was in Jebail (ancient Byblos) in the Lebanon, at the American mission school which he had discovered on his walking-tour, learning Arabic in the company of a number of women teachers who were to become his firm friends and, in the case of Mrs Rieder and Miss Fareedah el Akle, regular correspondents. Hogarth joined him there in February and they set off for Carchemish, travelling by way of Haifa, Deraa and Damascus (Lawrence was to know the last two in very different circumstances in the war), and reaching their destination in March.

Lawrence spent the best part of four digging seasons at Carchemish, first under Hogarth and then, from 1912, under Leonard Woolley. These were his most unclouded years. The skills he had first developed when as a schoolboy he had rubbed brasses and collected archaeological relics for the Ashmolean provided a useful foundation; he was well qualified as the expedition's photographer; and the experience of living off the land during his walking-tour had nurtured a natural talent for getting on with the local people, which he now exploited and developed as the expedition's principal employer of labour. When off duty there was much opportunity for practical jokes; high spirits were often the norm at Carchemish. Between digs he went off on long exploratory journeys, visiting castles, collecting Hittite seals for Hogarth, and pitting himself with relish against the challenges of terrain and climate. A companion on some of these journeys was a young Arab donkey-boy, Dahoum, of whom he became both close friend and mentor and whom he took home to Oxford in 1913, together with the site foreman Sheikh Hamoudi. The Arabs in their robes created a mild sensation among the towers and spires. C. F. Bell of the Ashmolean commissioned the distinguished artist Francis Dodd to come down to Oxford to draw Dahoum; an account of the occasion sent to its instigator in Italy, where he had gone on holiday, is one of several amusing and discursive letters to Bell which have only recently been released from a fifty-year embargo.

It has been suggested that Lawrence and Hogarth were engaged in espionage at this period and that the Carchemish dig was a cover for intelligence work; the fact that the Germans were building a massive bridge across the Euphrates hard by the British Museum site, as part of their Berlin–Baghdad railway, has been adduced in support. There is nothing in any new material to support this view, his brother A. W. Lawrence has always strongly discounted these allegations and certainly if Lawrence was so involved the burden lay lightly on him. However, in early 1914 he and Woolley *did* provide scholarly respectability for an essentially military survey, requested by Kitchener, of an unmapped part of Turkish-controlled Sinai — 'red herrings, to give an archaeological colour to a political job' was Lawrence's own neat definition of his and Woolley's role (letter to his mother 4 January 1914). This expedition and the experience of his Carchemish years left him well prepared for the wartime intelligence duties in which he would shortly be engaged.

There is such a wealth of previously unused material available from 1914 onwards and this early period has been so well covered in previous collections that it seemed best to reflect it with a relatively concise anthology — mainly of extracts, though some letters are published in full. From those collections I have taken examples of what seem to me good writing and observation, such as his accounts of Chartres, Athens and Constantinople, or his response to his first sight of the Mediterranean, or (in a letter now correctly dated September 1910) his *rêverie* about the magic of reading. In addition to republished material there are a number of hitherto unpublished letters, most of them in full: to C. F. Bell, as already described, to Miss Fareedah el Akle, to Mrs Rieder, to D. G. Hogarth, to James Elroy Flecker,[1] as well as one to his mother listing the expenses of his 1909 walking-tour and including the important summarising comment (it was the last letter of the journey): 'I won't repent this trip. It has been all wonderful, worth three times its cost.' I have also reinstated some passages suppressed by M. R. Lawrence when he edited his *Home Letters* (see General Introduction). This section contains, in a new letter to Fareedah el Akle dated 26 June 1911, a nice description of the contents of his letters to his family as he saw them: 'general affairs, with a dig in the ribs here, and a pin-prick there'. It was a description that would remain apposite throughout his life; small wonder that the sensitive M. R. Lawrence found certain digs and pin-pricks hard to take. One notable passage here restored shows that Lawrence was uncertain about the further development of his career. In the letter to his mother of 11 April 1911, in which he discussed future options and defended the dream he shared at that time with his Jesus College friend, Vyvyan Richards, of founding a William-Morris-style printing-press, he told his mother: 'I am not going to put all my energies into rubbish like writing history, or becoming an archaeologist. I would much rather write a novel even, or become a newspaper correspondent: — however there is still hope that Richards may pull the thing through.' The printing-press project was very dear to him and even survived the war years, but Lawrence as archaeologist, novelist and newspaper correspondent was never to be heard of again. The historian *did* survive, but as a chronicler of his own very personal history. As with so many men of his generation the war greatly changed the lives of those whom it did not destroy.

Almost all Lawrence's home letters are described here, as elsewhere in the book, as being written to his mother, even when there is no formal greeting to indicate that this is the case. The assumption seems a safe one, however. Such envelopes as have survived are normally addressed to Mrs Lawrence; in his letter of 2 July 1909 he begins: 'Dear Mother (the rest are understood)'; in his letter of 31 January 1911 he refers to her as his 'principal listener'; and the fact that he occasionally addresses a letter specifically to his father or to one of his brothers suggests that he generally assumed that she would be the prime reader of all letters not so assigned. This was to continue; even in his last years, writing to his mother and M. R. (Bob) Lawrence when the latter was a missionary in China, it was assumed that

---

1 This list originally included E. T. Leeds, but in May 1988 a volume of Lawrence's letters to Leeds, edited by J. M. Wilson, was published by the Whittington Press in a limited edition.

she was the principal recipient, but that Bob would read the letter in his turn.

HIS MOTHER
August 13, 1905   Fleece Hotel Colchester

Dear Mother

[. . .] We came here from Ipswich over a rather hilly road 18 miles long. Still we took two hours over it; and walked about six hills; a proceeding Father does not like. We are feeding splendidly. Father is much better and has not coughed since Lynn.[1]

I have had to give up Bures. We came by the other road because of the wind; still I hope to get Pebmarsh tomorrow;[2] and I got one yesterday so I'm not altogether mournful. I have sent off all my rubbings to Miss Powell; hope she'll like them. I expect you have Will with you now. Will you please tell him not to let you do more work than is necessary to keep you in condition? Also tickle Arnie when he gets up and when he goes to bed all from me. Tell him there are dozens of butterflies of all sorts about here, some Red Admirals; and a lot of other very queer ones. Ask Beadle[3] to come up here as he has never seen a Death's Head or some such insect. Norwich Museum he would have enjoyed. There was the largest collection of raptorial birds in existence 409 out of 470 species: I wonder if he'll shriek with horror when he hears that I did not look at them but went off and examined the Norman W.C.s. In the hall was a thrilling stuffed group a boa constrictor strangling a tiger. We hope to return to Oxford Wednesday. Kindly take heaps of love from me for yourself; and when you've had enough, divide the remainder into three portions, and give them to the three worms[4] you have with you. I wonder how the Doctor is enjoying Jerry.[5] Don't forget the Canon's birthday next Sunday.[6] We have had one

1 Lawrence's father suffered from bronchitis.
2 Bures (Suffolk) and Pebmarsh (Essex) were places where Lawrence had planned to make brass rubbings.
3 Beadle: his brother Will.
4 'The three worms you have with you': the other members of the family present at Polstead Road. 'Worms' was also used by Lawrence as a farewell, a salutation (e.g. 'accept my best worms'), or, in the singular, to denote the youngest member of the family, Arnold, who was frequently referred to as 'Worm' into his teens. In using the word Lawrence would also have been aware of its archaic meaning: serpent, snake or dragon.
5 Jerry: a dog. The doctor was presumably Dr A. G. Gibson, the Lawrence family physician, who lived nearby in the Banbury Road.
6 Canon Christopher of St Aldate's Church, Oxford: see Introduction to this section.

post card from Will, 1 from yourself and one letter from you. Loud snores to all. Love to yourself.

Ned

HL/Bodleian Reserve

HIS MOTHER
Friday, Aug 4, 1906   Le Clos Briant [Dinard]

Dear Mother
    I have arrived here quite right after an excellent crossing. The Kerrys almost missed the train at Oxford of course, and came to the boat just with a minute to spare.[1] The journey down to Southampton was uneventful, except for scares about the luggage going wrong. I rode straight to Netley,[2] and caused a spirit of eager enquiry to be manifested by the youth of Southampton. Netley is as fine as if not finer than I had imagined. It is certainly the finest ruin I have seen, and much the most picturesque. I do not think that the Chapter House and guest room can be equalled. [...]
    On board the boat I found my berth, and deposited all my spare goods, and then put on the extra thick coat (this information is for Mother). The Moon was full and glorious: Mr. Kerry and I stayed up till about 11.30 looking at it; I cannot say whether the cloud effects or the reflection on the water were the best but the 'ensemble' was perfect and left nothing to be desired. I never before understood properly Tennyson's
'Long glories of the Autumn Moon'[3]
but I see his reasons now for mentioning it so often, it was so different from the pale moon of the land. The moon was out from about seven to four, and there were heavy clouds with continuous lightning in the East. We only had about $\frac{1}{2}$ hour's rain. The sunrise was on the whole a failure, there was nothing so good as the sunset before. About 2 we passed between Sark and Jersey. Tell Chimp[4] I was not much impressed with the latter. It was all too dark and gloomy, for a residence; the only bright spot was the Corbière Light-house. St. Malo was reached before six, but we had to wait till seven before landing. The sea was very choppy and irregular with a strong swell around the Channel Islands. Everyone in the boat appears to

1 The Kerry family were friends and near neighbours of the Lawrences in Oxford.
2 i.e. Netley Abbey, a Cistercian house founded from the more famous Beaulieu Abbey in the 13th century.
3 From *Idylls of the King: The Passing of Arthur*; but Lawrence was misquoting — Tennyson wrote 'winter moon'.
4 Chimp: his brother Frank, who was born in Jersey.

have been sick with the exception of four or five, among whom Mr. K[erry] and myself were prominent. I found Mons. Chaignon[1] at the *Douane* (?);[2] we recognised each other at the same moment. He has hardly changed at all, if anything he is a trifle stouter. The customs people were chalking all the baggage as fast as it appeared, they do not seem to have opened any: there was a fearful crush; I should think there were 120 bicycles. [...] The Chaignons send all sorts of messages for Bob; it took me nearly ten minutes to explain all about the Brigade to them;[3] it was about the first thing they asked me. They also send dittos to you and the other nippers. Poor Hall[4] is not 1st in Locals after all. Love to yourself. (Don't do any work at all). To Father and to all the other worms down to the smallest. Just off to post. Ta Ta.

HL/Bodleian Reserve

HIS MOTHER
14 Août, 1906   Hotel du Commerce Guincamp

[...] Erquy is a bathing town so called, with enormous quarries of rose-coloured granite. We walked all over the quarry cliffs after eight, and the wind being high we enjoyed ourselves much. The cliffs were about 400 feet high, and commanded a good view. From Erquy, we rode to Château du Guildo, near Ploubalay. At Erquy when returning from bathing, I rode a measured half-kilo. on the sand in 40 seconds exactly. There was a gale behind me, and the sands were perfectly level and very fast, but still 30 miles per hour was distinctly good. I have never gone faster; of course my high gear was the one I rode. Father would like to come to stay at Erquy for a week, to do a little speed-work on the sands; he would not do it anywhere else, for the roads, like most Breton ones, are vile.
   [...]
   [With reference to touring in France. There is no doubt that people would cheat you if possible. When we did not get an accurate statement of accounts we got huge bills (this only happened twice). I have finished

---

1 The Lawrences had lived for a time in Brittany in the years before they settled in Oxford and had become particular friends of the Chaignon family, whom Lawrence used as a base and a point of contact during his visits to France.
2 *Douane*: French customs. The question mark is Lawrence's.
3 The Brigade: the Church Lads' Brigade at St Aldate's, of which both Bob and Ned were members.
4 Hall: E. F. Hall (1888–1986), a contemporary of Lawrence both at Oxford High School and Jesus College. Later a Canon of the Church of England. The 'Locals' were the Oxford Local Examinations.

up with nearly 39 francs over and have not cashed the sovereign Scroggs[1] brought. If you want an account of the expenditure during the trip, consult S. who kept the books. I thus spent some 61 francs in the eight days and this includes repairs 5 francs, and postcards with stamps, a gigantic item, although I only have about 8 p.c.'s over. We had no troubles, although I must get a new outer cover at once. (p.s. got a puncture today, S's front wheel) & will try a Dunlop Agency in St. Servan.] [...]

HL/Bodleian Reserve

HIS MOTHER
Friday morning [18 August 1906]   Dinard

[...] I see you want notes on the children here.[2] Pierre is rather more refined than the rest, but behaves worse than the baby of an English bargee. He is almost as tall as I am, and is very delicate, having overgrown his strength. Henri is a very boisterous imp, without a spark of delicacy, but what elderly spinsters call 'a thorough boy'. Dédée is very inquisitive, but rather nice. Lucienne is very loving and would be sweet if not so dirty, & Madelaine is terribly spoilt. The others are at present lumps of fat. Mr. Chaignon is short and inclined to stout, and is turning grey: he might be strong, and is not particularly interesting. Mme Chaignon is exceedingly nice, and easily includes in herself all the virtues of the rest of the family. I like her very much. The house is not so large as the stables, but my room is very nice. Yesterday [...] I bought and fixed a repair band over the weak spot in my tyre. I hope it will do for the present. [...]

Bodleian Reserve

1 Scroggs was the nickname of C. F. C. Beeson, friend of Lawrence at the Oxford High School, fellow brass-rubber and amateur archaeologist at home (they collaborated in collecting pottery, glass, coins etc. at building sites in Oxford and presenting them to the Ashmolean Museum) and occasional companion abroad.
2 i.e. the children of the Chaignon family. As no part of this passage appeared in *HL* it is credited only to the Bodleian Reserve, a practice that will be observed in such cases throughout the book.

HIS MOTHER
April 1907   Caerphilly

Dear Mother
    Here I am at my last Welsh castle, and, I think, in most respects my best.
[...]
    Caerphilly [...] is magnificent. The Horn-work is most interesting, and
the outworks could not be excelled, either for preservation or attractiveness.
There are no good photos to be obtained, and there have been none at any
time or at any castle I have visited. The conviction has been continually
growing stronger upon me, that I must tour round this part again with a
camera. Details which interest me, such as the moulding of a chimney piece,
or the shape of the flue, even the vaulting of a room, are always neglected
by the professional p.p.c. maker. [...]
    [Any person wishing to create an attraction or sensation in Wales may
appear without a hat. It is always sure to draw. Yesterday for instance 49
people told me that I had no hat (I thought this was obvious?) 6 told me I
belonged to the hatless brigade (there is a strong branch of it at Swansea)
hundreds (I counted 254 and then stopped) asked me where my hat was;
nearly as many asked me if I had lost it, and streetfuls yelled to me that I
hadn't got no 'at. I keep no account of Welsh remarks, but they must have
been almost as numerous as the English ones.]
    After ten days in Wales I ought to be able to sum up all the character,
habits, peculiarities, virtues, vices, and other points of the Welsh people. I
am sorry I cannot do this yet. They seem to me to be rather inquisitive,
[more dirty, and exceedingly ugly. I am at last discovering where I got my
large mouth from, it's a national peculiarity.]¹ At the same time they appear
honest; I have had no extortionate bills (which reminds me that I have over
£3 in hand). I have come to the conclusion that two meals a day with a
glass of milk at one o'clock, suit me better than three. At any rate I have
always felt fresh in this trip in spite of very hard journeys, and the number
of castles has not palled on me; I am fresh for any amount more and could
continue for months. I also feel stronger as the day goes on: with my
luggage left at home I could do 180 miles in the day with ease. [...]

HL/Bodleian Reserve

1 Lawrence rarely thought of himself as in any way Welsh, but he was particularly aware
  of his Welsh connection at this time in that his birth in Wales had qualified him to apply
  for the Meyricke Exhibition in History at Jesus College which he had won two months
  previously.

HIS MOTHER
Sunday 11 August 1907   Evreux

Dear Mother

Father is out, and so I am at last writing to you. I would have written before, but was so busy taking photos, etc. at Château Gaillard. Beauvais was a wonderful place, and I left it with great regret for Gisors which was disappointing, (a large castle, but all the towers locked up), from Gisors we came to Petit Andelys. The Château Gaillard was so magnificent, and the post cards so abominable, that I stopped there an extra day, & did nothing but photograph, from 6.0 a.m. to 7.0 p.m. I took ten altogether, and if all are successful, I will have a wonderful series. I will certainly have to start a book. Some of them were very difficult to take, and the whole day was very hard. I think Pt. Andelys would be a good place to stop at. The hotel is cheap, and very pleasant. The Seine runs near the back door, & the bathing is excellent, from a little wooded island in the centre of the river. There are plenty of hills within sight, & many interesting places. Also the scenery all along the river is exceedingly fine. Long strings of barges pulled by a steam-tug pass the hotel occasionally, and the whole place is over-shadowed by the hills with the ruins of the Château. I have talked so much about this to you that you must know it all by heart, so I had better content myself with saying that its plan is marvellous, the execution wonderful, and the situation perfect. The whole construction bears the unmistakable stamp of genius. Richard I must have been a far greater man than we usually consider him: he must have been a great strategist and a great engineer, as well as a great man-at-arms. [...]

HL/Bodleian Reserve

HIS MOTHER
26 August 1907   Le Mont St Michel[1]

Dear Mother

Here I am at last about to spend a night at the Mont. The dream of years is fulfilled. It is a perfect evening; the tide is high, and comes some 20 feet up the street. In addition the stars are out most beautifully, and the moon is, they say, just about to rise. The phosphorescence in the water interests

1 Fortress, monastery and town poised on top of a tiny precipitous off-shore island on the frontier between Normandy and Brittany, Mont St Michel was precisely the kind of place to excite Lawrence as historian and photographer. Four of his photographs of it — including a telephoto shot from fifteen miles off — are included in *HL*.

me especially: I have only seen it once or twice before, and never so well as tonight. The whole sea, when oars are dipped into it, seems to blaze, for several feet around. I rode here from Dinan, getting Frank's P.C. in St. Malo on my way. As you do not say you want anything, I will not bring back more than a cider-jug for Arnie. It is just large enough to hold all the cider he will ever want, and is a reddish-brown tint. (This news is for him). I am bringing it because there are none of the stamps which he wanted to be bought.

With Dinan and the Rance I am entirely in love. The Rue de Jersual, from the old bridge to the 'place,' is perfect: the river is most lovely. Above the town it becomes very quiet and peaceful, like the Thames: lined with Aspens & Lombardy poplars. When you add waterlilies, willows, and an occasional high bank, crowned with a quaint farmhouse or château, you have a fair idea of the characteristics of the stream. With its bathing, (excellent they tell me) its boating (they have some of Salter's boats)[1] and its beauty, I think it should suit the entire family. Suppose we transport ourselves thither some Autumn?

Since I left Father (to return somewhat on my travels) I have had a very wonderful time. It began at Fougères, which I saw by moonlight, and a more exquisite sight I have seldom seen. That castle is quite above and beyond words. It pollutes it to mention any but Château Gaillard, Pembroke, and Caerphilly in the same breath, and I am not sure but that Fougères is the finest of them all. The Tour des Gobelins is six stories in height, and circular. It stands on a granite cliff 80 feet high, and in the moonlight had a marvellous effect. It set off the strength of the Melusine, a tower near, with an enormous expanded base. The talus shoots right out like the Keep of Ch. Gaillard. Beyond the Melusine, after a hundred yards of machicolated curtain, come Raoul and Yrienne, two wonderful chefs-d'œuvre of the military architect. They are semi-circular bastions, projecting some 70 feet from the wall, are over 80 feet in diameter, and more than that in height; neither has a window or projection in the face, and over against them leans the Spire of St. Sulpice the most crooked, and the thinnest in Bretagne. I would have given anything to have been able to sketch or paint these things as I saw them. I really must return to Fougères soon, and do justice to the whole. The neglect in which it has been left by the guide-books is abominable.

From Fougères I glided S.E. to Le Mans, to photograph the effigy of Mrs. Richard I., Berengaria, in the cathedral there. The Apse and Nave of the building were splendid: the former especially. From Le Mans I rode to Saumur, via Le Lude, a most splendid Renaissance Château, unhappily private. Saumur itself is still in parts as Balzac painted it in *Eugénie Grandet*,

1 Salter's was and still is the best known Oxford boat-hire firm.

though the main streets have been rebuilt. The Castle is a military store-house, and the photos of Fontevrault were not as good as I had wished. I slept that night at Angers. On this stretch one of the small nuts holding the bolt that joins the chain fell off and the bolt, fortunately striking the crank & making a noise, was almost falling out.

Angers was a very quaint town, spoilt by electric trams. The exteriors of the castle & of the prefecture were interesting (nothing at all inside), and the cathedral, roofed as it was in domes, was a new style for me in architecture.

From Angers I rode the next day, through Lion D'Angers, where I was asked for my 'permit', to Rennes, and so on to St. Malo & Dinard. The vineyards were quaint but monotonous. At Dinard I tried 5 hotels & all were full. As it was by then 8 p.m. I went to the Chaignons, & strolled in whilst they were at dinner. When I spoke & revealed myself there was a most enthusiastic scene: all yelled welcome at once, they insisted on my staying to dinner, & sleeping there, and, whilst sending all sorts of messages to you, told me that I was always a friend there: that I was always welcome & was to come in whenever I could. They were quite upset at the idea of my going off next day. M. Corbeil was with them, & collapsed when he heard where I had come from. I have given them a topic of conversation for a week. Deux cent cinquante kilomètres, Ah la-la, qu'il est merveilleux. Deux cent cinquante kilomètres. [. . .]

HL/Bodleian Reserve

Lawrence's most challenging, and rewarding, bicycle ride took place in the summer of 1908 when he achieved a two-thousand-mile exploration of France, beginning and ending in Normandy and reaching as far south as the Mediterranean.

HIS MOTHER
Sunday August 2 1908   Aigues-Mortes

Dear Mother
I had better begin from my last letter before Vézélay.[1] This I found superb but rather in sculpture than in proportions.[. . .] From Vézélay I rode

1 Vézélay, in Burgundy, was where St Bernard of Clairvaux preached to such effect that he inspired the Second Crusade.

to Nevers, arriving on Friday. It is a quaint rather than beautiful town, with a good Renaissance ducal palace, & a fine cathedral. I telephoned from here to Dunlop in Paris for a new tyre, which after anxious waiting arrived all right on Monday: since then all has gone like a marriage bell in the way of punctures, and I am generally happy. The cost was however immense: — with telephoning: carriage: fitting etc., it cost nearly 20/–: result is I'm afraid I'll be short later on: in fact I am rather disgusted with my costs to date. The hotels all charge 2 f. for bed, & at least 2 for dinner (I don't like going to any but fairly decent places, alone, with money). My litre of milk staggers them for breakfast, (I always order it the night before, and it is amusing to watch their efforts to convince me I'm mistaken 'Monsieur does not mean a litre: it is too much' etc.), but not sufficiently to persuade them to charge less than 75 c. to 1 f. result 5 f. are gone by the morning: add some fruit or milk in the day, post cards (now total over 100) & postage, repair-bands, solution, tips for show places, an occasional bath etc. and you have a fair 7 f. per day: I had really hoped to do it cheaper. 6/– a day is absurd for one. (I have changed a note[1] quite successfully by the way: pocket proved admirable).

From Nevers I went by Moulins to Le Puy. Tell Father I had a 20 mile hill up into Le Puy. Part of my ride was up a superb gorge, with river foaming in the bottom, & rock & hill on each side: it was the finest scenery I have ever come across: truly the Auvergne is a wondrous district: but *not* one for a cycle: I'll take a walking tour there some day I hope. [...] From Le Puy I rode up for 10 miles more, (oh dear 'twas hot!) consoling myself with the idea that my sufferings were beyond the conception of antiquity, since they were a combination (in a similar climate) of those of Sisyphus who pushed a great weight up hill, of Tantalus who couldn't get anything to drink, or any fruit, and of Theseus who was doomed ever to remain sitting: — I got to the top at last, had 15 miles of up and down to St. Somebody-I-don't-want-to-meet-again, and then a rush down 4,000 feet to the Rhône. 'Twas down a valley, the road carved out of the side of the precipice, & most gloriously exciting: in fact so much so that with that & the heat I felt quite sick when I got to the bottom. I slept that night at Crussol, a fine xii. c. castle on a 500 feet precipice over the Rhône. Next day via Valence to Avignon, glorious with its town walls & papal palace, (Popes lived there 90 years, & built an enormous pile) & passed thence through Tarascon to Beaucaire, which I saluted for the sake of Nicolette,[2] into Arles. [...] From Arles I rode to Les Baux, a queer little ruined & dying town upon a lonely 'olive sandalled' mountain. Here I had a most delightful surprise. I was looking from the edge of a precipice down the

1 i.e. a £5 pound note.
2 A reference to the 13th-century romance *Aucassin et Nicolette*, set in Beaucaire.

valley far over the plain, watching the green changing into brown, & the brown into a grey line far away on the horizon, when suddenly the sun leaped from behind a cloud, & a sort of silver shiver passed over the grey: then I understood, & instinctively burst out with a cry of 'θαλασσα, θαλασσα'[1] that echoed down the valley, & startled an eagle from the opposite hill: it also startled two French tourists who came rushing up hoping to find another of the disgusting murders their papers make such a fuss about I suppose. They were disappointed when they heard it was 'only the Mediterranean'!

From Les Baux I descended to Arles, & thence to St. Gilles — Aigues-Mortes. I reached here late last night, & sent you a pencilled p.c. It is a lovely little place, an old old town, huddled along its old streets, with hardly a house outside its old walls, still absolutely unbroken, & hardly at all restored or in need of it. From it St. Louis started for his crusades, & it has seen innumerable events since. Today it is deserted by the world, & is decaying fast: its drawbacks are mosquitoes, (a new experience for me, curtains on all the beds), and the lack of a cheap hotel. It is however almost on the sea, and exceedingly pleasant, (above all if one could get acclimatised quickly to these brutes, I'm all one huge bite).[2] I bathed today in the sea, the great sea, the greatest in the world: you can imagine my feelings: [...]. I felt that at last I had reached the way to the South, and all the glorious East; Greece, Carthage, Egypt, Tyre, Syria, Italy, Spain, Sicily, Crete ... they were all there, and all within reach ... of me. I fancy I know now better than Keats what Cortes felt like, 'silent upon a peak in Darien'.[3] Oh I must get down here, — farther out — again! Really this getting to the sea has almost overturned my mental balance: I would accept a passage for Greece tomorrow: — and there I am going to Nîmes: — I suppose it cannot be helped: well I am glad to have got so far. [...]

HL/Bodleian Reserve

1 'Thalassa, Thalassa': 'The sea, the sea' — the famous cry of Xenophon's army of the Ten Thousand when on their journey back to Greece from Mesopotamia in 401 BC they caught their first glimpse of the Black Sea.
2 He became infected with malaria at this time and was to suffer recurring bouts of the disease throughout his life.
3 From Keats's sonnet *On first looking into Chapman's Homer*.

HIS MOTHER[1]
28 Août, 1908   Hotel de la Place Laigle

Dear Mother
   [...] I expected that Chartres would have been like most French Cathedrals spoilt by restoration, so I slipped out before breakfast to 'do' it. What I found I cannot describe — it is absolutely untouched & unspoilt, in superb preservation, & the noblest building (for Beauvais is only half a one) that I have ever seen, or expect to see. If only you could get an idea of its beauty, of its perfection, without going to look at it! Its date is late xiith & early xiii cent. It is not enormous; but the carvings on its 3 portals are as fine as the best of all Greek work. Till yesterday I would put no sculptors near the Greeks of the vth cent. Today the French of the early middle ages *may* be inferior, but I do not think so: nothing in imagination could be grander than that arrangement of three huge cavernous portals (30 odd feet deep), of gigantic height, with statues everywhere for pillars, bas-reliefs for plain surfaces, statuettes & canopies for mouldings. The whole wall of the cathedral is chased & wrought like a Florentine plaque, and by master hands! You may think the individual figures stiff — the details coarse — everything is hard & narrow I admit, but when you see the whole — when you can conceive at once the frame *and* the picture, then you must admit that nothing could be greater, except it were the Parthenon as it left the hands of Pheidias: it must be one of the noblest works of man, as it is the finest of the middle ages. One cannot describe it in anything but superlatives, and these seem so wretchedly formal that I am half tempted to scratch out everything that I have written: Chartres is Chartres: — that is, a gallery built by the sculptors to enclose a finer collection than the Elgin Marbles. I went in, as I said, before breakfast, & I left when dark: — all the day I was running from one door to another, finding in each something I thought finer than the one I had just left, and then returning to find that the finest was that in front of me — for it is a place absolutely impossible to imagine, or to recollect, at any rate for me: it is overwhelming, and when night came I was absolutely exhausted, drenched to the skin (it had poured all day) and yet with a feeling I had never had before in the same degree — as though I had found a path (a hard one) as far as the gates of Heaven, and had caught a glimpse of the inside, the gate being ajar. You will understand how I felt though I cannot express myself. Certainly

1 David Garnett thought this — Lawrence's response to a visit to Chartres Cathedral — 'the most beautiful and emotional of his early letters', but was refused permission to print it in his 1938 volume; he did, however, manage to insert it into the 1952 reprint of his *Selected Letters* and it was later published, without cuts, in *HL*. The core of the letter is reproduced here, only the opening paragraph (a brief summary of his travels since his previous letter) being omitted.

Chartres is the sight of a lifetime, a place truly in which to worship God. The middle ages were truer that way than ourselves, in spite of their narrowness and hardness and ignorance of the truth as we complacently put it: the truth doesn't matter a straw, if men only believe what they say or are willing to show that they do believe something. Chartres besides has the finest late xvi & early xvii bas-reliefs in the world, and is beautiful in its design & its proportions. I have bought all the picture post-cards, but they are of course hardly a ghost of the reality, nothing ever could be, though photography is best for such works. I took a photo myself of Philosophus, a most delightful little statuette, about 18 inches high: if not fogged, (I forgot to lock my camera, & somebody has fiddled with it), it may give one an idea of how the smallest parts of the building are finished with as much care as the centre-posts of the main doorways, and if Philosophus were of Greek marble there would be photographs of him in every album, between the Hermes of Praxiteles & the Sophocles of the Lateran. He is great work. I also tried to take a photo of the masterpiece, the Christ of the south portal, but that cannot be worth looking at. I expect I will burn my photos. of Chartres as soon as they are visible. Yet perhaps with care & time, one would get something worthy from a photograph. We must return there (I would want assistants) and spend a fortnight in pure happiness.

HL/Bodleian Reserve

Early in 1909, while planning his visit to the crusader castles of the Middle East, he wrote for advice to Charles Doughty, veteran traveller and author of *Arabia Deserta*, a classic work which he much admired. Doughty's reply was not encouraging: 'In July and August the heat is very severe and day and night, even at the altitude of Damascus (over 2000 feet), it is a land of squalor where a European can find evil refreshment.... The distances to be traversed are very great. You would have nothing to draw upon but the slight margin of strength which you bring with you from Europe....' Nevertheless Lawrence persevered and during his summer vacation undertook an 1100-mile walking-tour through Syria and Palestine, in the course of which he visited thirty-six out of some fifty castles on his proposed route and carried out the field research which enabled him to produce his impressive thesis.

August 13 1909   Tripoli (Tarabulus)

I have quite unexpectedly got an opportunity of sending you a line, so I will take it though there is nothing special to tell you: still you may be glad to have additional evidence that I am all right. I did not leave Beyrout till last Friday 6th & then went N. to the Nahr-el Kelb, the Dog River. [...] Then I went further N. (by the way I passed the place where S. George killed his dragon) to Jebail, crossing the river Adonis which at certain seasons runs blood-red. It used to be the centre of the Adonis worship of Aphica [?] and Byblus. Jebail is of course Byblus,[1] & I stayed there 3 or 4 days with Miss Holmes, the American missionary. She was most exceedingly kind in feeding me up, & as she had plenty of books & a marble-paved hall, with water ad lib. and trees (real green ones) in her garden I was very happy. [...]

[Miss Holmes told me one most striking thing — there exists among the Mohammedans today a secret sort of Christian, organised under a head in Damascus. She won the confidence of a customs-officer in Jebail, & one day he showed her a bible: she was astounded, & still more so when some other prominent members of the town came in, & there was, behind doors, singing of Christian hymns (*not* translations of European productions, but home-made chants) and a communion service administered by a layman. They would not tell her much, but naturally she has been put on the alert, & she has found that the sect is fairly large. She got an introduction to the head of it in Damascus but he would not see her: they fight very shy of intercourse with missionaries, on account of the row there would be. Still I think it is the best sign I have heard of in the country so far. A native Christian church is so much more likely to win than a foreign grafting, and with the new toleration the members can become bolder.[2] Miss Holmes, who is the best Arab linguist in the Mission (she has been half a lifetime in the country) thinks there are visible signs of the gradual decay of Islam. If so the American Mission has had the larger share.]
      [...]

HL/Bodleian Reserve

1 Byblus, or Byblos, was an ancient city of Phoenicia, the traditional birthplace of Adonis. The name would doubtless have had a special resonance for Lawrence in that the sale of Egyptian papyrus by Byblos merchants to the Greeks for book-making ultimately gave English such words as 'bible' and 'bibliography'.
2 Lawrence is here showing early signs of the view which he was to express with much force in later years when M. R. Lawrence was a medical missionary in China, that emergent nations should not be patronised by developed ones in the matter of religion and culture but should be left to find their own salvation.

29.8.1909   Latakia

Dear Mother
    Another chance for a note: this time hurried. I wrote last from Tripoli.
    I went thence to Aarka, & then to Kala'at el Hosn, passing one night on
a house roof, & the second in the house of an Arab noble, reputed, as I was
told next day, of the highest blood: a young man very lively, & rather wild,
living in a house like a fortress on top of a mountain: only approachable on
one side, & there a difficult staircase. If you keep this note I can tell you all
sorts of amusing things about him later: name Abdul Kerim. He had just
bought a Mauser, & blazed at everything with it. His bullets must have
caused terror to every villager within a mile around: I think he was a little
cracked.
    Then I got to Hosn, which is I think the finest castle in the world:[1]
certainly the most picturesque I have seen — quite marvellous: I stayed 3
days there, with the Kaimmakam, the governor: a most-civilised-French-
speaking - disciple - of - Herbert - Spencer - Free - Masonic - Mohammedan -
Young Turk:[2] very comfortable —.
    He sent an escort with me next day to Safita, a *Norman keep, with*
ORIGINAL *battlements*: the like is not in Europe: such a find. Again I slept
with Kaimmakam & Co. (Co. here means fleas) and next day I went on
again with a huge march, to two more castles, and a bed for the night in a
threshing floor, on a pile of tibn, chopped straw, listening to the Arabs
beating out their Dhurra[3] in the moonlight: they kept it up all night in
relays, till about 2 a.m. when they woke me up, & said they were all
exhausted, would I keep watch because there were thieves, & I was a Inglezi
& had a pistol: I obliged thinking it was humbug of the usual sort, (every
village distrusts its neighbour), but they told me in Tartus next day that
there really were not thieves, but *landlords* about! Isn't that charming? These
dear people wanted to hide the extent of their harvest. [...]
    No smoking yet, though here every man woman & child does: Latakia
tobacco, which Father knows all grows here: the peasants dry & smoke
their own, all in cigarettes: I will have such difficulty in becoming English
again, here I am Arab in habits & slip in talking from English to French &
Arabic unnoticing: yesterday I was 3 hours with an Orleannais, talking
French, & he thought at the end I was a 'compatriot'! How's that?
                                                        [Worms   Love

1 Usually known as Krak des Chevaliers.
2 Herbert Spencer (1820–1903) had won a wide reputation as a revolutionary philosopher;
   the Young Turks had carried out an armed, if bloodless, revolution against the Sultan of
   Turkey just over a year before Lawrence was writing, in July 1908.
3 Indian corn or millet.

This goes to Oxford. I expect Jersey is nearly over.]¹ I may manage a pencil scrawl from Antioch: but you may be happy now all my rough work is finished successfully: & my Thesis is I *think assured. Iradé invaluable.*²

DG/HL/Bodleian Reserve

HIS MOTHER
Sept. 22 1909   Aleppo

After all I am coming home at once, for lack of money. Of course you could send me more but I'd want new clothes, those I wear at present shall be left in Beyrout, I'd never get them past the sanitary inspection at P. Said: — new boots the present being 'porous', I've walked them to bits at any rate, & my feet lately have responded to it. They are all over cuts & chafes & blisters, & the smallest hole in this horrid climate rubs up in no time into a horrible sore. I can't imagine how many times I would have had blood poisoning already if it hadn't been for my boracic: but I want to rest the feet now or there will be something of the sort. To undertake further long walks would be imprudent, for even in new boots these holes would take long to heal. [...]

By the way it is remarkable that all this 3 months on most unaccustomed & most changing food & water my stomach has never been upset. That is the great bugbear of the European traveller in Turkey. I suppose my exercise etc. (I have walked 1100 miles) is responsible for my health.

I find an absurd canard in the Aleppo paper of a week ago: my murder near Aïntab (where I didn't go). I hope it has not been copied. The hotel people received me like a ghost. Mr. Edvard Lovance sounds like me.

Tell Will I have got about 24 Hittite seals & congratulate Arnie on his bicycle his tumbles & his handwriting. The P.O. had my letters here after all. They thought no apology necessary for their former mistake; but I got one after a little work. Am glad you are all right, & that Jersey was pleasant. 'So warm' indeed come out here & revel in 106° in the shade. Must finish now. Will spend 3 days Damascus (not a penny to spare) & then leave Beyrout 30th. Miss Holmes has offered me her purse: so I'll borrow if I run short at last. But not if I can help. Salaams.

                                                                Ned

HL/Bodleian Reserve

1 His mother had evidently been on a visit to Jersey, birthplace of his brother Frank.
2 Iradé: official authorisation to travel through Turkish-held territories. Lawrence had applied for his before leaving Oxford through Lord Curzon, at that time Chancellor of the University.

HIS MOTHER
Saturday 9 Oct [19]09   R.M.S. *Otway*

I am afraid I cannot write you any account of Eastern towns:[1] I don't know them well enough yet: but I thought I would send you a copy of the rough account I kept of my expenses, as they have been so great this trip. They are in round figures only, but I think nearly correct. You will see that living expenses in the hotels were enormous — £11.4.0 for 35 days — over 6/- a day. That is because the hotels are built for Europeans & rich merchants only, & are dear: also they have a vile system of 'pension' by which so much is charged whether one takes one's meals inside or not. So I couldn't usually follow my French trick of taking a room only & catering for myself. The usual charges were 8 francs a day.

Now I left Oxford with about £65 —

	£	s	d	
In London	6	0	0	fare from Oxford, 2 maps, a water bottle, & the Mauser pistol
On board		15	0	In tips, a subscription, & stamps at Gibraltar
P. Said	2	10	0	I stayed 5 days, & had extras.
To Beyrout	3	2	0	Steamer fares, & customs, port dues, etc.
In Beyrout	1	0	0	I stayed 3 days.
First tour	6	10	0	Includes a stay at Haifa & steamer fare: about 1 month in all
In Beyrout	3	10	0	I stayed 10 days & bought stamps etc.
To Aleppo	2	10	0	Second tour: about 5 weeks
In Aleppo	2	10	0	I stayed one week: a very dear place
Aleppo castle	1	0	0	Much formality to see castle & all sorts of officials with me
To Urfa				
carriage	8	0	0	2 men & 3 horses for a fortnight: tips to driver included
Food		4	6	
Tips on	1	0	0	Includes Euphrates boatmen etc.
way				
Camera	1	10	0	Well spent if it is recovered:[2] baksheesh of course
In Aleppo	1	10	0	I stayed 5 days
To Damascus	2	0	0	Railway fare
In Damascus		12	0	I stayed 3 days
To Beyrout	1	6	0	Railway fares
To Port Said	1	2	0	Steamer fare, deck passage
To London	12	0	0	Steamer fare, water rate, but includes Beyrout 12/- hotels P. Said hotel expenses 17/- a day
Hittite seals	6	0	0	Some of this I hope to get back
Tripoli	2	8	0	A mission

1 In a postscript to his previous letter he had written of his hope to spend a week or ten days in Damascus '& work up the details of town life' into an account for his family.
2 His camera had been stolen.

Urfa	3	3	0	A famine fund
Naples		7	0	A bronze head: too cheap & good to lose
In hand	1	0	0	Tips & train fare

| | 71 | 8 | 6 |

So you see I made £6   0   0

This was from the sale of my Mauser pistol (at a profit) in Beyrout on my departure (£5. 0. 0). The odd £1 is simply due to my crushing figures into the round. You see £11. 8. 0 is unnecessary expense: antiquities & charities: but the seals I came out to get, & the other people will do a lot with the money. I would only have spent it on 2nd class fares on rail (Syrian 3rd is beastly) & 2nd class on board. Still from Beyrout to P. Said is only 3 nights. The real bother was that I had to feed myself that time. The money in hand is just enough — but of course nobody will expect presents: Arnie the worm has had his. The stamps altogether came to 11/6. We will squander anything Mr. Hogarth pays me in riotous living to make up. I can't say when I return: Sat, or Sund they think: but she is a new boat (trial trip) with speed untried. Tell Will Naples Museum glorious, including bronze footballer. Worms to the rest of the party, & to Father, & yourself.

Ned

[...]
I hope Father found the College authorities agreeable: in any case I won't repent this trip. It has been all wonderful, worth three times its cost.
   Supplement for Will
   In a bronze foundry in Naples when searching for a 'footballer' (none to be got worthy under £2) I saw a Hypnos head,[1] very good work, but a bad cast, modern naturally. I asked price & tumbled down with it to 8 francs, little more than the value of the metal. You will admire it immensely: and I'll give you 5 minutes to find out the fault in the casting — The bronzes in the Naples museum are beyond words.

Bodleian Reserve

Lawrence was late back for the Michaelmas Term, but he had asked his father to call at Jesus College to make his apologies and he had also written to the college Principal, Sir John Rhys, explaining his situation and pleading 'four bouts of malaria when I had only reckoned on two'. A lecturer who

---

1 Hypnos was the Greek god of sleep.

was also a family friend described him on his return as 'thinned to the bone by privation'. Towards the end of term he wrote to Doughty informing him that his walking-tour had 'ended happily' and that he had found the castles he had visited 'so intensely interesting that I hope to return to the East for some little time'. Lawrence now settled to work on his thesis (which he entitled *The influence of the Crusades on European military architecture — to the end of the XIIth century*) and prepare for his final examinations. In the following summer he was one of a handful of students to be awarded a first in History.

HIS MOTHER
September 1910[1]   Hotel Bellevue Le Petit Andelys

[...] The sculptures of Rheims are almost perfect, it is not a Chartres, but wonderful all the same, I have got what PCs I could get: none worthy of course. Gisors I liked: Frank didn't. He is enjoying this place, because it has a river[2] and steam tugs, & an English family: so we will stay over Monday & let him get a little more of it. There is very safe bathing: & some boating in flat tubs of boats. [I took him over Chateau Gaillard this morning, & did my best to reconstruct it for him & make him interested. There were some sloe-bushes he preferred in the outer ward.]

The country here is altogether lovely: & the views more & more necessary: if I stayed very long I would take root. I sat up in the castle this morning a little after Frank went to dejeuner, & read below the keep. The colours in the water below me, & the sweep of the river under the cliffs were superb. Is there any chance of Will getting here this year? I can assure him he will find it repay any pains. The view has the same effect on people as a forest or a church: they talk in whispers.

The book I had was *Petit Jehan de Saintré*,[3] a xv Cent. novel of knightly manners — very good: — I have wanted to read it for a long time, but the Union[4] Copy was so badly printed that I had not the heart for it. Now I have found (for 1 f. 25) a series quite nicely typed on fairly good paper. So far I have only got 4 volumes, because they are rather much to carry: [as for the expense I saved that on food: — only 6 francs (and I reckoned to spend 3 frs a day on it).] It is altogether glorious to have found good French

1 Dated August 1910 in both *DG* and *HL* but September 1910 in the original.
2 The Seine. Cf. his letter of 11 August 1907.
3 By Antoine de la Sale (or Salle), c. 1386–c. 1460.
4 i.e. the Oxford Union.

books at last. I can read Molière & Racine & Corneille & Voltaire now: —
a whole new world. You know, I think, the joy of getting into a strange
country in a book: at home when I have shut my door & the town is in
bed — and I know that nothing, not even the dawn — can disturb me in
my curtains: only the slow crumbling of the coals in the fire: they get so
red & throw such splendid glimmerings on the Hypnos[1] & the brass-work.
And it is lovely too, after you have been wandering for hours in the forest
with Percivale or Sagramors le desirous[2] to open the door, and from over
the Cherwell to look at the sun glowering through the valley-mists. Why
does one not like things if there are other people about? Why cannot one
make one's books live except in the night, after hours of straining? and you
know they have to be your own books too, & you have to read them more
than once. I think they take in something of your personality, & your
environment also — you know a second hand book sometimes is so much
more flesh & blood than a new one. — and it is almost terrible to think that
your ideas, yourself in your books may be giving life to generations of
readers after you are forgotten. It is that specially which makes one need
good books: books that will be worthy of what you are going to put into
them. What would you think of a great sculptor who flung away his gifts
on modelling clay or sand? Imagination should be put into the most precious
caskets, & that is why one can only live in the future or the past, in Utopia,
or the wood beyond the World.[3]

Father won't know all this — but if you can get the right book at the
right time you taste joys — not only bodily, physical, but spiritual also,
which pass one out above and beyond one's miserable self, as it were
through a huge air, following the light of another man's thought. And you
can never be quite the old self again. You have forgotten a little bit: or
rather pushed it out with a little of the inspiration of what is immortal in
someone who has gone before you.

Ned

DG/HL/Bodleian Reserve

1 The head, bought in Naples, referred to in the previous letter.
2 A reference to Sir Thomas Malory's *Morte d'Arthur*, one of the great influential books of
Lawrence's youth; he carried a copy of it with him throughout his wartime campaigns.
3 A reference to William Morris's romance *The Wood Beyond the World,* published in 1894.
Morris was a powerful and formative influence in Lawrence's life, as writer, translator,
artist and printer of fine books.

E. T. LEEDS[1]

Nov. 2 1910   Grand Hotel du Nord Rouen

[...] It should create a good impression on your mind to know that I am in Rouen looking at Mediaeval Pots: Mr. Bell[2] got me letters from Mr. Salomon Reinach[3] that make me out to be a sort of god: and they all rush about the Museum here offering me keys and cupboards and cups of coffee: the last rather a bore.

Also Mr. Hogarth is going digging: and I am going out to Syria in a fortnight to make plain the valleys and level the mountains for his feet: — also to learn Arabic. The two occupations fit into one another splendidly.

These exhaust all my hopes: except that this wind will die down and give me a quieter crossing than I had yesterday. I was just feeling premonitions of internal crisis when Havre came in sight. I would, tho', not have been alone in my misfortune. *Vale*

.L.

Bodleian Reserve

Lawrence left for the Middle East in December 1910, his journey being made more enjoyable because the steamer on which he sailed through the Mediterranean, the S.S. *Saghalien*, suffered from persistent engine trouble, thus providing him with the opportunity for leisurely explorations of Naples, Athens and Constantinople. He was to remain in the Middle East for most of the next four years, returning only for occasional visits to England.

1 Edward Thurlow Leeds (1877–1955) was Assistant Keeper of the Department of Antiquities of the Ashmolean Museum; he succeeded D. G. Hogarth as Keeper of the Museum in 1928, holding the post until 1945. He had met Lawrence in 1908 and the friendship then begun was to produce a regular correspondence throughout Lawrence's years in the East. A note on the life of Leeds by D. B. Harden is published in the volume of Lawrence to Leeds referred to on p. 5.

2 C. F. Bell, one of Leeds's colleagues at the Ashmolean: see letters to him later in this section.

3 An eminent French scholar; he had been *Conservateur des Musées Nationaux* since 1886.

HIS MOTHER
Dec. 1910   Athens

[…] Just as we entered the Piræus the sun rose, & like magic turned the
black bars to gold, a wonderfully vivid gold of pillar and architrave and
pediment, against the shadowed slopes of Hymettus. That was the Acropolis
from a distance: — a mixture of all the reds & yellows you can think of
with white for the high-lights and brown-gold in the shadows. Of course
I got ashore at once, & plunged into the intolerable cesspit of the Piræus:
the place is a filthy drain for all the dregs of the capital, its only virtue that
it saves it from being a port. Before you reach Athens you pass through
green fields & over small streams, that effectually wash away the taste &
smell of the sea. The rail lands you in the midst of a very modern looking
town of squares & gardens, with a character partly French but not wholly
European or Asiatic; too bright for the one & too clean for the other. It
was above all things quiet, the quietest town imaginable, with few trams,
& those slow ones, no motors or bicycles & very few carts. The streets are
usually asphalt-paved, & there seemed hardly any dogs to bark and fight.
Even the vegetable-hawkers shouted like men, not like jackals or fog horns.
Everywhere were palm trees & mimosa, with green lawns. […] The quiet
was really almost uncanny, as I walked up the shallow valley below Mars
hill, & along the processional way to the gateway of the citadel. There were
no boys to bother one, no loud bellows'd leather sellers, only a misty
sunlight in which all Attica, Phaleron, Salamis, Eleusis, and the distant
Peloponnese lay motionless, 'drowned in deep peace', below the rock
platform of the Wingless Victory. To get there I had to climb up the white
marble staircase of the Propylea within the entrance gate. There were no
porters, no guides, no visitors, & so I walked through the doorway of the
Parthenon, and on into the inner part of it, without really remembering
where or who I was. A heaviness in the air made my eyes swim, & wrapped
up my senses: I only knew that I, a stranger, was walking on the floor of
the place I had most desired to see, the greatest temple of Athene, the palace
of art, and that I was counting her columns, and finding them what I
already knew. The building was familiar, not cold as in the drawings, but
complex, irregular, alive with curve and subtlety and perfectly preserved.
Every line of the mouldings, every minutest refinement in the sculptures
were evident in that light, and inevitable in their place. The Parthenon is
the protocathedral of the Hellenes. I believe I saw the Erectheum, and I
remember coming back to look again at the Propylea, and to stand again
beside the Niké Apteros: but then I came down again into the town, &
found it modern and a little different. It was as though one had turned from
the shades of the ancestors, to mix in the daily vocations of their sons: and
so only this about Athens, that there is an intoxication, a power of possession

in its ruins, & the memories that inhabit them, which entirely prevents anyone attempting to describe or to estimate them. There will never be a great book on Athens unless it is one by an enemy: no one who knew it could resist its spell, except by a violent attack upon its spirit, and who can attack it now of artists, when Tolstoy[1] is dead? He, and he alone, could have uprooted Greek culture in the world. I am coming back by Athens I think next year to stay a little time. For the present I am only confused with it: I do not know how much was Athens, and how much the colouring of my imagination upon it.

N.

DG/HL

VYVYAN RICHARDS[2]
Dec 15 [1910]   Constantinople

[...]
Constantinople is as much life as Athens stood for sleep. It is a huge town, crammed with people, who all live and eat, and sleep in the streets apparently. All day the huge Galata bridge, on boats over the Golden Horn is pressed with a multitude of people, all foot-passengers, jostling each other, going all ways apparently. One cannot stand an instant without being hustled all over the road by passers by, or walk forward a yard without dodging to one side or other to avoid a carriage, or a pack of mules, or only a porter, with two asses' burden on his shoulders. The colour and movement in the streets are insurpassable: — Damascus is not within a call of it: — and besides there are glorious-coloured mosques, in blue and gold and cream and green tiles, and yellow glazed pottery of *exactly the shapes in England in the xivth cent.,* and a street, a whole street, of the most divine copper-ware. The modern stuff is sometimes good, more often polished after making till the hammer marks are ground away, or even machine pressed but in all the shops are the old out of date shapes exchanged

---

1 Tolstoy, for whom Lawrence expressed the highest admiration, had died on 20 November 1910, aged 82.
2 See Introduction to this section: Richards was the most serious of three enthusiasts for fine book-printing with whom Lawrence discussed the idea of setting up a printing-press, the other two being C. F. C. Beeson and Leonard Green. He had first met Lawrence when the latter lived, briefly, in rooms at Jesus College, Richards being in his third year and Lawrence in his first. He became greatly attached to Lawrence and later wrote an admiring biography of him — *Portrait of T. E. Lawrence: The Lawrence of The Seven Pillars of Wisdom* — which was published in 1936.

for new, the wares of two or three generations back, perfect in shape and workmanship (before the French invasion), some bronze, some copper so heavy & thick, that they are not resold, but melted down, for the mere value of their metal. And I can't buy them, for I don't know Turkish: but I have bought a grammar, and started it: It won't be my fault if the hut is not full of old Turkish & Arab metal ware.

If you could only have seen the bronze water-cistern I saw yesterday.

DG

HIS MOTHER
Dec 31 1910   Jebail

[...] Miss Holmes is writing to you to say all is well with me: that went off last Tuesday, so you may get it first. She is flourishing, & her school: I came in for great Xmas festivities, which I kept out of mainly: Arabic now, with a little Antiquity: some 5 good flint saws: much prehistoric pottery.

Father should really come out here. Today, mid-winter, has been roasting hot, with a glaring sun, & clouds of flies & mosquitoes. We can pick ripe oranges in the gardens, and roses and violets in Miss Holmes' patch (facing N.): everything is green and flourishing, for there have been two or three showers since I landed. Still the heat, & the perfect calm, and the exquisite twilight effects are nearly equal to summer's. I need a sun-helmet, really. It is very sandy soil, & they say a golf-links is preparing on the seven miles of sand-dunes below Beyrout. I hope he is better in Wales, but it is not much good asking after his health, since all things will have changed before I get the reply: you must wire if it is to be of use.

Seven letters tonight: and some p.c.'s.

[...]

HL/Bodleian Reserve

HIS MOTHER
Jan 24 1911   Jebail

[...] We[1] both feel (at present) that printing is the best thing we can do, if we do it the best we can. That means though, (as it is an art), that it will be done only when we feel inclined. Very likely sometimes for long periods

---

1 Lawrence and Richards.

I will not touch a press at all. Richards, whose other interests are less militant, will probably do the bulk of the work. The losses (if any) will be borne by us both, according as we are in funds (we will approximate to a common purse): the profits will be seized upon as a glorious opportunity to reduce prices.

You will see, I think, that printing is not a business but a craft. We cannot sit down to it for so many hours a day, any more than one could paint a picture on that system. And besides such a scheme would be almost sure to interrupt *The Seven Pillars of Wisdom*[1] or my monumental work on the Crusades.

[...]

HL/Bodleian Reserve

HIS MOTHER
March 11 1911   Carchemish (Jerablus)

We have got here, & this is a hurried note to go off by the returning camelmen. We left Aleppo Thursday: this is Saturday, nothing of note on the journey except the flooded Sadjur: which was easily crossed tho', at a ford. I had no camera ready unfortunately. Mr. Hogarth drove & walked & rode: Thompson[2] rode & walked: I walked, except of course over the river.

Not much yet of course to say about this place. The mounds are enormous: but I'll send you a photo. or drawing later. We only got in about 4 o'clock: and have been unpacking since: eleven baggage horses, ten camels....

The head-man of the village, who is also the agent of the Liquorice Company that I ran into last time, has put the Co's house at our disposal. It is a big, stone-built, one storied place, with a court-yard adjoining: the roof will be good for sleeping on later in the year: at present the thermometer is 40° with a gale off those N.W. summits of the Taurus, that, snow-clad, were in view all this afternoon. We have bedding enough, good hap, for a host.

The village is about $\frac{3}{4}$ of a mile from the site, & the river: on high ground, so there is no possibility of fever in the hot weather, when or if it comes: snow here a few days ago: no skating on the river, worse luck.

1 Lawrence planned to use this title for a book he hoped to write about seven eastern cities; when this project failed—he destroyed the manuscript in 1914—he did not abandon the title. For his own account see his letter to Robin Buxton dated 22 September 1923.
2 R. Campbell Thompson (1876–1941), second in command to Hogarth.

As for the place: there is a high plateau in the corner N. of the Sadjur and W. of the Euphrates: this is some 500 feet above the river. We started on that this morning & then dropped gradually from foothill to foothill until we reached this village. It is a little place, of about 40 houses, very clean and fresh-looking, being all quite new, with a very fast-running spring on one side. I thought (and Mr. Hogarth said) that there was nothing but river-water in the place: as it is 'the most delicate fabrics may be washed without damage': the water is quite clear, fairly cool, and good-tasting. Its situation puts it out of the way of defilement.

The mound is about $\frac{3}{4}$ of a mile N. of the village: the river about $\frac{1}{2}$ mile to the E.: and it bends round until it washes the edge of the great 'Acropolis' hill.

Our unpacking was a lively sight: heaps & heaps of baggage animals of all sorts; horses, mules, donkeys, camels: about a dozen of our men, and perhaps 20 villagers, who swarmed out of their houses when we approached, & as soon as we had approved the house, all turned to under the orders of the little overseer, and cleared it out. It was full of camel-hides, & corn, poplar-poles and lentils. The last were impounded for the benefit of the expedition. I cater to some extent....

I want to go to bed now: we have had two very rough nights, and it is very cold. All quite well: I like the second-man Thompson, very much.

N.

[I think I should say a word about Father's letter: (which is not to hand at present). I do not much concern myself about the exact arrangements (one cannot at this distance): but I would prefer one on which Richards & himself agreed: if not let it be his own arrangement, since it is he who provides the money. Only it is not a gift or loan to Richards, as a person merely. It is an attempt to get started the press we both desire so much; the question whether Richards himself is approved or not does not enter the question hardly at all. I gathered that Florence[1] does not like him: his assumption of intellectual conceit tried her; but remember that people do not usually wear their inside skin out. I think myself that he is quite a heaven-sent partner.]

[...]

HL/Bodleian Reserve

1 Florence Messham, the Lawrence boys' former nurse.

E. T. LEEDS
Mar. 27 [1911]   Carchemish

Economy in letter writing! One must write to somebody, (one owes to 3
bodies); wherefore write to the meekest among them, and suggest he carry
out commissions: and you know it is really rather a privilege to get a line
at all, for we are busy out here.

Concerning digs: we are getting rather bored with bits of Hittite inscriptions that keep on turning up:[1] the only fun is squeezing 'em, which is my
particular part of the job. D.G.H. has nobly sacrificed his sponge to help
me: and really he didn't want a sponge: it was not as though there was
society here. Squeezing is rather good sport:[2] (I forgot to say that D.G.H.
has also given up his toothbrush for it: his teeth are mostly false, and so we
decided there was least need for his.) Next ... we haven't found anything
else, except a rude figure of a female (known as 'the lady') and another
broken figure or two: there is a lot of top hamper[3] and late stuff to clear,
and so many big stones that we go slow. Very little pottery, and no small
objects: (except myself). . . .

The second point should be the house: it is of stone, with mud floors
roof, and from the roof little bits drop all day and all night: and it is full
of birds that baptize the bald-heads at their leisure: my hair is still growing,
and every day I give thanks that I brought with me a few spare hairpins.

Then there are the cats: Father (who is only suffered, not encouraged);
he comes in at the holes in the roof and walls by night, and offends lewdly
in our beds. Then D.G.H. throws a boot towards it and hits Thompson,
and plants it in the bath, or knocks the light down: and when he has got
out and repaired damages he finds the cat in his bed when he lies down
again. So much for Father. Mother is plaintive, and rather a bore: she wails
aloud for food, usually about 2 a.m.: then she gets it, but in a tin: of late
she receives sympathy, in spite of one very irregular night, when she woke
me up with her claws over the face, and the rest of the expedition (who
sleep together, with piled revolvers) by trying to escape my yells by
jumping off the jam-tins through the window. She only knocked the tins
down of course, and fell short in the wash-basin. Of late Mother has been
in the family way, with Thompson a very gallant midwife. Her four kittens
are David George (a tab), Gregori (a black), Haj Wahid (ginger),[4] and R.

1 Lawrence and his colleagues were bored with Hittite inscriptions because they were
  incomprehensible at that date.
2 In archaeology to take a squeeze is to make a cast of an inscription or relief by packing
  it with wet paper etc. — hence the usefulness of Hogarth's sponge — which subsequently
  hardens.
3 Top hamper: archaeologically useless overburden.
4 Named after Gregori, chief foreman, and Haj Wahid, expedition cook.

Campbell, a sort of Scots Grey. They make a ghastly noise in the Expeditionary bedroom half the night: I am a tolerable sleeper, but the others get up
two or three times each, and draw beads on each other with revolvers. The
sanitary arrangements are primitive, and the spring-water distressingly
medicinal: so in the various excursions necessary (3 for D.G.H. 2 for R.C.T.
and sometimes one for myself) one slides silently past the muzzles of the
pistols, and past the sleeping Gregori with a hammer and a pick laid at his
bed-side, and past Haj Wahid snoring beside his Martini;[1] then one may
slip behind the corner of the house, and so be under cover from the Zaptiehs[2]
and their rifles. Some day one of these deadly weapons will go off, and the
Expedition will be advertising a vacancy.

The next point should be the baths: but there really isn't much to enlarge
upon. Really being in the Euphrates valley makes a canvas bath seem so
futile, though D.G.H. conquered this feeling last Sunday and the Sunday
but one before. I had a bath one Saturday. Thompson is rather fair-skinned,
and shaves regularly, so he has them more often. The personnel is many-
sided. I don't think much of its cooking, and ornamentally it is a failure,
but it can make mustard, and black paint, and bookshelves, and cigarettes,
and salads, and once in a way a jest. It has planted a garden, and hopes for
onions and chrysanthemums, and sunflowers and cabbages. The chief of it
has evolved a jerry and a clothes-line, and what-not (this latter end is for
the conventions and your imagination): It eats rather a lot, but all exes. are
paid, and how else are five bottles of cascara and castor oil and croton not
to be a sheer waste. Also it enjoys everything except the alarums and
excursions of the nights, and the getting up at sunrise: and it is in very
excellent health.

Will you assure Mrs. Poole[3] of this? (I mean the last phrase only ...
don't enter into details....) If we had some printing paper I would send
her some photographs of a Fellow and Demy of Magdalen[4] in difficult
situations.

[...]

Bodleian Reserve

1 Martini: the Martini-Henri, a breech-loading rifle.
2 Zaptieh: Turkish gendarme.
3 The wife of Lawrence's Oxford tutor R. L. Poole.
4 i.e. Hogarth and Lawrence.

HIS MOTHER
March 31 1911   Jerablus

[...] Today we are moving great stones: the remains of walls & houses are buried about $\frac{2}{3}$ of their height in fairly clean earth, but the upper few feet are filled up with rubble, and small rocks, with the ashlar masonry and concrete of the late Roman town. Whenever we break fresh ground dozens of these huge blocks have to be moved. Some of them weigh tons, and we have no blasting powder or stone-hammers with us. As a result they have to be hauled, prehistoric fashion, by brute force of men on ropes, helped to a small extent by crowbars. At this moment something over 60 men are tugging away above, each man yelling Yallah as he pulls: the row is tremendous, but the stones usually come away. Two men out of three presume to direct operations, and no one listens to any of them, they just obey Gregori's orders, and their shouting is only to employ their spare breath. Now they are raising the 'talul', the curiously vibrant, resonant wail of the Bedawi. It is a very penetrating, and very distinct cry; you feel in it some kinship with desert-life, with ghazzus[1] and camel-stampedes. (Meanwhile the stone has slipped & fallen back into the trench, and Gregori's Turkish is deserting him). Whenever he is excited he slips back into Greek in a high falsetto voice, that convulses our hoarse-throated men. [...]

My faculty of making & repairing things has recently demonstrated how to make paint (black & red) for marking antiques, how to render light-tight a dark slide, how to make a camera-obscura, how to re-worm a screw (difficult this without a die), how to refit a plane-table, and replace winding mechanism on a paraffin lamp. Also I have devised a derrick, and a complicated system of human-power jacks (out of poplar poles, & rope, and Arabs) which have succeeded in setting an Ishtar[2] on her legs again. The Romans or Assyrians had broken her off at the knees, and the men could not shift the slabs back again, with any delicacy: so Mr. Hogarth & myself set to, and with our brains, & the aid of 90 men, put all right again. Before this there had been 120 men playing about with the ropes quite ineffectually. [...]

DG/HL

1 Tribal raids.
2 Ishtar: goddess of love and fertility worshipped in Syria and Palestine, equivalent to the Greek Aphrodite.

HIS MOTHER
11 April 1911   Jerablus

[...] [Richards has been a little remiss in the business line I expect: of course he has no time to spare for it, with all the interest of type designing, and the annoyance of his schoolwork. I do not think a lease of less than 20 years would be sufficient: my own wishes would be at 30 or 40 to be altogether on the safe side. But I fear very much we will never get it done: in which case I fear my opportunities of doing something good that will count will be very small: at least I am not going to put all my energies into rubbish like writing history, or becoming an archaeologist. I would much rather write a novel even, or become a newspaper correspondent:—however there is still hope that Richards may pull the thing through: I am doing nothing to help out here, while he is going straight ahead through twice as much mess as we have any conception of, with no side interest whatever. There is something really great—and fine—about the man. One feels so selfish enjoying oneself out here when one might be in the fight. It is no laughing matter to be working against the 20th century.]

[...] Poor Father! his sons are not going to support his years by the gain of their professions & trades. One a missionary: one an artist of sorts and a wanderer after sensations; one thinking of lay education work: one in the army, & one too small to think.[1] None of us can ever afford to keep a wife: still the product of fairly healthy brains & tolerable bodies will not be all worthless in this world. One of us must surely get something of the unattainable we are all feeling after. That's a comfort: and we are all going for the same thing under different shapes: Do you know we illustrate the verse about heart, soul, mind, body? Will Arnie prove the strength that will make it all perfect & effective?

Frank's toes can (like other candidates) be operated on. Consult Dr. Gibson[2] if you do anyone. He knows the dodges of the red-tape fence. But let him in any case try for the Scholarship unless Mr. Cave[3] says it is not worth the continued preparation. The ordinary route into the Army is less pleasant than by Oxford & the O.T.C.[4]

Glad you sent Miss Holmes her cheque. She is doing a hard work, under great handicaps. If Will wants a little preliminary breathing time he might do far worse than try his hand at her boys' school. There is such need in Syria for taste, as well as good will. [Those lubberly vulgarians in the American College are undoing with both hands the good the Jesuits of Beyrout are trying to do, and all with the best intentions in the world. The

1 i.e. Bob, himself, Will, Frank, Arnold.
2 The family doctor.
3 A. W. Cave, Headmaster of the Oxford High School 1888–1925.
4 Officers' Training Corps.

result will be a sort of 'babu'[1] (ask Menon what that is)[2] if they are not checked by better example and better sympathy with the people. Dr. Bliss the President of the College is almost the only one of the Foreign Colony who seems to act on this idea: and he is almost single-handed, with a horrible Yankee staff to fight against. Not that there is any friction.] [...]

Digging is tremendous fun, & most exciting & interesting. The results so far are not nearly enough to justify a second season (I'll write about them soon) but the thing is (as I have said perhaps) like Pandora's box, with Hope in the last spit of earth. I have had some good pottery lately.

Mr. Hogarth returns next week: he hopes to get to Oxford about mid-May, & shortly after will publish interim report in *The Times*. I'll ask him to let you know when. He has been most exceedingly good to me all through: taught me a tremendous lot about everything from digging to Greek erotic verse: He'll help in my Meleager:[3] whom he enjoys also. [Worms & Euphrates fish (closely allied) to all.]

N

[...]

HL/Bodleian Reserve

HIS MOTHER
April 29 1911   Carchemish

[...] The most pleasing part of the day is when the breakfast hour gets near: from all the villages below us on the plain there come long lines of red and blue women & children, carrying bread in red-check handkerchiefs, and wooden measures full of leben[4] on their heads. The men are not tired then, and the heat is just pleasant, and they chatter about and jest & sing in very delightful style. A few of them bring shepherd's pipes, and make music of their sort. As a rule, they are not talkative: they will sit for minutes together at the house-door without a word: often coming out in the morning we have found 100 men grouped outside, wanting work, and have not heard a sound through the open window just above! The only time they get talkative is when they are about half-a-mile apart. A little companionable chat across Euphrates is a joy — except to one's ears near by, for sound

1 A term used for an Indian clerk writing in English, with only a superficial knowledge of the language.
2 An Indian student friend of his brother Will.
3 Meleager of Gadara, Greek poet of the late 2nd–early 1st century BC. His anthology of epigrams, *The Garland*, provided the core of the *Greek Anthology*.
4 Coagulated sour milk, a staple Arab drink.

carries tremendously in this region, and they bawl with their raucous voices. However not even Sheisho and Berkawi, two Kurd brothers, and the last in our employ, can talk over the noise of the flood at present: the other men gave up trying some days ago, and so the valley is at peace.

[...] Some of the workmen are rather fine-looking fellows: all of course are thin as sticks: and the majority small: there was no one within an inch of Mr. Hogarth's height: indeed the majority are hardly more than mine. Many shave their heads, others let their hair grow in long plaits, like Hittites. Today, Saturday, is pay day, and we knock off at 4, instead of 5, to give us time to get them paid. Each man, or nearly each man, gets an extra every week, according to the value of his finds. This little gamble appeals to them immensely.

[...]

HL/Bodleian Reserve

HIS MOTHER
23 May 1911   Carchemish

[...] Miss Gertrude Bell[1] called last Sunday, & we showed her all our finds, and she told us all hers. We parted with mutual expressions of esteem: but she told Thompson his ideas of digging were prehistoric: and so we had to squash her with a display of erudition. She was taken (in 5 minutes) over Byzantine, Crusader, Roman, Hittite, & French architecture (my part) and over Greek folk-lore, Assyrian architecture, & Mesopotamian Ethnology (by Thompson); Prehistoric pottery & telephoto lenses, Bronze Age metal technique, Meredith, Anatole France and the Octobrists (by me): the Young Turk movement, the construct state in Arabic, the price of riding camels, Assyrian burial-customs, and German methods of excavation with the Baghdad railway (by Thompson). This was a kind of hors d'œuvre: and when it was over (she was getting more respectful) we settled down each to seven or eight subjects & questioned her upon them. She was quite glad to have tea after an hour and a half, & on going told Thompson that he

1 Gertrude Bell (1868–1926): traveller, writer, archaeologist, mountaineer. She was already well known — and known to Lawrence — through such books as *The Desert and the Sown* (1907), an account of her journey into the Syrian interior. She was the first woman to reach the required standard for a first-class degree in History at Oxford (she had achieved this in 1888, the year of Lawrence's birth), but was not thereby entitled to a degree as no woman could be a member of the University. During the 1914–18 war she was a leading figure in military and political circles in Egypt and Mesopotamia. Afterwards she served first with the military administration and then with the Government of Iraq under the British Mandate.

had done wonders in his digging in the time, and that she thought *we* had got everything out of the place that could possibly have been got: she particularly admired the completeness of our note-books.

So we did for her. She was really too captious at first, coming straight from the German diggings at Kala'at Shirgat, where they lay down gravel paths, wherever they want to prove an ancient floor, & where they pile up their loose stones into walls of palaces. Our digs are I hope more accurate, if less perfect. They involve no 'reconstruction', which ruin all these Teutons. So we showed her that, & left her limp, but impressed. She is pleasant: about 36,[1] not beautiful, (except with a veil on, perhaps). It would have been most annoying if she had denounced our methods in print. I don't think she will.

[...]

DG/HL

D. G. HOGARTH[2]
June 8 [1911]   Carchemish

Your letters to Thompson & myself just come: very many thanks on account of the photographic notes: though I packed 16 of my films undeveloped: they may have become lost somehow. Will you send a list of the $\frac{1}{2}$ plate negatives, so that I may know what to take again?

Another matter. Thompson was calculating for another ten days here, and so I have taken 60 photos these last two weeks: all the pottery & small objects: except fragments of inscription & some reliefs. There are only about 4 dozen plates left, and subjects for most of these were booked.

I will have to revise most of these photographs now, for every day we find new things: I will use up the ones I have taken in developing (many thanks for the chemicals, they are admirable) and so will get at the right length of exposure. The results will thus be better: but I will want at least 3, and better 4, dozen of Wratten-Wainwright $\frac{1}{2}$ plates, as last times' [*sic*]. The Binocular camera has plenty still, for there has been little to do with

1 She was 43.
2 David George Hogarth (1862–1927) was the most important of Lawrence's Oxford mentors. Educated at Winchester and Magdalen College, Oxford (of which he became a Fellow), he explored Asia Minor 1887–94, was Director of the British School at Athens 1897–1900, became Keeper of the Ashmolean Museum in 1909 (holding the post until his death) and was appointed President of the Royal Geographical Society in 1925. He was also to be closely associated with Lawrence in the Middle East during the war.

it of late,[1] since I put in most of the day up here at the house, mending pottery, and photographing things. I have plenty of my own films now, for the prolongation of the diggings will take from me all chance of much castle-hunting this season. Small objects I have to take indoors of course. These great winds blow every day & every night, and in the open air a carefully arranged sheet of beads or whorls is sent rolling to the four airts [sic]. Even large pots tumble about.

[...]

The heat is not bad, and cannot be, as long as the winds stay cool: the idea of digging on is glorious, for there is really hope of several parts of the digs. That is Thompson's department tho! He is not quite at ease in all points: his bi-weekly letters depress him vastly: I expect that affair is not likely to survive this new shock of separation: and he is rather cut up about it,[2] though very determined that digs are better: is eating more than ever: swears that in hot weather one must constrain oneself to eat plenty of meat: we were provident not to throw away the covering stone of the last champagne grave on the mound.

[...] There does not seem to have been any Arab occupation of the site of any importance: but a long Byzantine one, following closely on the Roman, and coming down after 1000 AD. The remains of streets etc. belong to this last period. I don't think the Roman-Hellenist was much of a place.

Has Thompson told you that the arm & shoulder are the ones that fit? I have got 9 fragments all told on the block, which is nearly all there except the head of the back man. No other scrap of the great head has turned up: but it must be somewhere about: if we had a piece of body I think it would go on to the greaved legs.

The two basalt reliefs (the monstrous lion, double-headed, and the slab of bull-legged & lion headed people fighting) in the wall-line trench are the best we have found on the site: first-class work, as different as day from night compared with the chariots.

Those despised horses (180 now in my stable) are proving interesting: and fellow with them are some little humans of the style of the ruder, high-nosed bronzes, and a number of *females* grasping their breasts. They are all Hittite, I fancy, but what they are all doing I don't know.

[...]

Bodleian Reserve

1 Lawrence's 'binocular camera' has attracted the interest of those who support the supposition that he was involved in espionage at this time; he was however already using a telephoto lens during his travels as an undergraduate in France.
2 Thompson married following this first season at Carchemish and did not return.

HIS MOTHER
June 18 1911   Carchemish

[...] Our people are very curious and very simple, and yet with a fund of directness and child-humour about them that is very fine. I see much of this, for I sleep on the mound and start the work every day at sunrise, and the choosing of new men so falls to my lot. I take great care in the selection, utterly refusing all such as are solemn or over-polite, and yet we are continually bothered by blood feuds, by getting into the same trench men who have killed other's kin or run off with their wives. They at once prepare to settle up the score in kind, and we have to come down amid great shouting, and send one to another pit. There is no desire to kill, and public opinion does not insist on vengeance, if there is 50 feet of earth between the offender and the offended.
    [...]

HL

HIS MOTHER
June 24 1911   Carchemish

[...] The donkey boy mentioned above (Dahoum)[1] is an interesting character: he can read a few words (the only man in the district except the liquorice-king) of Arabic, and altogether has more intelligence than the rank & file. He talks of going into Aleppo to school with the money he has made out of us. I will try & keep an eye on him, to see what happens. He would be better in the country, only for the hideous grind of the continual forced labour, and the low level of the village minds. Fortunately there is no foreign influence as yet in the district: if only you had seen the ruination caused by the French influence, & to a lesser degree by the

1 Lawrence's friendship with Dahoum (whose real name was Ahmed) was to be an important one. In a footnote to Lawrence's 1911 *Diary of a Journey across the Euphrates* (included in *Oriental Assembly*) A. W. Lawrence wrote of him: 'It is believed that his personality supplied the largest element to the figure of S.A., to whom the *Seven Pillars of Wisdom* is dedicated.' He went on to quote, however, 'a Note of the Author's', i.e. of T.E.L.'s, to the effect that S.A. was 'An imaginary person of neutral sex'. By contrast when talking to Liddell Hart (*LHB*, p. 143) Lawrence stated that 'S. and A. were two different things, "S" a village in Syria, or property in it, and "A" personal.' Granted that Lawrence was not prone to simple straightforward answers and liked to keep his own counsel it seems likely that Dahoum was the 'personal', and probably the dominant, part of this equation. See also Lawrence's letters to G. J. Kidston dated 14 November 1919 (p. 168) and to R. A. M. Guy dated 25 December 1923 (p. 253).

American, you would never wish it extended. The perfectly hopeless vulgarity of the half-Europeanised Arab is appalling. Better a thousand times the Arab untouched. The foreigners come out here always to teach, whereas they had much better learn, for in everything but wits and know-ledge the Arab is generally the better man of the two.

I am not living in a tent: it is much too hot for that. I am only sleeping on the top of the mound. The river is swift, but quite pleasant for bathing: I have been in a few times: but at present it is not really warm (c. 90°). There are mosquitoes here about the house in plenty: on the top of the mound never, for the wind drives them off. I have written to the Canon.[1]
[...]

HL/Bodleian Reserve

MISS FAREEDAH EL AKLE[2]
June 26 [1911]   Carchemish

I think Mrs. Rieder[3] has the big [text unclear] with her: she said, in a very charming little letter she sent me, that you were extremely annoyed with me: your excuse for this most unchristian change of temper was that I had not written to you:

Now
I have twice tried to write to you in Arabic, and each time got as far as the serious part: then I was interrupted. One letter got six lines long, then waited about for weeks, and finally evanished. I am really most extremely sorry for having failed in my promise, if it was a promise, but at present we work 19 hours a day, in the open air mostly, & when we do get to the evening, we are too bothered to do more than write the perfunctory English scribble. I have read no Arabic since our first few weeks here, except your letters, & the last one took me about an hour!

Now
I didn't write to you in English, because you said in a letter of yours (in Arabic & English) that you didn't want a reply: and I always believe what some people say: you and Miss Holmes for some of them. Mrs. Rieder is

1 Canon Christopher of St Aldate's Church, Oxford.
2 A Christian Syrian schoolmistress who taught from 1911–14 in the American Mission School in Jebail and numbered Lawrence among her favourite pupils. Born in 1882 she was corresponding with Dr Mack about Lawrence in the late 1960s.
3 See next letter.

not that sort. So when you said you didn't want an answer, I supposed you didn't want an answer, and now Mrs. Rieder calls me names! It isn't fair of her at all. Do you know that in England we used to call you the fair sex? Are you horribly ashamed of yourself yet?

Now
I have written almost entirely to Miss Holmes, but my letters have been no more for her than for Noël:[1] they are like my letters home, general affairs, with a dig in the ribs here, and a pin-prick there. (I am talking of my brothers now: Miss Holmes' letters have not been blistering.) I wrote once to Mrs. Rieder in French, which I suppose you wouldn't much admire: at any rate she didn't. She said it wasn't French, but was very like me. If you can find out ask her what I am like.

Will you please tell Miss Aseem that I prostrate myself before her overcome by the affluence of her beneficence? That I wish her all the medicines in the world, and the fun of taking them? In fact I send my kind regards.

Now then, are apologies enough? Wouldn't you really be annoyed if you got a letter that did nothing else? It would be like a mutton chop that was all chop and no mutton.[...]

I have some thoughts of coming back to this district for the winter. Thompson & I may buy the site we are digging: it's about as big as Jebail, and the Baghdad railway will cross the river from it, and it's going for £33 — and make it a harbour of refuge for the district. There are a particularly villainous set of effendis about here, and we don't want our donkey boys flayed alive, and our workmen plundered while we are away.

It would be rather fun living alone in one of the villages: they are all mud-built you know, and quite pleasant. And the Arabic is such amusing stuff. If I could talk it like Dahoum (by the way what does the name Dahoum mean?)[2] you would never be tired of listening to me. I would say aitchfa for enough and bartchir for tomorrow: and lots more like that.

[...] Salaams to Miss Holmes, who will get a letter soon. I will be in Aleppo, returning to you, in six weeks from date. Nothing new found.

L.

Bodleian Reserve

1 Mrs Rieder's six-year-old son.
2 'Dahoum' means 'the dark one'. According to Leonard Woolley's *Dead Towns and Living Man* (1920) Dahoum's mother stated that he was very black at birth.

MRS RIEDER[1]
July 4 [1911]   Carchemish

[...] I have had quite a success with our donkey-boy,[2] who really is getting a glimmering of what a brain-storm is. He is beginning to use his reason as well as his instinct: He taught himself to read a little, so I had very exceptional material to work on but I made him read & write more than he ever did before. You know you cannot do much with a piece of stick & a scrap of dusty ground as materials. I am going to ask Miss Fareedah for a few simple books, amusing, for him to begin on. Remember he is to be left a Moslem. If you meet a man worth anything you might be good enough to remember this? A boy of 15 ... I would be vastly obliged.
    [...]

DG

MRS RIEDER
Am August 11, 1911[3]   Hotel Deutscher Hof Beirut

[...] What I wanted for the donkey boy was a history book or a geography which should be readable and yet Arab. I cannot give him such productions as those Miss Holmes uses, since nothing with a taste of 'Frangi'[4] shall enter Jerablus by my means. I have no wish to do more for the boy than give him a chance to help himself: 'education' I have had so much of, & it is such rot: saving your presence! The only stuff worth having is what you work out yourself. With which last heresy please be content a while. I will (probably ...) write from England.
                          Yours sincerely
                          T. E. Lawrence
    [...]

DG

Shortly after returning to Carchemish for his second season Lawrence, on the recommendation of Hogarth, spent some weeks in Egypt working under Flinders Petrie.

1 Mrs Rieder (or more strictly Mme André Rieder — she had married a Frenchman) taught languages at the American School at Jebail.
2 i.e. Dahoum.
3 Presumably Lawrence put the date in German because of the profession of the recipient and his current address.
4 Frangi, a corruption of 'Frankish', hence European.

MRS RIEDER
[Postmark 23.1.12]   Kafr Ammar
                        (which is 40 miles S. of Cairo, on the desert)

[...] No one but I would have achieved a letter at all from a Petrie dig.[1] A Petrie dig is a thing with a flavour of its own: tinned kidneys mingle with mummy-corpses and amulets in the soup: my bed is all gritty with prehistoric alabaster jars of unique types—and my feet at night keep the bread-box from the rats. For ten mornings in succession I have seen the sun rise as I breakfasted, and we come home at nightfall after lunching at the bottom of a 50 foot shaft, to draw pottery silhouettes or string bead-necklaces. In fact if I hadn't malaria to-day I could make a pretty story of it all: — only then I wouldn't have time. To begin with the Professor is the great man of the camp — He's about 5' 11" high, white haired, grey bearded, broad and active, with a voice that splits when excited, and a constant feverish speed of speech: he is a man of ideas and systems, from the right way to dig a temple to the only way to clean one's teeth. Also he only is right in all things: all his subs. have to take his number of sugar lumps in their tea, his species of jam with potted tongue, or be dismissed as official bound unprogressists. Further he is easy-tempered, full of humour, and fickle to a degree that makes him delightfully quaint, and a constant source of joy and amusement in his camp. [...]

About the digging: 'we' have stumbled on what is probably the richest and largest prehistoric cemetery in Egypt, and in our first week have dug out about 100 graves: these contain wooden coffins and bedsteads, boxes of alabaster jars, dozens of pots of new and known types, some little ivory, (spoons and gaming pieces and scraps of caskets) a good many bronze implements, axes, adzes, chisels, and other trifles. Also a good many baskets, and the shrouds and cloths in which the bodies were wrapped. We have found very few flints, and those not of the best, since the bronze was in general use. The graves are usually about 5 feet deep, and as all the soil is pure sand, digging is merely child's play. Owing to a hitch in his arrangements the Professor has all his workmen here, and so twice as many graves are found than we can record properly: with plenty of time it would be delightful, whereas now we are swamped with the multitude. We have about 900 pots (complete; — all broken ones are thrown away) about 120 alabasters, and a matter of twenty bedsteads. Also we have preserved a number of bodies

---

1 Flinders, later Sir Flinders Petrie (1853–1942), was an eminent British Egyptologist who carried out many important excavations in Egypt from 1884 onwards and held the Edwards Professorship of Egyptology at University College, London, from 1892–1933. He also excavated in Palestine and was the author of many books, both scholarly and popular, based on his work.

and skeletons complete by soaking them with boiling paraffin wax. These will go to Museums. [...]

DG

JAMES ELROY FLECKER[1]
Feb. 18 [1912][2]   Aleppo

Am still here! Of course when I got to Aleppo I found that the B.M.[3] idiots had sent me orders to buy the site and build the house, and had forgotten to provide the funds. Result, as I arrived with 16 piastres in my pocket, was a visit to Mr. Fontana,[4] and a borrowing of £10. With this I have scoured all Aleppo, buying Hittite seals. Huge sport! However, first of all, I went to Damascus, called on Devey at 10 a.m. and delivered the fish. He was overwhelmed with his sense of obligation to you, and turned out in pyjamas to tell me so. So our interview was short. Cavass, far-seeing man, turned up at the station to see me off. That's all for Damascus, except that I bought my 'lira' cylinder (Hitt.) for 10 frs. and had a little one (also Hitt.) thrown in. Good buying, and good objects.

Next — about things here. Fontana up to the ears in Greek anthology: Erotica of course: has spoken twice of your P.P. Cards of Italy. Have seen him four times. He received your salaams with the stomach of avidity and the bowel of satisfaction. What more could he do?

Have now over 20 Hittite seals: two of them superb Cappadocian-Hittite cylinders: love at first sight, but neither of them too dear. No bronzes, except one Hadad with a dealer, who will not descend below £4 Ottoman. This is causing me acute indigestion. Am sniffing at another glorious

1 James Elroy Flecker (1884–1915), poet and playwright. After reading Classics at Oxford he enrolled in the Levant Consular Service, spent two years studying Oriental Languages at Cambridge and then took up his first consular appointment in Constantinople in 1910. He and Lawrence met when he was in what was to be his second and final post, that of Vice-Consul at Beirut. His prime ambition always was to write and by this time he had already contributed to *Georgian Poetry*, published two volumes of verse and begun the play which was eventually to emerge as *Hassan* (see Lawrence's letter to his widow about the first London production of the play, dated 5 November 1923). He was, however, dogged by ill-health; he left the Middle East in 1913 and died of incurable tuberculosis two years later.
2 This letter, dated only 'Feb. 18' by Lawrence, is assigned to 1914 in the documentation of the Houghton Library at Harvard. However, Flecker was no longer in Beirut in 1914, in February 1913 Lawrence was in Sinai and comparison with other letters shows clearly that it dates from 1912.
3 B.M.: British Museum.
4 R. A. Fontana was the British Consul in Aleppo.

Cappadoc-Hitt. cylinder, aspersing its rarity: have been doing this for a week with a 50% effect so far: if the funds hold off much longer, I'll be begged to take it 'belash'.[1] On the whole, to buy antikas is sport, not commerce, and does no violence to one's sense of the instinctive glories of nature and the arts: — though that does not palliate the nature of the weather here, which is brumeginously [sic] humid.

There is a most beautiful Muristan[2] here, and I have reserved (by appointment) the most eligible-windowed room therein, for my retreat, when I shall have spent the tenth pound, and acquired the last thing Hittite in Aleppo. I look forward to closing there the evening of my days in dignity and retirement. Please tell D. G. Hogarth or C. L. Woolley[3] where they may find me, when they come to Aleppo next: Muristan el Wazir, top floor right on the staircase in the gate, Suk-es-Stamboul, Haleb. Letters care of Fontana. Woolley thinks he knew your son at Oxford, and that you may be useful: wherefore be warned, and don't lean towards altruism. Expect him about March 5, and warn him, if he goes to Jerablus, that he will find no roof to his head. I reserve for him the room beneath mine in my Muristan — and we can accommodate D. G. Hogarth at a pinch. In Albayiehs, with our narghilehs,[4] we will posture the wise men of Gotham.

Aleppo is all compact of colour, and sense of line: you inhale Orient in lungloads, and glut your appetite with silks and dyed fantasies of clothes. Today there came in through the busiest vault in the bazaar a long caravan of 100 mules of Baghdad, marching in line rhythmically to the boom of two huge iron bells swinging under the belly of the foremost. Bells nearly two feet high, with wooden clappers, introducing 100 mule-loads of the woven shawls and wine-coloured carpets of Bokhara! such wealth is intoxicating: and intoxicated I went and bought the bells. 'You hear them', said the mukari, 'a half-hour before the sight.' And I marched in triumph home,

---

1 'Belash': for nothing.
2 Or, more correctly 'Maristan', a Turkish word from the Persian used in Syria and Egypt for a mental hospital.
3 Leonard, later Sir Leonard Woolley (1880–1960), was in charge of the Carchemish dig from 1912–14. He was with Lawrence in the 1914 Sinai survey and served with him in Middle Eastern Intelligence during the war, though he spent the last two years of the war as a prisoner in Turkey. He later became well known for his excavations at Ur and for his books about his archaeological activities, e.g. Ur of the Chaldees and Digging up the Past.
4 narghile: oriental tobacco-pipe, hookah.

making the sound of a caravan from Baghdad: 'Oah, Oah', and the crowd
parted in the ways before me. Why are you staying in Beyrout? Come up!'[1]
                                                                    .L.

University of Harvard

HIS MOTHER
April 6, 1912   Carchemish

[...] The Germans are very friendly now, for we are allowing them to
clear away our dump-heaps of last year and this year free of charge. As we
want to dig under them in the near future we are doing ourselves a good
turn as well. The railway is too far away to disturb us.

    As for money, I have lots: about £40: in hand: or to be in hand shortly,
when Mr. Hogarth pays me for our seals. We have a very splendid
collection.

    Woolley gets on most excellently here. He is fresh enough from Egypt
to see the glory of the country and the people and the customs: I don't
think he will ever settle down in Egypt again. The men are as good this
year as last: splendid humorists: Bedouin for ever!
[...]
                                                                     N.

HL

A. W. LAWRENCE[2]
July 21, 1912

Ancient beast
    It is about a year since we wrote letters to one another: suppose we do
it again? It doesn't cost anything but time, and of time, do you know, I
have mints just now. This is the first time for years and years that I have
been able to sit down and think, and it is so precious a discovery: and one
that so many people want to take from you.
    [...]
    I have turned school-master, O tumult, and taught up to 11 times table

---

1 See Lawrence's *Note on Flecker* published in *Men in Print*, edited by A. W. Lawrence,
  (Golden Cockerel Press, 1940): 'This strange gawky figure [i.e. Flecker] felt the banishment
  of hot Beyrout, the steamy harbour, the formal consulate, the slow sourness of boiled
  cabbage which smelled through the hotel.' This final paragraph is written much in the
  known style of his correspondent, with whom Lawrence had discussed, *inter alia*, the
  revising of *Hassan*.
2 For a biographical note on A. W. Lawrence see p. 372.

a class whose average age was about seventeen. Then the house became a hospital, and I put an end to the local education authority. It was sad for they did so want to learn twelve times: It was a very wonderful school: everybody who got a table right got a lump of sugar each time. We finished two large tins! I took a class of four (including our Commissaire) in local history (special subject) and had the mollah of the district to listen to my lecture on geography. They can't make out why, if the world is really round, the people on the other side don't fall off. All this is stopped now and the head-master is reduced to writing nonsense to a worm.

[...] Have just been interrupted by a spider as big as a whale's nebula: bottled him in whiskey for you: such hooked teeth and toes: I took him for a crab when he knocked at the door and said 'come in'. Such a fright: Salaams to the world.

N.

DG

HIS MOTHER
22 Feb. 1913   Carchemish

[...] [M]y canoe has been 3 weeks in Beyrout, waiting till our agent there can find a spare moment to put it on the train for Aleppo,[1] and I have bought 6 carpets, two 16 feet long, and am short of money therefore ... and I don't know if we will dig or not this spring, and so I don't know if I will come back or not this summer....[...]

[At Aleppo I stayed five days more than I need, entertaining two naval officers who became partners in my iniquity of gun-running in Beyrout. The consular need of rifles involved myself, the Consul-General in Beyrout, Flecker, the Admiral at Malta, our Ambassador in Stamboul, two captains, and two lieutenants, besides innumerable cavasses,[2] in one common law-breaking. However Fontana got his stuff, and as he was too ill to entertain the porters, I had to trot them over Aleppo. And we did trot over it all, all day & all night, and out to Jerablus en prince, and back laded [?laden] with Babylonian gems, and Greek coins, & Roman bronzes, and Persian carpets and Arab pottery ... all going to a warship, a modern engine of

---

1 Lawrence had imported a canoe, equipped with an outboard motor, made by Salter's of Oxford, for use on the Euphrates.
2 Cavasses combined the functions of watchmen, messengers and orderlies at embassies and consulates.

efficiency and destruction ... what will their Captain say to their stuffed bags?][1]

Now all is peace, and I have been wandering up and down: ... forming a very beautiful collection of Hittite seals ... small but very select, and with some nice pieces of Roman bronze and glazed pottery as sidelines ... also I am in treaty for other carpets in the villages. Meanwhile I am making all day tarpaulin for our roofs, which leak, and repairing the house, and white-washing, and getting all into trim for a season in a week's time ... and perhaps all quite needlessly!

Salaams to Worm from the men here ... they rejoice in his socks, and all wear them themselves ostentatiously.

L.

HL/Bodleian Reserve

D. G. HOGARTH
End of February [1913]   Carchemish

I am getting garrulous, but no matter ... the Ottoman post will correct these faults: and besides I have got more seals, which I packed this evening to send to you: it is a pleasure to pack seals, even when there is no post in view ... and these are very nice seals: at least one is a beauty: button-like (feu bulla-bead), red stone, with characters incised ... not big, or sharp, or well cut, but you cannot have everything for your money as a rule.... I cannot even get one of your copper-plate posters from the greedy Leeds — though the number of seals presented by me, through forgetfulness to claim the purchase money, is legion —

Seriously, this last half-dozen, bought by me on the fringe of Abu Galgal, is very good. I rushed back, and have not been down again, because some villains began a dig at Deve Huyuk ... a Hittite cemetery of the last period, with Roman shaft tombs in between. The Hittite graves were full of great bronze spears and axes and swords, that the wretches have broken up and thrown away, because Madame Koch,[2] who is doing the dig, didn't buy such things. I got some good fibulae, which are yours, and not Kenyon's this time at all events ... (18 miles away) much better than the B.M. ones,

---

1 The reason for Lawrence's gun-running (his account of which was omitted from *HL*) was that R. A. Fontana, the Consul in Aleppo, feared that Aleppo might shortly be under attack from dissident Kurdish tribesmen, in which eventuality the Consulate might need means of self-defence. The naval vessel involved was H.M.S. *Medea*.

2 Madame Koch was an antiquities dealer — arguably not the most respectable member of her trade — in Aleppo.

some bracelets & ear-rings of bronze, a curious pot or two ... and as a sideline, some Roman glazed bottles, with associated Greek pottery, and a pleasant little lot of miscellanea ... tomorrow I return there to gather up, I hope, Hittite bronze weapons in sheaves: — unless the police get there first. It is exciting digging: — a plunge down a shaft at night, the smashing of a stone door, and the hasty shovelling of all objects into a bag by lamp-light. One has to pay tolerably highly for glazed pottery, so I will probably buy no more ... glass is found, but very dear ... bronze is thought nothing of....

I found our house filthy with leaking roofs, and have been lighting great fires in all rooms, and rebuilding fallen walls, and whitewashing, and making tarpaulins to mend roofs. You have no idea (unless you too have tried) how hard it is to make three large tarpaulins from one tin of tar and one tin of pitch.

[...]

Salaam Dr. Cowley[1] from me: no time for Aramaic yet.

L.

Ashmolean Museum Oxford

D. G. HOGARTH
June 14 [1913]   Carchemish

I wrote to Leeds this afternoon, and thought it enough, but perhaps I'd better write to you as well. We got your letter of joy upon the sculptures of the wall of animals and the King's gate. They are splendid, aren't they. For the photographs are very unsatisfactory so far as making them pretty goes. The carving on the captains is very soft, and delicate. The king & queen are not so good, from my point of view ... a little hard: the children are ugly, but very well done. The slab of dancers, for an archaic piece is also very fine: and there is probably quite a good lot more to find thereabouts.

[...]

I'm sorry you didn't like my last lot of seals, those from Marcopoli. Leeds says they arrived without documentation, but I expect that has been set right. I am almost sure they are all genuine, and I thought them rather a nice set. After all three of them are inscribed spheroids, and the cylinder (dated, as it may be in a little) is far and away the best cut of that period that I have ever come across. I'm rather wild at having paid so much for

1 Of the Bodleian Library: see letter to him dated 29 October 1914.

them since they are not up to your mark: and you are short this year.
[...]
    I think I had better not buy anything else in Aleppo this season, unless
it is something quite necessary to you. In any case, putting the lot together,
you have got very good ones from me this year, though very dear also.
But when I do come across a very fine one, I feel so disinclined to let it go.
I'd much rather give it you half price?
    You recommend selectiveness in buying ... for a long time I have not
been buying $\frac{1}{4}$ of the seals offered to me: only if I thought they were very
good, or had something not quite regular in their shape or design.
    I expect to get back about mid-July, & may bring the Hoja[1] & Dahoum
with me: which will shock you!

                                                                    .L.

Bodleian Reserve

Lawrence duly brought his Arab friends Dahoum and Sheikh Hamoudi to
Oxford. For their impressions of England see his letter to his mother of
30 September 1913. They in their turn impressed Lawrence's friends, among
them C. F. Bell, who arranged for the artist Francis Dodd to paint a
portrait — or portraits — of Dahoum.

C. F. BELL[2]
12 Aug. 1913   2 Polstead Road Oxford

Dear Mr. Bell
    It's rather late, but I think I ought to scribble you a line to tell you of
today's happenings.[3] Dodd[4] turned up smiling in the morning, and got to
work like a steam engine: — black & white, with little faint lines of colour
running up and down in it. No 1 was finished by midday, and was splendid:
Dahoum sitting down, with his most-interested-possible expression ... he

1 The site foreman, Sheikh Hamoudi.
2 Charles Francis Bell (1871–1966) was Keeper of the Department of Fine Art at the
  Ashmolean 1909–31; he was also, like Hogarth, a Fellow of Magdalen College. He was
  a Trustee of the National Portrait Gallery 1910–40.
3 Bell had brought about the 'happenings' here described — the portraits of Dahoum as a
  present for Lawrence — but was on holiday in Florence when they took place.
4 Francis Dodd (1874–1949) had had an extensive artistic training in Glasgow, Paris and
  Italy and was becoming known as a portrait painter. He was later an official war artist,
  one of his notable achievements being a series of portraits of generals of the British Army.

thought it great sport — said he never knew he was so good-looking — and I think he was about right. He had dropped his sulkiness for a patch.

No 2 was almost a failure. Dodd gave it up half-finished.

No 3, standing, was glorious. My brother came to the door with some people, and Dahoum just at the critical moment looked round a little bit annoyed, to see what the dickens the matter was. Dodd got him on the instant, and promptly stopped work in the funk of hurting it. It is an absolute inspiration: no colour, 'cause it was perfect as it was, unfinished.

I raved over it, and Dodd therefore gave No 1 to Dahoum, who in some unknown way had asked him for one of them. I left No 3 — the best, most pleasing though not the most 'pleasant' — with Dodd, to be sent you. Really it's worth looking at.

Dahoum is taking his out to Carchemish to show his people. I think I shall steal it later, since he says with them it will be only a nine-days wonder, and then done with. It's a most splendid thing: — though not so entirely the boy as No 3. Behold there isn't any room left for you![1] Which is a blessing, since I am not good at thanking people politely. It really was most awfully good of you: you got the right man absolutely, and the results are joyful.... How in the world did you ever dream of getting it done.

Good-night!
T.E.L.

British Library

HIS MOTHER
30 September 1913   Baron's Hotel Aleppo

[...] You are obviously interested to hear what the Arabs think of England. Unfortunately they are too intelligent to be ridiculous about it. They describe it as a garden, empty of villages, with the people crowded into frequent towns. The towns wonderfully peaceful and populous, the houses very high: the tube railways are to them a source of stumbling. They tell the villagers that Syria is a small poor country, very likely to be coveted by us tree-lovers ... and that the Arabs are too few to count in world-politics. All of this is very proper. They also estimate the value and quality of the food they ate in England:... and feel relieved at their discovery of the true end of the collecting of antiquities. Concerning ourselves, they praise Will and Arnie ... Mr. Bell and Sir Arthur Evans:[2] in this order.

1 i.e. on the page of notepaper.
2 Sir Arthur Evans (1851–1941), British archaeologist, famous particularly for his excavations in Crete, but also well known in archaeological circles for his reorganisation of the Ashmolean Museum, Oxford, of which he was Keeper 1884–96, making it into the finest museum in England outside national collections.

They were very pleased to see Will[1] again in Jerabîs.[2] Both went with him to Busrawi's camp.

[...]

HL

C. F. BELL
Dec. 10 1913   Carchemish

I think you would laugh till your 'dome-like stomach' cracked, if you could see us now. Woolley is sitting at a table, dressed in white flannel, not spotless, writing to Basil Blackwell[3] with a photograph of Dahoum propped up against the inkpot to console and inspire him: and I am sitting as close as I can to a fire of olive logs in the fireplace, dressed entirely in black and white with a cloth of gold cloak, writing to you, with a squeeze of a Hittite inscription to inspire *me*. Our room is about 30 feet long, and so between us there is about twenty five feet of very rough mosaic, starred with carpets: one would think we had had a row: but it is only because each of us is so dazzlingly lovely that we put one another out.

I got a letter from you a day or two ago, in which you had survived the little saddle-bag pieces of rug that Dahoum sent you. I am glad you don't object to them over much: and told him so: for really I was afraid that your prolonged silence was due to your difficulty in digesting such hairy morsels.[4] All is well apparently. What is a Zoilist?[5]

I wrote to you a few days or weeks back, I fancy, which should absolve me the need of writing this time: but it seems it doesn't.

You jeer at our quantities of rugs — but we have not enough even to cover the nakedness of this floor: we have to eke them out with goat-hair tent-cloth.

Digs are finished: we spent two days in Kurd country looking at Hittite monuments, and shivering with cold: and tomorrow we go down to Aleppo to look round about for things Hittite for Hogarth. We have not

---

1 Will Lawrence was staying for a time with his brother, before going on to India to take up a teaching post.
2 i.e. Jerablus: Lawrence was using the Arabic form.
3 Woolley had been a devoted friend of Basil, later Sir Basil Blackwell, son and successor of the founder of Blackwell's bookshops, Oxford, when the latter was a Postmaster (Scholar) at Merton College.
4 Far from merely tolerating the 'pieces of rug' sent to him by Dahoum as a present, Bell thought them 'very pretty' and made them into floor cushions which he greatly prized.
5 A zoilist is a malignant or censorious critic; from Zoilus, the grammarian and critic of Homer.

got the remotest little thing as a present (Xmas) to cheer him up. Please tell him that on Christmas Day I hope to dig Hamman, with Woolley: it will be great fun taking notes in a blizzard, for we have a real winter here.

A stupid letter: obviously a Hittite inscription is not a good inspiration: I'll take away the photo Woolley is gazing at, and send it to you as an appendix. It isn't good, since the drawing is in colour, and under glass: but it will do till I bring the original home: did I tell you that I bought it off Dahoum with a gun and a knife, with great difficulty? He likes it over much.

Salaam Leeds from me

E.L.

British Library

MISS FAREEDAH EL AKLE

Dec. 10 1913   Carchemish

Dear Miss Fareedah

I got your letter two or three days ago — but I had already heard from Mrs. Rieder that you were off to Damascus with Miss Hoel,[1] so it was not such great news. I am sorry you do not like the place. Damascus always seemed to me to *have been* such a splendid town. Those great mosques and khans and baths are wonderful, and the ruins of the bazaars: also the crowds of people in the town, of all the races of the earth, are rather wonderful too: Don't you think so? or do you want open country and a sea breeze?

[...]

My brother was in Damascus a month ago: I suppose you didn't see him?

Dahoum returns your salaams, with interest: which is forbidden him by his law.

Salaam Miss Hoel from me.

T.E.L.

Bodleian Reserve

1 Presumably a member of staff at the American Mission School.

MISS FAREEDAH EL AKLE
Dec. 26. [1913]   Carchemish

Dear Miss Fareedah

[...] We[1] are coming down to Beyrout next week, (where you probably are) and pass straight on to Jaffa, where we land, and go off South, from Gaza to Petra, with an expedition mapping the country.[2] We end up at Petra, I believe, and if so will take the Hedjaz line up to Damascus, in the first days of March: We will not stop more than a couple of days in Damascus, since we are supposed to begin to dig here in the first week of March. Altogether, you see, we are rather busy.

Dahoum comes South with us.... So if you do not run away too quickly from Damascus, you will see us all three together. Miss Hoel thinks Mr. Woolley is just like me: which saddens me, because I think him ugly.

Salaam me to Miss Hoel: prettily.

Yrs
T. E. Lawrence

Bodleian Reserve

C. F. BELL
Dec. 26 1913   Carchemish

Dear Bell ...

I owe you a letter or two I fancy: at any rate, if I don't you will owe me one which is better.

Woolley got a letter from you yesterday, with a glorious account of the Martyrs Memorial-hat.[3] I sent the extracts to Flecker, who had written to

1 We: Lawrence and Woolley.
2 See Introduction to this section (p. 4). The survey of Sinai in which Lawrence and Woolley were to take part had been initiated by Lord Kitchener, at this time British Agent and Consul-General in Egypt. Since the territory in question was under Turkish rule, it was thought that permission would be the more easily gained if it could be described as having an archaeological purpose. The expedition was therefore officially sponsored by the Palestine Exploration Fund for which the two archaeologists were instructed to produce a report for publication. This report duly appeared in 1915 under the title *The Wilderness of Zin*. The director of the survey was Captain Stewart F. Newcombe of the Royal Engineers, who was to become Lawrence's lifelong friend and to play a distinguished part in the Arabian campaign.
3 Bell's notes explain what so delighted Lawrence and Woolley. A Balliol undergraduate had put a chamber pot on the pinnacle just below the cross which tops the Martyrs' Memorial in St Giles, Oxford. Since it was made of enamelled iron, attempts to shoot it off failed and a steeplejack had been brought in to effect its removal. This had been achieved at midday, with all surrounding spaces, including the balconies and windows of the great Gallery of the Ashmolean, crowded with cheering spectators.

me asking for something cheerful. He is on a hill-top in Switzerland eating sour milk and sleeping in [sic] a verandah, being cured of consumption. Which cure usually remains incomplete.

Our Xmas festivities were yesterday: on Xmas Eve Woolley went out into the outer quad, (outer at my request) and sang two short carols, and 'Auld Lang Syne'. The effect was really beautiful, from a little distance: near at hand it was a little strong: there had been 15 pigeons in a house in the quad — and there are now only five, of which the black one has a broken leg. I found the cat groaning about midnight and put it out of its misery. The misery was so great that it ended only at the eleventh bullet.

We are going off tomorrow or the next day, to Jaffa: thence to Gaza and Petra on a P.E.F. survey:[1] it may be fun ... requirements are Arabic and an archaeological eye!

We have for the last week had a horrible time of it at night: after dinner and tea and hot baths we have gone out in a drizzle wrapped in white sheep-skin (Woolley's stinks like it, too) and have repassed charcoal braziers before the face of slabs to dry them (under tents): focused them and photographed them with flash-lights: when it was only a damp drizzle we did not mind it so much: when there was a strong cold wind driving sleet or mist into our faces, and scattering the flash-powder, we didn't like it ... or when it was fine & dry, and freezing hard, with a snow-wind coming off the Taurus so cold that we could hardly turn the screws of the camera.

Why do it? Because D.G.H. is sitting in the Ashmolean, over a coke furnace, and cursing our slowness in getting out those negatives: and here also the sun shineth not even at noonday. And we have no coke fire ... only a beaten copper hood and hearth (beaten with a 2 inch hammer) on which flame olive trunks:

Still in a wcek we will be too warm. Woolley says you will be sending me some snakes.... I clean forgot the Turkish customs ... they will think you did it on purpose ... or that I did. However perhaps they won't open them. Dahoum comes south with Woolley & me ... so that we will not find them till March. No matter.

Do you know Albert de Samain? a Frenchman: Flecker recommends him in a breath with Heredia?[2]

.L.

British Library

1 P.E.F.: the Palestine Exploration Fund.
2 Albert Samain (1858–1900) published three volumes of poetry in the 1890s; José-Maria de Hérédia (1842–1905) published three volumes of poetry between 1887 and 1894. Both were, *inter alia*, adept at the dramatic historical sonnet: cf. the former's *Cléopâtre* with the latter's *Antoine et Cléopâtre*.

HIS MOTHER
Jan 4 1914   At sea

I wrote to you from Aleppo, saying that I would write again when it became possible. Well, we ran down to Beyrout, getting a letter and a telegram on the way, which showed us that we must catch the first steamer to Jaffa, and then run down quickly to Gaza, and after seeing the consul there, go inland to Beersheba, and thence as local advice directed. There are a certain number of R.E.'s[1] thereabouts, beginning the survey. We are obviously only meant as red herrings, to give an archaeological colour to a political job.

[...] We have Dahoum with us, and are warned that we may have to ride camels some of the time: otherwise we are as ignorant of our supposed work as we were at first. I sent off from Beyrout to Mr. Hogarth a little cylinder seal: of prettily veined stone. I hope he will send it up to you and that you, if it seems to you worthless, will hand it on to Mrs. Rieder. It is Persian, about the time of Darius, or a little later perhaps. Now I want to go to sleep. There is no saying when I can write next: certainly not for a week or so.

                                        N.

Got ashore: & going off today at midday for Ashdod.

HL

E. T. LEEDS
Jan 24 [1914]   El Aûga

A quaint place to write to you from, this, a little lost Gov. station on the frontier line of Egypt and Syria. Still the spirit moves me.

To appreciate as you should our exploits in getting here, you would have had to follow our steps day by day. That I spare you: over the consequences of much riding of camels I draw thick veils: but take it as a summing up that we are very unhappy: Woolley is the more uncomfortable, since he is a flesh-potter: I can travel on a thistle, and sleep in a cloak on the ground. Woolley can't, or at least, is only learning to, quite slowly.

Our cook can't grasp a word of English, which explains his continued presence with us: after Woolley in a clear tone last Thursday had expressed his desire (in front of the whole camp) to bugger him with a rough stick.

---

1 Royal Engineers.

(Don't brag of this to D.G.H. he is too proper: C.F.B. will appreciate the inner meaning of Woolley's apparent wastefulness.)

Our menu is a broad one: we eat bread and eggs: and Turkish delight. Only yesterday we finished the eggs, and the nearest hens are three days journey to the N. If only a camel would start laying we would be in Paradise tomorrow.

We have evolved rather a sporting dinner: Woolley you know likes a many storied edifice.

Hors d'oeuvre

The waiter (Dahoum) brings in on the lid of a petrol box half a dozen squares of Turkish delight,

Soup
Bread soup
Then
Turkish delight on toast
Then until yesterday
Eggs
Then, sweet ...
Turkish delight
Dessert
Turkish delight.

Of course the bread is ad lib. You can see by this the perfectly delirious time we are having out here. It is weeks (or ten days) since we saw an Arab encampment: and the 'shop' in this place, much looked forward to for the last week, of eatables sells only Turkish Delight. Foul stuff: I don't want much more of it.

However other stores for us may turn up tomorrow:

Not a sign or smell of Israelites wandering about here: only on the old road from Gaza to Akaba did we find two little scraps of early pottery; we are doing the P.E.F. in the eye. Fancy our transforming a hill fort of the Amorites into a Byzantine monastery! Sounds almost impious, doesn't it.

.L.

Bodleian Reserve

E. T. LEEDS[1]

Feb. 28 [1914]   Hotel D'Angleterre Damas Syrie

Months since I wrote to you, and oceans have passed over my head since then, though alas! all the rest of me yet requires washing. Where was I? Aha ... I got down to Akabah alone and on foot, since my idiot camels went astray. Alone in Arabia! However, it was only a day and a night, but by jove, I was glad to see a tent (not mine) at the end of it. 48 hrs later, up came my camels, not smiling in the least.

Kaimmakam of Akaba was a bad man.[2] He had (or said he had) no news of us and our little games: and so he forbade Newcombe to map, and me to photograph or archaeologise. I photographed what I could, I archaeologised everywhere. In especial there was an island, said to be full of meat. The Bay of Akaba is full of sharks, hungry sharks (shivers) and the island was half a mile off shore. So, of course I engaged a boat ... and it never came, for the boatman went to prison at once. That looked to me a chance of a cheap sail, so I carried off the manless boat ... but a squad of police cut me off and robbed me of my treasure. I was alone alas! Well, I sent word to the Kaimmakam that upon his head was the forbidding me to go, and he said yes ... and while his police were carrying our mutual recriminations I puffed a zinc tank full of air, tied to its tail another for Dahoum, and one for a camera and tape and things ... and splashed off for the island with a couple of planks as paddles. The police returning a little later found my fleet sailing slowly seawards, and they had no boat, and no zinc tanks, and so could only weep while we worked. I had tied Dahoum to my tail, since I felt that any intelligent shark would leave me in the cold, but the whole squadron sailed across safely, saw, judged and condemned the ruins as uninteresting,[3] and splashed homewards, very cold and very tired: there was a most unkind breeze in our teeth, and the return took hours. Kaimmakam was informed of his fate, and cursed my religion: he attached to me in revenge a lieutenant and a half company of soldiers to keep me always in sight. [...] It's a long story ... they had camels, and couldn't walk and couldn't climb as fast as self and Dahoum ... and we walked them out of water, and they were hungry, and we dodged up valleys and slipped their trails; until the desired happened and the last one left us, and I spent a splendid morning all in peace on top of Aaron's tomb in Mount Hor. Perfect peace without ... rather a strained situation within, mitigated partly by a sweet rain-pool, partly by the finding of my tents next afternoon after a two-day absence. I shot a partridge on the hill at dawn, and we

1 This letter was published in *DG* but with the recipient described as 'A Friend'.
2 The Turkish Governor of Akaba.
3 In *The Wilderness of Zin*, however, he described the island as a 'point of capital interest' and gave a detailed account of its fortifications.

cooked it over brushwood, and ate half each. A very good partridge but a small one. The night just under the hill-top was bitterly cold, with a huge wind and blinding squalls of rain. We curled up in a knot under a not-sufficiently-overhanging-rock and packed our sheepskin cloaks under and over and round us, and still were as cold and cross as bears. Not thirsty though, at all.

We had luck, since we found the two great cross-roads through the hills of the Arabah, that serve modern raiding parties entering Sinai, and which served the Israelites a bit earlier. Nobody would show them us, of the Arabs, which accounts for our rather insane wanderings without a guide ... but we did it all well.

[...]

Petra, O Leeds, is the most wonderful place in the world, not for the sake of its ruins, which are quite a secondary affair, but for the colour of its rocks, all red and black and grey with streaks of green and blue, in little wriggly lines ... and for the shape of its cliffs and crags and pinnacles, and for the wonderful gorge it has, always running deep in spring-water, full of oleanders, and ivy and ferns, and only just wide enough for a camel at a time, and a couple of miles long. But I have read hosts of most beautifully written accounts of it, and they give one no idea of it at all ... and I am sure I cannot write nearly as nicely as they have ... so you will never know what Petra is like, unless you come out here.... Only be assured that till you have seen it you have not had the glimmering of an idea how beautiful a place can be.

[...]

DG

The 1914 season at Carchemish was a brief one. Hogarth came to visit the site in May and shortly afterwards Woolley and Lawrence closed down the dig and returned to England to write up their accounts of the Sinai survey. Lawrence was not to return to the place where he had spent the happiest years of his life. On 28 June Archduke Franz Ferdinand of Austria and his wife were assassinated at Sarajevo and within weeks the First World War had begun.

2 · THE WAR YEARS

1914–18

The outbreak of war in August 1914 found Lawrence in England. There is some confusion as to whether he volunteered for military service and was rejected because of his lack of height; arguably he implied as much to John Buchan in a letter from India in 1927 (see p. 335), but when Liddell Hart, researching his 1934 biography of Lawrence, wrote to him asking 'When and where was it you tried unsuccessfully to enlist?', he replied, 'I did not try to enlist.' In the event, it was his connection with Middle Eastern archaeology and with the Sinai survey which led to him finding suitable war work. After he and Woolley had discharged their duty to the Palestine Exploration Fund and to Kitchener by completing *The Wilderness of Zin*, Woolley obtained a commission in the Royal Artillery while Lawrence was enrolled by MO4 — the geographical division of Military Intelligence, based in the War Office in London. He began as a civilian but was soon offered a commission, becoming a Second Lieutenant on the special list (i.e. an officer without regimental affiliation) on 26 October 1914.

Turkey became a belligerent, on the side of Germany and the Austro-Hungarian Empire, on 29 October. Before the year was out Lawrence was in Cairo, a member of a swiftly assembled Intelligence Department which included not only former colleagues like Newcombe and Woolley (the latter seconded from the Artillery), but also other men of calibre like the Hon. Aubrey Herbert and George Lloyd (both of them Members of Parliament) and Philip Graves of *The Times*. His principal function was that of map officer, but he was also involved in general Intelligence assessment and became an expert on such subjects as the disposition and strength of Turkish forces. All this was important work, but he was essentially deskbound; and when in 1915 first his brother Frank and then his brother Will lost their lives in France, he began to feel increasingly ill at ease. He wrote to Leeds in November 1915: 'It doesn't seem right, somehow, that I should go on living peacefully in Cairo.'

He was briefly in a war-zone in March 1916 when he was sent to Mesopotamia to help in negotiations with the Turks regarding a British force which was trapped by Turkish forces at Kut-el-Amara on the River Tigris. Aubrey Herbert was one of two other partners in this enterprise, of which the purpose was to discuss on what terms the Turks would lift their siege. By the time they reached the enemy lines and met the Turkish commander their task was rather that of trying to achieve the best terms of surrender. On his journey back to Cairo Lawrence wrote a report condemning British organisation and generalship in Mesopotamia which was substantially borne out by the inquiry which Herbert won later that year from Parliament. His report was so outspoken that it was thought advisable to have it somewhat doctored before it was shown to the Commander-in-Chief in Egypt, Sir Archibald Murray. Before there could be any serious repercussions which might have affected Lawrence's position, the initiation of the Arab Revolt against the Turks by the Grand Sherif Hussein of Mecca in June 1916 opened a major new phase in the war. This was to provide Lawrence with the opportunity to exchange his Cairo desk for 'field-work' in the desert.

The letters of this early period frequently reflect the mood of frustration bred in him by almost two years of a largely paper war. 'We have no adventures, except with the pen,' he writes to C. F. Bell in April 1915 (in a letter which includes his fullest and most caustic account of his way of life in Cairo). 'One would be so much happier, I think, in a trench, where one hadn't to worry out politics & informations [sic] all the day.' Or again, 'I am going to be in Cairo till I die,' he writes to Mrs Hasluck in February 1916. 'Yesterday I was looking over samples of pyramids at an undertaker's with a view to choosing my style. I like the stepped ones best.' But there are other letters which show him in more buoyant mood, such as the two wide-ranging, light-hearted and, here and there, slightly outrageous surveys of the Middle Eastern situation written to George Lloyd while the latter was on active service in Gallipoli (29 June and 19 September 1915). 'Seriously, we were very cut up about getting no news of you,' he writes in the earlier letter, '& we think the Staff above the rank of Captain are shits.' 'I haven't much right to tell you all this,' he admits in the second one; 'inform Deedes, if he's trusty, & then use it for bumf or burn it.' Fortunately Lloyd did neither.

Even before the Revolt began he had been much involved in Arabian Intelligence and in early June 1916 he became the first editor of a regular publication, produced to high printing standards, called the *Arab Bulletin*, which was to run to well over a hundred numbers and of which the principal editor was to be D. G. Hogarth. One of its regular features was to be reports, often long and generally very well written, by the field officers of the Arab Bureau, of which Lawrence was soon to be a distinguished member.[1]

---

1 Hogarth wrote in the 100th edition: 'Since it was as easy to write in decent English as in bad, and much more agreeable, the *Arab Bulletin* had from the first a literary tinge not always present in Intelligence Summaries.'

In October 1916 Lawrence accompanied Ronald Storrs, the Oriental Secretary of the High Commissioner in Egypt, on a visit to Sherif Abdulla, one of the four sons of the Grand Sherif Hussein of Mecca, at Jidda in Arabia. (Hussein's sons, Ali, Abdulla, Feisal and Zeid, were his field-commanders in the Arabs' armed struggle against Turkey, which was now being conducted with the support of Britain and France.) When Storrs returned to Egypt Lawrence stayed on to assess the situation, and in particular to decide which of the four sons was the leader most likely to succeed, or, as he would put it in *Seven Pillars of Wisdom*, 'the leader who would bring the Arab revolt to full glory'. Having met Abdulla at Jidda and Ali at Rabegh (Zeid at eighteen was scarcely in the running) he rode inland by camel to Wadi Safra, where he met Feisal, by whom he was immediately impressed. He later wrote: 'I felt at first glance that this was the man I had come to Arabia to seek.' The reports both written and oral which he made following this crucial meeting with Feisal virtually guaranteed — though that was not his specific intention — that he would be sent back to Arabia to work with Feisal as liaison officer and adviser. He performed this role with significant variations for the rest of the war, gradually assuming more power and independence. The capture in July 1917 of the strategically important port of Akaba, by an Arab force led by Sherif Nasir of Medina and the veteran Howeitat chief Auda abu Tayi, with Lawrence as accompanying British officer, brought about a major shift in the Arab war and in Lawrence's career. The Arabs would thenceforward conduct their campaign in close alliance with the British, who were now under the dynamic General Sir Edmund Allenby, as the right wing of an advancing army. When Lawrence, arriving in Cairo with news of the fall of Akaba, was sent to meet the new Commander-in-Chief, he and Allenby very quickly came to an understanding, with the result that Allenby virtually gave Lawrence a free hand in Arabia, while Lawrence worked as best he could to harmonise Arab actions with Allenby's overall strategy.

Lawrence wrote very few personal letters in this important second period of the war. There are long gaps between his letters home, and evidently some he sent did not arrive, either because they were censored or, to use his own term, 'submarined'. I have included almost all that have survived, because, though he was restricted in what he could tell his family of his activities, they often convey simply and clearly the gist of what he had been doing and something, though far from all, of his state of mind at the time of writing. (It is the home letters, for example, which produce such quotable sentences as 'I have become a monomaniac about the job in hand', or 'there are few people who have damaged railways as much as I have'; similarly it is there that he produces some nice definitions of his role in the later stages of the war, as when he writes, 'the situation out here is full of surprise turns, and my finger is one of those helping to mix the pie', or when he describes himself, in a throw-away phrase, as 'an Emir of sorts'.) I have also been able to include some letters to E. T. Leeds, of which only a handful were available to Garnett, and then with the recipient's name disguised, which indicate the darker side of his mind, and reveal hints of the sense of guilt at the Allies' ultimate intentions towards the Arabs which was to ruin his peace of mind throughout most of the campaign. This guilt is shown incontrovertibly in the message which he drafted but did not send to his Intelligence head, Brigadier-General Clayton, printed on p. 111. Yet another mood, that of wistfulness for a lost world ('Very many thanks for writing. It has opened a very precious casement') informs the long and moving letter to Vyvyan Richards of July 1918, reprinted here from Garnett.

However, the most interesting and important war letters published in this book are those he wrote from the field to his friends and masters, letters which necessarily contain obscure military or political references (or, sometimes, a wealth of Arabic names) but which nevertheless communicate because they are hallmarked by Lawrence's accustomed vigour, clarity and forthrightness. These letters — to which I have added extracts from one or two reports which were not intended for or not used by the *Arab Bulletin*[1] — were not in the public domain when Garnett made his selection and, so far as I am aware, apart from occasional sparse quotation have not been published since. Writing to Robert Graves in 1927 when the latter was working on his biography of him, Lawrence wrote: 'All the documents of the Arab Revolt are in the archives of the Foreign Office, and will soon be available to students, who will be able to cross-check my yarns. I expect them to find small errors, and to agree generally with the main current of my narrative.' I believe these letters, patchy as they are and the survivors, I feel sure, of numerous letters lost, go with rather than against Lawrence's claim. They certainly throw some considerable light on his grasp of the essentials and the details of the Arab campaign, and indicate what has been called into question by some of his more critical biographers (notably of course Richard Aldington), the central importance of his role.

---

1 There seems no virtue in reprinting any of Lawrence's reports which were published in the *Arab Bulletin* as they were collected in a fine edition produced by the Golden Cockerel Press in 1939 under the title *Secret Despatches from Arabia*, edited by A. W. Lawrence. More recently the whole of the *Bulletin* has been reissued in facsimile.

DR A. E. COWLEY[1]
29 Oct. 1914   [War Office London]

[...] You ask when I am coming down ... I don't know. You see, there is only the Head of the Department (Col. Hedley)[2] left now, with myself to run errands: and so things are really a little short. Before the war there were six little men to help him, and there's more to do now.

I don't know if one gets days off ... as an exceptional favour I think one can, but I don't like such things. And working all days a week till 7 or 8 p.m. doesn't leave much time for the humanities. I disapprove of London on eighteen counts, of which most are explicit, but they take a long time. London seems curiously unmoved.

Sala'am me to Mrs. Cowley. Please tell her that I also talk French to Belgians, the subject of conversation being lithography.[3] It is very hard to get the hang of their terms: especially as in English I don't very well know what a rotary rubber-bed offset machine really is.

[...]

Bodleian Reserve

E. T. LEEDS
Mond. [16 November 1914]   [War Office London]

Dear Leeds

I was to have gone to Egypt on Sat last: only the G.O.C. there wired to the W.O. and asked for a road-report on Sinai that they were supposed to have.

Well, of course they hadn't got it — not a bit of it. So they came to me, and said 'write it.'

I thought to kill two or three birds with my stone, so I offered 'em the wilderness of Sin ... they took it and asked for more. So I'm writing a report from the military point of view of a country I don't know, and haven't visited yet. One of the minor terrors is, that later on I'm to get my

---

1 Dr Arthur Cowley (1861–1931) was Sub-Librarian of the Bodleian Library, Oxford, 1900–19 and Librarian 1919–31. He was knighted shortly before his death.
2 Colonel Coote Hedley was head of MO4, the geographical division of Military Intelligence.
3 In the second half of 1914 London was swarming with refugees from Belgium, through which country the Germans had marched in order to attack France in the opening moves of the war.

own book, and guide myself over the country with it. It will be a lesson in humility, I hope.

It's rather hard luck though, to have devilled my way all over Sinai, and then to have to write two books about it, gratis. And this second one is an awful sweat, for it has to be done against time, and the maps are not yet drawn. So I have to oversee them also, and try and correlate the two. It will not astonish you to hear that I have found a grey hair on my pillow this morning.

The W.O. people are very easily to be deceived into a respect for special knowledge loudly declared aren't they?

I'm to go out on Sat. next, I am told. I don't care, but I'm sure somebody will ask the W.O. for an epic poem on Sinai about next Friday, and I'll be turned on to that, gratis.

No matter....

I hope to see you on Friday, if you aren't ill. You might tell C.F.B. if you see him.

This month up here has been great sport. I reckon that it will take my successor months to get over the effect of my official letters on several occasions. He has gone down to Southampton today to placate the Ordnance Survey over my criticism of their suggested route of the Exodus. They nearly fused the telephone between 'em yesterday.

L.

Bodleian Reserve

JAMES ELROY FLECKER[1]
Dec. 3 [1914]

[War Office London]

Dear Flecker

I should have written very long ago ... but I have been for weeks up at the War Office working day, & half-night, at Sinai and Syria ... maps, & reports: nothing very exciting, but a little grind. Now it is all over, and on Tuesday I start E.[2] Woolley goes on Saturday.

About your people ... I have lost touch of Oxford. Roberts has enlisted. Cheesman is officer in an infantry regt. — I can't find out which, but will

---

1 Flecker (see note to letter of 18 February 1912) was terminally ill at Davos in Switzerland at this time. He died on 3 January 1915.
2 E: East.

ask further. Beazley can't get anything to do, because he's short-sighted.[1]

Not many dons have taken commissions — but 95% of the undergrads. have taken or applied for them. Next term Oxford will come to an end, I think. This term there are about a thousand up.

The war goes well, though too slowly. The Christians in Beyrout have been getting very restive, & the Moslems there are getting out. Quaint business, fighting.

Peaceful poems about willow-lined water-ways, & dreaming spires, and bells, are quite the things. Best war poems are written in peace-time. The converse should be true. Good luck to your pen.

Don't reply to this. I'll write again from Egypt.

In case of need Address TEL. G.H.Q. British Army Occupation Egypt.[2]

University of Harvard

Lawrence, together with Newcombe, finally left for Cairo on 9 December 1914.

E. T. LEEDS
24/12/1914   Intelligence Dept War Office Cairo

You see this is what we are. There wasn't an Intelligence Office, and so we set to, and are going to make them one; today we got the Office, and we all have the Intelligence: it is only a simple process of combining the two. However we have to complicate it by wireless and paid agents (beautiful words) and air reconnaissance and light of nature. All the time you know light of nature would write such a much more beautiful report by himself. But he must hamper himself with greasy Armenians, and unintelligent camel drivers.

---

1 Cyril Roberts, G. L. Cheesman and J. D. Beazley were close friends of Flecker's from his Oxford days, though he had met Roberts earlier. Cheesman had joined the Hampshire Regiment on the outbreak of war; he was killed in action at Gallipoli in 1915. Beazley became a brilliant Greek scholar and was later knighted. All these men shared a passion for poetry; see Lawrence's letter of May 1927 to Sydney Cockerell (*DG* 309): 'Beazley is a very wonderful fellow, who has written almost the best poems that ever came out of Oxford. [...] If it hadn't been for that accursed Greek art he'd have been a very fine poet.'
2 There is no signature; this line is written at the head of the letter.

Newcombe is Director . . . a magnificent but unpaid position. If Maxwell[1] didn't object to Staff we'd all be It: as it is we do the work, much cheaper . . . the Gods alone know what our pay is to be . . . for me I'm broke already, so have only a lack-lustre interest in the thing.

Woolley looks after personnel . . . is sweet to callers in many tongues, and keeps lists of persons useful or objectionable. One Lloyd who is an M.P. of sorts and otherwise not bad looks after Mesopotamia . . . and Aubrey Herbert who is a quaint person looks after Turkish politics:[2] between them in their spare time they locate the Turkish army, which is a job calling for magnifiers. One Hay does the Tripoli side of Egypt . . . And I am bottle-washer and office boy pencil-sharpener and pen wiper . . . and I think I have more to do than others of the faculty. If we can get somebody to grapple with the telephone (which burbles continuously) I will be as happy and as lazy as I want to be.

Perhaps someday there will be work to do . . . but Carchemish seems a most doleful way away.

Salute C. F. B. I'll write to him a letter as soon as I do something . . . I don't see any good in fooling him this way. I must write too to D. G. H. If any of our agents show promise I'll give them a card to Marcopoli in Aleppo, and pick him up a few easy spheroids.

Meanwhile — bed.

.L.

Bodleian Reserve

HIS MOTHER

12/2/15   Intelligence Office Cairo

Well, here goes for another empty letter: my bicycle is here: very many thanks for getting it out so quickly: I wish the W.O. would send out maps equally promptly.

You ask about the other people in the Office: well Newcombe and Woolley you have heard of. There is Hough ex-consul at Jaffa . . . pleasant

1 General Sir John Maxwell was the British Commander-in-Chief, Egypt, at the outbreak of war.
2 Both George Lloyd (1879–1941) and the Hon. Aubrey Herbert (1880–1923) were Unionist M.P.s, Lloyd for West Staffordshire, Herbert for South Somerset. Lloyd later became Governor of Bombay and, as Lord Lloyd, High Commissioner for Egypt. Aubrey Herbert, traveller, linguist and a man of powerful if eccentric personality, was John Buchan's model for his upper-class hero Sandy Arbuthnot, Lord Clanroyden — alias 'Greenmantle'. Both Lloyd and Herbert were to become lifelong friends of Lawrence.

and nothing more: there is Lloyd, an M.P. (I should think probably Conservative, but you never know) who is a director of a bank, and used to be Attaché at Constantinople. He is Welsh, but sorry for it: small, dark, very amusing ... speaks Turkish well, and French, German & Italian: some Spanish, Arabic & Hindustani ... also Russian. He is quite pleasant, but exceedingly noisy. Then there is Aubrey Herbert, who is a joke, but a very nice one: he is too short-sighted to read or recognise anyone: speaks Turkish well, Albanian, French, Italian, Arabic, German ... was for a time chairman of the Balkan League, of the Committee of Union and Progress, and of the Albanian Revolution Committee. He fought through the Yemen wars, and the Balkan wars with the Turks, & is friends with them all. Then there is Père Jaussen, a French Dominican monk, of Jerusalem. He speaks Arabic wonderfully well, and preceded us in wanderings in Sinai. We praise his work very highly in *The Wilderness of Zin*. He is very amusing, & very clever: and very useful as interpreter. ...

There is also Graves, *Times* correspondent,[1] and very learned in the Turkish army organisation. I think that is about all. We meet very few other people, except officers on business ... see a good deal of them, from General Maxwell downwards. He is a very queer person: almost weirdly good-natured, very cheerful, with a mysterious gift of prophesying what will happen, and a marvellous carelessness about what might happen. There couldn't be a better person to command in Egypt. He takes the whole job as a splendid joke.

The Turks are off for the time being. The troops that attacked us last week were from Smyrna (Turks) and from Nablous & Jerusalem & Gaza: there were no men from Aleppo, and very few from Damascus: our prisoners are very comfortable, and very content here: when they have been a few weeks in idleness they will be less pleased.

Lady Evelyn Cobbold turned up, on her usual winter visit to Egypt. ... I am to have dinner with her tonight.[2]

Dr. Mackinnon[3] is here: he is doing medical work, and Dr. Scrimgeour of Nazareth is looking after the prisoners: Cox[4] is being paid 15/– a day for me: so I hope that my account there will be clear: There are no carpets in Cairo that I want to buy: you don't get good ones under £50 here: so don't expect anything at present ... perhaps when I get back to Carchemish?

N.

HL/Bodleian Reserve

1 Philip Graves, half-brother of the poet Robert Graves.
2 Lawrence had met Lady Evelyn Cobbold at Petra on the last leg of the Sinai survey. She had lent him the money to return by the Hejaz Railway to Damascus.
3 A medical missionary formerly based in Damascus.
4 Cox and Kings were bankers to the Army in Egypt.

C. F. BELL
18.4.15   Military Intelligence Office War Office Cairo
                          Telegraphic Address 'Mukhabarat' Telephone No. 996

I know: — it's months since I wrote to Leeds, & so he is cursing: — and it's longer since I wrote to you, and I am like Allan in all respects except colour of hair. But in my case simply I am ashamed to write. Because I sit here all day long, looking like this notepaper. Telephone 996 and 2263 Cairo: Telegraphic address Mukhabarat ... so much for my Intelligence side; I am also officer in charge of Maps: telephones 3621, 3622, 1153, 3647. Telegraphic address Maps, Cairo. There you have it all. Is that anything to be proud of?

We came out here in mid-December: Woolley has now gone off to Port Said, where he runs about in a motor launch, & does exhibition work on hydroplanes and French battleships. He is an authority on prize law, and has taken prisoners.

Newcombe & I remain here. We are made base for the Mediterranean Expedition:— and we are I.O.[1] for Egypt: The first consists in maps, maps, maps, hundreds of thousands of them, to be drawn, & printed, & packed up & sent off:— my job:— also in keeping track of Turkish army movements, which is like hunting an inebriated needle with St. Vitus through whole fields of hay: & for it we send violent & rude telegrams to Sofia, Belgrade, Petrograd, Athens, Basra, & Tiflis. The last sounds rather a decent place. We then file up all these telegrams & our own ideas into a book, called the Turkish Army Handbook, now in its fourth edition. A very dull volume, with an extensive circulation (third thousand) [sic].

Then we do funny little pamphlets telling our soldiers how to speak to a Greek, & compendia of Turkish manners: and we advise all sorts of people in power on geographical points. The ignorance of these people would give them impossible-ever-to-sit-down-again experiences in a preparatory school. 'Who does Crete belong to?' 'Where is Piraeus?'

We edit a daily newspaper[2], absolutely uncensored, for the edification of 28 generals: the circulation increases automatically as they invent new generals. This paper is my only joy: one can give the Turkish point of view (in imaginary conversations with prisoners) of the proceedings of admirals & generals one dislikes: and I rub it in, in my capacity as editor-in-chief. There is also a weekly letter to 'Mother' (the London W.O.) in which one japes on a grander scale yet. Last week I sent them an extract from a Greek paper of Smyrna, freely translated, which compared our fleet at Smyrna, in its efforts at blocking the harbour, to an excited gentleman — but I don't

1 Intelligence Office.
2 i.e. a daily Intelligence Summary.

think this is quite fit for your ears. It was elaborate, & very long.

Well, well, you see we have no adventures, except with the pen, and those one can create in peace time outside an office. Cairo is unutterable things. I took a day off last month, & went & looked at it: no more: — and to think that — this folly apart — one would have been living on that mound in the bend of the Euphrates, in a clean place, with decent people not too far off. I wonder if one will ever settle down again & take interest in proper things. Newcombe — did you meet him — is a most heavenly person. He runs all the spies, & curses all the subordinates who don't do their duty, & takes off the raw edges of generals and things. Without that I should have gone mad, I think. One would be so much happier, I fancy, in a trench, where one hadn't to worry out politics & informations all the day.

TEL.

British Library

HIS PARENTS
4.6.15   Military Intelligence Office Cairo

I haven't written since I got your wire as I was waiting for details.[1] Today I got Father's two letters. They are very comfortable reading: — and I hope that when I die there will be nothing more to regret. The only thing I feel a little is, that there was no need surely to go into mourning for him? I cannot see any cause at all — in any case to die for one's country is a sort of privilege: Mother & you will find it more painful & harder to live for it, than he did to die: but I think that at this time it is one's duty to show no signs that would distress others: and to appear bereaved is surely under this condemnation.

So please, keep a brave face to the world: we cannot all go fighting: but we can do that, which is in the same kind.

N.

HL/Bodleian Reserve

---

1 Written following the death of his brother Frank, who had been serving in France as a Second Lieutenant of the 1st Gloucesters. He was killed on 9 May by shellfire when leading his men up to the front preparatory to an attack. He was 22.

HIS MOTHER
[Undated]   Military Intelligence Office Cairo

Poor dear mother

I got your letter this morning, & it has grieved me very much. You <u>will</u> never never understand any of us after we are grown up a little. <u>Don't</u> you ever feel that we love you without our telling you so? — I feel such a contemptible worm for having to write this way about things. If you only knew that if one thinks deeply about anything one would rather die than say anything about it. You know men do nearly all die laughing, because they know death is very terrible, & a thing to be forgotten till after it has come.

There, put that aside, & bear a brave face to the world about Frank. In a time of such fearful stress in our country it is one's duty to watch very carefully lest one of the weaker ones be offended: and you know we were always the stronger, & if they see you broken down they will all grow fearful about their ones at the front.

Frank's last letter is a very fine one, & leaves no regret behind it.[1]

Out here we do nothing. There is an official inertia against which one is very powerless. But I don't think we are going to have to wait much longer.

I didn't go to say good-bye to Frank because he would rather I didn't, & I knew there was little chance of my seeing him again; in which case we were better without a parting.

                                                             TEL

HL/Bodleian Reserve

CAPTAIN GEORGE LLOYD
29.6.15   Military Intelligence Office War Office Cairo

Dear Lloyd

Your 'after the storm' letter arrived today with Stepan Effendi. Mine was written at 117° in the shade, & a scirocco blowing, which was stronger than your dust storm, & hotter. Seriously, we were very cut up about

---

1 Frank's last letter, begun on 1 May 1915 and updated three times over the following week, contained this passage (expressing attitudes widely held and understood at the time): 'I am writing this letter on the hypothesis that I have been killed, so will treat it in that way. I am glad I have died, not so much for my country, as for all the many wrongs by which the war was mainly commenced and also which it inspired. The purpose for it all I do not think can be seen by us in this life but there is a purpose all the same.'

getting no news of you, & we think the Staff above the rank of Captain are shits.[1] Now for business. That Bagdad Expedition did a very good thing. It attacked Rota,[2] & captured 3 field guns, & then sent a gunboat with some officers & 88 men, up river top speed. They overhauled a Turkish gunboat burning palm logs, & so bagged 3 more guns, & then steamed into Amara. There they caused some astonishment ashore & bagged another river steamer. Their guns cut off retirement from Amara up the Persian bank, & so the Vali, & Seif el Din, Commandant of the C. P. Fire Brigade,[3] surrendered with 1400 merry men, 3 German officers & much machine guns, & a little Field Artillery. The 88 men lay low, & next morning there came in the advance guard (1500 strong) of the army of Mohammud Pasha Daghestani, who had been threatening Ahwaz. Vanguard found itself girt about with machine guns & challenged in English — so surrendered before it counted its opponents. The main Daghestani army unfortunately got warning & went by another road in a terrific hurry.[4]

Ajaimi's tribesmen (who had been flirting with the Turks) came in to make their peace, and offered two gory heads of German officers as a proof of sincerity & repentance. There was a 6th German in Mesopotamia, & he's missing.

Now for Arabia. We have made a quite fit & proper treaty with Idrisi, & Home[5] has ratified it. Only I'm afraid he's not ambitious of anything more than Assir, & a riotous battle with the Imam's tribesmen.[6] I wanted him to have ambitions on the Hedjaz, & to go & do a more than Wahabi purge of the Haramain! no luck there;[7]

Ibn Saoud has made peace with Ibn Rashid:[8] Ibn Rashid promises to be no more impudent, & to look kindly on our progress in Irak. Also to chasten the Ibn Hamad who were against us. Ibn Saoud is now making a treaty with India, the spirit of which is unknown here at present.

---

1 Lloyd was on active service in Gallipoli at this time; hence the anxiety about him expressed in the letter's first paragraph.

2 Ruta Creek on the Tigris, which had been mined by the Turks.

3 C. P. Fire Brigade: Constantinople Fire Brigade, whose name belied the fact that they were picked troops.

4 The exploit which so excited Lawrence, a foray by a British force up the River Tigris in Mesopotamia in May/June 1915, was to become known as 'Townshend's Regatta', after the name of the senior officer involved, Major-General Charles Townshend.

5 Home: the British Foreign Office.

6 Imam: the ruler of Yemen.

7 A difficult paragraph: Idrisi was a young Arab leader whom Lawrence had seen as leader of an Arab revolt against the Turks. He had signed a treaty with the British Resident in Aden in the previous month. Wahabi: a reference to the fundamentalist Islamic teachings of an 18th-century holy man, Mohammed ibn Abdul Wahab. Haramain: two holy cities, i.e. Mecca and Medina.

8 Abdul Aziz ibn Saud, Emir of Riyadh (now capital of Saudi Arabia), was well disposed towards the British; ibn Rashid was the head of the pro-Turkish rival house at Hail.

Otherwise? Well, we nearly sent a Camel brigade to Sheikh Said to capture it, because some sporting gunner there was having pot-shots at Perim lighthouse. Fortunately K. didn't want it, because Perim lighthouse doesn't really matter as much as a brigade.[1]

The Canal holds out nervously.[2] It expects an attack every full moon, & when it is dark also: & continually pretends to us that the Turks are coming on. It is divided by us. Fact is 3000 men at Arish, 1000 at Nekhl, 1000 at Beersheba, & the rest behind Jaffa, Haifa & Beyrout. And as the coal of Syria is out they are ruining their engines with lignite & olive logs.

We apostasised from your creed (as a revenge for no news) & planned a gaudy attack on Aleppo. It was to begin at Lattakia, push up the road to Jisr Shogr on the Orontes, & thence raid Aleppo & Hama, & come home by way of Hamman & Beilan: force: — 6000 infantry to hold the Latakia hill-crescent, & 2 divisions of cavalry to do the raiding.

Sat on: lack of cavalry: though someone regretted that it seemed the only chance in this war for good use of horse.

Syria is a horrid wash-out, & we all sit here & cipher & decipher telegrams, & print maps, & wonder when you will push. Apparently you will now, or when your new men come. Which is a new reason for capturing more Asiatic maps & a few of other parts of the world.

By the way, it isn't necessary for G.H.Q. to sit on new maps till it has a set, & then send them all down for *immediate* reproduction. We can draw piecemeal, & so perhaps not work overtime at 110° in the drawing office, & 119° in the Printing Office: as last week. The above paragraph is a grouse.

Incidentally most of the Printing Office are now dead. That is why Cairns, your printer, is wanted back. The photographer is dead also, and one draughtsman.

Oppenheim — damned rat — is in Syria. He will probably cause an anti-German rising if he behaves as usual.[3]

I wish you were back here. One learns so little of what is happening at home & in politics from Newcombe!

I'll come up your way shortly: BORED.

Yrs

TEL.

Churchill College Cambridge

---

1 K: Kitchener. Perim is an island, at this time a British territory, two miles off the coast of Arabia at the southern end of the Red Sea.
2 The Suez Canal.
3 Oppenheim: Baron von Oppenheim, German archaeologist, and chief of the Kaiser's Intelligence Service in the Middle East; known in Cairo as 'The Spy'.

W. G. LAWRENCE
17.7.15   Military Intelligence Office War Office Cairo

[...] Your job—revolver practice sounds pleasant.[1] We live in offices and in railway trains: also interviewing Turkish prisoners, & supplying information on any subject that crops up. No civil work however and much map-drawing & geography, both of which please me.

Frank's death was as you say a shock, because it was so unexpected. I don't think one can regret it overmuch, because it is a very good way to take, after all. The hugeness of this war has made one change one's perspective, I think, and I for one can hardly see details at all. We are a sort of Levant Foreign Office, and can think of nothing else. I wonder when it will all end and peace follow?

All the relief I get [is] in *The Greek Anthology*, Heredia, Morris & a few others! Do you?

DG

CAPTAIN GEORGE LLOYD
19.9.15   Military Intelligence Office War Office Cairo

Dear Lloyd

You don't in the least deserve a pearl such as this letter will prove: — you are perverse, absolutely perverse about that 25th Division. ANZAC never took a prisoner from it, and it was all in Syria till Mid-July. Your suggestion that part was in the Peninsula & went back to C.P.[2] to welcome its friends is an enormity. However let's forget that.[3]

We wire to Basra regularly, & tell them that you want news of them, & they sit on their tails, & won't say a word. All I know beyond the Bulletin is, that they say they are advancing against Kut el Amara, & that their Headquarters have moved from Basra to Amara.

Got a wire from you today about Sherif's information. The XIIth A.C. as you should remember (& would had you not left this office—see what

---

1 Will had returned to England from India in March 1915 and was a Second Lieutenant in the Oxford and Bucks Light Infantry.
2 Constantinople.
3 Lawrence was an expert on the disposition of Turkish forces throughout the Ottoman Empire: hence his bantering tone to Lloyd, who had plainly been in error in regard to the recent moves of the Turkish 25th division. ANZAC is the standard abbreviation for the Australian and New Zealand Army Corps which won a heroic reputation for its performance at Gallipoli—'the Peninsula', as Lawrence calls it here. Lloyd was attached at this period to the staff of the ANZAC commander, General Birdwood.

you lose!) came to Aleppo as a whole in Nov. December 1914. Fakhri was O.C.[1] Yasin Bey Chief of Staff.

Then in Jan 35th Division was sent to Basra, where we were violating the virginity of Irak ... and the 36th a little later went off to Mosul, & thence to Van region.

Fakhri, his staff, & his corps troops stayed behind in Aleppo & Hama, & began to feel lonely.

So they began to raise a new division or two for themselves out of the depots of the 6th A.C., which had gone to Constantinople, & didn't need any depots, as they were completing it from the recruiting areas of A.C. II and A.C. III.

Then the Arab movement became ominous, & Yasin Bey was sent up to Constantinople, where he became C.G.S. XVIIth A.C. There he is now.

Fakhri acted as deputy for Jemal in Aleppo for a time, & has now gone down to Damascus, where his headquarters probably are. He has got a German Staff officer to replace Yasin Bey: and he helps Azmi to curb Jemal's little aspirations. Isn't it heavenly of me to tell you all this?

Now about Sherif. His plans[2] are to slip into the Hedjaz, have a chat about tactics with the Sherif, slip out again, raise the 10 Syrian officers & the 600 rank & file we took on the canal, add to them 50 officers and 2000 men now in India, & drop into the Hedjaz heavily this time. Nuri Shaalan[3] has promised to help him, & can cut telegraph wires, tear up the Hedjaz line, & provide transport, which will enable them to proclaim the Sherif Khalifa,[4] & roll up Syria (with the help of Syrians) from the tail end. It will come off, if the first landing & attack on Medina succeed. The G.O.C.[5] is shy of it, Clayton is for it: I— but you will guess what I'm at: —

I haven't much right to tell you all this: inform Deedes,[6] if he's trusty, & then use it for bumf, or burn it. The Armenian affair may go through. Our stout men didn't 'see any advantage' in stirring up N. Syria—and so 4 divisions have been added thence to the Dardanelles army. The other 3

1 Fakhri Pasha and the XIIth Army Corps were subsequently to move to Medina, where they were to hold out successfully against the Arabs until after the armistice with Turkey in October 1918.

2 'His plans': Lawrence was referring to an Arab officer of the Turkish Army who had just deserted at Gallipoli. A prominent Arab nationalist, he was eager to meet Grand Sherif Hussein in the Hejaz with a view to discussing the practicalities of an Arab rebellion against the Turks. In the event he promised more than he could deliver, but plainly his plans enthused Lawrence and, no doubt, Lloyd.

3 Nuri Shaalan was the paramount chief of the Ruwalla tribe in northern Arabia; he would play an important part in the later stages of the Arabian campaign.

4 Khalifa: civil and religious leader.

5 G.O.C.: General Officer Commanding, i.e. Maxwell.

6 Captain Deedes, later Lieutenant-Colonel Sir Wyndham Deedes, was soon to join Military Intelligence in Cairo.

or 4 will follow, as soon as they raise scallywags to replace 'em, unless we some day do something. Couldn't your show point it out picturesquely to the G.S.?[1]

The Armenians of Jebel Musa (about 300 fighting men, with shot guns & black powder) put up a fight for about 6 weeks, & slew many Turks. They could have gone on indefinitely with arms & ammunition provided. The women & children of Armenian villages have all been expelled from Cilicia to Mesopotamia & Syria, but the men of fit age [have been] all sent into labour battalions. So N. Syria is full of married battalions of Armenians & Christians, fit men, with no relations or home ties. In addition there are many outlaws, Mohammedan & Christian, in the hills: — all of it good material for a rising backed by us: a few hundred men, a company or two of machine guns, 1000 rifles, & acceptance of Armenian offers of volunteers arriving daily from America, & we'll have all the Armenians & Cilicia in a horrible tangle. The G.O.C. is willing, & if you'll back up we can carry over the French & have a huge loot. Sherif in rear & Armenians in front: Baron von Oppenheim will hang:[2]—

The last touch is sheer, unmixed, professional, archaeological jealousy: —
Love
T.E.L.

Churchill College Cambridge

E.T. LEEDS
16.11.15   Military Intelligence Office Cairo

Dear Leeds

I have not written to you for ever so long ... I think really because there was nothing I had to say. It is partly being so busy here, that one's thoughts are all on the jobs one is doing, and one grudges doing anything else, and has no other interests, and partly because I'm rather low because first one and now another of my brothers has been killed.[3] Of course, I've been away a lot from them, & so it doesn't come on one like a shock at all ... but I rather dread Oxford and what it may be like if one comes back. Also

---

1 G.S.: General Staff.
2 See footnote to previous letter to Lloyd dated 29 June 1915 (p. 75).
3 The brother killed was Will, the one to whom he was closest both in age and interests. Will had transferred to the Royal Flying Corps in August 1915, becoming an observer. He was shot down on 23 October after being less than a week in France. He was officially posted 'Missing', but Lawrence, correctly, assumed the worst. His death was formally confirmed in the following May. He was 26.

they were both younger than I am, and it doesn't seem right, somehow, that I should go on living peacefully in Cairo.

However I haven't any right to treat you to all this.

Salute Bell from me: tell him it is what I have to do to Lieut-Commdr. Hogarth when I first meet him in the morning. It's very good to have him out here, stirring one up to all sorts of other ideas.

I wish one might have an end sometime.

Yours
T E Lawrence

Bodleian Reserve

MRS HASLUCK[1]
28.2.16   Army Headquarters The Force in Egypt Cairo

Dear Mrs. Hasluck

This is a reply to your letter of December 4! My manners at times astonish even myself.

[...]

We do nothing here except sit & think out harassing schemes of Arabian policy. My hair is getting very thin and grey. I hope you have found some excellent job, which will take all day and be interesting. I'm very sorry you did not come to Alexandria with the main body.

The plum pudding turned up, and was devoured mightily. It came a week late, & so was the only one in Egypt that did not go down with the *Persia*.[2] Many unkind things were said about us, but it was green jealousy only. Very many thanks indeed for the gift.

I am going to be in Cairo till I die. Yesterday I was looking over samples of pyramids at an undertaker's with a view to choosing my style. I like the stepped ones best.

I am a 2nd. Lieutenant ... and a Staff Captain, which explains the riddle. It's much better to use the archaeologist, as the first is cumbrous, and the second abominable.

Remember me to Hasluck if you hear from him: and my sincerest apologies to yourself for my delay in writing to you.

T E Lawrence

Bodleian Reserve

---

1 Mrs Hasluck: the wife of F. W. Hasluck, author of, among other works, *Athos and its Monasteries* (1924) and *Christianity and Islam under the Sultans* (1929).

2 The S.S. *Persia*, a troopship en route from England to India, had been torpedoed in the eastern Mediterranean on 30 December 1915 with heavy losses.

The following two letters were written during Lawrence's assignment to Mesopotamia in March to May 1916 discussed in the Introduction to this section (see p. 62). The first, to Mrs Rieder, written on the voyage out, is newly published; it contains among other things information to the effect that the railway bridge at Jerablus, which had been under construction throughout his years at Carchemish, had at last been completed. The second, to his mother, written on the way back (a letter so long that Lawrence wrote of it: 'I do not know how the Censor will find it in his heart to pass so Gargantuan a bale of manuscript') was published in *DG* and in full in *HL*. I have therefore reproduced — apart from the beginning and end — only those paragraphs relating to the central purpose of his mission, the negotiation with the Turkish commander besieging the trapped British force in Kut.

MRS RIEDER
End of March [1916]   Off Muskat[1]

Dear Mrs. Rieder

This is a reply to your letter of the beginning of the month. I'm writing on board, with Arabia in view on the left and Persia on the right. Arabia is the better. . . . Persia is all hills and looks wet.

I'm very sorry not to have written to you for so long. It is simply mental inertia. I am written out, and have nothing in my head but Arabian politics, Bagdad Railway, and such like emptinesses. If it was not that you ask me for news of the Railway I doubt whether even after ten days at sea I would have found words.

The old railway is complete from Constantinople to Kara Punar which is about 6 miles South of Bozanti, at the north end of the Cilician Gates. Then comes a stretch of about 20 miles under construction. There are difficult tunnels (35 of them) on this stretch, and it will take about one or two years to finish.

The line then runs from Dorak (about 18 miles N.E. of Tarsus) to Mamourie, which is about 8 miles N.E. of Osmanié, north of Alexandretta.

1 Lawrence was sailing to Basra on board the Canadian liner *Royal George*.

From Mamourie to Islahie there is another gap, of about 30 miles. This is due to a tunnel of 4882 metres long. It is finished, so far as boring is concerned, and should be open for traffic very shortly.

From Islahie the line runs on to Aleppo (or nearly there: — Aleppo is on a Y line from Muslimie) and from Aleppo out to Jerablus. The bridge there is in order, and finished. The wooden bridge was washed away, too late.

From Jerablus the line works through Tell Abaid (about 10 miles S. of Harran) to Ras el Ain, about 210 Kilometres E. of Jerablus. This is railhead, and the Company has no present intention to extend it.

I'm writing from memory, so I cannot give you the kilometre distance of each section: but you will be able to find most of the above places. One of the best maps (for N. Syria and Mesopotamia) is that in Max von Oppenheim's *Von Mittelmeer zum Tarsische Golf*, which is the best book on the area I know. For the Taurus section of the Railway (Karapunar to Dorak) there is an article by Newcombe in the R.G.S.[1] Journal for about September 1914.

The above information is all published in various places: this is for the information of the Censor, who has a tendency to snap up such details, and bore his Intelligence Officers by sending them in for 'information'.

We should get to Basra about Sunday: and I expect this letter will be posted there. I expect to stay ten days or a fortnight, and then return to Egypt. But in the Army one's programme is about as regular as a jumping cracker's.

Very many thanks for an electric torch (which is really the fons et origo of this note, and as usually tends to be a postscript; I think I am feminine by instinct). It has been most useful in this unexpected journey, and has probably further duty ahead of it before I see Egypt.

Will you, when next you write make clear to me the sex, name, and address of the sender? It is a relation of yours ... a hand-writing that looks prim, but is full of mysteries!

Please remember me to Noël. When I see him next he will be a budding undergraduate, with an incredible ignorance of Arabic, French & German!

Yours sincerely
T E Lawrence

Bodleian Reserve

1 R.G.S.: Royal Geographical Society.

HIS MOTHER
May 18 [1916]

We are at sea, somewhere off Aden, I suppose, so before it gets too late I am going to tell you something of what I saw in Mesopotamia. You must excuse the writing, because the ship is vibrating queerly.

[...]

Colonel Beach, one of the Mesopotamian Staff, Aubrey Herbert (who was with us in Cairo) and myself were sent up to see the Turkish Commander in Chief, and arrange the release, if possible, of Townshend's wounded. From our front trenches we waved a white flag vigorously: then we scrambled out, and walked about half-way across the 500 yards of deep meadow-grass between our lines & the Turkish trenches. Turkish officers came out to meet us, and we explained what we wanted. They were tired of shooting, so kept us sitting there with our flag as a temporary truce, while they told Halil Pasha we were coming — and eventually in the early afternoon we were taken blindfolded through their lines & about ten miles Westward till within four miles of Kut to his Headquarters. He is a nephew of Enver's, and suffered violent defeat in the Caucasus so they sent him to Mesopotamia as G.O.C. hoping he would make a reputation. He is about 32 or 33, very keen & energetic but not clever or intelligent I thought. He spoke French to us, and was very polite, but of course the cards were all in his hands, and we could not get much out of him. However he let about 1,000 wounded go without any condition but the release of as many Turks — which was all we could hope for.[1]

We spent the night in his camp, and they gave us a most excellent dinner in Turkish style — which was a novelty to Colonel Beach, but pleased Aubrey and myself. Next morning we looked at Kut in the distance, and then came back blindfolded as before. We took with us a couple of young Turkish officers, one the brother-in-law of Jemal Pasha, the other a nephew of Enver, and they afterwards went up to Kut from our camp in the hospital ships which removed the wounded. The ill feeling between Arabs and Turks has grown to such a degree that Halil cannot trust any of his Arabs in the firing line. [...][2] After that there was nothing for us to do, so the Headquarters ship turned round, and came down again to Basra. We got there about the 8th and I spent four or five days settling up things and then came away.

1 Their mission was to no avail. The British force in Kut surrendered while the talks with the Turkish commander, Halil Pasha, were in progress. Seventy per cent of the force perished while being force-marched to Turkey or during subsequent captivity; their commander, Major-General Townshend (of 'Townshend's Regatta' fame; see letter to Lloyd, 29 June 1915) spent the rest of the war as a prisoner in Constantinople.
2 Three lines omitted owing to unclear text.

This is an old Leyland liner, now a transport. There is only myself and a General Gillman on board. He is from near Abingdon and excellent company: we sit on the deck and write reports and notes all day, and sleep gigantically at night.

[...]

Hereafter I will again be nailed within that office at Cairo — the most interesting place there is till the Near East settles down. I am very pleased though to have had this sight of Mesopotamia in war time. It will be a wonderful country some day, when they regulate the floods, and dig out the irrigation ditches. Yet it will never be a really pleasant country, or a country where Europeans can live a normal life. In these respects, and in the matter of inhabitants, it must yield to the upper river, where we are.

I expect to find letters and papers knee-deep in Cairo when I return. The accumulation of two months business and pleasure will be awful to see — so do not look for immediate news of me.

Would you ask Gillman[1] to make me another pair of brown shoes like the last? Also please ask Arnie to send me out two books by Cunninghame Graham,[2] my Aristophanes, and a Bohn translation of Aristophanes. Latter can probably be bought second-hand from Blackwell. I would like my William of Tyre (*Estoire de Eracles*)[3] if the volumes are not too heavy for the post — and a Lucretius, if I have one. If Arnie likes any of these too well to part with let him send something else choice in their stead.

HL/Bodleian Reserve

June 1916 saw the launching of the Arab Revolt by Grand Sherif Hussein of Mecca and also the issue of the first edition of the *Arab Bulletin*; the latter event, dated 6 June, preceding the former by three days. Apart from his work on the *Bulletin* Lawrence's most noteworthy achievement in the first months of the Revolt was his highly professional contribution to the devising and production of new postage stamps for the Grand Sherif.

1 Gillman: shoemakers of Oxford.
2 R. B. Cunninghame Graham (1852–1936): Old Harrovian, anarchist, M.P., traveller, travel-writer, story-writer. Probably *Mogreb-el-Acksa* (1898), an account of Cunninghame Graham's attempt to reach the forbidden city of Tarudant in Morocco, was one of the books asked for by Lawrence in this letter. The two men corresponded after the war; there are five letters by Cunninghame Graham in *Letters to T. E. Lawrence*.
3 Guillaume de Tyre (c.1130–c.1186): Frenchman, prelate — he became Archbishop of Tyre in 1175 — and chronicler. His chief work. *Historia Rerum in Partibus Transmarinis Gestarum* (English title, *History of Deeds Done Beyond the Sea*) is one of the main authorities for the study of the Latin kingdom of the East in the 12th century.

July 1 [1916]   [Cairo]

Here goes for a letter to you, though there is little to say. The Reuter telegram on the revolt of the Sherif of Mecca I hope interested you. It has taken a year and a half to do, but now is going very well. It is so good to have helped a bit in making a new nation — and I hate the Turks so much that to see their own people turning on them is very grateful. I hope the movement increases, as it promises to do. You will understand how impossible it is for me to tell you what the work we do really consists of, for it is all this sort of thing. This revolt, if it succeeds will be the biggest thing in the Near East since 1550.

We carry on much as usual in the office, though Clayton has gone back to England for a couple of weeks, to talk over things with the Foreign Office. Mr. Hogarth still here, and in charge of Red Sea politics.

Tell Father I received his letter of the 14th of June, and will reply to it when I have time. The last two weeks we have lived in the middle of a storm of telegrams and conferences, and excursions, and to consider one's private affairs is not possible. The money may have come very opportunely, for the army here are very savage at being left out of the Arabia business, and I may have to cut adrift of them, which would reduce my pay a good deal.

I have gone out, with Mr. Hogarth, to live with an Irishman called MacDonnell,[1] who is one of our office. He has a house on the island in the Nile, where he normally lives with his family. They have gone to Alexandria, and we have freedom of the house. It is a change from the Hotel, and quiet.

I don't really think there is anything else I can tell you. I feel written out, for now I have two newspapers (both secret!) to edit,[2] for the information of Governors and Governments, and besides heaps of writing to do: — and it is enough. It is a very good thing everything goes on so well. As long as the show succeeds no very great difficulties will crop up. It is curious though how the jealousies and interferences of people on your own side give you far more work and anxiety than the enemy do. I have some very pretty maps in hand, and am drawing myself one of the country East of Damascus and Aleppo. Thanks to this war I know an incredible lot about the Near East. Our office is the clearing house through which every report and item affecting the Near East has to pass ... the mass of Stuff is amazing, and it all fits into itself like a most wonderful puzzle. If we had only begun in peace time there would have been almost nothing we had not known.

1 According to a letter to his mother not included in this selection Captain MacDonnell's special province in Military Intelligence was Tripolitania.
2 i.e. the daily intelligence reports and the *Arab Bulletin*.

Tell Mrs. Rieder that Dieb her coachman has been sentenced to some years imprisonment for insulting the Ottoman Government ... I think he will be only a few weeks there.

N.

HL/Bodleian Reserve

HIS MOTHER
22.7.16   [Cairo]

I'm afraid there is nothing to say this week either. William of Tyre, Cunninghame Graham and Aristophanes appeared duly. Very many thanks. One does not read them much, but the fact of their being on hand gives one a sense of security. It's like having a balance in books.

Clayton has got back. Everything here is going excellently, though as ever there is enough to do.

Arnie will be glad to hear I am printing stamps for the Sherif of Mecca. I'll send him some when they come out. Of course they are only a provisional issue. It's rather amusing, because one has long had ideas as to what a stamp should look like, and now one can put them roughly into practice. The worst is they can only be little designs, not engraved, so that the finer detail is not possible. I'm going to have flavoured gum on the back, so that one may lick without unpleasantness.

I saw Kerry a day or two ago, for a few minutes.[1] He is at Ismailia, with a post and telegraph company, I fancy or motor cyclist.

They have never heard of Hugh Whitelocke[2] here. I think he must be at Luxor. No news otherwise.

N.

[Please don't give any papers of Will's to Janet,[3] if possible, till I have seen them. There is no hurry about them. N.]

HL/Bodleian Reserve

1 A. H. G. Kerry was at the Oxford City High School with Lawrence, a boyhood visitor to the Lawrence household and a member of the Kerry family referred to in Lawrence's letter of 4 August 1906. He later became a housemaster at Eton.
2 Hugh Whitelocke: also an Oxonian friend: he served later in the Egyptian Expeditionary Force.
3 Janet Laurie: a friend of the family whom his brother Will had planned to marry. Lawrence himself had been an admirer of Janet in his undergraduate years and had actually proposed marriage to her himself. She later married Harvey Hallsmith and Lawrence became godfather to her first child.

Post out tonight, and as I did not write last week I must this week. I noticed from a recent letter that you had not heard of me for some time. I suppose a post must have dropped out in that sunk French steamer. Anyway I wrote.

I enclose 9 more stamps in this. The half and quarter piastre are not yet on sale.

Have been interrupted eleven times since last sentence. A telephone is useful but a nuisance.

I would like to know if my letters to you are opened? Two interruptions here.

Mr. Hogarth is due here on Friday, which will be pleasant. He is so entirely unprofessional that he acts like a breath of fresh air. (Telephone.) Here is a story for Worm.[1] Storrs,[2] of the British Residency, went down to Jidda lately with the Holy Carpet. When there he wanted to talk to the Sherif. So he went to the telephone, and rang up No. 1. Mecca, and began. In a few minutes he heard other voices on the line, so he told the Sherif that someone was trying to overhear their conversation. Sherif, very angry, rang up the Exchange, and ordered all telephones in the Hejaz to be cut off for half an hour. After which things went splendidly. The Sherif has a sense of humour, and is doing well. His weakness is in military operations. Four interruptions.

We have added a new man to our bunch, one Ormsby-Gore, an M.P.[3] ... seems good ... Ismailia come up soon and amalgamate with us. Then we are nearly 40 strong! There ought to be intelligence enough in the bunch to down Turkey — but unfortunately half of them are only door-posts and window frames! Things will go much more smoothly, though, when we are all in touch. (Telephone.) Worm should read Spenser as often as possible: not in larges doses (4 more interruptions) but for a few minutes at a time, and frequently. More interruptions — I think I must give this up. It is too hopeless trying to write when soldiers keep on rushing into one's room and throwing fresh papers into one's baskets. I have three baskets now, and three tables, and they are all about knee deep. (Telephone.)

When they get too bad I go out and see somebody somewhere else in the building (this place is nearly as big as the War Office) and come back

1 Transcribed as 'Arnie' in *HL*.
2 Ronald, later Sir Ronald Storrs (1881–1955), who was to become a lifelong friend of Lawrence, had been Oriental Secretary to the British Agency in Egypt since 1909. He had been much involved in negotiations with the Sherif of Mecca about the Arab Revolt.
3 William George Ormsby-Gore (1886–1964), later 4th Baron Harlech: Etonian, Unionist M.P. for Denbigh, later for Stafford.

and tear things up [and generally spiflicate things].[1]
More interruptions. I'm off. (Telephone).

N.

P.S. — This evening is worse than usual.

N.

HL/Bodleian Reserve

Lawrence arrived in Arabia on 16 October 1916, accompanying Ronald Storrs on his journey to Jidda to meet Sherif Abdulla.[2] Two days later he wrote his first operational report to Brigadier-General Clayton (printed on pp. 88–90), forerunner of many such reports to Clayton and others.

ERNEST DOWSON[3]
17.10.16   Jidda

Dear Dowson
    No point in writing to you: except to prove to you the existence of stamps! They are quite pleasantly received here. Some say that the design is rather out of date, and that a modern style (more like a cigarette picture) would be fitter. However, they are used, and well liked. In fact the half-piastre is sold out, in Jidda, and more than half have been wired for to Mecca.
    About the Survey. No progress, I'm afraid. I happened on Jidda at a very unfortunate moment, which I will explain to you at length some day. So Sherif Abdullah (I could not see S. Hussein)[4] could hardly be brought to a very fine point.
    I hope to have another go at him tomorrow.

1 The words 'and generally spiflicate things' are omitted in *HL* — one of many curious minor excisions by M. R. Lawrence, in this case because of his abhorrence of slang.
2 Abdulla (1882–1951), second son of the Grand Sherif Hussein, was Emir of Transjordan 1921–46 and King of Jordan 1946–51. He was assassinated in the Aqsa Mosque, Jerusalem. King Hussein of Jordan is his grandson.
3 Ernest, later Sir Ernest Dowson (1876–1950), was at this time Director-General of the Survey of Egypt, in which capacity he had been responsible for the printing of the recently issued Hejaz stamps.
4 S. Hussein: the Grand Sherif Hussein of Mecca, Abdulla's father. He had been a presence in the discussions at Jidda in which Lawrence had taken part, but not in person, by telephone. Born in 1853 or 4, he was (by self-proclamation) King of the Hejaz from 1916 until he abdicated in 1924; he died in Amman in 1931.

My regards to Mrs. Dowson.

Yours sincerely,
T. E. Lawrence

Bodleian Reserve

BRIGADIER-GENERAL GILBERT CLAYTON[1]
18/10/16

General Clayton

We spent about two and a half days at Jidda, about half of which was occupied with discussions with Sherif Abdullah. We got there just as Wilson[2] had received the telegram about the 'final' decision not to land a brigade at Rabegh (suggest you inform H.M.G. there are no 'final' decisions in war time, though I agree with this one!) and he was so taken up with the point that Syria was never mentioned.

Abdullah looks about thirty, and is very quiet in manner: all the same one could see that the decision against a Brigade was a heavy blow (mostly, I think, to his ambitions). He was very cut up at first, and tried to get the order changed, as he was afraid to inform his Father of it. I think it was pushing the principle a little too far, when they counter-ordered the aeroplanes! After all, I am going to land at Rabegh, and am just as much 'British troops' as they are.[3] However, that point can be pressed later if necessary. The Turkish planes, if they are handled by Turks will crash pretty soon, and their moral effect will then pass off.

The actual moment when the planes were called back was a particularly unfortunate one. They will never believe that the real reason was other than an excuse, I'm afraid.

I'm getting a few details on the sort of expenditure of Sherif Hussein.

---

1 Gilbert, later Sir Gilbert Clayton (1875–1929), was Lawrence's chief at Headquarters for most of the war; at this time he was B.G.G.S. (Brigadier-General, General Staff) Hejaz Operations, i.e. the senior staff officer involved in the Arabian campaign.

2 Lieutenant-Colonel C. E. Wilson, British Resident in Jidda.

3 The debate over the landing of an Allied Brigade in Arabia had two aspects: the reluctance of the British C-in-C Egypt to commit scarce resources, and the anxiety that the presence of Christian soldiers on sacred Moslem soil might cause a violent anti-Allied reaction in the Arab world and also — very important to the British — in India. Lawrence's impending visit to Rabegh had been agreed the previous day at Jidda during Storrs' conversations with Abdulla: he was to meet Ali, Hussein's eldest son, at Rabegh, and then ride inland to meet the third son, Feisal, at his camp in Wadi Safra. According to *Seven Pillars* Lawrence transmuted these visits into a mission to find the most promising leader among Hussein's sons; he was to find him in Feisal.

The old man is frightfully jealous of his purse-strings, and keeps his family annoyingly short. I think both Abdullah and Feisal should have allowances. The money question is going, I think, to be decisive: the Turks have been trying to circulate paper lately, which will be the end of them, if persisted in.

Sherif Hussein is obviously, from what everybody says, very clever, rather suspicious, and interferes in everything. But he is such an old dear that they only protest half-comically. He entertains royally, is accessible to everyone, very vigorous physically, and is perfect in all ceremonies. He is too mild to his enemies, but is respected the more by the people. He seems to be getting a little old, and looks upon his sons as boys not quite fit to act independently. Abdullah humours him, and tries to wheedle him round by diplomacy. Feisal[1] is a little impatient sometimes.

Aziz[2] has not taken me into his confidence, but is enormously interested in the Hejaz Railway, <u>North</u> of <u>Maan</u>. I cannot get him worked up to consider the El Ala-Medina stretch at all. All his questions are about the Hauran, Kerak, and the Nebk-Selemich region: even Aleppo sometimes. I fancy he may be trying to get up into the Rualla-Hauran country, not to do very much perhaps, but to sound the people, and cut the line. He will not take troops with him from Hejaz.

However, unless he asks my opinion I needn't take any notice of what I suspect, and indeed a diversion there might aid us in the end of November most powerfully. If he would blow up the Hama bridge, it would be safe to start excavating Beersheba!

Aziz suspects that all idea of an offensive from Medina has been abandoned by the Turks; however, he does not know much more about it than we do.

There is great need of some Intelligence work being done at Jidda. The opportunities are quite good, and at present there is no one to do them. If one stayed there, and worked, one would be able to appreciate the Hejaz situation quite well. There are some personal remarks here about Colonel Wilson which I won't write down. Will you please ask Storrs a few leading questions about him? Cornwallis regards me as prejudiced!

The tone of public opinion at Jidda is rollicking good-humour towards foreigners. It will however be quite a good thing when the French Political Mission goes.[3]

1 Third son of the Grand Sherif (1883–1933); later principal Arab delegate to the Paris Conference and King of Iraq from 1921 until his death.

2 Aziz Ali el Masri: competent Egyptian officer who soon faded from the Arabian scene but was thought at this stage to be a likely commander of Arab forces in the Hejaz. A pro-German in the Second World War.

3 Lawrence's view on French involvement in the Hejaz was shared by his superiors. The relationship between Lawrence and the Head of the French Military Mission to Jidda,

Jidda is a wonderful town, like gimcrack Elizabethan exaggerated. Storrs will give you some of the gems of our experience: most of it felt as though Gilbert was editing the Arabian nights, and adding footnotes! The most amusing atmosphere I've ever had.

T.E.L.

Bodleian Reserve

HIS MOTHER
18.11.16   Arab Bureau Savoy Hotel Cairo

This is only a scrawl to inform you what I wired: — namely that I have got back to Cairo. I left on October 13 from Cairo, reached Jidda on October 16, left there on October 19, for Rabegh. Left Rabegh on October 21, by camel; went up to Sherif Feisul's H.Q. at a place called Bir Abbas, half-way between Medina and the sea, about 100 miles North of Rabegh. After a few days there returned by road to Yenbo, and embarked on Nov. 1 for Jidda. On November 4 changed ships there, and went across to Port Sudan with Admiral Wemyss.[1] Reached Khartoum on November 7, and stayed with the Sirdar[2] till November 11, when I took train down the Nile to Halfa, then steamer to Asswan, and then by rail to Cairo.

At Asswan Hugh Whitelocke got into my carriage, and we were together as far as Luxor where he intended to stay a day to sightsee.

Since my return I have been extravagantly busy: — so much so that I cannot possibly write to you probably for two or three days yet. The day is one long series of interruptions.

I have now left G.H.Q. and joined the Arab Bureau,[3] which is under the Residency here. That is, the Sirdar is in charge of it, or will be very shortly.

Colonel Edouard Brémond, which was to continue after the war, was never to be an easy one, though he admired Brémond's military record (he had fought on the Somme) and in an early reference in *Seven Pillars* described him as 'the only real soldier in Hejaz'.

1 Admiral Sir Rosslyn Wemyss: Commander-in-Chief, East Indies and India, 1916–17, First Sea Lord 1917–19, created Baron 1919.
2 The Sirdar, i.e. Commander-in-Chief, of the Egyptian Army at this time was Sir Reginald Wingate; he was also (1899–1916) Governor-General of the Sudan. He was High Commissioner of Egypt 1917–19 and G.O.C. Hejaz Operations. Created Baron 1920.
3 The Arab Bureau had been established in February 1916 to deal specifically with Arabian problems and initiatives. It was under the control of the Foreign Office and (to quote Robert Graves, *Lawrence and the Arabs*, Chapter V) 'was run by a small group of men, some of them, like Lloyd and Hogarth, old friends of Lawrence's, who really knew something about the Arabs — and about the Turks'. It acted as a Staff and Intelligence Office for the Arabian campaign.

The atmosphere of being one's own master — or at any rate of being with people whose voices are not drowned by their grinding of axes — is pleasant. All very well.

N.

HL/Bodleian Reserve

By the time the following letter was written Lawrence was back in Arabia with the Sherifian forces, with whom he would serve for the rest of the war, though he would also make many visits to General Headquarters (in Egypt to begin with, later in Palestine) and to various other places, such as Suez, Jidda, Jerusalem, Beersheba, as occasion required. His appointment to Feisal was originally envisaged as a temporary one only, but it was so successful ('The value of Lawrence in the position which he has made for himself with Feisul is enormous': Brigadier-General Clayton to Major Hugh Pearson, 2 March 1917) that there was no thought of removing him. The successful relationship between him and Feisal —welding Arab vision and leadership with British enthusiasm and commitment — was to prove a powerful energising force throughout most of the campaign.

For a clear layman's introduction to the situation in which Lawrence now found himself, the reader is recommended to turn to his letter to his mother dated 12 February 1917.

DIRECTOR, ARAB BUREAU[1]

2.12.16   Yenbo

Director Arab Bureau

I got a wire from George Lloyd asking me to meet him at Yenbo. So I stopped till today. I am off now in half an hour to Feisal, who is at Kheif Hussein. No more news of the skirmish at Kheif. I hope to clear up that situation, and expect to be back on Monday night.

Garland[2] takes over my cipher. He is a most excellent man, and has won over everybody here. The very man for the place. His pupils seem to have

1 Major, later Sir Kinahan Cornwallis (1883–1959); Director Arab Bureau 1916–18.
2 Major Herbert Garland, attached to the Egyptian Army at this time with the rank of Bimbashi (equivalent to Major). Writer, metallurgist, inventor of the 'Garland' grenade and expert in explosives. Lawrence wrote of him in *Seven Pillars*: '... his knowledge of Arabic and freedom from the theories of the ordinary sapper-school enabled him to teach the art of demolition to unlettered Beduin in a quick and ready way.'

got on well on the Railway on the 29th.

Atmospherics here have been very bad, and so I have not been able to wire much.

Lloyd has arrived at the root of the matter, and his report will be worth seeing.[1]

Let me know Newcombe's movements.

TEL

Have been wildly rushed all day & yesterday mapping an aeroplane ground here.

PRO FO 882/7

DIRECTOR, ARAB BUREAU
5.12.16   [Yenbo]

[...] I had better preface by saying that I rode all Saturday night, had alarms and excursions all Sunday night, and rode again all last night, so my total of sleep is only three hours in the last three nights and I feel rather pessimistic. All the same, things are bad.[2] Henceforward much of the Harb will have to be ruled out. [...]

There is nothing now to prevent the Turks going South except Ali's anaemic force at Rabegh itself, the possibility of a recrudescence of the warlike spirit of the Harb in their rear, or the fear of Feisal behind them all. Feisal's position becomes difficult. He is cut off by the Wadi Safra from the Hejaz proper, and his power of cutting the Sultani road becomes remote.

1 Lloyd shortly produced a long *Report on the Hejas* [*sic*], dated 22 December 1916, covering all aspects of the Arab Revolt, political, military and economic, of which one keynote passage — with which Lawrence would have had full sympathy — reads as follows: 'It must ... be realised that whilst the Shereef is undoubtedly fully grateful and sensible for the sympathy and assistance which His Majesty's Government are giving him, he is yet quite acute enough to realise that he on his side is rendering important service to the British in this theatre of war. He recognises that his revolt is immobilising the best part of two Turkish divisions ... and that he with his tribesmen has been holding up as large a force as that which is engaged in Sinai. ... In consequence of this it is scarcely surprising that he feels that his own wishes and views should have weight with H.M.G., if not as an equal yet still as something more than a mere suppliant in receipt of favours.' (*PRO FO 686/6*)
2 Lawrence had arrived at Feisal's camp to find that he had suffered a severe setback at the hands of the Turks. In a surprise attack they had routed one of the main elements of Feisal's army, the levies of the Harb tribe. They had also set by the heels the smaller force under the command of Feisal's younger brother, Zeid, which had retreated in confusion towards Yenbo.

He is left with the Juheina only and they are a tribe with the seeds of trouble all present in them, in the jealousy of the Ibn Bedawi family of the hold Feisal is getting over their tribesmen. Feisal is the beau ideal of the tribal leader. I heard him address the head of one battalion last night before sending them out to an advanced position over the Turkish camp at Bir Said. He did not say much, no noise about it, but it was all exactly right and the people rushed over one another with joy to kiss his headrope when he finished. He has had a nasty knock in Zeid's retreat, and he realised perfectly well that it was the ruin of all his six months' work up here in the hills tying tribe to tribe and fixing each in its proper area. Yet he took it all in public as a joke, chaffing people on the way they had run away, jeering at them like children, but without in the least hurting their feelings and making the others feel that nothing much had happened that could not be put right. He is magnificent for to me privately he was most horribly cut up. [...]

Another thing, Feisal is out of his area here. He knows little more about Wadi Yenbo than we do. The names of places, sorts of roads and water supply are strange to him. He could still strike north, raise the Billi and Huweitat tribes and develop into South Syria, only he cannot do this while the Turkish force is free to attack Mecca in his absence.

I asked him about the effect on the tribes of the fall of Rabegh and Mecca.[1] It seems both have a great name among the tribes and he was not sure that the warlike feelings of the Juheina would survive the recovery of them by the Turks. Once he thought they would and then he thought they would not. Anyway he himself would not stick in the north and see Mecca fall. He swore he would come down by sea at once with the few Bisha and Hadtheil[2] that could come with him and die in defence of his people. On the other hand he does change his mind, and I estimate his personal prestige among the Arabs so great as to survive everything except actual and direct military disaster. If he loses Wadi Yenbo it will be greatly dimmed and he will go to Wadi Ais as a sort of fugitive and will lose Yenbo.

Feisal received me most cordially and I lived all the time with him in his tent or camp, so I had a very great insight into what he could do at a pinch.[3] If I was not such a physical rag I would tell you all about it.

                                                        T. E. Lawrence

1 Lawrence was asking what would happen *if* Rabegh and Mecca fell; they had not done so.
2 i.e. tribesmen from the vicinity of Mecca.
3 It was during this visit that Feisal made the request, to which Lawrence was happy to accede, that he should wear Arab clothes like his own while in his camp; one of the reasons given in *Seven Pillars* is that if so attired he could 'slip in and out of Feisal's tent without making a sensation which he had to explain away each time to strangers'.

P.S. Don't use any of above in bulletin or elsewhere, it is not just — because I am done up.

PRO FO 882/7

DIRECTOR, ARAB BUREAU
[c. 11 December 1916]

I am going down to Rabegh today to see Colonel Joyce and Major Ross.[1] I want to ask Colonel Joyce why he never sends me any information, and to get him to withdraw the Egyptian contingent, who are only a nuisance to us and the Arabs. I want to talk over the question of satisfactory air reconnaissance with Ross. He has four times tried to send a plane up here, and it has only once got through. That time its observation was a farce, so far as Yenbo was concerned, for he sent it up Wadi Safra from Bedr to near Bir Abbas, and then back to Waset, and up through Jebr to Nujeil, and so down over N. Mubarak to Yenbo. It was the end of a four-hour flight when they reached Yenbo, and the last half hour only was over an area of importance, and during that half-hour the men were too dazed to see anything. Also they only had the old map, and no notes on what places looked like, or what to look for. So they saw nothing, though they passed over Nakhl Mubarak during the battle.

I want them to come to Yenbo straight, and do their local reconnaissance on their way back to Rabegh, when we have primed them with what we want to know. If Ross cannot arrange this then the only thing to do will be to base a plane on Yenbo itself. The seaplanes have been doing yeoman work these last two days, bomb dropping on Bruka, and scouring the country.

My position at Yenbo is a little odd. I wire to Colonel Wilson only, and got a letter from him to say that I was in charge of supplies at Yenbo. That is not possible, for Abd el Kader, as agent of Sherif Feisul, runs the supply question ashore, and our interference would not be welcomed — and is not necessary. Whatever may be the position at Rabegh and Jidda, I can vouch that Yenbo is a most efficiently-run show. All that a 'supply officer' has to

1 Lieutenant-Colonel Pierce Joyce, who had been less than impressed by Lawrence at their first meeting in November 1916 (at Port Sudan when Lawrence was on his way to report to Sir Reginald Wingate in Khartoum), was soon to become his close ally and friend. 'Joyce worked for long beside me' (*Seven Pillars*, Chapter XVI). Major A. J. Ross was the Royal Flying Corps commander in the Hejaz.

do is to hand over the way-bills or whatever you call them, to Abd el Kader.[1]

I regard myself as primarily Intelligence officer, or liaison with Feisul. This was all right while Feisul was in the Interior, as they seem settled to have no one but myself in there. Only he is now in Yenbo, half-besieged, and in these circumstances Garland is much more use than I could be. For one thing, he is senior to me, and he is an expert on explosives and machinery. He digs their trenches, repairs their guns, teaches them musketry, machine gun work, signalling; gets on with them exceedingly well, always makes the best of things, and they all like him too. He is quite alive to intelligence work also, though he has not been in contact enough with things or documents to know much outside the immediate area here. Anyway he is the best man for Yenbo, and while he is here, I am wasting my time walking about with him. That is really why I am going down to Joyce, to see if he can suggest anything worth doing.[2]

Communication to & from Yenbo by wireless is very slow, for the naval work takes precedence, and Captain Boyle[3] wires a great deal of naval stuff, as well as intelligence reports, based on notes picked up by his interpreter, and from various telegrams. The interpreter is an Egyptian, and is not good.

Feisul has now swung round to the belief in a British force at Rabegh. I have wired this to you, and I see myself that his arguments have force. If Zeid had not been so slack, things would never have got to this pass.

[...]

T E Lawrence

Garland has written to you suggesting he have a few days' leave in Egypt. I hope this can be arranged, for he has done most admirable work here, and just at present all that is at a standstill.

.L.

PRO FO 882/6

1 Abd el Kader el Abdu (described by Lawrence in *Seven Pillars* as 'a well-informed, efficient, quiet and dignified person'), had only recently arrived in Yenbo from Mecca, where he had been Postmaster-General of the Hejaz at the time of the Hejaz stamps issue.
2 The problem of the division of labour between Lawrence and Garland was to be of short duration; Lawrence continued as adviser to Feisal as the latter's army moved northwards towards Syria, Garland spent much of the next two years carrying out valuable demolition and other work in the Hejaz.
3 Captain W. E. D. Boyle R.N. was Senior Naval Officer, Red Sea; later Admiral the Earl of Cork and Orrery.

HIS MOTHER
14.12.16 [Rabegh]

Am in Rabegh — half way between Jidda and Yenbo — tonight, & have just heard that a mail is closing for England. So as I did not write last one here goes this one. I cannot write you details till I reach Egypt, which will not be for some two weeks or so yet. Things very interesting at Yenbo, where is Sherif Feisul, one of the Sons of the Sherif of Mecca. I left there three days ago, and ran down to Jidda, to do a little business: am now going back, to stop a few days. Weather delightful, neither hot nor cold, with beautiful winds.

This letter will probably reach you a little after Christmas. I hope it will not be too wet again. All today I have been discussing Arabian geography & politics, which are the local topics. One has forgotten that there are other wars on.

If that silk headcloth with the silver ducks on it — last used I believe as a table-cloth — still exists, will you send it out to me? Such things are hard to get here now.

N.

This is not a letter: only a substitute for a field post card.

N.

HL/Bodleian Reserve

COLONEL C. E. WILSON[1]
19th December 1916 Yenbo

I am taking the opportunity of Mr. Garland's leaving Yenbo for Cairo on leave to send you some notes on local conditions here. I hope it will be arranged that he returns here when his leave expires; his knowledge of tools and arms has been invaluable, and when Feisul is able to restore communication with the Hejaz Railway, it will be possible for him to go up there and direct his explosive parties personally. Everybody ashore likes him.

[...]

Mr Garland will speak to you about the question of guns for the Sherif's

---

1 As British Resident in Jidda, Wilson had met Lawrence at the time of the Storrs-/-Abdulla conversations and had not been impressed; he later reported, however, on the 'great value' of his services to the campaign and on his 'pluck and endurance' (official report: 28 May 1917).

troops. I personally feel strongly that the inferior quality of these troops demands a superfine technical equipment. They have not the tactical skill to make an inferior gun, by superior handling, equal to the better gun of their enemies. Unless we can give them weapons in which they have confidence they will not be capable of meeting the Turkish artillery. When with Feisul in November I wrote down to Colonel Parker, and asked for a battery of British field guns, latest pattern, with telescopic sights. The guns supplied to Feisul are two German-made fifteen-pounder guns, very much worn, without telescopic sights or range-tables, with defective fuses and ammunition, and lacking essential parts of elevating gear, etc. I think that a battery of used 18-pounders, with complete equipment, should be supplied to replace them.

[...]

I think the Arab forces have made a fair show. The night that Turks were rumoured to be within a few miles the garrison was called out about 10 p.m. by means of criers sent round the streets. The men all turned out without visible excitement, and proceeded to their posts round the town wall without making a noise, or firing a shot. This is in contrast to their usual waste of ammunition without excuse, and shows an intention of rising to an emergency. The sentries have also kept a fairly good watch, and the outpost lines have been maintained steadily by day and night, at considerable distances outside the walls. The attitude towards ourselves of the Syrian and Mesopotamian officers in the army has been good. I have detected no signs of professional or political jealousy, except as regards the Egyptians.

[...]

There was a fight three days ago between 300 Ageyl and 400 Hadheyl, over a question of camels. About 1000 rounds were fired, and two men were killed and six wounded. The fight was checked by Feisul himself, who went out bare-headed and bare-footed, as he happened to be, and made peace at once. Some bullets struck the Monitor (M.31) in the harbour, and narrowly missed wounding or killing some of her crew. Sherif Feisul came off, when the matter was pointed out to him by Captain Boyle, and expressed his regret. The prompt quelling of the disturbance gives, I think, a good illustration of his personal prestige among his followers, since the affair was taking large proportions.

Rumours are current on the ships that British rifles can be bought cheaply ashore. I have tried to verify these, but without success and I think they are generally false, though isolated instances of men anxious to get rid of their arms may have occurred. The British rifle is highly prized.

T. E. Lawrence

PRO FO 882/6

MAJOR KINAHAN CORNWALLIS
27.12.16   [Yenbo]

Dear K.C.

It has been very good of you to send those two wires about Abd el Kader's son. The old man is more than grateful, and I am sure that he deserves it! He does everything in Yenbo, and is the best disposed person towards us I have struck.[1] I fear I am irregular & bad in reporting things to you. There has been so little worth sending of late.

If I am to stay here I will need all sorts of things. Have you any news of Newcombe? The situation is so interesting that I think I will fail to come back. I want to rub off my British habits & go off with Feisul for a bit. Amusing job, and all new country. When I have someone to take over here from me I'll go off. Wadi Ais is the unknown area of N. Hejaz, and I want to drop up and see it — anything behind Rudhwa will be worth while.

I enclose a file of papers: will you distribute them to the wise and the foolish? The map corrections are filthy, but I got so tired of making copies for everyone that you only get the original—unless the Flying people performed according to their promises and sent you a proper copy. However Dowson will, inshallah, make it out. I want it embodied, not in 3rd. Ed. Medina–Mecca, but in the 1st. Edn. <u>Medina</u>. A map showing Wejh and the Railway is an absolute necessity. Hogarth will find you Huber or Wallin — Burton is the other source. Let it be the full size & shape of the final sheet.

The 3rd. Medina–Mecca will then be a future issue, including probably a further revise of the Wadi Yenbo, and the new R.F.C. work Fina-Gaha etc. Ask Dowson to press the drawing of the Medina sheet. It should be very rough, and sketchy.

Am glad Bray[2] is back. I wonder what the next week will bring forth, here and there. Somehow I do not believe in a Turkish advance on Mecca, though they could, if they wished.

Wilson will send you a note on Dhurmish of Akaba. About Faiz, I thought you would try to bag him: he is a very unusual person. Don't get him caught by the Turks as a spy!

Send me a Hejaz Handbook some day, and an *Arab Bulletin* later than 31. You know they had no copy of my route-notes in Rabegh. They would have been useful to R.F.C.[3]

1 Abd el Kader el Abdu: see p. 95.
2 Captain, later Major N.N.E. Bray, Indian Army. Worked for Arab Bureau 1916. Subsequently emerged as a critic of Lawrence's role in Arabia notably in his book *Shifting Sands* published in 1934. See letter to Mrs Charlotte Shaw December 1934 (headed 'Monday night late'), p. 507.
3 R.F.C.: Royal Flying Corps.

Wedgwood Benn of the *Ben-My-Chree*[1] has got 200 negatives of the Muller party murdered near Jidda. They include a lot of Yemen things. Get them, if you can. Limbery gave them to him.

TEL

Will you get from Citadel & send down to Abd el Kader a leather portfolio of E[gyptian] Govt pattern. It should be 3 times as long as the paper is high. Present from me.

TEL

PRO FO 882/6

The most important development in the Arabian campaign in early 1917 was the advance of Feisal's army from Yenbo to Wejh, 180 miles to the north on the Red Sea coast. The move, closely supported by the Royal Navy, had the twin virtue of taking the war to the enemy and exposing more of the Hejaz Railway to attack; and of providing a vital psychological boost to Arab pride and thus increasing the incentive to tribes not yet involved to rally to the Revolt. 'We wanted this march, which would be in its way a closing act of the war in Northern Hejaz, to send a rumour through the length and breadth of Western Arabia. It was to be the biggest action of the Arabs in their memory; dismissing those who saw it to their homes, with a sense that their world had changed indeed; so that there would be no more silly defections and jealousies of clans behind us in future, to cripple us with family politics in the middle of our fighting.' (*Seven Pillars of Wisdom*, Chapter XXII)

Feisal left Yenbo on 3 January and reached Wejh on the 25th.

1 William Wedgwood Benn, later Lord Stansgate (1877–1960), father of Anthony Wedgwood Benn (Tony Benn M.P.). The *Ben-My-Chree* was a seaplane carrier, converted from a cross-channel steamer; she was sunk by Turkish shore batteries in 1917. Wedgwood Benn described his wartime experiences in his book *In the Side Shows*, by Captain Wedgwood Benn D.S.O. D.F.C. M.P., published in 1919.

COLONEL C. E. WILSON[1]
5.1.17   [Yenbo]

I have just come in from Feisul, and the *Race Fisher*[2] is leaving in half an hour. So I am sending a hurried note on Northern Politics.

As I reported to Captain Bray, Ibn Sheddad, Feisul's self-appointed messenger to the North (he is a Beni Wahab sheikh) left about Nov. 15 for Jauf. He got there in 12 days hard riding, without incident. In Jauf he found Nuri, Nawaf, Fawaz, and Sinaitan.[3] They held a committee meeting & came to the decision that they would break off all relations with the Turkish government at once. They will not however commit themselves to an active policy, until Feisul has established himself at El Ula,[4] and has opened up direct communication with them. This involves his occupying Teima, and blocking out Shammar Ghazzua — which Nawaf will not undertake. Teima is held by Abu Rumman for Ibn Rashid with seven men: — and offers to surrender to 8 — but Nawaf will not move against Ibn Rashid as yet.

The reasons that influence the Aneza sheikhs are those of ammunition (they have Martini & Gras guns) barley, and wheat. Jauf produces enough dates for the tribes, and some over, which are sent to Damascus. El Ula is the first possible point with which they can have direct contact with supplies from the Sherif.

The tone of the messages sent by Nuri and Nawaf to Feisul is excellent. They are quite ready to do their work, as soon as it gives a fair chance of success.

[...]

Feisul will not send ibn Sheddad North again, except from El Ula, when he has reached there himself. Matters stand over till then.

[...]

T E Lawrence

Feisul asks for	10 valises & flea-bags (for himself & staff: it is very cold here)
	1 Attaché case (a leather case with two locks about 18 inches long, & flat, for confidential papers)
All recommended by me, and urgent	1 sleeping tent, for himself. To be small and double if possible: big enough for a bed, and sitting ground for five or six people round a tray. We

1 The letter is addressed to Colonel Wilson, but with a note by Lawrence at the head of the page: '(Copy sent: this direct Cairo to save time).'
2 The *Race Fisher* was a fleet messenger ship, one of five employed on the East India & Egypt Station.
3 Sheikhs of the Ruwalla tribe.
4 El Ula: a station on the Hejaz Railway, about a hundred miles to the north-east of Wejh.

all feed in his tent together. The Survey[1] can make
this tent, if none are available. Strong ropes, and
double set pegs, iron & wood.
3 batteries of Q.F.[2] Mountain Guns.
1 battery of 18 pounders.
Also please send me 4 sets of 1/250000 of Syria, and 1/500000 of Maan
etc. (MAPS) Also one R.G.S. 1/200000 Syria Mesopotamia, etc.

TEL

PRO FO 882/6

HIS MOTHER
16.1.17   Umm Lejj

I have not written for a fortnight, for at first I was up country hopping
about on a camel, and later there was no post-boat. You see we have no
mail-steamers, but depend entirely on the Navy for our communications,
and they go about their business strictly. However, in any case you know
that I am completely well. I have got leave to stay down here a fortnight
longer, because things here are interesting, and new. Life in Yenbo was
varied, because I lived always on ships, and while there was always a ship,
it was sometimes one and sometimes another sort of ship. Some were
luxurious, some warlike, & some very plain — but all different. This place
you will not find on any map, unless you buy the northern sheets of the
Red Sea Admiralty charts (I don't recommend them!): any way, it is about
100 miles North of Yenbo, and is a little group of three villages (about 40
houses in each) on a plain about a mile square under red granite hills. As it
is spring just now the valleys and slopes are sprinkled with a pale green,
and things are beautiful. The weather is just warm enough to be too hot at
midday, but cold at night. I'm on a ship, as usual.

Sherif Feisul (3rd Son of Sherif of Mecca), to whom I am attached, is
about 31, tall, slight, lively, well-educated. He is charming towards me,
and we get on perfectly together. He has a tremendous reputation in the
Arab world as a leader of men, and a diplomat. His strong point is handling
tribes: he has the manner that gets on perfectly with tribesmen, and they
all love him. At present he is governing a patch of country about as large
as Wales, and doing it efficiently. I have taken some good photographs of
things here (Arab forces and villages and things), and will send you copies
when I can get prints made. That will not be till about the end of the
month, when I go to Cairo.

1 The Survey of Egypt, headed by Dowson.
2 Q.F.: quick-firing.

My Arabic is getting quite fluent again! I nearly forgot it in Egypt, where I never spoke for fear of picking up the awful Egyptian accent and vocabulary. A few months more of this, and I'll be a qualified Arabian. I wish I had not to go back to Egypt. Any way I have had a change.

                                                            N.

HL/Bodleian Reserve

LIEUTENANT-COLONEL S. F. NEWCOMBE[1]
17.1.17   [Um Lejj]

Dear S.F.N.

So I miss you by a day! I'm very sick, but it was either that or miss Wadi Hamdh, with the foreknowledge that I may never see Wadi Hamdh again, and that I will certainly see you at Wejh.[2]

I prepared Feisal (who is an absolute ripper) carefully for you, and had him well wound up to meet you on the morrow — and after all I took Vickery out with me instead.[3] It won't do, you know, that sort of thing.

This show is splendid: you cannot imagine greater fun for us, greater vexation and fury for the Turks. We win hands down if we keep the Arabs simple ... to add to them heavy luxuries will only wreck their show, and guerilla does it. It's a sort of *guerre de course*, with the courses all reversed. But the life and fun and movement of it are extreme.

I'm awfully glad you have come out ... you'll find it as good as I say and better — especially after you have met me. With which modest — but not senseless, saying — sleep. Boyle is good ... proud of his profession, but white, and itching for a show.[4] Try and get him a little game at Wejh. I'd like him to land N. of the town, & work along the sand-hills into the camp.

Vickery had a funny idea that nothing had yet been done out here. It's not true: may I suggest that by effacing yourself for the first part, and making friends with the head men before you start pulling them about, you will find your way very much easier? They tried the forceful game at

1 Later that year Colonel Newcombe's camel saddle-bag containing this letter and other documents was taken by a Turkish officer, Ismet Karadoyan Bey, at Qaleat Al Zumarrad on the Hejaz Railway after a skirmish between Arab and Turkish patrols. The two officers corresponded after the war and Newcombe's papers were returned to him.
2 Lawrence was writing during the march to Wejh.
3 Major Charles Vickery was a regular gunnery officer of considerable experience (he had served in the South African War, had spent five years with the Egyptian Army and had recently been at Gallipoli) whose military expertise Lawrence respected but with whom he differed over policy and tactics.
4 Captain Boyle was in charge of the seaborne force involved in the move to Wejh.

Rabegh—and have spoiled all the show. After all, it's an Arab war, and we are only contributing materials—and the Arabs have the right to go their own way and run things as they please. We are only guests.

Shall look forward to the 23rd beyond measure.[1]

L.

St Antony's College Oxford

HIS MOTHER

31.1.17   Arab Bureau Savoy Hotel Cairo

Am back in Cairo, though only for a few days. Left Yenbo about a fortnight ago, for Um Lejj, by sea. Landed at Um Lejj and came up by land to Wejh, which we took without fighting.[2] A landing party from the ships had practically done the work the day before. I snatched a week's leave, to come up here and buy some things, before going off to Sherif Feisul again.

As I have not had any letters lately (due to my moving about, and the difficulty of posts in the Red Sea) I cannot answer any particular questions. Things in Arabia are very pleasant, though the job I have is rather a responsible one, and sometimes it is a little heavy to see which way one ought to act. I am getting rather old with it all, I think! However it is very nice to be out of the office, with some field work in hand, and the position I have is such a queer one—I do not suppose that any Englishman before ever had such a place.

All of which is rather tantalising reading to you, because I cannot enter into details. I act as a sort of adviser to Sherif Feisul, and as we are on the best of terms, the job is a wide and pleasant one. I live with him, in his tent, so our food and things (if you will continue to be keen on such rubbish!) is as good as the Hejaz can afford. Personally I am more and more convinced that it doesn't matter a straw what you eat or drink, so long as you do not do either oftener than you feel inclined.

It has been very cold down there lately: the thermometer one morning

1 In fact Newcombe joined Lawrence in the desert on the 18th, the day after this letter was written.
2 There was no fighting by Feisal's army, but there was by the landing force, which included tribesmen, of whom twenty were killed. A British lieutenant of the Royal Flying Corps also died. Lawrence, who believed Wejh could have been forced to surrender without any show of force in a matter of days, was angered by what seemed to him pointless losses. If the whole garrison of Wejh had escaped, 'it would not have mattered the value of an Arab life. We wanted Wejh as a base against the railway and to expand our front; the smashing and the killing in it had been wanton.' (*Seven Pillars*, Chapter XXVII)

was down to 50° which struck us as rather serious!

The war in Arabia is going on very well: the Arabs are very keen and patriotic, and the Turks are beginning to get really frightened. I hope to write a better letter tomorrow: this is only a scrawl to catch the mail.

N.

HL/Bodleian Reserve

HIS MOTHER
12.2.17   Wejh

Here I am, back in Wejh again, sitting in our funny house trying to write or think or work. I'm afraid there are too many interruptions for much success.

Newcombe is here, and I hope things are going well. I got a letter from Arnie the other day pleading for more news of what the Sherifian forces are doing. Well you know, it is not my fault. They do a great deal, but some people — not themselves — seem to wish to keep the progress of the campaign a secret. As a matter of fact progress is difficult. The Arabs of the Hejaz are all for the Sherif, some keenly enough to volunteer, others less keen, but all well-wishers. Only, they are tribesmen, and as such are rebellious by instinct. They hate the Turks, but they don't want to obey anyone's orders, and in consequence they turn out only as a mob of snipers or guerilla-fighters. They are wonderfully active, quite intelligent, and do what they do do fairly well. They are however not fit to meet disciplined troops in the open, and it will be a long time before they are.

These details will give you a fair idea of the sort of campaign it is. There is a bunch of about 12,000 Turks in Medina and the neighbourhood, clinging to certain important water-supplies and roads South and West of Medina, and surrounded, on all sides except the Railway, by Arabs. The Turks are also holding the Hejaz Railway, which we now threaten from Tebuk downwards, but not as yet in any force. The Arabs proved incapable of taking Medina, held by its present garrison, and the Medina garrison proved unable to advance through the Arabs against Mecca. So now we have shifted part of our forces North to this place, and the struggle for the Railway will probably be the feature of this second phase of the Hejaz Campaign.

The Arab Movement is a curious thing. It is really very small and weak in its beginning, and anybody who had command of the sea could put an end to it in three or four days. It has however capacity for expansion — in the same degree — over a very wide area. It is as though you imagine a nation or agitation that may be very wide, but never very deep, since all the Arab countries are agricultural or pastoral, and all poor today, as a result of Turkish efforts in the past.

On the other hand the Arab Movement is shallow, not because the Arabs do not care, but because they are few — and in their smallness of number (which is imposed by their poverty of country) lies a good deal of their strength, for they are perhaps the most elusive enemy an army ever had, and inhabit one of the most trying countries in the world for civilised warfare.

So that on the whole you may write me down a reasonable optimist: I hope that the show may go as we wish, and that the Turkish flag may disappear from Arabia. It is indiscreet only to ask what Arabia is. It has an East and a West and a South border — but where or what it is on the top no man knoweth. I fancy myself it is up to the Arabs to find out! Talk about Palestine or Syria or Mesopotamia is not opportune, when these three countries — with every chance — have made no effort towards freedom for themselves.

I wonder what the censor will make of this letter? It may contain news for him, but I'm afraid precious little to the enemy! However you never know what they will do, and there is a 'Hush' policy over the Red Sea and Arabia which causes a good deal of amusement to the Arabs — and to us who are down here.

I hope to be able to send you some photographs of the Sherif and of Feisul and the rest of us shortly. Please wait in peace till then. Incidentally I'm to have no post towards you now for about ten days. Patience!

N.

HL/Bodleian Reserve

HIS MOTHER
25.2.17   Arab Bureau Savoy Hotel Cairo

Back in Cairo again for a few days — till the 28th to be exact. One does run about on this show! But as a matter of fact I have only come up to get some mules, and a wireless set, and a few such-like things.

Affairs are going a little slower than I had hoped, but there has been no suspicion of a set-back, and we are all well contented. I enclose a few photographs — as long as they are not published there is no harm in showing them to anyone. I have a lot more, but they have not been printed yet. They will give you an idea of the sort of country (in the oases) and the sort of people we have to do with. It is of course by far the most wonderful time I have had.

I don't know what to write about! What we will do when I get back I don't know exactly — and cannot say any how. Cairo is looking very gay, and everybody dances & goes to races as usual or more so — but after all, there is not, and never has been, war in Egypt.

The weather here is fresh — and in Wejh warmish. [...]

I got the headcloth safely, about a week ago, in Wejh,[1] together with news that Bob had gone to France.[2] As a matter of fact, you know, he will be rather glad afterwards that he has been ... and as it will be easier work, and healthier than his hospital work in London, I do not think that you have much cause to regret. Many thanks for the headcloth. [...]

I have now been made a Captain and Staff Captain again, which is amusing. It doesn't make any difference of course really, as I am never in uniform in Arabia, and nobody cares a straw what rank I hold, except that I am of Sherif Feisul's household.

Can't think of anything else to say, as have become a monomaniac about the job in hand, and have no interest or recollections except Arabian politics just now! It's amusing to think that this will suddenly come to an end one day, and I take up other work.

N.

HL/Bodleian Reserve

A FELLOW BRITISH OFFICER[3]

22.3.17   El Ain in Wadi Ais

I should have written before but have been ill. However things are quite alright now. Situation on line is stationary. Deserters come in daily and we have got a decent intelligence service with places right down to Medina. [...] The three aeroplanes in Medina have been burnt. I suspect they were bad ones, given up as useless therefore got rid of them and there are wild rumours in the place. Colonel Wilson asks that Ross be informed where we are. El Ain is about 10 miles West and South of Murubba in W. Ais on the 1/500,000 of Wejh as far as I can see. I did a compass traverse from Wejh but it was a shaky one. The road I came by was awful; hardly possible

---

1 See his letter home of 14.12.16.
2 M. R. Lawrence (Bob) served with the Royal Army Medical Corps in France from 1916–19.
3 This letter was preserved in typescript in a series of files containing papers, mainly carbon copies of letters and signals, apparently accumulated by Colonel Wilson. No addressee is given. The letter is an interesting one, being written on the seventh day of the ten days' illness in Abdulla's camp during which, according to Chapter XXXIII of *Seven Pillars*, Lawrence rethought the whole strategy of the Arab campaign. For Lawrence's account of conditions in Abdulla's camp and the reasons for his being there see next letter.

for camels. Am making headway steadily and hope to have a force of my own shortly. I want here two big railway moveable spanners and two wire cutters. There are supplies of each in the house at Wejh and Sherif Feisal will send them up.

Please see Sidi[1] Feisul for me and tell him I have not been able to do my job here because I have been ill. I hope to go down to the railway tomorrow for a preliminary reconnaissance and after that will be able to say what can be done, but in any case I will stay here a bit as it is most important that the Turks should not be able to concentrate much of their Medina force at El-Ula against him, and I am afraid if I do not stay here not much will be done.

Please beg him not to remain in Wejh unless it is absolutely necessary. The effect both on Arabs and Turks of knowing him to be near the line would be very great, and if he left his heavy baggage in Wejh he could fall back on it in case of need, quickly.

He has aeroplanes now and Wejh is very easy to defend. Also if the Turks pushed West from El-Ula I would get Sidi Abdulla to march up the line towards El-Ula which would have the effect of bringing the Turks back.

In fact I hope most strongly to find him at Jayadah or Ainsheifa soon.

Lawrence

PRO FO 686/6

COLONEL C. E. WILSON[2]
16.4.17   Wedj

[...] I had to stay in Abdulla's camp from March 15th to March 25th. On the way up I developed boils, which made camel riding uncomfortable, and on top of them first a short attack of dysentery, and then somewhat heavy malaria for about ten days. This combination pulled me down rather, so that I was unable either to walk or ride. I think, however, that even had I been fit I would have been unable to get Sidi Abdulla to take action much sooner than was actually the case.

---

1 Sidi: the customary honorific title used for the four sons of Grand Sherif Hussein (lit. 'my lord').

2 A brief summary of the contents of this report, with some direct quotations, appeared in the *Arab Bulletin* of 23 May, under the title 'In Sherif Abdullah's Camp'. It should be stressed that though Lawrence's account of Abdulla as a military leader was critical he had been sent out specifically 'to find out why he [Abdulla] had done nothing for two months' (see *Seven Pillars*, Chapter XXXI) and to stimulate him into action; and that he balanced his criticisms by paying tribute to Abdulla as the 'head and cause' of the Revolt, he having been the chief Arab negotiator with the British from 1914 onwards.

The conditions in his camp were, I thought, unsatisfactory. He had a force of about 3,000 men, mostly Ateiba. They seem to me very inferior as fighting men, to the Harb and Juheina.[1] [...] Access to the camp is nearly limited to his intimates, and he spends very little time with visiting Sheikhs or deputations. The business arrangements of supplies, equipment, money, accounts, and secretarial work generally are in the hands of Sheikh Othman, a Yemeni scholar, much over-worked and without even a clerk to assist him. Sidi Abdulla exercises little or no supervision and Shakir,[2] though he does a certain amount, hardly replaces him. Abdulla himself spends his time in reading the Arabic newspapers, in eating, and sleeping, and especially in jesting with one Mohamed Hassan, an old Yemeni from Taif, nominally Muedh Dhin[3] in the camp, but whom Abdulla introduced to me as his Karageuz (Punch). Abdulla and his friends spend much of the day and all the evening in playing practical jokes on Mohamed Hassan. These take the form usually of stabbing him with thorns, stoning him, or setting him on fire. The jests are somewhat elaborate: the day before I arrived Abdulla set a coffee pot on his head, and pierced it three times with shots from his rifle at 20 yards. Mohamed Hassan was then given £30 reward for his patience. Sidi Abdulla is fond of rifle practice, and also of Arabic poetry. Reciters from the camp while away much of his time with songs and dances.

He takes great interest in the war in Europe, and follows the operations on the Somme, and the general course of European politics most closely. I was surprised to find that he knew the family relationships of the Royal Houses of Europe, and the names and characters of their ministers. He takes little interest in the war in the Hedjaz. He considers the Arab position as assured with Syria and Iraq irrevocably pledged to the Arabs by Great Britain's signed agreements, and for himself looks particularly to the Yemen. He regards this, rather than Syria, as the future basis of strength of the Arab movement, and intends, as soon as set free from the boredom of these Northern operations, to chase Muhieddin out of Ibha, Idrissi out of Arabia and compel the Imam to the position of a feudatory. This sounds a large operation, but Abdulla is convinced of its practicability, and has even worked out the details of his actions. [...]

For the actual work for which I have come to this camp, Sidi Abdulla's attitude was hardly favourable. His Ateiba knew nothing of the country in which they were, — and their Sheikhs are non-entities. He had only a handful of Juheina with him and, led away by Shakir's tastes, scarcely desired more. Of his five machine guns only two were effective for lack [of] armourers or spares; he had no artillery officers, and till Feisal stripped himself of two of his four 2.95 mountain guns in Abdulla's favour, no

1 Men of the Harb and Juheina tribes formed a substantial part of Feisal's force at this time.
2 Sherif Shakir ibn Zaid was Abdulla's second in command.
3 Caller to prayer.

artillery except 2 small and very uncertain howitzers. His regular troops (70 Syrian deserters, the gunners and machine gunners) lack nearly all equipment, and he had taken no steps to help them. His Ateiba were two months in arrears of pay, simply through laisser faire, for the gold was present in the camp to pay them up in full. He understands very little about military operations, and the only officer in the camp, Sidi Raho, the Algerian Captain,[1] is either unable, or unwilling to persuade him to move. Since his arrival in Wadi Ais Sidi Abdulla had not ordered any attack on the railway. [...]

As it was impossible to arrange a proper routine of destruction of the railway at once with Sidi Abdulla, I began by some isolated efforts against various points. I give a rough list below, but cannot guarantee the dates since I got mixed up during my stay:

March 24th	Bueir	60 rails dynamited and telegraph cut.
March 25th	Abu el-Naam	25 rails dynamited, water tower, 2 station buildings seriously damaged by shell fire, 7 box-waggons and wood store and tents destroyed by fire, telegraph cut, engine and bogie damaged.
March 27th	Istal Antar	15 rails dynamited and telegraph cut.
March 29th	Jedhah	10 rails dynamited, telegraph cut, 5 Turks killed.
March 31st	Bueir	5 rails dynamited, telegraph cut.
April 3rd	Hediah	11 rails dynamited, telegraph cut.
April 5th	Mudahrij	200 railway [sic] blown up, 4-arched bridge destroyed, telegraph cut.
April 6th	Mudahrij	Locomotive mined and put out of action temporarily.
April 6th	Bueir	22 rails cut, culvert blown up, telegraph cut.

The Turks lost about 36 killed and we took some 70 prisoners and deserters during the operations.

[...]

The Turks search the line very carefully by daylight before a locomotive passes. A trolley came first, and then an infantry patrol of 11 men, of whom three were each side of the way, looking for tracks and fire on the way itself, walking bent double, scanning the line for signs of disturbance. For this reason tracks should be made through (i.e. both E . and W. of the line as though by a party crossing over) and the burying of the charges and fuse should be done most carefully. The railway is well laid, ballasting ample, and earth work and bridging solid. The rails are very light, and badly worn, and the sleepers (all steel) light in section and shallow. The heads of many

---

1 Algerian officer in the French Army, a member of the staff of the head of the French mission to the Hejaz, Colonel Edouard Brémond.

bolts have been buried to prevent loosening of the nuts, which makes it impossible to undo them with any ordinary short wrench.

[...]

I came back to Wedj on receipt of the pressing letter of Sidi Feisul (attached).[1] He was very annoyed with me for staying so long and is I think in a nervous and exhausted state. This will however right itself as soon as he leaves Wedj which will be shortly. [...]

T. E. Lawrence

I hope that in making the above strictures on Sidi Abdulla's behaviour, I have not given the impression that there is anything between us, he treated me like a Prince, and we parted most excellent friends in spite of my having said some rather strong things about the tone of his camp. I had come straight from Feisal's headquarters where one lives in a continual atmosphere of effort and high thinking towards the better conduct of the war — and the contrast with this of Abdulla's pleasure-loving laughing entourage was too great to be pleasant. One must remember however that Abdulla is the head and cause of the Hedjaz revolt and neither his sincerity nor his earnestness can be called in question. I do think, however, that he is incapable as a military commander and unfit to be trusted, alone, with important commissions of an active sort.

He did a great deal for me: — paid up the Ateiba, took an interest in his guns and machine guns, sent out his dynamite parties and began to prepare for a general move towards the line.

[...]

PRO FO 882/6

Over the next few months Lawrence wrote a number of reports for the *Arab Bulletin* but, apparently, very few letters; in his 'home letters' there is a gap of almost six months, though some may well have gone astray. This lacuna is scarcely surprising, however, as he was much on the move. From leaving Wejh in early May until arriving in Akaba in early July he was deep in the desert, far from any convenient naval transport or fleet messenger ship. He was also much preoccupied with the moral aspects of the campaign in which he was engaged. It was at this time that his sense of guilt at what

---

1 Feisal's letter, addressed to 'My Dear affectionate friend' and signed 'Your affectionate friend, Feisal', gives some indication of the importance which the Emir attached to Lawrence: e.g. 'I am waiting for your coming because I have many things to tell you. The destruction of the railway is easy. Major Garland has arrived and we can send him for this purpose.... You are much needed here more than the destruction of the line because I am in a very great complication which I had never expected,' etc.

he saw as British and French duplicity in regard to the political aspirations of the Arabs drove him to write the message, drafted but not sent, which follows. The letters that follow, written after the seizure of Akaba and his crucial meeting with Allenby, show him to all intents and purposes back in total control. In particular his letters to Clayton suggest a man in full grip of the situation, dealing professionally and confidently with everything from strategy to supplies, mindful of the smallest detail which might bring future advantage. His letters home are buoyant and cheerful; the campaign may be the 'maddest' ever run, but it will be 'imperishable fun to look back upon' (27 August). Only to Leeds—as he would also to Vyvyan Richards in the following year—does he present a different face.

BRIGADIER-GENERAL CLAYTON
[June 1917]

Clayton. I've decided to go off alone to Damascus, hoping to get killed on the way: for all sakes try and clear up this show before it goes further. We are calling them to fight for us on a lie, and I can't stand it.[1]

British Library

1 This message, found heavily pencilled over in one of Lawrence's wartime diaries and deciphered under special lighting and magnification, has been previously quoted by J. M. Wilson (who found it) in *Minorities*, p. 33 and John E. Mack, *A Prince of Our Disorder*, p. 182. Lawrence was using an Army signal pad at this time to scribble various diary notes and the message is written as though it were a normal signal; second thoughts evidently brought about his attempt to destroy it. It is relevant to two much discussed subjects: first, his sense of guilt arising from his belief that the Arabs were fighting on the basis of promises of independence which the Allies did not intend to keep; and second, the daring reconnaissance journey which he undertook to Damascus through enemy-held territory in June 1917 for which he received the unstinting admiration of his military superiors but about which he afterwards said or wrote very little. The Arab historian, Suleiman Mousa, considers the journey, and the report which followed it (published as *DG* 97) fabrications. However, none of Lawrence's colleagues at the time saw any reason to doubt his account of the distances he had allegedly covered or the discussions with tribal and other leaders he claimed to have held. This unsent message raises the possibility of a more credible interpretation of his reticence about this disputed journey: that he undertook it in a disturbed state of mind more concerned about his own attitudes than the task in hand. Lawrence refers to the journey in *Seven Pillars of Wisdom*, Chapter XLVIII; the published account omits, however, an important passage which occurs in the draft version of the book printed privately for him by the *Oxford Times*: 'Accordingly on this march I took risks with the set hope of proving myself unworthy to be the Arab assurance of final victory. A bodily wound would have been a grateful vent for my internal perplexities, a mouth through which my troubles might have found relief.'

COLONEL C. E. WILSON
30th July, 1917   Jeddah

On July 29th the Sherif sent a message asking me to come and see him and in the course of a long private conversation he gave me his views of the Sykes-Picot Mission.[1] The main points were that he had altogether refused to permit any French annexation of Beyrout and the Lebanon. 'They are Arab countries but I will neither take them myself nor permit anyone else to take them. They have deserved independence and it is my duty to see they get it.'

He said that he refused a detailed discussion of boundaries, on the grounds that hostilities between Turkey and the Allies still continue, and all decisions taken now would necessarily have to be modified in accordance with the actual results of military operations, for which he must have an absolutely free hand. 'If advisable we will pursue the Turks to Constantinople and Erzeroum [sic] — so why talk about Beyrout, Aleppo, and Hail.'

He is extremely pleased to have trapped M. Picot into the admission that France will be satisfied in Syria with the position Great Britain desires in Iraq. That he says, means a temporary occupation of the country for strategical and political reasons (with probably an annual grant to the Sherif in compensation and recognition) and concessions in the way of public works. 'I was ready without being asked to guard their interests in the existing railways, and assist their schools: but the Hedjaz and Syria are like the palm and fingers of one hand, and I could not have consented to the amputation of any finger or part of a finger without leaving myself a cripple.'

In conclusion the Sherif remarked on the shortness and informality of conversations, the absence of written documents, and the fact that the only change in the situation caused by the meeting, was the French renunciation of the ideas of annexation, permanent occupation, or suzerainty of any part of Syria — 'but this we did not embody in a formal treaty, as the war is not finished. I merely read out my acceptance of the formula "as the British in Iraq" proposed to me by M. Picot, since Sir Mark Sykes assured me that it would put a satisfactory conclusion to the discussion.'

T. E. Lawrence, Capt.[2]

PRO FO 882/12

1 Grand Sherif Hussein, by this time self-proclaimed King of the Hejaz, had just been visited by Sir Mark Sykes and M. Georges Picot, co-devisers of the Sykes-Picot agreement of 1916, whereby the Allies (including at this stage Russia) secretly colluded over the disposition of the territories of the Ottoman Empire after the war. Included in the agreement was the proposal that France should have a dominant interest in Syria, while Britain had a dominant interest in Mesopotamia (Iraq).

2 This report was despatched on the following day to the High Commissioner for Egypt, Sir

HIS MOTHER
12.8.17   Arab Bureau Savoy Hotel Cairo

This is only a note, to catch what I believe is a post. I'm sending some photographs in hope that they will arrive: of course they are not mine, but some R.F.C.[1] people who had taken them sent me copies. I've sent you a lot, one time and another, but I don't suppose many get through. I cannot send any enlargements, for printing paper is scarce.

Went down to Jidda a month ago, and saw Feisul at Wejh, and the Sherif himself at Jidda, and discussed things with them. Results satisfactory on the whole. I had never met the Sherif himself before, and liked him exceedingly: a very simple straightforward old man, clever enough too, but knowing so little. Upon us as a people is the responsibility of having made him a ruling power, and he is pitifully unfit for the rough and tumble of forming a new administration out of the ruins of the Turkish system. We will have to help him and his sons, and of the sons only Feisul and Zeid will play square to us. Abdulla is an intriguer, and poor Sidi Ali, the eldest son is a religious fanatic, and will be the tool of evil spirits. I do hope we play them fair.

I'm now going back to Akaba to look round at the country there: will start about the 16th from here. The average length of my last five visits to Cairo has been about 5 days! However it is more restful in Arabia, because one feels so nervous of what may happen if one goes away.

I cannot ask for leave, as I know there is so much to do down there, and no one to do it. If I asked I would probably get it, but it would not be right at present. If ever things get safe there, it will be possible to rest. You know there are very few of us on the job.

N.

Reginald Wingate, with an accompanying letter by Colonel Wilson, marked SECRET, in which he wrote: 'I have the honour to forward herewith for Your Excellency's information a note by Captain Lawrence on a private conversation he had with the Sherif on July 29th.' What concerned Wilson, rightly as events turned out, was his 'fear of a misunderstanding' on the part of the Sherif 'as to what was, or what was not, agreed upon at the meeting between Sir Mark Sykes, Monsieur Picot and the Sherif'. Certainly the idea that the French would be content with a transient relationship with Syria was an erroneous one; indeed the repercussions of Sykes-Picot were not only to cause much disaffection and dismay to the Arabs later but were in addition crucial in forming Lawrence's ambivalent attitude to the Arab struggle. The report is also a significant pointer to Lawrence's role at this time; the fact that although only a Captain he was invited to a private conversation with the senior figure on the Arab side suggests that he was seen as the Arabs' best interlocutor among the British officers attached to the Revolt, through whom Hussein's words would reach high places.

1 Royal Flying Corps.

About writing: — please try to realise that one's thoughts for nearly two years have been fixed on one object. We have realised part of the scheme, & the situation is critical but hopeful. In the circumstances one has become a monomaniac, unable to do or think about anything else — and of the one thing I cannot write to you.

                                                                    N.

HL/Bodleian Reserve

BRIGADIER-GENERAL GILBERT CLAYTON
[Undated: ? between 23 and 27 August 1917]   [Akaba]

General Clayton
    Please excuse the ink: I'm writing under difficulties.
    When we reached Akaba on Aug. 17 I found that one caravan of bombs had already gone to Kuntilla, and a second was just leaving. I arranged with Sherif Nasir[1] to send the balance next day, and on the 21st I went to Kuntilla myself, & saw the dump in position and the landing sign out. Ten Ageyl, under Shawish Daoud are holding the police post there pending the arrival of the aeroplanes.
    On the way to Kuntilla we met 14 parties of Beduins from both sides of the old Turk–Egyptian border, coming in to Akaba to salute Sherif Nasir. I think it all points to a decided move of Sinai opinion towards the Sherif, & away from the Turk. Nasir and Feisul are trying to persuade them that their new orientation involves friendship with the British. The Arabs seem rather prejudiced however.
    Please tell Captain G. Lloyd that Jeddua ibn Sufi is being sounded in the sense agreed upon between us.
    Sergt. 'Lewis' and Corporal 'Stokes'[2] are doing most excellent work training their Beduin in gun & machine gun work. I think the results will be very good. Would you please inform Major Hulton (O.B. G.H.Q.)[3]

1 Sherif Nasir of Medina, a leading figure on the Arab side, commander of the Akaba expedition and of the Arab entry into Damascus.
2 'Their names may have been Yells and Brooke, but became Lewis and Stokes after their jealously-loved tools.' (*Seven Pillars*, Chapter LX) Yells, who was Australian, was a Sergeant-Intructor in the Lewis gun: Brook (not Brooke) was an instructor, later also a Sergeant, in the Stokes trench-mortar.
3 Ordnance Branch, General Headquarters.

that I wish to keep them a little longer, since the training is not complete.

There is no news from the Guwaira area. A Turkish cavalry patrol visited Delagha, but was driven out with some loss by the Bedu, who have recently sent 40 captured mules here. I should not be astonished by a Turk occupation of Delagha, with a view towards Gharandel, to cut us off from W. Musa.

Jaafar Pasha[1] is taking over Akaba defence, which involves the maintenance of posts at Guwaira & Gharandel, Ghadian, etc. This sets free the Abu Tayu for extended raiding.

Please tell Major Lefroy that the Receiving set picks up Cairo easily, using the raised aerial. The ground aerial is not acute enough. The *Humber*[2] also picks up his messages to me. As his code is much safer than any Naval cipher, I would like disguised Y wires sent to me in his code for preference. I will not wire back in it, unless absolutely necessary. W. T.[3] from Akaba to Egypt is not good. The *Humber* cannot call anything in Egypt. I wonder if Major Lefroy could suggest anything. They can work up to 1000 metres length, on a 3 kilowatt power, but have a very low aerial. I have given Lieut. Feilding £2 from my secret service money. He will return this to you in Cairo.

Colonel Wilson arranged with Sherif Feisul to get him an extra £25000 by the first ship, from the £200000 grant. I hope this will be enough for the present. The £1000 bag in Major Cornwallis' safe might be sent as part of this.

Sherif Feisul is anxious to get here the prisoners willing to join his army from the P.O.W. camp in Egypt. He asks for them without equipment or extra training. Nessib el Bekri,[4] going to Egypt on *Hardinge*[5], can bring the draft down. I hope this question may be settled in this way — or that the Bekris after trying the men, may report 'none willing'.

1 Jaafar Pasha was a Baghdadi officer who had served in the German and Turkish armies; captured by the British and on parole in Cairo (following an escape in which he had been injured) he volunteered to serve on the Allied side when he heard of the outbreak of the Arab Revolt. He later served as Minister of Defence and Prime Minister under Feisal when the latter was King of Iraq, and was assassinated in 1935.

2 H.M.S. *Humber* was a monitor (i.e. a warship built principally for bombardment of enemy shore defences), described by Clayton in a letter to Lieutenant-Colonel Joyce as 'the main defence of the place [i.e. Akaba], commanding as she does, with her gun-fire, the whole of the available water' (18 September 1917: *PRO FO 882/7*).

3 W.T.: Wireless Telegraphy.

4 Nessib el Bekri (also spelled Nesib or Nasib by Lawrence) is described in *Seven Pillars*, (Chapter XXIV) as 'a Damascene land-owner, and Feisal's host in Syria (i.e. during Feisal's stay in Damascus before the Revolt), now exiled from his country with a death-sentence over him'. He served on Feisal's staff. He and Lawrence did not always see eye to eye; they had, for example, clashed over the purpose of the Akaba expedition. See *Seven Pillars*, Chapter XLVIII.

5 H.M.S. *Hardinge* was an armed Royal India Mail steamer attached to the Red Sea Fleet and used to transport troops and supplies.

Feisul suggests that the Egyptian Red Crescent might send a commission, or funds, for the relief of Syrians deported to Asia Minor. He has reason to believe that they are badly treated. Do you think it would be possible to arrange this?

Auda abu Tayi wants a set of false teeth.[1] The ship's doctors question their ability to cast his mouth in wax. Could a dental assistant be sent down from Egypt to do what is possible here? For all reasons it is not desirable to let Auda go away to Egypt for long.   .

T E Lawrence

PRO FO 882/7

HIS MOTHER
27.8.17   [Akaba]

This is written in a tent full of flies at Akaba, and the boat is leaving this afternoon. There is as usual nothing to say. I got here on the 17th of August, and found all as I had left it, except that my milk-camel has run dry: a nuisance this, because it will take me time to find another. I have too much to do, little patience to do it with, and yet things are going tolerably well. It is much more facile doing daily work as a cog of a machine, than it is running a campaign by yourself. However it's the maddest campaign ever run, which is saying quite a little lot, and if it ever works out to a conclusion will be imperishable fun to look back upon. For the moment it is heavy and slow, weary work, with no peace for the unfortunate begetter of it anywhere.

Newcombe is in Egypt ill; (nerves mostly). I've lost sight of everybody else. By the way I have returned to the Egypt Expeditionary Force, and should properly have no more to do with the Arab Bureau: but so eccentric a show as ours is doesn't do anything normal. Wherefore please address me as before, and don't put any fancy letters before or after my name. These things are not done by my intention, and therefore one can hardly count them.

I'm very glad you saw Mr. Hogarth. He will have probably given you a better idea than anyone else could give you of what we are really trying at. It consists of making bricks without straw or mud: — all right when it is a hobby, as with me, but vexatious for other people asked to do it as a job. By the way isn't it odd that (bar school), which was part nightmare

---

1 Auda abu Tayi, legendary chief of the Howeitat, who had ridden with Lawrence to Akaba, had smashed his previous set of false teeth because they were Turkish. See *Seven Pillars*, Chapter XXXVIII.

& part nuisance, everything I've done has been first hobby and then business. It's an odd fortune, which no one else could say, because everybody else plays games. It was a mercy that I broke my leg long ago, and settled to sit down the rest of my days.

Tell Arnie never to use an adjective that does not properly express what he means: slang reduces one to a single note, which is fatal.

N.

Some stamps enclosed.

HL/Bodleian Reserve

BRIGADIER-GENERAL GILBERT CLAYTON
27.8.17   [Akaba]

General Clayton

The *Race Fisher* is leaving for Egypt today, and I am writing to you again, since I may not have another opportunity for post for some time. The situation here has not changed in any way. I have stayed on in Akaba at Feisul's request, since he is altogether overwhelmed by the crowd of visitors, the new conditions, and the local difficulties arising. He is in very poor health, which makes things difficult.

Operations

The Abu Tayi[1] are owed two months' wages. Till they receive this we can hardly ask them to undertake a new job. However they will be the first charge on the funds the *Hardinge* is bringing, and we will then undertake the Railway between Maan and Mudowwara. There are seven waterless stations here, and I have hope that with the Stokes and Lewis guns we may be able to do something fairly serious to the line. If we can make a big break I will do my best to maintain it, since the need for shutting down Wejh altogether is becoming urgent.

As soon as the Railway attack is begun a force of 'regulars' will enter the Shobek-Kerak hills, & try to occupy them.

If these operations are part-successful, the Turkish force at Fuweileh[2] will probably be withdrawn, or reduced, and our position at Akaba then becomes safe. We cannot attack Fuweileh, and its retention in force by the Turks after the rains would be serious. At the same time I have little fear of anything unfortunate happening, since by extended threats on the

1 i.e. Auda's men.
2 A Turkish-held block-house some fifty miles north-east of Akaba, near the important railway strong-point of Maan.

Railway we can force the Turks to increase their forces there, and I believe that the Hejaz line is already working to full capacity to support the troops now between Deraat and Medain Salih. For this reason I do not think they can at once defend it, & attack Akaba on the necessary scale.

Captain MacIndoe[1] has shown me a report he has written on the local military situation. The facts are, I think, correctly stated, but he appears to overrate the man-power factor in this area. I have found hitherto that questions of Railway capacity, traffic conditions, camels, water and roads count for far more than the quantity or quality of troops on each side. To send the Camel Corps down to Akaba at present, and to attack the Railway with it, would, I am convinced, subtract from the Sherif such Beduin as are helping him now, and involve almost a certainty of conflict between the Arabs and our camel corps. One squabble between a trooper and an Arab, or an incident with Beduin women, would bring on general hostilities. An Arab victory next month, or an Arab defeat, might modify their present attitude. In the latter case (as in the Rabegh question) it might be too late to prevent disaster: but I would prefer personally to run this risk rather than incur the certainty of trouble by bringing down Imperial troops now. If Imperial troops are sent, to carry out an offensive against the Railway, sufficient supports must be sent to hold their L. of C.[2] in view of the probability of Beduin raids against them, and the Wadi Itm is not an easy line to guarantee in such case. However I take it that no modification of the policy agreed upon in Cairo will be decided upon, without my being given an opportunity of putting forward my views in detail.[3]

Supplies

This is a very difficult question just now. Feisul is dealing with it as vigorously as possible, and it may be modified by a success in the Kerak hills. It seems however as if we had underrated the local requirements. A list of the inscribed Beduin camel men was brought in yesterday, complete, and amounted to 22000 men. I have not seen a quarter of this total, and the lists are being revised today. I will send the new total if finished before the steamer sails steams. The true number will not be known till pay-day. Besides the men now inscribed there are hundreds (almost thousands) of others coming in daily. The slide of Arabs towards the Sherif was obvious when Nasir was here, and has become immense, almost impossible, since Feisul arrived. He is unable even to see all the head sheikhs of the new-

---

1 Captain J. D. MacIndoe, Scots Guards, had been appointed as General Staff Officer (G.S.O. 3), Hejaz Operations, in January 1917.
2 L. of C.: Line of Communication.
3 Two companies of the Imperial Camel Corps *were* used for a specific limited operation against the Hejaz Railway a year later in August 1918.

comers. All have to be fed while here, and for the return journey, & the imposition (quite unavoidable) is very serious.

In addition to the rations of the fighting men the Howeitat point out that their families are starving. Feisul tells them to go & buy food for them, & they retort that there is nothing for sale in Akaba. If flour, rice and coffee & sugar were for sale here we could turn over thousands per week: it would save a huge waste of rations and simplify the supply question generally. I know that the transport is a difficulty almost insurmountable, but if by any chance an extraordinary call of the Khedival line from Jedda could be arranged for Akaba it would be a great relief. Feisul says there are many Jidda merchants with foodstuff for sale who would come here at once. At present, thanks to Nasir's having had to give rations to the Arabs' families there remain in store at Akaba 531 bags of flour, & 812 of rice, only. There is enough coffee and sugar, and 863 bags of barley, which is good — but the flour will hardly last us till the September amounts arrive, unless they arrive punctually. It is now impossible to supply the up-country troops, and in consequence Ibn Nueir, Gasim abu Dumeig, and Mifleh abu Rikeiba, with their Arabs, have had to go in to Maan to surrender to the Turks. They went unwillingly, but it is rather a blow to the Arab prestige up at Guweira.

The August allowance, which was I believe calculated on 10000 heads, proves to have been just right, so far as the Howeitat are concerned. What is breaking down the situation is

    (a) the need of keeping a reserve till the September allowance is notified

    (b) the arrival here of Sherif Maalla with Shadli Alayan

    (c) the visitors from the North.

(a) is unavoidable, till a reserve dump can be established under Captain Goslett[1] here (b) means 2000 extra mouths, (c) is an indefinite and floating quantity, at present in the neighbourhood of 2500 a day, but liable to irregular increase. I am afraid the provision of food on sale, promptly, at Akaba will appear to you too difficult to establish. Its great value, to me, would be that we would have an immediate touchstone to show whether the present apparent need is real or not. The Howeitat swear they are starving, & produce piteous evidences of it: but I suspect a good deal of it is mere begging, as they know that any food that they may extract this way will be gratis. I doubt their spending very much of their wages on food, if it was for sale at a stiff price. There is no doubt though, that the strangers would, since they are in real want.

---

1 Captain, later Major, Raymond Goslett was supply officer at Akaba, having performed a similar function earlier at Wejh: 'the London business man who had made chaotic Wejh so prim'. (*Seven Pillars*, Chapter LVII)

Jaafar Pasha[1]
Is on the whole fairly sensible, I think, & shows more comprehension of
the Arab point of view than any of the other Syrian officers. Captain
MacIndoe criticises his force rather bitterly, but their real object is not so
much to engage Turkish forces on equal terms, as to stiffen the Beduin
resistance, by providing the comforting spectacle of a trained reserve, and
to impress the Turks with the fact that behind the Beduin screen lies an
unknown quantity, which must be disposed of before they can conquer
Akaba. The Turkish C. in C. cannot risk arriving here with less than 2000
men, because Jaafar has 2000 men: their quality, so long as it is not proved
bad by premature action, has of necessity to be estimated by the Turks as
good. Of course it would be nice and much simpler for us if the Arab
movement emerged from the bluff-and-mountain-pass stage, and became
a calculable military problem: but it hasn't yet, & isn't likely to. Jaafar's
force is serving its moral purpose admirably, & if he can find reliable officers
to handle the men tactfully & improve their discipline, it may become of
practical value in the near future. Most of the Syrian officers are such blind
prejudiced fools.

I don't think that any appreciation of the Arab situation will be of much
use to you, unless its author can see for himself the difference between a
national rising and a campaign.

I'm writing to Cornwallis for some trifles for Sherifs & Sheikhs. I have
asked for such things before, and will have to again. The cost will never
be very large, and even if it was, and I spent say 5% of the Syrian grant on
these private supplies, yet I fancy it would pay me. We want the Arabs to
keep step with our tune in this next affair, and to do that they must (or
their heads must) dance when we pipe. This means being on easy terms
with them all. Please explain, if necessary, to E.E.F.[2] that a gold watch may
sometimes carry further than a hundred rifles.

                                                              T E Lawrence

PRO FO 882/7

1 See previous letter to Clayton, p. 115, footnote 1.
2 The Egyptian Expeditionary Force: i.e. the main Allied army under General Allenby.

COLONEL C. E. WILSON
2.9.17   [Akaba]

[...] The Hejaz show is a quaint one, the like of which has hardly been on earth before, and no one not of it can appreciate how difficult it is to run. However it has gone forward, and history will call it a success: but I hope that the difficulties it has had to contend with will be equally clear. All my memories of it are pleasant (largely due to you,[1] of course, for on the face things should not be so), and if ever I can get my book on it out, I'll try to make other people see it.[2] They do not seem always to appreciate that while we hop about the Railway and places smashing things up, and enjoying ourselves, someone else has to sit and stew in Jidda keeping the head of the affair on the rails. You would be glad to hear sometimes how Feisul and the rest speak of you.
      [...]

DG

HIS PARENTS
5.9.17   Akaba

Got a letter of August 9 from you, which shows you never got a letter I sent you some time in July (12th I think) telling you what had happened on the way to Akaba. As a matter of fact it was a poor sort of letter, because I was rather doubtful how much to say. Either I said too much, or the ship sank.

I'm now off for a trip inland, lasting for about 3 weeks I expect, so this is the end of letters for the time being: indeed it's only as camels are late that I can write this anyhow.

Since July 10, when I got to Egypt from Akaba I have been to Wejh, Jidda, Yenbo, Akaba, up country, back to Egypt, to Alexandria, up to Akaba again, up country, back, & am now going up again — So you see it is a mobile sort of life, this.

Tell Mother they asked for that twopenny thing she likes, but fortunately didn't get it.[3] All these letters & things are so many nuisances afterwards,

1 Notwithstanding the criticism of some of his biographers, Lawrence was always ready to acknowledge the part which others played in the Revolt.
2 Evidence that Lawrence was already contemplating writing the book which would eventually emerge as *Seven Pillars of Wisdom.*
3 He had been recommended for a Victoria Cross on account of his reconnaissance journey through Syria but was appointed a C.B. (Companion of the Order of the Bath), Military Division, instead.

& I'll never wear or use any of them. Please don't, either. My address is simply T.E.L., no titles please.

In reply to Father's query, Yes, I have boils, lots of them. They began in March, & will go on till I have time to get to Egypt and be inoculated. Only I am usually too rushed in Cairo to get anything of my own done. Am very fit and cheerful enough when things are not too hectic. Going up country is always a relief, because then there is only one thing at a time to do.

Is Elsie Hutchins married?[1] I have had a letter signed Elsie, & think it must be from her. Will you get me Janet's address again, I've lost it?[2]

Cheque enclosed for £300. Will you ask Father to invest it for me? I can't do anything out here: Ask him to put it in the most obvious thing, without troubling himself — or keep it, if you want money.

Am off now.
N.

HL/Bodleian Reserve

HIS MOTHER
Sept. 24 1917   Akaba

Writing to you isn't very hopeful, since it is clear that you never get any of my letters. However I'll go on doing it, and some day one may get through. Would you like me to have a weekly telegram sent from Cairo telling you all well? I could arrange it easily enough. It's really a little serious that you should have received no letters between my wires. I sent the second one when I got back to Egypt from a visit to the Hejaz, because I had just had a note to say you had had no letters for two months, or some odd time.

By the way have any of my letters ever been opened by censor?

I'm now back in Akaba, after having had a little trip up country to the Railway, for the last fortnight. We met all sorts of difficulties, mostly political, but in the end bagged two locomotives and blew them up, after driving out the troops behind them. It was the usual Arab show, done at

1 Elsie Hutchins had been a near neighbour and playmate of the Lawrence boys in Oxford days: her married name was Ryman.
2 Janet Laurie: see letter home of 22.7.16.

no cost to us, expensive for the Turks, but not decisive in any way, as it is a raid and not a sustained operation.[1]

There are few people alive who have damaged railways as much as I have at any rate. Father may add this to the qualifications that I will possess for employment after the war! However, seriously, do remember that thanks to him I'm now independent, so far as money is concerned, of any employment whatever, and therefore I'll get back on to that printing-press scheme as soon as I am free. After all, you can't say that I haven't seen something of the world by now, and I can honestly say that I have never seen anyone doing anything so useful as the man who prints good books.

So don't worry about my future — and for my present don't put either Major or C.B. or any other letters (past present or future) after my name when writing to me. These sorts of things are only nuisances to a person with £250 a year, & the intention of not having more, and the less they are used the better. I'm sending back all private letters so addressed.

Do you remember a very light dusty-amber silk cloak I brought back with me once from Aleppo? If it is not in use, I would be very glad to have it sent to me. Arab clothes are hard to find now-a-days, with manufacture and transport thrown out of gear.

I got a letter from Bob the other day & news that Arnie has been excused responsions.[2] Also it proves that the anonymous thanks for a carpet was Elsie Hutchins! I'm glad she is married.

Do you know I have not written a private letter to anyone but you for over a year? It is a wonderful thing to have kept so free of everything. Here am I at thirty with no label and no profession — and perfectly quiet. I'm more grateful to Father than I can say.

N.

HL/Bodleian Reserve

1 Lawrence's official report describing this 'show' was printed in edition 65 of the *Arab Bulletin* under the title 'The Raid at Harret Ammar'. The *Bulletin* added a footnote on Turkish casualties, to the effect that the Turks admitted losing 27 killed and 42 wounded. The following two letters also include descriptions of the event, that to E. T. Leeds — in peaceful faraway Oxford — being markedly different in tone from the distinctly jaunty account to Stirling.
2 Responsions: qualifying examinations for entry into Oxford University.

E. T. LEEDS[1]
Sept 24. '17   Akaba

Dear Leeds

I'm sorry, but I felt the usual abrupt beginning would be too much for
your nerves, and that you would fall exhausted on to the floor of your
gallery, without even a Turkish carpet to break the shock of my writing
at last. What can have happened? I was pondering last night how for a year
I had written no private letter (except to my people, and those don't count,
for my mails are sunk or censored!) and today I go and break the habit.
Perhaps it's because it was a habit, and I'm getting old and stiff (not to say
tired, for every year out in Arabia counts ten) and habits must be nipped
in their shells.

I'm in Akaba for two days — that for me spells civilisation, though it
doesn't mean other than Arab togs and food, but it means you lunch where
you dined, and not further on — and therefore happy. The last stunt has
been a few days on the Hejaz Railway, in which I potted a train with two
engines (oh, the Gods were kind) and we killed superior numbers, and I
got a good Baluch prayer-rug and lost all my kit, and nearly my little self.

I'm not going to last out this game much longer: nerves going and
temper wearing thin, and one wants an unlimited account of both. However
while it lasts it's a show between Gilbert and Carroll, and one can retire on
it, with that feeling of repletion that comes after a hearty meal. By the way
hearty meals are like the chopped snow that one scatters over one's bowl
of grapes in Damascus at midsummer. Ripping, to write about —

This letter isn't going to do you much good, for the amount of information it contains would go on a pin's head and roll about. However it's
not a correspondence, but a discourse held with the only person to whom
I have ever written regularly, and one whom I have shamefully ill-used by
not writing to more frequently. On a show so narrow and voracious as this
one loses one's past and one's balance, and becomes hopelessly self-centred.
I don't think I ever think except about shop, and I'm quite certain I never
do anything else. That must be my excuse for dropping everyone, and I
hope when the nightmare ends that I will wake up and become alive again.
This killing and killing of Turks is horrible. When you charge in at the
finish and find them all over the place in bits, and still alive many of them,
and know that you have done hundreds in the same way before and must
do hundreds more if you can.

[...]

DG

1 Published in DG but without disclosing Leeds's name: he was described as 'A Friend'.

MAJOR W. F. STIRLING[1]
25 September 1917   Akaba

Dear Stirling
    Very many thanks! Though I think people are prone to ascribe to me
what the Arabs do (very efficiently, if oddly) on their own. I have a heavenly
temper, great natural modesty, and the art of window-dressing (the last
sentence is composed for the benefit of Holdich.[2] Please read it to him, and
ask him who is meant!).
    Seriously, the Arabs put up a surprisingly good show, and as the only
Englishman and historian, I get more than my share of notoriety. I don't
think it my fault. One must send in a report, and what more is to be done?
    The report you ask to see. As a matter of fact I handed it to Clayton
whose eyebrows went high (some of it was comic, some scurrilous, some
betrayed horrible secrets) and who sat on it. I don't think anyone in the
Savoy[3] ever saw it, whole. It certainly never went to H.C. or W.O. or
F.O.,[4] and I'm too tender-hearted to ask after it now. It was a MS document
of three pages, and compressed two months march into it: rather dull,
except to one who knew Syrian politics.[5] A note I scribbled in the train on
a mounted scrap we had, near Maan, appeared (with cuts) in the *Arab
Bulletin*, about No. 57, or 58. I haven't it by me, but old Cornwallis would
show it to you if you ever got to Cairo: or G. Lloyd, or Nugent.
    It is all ancient history now. The last stunt was the hold up of a train.
It had two locomotives, and we gutted one with an electric mine. This
rather jumbled up the trucks, which were full of Turks shooting at us. We
had a Lewis, and flung bullets through the sides. So they hopped out and
took cover behind the embankment, and shot at us between the wheels, at
50 yards. Then we tried a Stokes gun, and two beautiful shots dropped
right in the middle of them. They couldn't stand that (12 died on the spot)
and bolted away to the East across a 100 yard belt of open sand into some

---

1 Stirling was about to join the Sherifian forces in the desert, his principal task, to quote
   his autobiography *Safety Last*, being that of building 'a proper Arab Army, a force
   composed of Iraqis, Palestinians and Syrians, most of whom were released prisoners of
   war'. Stirling was to be Chief Staff Officer. He remained in the Arabian war-theatre for
   the rest of the war and entered Damascus with Lawrence in October 1918.
2 Lieutenant-Colonel G. W. Holdich: a staff officer in Cairo with whom Lawrence did not
   see eye to eye. See *Seven Pillars*, Chapter VII.
3 The Hotel Savoy, Cairo, housed British Military Headquarters.
4 H. C., W. O., F. O.: High Commissioner, War Office, Foreign Office.
5 The report referred to is that describing the Akaba expedition and Lawrence's reconnaissance journey into northern Syria in June 1917. It is printed in *DG*, and also in Garnett's
   Selected Letters and his *Essential T. E. Lawrence*. A typed copy of the original is held in the
   Public Record Office in *FO 882/16*.

scrub. Unfortunately for them the Lewis covered the open stretch. The whole job took ten minutes, and they lost 70 killed, 30 wounded, 80 prisoners and about 25 got away. Of my hundred Howeitat and two British NCO's there was one (Arab) killed, and four (Arabs) wounded.

The Turks then nearly cut us off as we looted the train, and I lost some baggage, and nearly myself. My loot is a superfine red Baluch prayer-rug.

I hope this sounds the fun it is. The only pity is the sweat to work them up, and the wild scramble while it lasts. It's the most amateurish, Buffalo Billy sort of performance, and the only people who do it well are the Bedouin. Only you will think it heaven, because there aren't any returns, or orders, or superiors, or inferiors; no doctors, no accounts, no meals, and no drinks.

Yours ever

T. E. Lawrence

Give my salaams to Holdich, and tell him to sprint, or we'll be in Damascus first.

J. M. Wilson/University of Texas

The following letter to Clayton was written as Lawrence was about to set off on one of his most important operations: a raid deep into enemy territory the principal purpose of which was, at Allenby's request, to blow up a key bridge in the Yarmuk Valley (just to the east of the Sea of Galilee) which carried the railway line linking the Hejaz Railway with the Palestinian coast. The attempt, carried out on the night of 8 November, did not succeed, as the subsequent letter to Colonel Joyce makes clear; but the letter does *not* make clear the extent of his disappointment at letting down his Chief. See *Seven Pillars*, Chapter LXXVI in which the page describing the *débâcle* is headed 'THE CUP SLIPS' and which ends with the statement: 'Our minds were sick with failure, and our bodies tired after nearly a hundred miles over bad country in bad conditions, between sunset and sunset, without halt or food.' After compensating for this major setback with attacks on the railway, the raiding force retired to Azrak, the ancient Arab fort and oasis in the desert to the east of Amman.

BRIGADIER-GENERAL GILBERT CLAYTON
24.10.17   Akaba

Dear General Clayton

A hurried note because I leave today at 2 p.m. and everything is still undone.

About Arab Legion.[1] Feisal will believe himself let down if they do not come by *Hardinge*. Their training is not so important as the prevention of this. Also the cholera trouble is a new reason for putting into Akaba at once as many reinforcements as you can.

The same applies to the Armoured Cars.[2] Even if everything is unfinished about them, something should come down in the *Hardinge*. They will be a great comfort here, and there are probably going to be panics and attacks by the Arabs from here soon.

Please send Izzet el Mukaddam to Akaba by *Hardinge*. He is wanted in the North.

I asked for nine exploders: only four have been sent, so I have had to rearrange plans somewhat. If others are available, they would be very useful. Also about the cable. I received at first 400 yards thick single cable (doubled this makes 200 yards of line) and after using it wired for 1000 yards light twin cable. You sent 500 yards of the old thick single in reply. Then I came up to G.H.Q. and saw you & Gen. Manifold, chose two good light wires, & asked for 4000 yards of them. In reply you have sent 650 yards of the old thick single line. The total length received is therefore only 1500 yards (750 when doubled) which is not enough for the 6 exploders in Akaba, or for the five more on order when they arrive: — and this thick single cable really hampers one seriously. Of course if there is no other we will make it do.

Then about Indian mountain guns. The two for Nuri[3] were never sent. Please send four now, for Feisul. We can use them on Bedouin raids, and so keep our remaining E.A.Q.F. guns for the regulars. I hope they may be put on the *Hardinge*.

The remainder of the special grant will no doubt have been sent off before this letter comes. Nasir & Zeid[4] (when he gets to Akaba — Colonel Wilson misreading a telegram from Cairo thought Akaba was blockaded

---

1 The Arab Legion was a force raised from Arab prisoners-of-war who had been members of the Turkish Army.

2 The (British) Hejaz Armoured Car Company was to play an important part in the campaign in 1918; its members were listed by name in Appendix I of *Seven Pillars*.

3 Nuri Said was Chief-of-Staff to General Jaafar, the commander of Feisal's regular force. He was later to serve as Prime Minister of Iraq no fewer than fourteen times and to lose his life when Feisal's grandson Feisal II was overthrown in 1958.

4 Zeid: King Hussein's youngest son.

& no one might land!) will bring it North with them on the 31st.

Colonel Wilson is writing to you about the £25,000 Wejh money taken off by Feisul at Akaba. The sight of £45,000 going into Wejh that month, to pay the Billi, was too much for us. I think we made better use of the £25,000 here!

I am taking Lieut. Wood, R.E. with me up country: It makes for insurance in case of accident on the job.

It's not my job — but I hope that Basset's appointment in Jedda is only temporary. G.L. will be back soon, & will give you all news we have.[1]

Yours sincerely
T.E. Lawrence

HL/Bodleian Reserve

COLONEL PIERCE JOYCE[2]

13.11.17   [Azrak]

Dear Joyce

Please tell Feisul we rode to El Jefer, and found Zaal and the Abu Tayi afraid to come with us. Sherif Ali[3] and Auda did their best to work them up, but they were not for it. The Abu Tayi have almost revolted against Auda, and I doubt whether we shall see much more good from them: they have seen too much good from us.

Thence we went to Bair, where we found Mifleh ibn Zebn. He with Fahad and Adhub ibn Zebn went with us, and did most splendidly. I think them three of the best Arab sheikhs I have met. Fahad was badly hit in the face in the train scrimmage, but will, I hope, recover.

From Bair we rode to Azrak where we met the Serahin. Sheikh Mifleh

---

1 G.L. was George Lloyd. For new light on the first part of this expedition see *Lord Lloyd and the Decline of the British Empire* by John Charmley, 1987, Chapter 9. Lloyd left on 29 October although he would have preferred to continue; however, as Lloyd noted in a diary of his journey, 'Lawrence said definitely that he thought it was useless and that although he did not pretend that he would not like me to come he felt that any additional individual who was not an expert at the actual demolition only added to the risk. He would like me best to go home to England for he felt that there was a risk that all his work could be ruined politically in Whitehall and he thought I could save this; failing this he would like me to rejoin him either in the north or in Kerah as soon as the bridge job was over, but he wanted me to tell Clayton that he did not want anyone else with him.'

2 Pierce Joyce was a regular officer of the Connaught Rangers; he was now based at Akaba and he and Lawrence were collaborating in organising the Arabian campaign. Lawrence wrote later: 'It was Joyce who ran the main line of the Revolt, while I was off on raids.'

3 Sherif Ali: Ali ibn Hussein el Harith (or, more correctly, el Harthi), Arab commander of the expedition and a close friend of Lawrence; the Sheikh portrayed by Omar Sharif in the film *Lawrence of Arabia*.

ibn Bali rode with us to the bridge, and did his best, but he and his tribe are not in it with the Beni Sakhr.

Emir Abd el Kadir came with us to Azrak, where we made the plan of attack on the bridge at Tell el Shehab. He said he would come with us, and we had no idea anything was wrong, but the same day he rode off (without warning either Ali or myself or the Arabs with us) to Salkhad, where he is still sitting. Tell Feisul I think he was afraid: much talk, and little doing, in his way. Neither Ali nor myself gave him any offence.

Tell el Shehab[1] is a splendid bridge to destroy, but those Serahin threw away all my explosive when the firing began, & so I can do nothing — If the Turks have not increased their guard we can do it later: but I am very sick at losing it so stupidly. The Bedu cannot take the bridge, but can reach it: the Indians can take it, but cannot reach it!

From Tell el Shehab we turned back to the Railway south of Deraa, and destroyed two locomotives. We must have killed about 100 Turks too. It was a most risky performance but came off all right. Little Ali is a very plucky youth, and came to my rescue on each occasion very dashingly. He will certainly get himself killed unless he continues to travel with a person as skilful and cautious as myself. Besides being in the thick of it when anything happens he keeps very good control of the Arabs on the march, and has been very decent to me — I think he is quite in the front rank of Sherifs — but he really must go easy with himself, or I will want a successor to travel with!

Please give Feisul (& Snagge)[2] any extracts you like from the report to Clayton enclosed.[3] Tell him the whole country of the Hauran fellahin is slipping towards him, and they only require arms, money and a shock to get all moving together. We can get no news of what happened at Gaza.

I think the attached might go to the Press.[4] Ali deserves a mention, for he is a very uncommon youth. My personal requests in another paper.[5]

Yours
T E Lawrence

DG

1 Tell el Shehab: the bridge in the Yarmuk Valley which was the special target of the raid. Its destruction had been requested by Allenby, so that the failure to achieve this was a deep blow to Lawrence's professionalism and pride.
2 Snagge: Captain A. L. Snagge R.N., naval commander at Akaba.
3 The report referred to was published in the *Arab Bulletin* of 16 December under the title 'A Raid'.
4 The attached was a brief report, as follows: 'On November the eleventh a detachment of the Northern Army of Sherif Feisul, under the command of Sherif Ali ibn Hussein el Harith, attacked the Railway and troop trains between Deraat and Amman. Two locomotives and some coaches were completely destroyed, and a bridge blown up. The Turks lost heavily in killed and wounded. The Arabs lost seven men.'
5 Lawrence's 'personal requests' were for explosives, detonators, fuses and guns.

HIS MOTHER
14.11.17   Azrak[1]

I wonder if you can find this place: — it's out in the desert between Deraat
and Amman — and if you do find it you will think it a most improbable
place to live at.

Living however is quite easy and comfortable here. We are in an old
fort with stone roofs and floors, and stone doors of the sort they used in
Bashan. It is a bit out of repair, but is improving in that respect every
day.[2]

I do not know what its postal arrangements are like: at least they begin
with about ten days on a camel of mine, and after that the ordinary risks
of letters now-a-days. Your chances of getting it are therefore a little thin,
it seems to me.

I go on writing and writing and it has no effect: every letter I get from
you says that you have not heard from me since last time: very disheartening,
since writing is always a risk (if our friends get this letter they will pay me
a visit) and often difficult. Meanwhile it is restful. I am staying here a few
days; resting my camels, and then will have another fling. Last 'fling' was
two railway engines. One burst into fragments, & the other fell on the first.
Quite a successful moment!

If you see a note in print saying that 'A detachment of the N. army of
Sherif Feisul etc.' Then that's me ... the rest is anonymous.

In case my last three letters have fallen through, please tell Arnie that his
plan is excellent. I told the people concerned in Cairo, and either Mr.
Hogarth or myself can get it arranged quite easily if the time comes.
Personally I don't expect it will, but I always was an optimist.

I wonder if Gillman could make me another pair of brown shoes? There
may be regulations against export, so he should find out first. I do not often
wear shoes, but they come in handy sometimes in reserve. I sent you a
cheque for £300 some weeks ago, and asked for Janet's address. Did you
get them and if not will you let me know?

---

1 Azrak in Arabic means blue, doubtless a reference to the colour of its numerous lakes and
   pools under a clear sky.
2 For a somewhat more eloquent description of Azrak — which plainly caught Lawrence's
   imagination — see *Seven Pillars*, Chapter LXXV. 'Of Azrak, as of Rumm, one said
   "Numen inest" [Divinity is here]. Both were magically haunted: but whereas Rumm was
   vast and echoing and God-like, Azrak's unfathomable silence was steeped in knowledge
   of wandering poets, champions, lost kingdoms, all the crime and chivalry and dead
   magnificence of Hira and Ghassan. Each stone or blade of it was radiant with half-
   memory of the luminous silky Eden, which had passed so long ago.'

There, this letter has been 3 days in writing, & I have done all the rest of the work meanwhile.

T. E. Lawrence

HL/Bodleian Reserve

On 20–21 November 1917 Lawrence underwent the ordeal that was to affect him for the rest of his life: his capture, beating and rape at Deraa (as described in Chapter LXXX of *Seven Pillars*). There appears to be no wartime reference to this episode. It is however summarised in a report written after the war during his visit to Cairo in June 1919 (see Part 3, p. 165) and it is touched on, if sparingly, in his later letters: e.g. to Edward Garnett, 22 August 1922; to Charlotte Shaw, 26 March 1924 and 26 December 1925; to E. M. Forster, 21 December 1927. Three weeks after Deraa he was present at the official entry into Jerusalem, which was seized from the Turks in early December. His letter to Leeds after this event (15 December 1917) shows that he was beginning to realise that the war had changed his life irrevocably: 'after being a sort of king-maker one will not be allowed to go digging quietly again. Nuisance.'

HIS PARENTS

14.12.17   The Residency Cairo

Well here I am in Cairo again, for two nights, coming from Akaba via Jerusalem. I was in fortune, getting to Jerusalem just in time for the official entry of General Allenby.[1] It was impressive in its way — no show, but an accompaniment of machine gun & anti-aircraft fire, with aeroplanes circling over us continually. Jerusalem has not been taken for so long: nor has it ever fallen so tamely before. These modern wars of large armies and long-range weapons are quite unfitted for the historic battlefields.

I wrote to you last from Azrak, about the time we blew up Jemal Pasha,

1 Jerusalem fell to Allenby on 9 December 1917 and the official entry took place on the 11th. Lawrence's participation in the latter event was due to Allenby, who, according to *Seven Pillars*, 'was good enough, although I had done nothing for the success, to let Clayton take me along as staff officer of the day. The personal Staff tricked me out in their spare clothes till I looked like a Major of the British Army.' Lawrence appears fleetingly in the newsreel film of the occasion, a diminutive, distant but clearly recognisable figure.

and let him slip away from us. After that I stayed for ten days or so there, and then rode down to Akaba in 3 days: good going, tell Arnie: none of his old horses would do so much as my old camel. At Akaba I had a few days motoring, prospecting the hills and valleys for a way Eastward for our cars: and then came up to H.Q. to see the authorities and learn the news-to-be.

Tomorrow I go off again to Akaba, for a run towards Jauf, if you know where that is. Mother will be amused to learn that they are going to send me to England for a few days in the spring, if all works well till then: so this is my last trip, possibly. Don't bank on it, as the situation out here is full of surprise turns, and my finger is one of those helping to mix the pie. An odd life, but it pleases me, on the whole.

I got that little cloak all well — many thanks; the Near East used to make all these wonderful things, but the interruption of trade routes and the call of military service hamper it now, and one's needs are every day more and more difficult to meet. I'm an Emir of sorts, and have to live up to the title.

I see A.[1] is getting slowly up the obstacles of many exams. They are silly things, terrible to the conscientious, but profitable to the one who can display his goods to effect, without leaving holes visible. As real tests they are illusory. So long as you can read good books in the languages they affect, that's enough for education: but it adds greatly to your pleasure if you have memory enough to remember the why & wherefore of the waxing and waning of peoples, and to trace the slow washing up & down of event upon event. In that way I think history is the only knowledge of the easy man. It seems to me that is enough of didactic.

Mr. Hogarth is here in Cairo, acting as our base of information. He is one of the people whom the Arabs would have great difficulty in doing without. The blank in knowledge when he goes back to England is always great. Pirie-Gordon[2] is coming out, to write popular articles on the Arab war for the home papers — so soon you will know all about it. Secrecy was necessary while the fight was a life and death one in the Hejaz: but since the opening of Akaba the stress has been eased, and today we are as comfortable as any front. As public sympathy is desirable, we must try and enlist on our side a favourable press. A. will be content, but must take it as said that it was quite impossible before. This show of ours began with all against it, and has had first to make itself acceptable to the elect. They converted, we can afford to appeal to a wider circle. It is not much use trying, with a J pen, to tell you how we are going to do it.

Many thanks to Father for investing that cheque of mine. When I stay out in Arabia for months on end I spend comparatively little, for the

1 Arnold Lawrence.
2 C. H. C. Pirie-Gordon was an archaeologist friend from Lawrence's university days.

Government buys my camels, & the Sherif pays the men. I have only clothes (cheap things Arab clothes) and personal presents to pay for. On the other hand, when I get to Cairo I have many commissions, from Arab sheikhs, for things they want — and if they have been useful, or will be useful, they get them free of charge! My acquaintances are legion, or the whole population from Rabegh to Deraa, and the burden correspondingly heavy. However they have just raised my pay, by pushing me up the roll of Staff appointments. I'm now called a G.S.O.2.[1] The French Government has stuck another medal on to me: a croix de guerre this time. I wish they would not bother, but they never consult one before doing these things. At least I have never accepted one, and will never wear one or allow one to be conferred on me openly. One cannot do more, for these notices are published in the Press first thing, and to counter-announce that one refused it, would create more publicity than the award itself. I am afraid you will be rather disgusted, but it is not my fault, and by lying low and simply not taking the things when given me, I avoid ever really getting them.

This letter should get to you about Christmas time, I suppose, as few mails have been sunk of late. That will mean that you are getting at least fortnightly letters from me, which should put off any anxiety you might otherwise feel. Mr. Hogarth of course hears of me every few days, so that his information is much fuller than anything I can ever give you.

I'm in the proud position of having kept a diary all the year 1917. To date, it is rather a brief one, consisting only of the name of the place where I sleep the night of each day: and the best thing about it is the disclosure that ten successive nights in one place is the maximum stop in the 12 months, and the roll of places slept in is about 200. This makes it not astonishing that my Arabic is nomadic! I hope A. is getting on with his army subjects. It would be a useful thing to know how to drive a car, but judging from the papers there must be fewer cars in Oxford than in Akaba.

He should keep an eye on the illustrated papers soon. They are going to get an occasional photograph from us, to help keep the Sherif (and Feisul above all) before the public eye. The Arab Bureau have about 500 excellent prints, and so the selection may be a good one. Some of them you will probably have already had, as I remember sending you some of the best. I'm also sending you a sheet of Hejaz 1 piastre stamps. You said you had not received any of this value. These are of course 1st edition, and are worth

1 General Staff Officer, grade 2.

a good deal more than you would expect! Lady Wingate gave them to me, for of course it is impossible to find them anywhere for sale.

Here endeth this letter.

N.

HL/Bodleian Reserve

E. T. LEEDS

15.12.17   The Residency Cairo [erased]

I suppose it was because your pen was a thin one: anyhow your letter gave me an impression of London in gloom. It's what all the papers say, and is terrible.[1] I hope you are bearing up.

About stuff here. Jerusalem cheered all of us mightily. Casualties were so few, and the booty so immense. I was in the official entry, and going up there we found the whole countryside strewn with the old store-heaps of the Turks. Twenty million rounds of SAA,[2] and uncounted shells. Also there are thousands of deserters, and God knows what amount of stuff looted by the villagers before we came. It is the loss of the accumulated stores of two years to them: and it will take them six months to pile up such another lot, if they can concentrate all their efforts on the job. In actual prisoners, and in killed and wounded the show was not over great—but then there were not many Turks to begin with—and very few to end with.

Commend me to ffoulkes. I heard of his Tower catalogue. I've got a trophy he would like for his War Museum.[3] The Turks took four of the short Lee Enfield rifles taken at Gallipoli, and engraved them in gold on the chamber 'Part of our booty in the battles for the Dardanelles' in a most beautiful Turkish script. Deeply cut by hand, and then gold wire beaten in. Four of these rifles were sent, one to each of the sons of the Sherif of Mecca. I carry Feisul's, which he gave me (it's a 1st Essex gun) and I'm trying to get Zeid's, which I'll send C.J.ff if I win. They form admirable gifts, tell him. Ali has one, but Abdulla's has been given to Ronald Storrs, oriental secretary to the Residency here.

The idea seemed so good that I'm doing some Turkish rifles, with

1 Late 1917 had been a bad time for war news: huge casualties and little territorial gain in Flanders, the Central Powers successful in Italy, Russia out of the war following the Bolshevik Revolution. The best news was from the Middle East where the British had seized Baghdad and Jerusalem.

2 SAA: small arms ammunition.

3 Charles John ffoulkes (1868–1947), one-time lecturer on armour and mediaeval subjects at Oxford, was Curator of the Armouries of the Tower of London from 1913–35 and first Curator and Secretary of the Imperial War Museum — which was founded in March 1917 — from 1917–33. His 'Tower catalogue' was doubtless his *Survey and Inventory of the Tower of London*, published 1917.

inscriptions in Arabic, presents from Feisul to R.N. officers who have helped him. There will be seven of these, in all, if I complete my programme.

It's very good of you to go on helping the brutal and licentious after the B. and L. way they have treated you. I don't know why we should do things in that sort of way. Give an Easterner who is not a hereditary grandee, power, and he is a tyrant in a week. Are we the same, or is it only our stupidity? Bad men, or bad manners?

It's very nice to hear about sack-bottles and tokens again, for one is getting terribly bound up in Eastern politics, and must keep free. I've never been labelled yet, and yet I fear that they are going to call me an Arabian now. As soon as war ends I'm going to build a railway in S. America, or dig up a S. African gold-field, to emancipate myself. Carchemish will either be hostile (Turks will never let me in again) or friendly (Arab), and after being a sort of king-maker one will not be allowed to go digging quietly again. Nuisance. However the war isn't over yet, and perhaps one needn't worry one's head too soon about it.

Saw D.G.H. yesterday. All well here and there.

.L.

Bodleian Reserve

'Don't expect any letter from me for a time now,' he wrote to his mother on 8 January 1918. 'I'll be very busy, and quite away from touch with Egypt.' It is a keynote statement for the last year of the war, which would include his one conventional battle at Tafileh in January (fought in the hills to the south of the Dead Sea during an attempt, later abandoned, to link with Allenby's forces in the Jordan Valley); his promotion to Lieutenant-Colonel in March; his first encounters with Lowell Thomas, the American publicist who would ultimately convert him into 'Lawrence of Arabia' (there are, however, no references to Thomas in his war letters); and finally — the climax of two years of strenuous effort — the advance on Damascus in September–October in collaboration with Allenby's north-ward thrust through Palestine.

Only seven home letters have survived (he managed only one brief message between the end of March and mid-July) and his letters relating to the war are equally few and far between, though they include some of great interest. There are two important ones to Clayton, particularly that of 12 February, which is very illuminating on the matter of his perception of the nature of his role in the Revolt ('I do my best to keep in the background, but cannot' etc.); and which also shows that it was he who assumed the task of persuading the most effective of all the Arab leaders,

Feisal, to go along 'for the duration of the war at least' with Britain's pro-Zionist Balfour Declaration of November 1917. There are three letters to, and carefully preserved by, the then Governor of Beersheba, Mr A. F. Nayton, given to Lawrence's brother in 1946. In addition, there is Lawrence's only known letter written in Arabic, dated 'Ramadan 17, 1336–June 25, 1918', to none other than King Hussein of the Hejaz himself, encouraging him to continue his support and informing him: 'Had it not been for your courage in ordering Sidi Feisal to leave Medina and proceed to Wejh and Akaba, the Arab movement would not have been as completely successful as it is today.' Finally, there are two despatches from the last phase of the campaign.

HIS MOTHER
8.1.18   Akaba

In this country one's movements never work out as planned: in proof of that, here I am in Akaba again after quite a short excursion up country. I wrote to you last from Cairo, I fancy, and prophesied that I would be a long time away! Tomorrow perhaps we will get off about midday, to go up towards the Dead Sea, on the East side. It is beautiful country, but too hilly for pleasure. Today I'm busy buying some new riding camels, and saddles and saddle-bags.

I looked through the last few letters received, but I don't think there is anything requiring answer. Newcombe, about whom you asked, has been taken prisoner, and is now probably in Asia Minor. He was working with the army in Palestine when he was caught.[1]

Posts have been a little disorganized lately, for the last letters from England are dated November 9: however one knows that had there been anything wrong there would have been telegrams about. It is only good news which is not worth spending money on: you hear the bad too soon.

This Akaba is a curious climate. On the coast we have a typical Red Sea winter, which at its worst is like a fine October day, and at its best is like summer weather. No rain to speak of, not much wind, and persistent sunshine. If you go thirty miles up country at once you get into cold wet weather; with white frosts at night. If you go 20 miles further East you find yourself in miserable snow-drifts, and a wind sharp enough to blow through a sheepskin. Next day you are in Akaba again, and thoroughly warm.

1 Newcombe had been captured in early November 1917 when a scratch camel force under his command, with which he had been harassing the Turks in southern Palestine, was attacked by no fewer than six Turkish battalions. His force held out resolutely, only surrendering after sustaining heavy casualties and having exhausted all its ammunition. He spent the rest of the war as a prisoner of the Turks.

I'm sending you a photograph or two with this letter: none of them are very interesting, but some day we may be glad of them. The Arab Bureau, to which Mr. Hogarth belongs, has a wonderful collection of Arabian photographs, of which I want a few published in the *Illustrated London News*. They include a rather impressive snap of Feisul himself, getting into a car at Wejh, and some of his bodyguard, taken by me from the saddle, as I was riding in Wadi Yenbo with them and him. It would take a great painter, of course, to do justice to the astonishing life and movement of the Bedouin armies, because half the virtue of them lies in the colours of the clothes and saddle trappings. The best saddle-bags are made in the Persian Gulf, on the Eastern shore of Arabia, and are as vivid and barbaric as you please.

One of the prints to appear, showing the Sherifian camp at dawn, in Wadi Yenbo, was taken by me at 6 a.m. in January last, and is a very beautiful picture. Most sunrise pictures are taken at sunset, but this one is really a success.

There, I have an article to write for an Intelligence Report published in Egypt, and much else to do. Don't expect any letter from me for a time now. I'll be very busy, and quite away from touch with Egypt.

N.

HL/Bodleian Reserve

MILITARY GOVERNOR, BEERSHEBA[1]

22.1.18   Tafileh

Commandant Beersheba

The bearer of this letter,[2] Sheikh Jeddua el Sufi, is the nephew of Hamad

---

1 Behind this letter lay the problem, faced throughout the campaign by Lawrence, of finding the necessary gold to keep the Arab armies in the field. The sequel to it is described in a note by the recipient, Mr A. F. Nayton, Military Governor Beersheba District in 1918, to A. W. Lawrence dated 9 January 1946: 'I did not consider Jeddua to be a safe enough messenger to carry a large amount of gold and informed T. E. L. accordingly. As a result your brother himself came across to Beersheba and spent a couple of nights with me there. He travelled, as usual, with some twenty of his personal bodyguard, a queer mixture of "toughs" from numerous tribes, all beautifully mounted on first-class riding camels. As you know the Turks had put a high price on T. E. L.'s head and in the first place your brother considered it safer to camp in the midst of his guard at some distance from my headquarters. He was persuaded, however, to stay in our mess and seemed to enjoy the somewhat primitive amenities which enabled him to have a hot bath and some English food! Once we had overcome his shyness he entertained us for hours with accounts of his varied experiences with our Arab allies.

  'He collected his gold and rode off "into the blue" far too soon for our liking. Of T. E. L.'s so many admirable qualities the one that has always appealed to me most was the infinite patience with which he handled the Arabs, notwithstanding the many disappointments and the innumerable times he was "let down" by them.'

2 See next letter, to Brigadier-General Clayton.

el Sufi, the former head sheikh of Beersheba district, and now one of the adherents of Sherif Feisul. I have asked Jeddua to go in to you with the letter enclosed, for General Clayton, and assured him that he will be well treated in Beersheba, and given supplies, if necessary, for himself, his men, and his animals, so long as he remains. In the letter to General Clayton I have asked him to get G.H.Q. to telephone you to this effect. Until that confirmation arrives I hope you will be able to provide him with what is necessary, on your own authority. I have asked General Clayton, in the letter enclosed, for £30000 in gold, which Jeddua will bring back to me here; (he is quite trustworthy); but to get the necessary authority, and to send the money to Beersheba from Cairo, will, I expect take at least five days. Jeddua should return here as soon as it arrives, and I would suggest that if possible he retain his arms, while waiting. You will find him on his best behaviour.

T E Lawrence

I would be most obliged if the letter to General Clayton could be sent forward as quickly as possible, and that he be advised by telephone or telegraph, of the arrival of Jeddua with a letter from me for him. I do not think that Jeddua himself need go up to G.H.Q. in any case, though that of course would be for General Clayton himself to decide.

[On back of envelope containing letter] The specie, when it arrives, please divide up into its bags of £1000 each, and put each into a camel sack of the type enclosed. The wooden cases are too heavy for transport by the Kurnub roads. The sacks can be made in Beersheba, I expect.

Bodleian Reserve

BRIGADIER-GENERAL GILBERT CLAYTON
22/1/18   Tafileh

General Clayton
   I am sending this letter in to you by Jeddua el Sufi, to Beersheba. Will you please as soon as it arrives, get G.H.Q. to telephone to the O.C. there

to treat him well. He will have about 15 men and animals with him, and should be given supplies by us for them as long as he has to remain there. I am asking the Commandant to do this temporarily, till your approval reaches him.

Affairs are in rather a curious state here. The place surrendered (after two false reports and a little fighting at the last) on the 15th. The local people are divided into two very bitterly opposed factions, and are therefore terrified of each other and of us. There is shooting up and down the streets every night, and general tension.

[...] Zeid is rather distressed by the packet of troubles we are come in for (amongst other things a colony of besieged Moors and a swarm of destitute, but very well fed, Armenians) and is pulled here and there by all sorts of eager new-comers all intriguing against one another like cats.

I am really sending in Jeddua for money. The figures of tribal wages given Zeid at Guweira prove rather inadequate (i.e. the Sakhur get £22000, and not £6000) and we are going to be out of funds perhaps before we take Kerak, even. Can you send me, via Jeddua £30000 special grant? This will be quicker than fetching from Akaba, even if there was the money at Akaba.

As for operations: Jaafar Pasha was up here, wanting the Beduin all to go from here to the Railway, and 'cut it'. Which is all very well, but not possible in the present state of affairs. We have sent Sherif Abdulla, with Hamad el Sufi, and locals, to El Mezraa, to block any leakage of supplies from Kerak, Westward, and Mastur goes today to Wadi el Hesa, to block it on the South. The Sakhur left this morning for Bair, to move slowly up to just N.E. of Katrane, and thence dash at Madeba as soon as Kerak falls, or we get to Hamman el Zerka. Which plan we adopt depends on the reply of the Kerak people to messengers sent them yesterday. Rifaifan, the head of the Majalli, is pro-Turk, and will, I hope, hop it. Hussein el Tura, the other headlight, is secretly pro-Sherif and may call up enough courage to take a visible plunge. If so, Kerak should fall in about 4 days time and Madeba almost simultaneously. If not, there will be a delay. We can enlist 500 Tafileh men, and move up the East coast of the Dead Sea to Hamman el Zerka, and then call in the Sukhur to help. I would prefer the first course. For the second the extra £30000 is necessary and that will take, I calculate, 10 days to reach us.

[...]

T. E. Lawrence

PRO FO 882/7

HIS MOTHER
Feb. 6, 1918   [Guweira]

Excuse a scrawl: this is only to say that I am here and quite fit: in Guweira, a place 35 miles NE of Akaba. I have come down for a night to see Feisul, from Tafileh, where I have been for the last few days.

No news from you for a long time, and no opportunity, I expect, of hearing from you for some time yet. General Clayton has, I believe, wired for Arnie — but I do not know in what terms, why, or what the answer has been. If I hear of him in Cairo, I'll try to cut across for a day or two and fix things up with him. He must spend at least some months there.

We had a fight north of Tafileh the other day — the Turks attacked us and we annihilated them. Took 23 machine guns & two guns, all in working order. Our loss 20 killed, theirs about 400.[1] I am now off again, buying camels in the Eastern desert, round Wadi Sirhan and Jauf.

Weather bitterly cold, with persistent snow and rain, but not likely to endure much longer. The coast & Dead Sea are warm, but our work lies on the plateau, 4,000 or 5,000 feet up.

N.

Stamps enclosed are part of Tafileh post office, all surcharged Peninsula of Sinai!

HL/Bodleian Reserve

BRIGADIER-GENERAL GILBERT CLAYTON
12th February 1918   Tafileh

Dear General Clayton
I found your letter last night when I arrived from Guweira. The gold had already reached there when I got there, and is on the way up.[2] The roads are awful — mud, snow and slush — and of the 19 riders who left, only 7 got through. The others will come in gradually as the conditions improve. One must reckon on ten days now, from Guweira to Tafileh.

I have numbered your paragraphs, for convenience.

---

1 The Battle of Tafileh took place on 25 January. Lawrence was far more disturbed about the battle, which he felt was an unnecessary one, with unnecessary casualties, than this letter suggests. See *Seven Pillars*, Chapters LXXXV–LXXXVI.
2 Lawrence had been to Guweira to organise a subsidy of £30,000 in gold sovereigns for Zeid's army (Zeid had been the nominal commander at the Battle of Tafileh), travelling each way through appalling wintry weather.

(1) Your sending back Jeddua so well pleased with us, has had an excellent effect. I am very glad he went. [...]

(2) [...] The I.C.C. could not work across W. Arabia unless they could do without supply columns, or feed from Akaba. I am still against their use, except as last resort if the Arabs fail, and I think they would have to be re-modelled (e.g. put on graze feed) in any case, before they came across.[1] I have given Deedes' officer[2] a few summary notes, but I know they will not be considered enough. If Intelligence still press, get them to send an officer to look. I'll send any escort he wants, to Hebron or Beersheba.

(3) I'm very glad X[2] (I can't remember his name) came. I enclose a letter to Deedes, about his scheme. If you agree, please send it on.

(4) Zeid hummed and hawed, and threw away his chance of making profit from it. He had the country from Madeba at his feet. These Arabs are the most ghastly material to build into a design.

[...]

(6) This £30,000 will last the N. tribes this month, and leave enough over to carry us on into the middle of March.[3] The Sukhur cost £26,000 a month, Ibn Jazi £4000, Abu Tayi £7000, Howeitat oddments £3500. Cost of living for regular soldier in Tafileh about £1 a week. If the situation does not change Zeid will spend about £45,000 a month and Feisul about £50,000, for the next two months. If we take Madeba, add about £4000 a month. I hope to spend about £15,000 on camels, shortly, extra, as agreed with Dawnay[4] in Guweira: otherwise we are wasting about £20,000 a month on an unemployable regular army. The Azrak camel contract will be extra, and by then I hope the railway will be cut, and £16,000 a month saved in wages. However, I have prophesied many times, and each time wrongly, so am getting shy. If the Arabs had any common spirit, they would have been in Damascus last autumn.

1 I.C.C.: Imperial Camel Corps. Two companies of them *were* used, with Lawrence's agreement and support, for a specific brief operation in the desert in the summer of 1918.

2 'Deedes' officer', or X (see next paragraph), was Lieutenant Alec Kirkbride, Royal Engineers, later Sir Alec Kirkbride, British Resident in Transjordan. He had been sent by Lieutenant-Colonel (later Sir Wyndham) Deedes, to investigate the possibility of supplying some of the needs of the Arab armies direct from Palestine instead of the normal route through Suez and Akaba. He was with Lawrence in the final advance on, and occupation of, Damascus.

3 This was an incorrect prediction. When Lawrence returned to Tafileh a week later after a reconnaissance towards the Jordan Valley, he found that Zeid had disposed of all the gold for past services and had none for future ones. There was thus no possibility of continuing with the next stage of Arab operations as agreed between himself and Allenby. For Lawrence's reaction to this development see p. 144.

4 Colonel Alan Dawnay (1888–1938) Old Etonian and officer of the Coldstream Guards, served with Lawrence in the desert in 1918. See *Seven Pillars*, Chapter XCII: 'Dawnay was Allenby's greatest gift to us — greater than thousands of baggage camels.' The two men became friends and, later, regular correspondents.

[...]

(8) Zeid having lost his frontal chance, I am stirring up the Sukhur to cut across the line by Ziza, and raise Cain about Madeba, W. Sirr, Chor el Riba. If I get them to taste I'll ride with them, but I am getting shy of adventures. I'm in an extraordinary position just now, vis à vis the Sherifs and the tribes, and sooner or later must go bust. I do my best to keep in the background, but cannot, and some day everybody will combine and down me. It is impossible for a foreigner to run another people of their own free will, indefinitely, and my innings has been a fairly long one.

[...]

(12) For the Jews, when I see Feisul next I'll talk to him, and the Arab attitude shall be sympathetic, for the duration of the war at least.[1] Only please remember that he is under the old man, and cannot involve the Arab kingdom by himself. If we get Madeba he will come to Jerusalem and all the Jews there will report him friendly. That will probably do all you need, without public commitment, which is rather beyond my province.

[...]

L.

PRO FO 882/7

MILITARY GOVERNOR, BEERSHEBA DISTRICT
16.2.18 El Ghor el Safiye

Commander Bir Seba

Please inform G.H.Q. (General Clayton) that the Turks sent a launch to Mezraa, towed the broken launch and dhows into deep water, and sank them. Mezraa remains in our hands. Sherif Abdulla is camped (10 tents) near some ruins in a garden bearing 326 from the N. point of Jebel Usdum and one mile from the E. beach of the Dead Sea. He has 100 Ageyl, 150 Ghawirneh, 100 Audat, and western details with him: also two machine guns. The fighting men with him are Ibrahim abu Irgeyig (very good), Jeddua el Sufi and Mohammed Gabbua of the Dhullam. The Audat sheikhs are second rank. Please inform Colonel Parker that the horse is a matter of some difficulty. Sherif Feisul gave it to one of his officers. Does he require

---

1 The Balfour Declaration of November 1917 had stated that the British Government viewed with favour the establishment of a Jewish national home in Palestine, provided the rights of people already living there (mostly Arabs) were not infringed — an impossible equation, as later history would show. Lawrence's task was to ensure that concern about this new development should not affect the Arabs', or more particularly, Feisal's, war-effort.

that horse, particularly, or would another of the Sherif's animals do? They are at his disposal, but not very good, I'm afraid. One Juma abu Seneima went to Khan Yunus with a letter from the Sherif, and has been arrested. Jeddua el Sufi is interceding for him. Could you push on his affair, and get him finished?[1]

Bearer Mohammed Ferhan is buying camels for the Sherifian forces. If you can help him in any way, without troubling yourself, please do. Our lack of transport would be comic if it was not such a nuisance.

Please inform Colonel Deedes that his officer,[2] with letters for General Clayton and himself, has gone to Akaba, and should reach there about Feb 18. Any messages for me may be sent by any decent Terabin Arab, c/o Sherif Abdulla ibn Hamza. Hamad and Jeddua are both with him, and so access is easy. Tafileh is only 5 hours further. I return to Tafileh tomorrow, and expect to move E from there a day later.

T. E. Lawrence

Bodleian Reserve

MILITARY GOVERNOR, BEERSHEBA DISTRICT
18.2.18   Tafileh

Governor Beersheba

The air attack on Katraneh[3] is reported to have been carried out by eleven aeroplanes, and to have caused great damage. Jemal Pasha, with the governor of Kerak rode thither at once with 500 cavalry, and none of them have yet returned. Hundreds of Kerak Arabs (including Faris, the head of the Butush) have come in to us in consequence, and things have greatly improved. If the raid could be repeated, we would profit still more, and if the castle at Kerak is a good mark bombs dropped there would probably bring over the Majalli, who are wavering.

A Sherifian ambush day before yesterday captured and killed a Turkish

---

1 In late January, urged by Lawrence, Sherif Abdulla el Fair (not to be confused with Abdulla, son of Hussein) had attacked and taken the little Dead Sea port of Mezraa (or El Mezra) capturing ten tons of grain and sixty prisoners; the launch and (six) dhows referred to, which they had found at anchor, had been scuttled — which explains why the Turks, having retrieved them, sank them. Liddell Hart in '*T. E. Lawrence' in Arabia and After* wrote (p. 277) that this 'interruption of the Turks' lines of supply pleased Lawrence far more than his own tactical victory' — i.e. Tafileh. The Turks had been lightering food supplies up the Dead Sea and the disruption of this traffic had been assigned to Lawrence by Allenby as an important objective.
2 Kirkbride.
3 A station on the Hejaz Railway.

patrol of 10 cavalry and 16 mule M.I. on the northern bank of Seil el Hesa. Above for General Clayton, by post, please.

T. E. Lawrence

Please send following to Colonel Parker.

If possible please send to Sherif Abdulla ibn Hamza two Terabin Arabs, Mohammed abu Mughasib, and Nassar Gelaidan, at present imprisoned in S. Palestine. They will take service with the Arab forces. If Nassar's camel can be released with him, it will be good.

T. E. Lawrence

Bodleian Reserve

Taken aback by Zeid's disclosure that he had no gold left to finance any further operations (see letter to Clayton dated 12 February 1918, footnote 3), Lawrence decided to place his future in Allenby's hands and rode to Beersheba to ask to be relieved of his duties. However, under persuasion by Hogarth and Clayton, and hearing that General Smuts, a member of Lloyd George's War Cabinet, had come out from London to expound important new plans, he relented and agreed to continue. He had no further dealings with Zeid, returning to his collaboration with Feisal, with whom he worked in more or less close association for the rest of the campaign.

HIS MOTHER
8.3.18   Cairo

Here I am in Cairo again. At Tafileh I had a difference of opinion with Sherif Zeid, the 4th son of the old man of Mecca, and left him for Beersheba. This was about the 22nd. I then went to Jerusalem, Ramleh, Jerusalem, Beersheba, Ismailia, Cairo, Suez, Akaba, Guweira, Akaba, Suez, and got back here last night. I hope to be here four nights.

This year promises to be more of a run about than last year even!

As for coming back — no, not possible now. The situation has changed since I came over, and I'm to go back till June at least. One rather expected that, I'm afraid.

I thought I had told you that Newcombe had left the Sherifian forces before he was captured? He never came to Akaba at all, but went to Palestine with the British.

No letters from you lately, except a November unit which I picked up at Akaba. By the way after this note don't expect any other from me till about the middle of April, for I'm going up country for a month, on an inspection trip.

They have now given me a D.S.O.[1] It's a pity all this good stuff is not sent to someone who would use it! Also apparently I'm a colonel of sorts.[2] Don't make any change in my address of course.

I wonder if you remember Young,[3] an Indian Army officer who came to Carchemish while Will was there? He has just come over to help our thing forward, I hope. He should be the right sort of man: the work is curious, and demands a sort of twisted tact, which many people do not seem to possess. We are very short-handed, and it will make things much easier if he fits in well.

Hugh Whitelocke has just joined the Egyptian Army I hear. They say he is somewhere in Cairo, so I may see him, but it is only a chance, as on these flying visits I rush about all day and do very little ordinary speech. It will be a comfort when this gipsy mode of life comes to an end. However thank goodness the worst of the winter is over. I had one very bad night out in the hills when my camel broke down in the snow drifts, and I had to dig a path out for it and lead it for miles down slippery snow-slopes. One's usual airy sort of white shirt and bare feet are better in summer than in winter. Of course the hill country east of the Dead Sea is very high, and one gets what frost and snow there is, anyhow.

There, I can't think of anything else cheerful to tell you about — except perhaps that three of my camels have had babies in the last few weeks. That makes me about thirty riding camels of my own, but then my bodyguard of servants is about 25, so there are not so many spare. I never have any baggage camels with me ... we carry what we need on our own animals.

Here by good fortune are some new photographs just to hand.

N.

HL/Bodleian Reserve

1 Distinguished Service Order, for his conduct at the Battle of Tafileh.
2 He was officially promoted from Temporary Major to Temporary Lieutenant-Colonel on 12 March.
3 Major, later Sir Hubert Young.

HIS MOTHER
28.3.18   Akaba

Well, I foretold a long trip, when I was in Cairo a few days ago, and here I am back in Akaba for two nights. Various things happened to delay my start — and indeed I may have one more chance of writing about a week hence, from further North.

News? none. We have lost so much by frost and snow and rain that movement has become difficult, and very unpleasant. There is however hope that the spring is coming. Yesterday was warm, but then Akaba always is.

About A. General Clayton asked me about him last time I was in Palestine. They did not wire for him, after all, as another man turned up, who will do for the present, and I knew he would rather not hurry things too much. As soon as I hear from you that he is ready to come out they will make an application for him to the War Office. For it to be successful he must be in the army, and an infantry regiment will be the easiest place, unless he gets a special list commission, which may not be still possible. I do not think there will be any difficulty about it at all, so long as he keeps up with his Arabic.

I saw Kerry the other day, and Hugh Whitelocke — the only people from Oxford seen for some little time. No matter: after four years of this sort of thing I am become altogether dried up, and till the business ends I can't do anything else either here or there. It will be a great comfort when one can lie down & sleep without having to think about things; and speak without having one's every word reported in half a hundred camps. This is a job too big for me.

                                        N.

HL/Bodleian Reserve

HIS MOTHER
12.5.18   Arab Bureau Savoy Hotel Cairo

I sent you a wire a week ago, as I passed through Cairo on my way up to Palestine. Since then I have been travelling at red hot speed, but tonight have finished. Tonight I am going to spend in Cairo, and I got here last night. It is the first time for six weeks that I have spent two nights running in one place.

I'll get letters from you tomorrow, and answer them at my leisure, because I expect I'll be here a week.

This is only a scrawl meanwhile. All is very well, and while we have not done all we want, we have done all that we could do by ourselves, and it is not at all bad.

N.

HL/Bodleian Reserve

KING HUSSEIN OF THE HEJAZ[1]
Ramadan 17, 1336–June 25, 1918

His Majesty King Hussein
   Probably, I am afraid, I told you some things uncertain about the Northern Army. I intend now to give you a brief account in order to eliminate any inconvenience which may have been caused by my repeated demand for assistance.

At Present.
There are now 4,000 Turkish soldiers at Ma'an entrenched in strong fortifications with cement machine gun points and many guns. There is a good supply of water and sufficient food for three months. Against this force stands Sidi Faisal's regular army of 3,500 with guns stronger than the Turks. The big guns are all placed opposite Ma'an supported by 700 infantry soldiers at Wahida about two hours from Ma'an, 800 at Jerdun and 600 at Jurf al-Darawish.
   The Turkish force at Jerdun is made up of 150, about 500 at Anaza and 400 at Jurf. The railway has been cut off to the south of Ma'an and between all the stations from Ma'an to Fareifra. The enemy can repair the railway between Ma'an and Fareifra within three weeks, but that between Ma'an and Mudawwara could not be repaired until after peace. No Turkish force could move through the destroyed sections.

Your Majesty will conclude from the above details the following:
(1) Feisal's force of 3,500 will not be able to occupy Ma'an in direct assault. No commander could attack nowadays an entrenched force if he has not under him at least twice or three times the surrounded force.
(2) Feisal cannot gather all his forces against Ma'an. The Turks want to lift the siege from Ma'an after the pilgrimage and on that account they moved a month ago their force from Jurf and Anaza in order to repair the railway but they were stopped and surrounded by the Arabs.

---

1 Written in Arabic, this letter eventually became the property of the King's youngest son, Emir Zeid.

No doubt your Majesty will recognise that your small Northern Army
has:
(1) Cut the railway between Syria and Hejaz permanently.
(2) Surrounded a superior force for three months at Ma'an.
(3) Stopped and surrounded the reinforcements of the enemy estimated at
half the strength of your army for six weeks at Jurf al-Darawish.

All this has been achieved by the 3,500 regular soldiers under the
command of Ja'afar Pasha. The bedouins are no good for a continued siege
and would not attack fortifications. The Huweitat, Beni Sakhr and other
tribes which are under the command of Sidi Feisal did not participate in
the operations of Ma'an.

The British General Staff is of the opinion that rarely has an army
accomplished what Ja'afar's army has, under the command of Emir Feisal
and the British Officers (Col. Joyce, Major Maynard and myself) who
helped to organize it. All the above mentioned are satisfied with their work
but we are a little afraid of the future.

The Future.
The first Turkish force was surrounded by Feisal at Jurf. The Turks are
bound to lift the siege upon Jurf as well as upon Ma'an within the next
two months. The strength of the Turkish army at Amman is estimated at
8,000 and it is possible that the German General Staff would send a third
of it from Katraneh to Ma'an.

Sidi Feisal's army is now doing so much more than any other army equal
in strength would do. When Katraneh forces advance, Feisal will be bound
to assemble his forces at Waheida, while the enemy is engaged in repairing
the railway between Fareifra and Ma'an. Sherif Nasir has now at Hesa 70
regulars and 400 bedouins and has done admirably well on your side, but
he cannot stand alone against 3,000 Turkish regulars.

After the railway to Ma'an is repaired, the Turks will be able to reinforce
Ma'an by infantry and means of transportation and then they will attack
Abu al-Lissan. The Arab fortifications there are in good condition and
therefore your army will probably be able to defend itself. Otherwise the
army should retreat to Guweira, a well fortified position which the Turks
will not be able to attack. Moreover they can neither attack Akaba nor be
able to repair the railway to Mudawwara.

As to Arab plans I can say nothing now but I must state that there will
be no successful results from a direct attack at the vanguard of the enemy.
Had it not been for your courage in ordering Sidi Feisal last year to leave
Medina and proceed to Wejh and Akaba, the Arab movement would not
have been completely successful as it is today.

In war it is more profitable for the Arabs to adopt the daring plan which
the enemy does not anticipate.

I have submitted to Sidi Feisal a plan which General Allenby might help us in implementing. If this plan succeeds, Ma'an and its garrison of 14,000 Turks is now locked in with no hope of escape to north, south, east or west.

I beg you Sir to burn this letter after reading it, because I am writing to you about matters which I should have disclosed to you orally.

I conclude begging you to be so kind as to accept my sincere respect and best wishes.

T. E. Lawrence[1]

British Library

VYVYAN RICHARDS[2]

15.VII.18   [Cairo]

Well, it was wonderful to see your writing again, and very difficult to read it: also pleasant to have a letter which doesn't begin 'Reference your F.S. 102487 b of the 45th inst.' Army prose is bad, and one has so much of it that one fears contamination.

I cannot write to anyone just now. Your letter came to me in Aba Lissan, a little hill-fort on the plateau of Arabia S.E. of the Dead Sea and I carried it with me down to Akaba, to Jidda and then here to answer. Yet with all that I have had it only a month and you wrote it three months ago. This letter will be submarined and then it is all over for another three years.

It always seemed to me that your eyes would prevent service for you, and that in consequence you might preserve your continuity. For myself. I have been so violently uprooted and plunged so deeply into a job too big for me, that everything feels unreal. I have dropped all I ever did, and live only as a thief of opportunity, snatching chances of the moment when and where I see them. My people have probably told you that the job is to foment an Arab rebellion against Turkey, and for that I have to try and hide my frankish exterior, and be as little out of the Arab picture as I can. So it's a kind of foreign stage, on which one plays day and night, in fancy dress, in a strange language with the price of failure on one's head if the part is not well filled.

---

1 Signature both in Arabic and English.
2 When Richards showed Lawrence this letter seven years later (in much changed circumstances), Lawrence found it interesting enough to copy for himself. He subsequently sent his copy to Charlotte Shaw apparently believing it to be the only surviving letter of his 'Arab period'. See letter to Charlotte Shaw, 29 March 1927, p. 320.

You guessed rightly that the Arab appealed to my imagination. It is the old old civilisation, which has refound itself clear of household gods and half the trappings which ours hastens to assume. The gospel of bareness in materials is a good one, and it involves apparently a sort of moral bareness too. They think for the moment and endeavour to slip through life without turning corners or climbing hills. In part it is a mental and moral fatigue, a race trained out: and to avoid difficulties they have to jettison so much that we think honourable and brave: and yet without in any way sharing their point of view I think I can understand it enough to look at myself and other foreigners from their direction, and without condemning it. I know I'm a stranger to them, and always will be: but I cannot believe them worse, any more than I could change to their ways.

This is a very long porch to explain why I'm always trying to blow up Railway trains and bridges instead of looking for the well at the world's end.[1] Anyway these years of detachment have cured me of any desire ever to do anything for myself. When they untie my bonds I will not find in me any spur to action. Though actually one never thinks of afterwards: the time from the beginning is like one of those dreams, seeming to last for aeons, out of which you wake up with a start, and find that it has left nothing in the mind. Only the different thing about this dream is that so many people do not wake up in life again.

I cannot imagine what my people can have told you. Until now we have only been preparing the groundwork and bases of our Revolt, and do not yet stand on the brink of action. Whether we are going to win or lose, when we do strike, I cannot ever persuade myself. The whole thing is such a play, and one cannot put conviction into one's day-dreams. If we succeed I will have done well with the materials given me, and that disposes of your 'lime-light'. If we fail and they have patience, then I suppose we will go on digging foundations. Achievement, if it comes, will be a great disillusionment, but not great enough to wake one up.

Your mind has evidently moved far since 1914. That is a privilege you have won by being kept out of the mist for so long. You'll find the rest of us aged undergraduates, possibly still not conscious of our unfitting grey hair. For that reason I cannot follow or return your steps. A house with no action entailed upon one, quiet, and liberty to think and abstain as one wills, yes, I think abstention, the leaving everything alone and watching the others still going past, is what I would choose today, if they ceased driving me. This may be only the reaction from four years opportunism, and is not worth trying to resolve into terms of geography and employment.

Of course the ideal is that of the lords who are still certainly expected,

---

1 A reference, which Richards would have appreciated, to William Morris's romance *The Well at the World's End.*

but the certainty is not for us, I'm afraid. Also for very few would the joy be so perfect as to be silent. Those words peace, silence, rest, take on a vividness amid noise and worry and weariness, like a lighted window in the dark. Yet what on earth is the good of a lighted window? and perhaps it is only because one is overborne and tired. You know when one marches across an interminable plain, a hill (which is still the worst hill on earth) is a banquet, and after searing heat, cold water takes on a quality (what would they have said without this word before?) impossible in the eyes of a fen-farmer. Probably I'm only a sensitised film, turned black or white by the objects projected on me: and if so what hope is there that next week or year, or tomorrow, can be prepared for today?

This is an idiot letter, and amounts to nothing except a cry for further change; which is idiocy, for I change my abode every day, and my job every two days, and my language every three days, and still remain always unsatisfied. I hate being in front, and I hate being back, and I don't like responsibility and I don't obey orders. Altogether no good just now. A long quiet like a purge, and then a contemplation and decision of future roads, that is what is to look forward to.

You want apparently some vivid colouring of an Arab's costume, or of a flying Turk, and we have it all, for that is part of the mise en scene of the successful raider, and hitherto I am that. My bodyguard of fifty Arab tribesmen, picked rioters from the young men of the deserts, are more splendid than a tulip-garden, and we ride like lunatics and with our Beduins pounce on unsuspecting Turks and destroy them in heaps: and it is all very gory and nasty after we close grips. I love the preparation and the journey, and loathe the physical fighting. Disguises and prices on one's head, and fancy exploits are all part of the pose. How to reconcile it with the Oxford pose I know not. Were we flamboyant there?

If you reply — you will perceive I have matting of the brain and your thoughts are in control, please tell me of Berry, and if possible Winkworth.[1] He was the man for all these things, because he would take a berserk beery pleasure in physical outposts.

Very many thanks for writing. It has opened a very precious casement.

L.

DG/British Library

1 Friends of their undergraduate days.

HIS MOTHER
15.7.18   Cairo

Well, this has been a long interruption of writing. I went off to Jidda, after the last letter, as soon as I had been to Alexandria (to see the High Commissioner) and to Palestine, to see General Allenby. At Jidda I had to stay several days, before I could get a boat back to Suez. It was an unprofitable journey, and I was not able to get anything done of my hopes. There were a great many local things however, which I saw, and which rather changed the outlook.

Then from Jidda we dashed up to Wejh, and thence to Suez: a bad trip, in a small boat, against a strong head wind. Took us 5 days. From Suez I came here for a night, then Alexandria, then Palestine, and have now come to anchor here for perhaps a week. It is very nice to have finished one part of the show. We begin something fresh next month, and the change will be a pleasant one.

Having said that much, that is all, I think, that I have got to say. You know I have nothing doing or to do which does not actually concern Feisul's campaign, and that I make a rule to write nothing about. I cannot talk about books because I don't read any, or about people, because I only meet the Staff who deal with our operations, or places, because most of them are not to be made public property. So there you are —

As I'm in the middle of the show, I have to be more careful than anybody else. Mr. Hogarth is coming back to England about the middle of August, and hopes to see you and explain something of how we get on. The communiqués in the press contain the least part of the truth. The two Sherifs down by Medina, Abdulla and Ali, allow their fancy very free play with their achievements, and keep on reporting that they have broken thousands of rails and bridges. The bridges are tiny culverts, and the breaks in the rails only shorten them a few inches. Besides they break usually only 10% of their published figures. The communiqués of Feisul's army are written by ourselves, or at least checked by us, and are more truthful.

One thing they have not brought out, I fancy, and which I can tell you, is that from Maan southward for 100 kilometres there are no Turks, and the 8 stations and all the rails and bridges have been smashed to atoms by us. This makes a break that I am sure they will not be able to repair so long as the war lasts, and thanks to it the very large body of troops from there to Medina are cut off from Turkey, as much as the little garrisons of Turks in South Arabia. Medina is a holy city, and the Arabs do not attack it: it has huge gardens and palm groves, and is quite self-supporting so far as food goes, so there is no definite reason why the troops there should ever surrender. We are not in any hurry about it, anyway, though the capture of the place might be a political gain to the Sherif.

There, I think that is enough talk. If I could think of anything more to say I would prolong it. The W.O. reply to our application for A. should arrive any day, and when it comes I will write again. We left it purposely till the vac.

N.

HL/Bodleian Reserve

Lawrence's war ended in a flurry of military and political action, as the Turks, heavily defeated by Allenby to the west of the Jordan and severely harassed by Feisal's Arab forces to the east, retreated in disarray leaving Damascus open to capture. He was one of the first to enter the city on 1 October, becoming briefly its '*de facto* Governor' (his own phrase), his purpose being to set up an Arab administration strong enough to survive the inevitable crises that would follow liberation. One of his first actions in Damascus was to throw out a provisional government set up as soon as the Turks left by two usurping Algerian brothers, Mohammed Said and Abd el Kadir, whom he saw as in many ways evil geniuses and betrayers of the Revolt.[1]

The following documents are from this final phase: a despatch written as the advance gained momentum and his last campaign despatch, written on the day of his entry into Damascus.

GENERAL STAFF, G.H.Q.
24.9.18   Um El Surab[2]

The Turks have given up the repair of the line, and are streaming up the Haj road to Deraa. In consequence we have closed down here. Sherif Feisal returns at once to Azrak. Saad El Skaini goes west with Rafa El Khoraisha to the Irbid district. Sherif Nasir and Nuri Shalaan move to Umtaiye, Taibe, Tafas, Sheikh Saad to place the army there, and get into contact with the British by way of the new El Al, Kefr Harib road.

The Turks are entrenching Deraa, but the country is such that they will inevitably be cut off there, if they delay, by your cavalry if they issue either by Beisan, Irbid or by Semakh — El Al roads. If we can get El Al quickly, we will secure you the latter at least.

1 On this subject see Lawrence's report to D.C.P.O., 28 June 1919 (p. 165).
2 On the road from Azrak to Deraa.

We spend to-night in Umtaiye, and would cross the railway near Tell Arar to-morrow night (25–26), if all goes well.

Will you please try and arrange the evacuation of the aerodrome here to-morrow. There are 2 mechanics, and some kit, and little or no petrol. We will leave the cars here till the planes leave. Till mid-day, therefore, the Bristols[1] here will do us. If it is possible, after mid-day on the 25th and throughout the 26th, we would like a continuous patrol of Deraa, dropping bombs as is possible, and if there is an important concentration of enemy on the line between Deraa and Ghazale, dropping a message to that effect on us. Our position will be between Umtaiye and Naeime, and we will lay out an H on the ground when we see a machine over us. We will put out the same sign at Sh. Saad next day if you like to send out to find us.

Please get £10,000 in gold to Ramleh to be drawn on by us in case of urgency. It can be replaced from the £100,000 in Akaba.

In case of need please communicate with Sherif Feisal at Azrak.

T. E. Lawrence

PRO WO 157/738

GENERAL STAFF, G.H.Q.

1.10.18   Damascus

Please forward following to Hedjaz Operations.

An Arab force left Deraa on September 29th under Sherif Nasir and Nuri Bey Said, following up the 4th Cavalry Division on the right flank. We marched up the Hedjaz Railway, and in the morning of September 30th came in contact with an enemy column of 2000 men with 4 guns retiring from Deraa. Our mounted men kept up a running fight with these till 4 p.m. when Sherif Nasir galloped ahead of them with 30 horse and threw himself into Khiara Chiftlik, South of Kiswe, to delay the enemy, as General Gregory's Brigade was just marching into Kham Denun. The Turks showed some fight but were shelled effectively by the British, and taken on the head and west flank by the British, while the Arabs hung on to their tail. The Arabs took about 600 prisoners, 14 machine guns and 3 guns.

From Kiswe the Sherif sent a mounted force forward to get contact with his followers in the gardens east of Damascus, to find that his local committee had hoisted the Arab flag and proclaimed the Emirate of Hussein of Mecca at 2.30 p.m.

1 i.e. Bristol F2B fighter aircraft.

Sherif Nasir with Major Stirling and myself moved into Damascus at 9 a.m. on October 1st amid scenes of extraordinary enthusiasm on the part of the local people. The streets were nearly impassable with the crowds, who yelled themselves hoarse, danced, cut themselves with swords and daggers and fired volleys into the air. Nasir, Nuri Shalaan, Auda abu Tayi and myself were cheered by name, covered with flowers, kissed indefinitely, and splashed with attar of roses from the house-tops.

On arrival at the Serai Shukri Pasha el Ayoubi was appointed Arab Military Governor, as all former civil employes [sic] had left with Jemal Pasha[1] on the previous day. Martial law was proclaimed, police organised, and the town picketed. The Rualla are behaving very well, but the Druses are troublesome.

I have no orders as to what political arrangements should be made in Damascus and will carry on as before till I hear further from you. If Arab military assistance is not required in further operations of the Desert Corps, I would like to return to Palestine as I feel that if I remain here longer, it will be very difficult for my successor.

T. E. Lawrence

G.O.C., Desert Mounted Corps has seen above, and agrees with my carrying on with the town administration until further instructions.

T.E.L.

The Arab Army since September 26th have taken 8000 prisoners and 120 machine guns.

PRO WO 157/738[2]

On 3 October the principals on the Allied side, Allenby and Feisal, reached Damascus. Lawrence asked Allenby's permission to go, which was granted. On the 4th he left, first for Egypt and then home. 'The old war is closing, and my use is gone,' he wrote from Cairo to the Base Commandant at Akaba, Major R. H. Scott, adding: 'We were an odd little set, and we have, I expect, changed History in the near East. I wonder how the Powers will let the Arabs get on.'[3]

1 The Turkish commander in Syria.
2 Published in *Allenby's Final Triumph*, by W.T. Massey (Constable, 1920).
3 Letter of 14 October 1918: published in *DG*.

3 · THE POLITICAL YEARS

1918–22

3   Introduction

Following the triumphal entry into Damascus, Lawrence returned home to England, exchanging the military for the political arena. Before the end of October he was arguing the Arabs' case before the Eastern Committee of the War Cabinet, at the same table as, among others, Lord Curzon (who was chairman), General Smuts, Lord Robert Cecil (Assistant Foreign Secretary), Edwin Montagu (Secretary of State for India) and Sir Mark Sykes. His reputation had gone before him, so that if there was a certain *naïveté* about the solutions he proposed for the problems of the Middle East he was nevertheless listened to with both respect and admiration. In early November, even before the official end of hostilities, he telegraphed with Foreign Office approval to King Hussein of the Hejaz urging that Feisal should be despatched to Paris as his representative at the peace talks which would soon follow. The French Government cavilled about Feisal's precise status but eventually he was allowed to sail for Europe. Lawrence was present as he stepped ashore from H.M.S. *Gloucester* at Marseilles on 24 November to be met by senior French officials, and the party was joined by Colonel Brémond, former Head of the French Military Mission to the Hejaz, on arrival at Lyons. Subsequently, after Feisal had been taken on a brief tour of the French battlefields without Lawrence (as a 'foreign hanger-on' — his own phrase — he was not made welcome), the two men spent much of December together in Britain. Notable meetings took place with the King and with the Zionist leader Chaim Weizmann, a meeting at which it seemed possible that Jewish and Arab aspirations might be reasonably harmonised.

In January 1919 Feisal and Lawrence went to Paris. Lawrence found that no seats had been assigned to Arab delegates but his intervention speedily produced the two necessary tickets. Frequently seen wearing an Arab head-dress with his British uniform, he was a public relations success — Gertrude Bell called him 'the most picturesque' figure at the conference — but French determination combined with Lloyd George's *realpolitik* gave the Arabs little chance. Woodrow Wilson's doctrine of 'self-determination' seemed to offer encouragement, but Arab aspirations were inevitably low in the pecking order of international concern after a war which had seen so massive a blood-letting in Europe. France, having suffered not only a huge loss of manpower but also four years of partial territorial occupation, needed to reassure herself by annexations elsewhere, and Syria, which she had long coveted, was the necessary consolation-prize. Feisal's removal from Damascus, where he was *de facto* ruler, was merely a matter of time. Lawrence found himself increasingly isolated and his pro-Arabism more and more unacceptable as British pragmatism and French determination found their inevitable accommodation. For much of 1919 and 1920 he waged an eloquent and hard-hitting campaign through letters and articles in the press, using his public reputation to gain publicity for his attacks on establishment policy and decisions.

Meanwhile, other factors were at work which complicated a psychological condition already overwrought after four years of war, two years of which he had lived at almost white heat. Early in 1919 he embarked on the long, draining task of writing and re-writing his account of the Arab campaign — the book which was to emerge as *Seven Pillars of Wisdom*; the work which would occupy him on and off until 1926. Oxford gave him a base and a sanctuary by electing him to a Research Fellowship of All Souls College, but he was not at ease in an academic environment and found it more congenial to write in a garret room in Barton Street, Westminster, loaned to him by his architect friend Herbert Baker; there he often wrote for hours at a time, taking only minimal nourishment and refreshing himself with solitary walks through the London streets. In mid-1919 the American publicist Lowell Thomas, after a successful season in New York, launched at the Royal Opera House, Covent Garden, his 'illustrated travelogue' about the Middle Eastern war which turned Lawrence almost overnight into a show-business celebrity. He would thenceforward always be known as 'Lawrence of Arabia'. Churchill brought him back into positive political work in 1921 and he spent some months in the Middle East helping to devise a settlement sufficiently fair to the Arabs for him to feel that he could leave the political milieu, which he had never found to his liking, with clean hands. Feisal was given a kingship, though of Iraq not Syria, while his brother Abdulla was installed as Emir in Transjordan. Later in 1921 Lawrence was again in the Middle East as Chief Political Representative in Transjordan before handing over to H. St J. B. Philby. He then returned to England where, his duty to Churchill discharged, he retired not only from politics, but also from normal life. To the amazement and dismay of many of his friends, in the summer of 1922 he enlisted under an assumed name — John Hume Ross — in the ranks of the Royal Air Force. He would never again hold any high office or play any important military or political role.

Compared with the years ahead this was a period when he wrote relatively few letters. Much of his energy went into verbal argument or in articles or memoranda — and he was, of course, writing *Seven Pillars*. There are only four known letters to his family (though he was frequently in Oxford he was also much away from it): one from Paris in 1919, two from Cairo in 1921, one from London in 1922. I have included all of these (if not all at full length) and I have reproduced a number of the personal letters of this period printed in Garnett; the political ones to newspapers, available not only in Garnett but also in Stanley and Rodelle Weintraub's *Evolution of a Revolt*, seemed less worthy of repetition. I have, however, tried to cast new light on his political activities by including three of the numerous forthright minutes written by him at the Peace Conference and most of the long and often eloquent cables he sent from Jidda in August and September 1921 when he was engaged in the difficult, indeed impossible, task of trying to persuade King Hussein of the Hejaz to accept Churchill's Middle Eastern settlement. 'This is the beastliest trip ever I had,' he wrote to Eric Kennington from Aden at this time.

Among other letters, some of them new, some republished, there are two to Fareedah el Akle, in which he writes interestingly if disenchantedly about the war, the Middle East and Lowell Thomas; one to Sir Archibald Murray, Allenby's predecessor as Commander-in-Chief in Cairo, in which he makes one of his rare approving comments about *Seven Pillars*: 'the story is in parts very odd and exciting [...] for it is not badly written, and is authoritative, in so far as it concerns myself'; and two to Ezra Pound about his hopes and fears as a writer, the second of which includes a dismissive reference to the poetry of his future critic-in-chief Richard Aldington. I have also printed the letter to the Foreign Office official G. J. Kidston, to whom he wrote outspokenly about his secret war aims, first published in the *Sunday Times* in 1968. In addition I have included a number of letters which he wrote when he was trying to persuade certain former participants in the Arab war to sit for the artists whom he had asked to collaborate in the production of his lavish subscribers' edition of his book. They show him apparently buoyant, even jesting, at a time when he was about to take his plunge into social and personal obscurity. Other recipients represented here who were not featured in Garnett include Geoffrey Dawson, then Editor of *The Times*, the artist Augustus John, the veteran traveller, poet and political radical Wilfred Scawen Blunt, and, already mentioned above, H. St J. B. Philby. There are also a number of letters to Sir Hugh Trenchard, Chief of the Air Staff, written on the eve of enlisting in the Air Force. Among the last letters in this section, previously published but certainly worthy of being re-used, are two to George Bernard Shaw which initiated the relationship with the Shaws which was to produce numerous letters to G. B. S. and, much more significantly, the intimate, long-sustained correspondence with his wife Charlotte.

GEOFFREY DAWSON[1]

Sunday [24 November 1918][2]   Carlton Hotel Pall Mall London

I'm afraid this is really meant by providence for the *Daily Mail*. I found I couldn't give you the original MSS and was kept busy till last night, and then wrote this at a sitting. It's a pity, because it begins decently, & drivels off into incidents. Please burn it.

Feisul will probably be in London on Thursday and then I'll try and arrange you something useful.

The points that strike me are that the Arabs came into the war without making a previous treaty with us, and have consistently refused to listen to the temptations of other powers. They have never had a press agent, or tried to make themselves out a case, but fought as hard as they could (I'll swear to that) and suffered hardships in their three campaigns and losses that would break up seasoned troops. They fought with ropes round their necks (Feisul had £20000 alive & £10000 dead on him. I the same: Nasir £10000 alive, & Ali el Harith £8000) and did it without, I believe any other very strong motive than a desire to see the Arabs free. It was rather an ordeal for as very venerable a person as Hussein to rebel, for he was at once most violently abused by the Moslem press in India & Turkey, on religious grounds.

Hussein took the headship of the Arabs because he was invited to, by all the Arab secret societies, as the one man whose pre-eminence was founded on an arbitrary reason — birth.

England spent about £10,000,000 in all on the Arabs, and two of the British staff were killed over it. More should have been but there were only about 20 of us all told.

The actual value of Arab alliances is a matter of opinion (posterity's opinion, probably) but the East has been rather impressed by our having taken the most unlikely material in the world, and pushed it to undreamed of success. And we have done it all without losing a grain of its good will!

There is a private matter which I would like to tell you — not for action. Sir Henry MacMahon [*sic*] did all the spadework of the entry of the Sherif

---

1 Geoffrey Dawson (1874–1944), born Robinson — he changed his name by Royal Licence in 1917 — was Editor of *The Times*, 1912–19 and 1923–41.

2 The date is assumed from the fact that three articles by Lawrence (described as 'A Correspondent') appeared in *The Times* during the following week, one entitled 'The Arab Campaign' on 26 November, two entitled 'The Arab Epic' on 27 and 28 November.

into the war, and was sacked (largely for it) when things got bad in the early days of the rising. Now Wingate says he did it. It was really MacMahon advised by Storrs, Clayton, & perhaps myself.

The Sherifian solution for the Near East is Irak (Bagdad to us) like Egypt, under the British, with nominal Arab prince: Jezireh (Mosul to Diarbehir & Birejek) Arab-Kurd province of Irak, under separate constitution, with nominal Arab prince: Syria (port of Tripoli) independent under Feisul: it has fought for it, and deserves preferential treatment. Palestine British protectorate, with some scope for Jewish expansion. They would like the French to take over the business of the Armenians (Cilicia, & the six vilayets.)[1]

The old Sherif wants to be prayed for in Mosques on Friday. He is, already, in Syria, and in parts of Mesopotamia, and will be generally if we leave things alone.

T. E. Lawrence

Bodleian Reserve

HIS MOTHER
30.1.19   Hotel Majestic Paris

I got your letter yesterday, and will answer it this morning, while waiting up here for breakfast. I'm living at the Continental, which is half an hour's walk from the Majestic and Astoria, the British quarters, and this morning I found a taxi, which is a rare thing. In consequence I have ten unexpected minutes.

About work — it is going on well. I have seen 10 American newspaper men, and given them all interviews, which went a long way. Also President Wilson, and the other people who have influence. The affair is nearly over, I suspect. Another fortnight, perhaps.

Everybody seems to be here, and of course it is a busy time. I have had, personally, one meal in my hotel since I got to Paris! That was with Newcombe, who turned up unexpectedly.

Bliss, of the Beyrout College is here,[2] and proving a very valuable assistant of the Arab cause. Tell A.[3] I haven't seen a bookshop yet. I cannot

---

1 The old Turkish provinces.
2 Dr Howard S. Bliss, President of the American University at Beirut, whom Lawrence had met before the war (see his letter home of 11 April 1911), had been officially invited by the United States to produce evidence on the Syrian question.
3 A.: Arnold Lawrence.

come to England to meet Bob, but if he came to Paris could see him. I'm always in my room (98, at the Continental) before 10 a.m. (unless out at breakfast as today) and after 11.30 p.m.

N.[1]

HL/Bodleian Reserve

SIR LOUIS MALLET[2]

22.4.19   [Paris]

Sherif Feisal asks me to tell you that some of his Mesopotamian officers will wish shortly to return home. These men are mostly convinced that Abdulla should become Emir of Bagdad, and will inevitably say so on their return.[3] Feisal will not of course send with them, or make, any expression of his own opinion on the matter. He cannot on the other hand instruct them to keep silent on the point. They are officers who have served us and him very well, and are mostly very pro-British. He cannot without suspicion keep them in Syria indefinitely, but he does not want them to go back to Mesopotamia without our knowing of them, and of their opinions and probable course of action on arrival. Indeed he would be glad to have our assurance that they will not be hindered so long as their behaviour is reasonable — and that their beliefs will not be considered seditious.

I need hardly say that they all expect and want a British mandate in Mesopotamia.

T E Lawrence

PRO FO 608/92

1 This was the last letter home written to both his parents. His father died in early April, victim of the great influenza epidemic of 1918–19. His mother was to outlive his father by 40 years, dying in November 1959, aged 98.

2 Sir Louis Mallet was a senior member of the British Delegation to the Peace Conference. Lawrence's memorandum evidently failed to reach its destination as swiftly as he intended, for it carries the footnote: 'I saw this for the first time on June 1, 19 L Mallet.'

3 Lawrence was still campaigning at this time for the political solution which he had put to Lord Curzon's cabinet committee in October 1918: namely that Feisal should be ruler of Syria and Abdulla ruler of Mesopotamia — a scheme which had aroused much hostility in the India Office and was becoming equally unpopular with the Foreign Office.

3.5.19   [Paris]

In a nutshell, nothing has passed.[1] Clemenceau tried to make a bargain with Feisal, to acknowledge the independence of Syria in return for Feisal's statement that France was the only qualified mandatory.

Feisal refused. He said first that it wasn't true. France hardly understood the mandatory system. Secondly, if he said so he would only have to go away to Mecca, since he could not make his people agree with him. The French had now, by means of the commission, to deal with the people, not with him.[2]

Thirdly, that a statement that the French refused to admit the independence of Syria would help him. They had admitted it in the declaration of Nov 1918: in the Sykes-Picot, and it was the first clause of the mandate they were hoping for. Therefore it was not worth paying a lie for.

                                                                    TEL

PRO FO 608/93

In May 1919 Lawrence joined an experimental flight of Handley Page bombers bound for Egypt; his intention was to visit Cairo and collect his wartime reports and other personal effects. The aircraft in which he was travelling crashed at Rome during an attempt at a night landing without the necessary landing lights. The two pilots were killed; Lawrence received minor injuries but was able shortly to continue his journey. He was helped out of the wreckage by Aircraftman Daw, a letter of gratitude to whom is printed on p. 167. In Cairo he wrote the important report which follows, about the two Algerian brothers whom he had deposed on his arrival in Damascus, one of whom he held in part responsible for his ill-treatment at Deraa (see p. 153).

1 From a memorandum headed 'Relations between Emir Feisal and the French Govt' containing a request to Lawrence to clarify 'what did actually pass' in the recent conversations and correspondence between Feisal and M. Clemenceau, the French Premier, about the future of Syria. Basically neither Feisal nor Lawrence trusted French intentions and Feisal had returned to Syria on 23 April without having arrived at any understanding.
2 The Inter-Allied Commission proposed by President Woodrow Wilson to ascertain the wishes of the local inhabitants in those areas of the Middle East which were in dispute. In the event the commission that went out consisted of just two Americans (Messrs King and Crane) and its findings were ignored.

DEPUTY CHIEF POLITICAL OFFICER, CAIRO[1]
June 28 1919   Grand Continental Hotel Cairo

D.C.P.O.

I want to begin at the beginning about this as to do so will probably put the question at rest for good.

These brothers Mohammed Said and Abd el Kadir w re judged insane in 1911, but escaped detention in asylums by free use of their wealth. Mohammed Said holds a world's record for three successive fatal pistol accidents. He accompanied the propaganda mission of FROBENIUS[2] to the Red Sea for the Sudan in 1915, but turned back from Kunfida as Frobenius did not treat him with sufficient dignity. He was then removed to Brusa with his brothers, and kept under loose surveillance. The Ottoman Government soon decided that they might be useful, and Abd el Kadir offered to run a counter-Sherifian Arab propaganda under Abbas Hilmi against the British in Egypt. He was accordingly released from Brusa and sent down to Damascus. Thence he made a sham escape to Feisal, and went on to Mecca (in October 1917). He persuaded Hussein that he was a man of first importance in Syria, and was commended by him to Feisal. He returned to Akaba in the end of October 1917, and was sent up by Feisal with Ali ibn Hussein and me, to try and cut the Deraa bridges behind von Kress during Allenby's Jerusalem push.

Abd el Kadir was a fanatical Moslem, and had been much annoyed by the Sherifs' friendship with the British. He tried to persuade Ali & me to base ourselves in his Jaulan villages to cut the line, promising us the help of the Algerian peasantry. We refused this plan (he intended to betray us) and he pretended to be annoyed, and deserted one night from Azrak. He rode into Jebel Druse, to Salkhad where Feisal had an adherent in Hussein el Atrash. Abd el Kadir stayed with him for three days, talking bombastic rot about the Turks, and trying to provoke Hussein el Atrash to rise. He intended to denounce him when he did so. Hussein was too wily to be taken in, and Abd el Kadir slipped away from his house one night, and rode in to the Turks at Deraa. He told them the results of his mission, and especially that Ali & I were going for the Yarmuk bridge that week. The Turks ordered out cavalry to intercept us, but we made our attempt that very night, failed, and slipped back before the Turkish cordon was complete. Abd el Kadir then went to Damascus. I went in to Deraa in disguise to spy out the defences, was caught, and identified by Hajim Bey the Governor by virtue of Abd el Kadir's descriptions of me. (I learnt all about his treachery from Hajim's conversation, and from my guards.) Hajim was an

1 This post had been held since earlier in the year by Lawrence's wartime colleague Major W. F. Stirling.
2 Frobenius had been head of a German military mission in the Middle East.

ardent paederast and took a fancy to me. So he kept me under guard till night, and then tried to have me. I was unwilling, and prevailed after some difficulty. Hajim sent me to the hospital, and I escaped before dawn, being not as hurt as he thought. He was so ashamed of the muddle he had made that he hushed the whole thing up, and never reported my capture & escape. I got back to Azrak very annoyed with Abd el Kadir, and rode down to Akaba. Mohammed Said now came across to Feisal with false friendly letters from Jemal[1] in answer to some Feisal had sent to him with my approval. Just before he came Ali Riza sent a note to Feisal to say that Mohammed Said was coming to make anti-Arab propaganda among the officers of the Arab army. So we isolated him, and in disgust he only stayed two days in the camp.

Abd el Kadir now became Jemal's confidential adviser on Arab questions and raised volunteers for him. These fought the British in the first & second Amman raids, and did well for the Turks.

When September 1918 came, and Feisal's flying column attacked Deraa district, Abd el Kadir at once transferred his volunteers to the Hauran, and garrisoned the Railway against us. We captured a lot of them, and they told us of all his efforts against us. When the Turkish *débâcle* came Abd el Kadir ran away quickly to Damascus, and as soon as the Turks had gone, took forcible control of the local government, in virtue of the remains of his Algerian volunteers.

When Nasr & I arrived Abd el Kadir & Mohammed Said were sitting in the Serail with their armed servants. Feisal had begged me to get rid of them, so I told them to go, and that Shukri el Ayubi would be military governor till Ali Riza returned. Abd el Kadir refused to go, and tried to stab me in the council chamber. Auda knocked him down, & Nuri Shaalan offered me the help of the Rualla to put him out. Mohammed Said & Abd el Kadir then went away, breathing vengeance against me as a Christian. I thought they would be quiet, but that night they called a secret meeting of their Algerians & the Druses, & begged them to strike one blow for the faith before the British arrived. I heard of this, warned General Nuri Said, and borrowed the Rualla from Nuri Shaalan. With the latter I rushed Abd el Kadir's house, and took him, while Nuri Said cleared the Druses out of the streets. I meant to shoot the two brothers, so interned Abd el Kadir in the Town Hall till I should have caught Mohammed Said. Before I had done so Feisal arrived, and said that like a new Sultan he would issue a general amnesty. So Abd el Kadir escaped again. He got some of his men to shoot at me that same day, but I won.

(Later on Abd el Kadir broke out again, and went for Feisal's house, & was shot, I believe by one of the sentries. This was after I left.)

1 See p. 155 note 1.

If ever two people deserved hanging or shooting in Syria they were these two brothers, and I very much regret that Mohammed Said has been given so much rope. Feisal has asked several times for his internment. He is the only real pan-Islamist in Damascus, and in his insanity is capable of any folly or crime against us.

T.E.Lawrence

University of Texas

FREDERICK J. DAW
5.7.[19]19   [Cairo]

Dear Dawes [*sic*]
   Will you buy yourself some trifle to remind you of our rather rough landing together at Rome? I was not at all comfortable hanging up in the wreck, and felt very grateful to you for digging me out.[1]

Yours sincerely
T E Lawrence

Bodleian Reserve

FROM A PEACE CONFERENCE MEMORANDUM[2]
[18 or 19 July 1919]   [Paris]

Some of these officers are resigning from the Arab Army, and in that case they will presumably return to Mesopotamia as private citizens. As they are all the men in Mesopotamia who had the courage to fight for their country, I regret that they are apparently going to be driven into opposition to our administration there. It is curious that men useful (indeed necessary) to Allenby in Syria should be 'spreaders of undesirable propaganda' in Mesopotamia. I prefer the terms of Lord Curzon's letter of June 16.[3]

TEL

PRO FO 608/92

1 Daw was an Aircraftman of the R.A.F. The letter was accompanied by a cheque for £10.
2 This is Lawrence's note on a memorandum circulated for comment entitled 'Return of Feisal's Officers to Mesopotamia', dated 18 July, which quoted a Foreign Office telegram of 17 July stating 'that it is inadvisable to give official countenance to the spread of undesirable propaganda in Mesopotamia'. Lawrence had already made clear his thoughts on this subject in his note to Sir Louis Mallet dated 22 April 1919 (see p. 163).
3 The 'letter of June 16' giving Lord Curzon's views stated that 'his Lordship would deprecate any appearance on the part of His Majesty's Government of putting obstacles in the way of the return to their native country of men who have volunteered for service in the Allied cause and have been of such assistance to the Allied operation in Syria'.

VYVYAN RICHARDS
1. Sept. [1919]   2 Polstead Road [Oxford]

[...] I'm out of the army today: and today I have paid for 5 acres 2 rods 30 poles of Pole Hill:[1] that is the whole upper field, down to the rudimentary hedge. I haven't yet got the conveyance, so am not yet the legal owner, but they cannot draw back from the bargain, and as far as I'm concerned it's finished. I feel years more settled in mind, and hope that we will acquire merit there together. When we meet next (or even before) we'll have to make up our serious minds how to tackle Gardiner. I have not yet been able to buy the hedge from the Chingford Estate, and am so short of funds temporarily that I am not pressing them vigorously.

I hope to have about £300 more in six weeks time, and we must then interview builders. The anti-aircraft station fate is still uncertain. The Air Ministry and the War Office cannot decide who is in charge of London air defence. I just thought I'd write and tell you of the Hill: and also that I've borrowed your Bradley.[2] I'm not studying it, but find gobbets (e.g. the discussion of space) most stimulating and suggestive. How pleased Bradley would be if he knew I approved of it. a rivederci.

                                                                        L.

DG

G. J. KIDSTON[3]
[14 November 1919][4]

Dear Kidston
    You asked me 'Why' today, and I'm going to tell you exactly what my motives in the Arab affair were, in order of strength:

1 Pole Hill was a property in Essex where he planned to set up a printing-press with Vyvyan Richards.
2 F. H. Bradley, brother of the noted Shakespearian scholar A. C. Bradley, was the author of several influential works on metaphysics and logic.
3 A member of the Eastern Section of the Foreign Office who had asked Lawrence about his motives during the war.
4 I have retained the date given in the Sunday Times of 16 June 1968 in which this letter was first published, but internal evidence suggests that it was probably written much earlier in 1919. It is also published in Knightley and Simpson's The Secret Lives of Lawrence of Arabia.

(i) Personal. I liked a particular Arab very much, and I thought that freedom for the race would be an acceptable present.[1]

(ii) Patriotic. I wanted to help win the war, and Arab help reduced Allenby's losses by thousands.

(iii) Intellectual curiosity. I wanted to feel what it was like to be the mainspring of a national movement, and to have some millions of people expressing themselves through me: and being a half-poet, I don't value material things much. Sensation and mind seem to me much greater, and the ideal, such a thing as the impulse that took us into Damascus, the only thing worth doing.

(iv) Ambition. You know how Lionel Curtis[2] has made his conception of the Empire — a Commonwealth of free peoples — generally accepted. I wanted to widen that idea beyond the Anglo-Saxon shape, and form a new nation of thinking people, all acclaiming our freedom, and demanding admittance into our Empire. There is, to my eyes, no other road for Egypt and India in the end, and I would have made their path easier, by creating an Arab Dominion in the Empire.

I don't think there are any other reasons. You are sufficiently Scotch to understand my analysing my own mind so formally. The process intended was to take Damascus, and run it (as anyone fully knowing the East and West could run it), as an independent ally of G[reat] B[ritain]. Then to turn on Hejaz and conquer it: then to project the semi-educated Syrians on Yemen, and build that up quickly (without Yemen there is no re-birth for the Arabs) and finally to receive Mesopotamia into the block so made: all this could be done in thirty years directed effort, and without impairing British holdings. It is only the substitute of a 999 years' lease for a complete sale.[3]

Now look what happened when we took Damascus:—

Motive (i) I found had died some weeks before: so my gift was wasted, and my future doings indifferent on that count.

1 Presumably a reference to Dahoum.

2 Lionel Curtis (1872–1955): Fellow of All Souls College, Lecturer in Colonial History, former member of the Transvaal Legislative Council, barrister, civil servant, editor and author. From 1923 one of Lawrence's most constant correspondents.

3 The previous paragraph suggests a vision of the Empire not unlike the present British Commonwealth; compare his letter to Lord Curzon of 27 September 1919 (in DG, not reprinted here) in which he wrote: 'My own ambition is that the Arabs should be our first brown dominion, and not our last brown colony.' This paragraph appears to suggest that such a Dominion should be formed by conquest; but again see the letter to Curzon which makes the same point but less dramatically: 'It seems to me inevitable that the next stage of the Arab Movement will be the transfer of the Hejaz towns to Damascus in the same relation as they formerly stood to Turkey.' For other variations on this theme see the last page of Seven Pillars and the famous passage beginning 'All men dream...' in the Introductory Chapter.

Motive (ii). This was achieved, for Turkey was broken, and the central powers were so unified that to break one was to break all.

Motive (iii). This was romantic mainly, and one never repeats a sensation. When I rode into Damascus the whole country-side was on fire with enthusiasm, and in the town a hundred thousand people shouted my name. Success always kills hope by surfeit.

Motive (iv). This remained, but it was not strong enough to make me stay. I asked Allenby for leave, and when he gave it me, came straight home. It's the dying remains of this weakest of all my reasons which made me put up a half-fight for Feisal in Paris and elsewhere, and which occasionally drives me into your room to jest about what might be done.

If you want to make me work again you would have to re-create motives (ii) and (iii). As you are not God, Motive (i) is beyond your power.

I'm not conscious of having done a crooked thing to anyone since I began to push the Arab Movement, though I prostituted myself in Arab Service. For an Englishman to put himself at the disposal of a red race is to sell himself to a brute, like Swift's Houyhnhnms.[1] However my body and soul were my own, and no one can reproach me for what I do to them: and to all the rest of you I'm clean. When you have got as far as this, please burn it all. I've never told anyone before, and may not again, because it isn't nice to open oneself out. I laugh at myself because giving up has made me look so futile.

T.E.L.

Bodleian Reserve[2]

---

1 In the fourth part of *Gulliver's Travels* the Houyhnhnms, a race of noble and rational horses, are contrasted with the Yahoos, who are human-shaped but brutish in their behaviour. See Chapter I of *Seven Pillars*, where the same idea occurs: 'A man who gives himself to be a possession of aliens leads a Yahoo life, having bartered his soul to a brute-master.'

2 Published in the *Sunday Times* on 16 June 1968; also in Knightley and Simpson's *The Secret Lives of Lawrence of Arabia* (Nelson, 1969).

H. ST J. B. PHILBY[1]

21.11.19   [All Souls College Oxford]

Dear Philby

I'll drop in on Monday evening about 5.30: if you don't put me off meanwhile. Please do so like a shot if anything turns up, for I have ample leisure.

Yours sincerely
T E Lawrence

Also please don't call me Colonel. That folly died months ago.

L.

Then the ostrich egg. That's another remissness. I'll call for it next time I'm up. For the moment an economy fit is on me, and so I sit here and glower through my window at the quad: (you would call it a court).[2]

TEL

St Antony's College Oxford

SIR ARCHIBALD MURRAY[3]

10.1.20   2 Polstead Road Oxford

Dear Sir Archibald Murray

I am painfully aware of what Mr. Lowell Thomas is doing. He came out to Egypt on behalf of the American Government, spent a fortnight in Arabia (I saw him twice in that time) and there he seems to have realised my 'star' value on the film. Anyway since he has been lecturing in America & London, & has written a series of six articles about me, for American & English publication. They are as rank as possible, and are making life very difficult for me, as I have neither the money nor the wish to maintain my constant character as the mountebank he makes me.

He has a lot of correct information, & fills it out with stories picked up

1 Harry St John Bridger Philby (1885–1960): explorer, orientalist, member of the Indian Civil Service, father of the spy, Kim Philby. Philby had led the British political mission to central Arabia in 1917–18, but the two men did not meet until June 1919, when Lawrence reached Crete during his prolonged flight to Egypt; it was in Philby's aircraft that he finally reached Cairo.
2 Oxford quadrangle is Cambridge court; Philby had been at Trinity College, Cambridge.
3 Sir Archibald Murray (1860–1945) was the Commander-in-Chief Egyptian Expeditionary Force from early 1916 to mid-1917, when he was succeeded by General Allenby.

from officers, & by imagination. In your case you are saddled with what Holdich[1] did (when I went to Arabia I had never seen you, & I don't suppose you had ever heard of me: we first met in Cairo when I came back from Yenbo) and I wish I could escape so lightly. My impressions when I saw General Allenby were mixed, for after considerable difficulties (you may remember a conference in Ismailia, when you were not very kind!) what we had done & said had persuaded you & General Lynden Bell,[2] and you had sent a report to London supporting the Arab affair warmly. Then you were recalled, & I wondered how Allenby would look on us. As a matter of fact he was magnificent.

Lowell Thomas asked me to correct his proofs: but this I decided was impossible, since I could not possibly pass one tenth of it, & he was making his living out of it. He then asked me what view I would take about misstatements, & I said that I would confirm or deny nothing in public. The stuff was to me too obvious journalism to weigh very deep with anyone serious. If you wish I will write to him and correct the remarks about you: but I would point out that I am sitting still while he calls me an Irishman, and a Prince of Mecca and other beastlinesses, and it seems hardly possible to begin putting it straight.

I am very glad you wrote to me, because I have been wondering for some time about writing to you. I put on paper my account of what happened to me in Arabia some time ago, but had it stolen from me, and am therefore doing it again, rather differently.[3] It seems to me unfit for publication, but if published it will have some success (for the story is in parts very odd and exciting — there were many strange things) and will probably last a long time, & influence other accounts in the future, for it is not badly written, & is authoritative, in so far as it concerns myself.

You are mentioned inevitably, by name five or six times, (not always perhaps just as you would have put things, but to my information, correctly) and I wondered whether you would agree to look it over in MSS. The

---

1 Colonel Holdich: see p. 125 note 2.
2 General Lynden Bell had been Murray's Chief-of-Staff.
3 The first version of *Seven Pillars* went missing at Reading Station (between London and Oxford) in November 1919. See Liddell Hart's notes on a conversation with Lawrence dated 1 August 1933: 'Details of loss of 1st [version]: On train journey from London to Oxford. Went into refreshment room at Reading, and put bag under table. Left it. Phoned up from Oxford an hour later, but no sign of missing bag — it was a bank messenger's bag, the "thing they carried gold in".... (It was manuscript — on loose-leaf ledger; blank sheets, not ruled. Only wrote one side of page. None of it was ever typed.) T. E. wonders — Did fancy (involuntarily) play with it?' (*T. E. Lawrence to His Biographers*, Part II, p. 145) 'Surely an invitation to theft' was Dr Mack's comment on this account. However, A. W. Lawrence firmly refutes any suggestion that he deliberately put the manuscript at risk: 'To me it is inconceivable that the bag can have been lost "accidentally on purpose".' (Letter to me, 29 November 1987)

labour would not be great, for I could mark the places concerning you, and I rather want everybody mentioned to see it, in case of accident. It sounds like blackmail, but I fear there is nothing worth paying for, and I do not think there is anything that will annoy you too much. If there was, and it was possible, I would knock it out.[1]

As I said, the first draft was stolen, & the second is not finished, so this letter is a little too soon: but if you will be so kind as to allow me to send it to you, then there need be no delay when it is ready.

Please write to me if you want [the] Lowell Thomas thing altered (it will probably come out in book form, & I suppose in French & Arabic & Chinese & Esperanto also), and I will see that it is done at once. I don't pay him ... but I could kick his card-house down if I got annoyed, & so he has to be polite. As a matter of fact he is a very decent fellow — but an American journalist, scooping.

Yours sincerely
T E Lawrence

Please address Mr. now. My colonel days are over!

University of Harvard

MISS FAREEDAH EL AKLE
Feb.16 [1920]

Dear Miss Faridah

Of course I'll write to you: why did you ever think I wouldn't? It was only bad manners for the man to begin the correspondence with the lady.[2]

I was very glad to have your news at last. Mrs Rieder told me you were alive & well, and this was good news after all the horrors of the war in Syria. At any rate, however bad things are now they were worse then.

Please thank the Jabail people from me: though I fear I did very little, & that little has been misunderstood.

[...] Feisal is a very nice fellow, much too good for the horrible trade

---

1 I am not aware that Murray took up Lawrence's offer, but if he had done so he might have been less than pleased. See letter to C. E. Wilson dated 19 February 1926: 'I've shortened the new edition [...] by [...] making two words do for six. Where Archie Murray was described as "jealous, spiteful, bad-tempered, vicious, clever, quick & narrow" he is now called "feminine & feline".'

2 Miss el Akle wrote in reply to Lawrence's opening gambit: 'So you expect the lady to start the correspondence! And what if she happens to be an oriental being, whose customs and ways are just the reverse of yours???'

of politics, and too weak to do the right thing just now. However we are going to do our duty in Mesopotamia, so if you live out your proper life (this is, I believe, if you eat a lot and work a little) you will see everything come true. It is going to take many years.

For myself, I have stopped all my work, and am just wandering about London thinking. It sounds rather silly, but in reality it is a very happy business. I hope you will be able to come to England some day, as we always talked about. You would find it so odd, so small & so crowded.

If you want to write to me, you will be wisest to write to Oxford. Better not write politics, because they may look at your letters.

There is no book [title in Arabic]: an American has told a lot of lies about me, that's all. And I'm afraid I can't ever come to Syria again. Because I failed.[1]

L.

Bodleian Reserve

COLONEL S. F. NEWCOMBE
16.2.20

Dear S.F.

I owe you five letters! At first it wasn't worth while for you were reported to me in one week as at Aleppo, Azrak, Bagdad & Cairo: and then it became a habit.

However the arrival of a smaller (I hope not cheaper) edition[2] is an occasion for a bookworm like myself. The editio princeps always has a special value: but in some cases (Shakespeare folios e.g.) new matter is embodied in the reprints, which gives them a market reputation little, if any, less than original. At the same time collectors, and especially collectors of sentiment, always prefer the genuine article.

However Mrs. Newcombe will regard the graft as the first. These things, as Solomon quoted from Adam's table-talk, depend on the point of view. Please give her my heartiest congratulations.

Then about business. Of course Lawrence may have been the name of your absolutely favourite cousin or aunt, (observe my adroitness in *sex*), and if so I will be dropping an immodest brick by blushing — but if it isn't, aren't you handicapping 'it'? In the history of the world (cheap edition)

1 Miss el Akle replied: 'You say "you failed". Is it meekness on your part to say that? After all that you have achieved, you may have failed in letting others see what you think is right. The failure, therefore, is on their side, and not yours.'
2 Colonel Newcombe's son, Stuart Lawrence Newcombe, had just been born.

I'm a sublimated Aladdin, the thousand and second Knight, a Strand-Magazine strummer. In the eyes of 'those who know'[1] I failed badly in attempting a piece of work which a little more resolution would have pushed through, or left un-touched. So either case it is bad for the sprig, unless, as I said, there is a really decent aunt.

As for god-fathering him, I asked two or three people what it meant, & their words were ribald. Perhaps it is because people near me lose that sense of mystery which distance gives. Or else it was because they didn't know it was you — or at least yours. Anyhow I can't find out what it means, and so I shall be delighted to take it on. Everybody agrees it means a silver mug — but tell me first if his complexion is red or white: I wouldn't commit a colour-discord.

Give Rose my ἀγάπη you will know what to say ... something neat, & not too Newcomian. As for the rugs, please take any that seem worthy to you. There were two Afghans in the Arab Bureau, & a big (and not bad but thin) Shiraz, in the Savoy.

I have abandoned Oxford, & wander about town from a bedroom in Pimlico, (temporary, for Bethnal Green is nicer to the nose) looking at the stars. It is nicer than looking at Lord Curzon.

Please give Mrs. Newcombe my very best regards. How odd it must be having married you. Tell her my letter wasn't fit for her to see.

L.

Hogarth sends his warmest congrats. to all three.

Seriously I am changing my own name, to be more quiet, and wish I could change my face, to be more lovely, & beloved!

DG

AUGUSTUS JOHN[2]
19.3.20

Dear John
    Really I'm hotter stuff than I thought: the wrathful portrait went off at

1 'Those who know': Garnett presumed that Lawrence was quoting Dante (*Inferno*, Canto IV) on Aristotle: 'Il maestro di color che sanno' — 'The master of those that know'; but as a great reader of Tennyson Lawrence might well have had in mind the latter's description of Francis Bacon in *The Palace of Art*: 'large-browed Verulam/The first of those who know'. Very probably he was consciously echoing both these sources.
2 Augustus John (1878–1961) had been an official artist at the Paris Peace Conference and it was there that he had met Lawrence. This letter was a response to John's exhibition entitled *Types* which had opened at the Alpine Club Art Gallery, London, in early March 1920. Among the 'types' were portraits of the father of the modern British Navy Lord Fisher, the Assistant Foreign Secretary Lord Robert Cecil, and George Bernard Shaw; and there were two portraits of Lawrence and two of Feisal. The so-called 'wrathful portrait'

top speed for a thousand to a *Duke*! That puts me for the moment easily at the head of the field in your selling plate. Of course I know you will naturally think the glory is yours — but I believe it's due to the exceeding beauty of my face.

May I write to Orpen[1] and say what a pity I think it that you troubled to paint 38 other people? It means of course a pity from the commercial point of view only, for there is no doubt the others set me off! What do artists' models of the best sort fetch per hour (or perhaps per job, for I might fall on a Cézanne, and I don't want to get rich)? It seems to me that I have a *future*.

I went to your show last Thursday, with Lionel Curtis. We were admiring me, and a person with a military moustache joined us, and blurted out to us: 'Looks a bloody sort of creature doesn't he?' Curtis with some verve said 'Yes'. I looked very pink.

Yours
TEL

Tate Gallery Archives London[2]

F. N. DOUBLEDAY[3]
29.3.20

[...]
Unless I am starving (involuntary) there will be no London publisher. My whole object is to make the money in U.S.A. and so avoid the notoriety of being on sale in England. One gets, inshallah, the goods without the publicity.

(see first paragraph) was bought by the Duke of Westminster, who later in 1920 presented it to the Tate Gallery. It was reproduced in black and white on p. 126 of the 1935 edition of *Seven Pillars of Wisdom* (it also appears on the dust-cover of *A Touch of Genius*, my 'life' of Lawrence written in collaboration with Julia Cave). A copy of it hangs in the Hall of Jesus College, Oxford.

1 Sir William Orpen (1878–1931) had been a war artist on the Western Front and had also been present at the Paris Peace Conference, where he had met and portrayed Lawrence. Robert Graves saw in Orpen's portrait 'a sort of street urchin furtiveness' which he recognised and endorsed, but Lawrence much preferred John's interpretation of him to Orpen's.

2 Microfiche TAM 21G (64/67).

3 Frank Nelson Doubleday was head of the American publishing house which would eventually publish *Seven Pillars*. He and Lawrence had met at a dinner party in London in December 1918 and subsequently at the Paris Peace Conference.

Please thank Mrs. Doubleday for her letter: and assure her that I would have answered it by cable, only that she called me Colonel, which is an antique, red-faced, shrivelled man, with a white moustache: quite horrible.
[...]

Yours sincerely
T.E. Lawrence

Bodleian Reserve

ROBERT GRAVES[1]

15.IV.20   [All Souls College Oxford]

Dear Graves

I am settled in All Souls for five or six weeks: and owe you a letter and many thanks for your blue booklet:[2] do look me up when you first can: I'd like to see you any time day or night, though we won't dine in College — too heavy that for my taste.

If you could warn me before you come it would be prudent, since my movements are as odd as my manners. Suppose you begin with a lunch any day except the 21st?

Yours ever
T E Lawrence

(No longer a Colonel, please!)

University of Harvard

---

1 Robert Graves (1895–1985): poet, novelist, writer of one of the undisputed classics of the Great War *Goodbye to All That*, and, in 1927, author of the first popular biography of Lawrence by a British author, *Lawrence and the Arabs* (Cape, 1927). At this time although 24 and married he was an Oxford undergraduate at St John's College. The two men had met at a guest-night at All Souls in the course of which, during a discussion about Greek poetry, Lawrence had said: 'You must be Graves the poet? I read a book of yours in Egypt in 1917 and thought it pretty good.' This was the start of a long though not always untroubled friendship.
2 Graves's book of poems *Country Sentiment*, published by Martin Secker in England and by Knopf in America in March 1920.

EZRA POUND[1]
Sunday [April 1920]   All Souls College Oxford

Dear Pound

Your letter has confused me. I'd very much like to write, especially to make money, (regretting exceedingly that it must be prose which is only half-price), but there are difficulties.

First of all I haven't even a wish to feel the existence of a vortex — if I had one I'd try to get it cut out: — and so I fear that my writing would not be to your standard. Of course *The Dial* may be ordinary, but I haven't seen it, and so it is likely to resemble *Blast*.[2]

That leads up to difficulty the second. You'll say you don't care a — what I write, so long as I sign it by my name, which has a certain value as advertisement.

True, but I won't use it therefore.[3] Here in Oxford I'm still Lawrence (not Colonel, please), but in London I've changed it, for peace and cleanliness, and I couldn't dream of printing anything over it.

Wherefore it seems to me I'm no good to you. The cinema doesn't in the least represent the truth, and what I do truly, must therefore sail under other than cinema colours.

I came down here (penniless!) last Thursday after a six months' very pleasant loaf in London: and here I'll stay till quarter-day (June) and then back to London. They give me credit in this establishment.

Congratulations on going to Italy. You'll be a millionaire there on small

1 Ezra Pound, controversial American poet (1885–1972), had been long prominent in English literary circles, though he was shortly to move to Paris and then to settle more or less permanently in Italy. He was co-founder of the Imagist school of poetry (with Richard Aldington and Hilda Doolittle), and author of the *Cantos* and other volumes of poetry. Lawrence was writing in reply to a letter by Pound dated 20 April 1920 (addressed in characteristic style to 'My dear Hadji ben Abt el Bakshish, Prince de Meque, Two-Sworded Samurai' etc.) in which the subject of Lawrence's contributing to the American literary magazine *The Dial*, famous for publishing many of the most distinguished writers of the day, was discussed.

2 In referring to 'a vortex' and to *Blast*, Lawrence was alluding to the aggressive literary movement known as Vorticism of which Pound was a leading member and which had expressed its literary philosophy in a magazine entitled *Blast*, edited by Pound and Wyndham Lewis.

3 On the matter of his wish to write anonymously Pound had commented: 'Also I don't care a saffron ... whether you use your name or not; only if you don't you will be under the shameful and ignominious necessity of writing something which will interest the editor.' He added: 'In sending copy to America, let me caution you to use an incognito as well as a pseudonym ... My bright compatriots are quite capable of printing an article by Mr Smith, and then printing a leetle note at the end of the number saying "The article by Mr Smith is really written by the distinguished Sheik-tamer and Tiger-baiter etc ... who for reasons of modesty has concealed himself 'neath the name of Smith-Yapper".' See also Lawrence's letter to Pound dated 20 August 1920.

outgoings, and it's going to be beautifully warm. I wish I could leave England for a long spell. No such luck.

Yours sincerely
T E Lawrence

Bodleian Reserve[1]

H. ST J. B. PHILBY
21 May [1920]   All Souls

Dear Philby
    A word of explanation about this. It happens to be — politically — the right moment for pressure towards a new Middle East Department, since some re-shuffling of spheres is certain to happen quite soon: and the enclosed is a step taken under advice, to add pressure from outside, to what is going on inside.
    They have asked me to get your name on the list: other 'experts' invited are Hogarth, Curtis, Toynbee, & myself. I have no doubt you will agree, so I won't bother to argue. It is a step necessary before a new policy can be put in force, and when we get it through, then we'll have to open up a battery of advice on the new men.
    There are five peers in it (pour encourager . . .) and two or three of each H. of C. group — Maclean & Benn: Lord R. Cecil & Aubrey Herbert: Hoare & Elliott: Yate & Glyn: Clynes & Barnes: all chosen for 'weight' reasons in the present balance of power.
    Curzon is of course the enemy: but he's not a very bold enemy, & won't like a rift in his family showing up: I have good hopes of it.[2]

Yours
E.L.

I called on Wed: but vainly: will try again next week.
[. . .]

St Antony's College Oxford

---

1 This and a later letter to Pound (p. 181) were published in the literary magazine *Nine* in 1950.
2 Philby joined Lawrence's distinguished lobby, which duly approached Lord Curzon, who was Foreign Secretary. Elizabeth Monroe's biography of Philby gives the background to this initiative: 'Delay over framing a peace treaty with Turkey, caused partly by President Wilson's stroke, and consequent uncertainty over American intentions in the Middle East, gave scope for much amateur planning of the Arab future. Philby, always ready to

WILFRED SCAWEN BLUNT[1]

10.8.20   All Souls College Oxford

Dear Mr. Blunt

This letter is so long delayed that it is very hard to write: but I felt for a
long time that it would be butting in on you, and then when I saw the
note you sent to Philby, I felt I might risk it.

Unfortunately I have been driven down into Oxford (here I live on
credit: elsewhere I need cash!) and will be here probably for another month.
I'd very much like to come down and see you, and if you'll let me write
again when it is possible for me to say what time, I'll be very much obliged.

                                                           Yours sincerely
                                                           T E Lawrence[2]

Fitzwilliam Museum Cambridge

---

join campaigns that interested him, found himself in demand on committees and deputations.... He joined a deputation collected by T. E. Lawrence to rescue the Middle East
from the "pernicious grasp" of the India Office and Foreign Office. This group asked
Curzon for a "semi-diplomatic, semi-administrative clearing house" that would put an
end to clashes over British policy in the Arab world between rival political governments.
With Lord Robert Cecil, D. G. Hogarth, Lionel Curtis, Arnold Toynbee, T. E. Lawrence,
Aubrey Herbert and politicians of all three political parties "chosen for weight reasons",
Philby called at the Foreign Office to lobby for this change, only to be defeated by
Curzon's "Indian outlook".' (*Philby of Arabia*, 1973, p. 103) However, the defeat was not
total in that Middle East affairs *were* transferred from the Foreign and India Offices in
1921, but not to a separate department; to the Colonial Office under Churchill as Colonial
Secretary, where he asked Lawrence to join him.

1 Wilfred Scawen Blunt (1840–1922) was a man of many parts: famous traveller, anti-
imperialist, supporter of Egyptian nationalism and Irish Home Rule (he was briefly
imprisoned in 1888 while agitating for the latter cause), poet, historian, biographer, and
diarist. At this time a veteran of 80 he was living in retirement at Newbuildings Place,
Southwater, Sussex.

2 Blunt replied: 'Any one who can talk to me of Arabia & the desert life finds a free seat
at my coffee hearth & you especially who know so much.' Blunt's reply is printed in full
in *Letters to T. E. Lawrence*, edited by A. W. Lawrence.

EZRA POUND[1]
20.8.20   All Souls College Oxford

O E — P!

For twenty days I have been faced by your letter: each day I read a new name of a contributor to *The Dial*: but there is surely no place for me in that galaxy? Of course Joyce can write (and does, just occasionally): you can write (and do): T. S. Eliot ... perhaps: but the people I like are so different, Hodgson; Sassoon: D. H. Lawrence: Manning: Conrad: [...] but do you see the point? I'm academic idyllic, romantic: you breathe commas and exclamation marks. We ought not to exist together on one earth, but the earth is so broad-minded that she doesn't care.

I've written in the *Round Table*: in the *Times*: in the *Daily Herald*: in the *Army Quarterly* (all anonymous). I've never read any Fritz Vanderpyl: I don't feel as though I must: where can I see *The Dial* free of charge because I'm broke to the world, and can't buy it: surely R. Aldington[2] and W. B. Yeats[3] are no good?

                                                                    E.L.

Bodleian Reserve

WILLIAM ROTHENSTEIN[4]
27.9.20   All Souls College Oxford

Dear Rothenstein

I've behaved rottenly in not answering your first card: only I made a vow not to write before I'd finished a job I was doing — and I have not finished it yet.

On the same account I can't come up to London till next month — October 1 or 2 probably, but then I'll be there for some weeks, and that will give you a tremendous chance. I'm sorry for the delay ... but it is

---

1 See previous letter to Pound of April 1920, p. 178.
2 An interesting comment on the poet and novelist who was to become, thirty-five years later, Lawrence's bitterest critic.
3 For a later, different view of Yeats see p. 466.
4 Later Sir William Rothenstein (1872–1945: knighted 1931): artist, trained at the Slade School London and later in Paris, where he knew Degas and Toulouse-Lautrec; official war artist with British and Canadian Forces in the First World War. He and Lawrence met in London in the autumn of 1920 and shortly afterwards Rothenstein began a painting of him in Arab dress. The letter is about the arrangements for the necessary sittings. Rothenstein wrote of him in *Lawrence by His Friends*: 'Generous with his time, he never seemed to object to standing for hours together.'

beyond my power to alter for the moment.

The world is still running on top-gear, apparently, and that makes quietists like myself nearly breathless: however, perhaps it's better than being dull. Only (ridiculus mus) it breaks up my work horribly!

Yours sincerely
T.E.L.

I have about a thousand unanswered letters: so instead of cursing my slowness, you should be singing for joy of getting even a fortnight-old word.

L.

Bodleian Reserve

CHARLES DOUGHTY

October 4 1920   All Souls College Oxford

Dear Mr. Doughty

I'm very glad that *Arabia Deserta* is being pushed so fast. It will be a great thing to have it on the market once more: though I regret the price, which seems terribly high.[1]

It is good that you should look over the proofs: the first edition had singularly few misprints, and it will be a pity if the second falls below it in accuracy.

Your preface will add very much to the understanding of the book, and I look forward to reading it.

I wish I could say the same about my miserable effort. They asked me for 5000 words, and I managed it at last: but it was as difficult a thing as I have tackled, and the whole affair is in shocking taste. Of course *Arabia Deserta* cannot be prefaced by anyone but the author. The Medici people were interested only in their American sales, in which my name will be useful, for I have had better advertisements there than you have had: but the people who like *Arabia* will find my thing a blemish, and will be

---

1 Lawrence had been for many years an admirer of Doughty's classic work, *Travels in Arabia Deserta*, which he had read avidly as a boy and had found of considerable value during the war. However, it had long been out of print and he had therefore launched a personal campaign to have it republished. His first thought was to have this done by the Egyptian Survey Department which had printed the *Arab Bulletin*, but in the end it was published more effectively and nearer home by the Medici Society in association with Jonathan Cape. The price of his achieving this ambition was that he was required to write an Introduction — the 'miserable effort' referred to in the fourth paragraph.

annoyed with me for writing it, and with you for letting me write it!

However time will cure all these things: and I'll make sure that my note appears only in the second edition!

Yours sincerely
T. E. Lawrence

If possible I will come down to Eastbourne and see you at the end of next term. October and November are very busy months for me.

L.

Bodleian Reserve

MISS FAREEDAH EL AKLE
January 3 [1921]

Dear Miss Fareedah

I wonder how many letters from you to me have gone astray? You mention one in April. I don't know when it was, but long ago I got one, and answered it! I distinctly remember that, as I was proud of it, for I very seldom write letters.

[...]

Don't take what is said in *Asia* too accurately.[1] L. Thomas was never up country with me at all (and only ten days in Arabia, far behind the front) and his stories of fighting & riding are second-hand. The Arab war was not nearly as silly as he makes out: and I was not in charge of it, or even very prominent. Only I was in fancy dress, & so I made a good 'star' for his film. Dahoum died some years ago, during the war, of fever.[2]

No, I don't see Mrs. Rieder nowadays, & I haven't seen Noel since he was in Jebail. I expect he's grown up now. Mrs. Rieder lives in London I think. I saw her once in Paris in 1919.

I didn't see Miss Holmes' book. You know I'm busy at book-printing now, and read very little. Also I've forgotten all the Arabic I ever knew — reading or writing, that is: probably I could still talk it, if I ever met an Arab, but I haven't seen one since July 1919 — which you remember was not very much: not as much as it should have been, in view of the excellence of my teachers.

My best address is   All Souls College
Oxford

1 *Asia*: journal of the American Asiatic Society of New York, which had published articles by Lowell Thomas about Lawrence.
2 Miss el Akle had asked for information about Dahoum.

and I'm Mr. Lawrence now! There is no reason why the post should be bad.

I've long given up politics.

Yours sincerely
TEL

Bodleian Reserve

Lawrence had found a friend and admirer in the former war artist Eric Kennington whom he had invited to help with the provision of illustrations for his book and the two men had planned a visit to the Middle East, so that Kennington could meet and draw portraits of some of Lawrence's Arab comrades-in-arms. In the end, however, Kennington went on his own while Lawrence, persuaded by Churchill to join him at the Colonial Office, travelled with his new chief to Egypt for the Cairo Conference.

WILFRED SCAWEN BLUNT
2.3.21

Dear Mr. Blunt

It's very good of you to have written to me. I'm only sorry that the short time will not let me come & see you, or write to you properly.[1] We start tomorrow, or rather this morning for Cairo, for that odd conference, where I'll either get my way or resign — or even do both things!

It's the Colonial Office: Winston is a new and very keen mind on the Middle East business, & I hope will take it the right way. It's a very great chance given me.[1]

Yours sincerely
T E Lawrence

Fitzwilliam Museum Cambridge

1 Blunt had written to him on 26 February 1921: 'A line to congratulate you on having forced your policy on the Foreign (or is it the Colonial) Office & I should be glad to have another talk with you before you leave England again for the East.' (*Letters to T. E. Lawrence*, edited by A. W. Lawrence)

HIS MOTHER
March 20, 1921   Semiramis Hotel Cairo

We got here about a fortnight ago: and it has been one of the longest fortnights I ever lived: started about March 3, & went via Marseilles & Alexandria. Eight days out.

Here we live in a marble & bronze hotel, very expensive & luxurious: horrible place: makes me Bolshevik. Everybody Middle East is here, except Joyce & Hogarth. We have done a lot of work, which is almost finished. Day after tomorrow we go to Jerusalem for a week: after that don't know: perhaps home: perhaps I return to Egypt for a further fortnight.

Kennington has gone to Damascus.

Can't tell you anything else. Have seen Allenby several times, he's very fit: Kennington drew him, & Ironside[1] & me: wanted to draw Gertrude,[2] but hadn't time.

We're a very happy family: agreed upon everything important: and the trifles are laughed at.

Hope A is better.

N.

HL/Bodleian Reserve

HIS MOTHER
April 12 [1921]   Grand Continental Hotel Cairo

Back here in Cairo for two days: have been moving rapidly since I last wrote. We went from Cairo about March 25 to Jerusalem, stopping at Gaza on the way. Two days later I was driven over by car to Salt, across Jordan, where I met Abdulla, Feisal's brother, who drove back to Jerusalem with me. It was an amusing performance, for the people of Salt & Jerusalem were very enthusiastic & excited, & nearly mobbed the car in their anxiety to welcome Abdulla.

From Jerusalem I went, on the 31st back to Amman by car, through Salt. The country across Jordan is all in spring, and the grass & flowers are beautiful. On this side of Jordan the rains have not been very good, & things are too dry already.

Spent eight days in Amman, living with Abdulla in his camp. It was

1 General Sir Edmund Ironside.
2 Gertrude Bell.

rather like the life in war time, with hundreds of Bedouin coming & going, & a general atmosphere of newness in the air. However the difference was that now everybody is trying to be peaceful.

On Saturday last I ran back to Jerusalem by car (it takes six hours from Amman) & on Sunday I went down to Ramleh, on the coast plain near Jaffa, where our aerodrome is, & flew with four machines to Amman. Abdulla had been longing for aeroplanes, & gave us a great reception & a large lunch. Then we went back to Ramleh, & I went up to Jerusalem to dinner.

Next morning they drove me down to Ramleh, where another four machines took me in to Egypt: and here I have been yesterday and today.

Tonight I'm off to Jerusalem again, and after three days there to Amman, with Sir H. Samuel,[1] who is going over to call on Abdulla, & who will probably stay two nights. Some of his party want to see Petra, so perhaps after that I'll go down there for a night or two to show them round. That ought to finish my jobs out here. I'll be very glad to get back. Would you tell Hogarth of my movements? I haven't written to anyone since I left, & he may be back by now.

N

I am trying to buy him some bronze weapons from tombs on Philistine plain, axes and daggers.

HL/Bodleian Reserve

Lawrence came home for some weeks in the early spring and summer of 1921, returning east in early July having been appointed a plenipotentiary under the great seal of England for his next mission, to the Hejaz.

MRS RIEDER
7.7.21   Colonial Office

Dear Mrs. Rieder
   Tonight when I was clearing up my papers before leaving for the East, out popped your letter. It's two months old, so has no doubt settled itself meanwhile. I rejoice that Noel is snatched from science, though only late

---

1 Sir Herbert Samuel (1870–1963), later Lord Samuel, was at this time British High Commissioner for Palestine.

in life: but it might have been too late. As for modern languages, there's only one worth studying: English: that I am aware of: but it's better than science: even if he learns French.

Apropos of France: I'm not anti-French any more. Feisal has swept Mesopotamia, & that is amends for his scurvy treatment in Paris. Do you know that proverb about when you need a long spoon? I laugh every now & then in Whitehall, and the Whitehalled think me mad.

Very sorry for the delay: but my advice never was worth anything.

Yours
E.L.

Bodleian Reserve

WILFRED SCAWEN BLUNT
7.7.21   Colonial Office

Dear Mr. Blunt

I kept your letter for some days, in the hopes that I would have a free time, or that the train service would get better. Unfortunately neither happened, & I have to start tomorrow. I'm exceedingly sorry. I go straight to Jidda, to see King Hussein, & then perhaps to Yemen: return probably in two months, & will then call. Very many more apologies

Yours sincerely
T E Lawrence

The last ten days I've been a shuttle cock, tossed between the Colonial & Foreign Offices, & much distracted & annoyed by it all. Please forgive my apparent rudeness.

Fitzwilliam Museum Cambridge

Lawrence spent much of August and September 1921 in Jidda, attempting to persuade King Hussein of the Hejaz, now grown old and difficult, to accept the political settlement proposed at Cairo and already accepted by Feisal and Abdulla — a task the problems of which are made clear by the following cables. He later told a Tank Corps colleague 'that his visit to the Hejaz in 1921 had been almost too much for him and that the mental strain to which he was subjected during the negotiations had been worse than anything he had known during the campaign', i.e. during the war. His performance at this time has not endeared him to Arab historians, though it can be said in his defence that the new settlement coincided far more with Arab aspirations than that which had emerged out of the hard-headed negotiations in Paris.

Hussein was ousted by Ibn Saud in 1924 and spent the rest of his life in exile, a sad end to the career of the instigator of the Arab Revolt.

CABLE TO FOREIGN OFFICE
2.8.1921

LAWRENCE, JEDDAH, TO PRODROME, LONDON

Have had several meetings with King, who has not referred[1] to the draft treaty since he saw it. He urged his claims to Kingship of Mesopotamia, but collapsed and gave up idea when I discussed practical effect of move. He has announced his abandonment of position founded on McMahon letters,[2] but raises absurd new ideas daily. Old man is conceited to a degree, greedy, and stupid, but very friendly, and protests devotion to our interests. His entourage are anti-British, except for Fuad el Khatib and Zeid,[3] who are helping us continually, and all sorts of interests are begging him not to conclude any treaty. However he shows such reluctance to quarrel with me that I suspect his own mind to be divided: but until he introduces subject of Treaty again I cannot say whether there is any hope of it. If he could be kept here for a month he would become biddable: but he will go off the rails as soon as he is back in Mecca. He has suggested my returning after the pilgrimage.[4] I will not do so unless he accepts the principle of a treaty now.

PRO FO 686/93

1 'Refused' in original text.
2 Sir Henry McMahon, then High Commissioner for Egypt, had corresponded with Hussein in 1915; his most important letter, dated 24 October 1915, had stated that Britain, subject to certain reservations, was 'prepared to recognise and support the independence of the Arabs'. The McMahon-Hussein understandings had been superseded by the Sykes-Picot agreement.
3 Hussein's youngest son.
4 i.e. the annual pilgrimage to Mecca.

CABLE TO FOREIGN OFFICE
4.8.1921

LAWRENCE, JEDDAH, TO PRODROME, LONDON

Have had more conversations with the King. He was only playing with me so I changed tactics and forced him to make exact statements. After some questions he made clear that he refused absolutely all notion of making a treaty but expected acknowledgement of his kingship in Mesopotamia and Palestine, priority over all rulers in Arabia who were to be confined to their pre-war boundaries, and cession to himself of Asir and Hodeida. His ambitions are as large as his conceit, and he showed unpleasant jealousy of his sons.

I gave him my candid opinion of his character and capacity. There was a scene, remarkable to me in that not only the Foreign Secretary but the King also burst into tears. I walked out with parting remarks which brought Zeid to me last night with a rough draft of a treaty based on ours for my consideration.

The King is weaker than I thought, and could, I think, be bullied into nearly complete surrender. Reason is entirely wasted on him since he believes himself all-wise and all-competent, and is flattered by his entourage in every idiotic thing he does. The difficulties of using force are the short time, and the fear that if I hurt him too much he will sulk in Mecca. I will not be able to finish anything before the pilgrimage, but his draft, if he submits it formally to me today, will give me grounds for returning here at the end of the month.

PRO FO 686/93

CABLE TO BRITISH HIGH COMMISSIONER, BAGHDAD
8.8.1921

LAWRENCE, JEDDAH, TO HIGHCOM, BAGHDAD

Hussein's telegram may now be delivered with message from me that King is gradually coming round to our point of view, and has been provisionally paid a month's subsidy in consequence. The negotiations have been difficult.

PRO FO 686/93

ERIC KENNINGTON [1]

25.8.21   Aden

Dear Kennington

After all the mail delayed two days: but there was no profit for you in them. I had to go up country, and could not write your note any better than it was.

This is muck:[2] but it has the advantage either

  (i) Of getting home a week early, and so giving you time to get someone proper to write an alternative

or (ii) Of being four times too long, and so giving you room to select the least bad.

It's altogether yours, to reject, shorten, cut about, add to, rearrange, correct. There's no good in it: and I'll be glad if you kill it.

However if I remember the Leicester they only put about three lines in front of the catalogue of names: and there are three not good, but harmless lines in this: I'd cut it down to that myself, but I'm bothered if I know which three they are. I hope to be back soon: with Abdulla: news to you later.

                                                                E.L.

This is the beastliest trip ever I had: but thank the Lord I took no dress clothes.

Bodleian Reserve

CABLE TO FOREIGN OFFICE

7.9.1921

              LAWRENCE, JEDDAH, TO PRODROME, LONDON

On my return King went back on his decision and demanded

1 Eric Henri Kennington (1888–1960): artist and sculptor, official war artist 1916–19 and 1940–43.
2 Lawrence enclosed with the letter his Introduction to the catalogue of Kennington's Arab portraits being shown at the Leicester Galleries. Written at the time when he was engaged in a dispiriting struggle with their leader, he shows in it a great affection for the individual Arab warriors with whom he fought: e.g. '[T]he desert is full of legends and songs of their fighting [...] and personally I am very content to have had a share in causing to be made these records of their faces while the knowledge of what they did is fresh in men's minds.' The full text of the Introduction is in *The Essential T. E. Lawrence*, edited by David Garnett.

(1) Return of all states in Arabia except his to their pre-war boundaries.
(2) Cession to him of all areas so vacated.
(3) Right to appoint all Cadis and Muftis[1] in Arabia, Mesopotamia, Palestine.
(4) Recognition of his supremacy over all Arab rulers everywhere.

My reply made him send for a dagger and swear to abdicate and kill himself. I said we would continue negotiations with his successor. Ali then took a strong line, and formed a committee of himself, Zeid, Haddad, and Fuad, to discuss with me. Things are now going in most friendly and rational way. King is not formally superseded but has certainly lost much of his power. The sons report to him and the Queen, who is of our party, lectures him at night. I look upon the assumption of responsibility by Ali as a most happy event and am taking the opportunity to get his ideas on paper concerning all outstanding Arab questions without committing either side in any way. We will go on with Treaty in two or three days.

[...]

PRO FO 686/93

CABLE TO FOREIGN OFFICE
22.9.1921

LAWRENCE, JEDDAH, TO PRODROME, LONDON

King Hussein had approved each clause of Treaty and announced publicly his forthcoming signature of it. When Ali presented him text for ratification he shouted and struck at him, and then sent us eight contradictory sets of prior conditions and stipulations all unacceptable. Ali says the old man is mad, and is preparing with Zeid to obtain his formal abdication. Ali and Zeid have behaved splendidly, and they may change things in the next weeks. Have left Marshall[2] text of Treaty, and if King climbs down he will receive his signature: but meanwhile, or till I reach England and report I suggest that no changes or new lines of policy be taken by you. Have asked King to return the eighty thousand rupees paid him in advance of subsidy on his promise to sign.

PRO FO 686/93

1 Cadis: civil judges. Muftis: expounders of Islamic law.
2 W. E. Marshall, the British Minister at Jidda; he had served with Lawrence as a doctor in the Arab campaign.

ERIC KENNINGTON
1 October [1921]   Grand Continental Hotel Cairo

[...] The reasons for stopping work are three. I don't know their order of magnitude. A lump of money I was expecting has not (probably will not) come. My house in Epping has been burnt down. In the leisure hours of this trip I have read the manuscript of my book; and condemned it. Not good enough to publish, because it's not as good as I can make it (unless I deceive myself).

[...]
What more? Nothing. I'm bored stiff: and very tired, and a little ill, and sorry to see how mean some people I wanted to respect have grown. The War was good by drawing over our depths that hot surface wish to do or win something. So the cargo of the ship was unseen, and not thought of. This life goes on till February 28 next year. Au revoir.

                                                              TL

Liddell Hart Centre for Military Studies, King's College London

SIR HUGH TRENCHARD[1]
[January 1922]

You know I'm trying to leave Winston on March the first. Then I want about two months to myself, and then I'd like to join the R.A.F. — in the ranks, of course.[2]

I can't do this without your help. I'm 33 and not skilled in the senses you want. Probably I couldn't pass your medical. It's odd being too old for the job I want when hitherto I've always been too young for the job I did. However my health is good: I'm always in physical and mental training, and I don't personally believe that I'd be below the average of your recruits in either respect. If you think so that will end it.

You'll wonder what I'm at. The matter is that since I was 16 I've been writing: never satisfying myself technically but steadily getting better. My last book on Arabia is nearly good. I see the sort of subject I need in the beginning of your Force ... and the best place to see a thing from is the ground. It wouldn't 'write' from the officer level.

---

1 Hugh Montague Trenchard (1873–1956), the acknowledged 'father' of the Royal Air Force, was to be a considerable benefactor to Lawrence from this time forward. He was created a baronet in 1919 and raised to the peerage in 1930.
2 Lawrence had met Trenchard at the Cairo Conference and had already broached the idea of his joining the Air Force as an ordinary airman at some future time.

I haven't told anyone, till I know your opinion; and probably not then, for the newspapers used to run after me and I like being private. People wouldn't understand.

It's an odd request this, hardly proper perhaps, but it may be one of the exceptions you make sometimes. It is asking you to use your influence to get me past the Recruiting Officer!

Apologies for making it: if you say no I'll be more amused than hurt.

Yours sincerely
T.E. Lawrence

R.A.F. Museum Hendon

HIS MOTHER
15 February 1922   [14 Barton Street London][1]

[...] [About the ring, don't worry. Nothing mankind has yet made is worth any regret. If you need another send me word, & I'll send you some. There are thousands in London and their newness doesn't matter: for when you lose a thing there is no rhyme or reason in losing its associations also. You can transfer them to your finger itself, or to something else, for your imagination made them, & is all powerful over them & you.]

[...]

I'm perfectly well, & very comfortable in Barton Street which is quite beautiful. The quiet of so little a place in the middle of a great mess has to be experienced a thousand times before it is properly felt. I will be very sorry to leave, when I have to leave, but it's altogether too pleasant to be allowed to go on too long. [...]

My own plans are still doubtful. I asked Winston to let me go, and he was not very willing: indeed he didn't want it. I told him I was open to hold on for a little till his first difficulties were over (there are new things happening just now), but not in a formal appointment. Probably I'll get leave on the first of March, & not go back again, unless that Paris idea comes further: or some other odd notion. There was a question of me for Egypt, if Allenby came away: but that of course I wouldn't accept. I don't think ever again to govern anything.[2]

1 Herbert Baker's house in Westminster: see p. 159.
2 This hint that he had been thought of as a successor to Allenby as High Commissioner of Egypt was ridiculed by Richard Aldington but Lawrence certainly believed this to be the case. When Allenby's successor Lord Lloyd was forced to resign in 1929 Lawrence wrote to Lady Astor: ' "There but for the grace of God", say I.' (29 July 1929: not printed in this book).

If I get away finally from the Colonial Office about May my plans are to do nothing for a little, & then perhaps to consider the Air Force. Of course I'm too old to join it, but I think that the life & the odd mind (or lack of mind) there, might give me a subject to write about. This long-drawn-out battle over my narrative of the campaigns of Feisal has put an ink fever into me. I find myself always going about trying to fit words to the sights & sounds in the world outside me.

However all this remains uncertain, and will remain uncertain for me till I do it. That's a new course I have: of trying to prevent myself making up my mind till afterwards, when the need of action is over.

Let me know what you yourselves do, please, now & then. It's odd you know how impossible it is to be altogether alone. It's the one experience that humanity has never really worked towards: and I'm quite sure that we can only manage it in a crowded place. The difficulty is to keep oneself untouched in a crowd: so many people try to speak to you or touch you: and you're like electricity, in that one touch discharges all the virtue you have stored up.

However these things don't really matter.

N.

I'm afraid this letter's very scrappy: but I've answered the points in your last as they arose.

HL/Bodleian Reserve

SIR HUGH TRENCHARD
July 2 1922   Colonial Office

Dear Sir Hugh Trenchard
   Winston has agreed to let me go after next Tuesday. I have not told him what I want to do next, as since I first wrote to you Geddes[1] has happened, and may make impossible for you what you then thought possible.
   If there is still a chance of it may I come and see you?[2]

---

1 Sir Eric Geddes had presided over a committee on government expenditure which had reported in February 1922, proposing swingeing cuts in, *inter alia*, education, public health and the armed services.
2 Trenchard invited Lawrence to stay the night with him at his home at Barnet in Hertfordshire so that they could talk the matter over with no one else present apart from Lady Trenchard. Trenchard later told A. W. Lawrence that he tried to persuade T.E.L. that he could achieve more in the R.A.F. in a more responsible position, 'but he was so insistent that I eventually agreed'.

                                        Yours sincerely
                                        T.E. Lawrence

R.A.F. Museum Hendon

ERIC KENNINGTON
Monday [10 July 1922]

Dear Kennington
    It's abnormally good of you to offer the cottage. A month ago I'd have
leaped at it. On Saturday a man offered to help me to a job which I have
wanted to do since 1919. I don't know if it will come off yet or not: but I
think it will: and in that case it will hold me in London for at least a year.
No money in it, but keep, and very interesting work.[1]
    So I'll refuse yours on the chance of this other thing's coming my way.
Very many thanks indeed.
    The cuttings are very good. Why did no one curse you?
                                        E.L.

Bodleian Reserve

SIR HUGH TRENCHARD
21.VII.22   14 Barton Street S.W.1

Dear Sir Hugh
    Winston very agreeable. I hope your lord was the same.[2] In which case —
about August 9?
                                        Yours sincerely
                                        T.E. Lawrence

R.A.F. Museum Hendon

Events proceeded at a somewhat slower pace than that envisaged by Lawrence in the preceding letter to Trenchard. He and Trenchard met at the
Air Ministry on 14 August, when he was informed that his enlistment

1 Doubtless a reference to his impending enlistment. There are numerous others in the
  letters he wrote at this time.
2 The Air Minister — Trenchard's 'lord' — was Captain F. E. Guest.

would be arranged by Air Vice-Marshal Sir Oliver Swann, member of the Air Council for Personnel. Swann shortly afterwards nominated 21 August as the day for this to take place; the date was subsequently changed to 30 August at Lawrence's request.

COLONEL S. F. NEWCOMBE
22.7.22   14 Barton Street S.W.1

I found a wingless angel called Macintosh (tears in Heaven over that!) who offers to forward your letters.

This is to say that I've started a collection of heads of Englishmen of character, connected with the Arab Revolt.

Vickery is not in it:[1] you are. But I haven't got your head. Will you let me get it?

There's a young cubist artist called Roberts.[2] Very gifted & good. He'll make it look like a problem in Euclid. You'll love it. So'll I. He's in London: & will draw you when you can give him two hours. Line only: no paint or colour.

I'm aiming at 12 heads: all different men, all different artists: all schools except the Royal Academy. A huge joke. Eventual illustrations for my eventual book.

Mrs. N. will hate it (the drawing) but wives & mothers always do. She shouldn't interfere: it's not her baby (or b.b.) who's to suffer.

Are you willing? 'Cause if so please tell me when you'll be next in London: & I'll fix up Roberts or another to meet you: lunch; & off with your head.

E.L.

Bodleian Reserve

1 He had clashed with Vickery at the time of Feisal's advance to Wejh, as Newcombe would have recalled. See p. 102 note 3.
2 William Roberts served as a war artist in the two World Wars. When Lawrence invited him to contribute to *Seven Pillars* he was a struggling 27-year-old. He later became an R.A. (Royal Academician).

WILFRED SCAWEN BLUNT
23.7.22   14 Barton Street Westminster

Dear Mr. Blunt
Yes, I got away, later than I intended, but I liked Winston so much, and
have such respect for him that I was determined to leave only with his
good-will: — and he took a long time to persuade! Otherwise I would have
been free in February.[1] I'd like to see you again, and hope that you are now
more comfortable in yourself than when I came down last. It can only be
a day visit, I'm afraid. Would next Friday, by the 10.26 at Southwater, suit
you? If not, then any day of the following week.
                                             Yours sincerely
                                             T E Lawrence

Fitzwilliam Museum Cambridge

COLONEL S. F. NEWCOMBE
Sunday [?August 1922]

Munificence
He made a great drawing of it: it's a very splendid work of art: better
so than as portrait: because he's turned you from flesh into metal, & made
you so fierce & warlike that my blood runs cold to see it. It's uncannily
like, & yet so much harder. Perhaps it's the being drawn which drew you
so much together: or else it's family cares. Any way time will make your
face like that, & will leave the hair only a regretted memory. *Who brushed
it?*
   [. . .] It's hard for a youngster to be so great an artist, & to know it, & to
be unable to sell anything. However his head of you marks a step in advance
of anything he's done to date. It ought to go to the Tate Gallery. I suppose
you don't mind it's bearing your name if shown? I took it to Kennington,
who wondered at it. I'll get Roberts to do two or three others: because by
itself it would look too pointedly excellent.
   Do you hate it? and did Mrs N.? Some day I'll have prints of it for you.
                                             T.E.L.

Do tell Boyle when he comes back, what he's missed: & say that if he'll let

1 Blunt had written to Lawrence, on reading his letter of resignation in the *Morning Post*:
  'I congratulate you on having been true to your word and broken your official bondage.
  Liberty is the only thing worth a wise man's fighting for in public life.' (*Letters to T. E.
  Lawrence*, edited by A. W. Lawrence) Blunt was unwell at this time; he died some weeks
  later, on 10 September 1922.

you know dates, I'll send someone down later to have a dab at him.

However it won't be as good as yours.

Bodleian Reserve

BRIGADIER-GENERAL SIR GILBERT CLAYTON
15–8–22　　　　　　　　　　　　　　14 Barton Street Westminster

Dear General Clayton

I wrote a book about that dog-fight of ours in Arabia. It is not for present publication, partly because it's too human a document for me to disclose, partly because of the personalities in it, partly because it is not good enough to fit my conceit of myself. The last is a weak point, but the first in my mind: though it is difficult to judge of one's own work. Hogarth is reading it, as an insurance against inaccuracies.

You come into it: not very much, not as much as you should, but the thing is only a narrative of my private accidents. However, you had a share in them, & that's why I am writing to you. I want a drawing of you for one of the illustrations. Decent pictures will cover up a multitude of faults in their book: so I'm rather putting myself about to collect some. Kennington went East for me, & did about twenty Arabs: and I want about a dozen Englishmen to balance them.

English people all look alike, in dress anyway: so to make an extra variety I'm out to have the dozen drawn by different artists. They include Newcombe, Alan Dawnay, Hogarth, Boyle (R.N.), Brodie, Bartholomew, & that sort of person.

The best man I think to do you, if you agree to sit, will be William Nicholson,[1] of Apple Tree Yard, between Jermyn Street & St. James Square. He's a very subtle & very talented person. I've talked to him about you, & he thinks you sound good for a wood-cut. These he has done many of, & is famous for. He suggests September as the best time for it. It would probably take two sittings, I expect, about 2 hours each. You would find it boring, but the result would be interesting. I hope you will agree to it. If you do, I'll put Nicholson in touch with you when the month comes. I am going away myself.

　　　　　　　　　　　　　　　　　　Yours sincerely
　　　　　　　　　　　　　　　　　　T E Lawrence

By the way, the wood–block would of course be my property: but I think

1 William, later Sir William Nicholson, illustrator, poster designer, even costume-designer (e.g. for the first production of J. M. Barrie's *Peter Pan*), won his principal reputation as a portrait painter. He duly produced a portrait of Clayton for *Seven Pillars*. He was the father of the noted abstract painter Ben Nicholson and father-in-law of Robert Graves.

there is no chance of its being published for years, so that the publicity will be nil. Lady Clayton will be amused to have a few proofs pulled of it: after which I'd have it stored away.

E.L.

Bodleian Reserve

BERNARD SHAW[1]
17.VIII.22   14 Barton Street Westminster

Dear Mr. Shaw

You will be puzzled at my writing to you: but Cockerell some months ago took me round to you and introduced me, and you did not talk too formidably.[2]

I want to ask you two questions: the first one, 'Do you still read books?', doesn't require an answer. If you still go on reading I'm going to put the second question: if you don't, then please skip the two inside pages of this note and carry over to my signature at the end, and burn it all without replying. I hate letter-writing as much as I can, and so, probably, do you.

My real wish is to ask if you will read, or try to read, a book which I have written. It's about the war, which will put you off, to start with, and there are technical unpleasantnesses about it. For instance it is very long: about 300,000 words I suspect, though I have not counted them. I have very little money and do not wish to publish it: however it had to be printed, so I got it done on a lino. press, in a newspaper office.[3] That means it's beastly to look at, two columns on a quarto page, small newspaper type which hurts your eyes, and dozens of misprints, corrected roughly in ink:

1 George Bernard Shaw (1856–1950): Irish-born playwright, critic, Socialist thinker, personality and wit, Shaw was at this time a veteran of 67 with a reputation as a successful dramatist going back to the 1890s.
2 Sydney Cockerell, Curator of the Fitzwilliam Museum, Cambridge, had introduced Lawrence to Shaw earlier in the year following a lunch at which Lawrence and Cockerell had discussed how they could help Charles Doughty, the author of *Arabia Deserta*, who was in financial difficulties. Cockerell was due to call at Shaw's home in Adelphi Terrace to pick up a portrait of Shaw for his Museum and suggested that Lawrence should accompany him. Lawrence demurred but consented to go along when Cockerell pointed out that it being Saturday the Shaws would almost certainly be away at their country retreat at Ayot St Lawrence. The Shaws, however, were at home. It was on the strength of this casual encounter that Lawrence decided to ask Shaw to read *Seven Pillars*.
3 The newspaper office was that of the *Oxford Times*; the text thus produced became known as the 'Oxford' version. Eight copies were printed, of which five were bound for circulation to friends and a sixth was given to Edward Garnett for his proposed abridgement.

for only five copies exist, and I could not afford a proof. The punctuation is entirely the compositor's fancy: and he had an odd fancy, especially on Mondays.

That's the worst to be said on the material side. So far as concerns myself you must be told, before you commit yourself to saying 'yes', that I'm not a writer, and successfully passed the age of 30 without having wanted to write anything. I was brought up as a professional historian, which means the worship of original documents. To my astonishment, after peace came I found I was myself the sole person who knew what had happened in Arabia during the war: and the only literate person in the Arab Army. So it became a professional duty to record what happened. I started out to do it plainly and simply, much as a baby thinks it's easy to talk: and then I found myself bogged in a confusion of ways of saying the easiest things, and unable to describe the plainest places: and then problems of conduct came along, and the people with me had to be characterised: — in fact I got fairly into it, and the job became too much for me. *Your* first book was not perfect, though it was a subject you had chosen for yourself, and you had an itch to write!

In my case, I have, I believe, taken refuge in second-hand words: I mean, I think I've borrowed expressions and adjectives and ideas from everybody I have ever read, and cut them down to my own size, and stitched them together again. My tastes are daily mailish, so there's enough piffle and romance and wooliness to make a realist sick. There's a lot of half-baked thinking, some cheap disgust and complaint (the fighting fronts were mainly hysterical, you know, where they weren't professional, and I'm not the least a proper soldier): in fact all the sham stuff you have spent your life trying to prick. If you read my thing, it will show you that your prefaces have been written in vain, if I'm a fair sample of my generation. This might make you laugh, if the thing was amusingly written: but it's long-winded, and pretentious, and dull to the point where I can no longer bear to look at it myself. I chose that moment to have it printed!

You'll wonder, why if all this is true (and I think it is) I want any decent person still more a person like yourself★ to read it. Well, it's because it is history, and I'm shamed for ever if I am the sole chronicler of an event, and fail to chronicle it: and yet unless what I've written can be made better I'll burn it. My own disgust with it is so great that I no longer believe it worth trying to improve (or possible to improve). If you read it or part of it and came to the same conclusion, you would give me courage to strike the match: whereas now I distrust my own judgement, and it seems cruel to destroy a thing on which I have worked my hardest for three years. While if you said that parts were rubbish, and other parts not so bad, and parts of it possible, (and distinguished those parts variously) then your standards might enable me to clear up mine, and give me energy enough to tackle the job again. (If you say it is all possible then I will reluctantly get rid of your own books from my shelves.)

All this is very unfair — or would be, if you knew me: but deleting that twenty minutes with Cockerell we are utter strangers, and likely to remain so, and therefore there is no pressure on you to answer this letter at all. I won't be in the least astonished (indeed I'll write another of the same sort to a man called Orage[1] whom I have never met, but whose criticism I enjoy): and my opinion of you will go up. Yours with many apologies

T E Lawrence

Incidentally: I don't want people to know that the book exists. So whether you reply or not, I hope you will not talk of it.

* ambiguous: but I wanted to avoid expressing my liking for your work.

DG

EDWARD GARNETT[2]

22.VIII.22   [Postmarked London S.W.1]

I should have warned you before I sent it (only it seemed so remote a contingency) that if your opinion was favourable it would be wasted on me. Perhaps as you haven't yet finished it, this is still not too rude to say. The thing is spotted in nearly every line with blemishes of style, and while my critical sense doesn't reach as far as subject matter and construction, I judge them equally bad, by analogy.

So please don't consider the point of publication. That never came into my mind when writing it: indeed I don't know for whom I wrote it, unless it was for myself. When it came to the point of printing it, several passages had to come out, for fear of the compositor, and I cannot imagine showing it except to a few minds (like yours) already prejudged to kindness.

If that Deraa incident whose treatment you call severe and serene (the

---

1 A. R. Orage (1875–1934), editor of *The New Age*. See also note to letter to Ezra Pound dated 7 December 1934 (p. 505).

2 Edward Garnett (1868–1936) was the father of David Garnett. A novelist and critic in his own right, he was most famous as a publisher's reader — notably for Jonathan Cape — and as an encourager of important writers, among them E. M. Forster, Joseph Conrad and D. H. Lawrence. T. E. Lawrence summed up something of Garnett's gift in a sentence from his last letter to him in 1934: 'Your criticisms have always gone personally from you to the artist, instead of being exhibition pieces to catch the public eye on the way.' He was to devote much time and energy to fostering Lawrence as a writer — a far from easy task.

second sounds like a quaint failure to get my impressions across, but I know what you feel) had happened to yourself you would not have recorded it. I have a face of brass perhaps, but I put it into print very reluctantly, last of all the pages I sent to the press. For weeks I wanted to burn it in the manuscript: because I could not tell the story face to face with anyone, and I think I'll feel sorry, when I next meet you, that you know it. The sort of man I have always mixed with doesn't so give himself away.

I shall hope for help from your pencilled notes, and am very grateful for your goodness in reading it, and for what praise you have given it: only please don't do more, because it only underlines what I know to be my failure. Hitherto I've always managed, usually without trying my hardest, to do anything I wanted in life: and it has bumped me down, rather, to have gone wrong in this thing, after three or four years top-effort. That shows the difference between mere brick-laying and creative work. It's what I told Nicholson and yourself that day in Piccadilly: there's no absolute in the imaginative world, and so journeymen like myself are confused and miserable in it.

I'm afraid this is a very affected note: but your letter has upset me. Sorry.

E.L.

The other passage you mention, where the tommies went wrong.[1] — I may be in order exhibiting myself: but how can I give them away? They were such decent fellows, and we treated them so poorly.

When you have had enough of it I'd like to come down and ask you some technical questions.

DG

BERNARD SHAW
27.VIII.22   14 Barton St Westminster

[...]

I'd like you to read it [...] partly because you are you: partly because I may profit by your reading it, if I have a chance to talk to you soon after, before you have got over it. You see the war was, for us who were in it, an overwrought time, in which we lost our normal footing. I wrote this thing in the war atmosphere, and believe that it is stinking with it. Also there is a good deal of cruelty, and some excitement. All these things, in a

---

1 A reference to a passage which Lawrence decided to delete describing the punishment of a British soldier and an Arab who had been arrested for having homosexual relations.

beginner's hands, tend to force him over the edge, and I suspect there is much over-writing. You have the finest cure for flatulence, and I have great hopes that you will laugh at parts of what I meant to be solemn: and if I can get at you before you have forgotten which they are, then I'll have a chance to make it better.

You'll be amused at my amateur method of getting help: and at my having a standard of work: but it's the only book I'll write, and so I want it to be tolerable.

[...]

DG

4 · FIRST YEARS IN THE RANKS

1922–26

4 Introduction

Lawrence joined the Royal Air Force as 352087 Aircraftman John Hume Ross on 30 August 1922. During his basic training at Uxbridge he compiled the notes and observations which were to form the core of his second famous literary work, *The Mint*. Early in November he was sent to the R.A.F. School of Photography at Farnborough. On 27 December the fact that a 'Famous War Hero' was lurking in the ranks under an assumed name was revealed as a front page story in the *Daily Express*. On 23 January 1923 he became a civilian again, dismissed, as he wrote a week later to the Editor of the *Observer*, J. L. Garvin, 'for possessing too large a publicity factor to be decent in an A.C.2'. Yet by March he was in the ranks again, this time as a Private in the Army, and with a new alias, T. E. Shaw.

He was posted to the Tank Corps Training School at Bovington in Dorset, where he remained for over two years, frequently railing at Army life and campaigning throughout to return to the Air Force, even at one time hinting at suicide unless he got his way. Without Bovington, however, he would not have forged some of his most important friendships, with Tank Corps men on the one hand or, for example, Mr and Mrs Thomas Hardy on the other. Without Bovington too there would have been no Clouds Hill, the half-derelict cottage a mile and a half from the camp which was to be his home and his sanctuary for the rest of his life and which he spent much energy and imagination in improving. Clouds Hill soon became a venue where people from a wide range of backgrounds forgathered, with writers and artists mingling easily with men in khaki or Air Force blue, and the rankers as likely as the aesthetes to be curled up with a book of poems or a literary novel. 'What was Clouds' Hill?' Lawrence wrote to Mrs Shaw on 31 August 1924, after a night in which records of the Choral Symphony had alternated with tea-drinkings until 2 a.m. and Jock Chambers of the R.A.F. had read *Back to Methuselah* whenever there was an interval: 'A sort of mixed grill, I fancy: but very good. Everybody is beginning to fall in love with it. The air of it is peaceful: and the fire burns so well.'

206

All this, however, was not enough to reconcile him to life in a service for which he could feel no affection. He punctuated his Tank Corps years with pleas to the Chief of the Air Staff, Sir Hugh Trenchard: 'February is "supplication month" ...' he wrote in early 1925, 'so for the third time of asking — Have I no chance of re-enlistment in the R.A.F., or transfer? It remains my only hope and ambition, dreamed of every week, nearly every day.' At last in August he was readmitted to the R.A.F. and sent to the Cadet College at Cranwell in Lincolnshire — though not, of course, as a Cadet, but as an ordinary Aircraftman. He stayed there until late 1926, when he sailed by troopship for India.

Throughout this period he was working intermittently on *Seven Pillars of Wisdom*; by the time he left for India his lavishly printed and illustrated subscribers' edition was completed and the popular abridgement entitled *Revolt in the Desert* was awaiting publication. That this latter event would inevitably lead to another upsurge of publicity and myth-making led to his request to be posted abroad.

This is an important period for letters — the beginning of the high tide which was only to subside, and that far from completely, in the last weeks of his life. The circulation of the 'Oxford' text of *Seven Pillars* inevitably prompted many exchanges; two letters worth singling out are the undated letter to Vyvyan Richards written early in 1923 and the letter to Colonel Wavell dated 11 May 1923. The Charlotte Shaw correspondence — candid, confessional, written with a sense of style and ranging widely over life and literature — began shortly after he reached Bovington. Bovington also produced a series to Lionel Curtis, five in all, between March and June 1923, which David Garnett described as 'the most revealing letters of Lawrence's I know'. While it is true that Garnett could not compare them with those to Charlotte Shaw, being denied access despite his best efforts to persuade, he was certainly right in making high claims for them, for not only are they remarkable pieces of writing but they are also a most vivid portrait of a mind on the edge of despair. Lawrence began almost lightly, proposing a series of letters 'more splendid' than Daudet's *Lettres de mon moulin*; by the time they ended they had become a composite statement more comparable in tone to Wilde's *De Profundis*. They are all reprinted here (one somewhat shortened), though whereas Garnett ran them as a complete sequence I have interleaved them with letters to other recipients.

As elsewhere in this selection I have included some of the best of Garnett but there are many new letters too: outspoken to R. D. Blumenfeld of the *Daily Express*, frank and depressed to Alan Dawnay, affectionate to R. A. M. Guy. There are also some revealing letters to E. M. Forster and one to Vyvyan Richards, dated 26 June 1924, in which he writes on a subject with which he deals rarely: his beliefs. 'My new feeling (a dreaded conviction is looming up in the near distance) is that the basis of life, the *raison d'être* of us, the springs of our actions, our ideals, ambitions, hopes are carnal as our lusts: & that the appositions of mind & body, of flesh & spirit, are delusions of our timid selves.' This is a comparatively brief aside in a letter on a number of themes, but the period also includes a long letter written in a mood of such unhappiness and disillusion that it has been fittingly described as the bitterest letter he ever wrote; this is his letter to Charlotte Shaw sent from Cranwell after his meeting with Lord Winterton and King Feisal of Iraq at Winterton's country house in September 1925 (see p. 289).

Although not evident from his letters, it was during his Bovington years that, according to revelations made in the *Sunday Times* in 1968, he first submitted himself to severe beatings administered by a young Scotsman, John Bruce. Bruce is mentioned in only two letters in this collection: one to Charlotte Shaw dated 19 July 1924, printed here for the first time, and one to the American publisher F. N. Doubleday dated 18 September 1930, republished here from Garnett (in Part 6), in which he is referred to as 'Jock, the roughest diamond of our Tank Corps hut in 1923'.

AIR VICE-MARSHAL SIR OLIVER SWANN[1]
1.IX.22   [R.A.F. Uxbridge]

Dear Swann

I can't ask the corporal how an aircraft hand addresses an air-vice-marshal: — so please take this letter as a work of my late existence! I hadn't meant to write, except when I changed station, but the mess I made of Henrietta St.[2] demands an apology. I thought I was fitter: but when it came to the point, walked up and down the street in a blue funk, and finally went in with my nerves dithering, and my heart dancing. My teeth never were any good, so the doctors threw me straight downstairs again. There Dexter[3] caught me, and lent me what was no doubt his right hand to steer me past the medical, and through other rocks of square roots and essays and decimals. However I was obviously incapable of getting through on my

1 Swann, as already indicated on p. 195-6, had been instructed by Trenchard to arrange Lawrence's entry into the R.A.F. but he had done so without enthusiasm ('I disliked the whole business, with its secrecy and subterfuge') and had met Lawrence once only at the Air Ministry. He was therefore somewhat surprised at the tone of this and several other letters which Lawrence subsequently wrote to him from which, Swann told Garnett, 'one would think ... that I was a close correspondent of Lawrence's, possibly even a friend of his'.
2 Henrietta Street was the site of the R.A.F. recruiting office where Lawrence enlisted; his enlistment is described in the opening chapter of *The Mint*.
3 A Flight Lieutenant to whom Lawrence had been instructed to report.

own, so he got another chit from you, and that did the trick satisfactorily. If I'd known I was such a wreck I'd have gone off and recovered before [join]ing up: now the cure and the experiment must proceed together. I'm not very certain of myself, for the crudities, which aren't as bad as I expected, worry me far more than I expected: and physically I can only just scrape through the days. However they are a cheerful crowd; and the N.C.O.s behave with extraordinary gentleness to us (there's no other word fits their tone — except on the square, from which good Lord deliver us!) and I enjoy usually one hour of the sixteen, and often laugh in bed after lights out. If I can get able to sleep, and to eat the food, and to go through the P.T.[1] I'll be all right. The present worry is 90% nerves.

Would you tell the C.A.S.[2] that he's given me the completest change any mortal has had since Nebuchadnezzar: and that so far as I'm concerned it's to go on? Fortunately I told him I wasn't sure how long I could stick it, so that there is always a bridge — but it isn't required yet, and I hope won't be: only it's a comforting thought for the fifteen bad hours.

As for the special reason for which I came in — there's masses of gorgeous stuff lying about: but the scale of it is heart-rending. I found the Arab Revolt too big to write about, and chose this as a smaller subject to write about: but you'd have to be a man and a half to tackle it at all decently.

I must say you have an amazing good crowd in the ranks: as a new force it ought to be pretty alive: but its keenness and life is better than I dreamed of.

In case I'm wanted by the Colonial Office I'll send you a note as often as I change station: but not more unless I want something, which will be a sad event. Less than two years won't do what I planned, in my present opinion: and they all say that things are easier outside Uxbridge. Also I'll have got used to being a dog's body.

Please tell the C.A.S. that I'm delighted, and most grateful to him and to you for what you have done. Don't bother to keep an eye on what happens to me.

Yours sincerely
T E Lawrence

I've re-read this letter: it gives too dismal an impression. It's only the sudden change from independence to dish-washing, and from mental to physical living which has been too much for my strength. And I'd harmed my health more than I thought by these three years trying to write a war book. It's hard to squeeze the last drop out of your memories of two years, and I sweated myself blind trying to make it as good as possible. Result that I

---

1 P.T.: Physical Training.
2 C.A.S.: Chief of Air Staff, i.e. Trenchard.

leap into the air when spoken to unexpectedly, and can't reply a word: only stand there shivering! And it's hard not to give oneself away at such moments. The actual conditions are better than I thought.

E.L.

DG

EDWARD GARNETT
Monday 9.x.22   [R.A.F. Uxbridge]

[...] It's good of you to (or rather that you should) like my effort more on the re-reading. My test for a book is that one should finish it each time with a mind to read it again — some day. It's particularly interesting that the last fifty pages seem to you alive: I've never been able to see them at all: always by the time I have got so far my eyes have carried forward to the end, and I've gone through the last fighting like a dream. Those pages have been worked at very hard, but I've never got them in perspective: and I've always had a lurking fear that they were flatter than the vith and viith parts (the failure of the bridge and the winter war) and formed an anticlimax — a weak ending. It was impossible for me to last out so long a writing with my wits about me: and I've feared that there would be found no reader long-winded enough to get there either. Your judgment that the book is in excess, as regards lengths, is also, I judge, true as regards intensity and breadth. I've had no pity on myself writing it — nor on my readers reading it. There's a clamour of force in it which deafens. A better artist would have given the effect of a fortissimo with less instrumentality. It's unskilled craftsmen who are profuse.

What you say about the oddity of my brain doesn't surprise me — but it helps to explain the apartness of myself here in this noisy barrack room. I might be one dragon-fly in a world of wasps — or one wasp among the dragon-flies! It's not a comfortable place: but if the oddity of my standing produces a fresh-feeling book, I suppose I shouldn't grouse about my luck.

The personal chapter clearly bothers you.[1] A man (a metaphysician by nature, who was at Oxford with me and knows me very well)[2] read it, and told me that it stood out as the finest chapter in the book. I tend more to your opinion: it's not meant for the ordinary intelligences, and *must* mislead them: but to set it out in plain English would be very painful. However six months away from it, and then a fresh approach may work a change in

1 Chapter CIII: *Myself.*
2 Vyvyan Richards.

my feeling towards it: may even give me energy to re-write it. At present nothing sounds less probable. I don't even feel capable (though I'd love to) of writing a fresh book on this place. I've made some rather poor notes, which show me how hard it would be to bring off a picture of the R.A.F. Depot.

I wonder how the reduction seems to you now.[1] If you get it to 150,000 and satisfy yourself, and then I take out 20,000 or so, that should do the trick. What an odd book it will be! It's over-good of you to attempt such a business. I decided yesterday in church (church-parade!) that I ought to publish nothing. Today I feel inclined to publish. Am I neurasthenic or just feeble-willed?

I'm afraid I can't come away, even for a day.

E. L.

(Glad you like Auda, I did!)

DG

R.D. BLUMENFELD[2]   14 Barton Street SW1
11.XI.22

Dear Blumenfeld

This letter has got to be indiscreet — shockingly so, when one thinks how the *Daily Mail* gave away the poison in the chocolates — please keep it as a personal one, from me to you.

When Winston at last let me go — it took four months work to make him: I refused salary, & begged for release each time I saw him, etc. — I found I was quite on the rocks: and so I enlisted, as a quick and easy way of keeping alive, and alive I am, in the ranks, & not always miserable. It's a varied life, often very bad, but with spots of light, very exciting and full of freshness. You know I was always odd, & my tastes my own. Also the

1 Edward Garnett had offered to produce an abridged version of *Seven Pillars*.
2 Born in the U.S.A., R. D. Blumenfeld (1864–1948) was Editor of the *Daily Express* from 1902–32. Lawrence had written two articles for the *Express* in May 1920 for which he refused to accept payment, whereupon Blumenfeld sent him a rare copy of the *Arabian Nights*. Lawrence thanked him but explained that he felt uncomfortable about Blumenfeld's generosity since by publishing his articles the *Express* had 'achieved some things I wanted very much, and I am still therefore deeply in your debt'. He added: 'Unfortunately I cannot pay my side of it with beautiful books — but please let me know any time I can be of use to you.' Blumenfeld had at last taken up Lawrence's offer, only to find that the latter was no longer in either a position or a frame of mind to accept any journalistic commission.

only way I could escape politics entirely was to cut myself sharply off from my former way of living: and making a living with one's fingers is joyful work, & as clean as possible, after politics — to which not even the *Express* shall drag me back!

No reflection on Winston, who's a great man, & for whom I have not merely admiration, but a very great liking. If we get out of the Middle East Mandates with credit, it will be by Winston's bridge. The man's as brave as six, as good-humoured, shrewd, self-confident, & considerate as a statesman can be: & several times I've seen him chuck the statesmanlike course and do the honest thing instead.

I use Barton Street as an address, & either call there, or have my letters sent away to barracks for me. You will understand that I'm no more master of my time, & can't come up: nor can I write very much down here: nor have I the will to write much. I wore my nerves into a mop, finishing my war journal of events in Arabia. It ended as a very long book, indiscreet in the personal, political, & military spheres, & a complete picture of myself! Anyway it shan't be published in its entirety: but I'm tired of having written so much, & prefer to play about with rifles meanwhile.

Do keep this news to yourself. No one in camp knows who I am, & I don't want them to.

Yours sincerely
T E Lawrence

Bodleian Reserve

WINSTON CHURCHILL
18 November 22

Dear Mr Churchill

This is a difficult letter to write — because it follows on many unwritten ones. First I wanted to say how sorry I was when you fell ill, and again when you had to have an operation. Then I should have written to say I was sorry when the Government resigned. I meant to write & congratulate you on getting better: but before I could do that you were in Dundee and making speeches. Lastly I should write to say that I'm sorry the poll went against you[1] but I want to wash out all these lost opportunities, & to give you instead my hope that you will rest a little: six months perhaps. There is that book of memoirs to be made not merely worth £30,000, but of permanent value. Your life of Lord Randolph shows what you could do

---

1 Churchill had lost his seat at Dundee in the General Election of 15 November.

with memoirs. Then there is the painting to work at, but I feel that you are sure to do that anyhow: but the first essential seems to me a holiday for you. It sounds like preaching from a younger to an elder (and is worse still when the younger is an airman-recruit!) but you have the advantage of twenty years over nearly all your political rivals: and physically you are as strong as any three of them (do you remember your camel-trotting at Giza, when you wore out all your escort, except myself, & I'm not a fair competitor at that!) and in guts and power and speech you can roll over anyone bar Lloyd George: so that you can (or should) really not be in any hurry.

Of course I know that your fighting sense is urging you to get back into the scrimmage at the first moment: but it would be better for your forces to rest & rearrange them: & not bad tactics to disengage a little. The public won't forget you soon, & you will be in a position to choose your new position and line of action more freely, for an interval. I needn't say that I'm at your disposal when you need me — or rather if ever you do.[1] I've had lots of chiefs in my time, but never one before who really was my chief. The others have needed help at all times: you only when you want it: — and let me say that if your tools in the rest of your career to date had been of my temper you would have been now too big, probably, for the country to employ! That's a modest estimate of myself, but you know it doubles the good of a subordinate to feel that his chief is better than himself.

Yours sincerely
T. E. Lawrence

By the way, I've got keen on the RAF and propose to stick to it for the present.

Churchill Papers[2]

R. D. BLUMENFELD
24.XI.22   [Farnborough]

Dear Blumenfeld

Your offer is a generous and very kind one: and you will think me quixotic in refusing it: but I ran away here partly to escape the responsibility of head-work: and the *Daily Express* would expect me to take it up again.

1 In a letter of 17 July 1922 Churchill had written to Lawrence stating he very much regretted his departure from the Colonial Office and adding 'Still, I feel I can count upon you at any time when a need may arise.'
2 Printed in *Winston S. Churchill* by Martin Gilbert, Companion Part 3 to Volume IV.

Had I fewer wits I would have been a merrier person. My best thanks all the same.

No, please don't publish my eclipse. It will be common news one day, but the later the better for my peace in the ranks:[1] and I'd be sorry to have to render reasons for it. As you say, it reads like cheap melodrama, and my life so far has been that, nearly since the odd circumstances of my birth. Some day I'll tell you stories about myself—if you will hear them.

Meanwhile I'm excogitating a new book—in no way personal—on the spirit of the Air Force;[2] a most remarkable body: and am hoping to take advantage of my obscurity to produce an abridgement of my old war-book on Arabia. This latter book I printed privately (5 copies) a while ago: and if the abridgement is approved by a publisher I'll find myself rich—according to my standard. Whether I'll continue in the R.A.F. then, or return to London life—I don't know.

I hope the nursing home (now half over, I suppose, for my post comes spasmodically, with long delays) will go prosperously for you. It's beastly, the being in any way ill. By the way don't you think it's good for me at my great age, after a ragged life, after seven bad air-crashes, after nine war-wounds, and many peace-ones, to be able to enlist and hold my own with a lusty crowd? I'm contented with myself.

Yours ever
T. E. Lawrence

Bodleian Reserve

BERNARD SHAW

30.XI.22   14 Barton Street

Dear Mr. Shaw

I'm afraid you are either making a labour of it,[3] or you don't want to tell me that it's rubbish. I don't want to bore you (nice of me!) and if you

---

1 It was the *Daily Express* which *did* publish Lawrence's 'eclipse', just over a month later while Blumenfeld was away ill.
2 The 'new book' would eventually emerge as *The Mint*.
3 In an annotation to this letter dated 7 July 1940 G.B.S. wrote: ' "it" is the *Seven Pillars*: one of the early copies that he got printed in double columns at a newspaper office. I had to cut out or rewrite several passages that were outrageously libellous. He showed these passages, with my revisions, to the victims, and expected them to be amused!' See for example Lawrence's letter to Sir Archibald Murray dated 10 January 1920 and footnote 1 on p. 173.

say it's not I'll agree with you & cackle with pleasure at finding my judgement doubled.

Please laugh & chuck it!¹

Yours sincerely

T. E. Lawrence

Jesus College Oxford

BERNARD SHAW

27.XII.22   [R.A.F. Farnborough]

Dear Mr. Shaw

Your letter reached me on Christmas day, and has interested me immensely — especially one phrase. No doubt it was used to help me with Constable's² (gratitude etc.) and it's immodest of me to refer to it — but you say that it's a great book. Physically, yes: in subject, yes: an outsider seeing the inside of a national movement is given an enormous subject: but is it good in treatment? I care very much for this, as it's been my ambition all my life to write something intrinsically good. I can't believe that I've done it, for it's the hardest thing in the world, and I've had such success in other lines that it's greedy to expect goodness in so technical a matter. However your phrase makes me hope a bit: will you let me know your honest opinion as to whether it is well done or not? When I was actually writing it I got worked up and wrote hardly: but in the between-spells the whole performance seemed miserable, and when I finished it I nearly burned the whole thing for the third time. The contrast between what I meant and felt I could do, and the truth of what my weakness had let me do was so pitiful. You see, there's that feeling at the back of my mind that if I really tried, sat down and wrung my mind out, the result would be on an altogether higher plane. I funk this extreme effort, for I half-killed myself as it was, doing the present draft: and I'd willingly dodge out of it. Isn't it treated wrongly? I mean, shouldn't it be objective, without the first-person-singular? And is there any style in my writing at all? Anything recognisably individual?

---

1 Shaw replied on 1 December: 'Patience, patience: do not again shoot your willing camel through the head' — Lawrence had killed his own camel in the excitement of action at Aba el Lissan just before the seizure of Akaba — adding that he had not read *Seven Pillars* yet but that his wife had 'ploughed through it from Alpha to Omega'. For the text of this and other letters by G.B.S. to Lawrence see *Letters to T.E. Lawrence*, edited by A.W. Lawrence.

2 Constable's: Bernard Shaw's publishers.

Apologies for bothering your eminence with 'prentice questions: but I'm mad-keen to know, even if it's to know the worst.

[...]

You ask for details of what I'm doing in the R.A.F. Today I scrubbed the kitchen out in the morning, and loafed all the afternoon, and spent the evening writing to G. B. S. Yesterday I washed up the dishes in the sergeants' mess in the morning (messy feeders, sergeants: plates were all butter and tomato sauce, and the washing water was cold) and rode to Oxford in the afternoon on my motor-bike, and called on Hogarth to discuss the abridgement of the Arabian book. It being Christmas we do fatigues in the morning, and holiday in the afternoon. Normally I'm an 'aerial photographer, under training': it doesn't mean flying, but developing the officers' negatives after they land: and the 'under-training' part means that I'm a recruit, and therefore liable to all sorts of mis-employment. For three weeks I was an errand-boy. I've also been dustman, and clerk, and pig-stye-cleaner, and housemaid, and scullion, and camp-cinema-attendant. Anything does for airmen recruits: but the life isn't so bad, when the first crudeness works off. We have a bed each, and suffer all sorts of penalties unless they are 25 inches apart: twelve of us in a room. Life is very common, besides being daily. Much good humour, very little wit, but a great friendliness. They treat my past as a joke, and forgive it me lightly. The officers fight shy of me: but I behave demurely, and give no trouble.

Yours sincerely

T E Lawrence

DG

The preceding letter to Bernard Shaw was written on the day on which the *Daily Express* disclosed Lawrence's presence in the Air Force in a story headlined 'UNCROWNED KING' AS PRIVATE SOLDIER. There was more in the centre pages and more again on the following day under such headlines as PRINCE OF MECCA ON RIFLE PARADE. The press came down to look for Lawrence at Farnborough where, to quote David Garnett, he was 'valiantly protected' by his friends in the ranks. The ultimate result of this sudden outburst of publicity was to be his expulsion from the R.A.F., but its more immediate consequence was his decision to stop the proposed publication of the abridged version of *Seven Pillars of Wisdom*.

BERNARD SHAW
2.i.23   Farnborough

Dear Mr. Shaw
   Our letters crossed. I'm sorry.
   It's most good of you to wish to help me, & I'm afraid I'm rather a
difficult person to help. The publication of the whole book seemed to me
an impossible business, for personal reasons. So I agreed to the abridgement,
which, as a censored article, was in essence dishonest. Then, the *Daily
Express* blew out that rubbish (not Cape's fault: it was written by one of
the officers here) & I felt that to publish anything now might look as though
I were using the R.A.F as an advertising stunt. So I've cancelled Cape's
contract (fortunately not completed, & so I hope there will be no damages
to pay) and have told him that nothing is to appear this year.
   About Doughty. It was a book which owing to its length (longer than
my effort) and its Arabic, & its cuts, was very expensive to re-set, and its
prospect of selling seemed problematical to all publishers, till Cape (then
with Lee-Warner) said that he would risk a 500 edition, at a price to cover
costs, if I'd write a preface.[1]
   I hate introductions to masterpieces (puff-introductions by pygmies: it's
like tourists cutting their names on the walls of Kenilworth) but there
seemed little chance of getting the book out without an effort by me in
that direction. I consulted Doughty, who very nobly agreed to suffer it: &
then I pieced together pages from my *Seven Pillars*, with some few lines
written expressly, & put asterisks where the separate fragments seemed to
jar together.
   Cape got his reward, for the 500 copies sold in about three months.
Doughty got £300 or so: everybody was satisfied: and I withdrew the puff,
which I hope will soon be decently forgotten. It's unpardonable, for the
lesser to praise the greater, & *Arabia Deserta* is a far greater book than the
Seven Pillars.
   Cape has since printed off another 500 *Arabia Deserta*s, & they are selling
slowly. Moulds have been made, & the book won't again be unprocurable.
That's a pious work to have done, & condones my offence of taste. This
long explanation is for Mrs. Shaw's benefit, as she is interested. If I had an
A.D. with my preface I'd send it: but I haven't!
   The cancellation of my book means that I stay in the R.A.F. for the time

---

1 The successful republication of Charles Doughty's masterpiece *Arabia Deserta*, with
   Lawrence's introduction, was a major factor in establishing Messrs Jonathan Cape as a
   publishing house. See Cape's contribution to *T.E. Lawrence by His Friends*.

being: and my address here (this isn't a tout for another letter!) is

I'm going to wash out that	352087 A.C.ii Ross
old name, which has too	B.3. Block
many war associations to	School of Photography
please me: and which isn't	R.A.F.
my real name, any more than Ross!	S. Farnborough
	Hants.

T E L.

University of Texas

RAYMOND SAVAGE[1]

7.1.23   R.A.F.   S Farnborough

Dear Savage

I came up yesterday and saw Cape and Garvin,[2] and made up my mind (is it final? The beastly thing has wobbled so that I despair of its remaining fixed for life) not to publish anything whatever: neither abridgement nor serial, nor full story: at least this year: and probably not so long as I remain in the R.A.F. I've written to Cape with this and told him. I needn't say how much I am ashamed of the trouble everyone has had, and will have, as a result of this decision: but it's the only one I can make.

You will probably want to say something, on your own account, to clear up the matter. I'd suggest, if so, your writing that 'Mr. Lawrence wrote his narrative in 1919: and later printed privately an edition of eight copies, which have been circulated among the people concerned; and that while he has no intention of publishing this version, he did recently agree provisionally, to the publication of an abridgement (one third of the original matter) by Mr. Jonathan Cape.'

The next stage is more difficult. You can either say, bluntly, that afterwards I withdrew from the negotiations: or that my service in the R.A.F. in my opinion precludes me from publication meanwhile: or that I'm too fed up with the *Daily Express* to endure the thought of giving away the remainder of myself to them.

Anyway, invent something, if you will, and if you want to: and let me see it before you publish it; and meanwhile tear up those contracts, and accept my very deepest apologies for the whole miserable business.

Yours ever

T. E. Lawrence

Bodleian Reserve

1 Lawrence's literary agent. During the war he had served on Allenby's staff; he later wrote a biography of his former chief under the title *Allenby of Armageddon*, published 1925.
2 J. L. Garvin, Editor of the *Observer*, who had hoped to serialise the abridged *Seven Pillars*. See letter to him dated 30 January 1923 (p. 221).

MRS CHARLOTTE SHAW[1]

8.1.23   R.A.F.

Dear 'Mrs. G.B.S.'

It's a wonderful letter, that of yours, and I've liked it beyond measure:[2] though my doubts as to the virtues of the *Seven Pillars* remain: indeed I'd be an insufferable creature if I was sure of it, for to me a good book is the best thing that can be done. However I'd been thinking it possibly a bad book, and your praise of it makes me more hopeful. At the same time, you know, it's more a storehouse than a book — has no unity, is too discursive, dispersed, heterogeneous. I've shot into it, as a builder into his yard, all the odds and ends of ideas which came to me during those years: indeed I suspect that it's a summary of myself to February 1920, and that people who read it will know me better than I know myself.

Since 1920 I've had new experiences, and it's partly that newness today which makes the *Seven Pillars* seem to me so inadequate to their theme. This last adventure in the R.A.F. is a chapter in itself. It would be hard to remain inhuman while jostling all days and nights in a crowd of clean and simple men. There is something here which in my life before I'd never met — had hardly dreamed of.

I explained my action with the Doughty preface in a letter to G.B.S. last week:[3] and have told him also that I've refused to sign my contract for any part of the *Seven Pillars*, to Cape or anyone else. I'd like to publish the whole, but that's as improbable as that I'd walk naked down Piccadilly: not that I'd like that either, but the whole is the only honest thing.

I showed my Mother your letter. She likes you now, because you praised my work, and mothers have (privately) an inordinate pride in sons. The

---

1 Born Charlotte Payne-Townsend (later changed to Payne-Townshend) in 1857, she married Bernard Shaw in 1898 and though their marriage was one of companionship only, it endured until her death in 1943. Though over thirty years older than Lawrence, she and Lawrence shared an Irish background, a mother-dominated childhood and a predisposition to celibacy and they were able to write to each other with a remarkable and sustained intimacy. (N.B. Strictly she should be named as Mrs Bernard Shaw but she is so frequently referred to as Mrs Charlotte Shaw in the Lawrencian context that I have adopted this form throughout.)

2 In a letter dated 31 December 1922 Charlotte Shaw had written: 'Now is it *conceivable*, *imaginable*, that a man who could write the *Seven Pillars* could have any doubts about it? . . . I devoured the book from cover to cover as soon as I got hold of it. I drove G.B.S. almost mad by insisting on reading him special bits when he was deep in something else. . . . [I]t is one of the most amazingly individual documents that has ever been written . . .' etc.

3 See letter to G.B.S. dated 2 January 1923 (p. 217).

horrors of the book strike her painfully, and she hates my having noted, or seen, such things.

Meinertzhagen saw his description, and laughed over it, not in any way annoyed.[1] There is an astonishing power in that man.

It's very good of you and G.B.S. to offer me your help. It would be invaluable if I was publishing: but today I feel that I won't. It was only lack of food which frightened me into consenting: and in the R.A.F. they give us quantities of food.

Yours sincerely
T. E. Lawrence

British Library

The following letter shows that at this critical period when his Air Force career had been put at risk by the *Daily Express* disclosures, Lawrence briefly contemplated as a serious possibility the idea, put to him by Robert Graves, of going to live with Graves and his wife Nancy Nicholson in Nepal.

Five days after refusing the offer he was discharged from the R.A.F.

ROBERT GRAVES
18.1.23

Dear R.G.

I've delayed, thinking about it: and thinking is slow in B block because people talk more readily. Now there is a sort of riot happening over by the fire: and so writing is made difficult.

The conclusion is that probably I won't.[2] The escape from what is nearly

---

1 Colonel Richard Meinertzhagen had served with Lawrence in the Middle East and also in Paris. He later presented a somewhat unflattering account of Lawrence in his *Middle East Diary 1917–1956*, published in 1959 but in his *Army Diary*, published in 1960, he wrote of him: 'I respected him, admired him and was devoted to him.'

2 The background to this letter is explained in *RGB*, though with the name of the country in question — Nepal — omitted. Graves wrote: 'I was troubled about his [Lawrence's] life in the ranks and felt that he ought to be rescued. Then I, and my family, had an invitation from the Foreign Minister of a certain remote Eastern principality to go there and live at the Government's expense: the invitation was extended to Lawrence. If he went, we went.' Lawrence's refusal meant that Graves and his family did not go either. 'The I.O.' was the India Office, at which Lord Winterton was Under-Secretary of State.

squalor here was attractive: and Nepal is out of the world (by the way passports won't be difficult: the I.O. will do that much for my sake. Lord Winterton was 'one of us' in Hejaz): but partly I came in here to eat dirt, till its taste is normal to me; and partly to avoid the current of other men's thinking; and in your hill-court there will be high thinking. My brain nearly went in Barton St. with the weariness of writing and re-writing that horrible book of mine: and I still am nervous & easily made frantic.

So I think I'm going to stay on in the R.A.F. which has the one great merit of showing me humanity very clear & clean. I've never lived commonly before, & I think to run away from the stress of it would be a failing.

I owe you a word about that book. It may be printed privately, in a limited subscription edition, next year. A sort of 15 guinea book, almost unprocurable. I hovered for a while this year with the notion of a censored version: but that seems dishonest, until the whole story is available.

I'm glad you're feeling easier. In mechanical jargon you've been 'revving' yourself too high for the last eighteen months. Such forced running means a very heavy fuel consumption, & is not true economy. Your 'philosopher' period as a poet is worth taking care for, since its product will surpass your lyrical.

Many thanks to Malik.[1] I very nearly came, but I wanted to too much for it to be a wholesome wish.

E.L.

University of Harvard/RGB

J. L. GARVIN[2]
30.1.23   14 Barton St S.W.1

Dear Garvin

I sent you the *Seven Pillars* from Farnborough last week: but within half an hour of that I'd got my dismissal from the R.A.F. for possessing too large a publicity factor to be decent in an A.C.2. Wherefore I've sent to Savage, who was the long-suffering man acting as my agent, & told him that the proposed publication again falls through.

You'll remember that after sleeping over my talk with you I cancelled

---

1 Malik (*sic*): Basanta Mallik, a graduate of Calcutta University and of Exeter College, Oxford, and later a post-graduate student at Balliol College, was the initiator of the invitation to Nepal.

2 James Louis Garvin (1868–1947) was Editor of the *Observer* 1908–42. He was one of the most influential journalists of his time. He was made a Companion of Honour in 1941.

all idea of publishing an abridgement. It seemed too dishonest a white-washing of the ugly side of the Arab business. Cape was miserable about it, so to comfort him I offered him the proceeds of serial publication with you. He countered with ideas of a limited subscription edition of the entire work, & I had provisionally accepted this, & was turning over the draft contract in my ruminant mind — when the new blow fell, & I wired to say that it was all over again. Since then I've been wandering about, rather address-less, but sooner or later I'll blow into Barton St, where Herbert Baker anyway will receive anything for me: so the *Seven Pillars* may well go there till I want them. You don't know any serious person who would like to buy one of the five copies of that inordinate work? Going very dear!

I hope that your eyes have refused to attempt the strain of its horrible print, & consequently that you haven't read it. If my marching order had come an hour earlier you wouldn't have been bothered.

What an unending nuisance being known is! I'm beginning to despair of ever getting away from my past.

Yours
T E Lawrence

University of Texas

H. W. BAILEY[1]

4.2.23   14 Barton Street Westminster

Dear Bailey

You must have given up hopes of me! But as a matter of fact, when that newspaper shriek about me came out, the Air Ministry got angry and gave me the sack, and I've been dodging about since after jobs.

My letters lay in a neglected heap at Farnborough for a long while, and were finally sent on to me by the Air Ministry. The idiot Press said that I'd enlisted in order to write a book about the War — but this was written three years ago and lies in a cupboard. The truth was that I was a little short of cash and still am, though things are looking better.

The address above will find me always (even if I go abroad in the near future as I expect), and I'd very much like to hear how you are and what you are doing. Please send me a line if you have time for it. Do you know by any chance, where Rolls, the tender-driver, is?[2]

I hear occasionally from most of the officers who were on our show, but

1 H.W. Bailey is listed in Appendix 1 of *Seven Pillars of Wisdom*, as being a member of the Machine Gun Corps in the Hejaz Armoured Car Company.

1 S.C. Rolls: see letter to him dated 10 June 1931 (p. 454).

very seldom from any of you; when we got to Damascus I hopped off like a scalded cat and swore that I'd never go back, so couldn't get any addresses. Lately they have been offering me command of armoured car units in Palestine; but I feel somehow that I don't want any more commissions.

It was very good of you to write to me.

Yours ever
J. H. Ross

People would bore me by calling me 'Colonel' Lawrence. So I changed it in 1920.

Marshall	The 'Doc' is British Minister to Hejaz. Lives at Jeddah.
Joyce	Is in Bagdad, military adviser to Feisal.
Goslett	Is in business in London.
Gilman	I last heard of married and an engineer in France.
Stirling	Is in Palestine.
Young	Is in the Colonial Office, London.
Kirkbride	Is in Palestine.
Junor	The flying man up at Azrak with us, was with me at Farnborough lately.
Wade and Dowsett	I haven't heard of for a long while.

Bodleian Reserve

VYVYAN RICHARDS
Thursday [early 1923]

The seal in which I bound the *S.P.* must have died of a surfeit of tomatoes. Isn't it a glorious colour.

I've been thinking over your letter: its praise is very welcome, because my feelings towards the *Seven Pillars* are mixed. Relatively it's a bad book, & gives me no pleasure. That's why your enjoyment of parts or elements of it gratifies me, as a sign that others can find in it something of what I failed to put into it in full measure. Positively I know that it's a good book: in the sense that it's better than most which have been written lately: but this only makes me yet sorrier that it isn't as good as my book should have been.

If you dig malevolently behind these last sentences you will realise that I have a tolerable opinion of myself. The criticisms of the book miss their aim in me, partly because I have made them all (& many others) in a far stronger sense, to myself: and the reason why the book isn't different is because my will-power to persevere with it failed. I don't know if it will return. A book dropped behind a man is so soon left behind.

Now for your points:—

You are intoxicated with the splendour of the story. That's as it should be. The story I have to tell is one of the most splendid ever given a man for writing.

Some things mar it for you. Please mark them marginally & I'll discuss them at leisure. You should not need so long to acquire my angle or need to acquire it at all.

Plain lapses. I can't have written hurtled. Wasn't it only hustled or something? and a misprint? Any way, please mark such points. In so long a book my head must sometimes have nodded.

Black marks on white paper. Deliberate, I'm afraid. We will discuss the fitness together.

Self-depreciation is a necessity with me.

More critic than artist. That's the analytic vein in me. Ineradicable. A critic in conscious creation is of course an artist. Ditto a blacksmith or a playwright. A critic is no more barred from creation than any other being. I'll say even that there's creative criticism: not literary nor artistic, but personal (biography) or ethical (Pater's *Imaginary Portraits*). To have an excess of creative over critical sense produces a Swinburne. To be excessively critical is to be like Rupert Brooke. The perfect artist is half-critic & half-creator.

Written history has never yet so nearly approached the unity of a work of art. Written history is inevitably long & must be judged by the standard of epic rather than lyric. The *Iliad* has only a fictitious unity. Gibbon at least as much. I suppose the *Peloponnesian War* has more unity than the average drama. Only perhaps you'd call it not true. I'll admit that modern history has seldom been 'composed' in the artistic sense. Trevelyan's Italian efforts perhaps. But modern history tries to be a science, not an art.

Your intelligence seems to limit instinctive experience before it is part of you. It at least tried to do this. I could have written a simple story, but only fraudulently, since by nature, & education & environment I'm complex. So I tried to make my reactions to experience as compound as they were in reality. I don't agree with your implied hint that simplicity is ethically better (when it would be false): or in any circumstances more artistic. A twice-swallowed oyster would be a double profit to the consumer.

The fine choice of adjective is a perpetual delight. I'm most glad of this, for I took great care with them: there's a fault or two however in every paragraph, but not other than I can correct in a week's care. These stylistic changes are easy & pleasant to make.

The purple passages even when they are meant to be purple. I suspect every purple passage is intentional. In my experience purple things are a conscious straining upward of the mind. Yes, too, it was & is very hard *to write about oneself* in action. I'm proposing to flatten off a good deal of the personal doing—and to eliminate (it comes easy) five out of six of the 'I's'. The book will gain in power by that much restraint. Already there's a lot, but I'm ambitious after power & want to knock my readers down with it.

Cut out all suggestions of self-depreciation. But I really do cut myself down, in all sincerity. I've been & am absurdly over-estimated. There are no supermen & I'm quite ordinary, & will say so whatever the artistic results. In that point I'm one of the few people who tell the truth about myself.

I might make it the perfect lyrical triumph. Yes but that was only the superficial aspect of the campaign, & it would be superficial to write it as a triumph. The word on my title page is ironic.[1]

The making of a great tragedy in its being not really my triumph. I tried to bring this out, just this side of egotism, as a second note running through the book after Chapter V, & increasing slowly towards the close. But it would be a fault in scale to represent the Arab Revolt mainly as a personal tragedy to me.

The stillness of absolute works of art. You admire these most. Which are they? Isn't it that you admire more than the category of history & biography, the category of whatever it is. I don't want to rack my head (in barrack room with the other 46 making a noise) to think of what they are. But honestly I doubt whether stillness is an 'absolute' element in works of supreme art. It seems to me a manner like another. My big books Rabelais, *Moby Dick, Karamazov*, leave their readers in a sweat. *Zarathustra* has his stillness. Of the poems there's no stillness in the *Cenci* (exhaustion rather) or in the *Oresteia*: or in *Lear*. Of the priests who serve one stands still, & eight move about & work for him: and there are religions full of movement. I think you are mistaking a preference for a principle.

There is a danger where one savours too much, of creating what one has found savoury in others. Have I done this? or do you suspect it too frequently? If so, please mark the spots.

I think Brooke's technique as good as Keats, but his sense of the taste of

---

1 *Seven Pillars* is sub-titled *A Triumph*.

words was less fine: and his native irony restrained him from the sugary-pictures of Keats. It restrained him too much, so that it was seldom musical: whereas Keats when his self-criticism held back from the sugar, had almost no likely fault to avoid. Art Creation is avoidance as much as it is presentation. And it's interesting to see Keats's growth in force (& decline in sweetness) from *Endymion* to *Hyperion*.

I agree that the *Seven Pillars* is too big for me: too big for most writers, I think. It's rather in the Titan class: books written at tiptoe, with a strain that dislocates the writer, & exhausts the reader out of sympathy. Such can't help being failures, because the graceful things are always those within our force: but as you conclude their cracks & imperfections serve an artistic end in themselves: a perfect-picture of a real man would be unreadable.

We ought to talk over the *S.P.* I'm coming up to London on Saturday next (2 p.m. in the hall of Charing Cross Underground probably). Your Sundays are busy, so you probably can't come: and perhaps I can't. If so I'll wire on Saturday saying No go. Don't bother to reply to this meanwhile. After Charing X I go on to Barton St. till about 7 p.m. If you come bring the book with you.

E.L.

Bodleian Reserve/University of Texas

Forbidden the Air Force, there was always the Army. Again Lawrence's connections in high places provided the solution to his dilemma. General Sir Philip Chetwode (later Field Marshal Chetwode) had commanded under Allenby and was now Adjutant-General to the Forces at the War Office. Apparently at the prompting of Colonel Alan Dawnay, close comrade of Lawrence in the last year of the war, Chetwode approached the Commandant of the Tank Corps, Colonel Sir Hugh Elles, who saw no difficulty in accepting Lawrence into his Training Centre at Bovington Camp, Dorset. Lawrence was allowed to enlist in the Tank Corps on a seven-year engagement, was given the number, rank and name of 7875698 Private T. E. Shaw and was posted to A Company of the Royal Tank Corps depot at Bovington with effect from 12 March 1923.

LIONEL CURTIS
19.3.23   [Bovington Camp]

Lorde

My mind moves me this morning to write you a whole series of letters, to be more splendid than the *Lettres de Mon Moulin*.[1] Nothing will come of it, but meanwhile this page grows blacker with the preliminaries.

What should the preliminaries be? A telling why I joined? As you know I don't know! Explaining it to Dawnay I said 'Mind-suicide': but that's only because I'm an incorrigible phraser. Do you, in reading my complete works, notice that tendency to do up small packets of words foppishly?

At the same time there's the reason why I have twice enlisted, in those same complete works: on my last night in Barton Street I read chapters 113 to 118, and saw implicit in them my late course. The months of politics with Winston were abnormal, and the R.A.F. and Army are natural. The Army (which I despise with all my mind) is more natural than the R.A.F.: for at Farnborough I grew suddenly on fire with the glory which the air should be, and set to work full steam to make the others vibrate to it like myself. I was winning too, when they chucked me out: indeed I rather suspect I was chucked out for that. It hurt the upper story that the ground-floor was grown too keen.

The Army seems safe against enthusiasm. It's a horrible life, and the other fellows fit it. I said to one 'They're the sort who instinctively fling stones at cats' ... and he said 'Why what do you throw?' You perceive that I'm not yet in the picture: but I will be in time. Seven years of this will make me impossible for anyone to suggest for a responsible position, and that self-degradation is my aim. I haven't the impulse and the conviction to fit what I know to be my power of moulding men and things: and so I always regret what I've created, when the leisure after creation lets me look back and see that the idea was secondhand.

This is a pompous start, and it should be a portentous series of letters: but there is excuse for it, since time moves slower here than elsewhere: and a man has only himself to think about. At reveille I feel like Adam, after a

---

1 Lawrence's letters to Lionel Curtis between March and June 1923 are among the most powerful that he ever wrote. See Introduction to this section (p. 207) and Lawrence's letter to Charlotte Shaw dated 18 August 1927 (p. 344) in which he wrote: 'When Graves [researching for Lawrence's biography] asked me about letters I told him that only you (for the recent period) and Lionel Curtis (for the Tank Corps period) held anything illuminating. Curtis' letters are essays in misery, for I felt like Lucifer just after his forced landing, at that stage of my career.' For Lionel Curtis see note to letter to G. J. Kidston dated 14 November 1919. *Lettres de mon moulin*, a book of sketches of life in Provence, is one of the most famous works of the nineteenth-century French writer Alphonse Daudet.

night's pondering: and my mind has malice enough rather to enjoy putting Adam through it.

Don't take seriously what I wrote about the other men, above. It's only at first that certain sides of them strike a little crudely. In time I'll join, concerning them, in Blake's astonishing cry 'Everything that is, is holy!' It seems to me one of the best words ever said. Philip Kerr[1] would agree with it (one of the engaging things about Philip is his agreement with my absence), but not many other reflective men come to the same conclusion without a web of mysticism to help them.

I'm not sure either that what I've said about my creations is quite true. I feel confident that Arabia and Trans-Jordan and Mesopotamia, *with what they will breed*, are nearly monumental enough for the seven years' labour of one head: because I knew what I was at, and the others only worked on instinct: and my other creation, that odd and interminable book ... do you know I'm absolutely hungry to know what people think of it—not when they are telling me, but what they tell to one another. Should I be in this secret case if I really thought it pernicious?

There again, perhaps there's a solution to be found in multiple personality. It's my reason which condemns the book and the revolt, and the new nationalities: because the only rational conclusion to human argument is pessimism such as Hardy's, a pessimism which is very much like the wintry heath, of bog and withered plants and stripped trees, about us. Our camp on its swelling in this desolation feels pustular, and we (all brown-bodied, with yellow spots down our front belly-line), must seem like the swarming germs of its fermentation. That's feeling, exterior-bred feeling, with reason harmonising it into a picture: but there's a deeper sense which remembers other landscapes, and the changes which summer will bring to this one: and to that sense nothing can be changeless: whereas the rational preference or advantage of pessimism is its finality, the eternity in which it ends: and if there isn't an eternity there cannot be a pessimism pure.

Lorde what a fog of words! What I would say is that reason proves there is no hope, and we therefore hope on, so to speak, on one leg of our minds: a dot and go one progress, which takes me Tuesday Thursday and Saturday and leaves me authentic on the other days. Quelle vie.

DG/All Souls College Oxford

1 Sir Philip Kerr (1882–1940), later 11th Marquess of Lothian. He was a friend of Lionel Curtis, with whom he had worked in South Africa after the Boer War in what became known as Milner's 'Kindergarten', i.e. the group of young admirers assisting Lord Milner when the latter was Governor of the Transvaal and the Orange Colony. Ambassador to the U.S.A. 1939–40.

ROBERT GRAVES
20.3.23   14 Barton Street

Dear R.G.

I've been some while wanting to write, & your note (which came to hand yesterday) is the last straw to weigh down my mind.

Sorry to have missed you in London: but my movings have been eccentric of late. The R.A.F. threw me out, eventually. Crime of too great publicity. Stainless character. I took the latter to the W.O. and persuaded them to let me enlist with them. So I'm now a recruit in the Tank Corps. Conditions tough, companions rough, self becoming rough too. However there is a certainty and a contentment in bed-rock.

I wanted to ask you ... we are near Dorchester, & I run about Dorset on wheels (when they take their eyes off us) ... do you think old Hardy would let me look at him? He's a proper poet & a fair novelist, in my judgment, & it would give me a feeling of another mile-stone passed if I might meet him. Yet to blow in upon him in khaki would not be an introduction. You know the old thing, don't you? What are my hopes?[1]

Youuurs
T.E.?[2]

University of Harvard/RGB

A. E. (JOCK) CHAMBERS[3]
21.3.23   [Bovington Camp]

[...] I liked B.iii and the R.A.F. and this army life feels very drab in comparison. Also you know we really were a decent crowd: and the present lot with me are the sort who'd always throw something at any cat they saw. It's a moral difference, I feel, and unless I can get over it I'll find myself solitary again.

1 Graves duly wrote to Thomas Hardy on Lawrence's behalf, and the latter soon became a favourite visitor at Hardy's Dorchester home, Max Gate.
2 I have followed Graves's transcription 'T.E.?', but the original signature is an almost indecipherable scrawl of which the first letter looks rather more like R than T, as though he had begun to write 'Ross' or, more simply, 'R' (as for example in his letter to Lionel Curtis on the following day), and then realised that this was not a formula he had used when writing to Graves. His letters to Graves were usually signed 'E. L.' or 'L.'
3 Jock Chambers had been the orderly of Lawrence's hut — B3 — at Farnborough, where the two men had soon become close friends. He had served in the Navy and the Army before joining the Air Force. He contributed to *T. E. Lawrence by His Friends* and remained a lifelong admirer and disciple, defending him against all detractors.

The camp is beautifully put — a wide heath, of flint & sand, with pines & oak-trees, & much rhododendron coming slowly into bloom. When the heather flowers in a few weeks there will be enough to please me.

One of my sorrows is the recruits' course (new name, naturally, new age, no previous service) & a consequent imprisonment in the camp for a month, being damnably shouted at.

[...]

Regard me to B3. My only present likeness to it is another corner bed!

Yours
R.

DG

R. A. M. GUY[1]

21.3.23   Bovington Camp

My rabbit

I do no good here. Out upon the army & all its clothes and food & words and works. You in the R. A. F. are as lucky as I thought myself in the old days, & as I used to tell you.

They give us great leisure. Five hours work a day on Monday and Thursday. Tuesday is an afternoon for sports. Wednesday is a half-day. On Friday our work is drawing pay, & wondering afterwards why they, out of all the possible payments in the world, should have given us just that little or that much. Saturday, needless to say, is Saturday: and Sunday is Sunday.

I'm going to dazzle you, if ever I see you again, with the perfection of my salute: while at slow marching! I march slower and slower: the whole camp agrees that my slow marching is slow. Though some idiots this afternoon were arguing as to whether it was marching. God help them, they are fools, & myself the solitary wise man in Dorset.

'Easter leave' did you say, in your exquisite letter? I get none. They dazzle us with the prospect of eight days' leave in August: — but to win that we must have done eighteen weeks upon the square, & must have reached, as a squad, the standard of finished squads. Horrors & horrors piled upon one another! Thanks be to God that I require no leave. Only, rabbit, I'm sorry, since that summer holiday in Oxford would have been perhaps a pleasure to you. There are no rabbits here (or at least no imitation ones)

1 Robert (Bob) Guy was a young Aircraftman with whom Lawrence developed an especially close friendship. See particularly his letter to Guy written on Christmas Day 1923 (p. 253).

and it would give me contentment to see your queer but jolly face again. There are men from Brum, but their accent isn't like yours (except when they miss an h) and their wishes are ordinary.

My attack upon you in the last letter was presumably a bad joke. I envy everyone who doesn't think continually.

Brough[1] is in London, & myself confined to camp.

R.

Tell Jock that soldiers are men like Jimmy Carr, & that I can't do the weight. I might sham A.C.II-ship, but this is too difficult.

I wasn't in Farnborough on Monday. Depot.

Bodleian Reserve

MRS THOMAS HARDY[2]

25.3.23   [Bovington Camp]

Dear Mrs. Hardy

A letter from Robert Graves (to whom I had written) tells me that I'm to get into communication with you. It feels rather barefaced, because I haven't any qualifications to justify my seeing Mr. Hardy: only I'd very much like to. *The Dynasts* & the other poems are so wholly good to my taste.

It adds to my hesitation that I'm a private in the Tank Corps, at Wool, and would have to come across in uniform. You may have feelings against soldiers. Also I'm therefore not master of my own time. They let us off on Wednesdays, Saturdays, and Sundays at noon: and I have a motor cycle so that getting over to Dorchester is only a matter of minutes. I must be in camp again at 9.30 p.m: but between that & noon on any one of those three days for the next three months I should be free, if you are good enough to offer me a time.

---

1 i.e. his motor-cycle: see p. 252n.
2 Florence Hardy, née Dugdale (1879–1937), was Thomas Hardy's second wife; they had married in 1914, two years after his first wife's death. She had met Hardy in 1907 when she volunteered to help him with the checking and revision of his verse-drama *The Dynasts*. Lawrence's relationship with the Hardys was to become not dissimilar to that with the Shaws — in each case he was seen to some extent as a kind of surrogate son. In each case too Lawrence's correspondent was the wife, not the husband. Lawrence invited himself through Graves into the Hardy home (Max Gate on the edge of Dorchester) but this was not seen in any way as an imposition. Both the Hardys became very fond of Lawrence, who also gained the reputation of being one of the few visitors to Max Gate who could cope with their terrifying dog Wessex.

The deepest apologies. I'm suggesting that you take a great deal of quite unwarrantable trouble.

Yours sincerely
T E Lawrence

In case you like R. G. enough to reply, please address me
        7875698 Pte T. E. Shaw   Hut F12   B Company   1st Depot
            Battalion   Tank Corps   Bovington Camp   Wool
I dropped the 'Lawrence' part of me six months ago.

Bodleian Reserve

LIONEL CURTIS
27.3.23   [Bovington Camp]

It seems to continue itself today, because I've been wondering about the other fellows in the hut. A main feeling they give me is of difference from the R.A.F. men. They were excited about our coming service. We talked and wondered of the future, almost exclusively. There was a constant recourse to imagination, and a constant rewarding of ourselves therefore. The fellows were decent, but so wrought up by hope that they were carried out of themselves, and I could not see them mattly. There was a sparkle round the squad.

Here every man has joined because he was down and out: and no one talks of the Army or of promotion, or of trades and accomplishments. We are all here unavoidably, in a last resort, and we assume this world's failure in one-another, so that pretence would not be merely laughed at, but as near an impossibility as anything human. We are social bed-rock, those unfit for life-by-competition: and each of us values the rest as cheap as he knows himself to be.

I suspect that this low estimation is very much the truth. There cannot be classes in England much more raw, more free of all that the upbringing of a lifetime has plastered over you and me. Can there be profit, or truth, in all these modes and sciences and arts of ours? The leisured world for hundreds, or perhaps thousands of years has been jealously working and recording the advance of each generation for the starting-point of the next — and here these masses are as animal, as carnal as were their ancestors before Plato and Christ and Shelley and Dostoevsky taught and thought. In this crowd it's made startlingly clear how short is the range of knowledge, and what poor conductors of it ordinary humans are. You and I know:

you have tried (Round Tabling[1] and by mouth) to tell all whom you can reach: and the end is here, a cimmerian darkness with bog-lights flitting wrongly through its gas.

The pity of it is, that you've got to take this black core of things in camp, this animality, on trust. It's a feeling, a spirit which colours every word and action, and I believe every thought, passing in Hut 12. Your mind is like a many-storied building, and you, its sole tenant, flit from floor to floor, from room to room, at the whim of your spirit's moment. (Not that the spirit has moments, but let it pass for the metaphor's sake). At will you can be gross, and enjoy coffee or a sardine, or rarefy yourself till the diaphancité [sic] of pure mathematics, or of a fluent design in line, is enough to feed you. Here—

I can't write it, because in literature such things haven't ever been, and can't be. To record the acts of Hut 12 would produce a moral-medical case-book, not a work of art but a document. It isn't the filth of it which hurts me, because you can't call filthy the pursuit of a bitch by a dog, or the mating of birds in springtime; and it's man's misfortune that he hasn't a mating season, but spreads his emotions and excitements through the year ... but I lie in bed night after night with this cat-calling carnality seething up and down the hut, fed by streams of fresh matter from twenty lecherous mouths ... and my mind aches with the rawness of it, knowing that it will cease only when the slow bugle calls for 'lights out' an hour or so hence ... and the waiting is so slow....

However the call comes always in the end, and suddenly at last, like God's providence, a dewfall of peace upon the camp ... but surely the world would be more clean if we were dead or mindless? We are all guilty alike, you know. You wouldn't exist, I wouldn't exist, without this carnality. Everything with flesh in its mixture is the achievement of a moment when the lusty thought of Hut 12 has passed to action and conceived: and isn't it true that the fault of birth rests somewhat on the child? I believe it's we who led our parents on to bear us, and it's our unborn children who make our flesh itch.

A filthy business all of it, and yet Hut 12 shows me the truth behind Freud. Sex is an integer in all of us, and the nearer nature we are, the more constantly, the more completely a product of that integer. These fellows are the reality, and you and I, the selves who used to meet in London and talk of fleshless things, are only the outward wrappings of a core like these fellows. They let light and air play always upon their selves, and consequently have grown very lustily, but have at the same time achieved health and strength in their growing. Whereas our wrappings and bandages

---

1 Lionel Curtis was Editor of *The Round Table*, a quarterly review of the politics of the British Commonwealth.

have stunted and deformed ourselves, and hardened them to an apparent insensitiveness ... but it's a callousness, a crippling, only to be yea-said by aesthetes who prefer clothes to bodies, surfaces to intentions.

These fellows have roots, which in us are rudimentary, or long cut off. Before I came I never visualised England except as an organism, an entity ... but these fellows are local, territorial. They all use dialects, and could be placed by their dialects, if necessary. However it isn't necessary, because each talks of his district, praises it, boasts of it, lives in the memory of it. We call each other 'Brum' or 'Coventry' or 'Cambridge', and the man who hasn't a 'place' is an outsider. They wrangle and fight over the virtues of their homes. Of solidarity, of a nation, of something ideal comprehending their familiar streets in itself — they haven't a notion.

Well, the conclusion of the first letter was that man, being a civil war, could not be harmonised or made logically whole ... and the end of this is that man, or mankind, being organic, a natural growth, is unteachable: cannot depart from his first grain and colour, nor exceed flesh, nor put forth anything not mortal and fleshly.

I fear not even my absence would reconcile Ph.K.[1] to this.

                                                                E.L.

DG/All Souls College Oxford

COLONEL A. P. WAVELL[2]

11.V.23   [Bovington Camp]

Dear Wavell

Many thanks for your letter: it pleased me, for though (as of a son) I can see and say no good of my book, yet I'm glad when others praise it. I hate it & like it by turns, & know that it's a good bit of writing, and often wish it wasn't. If I'd aimed less high I'd have hit my mark squarer, & made a better little thing of it. As it stands it's a great failure (lacking architecture, the balance of parts, coherence, stream-lining): and oddly enough among my favourite books are the other great failures — *Moby Dick*, *Also sprach Zarathustra*, *Pantagruel*, — books where the authors went up like a shoot of

1 Ph.K.: Philip Kerr (see note to letter of 19 March 1923, p. 228).
2 Colonel A.P. Wavell, later Field Marshal Earl Wavell of Cyrenaica (1883–1950), had been Chief of Staff of XXth Corps in Allenby's Palestine and Syria campaigns and was at this time Assistant Adjutant-General at the War Office. He and Lawrence had met in December 1917 on the occasion of the official entry into Jerusalem. See his contribution to *T.E. Lawrence by His Friends*, with its keynote statement: 'He [Lawrence] will always have his detractors. . . . They knew not the man.'

rockets, and burst.[1] I don't mean to put mine into that degree of the class: but it is to me as *Zarathustra* was to Nietzsche, something bigger than I could do.

Apart from literature, how does it strike you as history? It's hard to see another man's campaign—but you s̶a̶y̶ saw as much of mine as I saw of yours ... does my record of mine stand up, so to speak, upon its military feet? I've never posed as a soldier, & feel that the campaign side of the book may be technically weak. That's why I was glad you asked to read it, because I hope you'll have an opinion (critical not laudatory) on your professional side. Bartholomew made no comment. That's the worst of writing too long a book ... it gets beyond criticism, by being too r̶i̶c̶h̶ abounding in weak & strong points. Keep it a little longer if you wish, but not too long please, for a friend of mine (who wants it eagerly), has been waiting quite a while for a spare copy. Another fault of a long book: it circulates so slowly. There are only six copies, & three of them are on permanent loan to Hogarth, Alan Dawnay, & Kennington, the artist, who did some forty or fifty drawings of its contents for me. As for holding it private—well I've suffered more than I can bear of public discussion & praise, & the insufficiency & obliquity of it are like a nightmare of memory. To publish the whole book might cause a new clamour, for I don't hide from myself that it might be a successful book, as sales went. To censor it would mean practical re-writing, & I'm weary of the work put into it already: also it feels a little dishonest to hide parts of the truth. Further I remind myself that the feelings of some English, some French & some Arabs might be hurt by some of the things I tell of. Against these f̶e̶e̶l̶i̶n̶g̶s̶ instincts you have to set the vanity of an amateur who's tried to write, & would like to be in print as an author: and my need of money to live quietly upon. It's a nice calculation, with the balance just against, & so I bury all my talents!

When you have finished with it will you post it me? I'm now

> Pte. T. E. Shaw. 7875698
> Hut F. 12
> B. Coy.
> > 1st Depot Batt. Tank Corps
> > Bovington Camp
> > Wool
> > Dorset.

A horribly long address I'm afraid, but not my fault, though the coming here was: however I was decided not to touch politics again, & my untrained hands & wits failed to earn me a certain living: so after the R.A.F. chucked

---

1 *Moby Dick* was by Herman Melville, *Also sprach Zarathustra* was by Friedrich Wilhelm Nietzsche, *Pantagruel* was by François Rabelais.

me out I got Chetwode to let me into the army, where the work is so little
& so dull that all my mind's time is my own. Of course it gives me no
chance of coming to London. Don't tell people.

Yours ever
T.E.L.

Bodleian Reserve

LIONEL CURTIS

14.V.23   Tanktown

I should have written before, but a split thumb, and the sudden discovery
of the authorities that I belonged to a criminal class, have put me out of
the mood for subjective writing:— and since politics passed out of me the
only theme between us is myself.

There was one injustice in your letter. My crying-out here was not at
the foul talk. To me it's meaningless, unobjectionable, on a par with heedless
fair-talk. The R.A.F. was foul-mouthed, and the cleanest little mob of
fellows. These are foul-mouthed, and behind their mouths is a pervading
animality of spirit, whose unmixed bestiality frightens me and hurts me.
There is no criticism, indeed it's taken for granted as natural, that you
should job a woman's body, or hire out yourself, or abuse yourself in any
way. I cried out against it, partly in self-pity because I've condemned myself
to grow like them, and partly in premonition of failure, for my masochism
remains and will remain, only moral. Physically I can't do it: indeed I get
in denial the gratification they get in indulgence. I react against their
example into an abstention even more rigorous than of old. Everything
bodily is now hateful to me (and in my case hateful is the same as impossible).
In the sports lately (they vex us with set exercises) I was put down to jump,
and refused because it was an activity of the flesh. Afterwards to myself I
wondered if that was the reason, or was I afraid of failing ridiculously: so
I went down alone and privily cleared over twenty feet, and was sick of
mind at having tried because I was glad to find I still could jump. It's on a
par with the music for which I'm hungry. Henry Lamb[1] is in Poole, and
will play wonderfully to me if I go over: and I won't go, though I'm so
starved for rhythm that even a soldier's stumbling through a song on the
piano makes my blood run smooth (I refuse to hear it with my head).

This sort of thing must be madness, and sometimes I wonder how far
mad I am, and if a mad-house would not be my next (and merciful) stage.

---

1 Henry Lamb (1883–1960): artist, associate of the Bloomsbury group.

Merciful compared with this place, which hurts me, body and soul. It's terrible to hold myself voluntarily here: and yet I want to stay here till it no longer hurts me: till the burnt child no longer feels the fire. Do you think there have been many lay monks of my persuasion? One used to think that such frames of mind would have perished with the age of religion: and yet here they rise up, purely secular. It's a lurid flash into the Nitrian desert: seems almost to strip the sainthood from Anthony. How about Teresa?

I consume the day (and myself) brooding, and making phrases and reading and thinking again, galloping mentally down twenty divergent roads at once, as apart and alone as in Barton Street in my attic. I sleep less than ever, for the quietness of night imposes thinking on me: I eat breakfast only, and refuse every possible distraction and employment and exercise. When my mood gets too hot and I find myself wandering beyond control I pull out my motor-bike and hurl it top-speed through these unfit roads for hour after hour. My nerves are jaded and gone near dead, so that nothing less than hours of voluntary danger will prick them into life: and the 'life' they reach then is a melancholy joy at risking something worth exactly 2/9 a day.

It's odd, again, that craving for real risk: because in the gymnasium I funk jumping the horse, more than poison. That is physical, which is why it is: I'm ashamed of doing it and of not doing it, unwilling to do it: and most of all ashamed (afraid) of doing it well.

A nice, neurotic letter! What you've done to deserve its receipt God knows . . . perhaps you have listened to me too friendly-like at earlier times. Sorry, and all that. You are a kind of safety-valve perhaps. I wish you were an alienist, and could tell me where or how this ferment will end. It makes me miserable on top of all the curiosity and determination: and sets me so much aside that I hardly blame the powers for jumping on me with their dull punishments.

                                                                    L.

DG/All Souls College Oxford

MRS THOMAS HARDY
21.V.23

Dear Mrs. Hardy

I'm afraid I'll come on Saturday next at tea-time! De la Mare is known to me only by his books — but he should be delightful, if he lives up to them:[1] and most good people are better than their books.

It sounds greedy, always to come when you ask me: but your house is so wonderfully unlike this noisy room that it is difficult to resist, even for its own sake: and then there is Mr. Hardy, though you mustn't tell him so, for the thrill is too one-sided. He has seen so much of human-kind that he must be very tired of them: whereas for me he's Hardy, & I'd go a long way even to see the place where he had lived, let alone him living in it.

There, you will think me absurd: but still I'll arrive on Saturday!

Yours sincerely
T E Shaw

DG

COLONEL A. P. WAVELL

21.V.23   [Bovington Camp]

Dear Wavell

Many thanks for the book (which has gone forward to its next) and for your long letter. It's exactly the sort of thing which I wanted to read.

No, I don't feel confident militarily. All the while we fought I felt like a conjuror trying an insufficiently-rehearsed trick — surprised when it came out right. A succession of such chances gave me the feeling I was apt at the business: that's all.

[...]

As for the reply to raiding tactics. As you say, it's greater mobility than the attack. This needn't mean large drafts from the harassed G.O.C. If the Turks had put machine guns on three or four of their touring cars, & driven them on weekly patrol over the admirable going of the desert E. of Amman & Maan they would have put an absolute stop to our camel-parties, & so to our rebellion. It wouldn't have cost them 20 men or £20,000 ... *rightly applied*. They scraped up cavalry & armoured trains & camel corps & block-houses against us: because they didn't think hard enough.

[...]

There is one other thing of which every rebellion is mortally afraid — treachery. If instead of counter-propaganda (never effective on the con-servative side) the money had been put into buying the few venial men always to be found in a big movement, then they would have crippled us.

---

1 The poet and story-writer Walter de la Mare (1873–1956) was by this time well into the literary career which would bring him such honours as the C. H. (Companion of Honour), the O. M. (Order of Merit) and burial in St Paul's Cathedral.

We could only dare these intricate raids because we felt sure and safe. One well-informed traitor will spoil a national rising.

Bombing tribes is ineffective. I fancy that air-power may be effective against elaborate armies: but against irregulars it has no more than moral value. The Turks had plenty [of] machines, & used them freely against us — and never hurt us till the last phase, when we had brought 1000 of our regulars on the raid against Deraa. Guerrilla tactics are a complete muffing of air-force.

[…]

.L.

DG

LIONEL CURTIS
30.V.23

[…] You say my friends feel the absence of me — but personality (which it is my gift to you to exhibit) is of a short range, and in my experience has not touched more than ten or twelve friends at a time: and here I live with twenty very barren men, who feel my being with them. The hut is changed from what it used to be, and unlike what it would be (will be?) if I left. This isn't conceit, but a plain statement; for there would be a change if any one of us twenty was taken away: and I am richer and wider and more experienced than any of the others here. More of the world has passed over me in my 35 years than over all their twenties put together: and your gain, if you did gain by my return, would be their loss. It seems to me that the environment does not matter. Your circle does not draw from me (except superficially) more than theirs: indeed perhaps caenobite man influences as much as man social, for example is eternal, and the rings of its extending influence infinite.

For myself there are consolations. The perfect beauty of this place becomes tremendous, by its contrast with the life we lead, and the squalid huts we live in, and the noisy bullying authority of all our daily unloveliness. The nearly intolerable meanness of man is set in a circle of quiet heath, and budding trees, with the firm level bar of the Purbeck hills behind. The two worlds shout their difference in my ears. Then there is the irresponsibility: I have to answer here only for my cleanness of skin, cleanness of clothes, and a certain mechanical neatness of physical evolution upon the barrack-square. There has not been presented to me, since I have been here, a single choice: everything is ordained — except that harrowing choice of going away from here the moment my will to stay breaks down. With this exception it would be determinism complete — and perhaps in determinism complete there lies the perfect peace I have so longed for. Free-will I've tried, and rejected: authority I've rejected (not obedience, for that is my present effort, to find equality only in subordination. It is dominion whose taste I have been cloyed with): action I've rejected: and the intellectual life: and the receptive senses: and the battle of wits. They were all failures, and my reason tells me therefore that obedience, nescience, will also fail, since the roots of common failure must lie in myself — and yet in spite of reason I am trying it.

[...]

DG

ERIC KENNINGTON
27.VI.23   [Bovington Camp]

Dear Kennington

I'm a worm, a peccant worm: should have written months ago.

[...]

I'm very glad you are helping Roberts. He makes help difficult sometimes, and yet I feel that I would like the oyster if I had any tool strong enough to pry it open. Tell me some time what you think of his considered effort at me. He painted with astonishing certainty: not like John who put a new expression in [my] eyes and mouth on each sitting: but as though there was a fixity in my appearance and mood.[1]

Do I go further now? No, I don't think there is anything more to say. The army is loathsome: Dorsetshire beautiful: the work very light. So I can carry on here.

[...]

T.E.

Bodleian Reserve

1 Roberts's portrait of Lawrence — done in 1922 in oils and depicting him in Air Force uniform — is now in the possession of the Ashmolean Museum, Oxford.

LIONEL CURTIS
27.VI.22 [really 23]

Old thing, This correspondence nearly died: might have died if you had not asked whether I did not join for the sake of the others here. Of course I didn't: things are done in answer to a private urge — not one of altruism.

You've been talking to Hogarth about my discomfort in the Tank Corps: but you know I joined partly to make myself unemployable, or rather impossible, in my old trade: and the burning out of freewill and self-respect and delicacy from a nature as violent as mine is bound to hurt a bit. If I was firmer I wouldn't cry about it.

It isn't all misery here either. There is the famous motor-bike as a temporary escape. Last Sunday was fine, and another day-slave and myself went off with it after church-parade. Wells we got to, and very beautiful it was:— a grey sober town, stiffly built of prim houses, but with nothing of the artificial in it. Everything is used and lived in; and to make the xvth century habitable today they have put in sash-windows everywhere.

One 'close', the Vicar's close, was nearly the best, it was so cloistered off (even from its quietest of streets): and so grey and green: for the local limestone has turned very sad with time, and has crannied, so that its angles are living with flowers of many sorts: and each of the 'cells' in this close has a little grass-plot between it and the common path down the centre: and on these plots poppies stood in groups like women at a garden party. There was sunshine over it, and a still air, so that all the essence of the place was drawn out and condensed about our heads. It was a college-like place, and looked good to live in: so for a while the camp waiting here for me became an ungrateful thought. Hogarth had written, hoping to get me back into the R.A.F. and the prospect of such happiness had made the Army nearly intolerable. However that's over, easily, for I was only hoping against the knowledge that it wouldn't be possible.

Afterwards I trailed into the cathedral precinct, and lay there on the grass, and watched its huge west front, covered over with bad sculpture, but very correct and proper still, in the manner of the town. There is a remoteness about cathedrals now-a-days—: they are things I could not contribute to, if they were still a-building: and in front of Wells today there was a white-frocked child playing with a ball; the child was quite unconscious of the cathedral (feeling only the pleasure of smooth grass) but from my distance she was so small that she looked no more than a tumbling daisy at the tower-foot: I knew of course that she was animal: and I began in my hatred of animals to balance her against the cathedral: and knew then that I'd destroy the building to save her. That's as irrational as what happened on our coming here, when I swerved Snowy Wallis and myself at 60 m.p.h. on to the grass by the roadside, trying vainly to save a bird which dashed out its life against my side-car. And yet had the world been mine I'd have left out animal life upon it.

An old thing (it pleased me to call him Canon) doddered over and sat by me on the grass, and gave me a penny for my thoughts: and I told him (reading Huysmans[1] lately) that I was pondering over the contrasts of English and French cathedrals. Ours set in closes so tree-bound and stately and primly-kept that they serve as a narthex to the shrine: a narthex at Wells grander and more religious than the building proper. Whereas French cathedrals have their feet in market places, and booths and chimneys and placards and noise hem them in: so that in France you step from your workshop into the aisle, and in England you cannot even enter till the lawns have swept the street-dust from your feet. The old clergyman gave me another penny to read him the riddle and I did it crab-wise, by a quote from du Bellay,[2] and that Christchurch poem about Our Sovereign Lord the King.[3] He was a book-worm too, and we talked Verhaeren and Melville and Lucretius[4] together, with great pleasure on my part, and the vulgar relish that I was making a cockshy of his assurance that khaki covered nothing but primitive instincts.

He took me round the bishop's palace-garden, pumping me to learn how I endured camp life (living promiscuous seemed to his imagination horrible, and he by profession a shepherd of sheep!), and I hinted at the value of contrast which made all Wells crying-precious to me: and then we leaned over the wall and saw the fish in the moat, and it came upon me very hardly how excellent was their life. Fish are free of mankind you know, and are always perfectly suspended, without ache or activity of nerves, in their sheltering element.

We can get it, of course, when we earth-in our bodies, but it seems to me that we can only do that when they are worn out. It's a failure to kill them out of misery, for if there isn't any good or evil but only activity, and no pain or joy, only sensation: then we can't kill ourselves while we can yet feel. However I'd rather be the fish (did you ever read Rupert Brooke's 'And there shall be no earth in heaven', said fish' [sic])[5]

---

1 Joris Karl Huysmans was the author of an epic work on Chartres called *La Cathédrale* (1898); earlier he had won a reputation as a 'decadent' novelist and as such had exercised an important influence on Oscar Wilde.

2 Joachim du Bellay: 16th-century French poet.

3 A reference to the anonymous poem *Preparations* ('Yet if His Majesty, our sovereign lord ...'), found in a manuscript of Christ Church, Oxford, and printed in the *Oxford Book of English Verse*.

4 Emile Verhaeren, Belgian poet who published, in French, between 1883 and 1911; Herman Melville, American poet and novelist and author of one of Lawrence's favourite works *Moby Dick*; Lucretius, Roman poet and philosopher of the 1st century BC.

5 A reference to the last two lines of Rupert Brooke's *Heaven*: 'And in that Heaven of all their wish, There shall be no more land, say fish.'

or the little bird which had killed itself against me that morning.
   There, my letters always end in tears!

E.

DG/All Souls College Oxford

EDMUND BLUNDEN[1]
17.VII.23[2]

Dear Blunden
   It's a mirage, of course. I wrote my beastly thing in 1919: & by 1921 had
summoned up enough courage to print it (in an edition of six copies, run
off on an Oxford newspaper press). That is as far as it has gone, except that
something like a dozen people have read it. I have no intention of publishing
it: there has been far too much talk already. That poor purblind Lowell
Thomas creature imagined by talking that he was doing me no harm (and
making his fortune). The second possibility forced me to let him continue:
and he drove me out of sight, that I might avoid the disgust of being the
vulgar creature of his invention. Then I lost what little money I ever had,
& cut the two knots together by enlisting under another name. The Army
is not a rose-bed, but at any rate one is obscure in it: & here I propose to
stay.
   These details aren't for publication: but they will inform your discretion
of what to say if there is more chat. My respect for your work (and regret
that its excessive goodness drives you into shifts to earn food) is the cause
of my writing to you.

Yours sincerely
T E Lawrence

Lowell Thomas' story is a myth, built up on a very small foundation of
official information, & padded with gossip. He came out to Egypt on a
semi-official mission, & was allowed to see & hear things.

.L.

University of Texas

1 Edmund Blunden (1896–1974): poet, biographer and later, professor, both in Tokyo and
   Oxford. His reputation depended at this stage largely on his early volumes of poetry; his
   most famous work, *Undertones of War*, a distillation of his experiences as a trench-officer
   on the Western Front in the First World War, was to appear in 1928.
2 Lawrence actually dated this letter '17.VII.22', but the reference to his being in the Army
   makes clear that this is a mistake.

A. E. (JOCK) CHAMBERS
17.IX.23   [Bovington Camp]

Dear Jock
    [...] I'm no writer: can't write: wish I could see you: am home-sick
for the R.A.F. The army is more beastly than anything else which the wit
of man has made. Only of course it wasn't his wit that made it: it came
suddenly from him at midnight one moonless time, when he was taken
short.
    God be merciful to us sinners.

                                                                  R.

Bodleian Reserve

R A. M. GUY
17.IX.23

Rabbit, son
    It's true I don't write: can't write: am suffering from dryness of the brain
& decay of the natural affections: but I'm in the Army as a penance to kill
old Adam: so the more I neglect duties the deeper my satisfaction at my
increasing beastliness.
    They have stopped chasing me. I exist only for fatigues, which I perform
with a dull thoroughness; hardly Brough at all (it rusts in a shed): write
nothing of my own: but have translated two French novels lately, for gold.[1]
    Gold means paper. The second one, just finished, was done on your
account, for I had the ambition to send you a trifle for your birthday. My
pleasure in the R.A.F. was partly, largely, due to the pleasure I got from
your blue & yellow self: and I owe you a deep debt for many happy times.
    Now you tell me Birmingham is not going well, so I'm sending it
enclosed in this, hoping that you won't take offence. I made it in less than
a month, so that it is no great gift which I offer you.
    I wish we could meet again: though every R.A.F. uniform I see makes
me heart-sick.

                                                                  R.

University of Harvard

1 The translation he was completing at this time was that of the fairy story *Le Gigantesque*
  by Adrien le Corbeau, which was published by Cape the following year under the title
  The Forest Giant. He refers to two novels, however, presumably because he had agreed
  in the first instance to translate Mardrus's *Arabian Nights*, but another publisher had
  announced a forthcoming translation, with the result that the project had been abandoned.

ROBIN BUXTON[1]
22.IX.23

Dear Robin,

Glad you are reading the thing. Please don't inhibit yourself from scribbling comments of an insulting sort in the margins, made especially wide for the purpose. Your praise makes my stomach warm: but your criticisms are really helpful: whether in the field of morality, belles-lettres, tactics, or just manners. Down with them while you can!

The 'Seven Pillars of Wisdom' is a quotation from *Proverbs:*[2] it is used as title out of sentiment: for I wrote a youthful indiscretionary book, so called, in 1913 and burned it (as immature) in '14 when I enlisted. It recounted adventures in seven type-cities of the East (Cairo, Bagdad, Damascus etc) & arranged their characters into a descending cadence: a moral symphony. It was a queer book, upon whose difficulties I look back with a not ungrateful wryness: and in memory of it I named the new book, which will probably be the only one I ever write, & which sums up & exhausts me to the date of 1919.

S.A. was a person, now dead, regard for whom lay beneath my regard for the Arabic peoples. I don't propose to go into further detail thereupon.[3]

[...]

Have you read my account of the I.C.C. march? Please say honestly what parts of it, or of its tone, hurt your feelings. I was wrapped up in my burden in Arabia, & saw things only through its distorting prism: & so did third parties wrong. It wasn't meant: just the inevitable distraction of a commander whose spirit was at civil war within himself.

DG

---

1 Major Robin Buxton had commanded the two companies of the Imperial Camel Corps (the I.C.C. of the final paragraph) which had carried out a special mission in the desert in association with Lawrence in August 1918. He was now a banker with Martins Bank and Lawrence's financial adviser.
2 Proverbs 9, 1: 'Wisdom hath builded a house: she hath hewn out her seven pillars.'
3 See the dedicatory poem 'To S. A.' at the beginning of *Seven Pillars*.

LORD WINTERTON[1]
27.X.23   [Bovington Camp]

Dear Winterton

Sorry to have appeared to make mysteries: I didn't mean it: it's only that I'm not again returning to decent life, & feel a little less than proud of myself & my state. My constant address (as Lawrence — did you know that wasn't my real name?) is at 14 Barton St. Westminster, the house of Herbert Baker, one of the Delhi architects, & a supremely decent person. I used to live there, & his Staff still send my stuff on.

If you want to write to me directly you will have to call me

> 7875698 Pte. T. E. Shaw
> B. Company
> 1st Depot Battn.
> Tank Corps
> Bovington Camp
> Wool
> Dorset

and that's so complicated an address that few people use it. After the R.A.F. slung me out I didn't much care what happened: (the Air I was very keen on, & was enjoying more than anything I've ever done): so finally when broken in cash I enlisted, & have been quietly in Dorset since. Can't & don't pretend to like it, but it's better than the Colonial Office anyhow: for if I'm not making the world better (an immodest ambition of you politicals!) at least I'm not making it worse, as I used to do.

There is a sporting chance of my getting on a draft to India, armoured cars, which would deliver me from mud. I prefer sand & sun, even with scorpion-sauce.

You are lucky to get flying again. The very sight of a plane or of an airman makes me sort of homesick. If Hoare dies horribly some day you will know it's my bad wishes dogging him.[2]

This letter doesn't sound cheerful. Actually things aren't bad (when it's not raining, as now) for I've got an extravagant motor-bike, as fast as a hurricane, & hurl over S. W. England on it, pleasing myself at every sharp bend & bad place . . . and to be anonymous & out-of-sight & very speedy isn't a bad estate.

---

1 Edward, 6th Earl Winterton (1883–1962), at this time Under-Secretary of State for India, had served with Lawrence in the last phase of the Arab war.

2 Sir Samuel Hoare, later Lord Templewood (1880–1959), was at this time Secretary of State for Air. He was to prove the principal obstacle to Lawrence's readmission to the R.A.F.

Curtis is trying to get printed that fantastic book of mine: a privately subscribed edition, at a huge price. Don't buy one, unless you are suddenly enriched — I'll lend you mine, if it comes off. Your portrait by Roberts will be a decoration of it. He is having a show next month I believe, in Chelsea somewhere.

Yours ever
TE?

Bodleian Reserve

SIR HUGH TRENCHARD
2.XI.23   Bovington

Dear Sir Hugh

I'd like to,[1] very much: but there are two difficulties already in my view:—

(a) It is armistice day, and I do not know if leave will be given.

(b) I have a decent suit, but no dress clothes at all.

The leave I will ask for, but till Thursday next (Nov. 8) there will be no answer to the application. The clothes are beyond my power to provide: and I fear that Lady Trenchard might not approve a lounge suit at dinner. It depends on the other company probably. Please ask her before you reply.

[...]

The Army and Navy Club at six or six-thirty would suit me excellently and I hope it may come off. Undiluted Tank Corps is a disease. It is very good of you to ask me.

Yours sincerely
T.E.?[2]

R.A.F. Museum Hendon/HMH

1 i.e. go to dinner with Trenchard at his club.
2 Lawrence was told that it would be in order to wear his Private's uniform so the invitation was accepted.

LORD WINTERTON
5.XI.23   [Bovington Camp]

Dear Winterton

Thanks for wanting the book. There are some irreverencies in it concerning yourself. I don't know of course if the reprint idea will actually
take shape.

As for coming to the I.O.[1] — you know I'm in khaki, & can't show up
in that. The 'bike is often being laid up, since it is a costly item: and the
railway return fare is rather steep. However next time I reach London I'll
ring you up — if it's a week-day — and talk. The mischief is that they only
let us off on Sat. afternoon, till Sunday night ... and you don't (God be
thanked!) go to office in those hours.

Yes, I remain as cheerful as possible, & am very well: but it isn't a good
life. However perhaps Hoare will be thrown out next election. Get the Air
for yourself if so. Good job, as big as its holder, & the only one with growth
unlimited.

Yours ever
T E?

Bodleian Reserve

MRS HELLE FLECKER[2]
5.XI.23

Dear Mrs. Flecker

Well at last I saw *Hassan*, standing one week-end night behind the dress-
circle, where one could both see and hear. I liked the seeing best ... but it
is extraordinarily hard to write to you about the play. When that brute
intoned the Yasmin ghazel I wanted to kill him:[3] and he butchered the
prose just as horribly, and the others had no sense of style, and their voices

1 I. O.: India Office.
2 Mrs Hellé Flecker was the Greek-born widow of James Elroy Flecker. Lawrence had
been to the first production in English of Flecker's play *Hassan* at the Haymarket Theatre,
London. (It had been performed earlier in the year in German at Darmstadt.) The play
was produced by Basil Dean, the costumes and design were by George W. Harris and
the incidental music was by Frederick Delius. Opening on 20 September 1923 *Hassan*
was a considerable success, running for 281 performances.
3 The 'brute [who] intoned the Yasmin ghazel' — a 'ghazel' is a piece of oriental love
poetry — was the distinguished actor Henry Ainley, playing Hassan. Yasmin was played
by Cathleen Nesbitt. 'Yasmin, A Ghazel' had earlier appeared in Flecker's 1913 collection
The Golden Journey to Samarkand.

were false — all but Ishak's[1] — and it was cruelty to all those lovely lines ... and yet, and yet, the play came over and held not merely me but everybody else about me — everyone in the theatre, I think. It was a conquest of mind over matter ... and made me very proud of Flecker's strength.

The settings were beautiful. The man Harris who made the designs and Dean who I suppose oversaw the whole, have done splendidly: nothing in it tawdry, except perhaps the fountain in the court. The closing chant of Samarkand was fine, and Delius throughout superfine.

There hasn't I suppose been such a play in London before: and will not be again: and it is a very proud sight to have seen. Yet it's murder, complete murder.

I hope one more thing — a most important thing — that the job will pay. They have spent enormously upon it ... and I hope will reap as they deserve, and that some of their grains will fall by your wayside. Flecker would have liked that — would have cursed mightily if it hadn't come off — and would have wanted it even more in the actual circumstances.

My joining up was quite direct and plain. I hate the semi-politics to which my Eastern efforts in the war had seemed to doom me: and to break away from them, to make myself quite independent of them and their glamour, I changed my name, and had consequently to begin rather low down. I'm not worth much money apart from Arabia: and to that I'll not return. I won't even make money by publishing my beastly book upon the war-period, because that's all of a piece with it.

Wherefore I'm an oppressed private, hating the army and quite out of place in it: but growing more into my place and company, daily.

Yours sincerely
TEL...

Bodleian Reserve

A. E. (JOCK) CHAMBERS
5.XI.23   [Bovington Camp]

Dear Mahomet

[...] I'm not wholly resourceless in Bovington: found a ruined cottage near camp (a mile out) & took it for 2/6 a week.[2] Have roofed it & and am flooring it. At present one chair & a table there. Am hoping for a book

---

1 Ishak — minstrel to the Caliph of Bagdad — was played by Leon Quartermaine.
2 Clouds Hill.

case this week, & a bed next week but cash isn't too plentiful & needs are many. I'll let you know for week after next it might do you to stay in. There is firewood & you are good at bed-making. No floor-scrubbing.[1] Scruffy place. About a dozen good books already.

Too many people talking to me can't write.

R.

Bodleian Reserve

HIS MOTHER
22.11.23   [Bovington Camp]

A month has passed. This is going to Paoing.[2] You told me to write to Vancouver, which I did, no doubt too late to overtake you. Shanghai you did not mention, & I haven't written there. If I had, it would no doubt have been too late also.

You are fortunate to miss this November. It has been colder than any other in my memory. No news here or elsewhere. I sent you a Doughty by post the other day: & hope you get it. The postage was dear, & the book is rare, in that edition. Now Cape has brought out a £3.3.0 edition, of the complete book, on quite good paper. The identical print of course.

I am doing a little work for Cape, to fill up my odd moments: and Buxton (the banker) is looking for 100 subscribers of 30 guineas each, to make possible a private reprint of my book on Arabia. Hardy praised it, & makes me feel justified in giving it so much distribution. Of course there would be no reviews, no copies for public sale, & no profits.

I still see Hardy occasionally. John has painted (at my request) a very beautiful portrait of him. The old man is delighted, & Mrs. Hardy also. It is seldom that an artist is so fortunate in his sitter's eyes.

I've taken a little cottage (half ruinous) a mile from camp, & water-tighted it to act as a work-room for myself. There I hope in future to do my writing, which is becoming more & more a habit. No original stuff, of course: just translations. I hope not again to do anything of my own. It is not good for man to make things.

Nothing else I can think of to write.

I hope the journey is not still wearisome to you: but you must be looking

1 At their first meeting at R.A.F. Farnborough Chambers as hut-orderly had immediately ordered Lawrence to scrub his own bed-space.
2 In west China, to which Mrs Lawrence was travelling in order to live with her eldest son Bob, who had joined the China Inland Mission in 1921 and was now serving as a medical missionary.

forward to its end: yet, you know, these journeys don't really end, till we do.

N.

HL/Bodleian Reserve

ERIC KENNINGTON
13.12.23

Dear Kennington

At a meeting last Sunday Hogarth, Dawnay, Curtis, and I decided to produce 100 copies of the *Seven Pillars*, at 30 guineas a copy, if so many subscribers can be found.

I am to be solely responsible (that the law of libel, civil or criminal, may fall blunted on my penniless status as a private soldier), will pay all bills, and sign all papers and copies. Hogarth will help edit my proofs: you, edit my pictures (I hope).

Production to start as soon as £200 has been subscribed: ('starting' means sending four Arab pastels to W. & G.).[1]

Intending subscribers are to write to me (under any name), to

Clouds' Hill
Moreton
Dorset

for details and conditions. I'll reply personally to each.

If you know any unco' rich please try and pillage them.

I estimate the job might take a year at the shortest, two at the longest.

As for printer.

Aforesaid copyright act and law of libel will make advisable my being a nominal partner in the printing firm. To retire as soon as job is completed.

I want it done monotype, in eleven point or fourteen point, of a type approximating to O.F. Caslon, unleaded: with side-headings in side margin: no top-heading, lines not long, but print-panel taller than usual in quartos. The size of the page you know (it's the Ghalib[2] proof, anyway. I forget the dimensions).

Paper to be a *thin* decent rag brand, hand-made or machine-made of similar quality. Not perfectly bleached: — a tone of yellow or mud in it.

1 Whittingham & Griggs, The Chiswick Press, London.
2 Ghalib: one of 'Kennington's Arabs', i.e. one of his Arab portraits done for *Seven Pillars*.

Book will run between 300,000 and 330,000 words: preferably the lesser number.

Matter will be sent in in sheets of the book you have, hand-corrected (scissors and paste). So it will be a very legible M.S. to set up from.

Will you ask your printer how this proposition appeals to him ... what sample experimental type-panels and margins he would set up: how long he would be before he could start the job: how many words per week he would be prepared to set up: how many sheets he would be prepared to hold in type, what he would charge per thousand words? (I can't say per folio, because we haven't yet set up a dummy page).

I would interfere with the sample pages a good deal, with the accepted format very little. Author's corrections almost nil. Matter sent in regularly.

I've printed enough to have a conscience and regard for type-matter.

Yours
T.E.

Bodleian Reserve

MRS THOMAS HARDY
22.XII.23   [Bovington Camp]

Dear Mrs. Hardy

I waited to see if I could: and I'm afraid I can't. It's a good thing because it would feel intrusive to go to lunch on Christmas day. However I would probably have fallen to it, only that I'm without transport. The ancient & splendid bicycle was borrowed (without leave) by a villain, who rode her ignorantly, & left her, ruined, in a ditch.[1] It saved me the pang of selling the poor beast: but also it shuts me unhealthily close into camp:— and so I'm trying to persuade the maker of it to supply me with another!

I'll hope to see you and Mr. Hardy soon.

Yours sincerely
T E Shaw

Bodleian Reserve

1 This was the second of seven Brough motor-cycles owned by Lawrence between 1922 and 1935; an eighth was on order at the time of his death; the first had been badly damaged on 31 March 1923 during a return journey from London to Bovington. George Brough, their 'maker' as Lawrence calls him here, had been manufacturing motor-cycles since 1910; Lawrence called his machines George I, George II etc. in tribute to him. The two men did not meet until 1925, after which date they corresponded regularly. Lawrence was dubbed 'Broughy' Shaw by his fellow soldiers because of his addiction to Brough Superiors.

R. A. M. GUY
25.XII.23   Clouds Hill Moreton Dorset

Dear Poppet

Xmas, — spent alone in my new-old cottage — has been a quiet time of simple thinking. It seems to me that I've climbed down very far, from two years ago: and a little from a year ago. I was in the guard-room of Farnborough that night, & next day the newspapers blew up and destroyed my peace. So it's a bad anniversary, for me.

Yes, Trenchard writes to me sometimes, but it won't be to have me back. Baldwin, the Prime Minister, tried to persuade him, & failed. Trenchard is a very great man, & makes up his mind only once. In my case I think he was wrong, & I think he knows it. My fault, if I was at fault in my conduct at Farnborough, was not a big one, & I've paid for it in these ten months of misery here. However you will be tired of my dwelling so much on the same subject: the excuse is that my mind dwells on it every day, & many nights, for the R.A.F. is my best memory.

I'm glad you got your fortnight at home. You are become almost a sailor now, & such feel lost when their service ends, or when their leave-money is all spent. Try to be civil as well as naval and aerial. It's easier to be three things than two, because the intensity of each is less.

I'm seeing Bernard Shaw tomorrow, which will be a treat for me. You saw Russell[1] — well, he's the best fellow I can find in camp, and he's decent in suffering my fancies patiently: but I long for something a little hotter & stronger at times, something which goes further along my road & extends my mind a little. Brain-men like Hardy & Shaw do me that service, and therefore I love meeting them.

When I said 'This is the last' I meant that again for an overwhelming time we were going to be apart. Letters don't work, nor do casual meetings, for the shadow of the near end lies over them, so that the gaiety is forced & the talk foolish. You & me, we're very unmatched, & it took some process as slow & kindly as the barrack-room communion to weld us comfortably together. People aren't friends till they have said all they can say, and are able to sit together, at work or rest, hour-long without speaking.

We never got quite to that, but were nearer it daily ... and since S.A. died I haven't experienced any risk of that's happening.

That added an extra regret when Trenchard so firmly cut my vital cord. ...

Back on the old subject you see.

---

1 Private Arthur Russell, a young man from Coventry, was one of Lawrence's room-mates at Bovington and a frequent visitor to Clouds Hill. See next letter, to Russell's mother.

I hope you will enjoy the cruise & be contented some day with your job. Believe me, you're lucky.

Yours

R.

University of Harvard

MRS RUSSELL
25.XII.23   Camp

Dear Mrs. Russell

Does it feel queer to be Arthur's mother? Sometimes, I expect. He is rather an uncommon person.

I don't know, of course, what stories he has told you about me. The truth is that he gives up a good deal of his spare time to showing me about: and in return for his kindness I try to be as little tiresome to him as I can. The debt is all mine, to him.

Many thanks for your Xmas present. It was the only one I had, as it happened, and the cigarettes were very successful. They made me break my rule, or rather my habit, of not smoking. Years ago in France we used to get nothing but those 'Caporal' cigarettes, & so they brought back memories with them.

We have been, (Arthur & I) all day up here in a little cottage I have near camp, doing nothing but sitting still & talking. The Christmas in the other place[1] was a bit too merry for our tastes. A sober man feels such a fool when all the world around him is tipsy.

It's started raining now, which is hard luck on the others . . . and on me, for I've got to walk home a mile through it. Arthur's going to sleep here by himself, on the floor or the sofa; he says it'll be all right: anyway it is better than the guardroom where he has to doze away a night a week. He'll keep the fire going, & old Bill, my tenant, will snore away in the kitchen downstairs.

As for coming to Coventry — yes we mean to do that one week-end next year, when the evenings get longer and the roads drier. We'll come up by Brough, & that means you will hear us long before you see us. As he says 'I like a bike with a good healthy exhaust'.

1 i.e. Bovington. Though Lawrence gave 'Camp' as his address the letter was obviously written from Clouds Hill.

Again with many thanks

> Believe me
> Yours very sincerely
> 'Brough'

It's as good a name as any. I haven't a proper one. We call him 'Bullet' (his head) 'Cov' (his native town) 'Imp' (his manner) 'Infant' (his appearance). I once heard him called Russell, too.

University of Texas

MRS THOMAS HARDY

31.1.24   [Clouds Hill]

Dear Mrs. Hardy

I'm very sorry, but I cannot manage to get over by train: my fault I expect, though the army standard of conduct does ask too much of us.

If I had a bicycle I'd have managed it: and I'm getting one soon. The maker of the old marvel is sending me (on loan) one of his latest. So in a fortnight or so I'll again be blessed with the freedom of Dorset (not to mention Hants, Devon, Somerset, Wiltshire, and others). A pity that a fortnight is so long as fifteen days.

Till then it's Clouds Hill for me on my spare afternoons. If you or the Asquiths ('and' the Asquiths, rather, though I don't know them)[1] are at a loss for an excursion, and the day is lovely, then do take them over the great Heath, & call at the cottage going or coming. Some of the fellows are making it their habit to drop in: but mostly they are quiet men, & if they irked you I could drive them out, temporarily. You see the cottage is unlike camp, & it gives them a sense of healthy change to visit me, and I like them to like coming.

> Yours sincerely
> T E Shaw

Bodleian Reserve

1 Presumably Herbert Asquith (second son of H. H. Asquith, Liberal Prime Minister 1908–16) and his wife Lady Cynthia Asquith, who were friends of the Hardys. Lady Cynthia was also secretary to the writer Sir J. M. Barrie.

E. M. FORSTER[1]
20.2.24

I've been transferred from B. Company: so a man brought your letter over to me two nights ago just after I had gone to bed with a bout of malaria: and a miracle happened: the fever left me and I sat up in bed and read it all! This book is my only one, & I have a longing (which I seldom admit) to hear what men say of it.

In your case it is wonderful. Writers & painters aren't like other men. The meeting them intoxicates me with a strangeness which shows me how very far from being one of them I am. Of your work I only know *Howards End & Siren & Pharos:*[2] but that's enough to put you among the elect ... and yet you bother to write to me whole pages about my effort. No one else has done that for me;[3] and I'm abnormally grateful. Grateful even to the point of wishing for more — not written of course, but to ask you of some of the difficulties I've met. However you will be spared this probably. The army does not let me off at practical times.

Your division of books into the active and the passive pleased me. The fluid ones are those written by writers: and the static ones are those (the many more) written by imitators like me. The second have no justification of being, except the scarcity of the real thing ... and the need of books which shall be tools, ancillary. Works of art have their own life, and so aren't best fitted to be railway timetables, or dictionaries, or histories.

My thing was forced from me not as a poem, but as a complete narrative of what actually happened in the Arab Revolt. I didn't think of it till all was over, and it was compiled out of memory (squeezing the poor organ

1 Lawrence's friendship with the well-known novelist E. M. Forster (1879–1970) was of great importance to him; he saw him as an established writer with that hallmark of creativity which he feared he did not have himself. They had met briefly in 1921 at a lunch for Feisal at a Mayfair hotel, from which Forster took away the impression of a 'small fair-haired boy' who 'rapped out encouraging words about the Middle East'. They had now been brought together through their mutual friendship with Siegfried Sassoon, who had lent Forster a copy of *Seven Pillars*. If Lawrence valued Forster's comments on *his* book, Forster for his part found *Seven Pillars* a valuable aid to the task *he* was then engaged in — attempting to finish his most famous and successful novel *A Passage to India*. See P. N. Furbank, *E. M. Forster: A Life*, Volume II, p. 120: 'The book [*Seven Pillars*] affected him not only as a man but as a writer. He wrote the two final chapters of *A Passage to India* under its influence, completing them, and the novel, in a burst of confident energy.' Forster then wrote to Lawrence the detailed letter of criticism to which this letter was his reply. I have included eight of the letter's twelve paragraphs; the full text is in *DG*.

2 *The Story of the Siren* and *Pharos and Pharillon*. His novel *Howards End* (1910) had been very influential in establishing Forster's reputation.

3 As David Garnett noted at this point, 'Edward Garnett alone had been writing about *Seven Pillars of Wisdom* for months.'

with both hands, to force from it even the little lively detail that there is). If I invent one thing I'll spoil its raison d'être: and if there are invented conversations, or conversations reconstructed after five years, where will it be?

Also, you know, I feel profoundly dejected over it all. It reads to me inferior to nearly every book which I have found patience to read ... and that is many. If it is the best I can do with a pen, then it's better for me to hump a rifle or spade about; and I fear it's the best I can write. It went through four versions in the four years I struggled with it, and I gave it all my nights and days till I was nearly blind and mad. The failure of it was mainly what broke my nerve, and sent me into the R.A.F. ... where I found six months of full contentment. The Army is a sad substitute. However I'm off the point.

War and Peace is almost the largest book in the world. I've carried it whenever I had the transport, and ever wished it longer. But then Tolstoi was an enormous genius. While I was trying to write I analysed most of you, and found out, so far as it was within my fineness to see, what were your tricks of effect, the little reserves & omissions which gave you power to convey more than the print says. But it is hopeless to grapple with Tolstoi. The man is like yesterday's east wind, which brought tears when you faced it and numbed you meanwhile.

Your goodness in writing to me with such care shows that you think (or makes me think that you think) there's some hope in my writing. Yet the revise I'm going to give *The Seven Pillars* in the next ten months can be one of detail only: for the adventure is dead in me: and I think it is the only thing I'll ever try to write. The Army is a great assoiler ... and my two years of it has nearly cured me of the desire to work gratuitously. This means 'without self-satisfaction or money': the first I only get out of hot speed on a motor-bike. The second I never get. My own writing has brought me in eleven pounds since 1914. A scruple (absurd in view of the obliquity of the whole movement) prevented my taking pay while I was East: and prevents my taking profits on any part of the record of the adventure. I can make a little translating foreign novels: but it's not much, and painful work. The army is assured bread & butter ... and that feels better than a gamble outside. Also I feel disinclined to struggle again for a living. If I can't keep alive without much pain then I won't bother to do so at all.

I wonder why I'm writing all this to you. I think perhaps because you are a stranger, and have been interested in my addled egg. It was an extraordinary experience for me, the reading of your letter.

[...]

DG

SIR HUGH TRENCHARD
1.3.24

Dear Sir Hugh

Forgive me this letter. I'm ashamed of it already, since I know that you sacked me for good, and it's perverse of me not to take it so. Yet the hope of getting back into the R.A.F. is the main reason of my staying in the Army. I feel eligible, there, for transfer or re-enlistment. You once took over some Tank Corps fellows: and lately the change of Ministry heartened me: and I've served exactly a year in the Army now, & been found amenable to discipline. Don't say that the Army can more easily digest an oddity than can the R.A.F. It isn't true. The Air has twice the vitality — with good reason.

Whenever I get one of your letters I open it excitedly to see if your mind has changed. It seems to me so plain that the presence in the ranks of a man as keen on the Air as myself must be generally beneficial. Yesterday however you told me plainly, for the first time, that it was my gaiety which got me into trouble at Farnborough. I didn't know of it, & doubt it yet. Guilfoyle's neurasthenia made him imagine things.[1] He didn't amuse me — rather he made me sick and sorry. I don't like saying so (since part of the game is to take what happens in C.O.s) but I fancy he injured me out of deliberate fear. It wouldn't happen again, for not one in a hundred of your Squadron-Leaders is a nerve-wreck.

However on the whole I was happy at Farnborough, and so perhaps I did, unawares, walk about smiling. Surely not a great fault, & one easily put right. The superiors have lots of power over the ranks, in every service, including yours, and Guilfoyle could have made me cry (if he'd wished) by some sentence less than indefinite years in the Army. I don't mind the present discomfort (as long as I can hope to reach the R.A.F. at the end): but the filth is a pity, for no fellow can live so long in it & keep quite clean. I feel I'm not worth so much to your people as I was a year ago . . . but as I said before, I'm still worth having. It was a stimulant to the other A.C.s to have a man, relatively as experienced as me, content among them: and I liked them, which shows that it was all right. I still hear from many of them.

It's all difficult to write. If you'd been a stranger I could have persuaded you: but my liking for your Force and its maker make it impossible for me

---

1 Guilfoyle: Lawrence's C. O. at Farnborough, whom he blamed for giving him away to the press.

to plead properly. Do think of the many hiding-holes there are (India, Egypt and Mespot and seaplane-ships) before you tear this up![1]

Yours sincerely
TEL

R.A.F. Museum Hendon/HMH

MRS CHARLOTTE SHAW
16.3.24   Clouds Hill Moreton Dorset

Dear Mrs. Shaw

I've read *Joan, St. Joan* ... and want to say straight out that it is one of his best writings.[2] Don't take me as a play-judge. I know nothing of the stage, and don't care very much for it: a play to me is only a particular art-form like a sonnet: but as writing *Joan* is magnificent.

Some sea-change has come over G.B.S. in the last ten years. Perhaps it isn't new that he should be on the side of the angels — even when they are undisguised angels — but surely it's new that every one of his characters should be honest and kindly and even-minded? I like it, and find it essentially true, the more I see of men (almost I'm able to think gently of some sergeants ... they mean less than appears ... their official style has to be subtracted before you measure the manner and matter of their delivery): but people don't usually feel fair towards humanity till they are old and successful and ready to retire ... and G.B.S. isn't the third, and probably will never be the first ... just as I'll never be the second.

Seriously, it's done his art and heart good to get the doctrine of *Methuselah* off his breathing-works:[3] and the poet in him is now going to have a little dance. Did you note the balance of prose in the fighting parts of *Joan*? Take care: he may yet write an epic of blood-lust. All things are possible with a delivered evangelical.

Wonderful lines in *Joan* were on p. 26, where the Archb[ishop] rebukes the lap-dogs. Oh, I'd like to hear de Rais stamp out his desperate sane-face from that!

I shrink from Joan's very little dialect. It seems to me a literary manner, like italics: unworthy of an artist with Mr. Shaw's cut and sweep of spoken word. He gives Joan a loud simplicity without it ... and I'm a detester and despiser of bumpkins. The best men in the ranks aren't the bumpkin-

---

1 Air Vice-Marshal Philip Game, successor to Swann as the Air Council member for personnel, minuted favourably on Lawrence's plea to Trenchard, who took it up with the Air Minister Sir Samuel Hoare, but Hoare rejected it out of hand.
2 *Saint Joan* was first produced just ten days later on 26 March 1924 at the New Theatre, London, with Sybil Thorndike in the title-role.
3 *Back to Methuselah* was Shaw's previous play. A gigantic work taking three nights to perform, it was Shaw's favourite play, an opinion not widely shared.

spoken. A fellow worth listening to isn't the tyro, but the man who is trying once more, on top of ten thousand failures, to phrase precisely what his mind feels.

[...]

I found pp. 66–95 intolerable. The shadow of the tragedy at the end lay over the first pages, and made the so accurate historical 'placing' of the men a horror. Over these pages I galloped, to reach the crisis. Joan came in, and held her own, indeed increased her nobility. It was good to make her sign that confession ... and then she died, 'off'. I have a prejudice against the writer who leaves the reader to make his top-scene for him. *Hounds of Banba*[1] does it, in the story of the burning of the village ... but faces the struggle in the story of the man's funeral. I funked it, in the death of Farraj, my man:[2] faced it, in the plain narrative of my mishaps in Deraa the night I was captured.[3] Here in *St. Joan* the climax will be red light shining from the fire into the courtyard. Authors feel they aren't up to writing about so tremendous a thing, and so they put a row of dots, or swallow silently, and leave the poor reader to stuff up their gap with his cherished and grudged emotion. It's indirect art and direct shirking.

Of course if he'd dipped his pen in all his strength and written straight forward the play could never have been presented: but the more honour so. It would have cleaned us all to have *seen* Joan die.

The fifth act is pure genius. I wouldn't have a thought of it otherwise than written: I'm most thankful to you for letting me read it.

E.S.

[...] My bike will probably let me see one of its nights, if it goes properly. S. Thorndyke [*sic*] doesn't look like St. Joan, you know!

It was my fault that I didn't see you during *Methuselah*: but I was innocent of the ringing up. The grime and oiliness of those dark 150-mile dashes sandwiched in between laborious days were thick on me when I twice called: and the guardians of your entanglement couldn't pierce through them to see the harmless softness of my face: nor was my brogue strong enough. They were firm that neither you nor he ever saw anyone without appointment.

When G.B.S. scoffs at my fear of publicity he should go down the first half-flight of stairs and look at that gate and imagine himself without it ... imagine himself day-tenant of one-twentieth of a barrack-floor, and owner of the handkerchief and money in the pocket of his government suit!

T.E.S.

British Library

1 A novel by the Irish writer Daniel Corkery, published in 1920.
2 See *Seven Pillars*, Chapter XCIII.
3 See also Lawrence to Mrs Shaw, 26 March 1924 (p. 261).

MRS CHARLOTTE SHAW
26.3.24   Clouds Hill

O dear. I've gone and done it. Very very sorry. This 'to-be-envied' camp-life makes me rebound too high at times. Explanations.

(i)   Barrie. You justify him as a man. My attack is upon the artist. He writes with an eye upon the box-office, with an ear to please the very many. He succeeds: but must pay the price of annoying the few. It infuriates me when a fine writer (or painter) deliberately does the not-quite best. I don't mind dead silence. I can't stand Peter Panning or Arnold Bennetting.

(ii)   Belloc. Great gifts: *Path to Rome* a delightful saucy book. His historical work impudence. Half-truths or calculated lies, served out to the public brilliantly. It's like putting a fine sauce over diseased ill-cooked meat. Done for money. Caddish, I call that.

(iii)   Lowell Thomas. Not to be condemned like B & B & B.[1] He's a born vulgarian, who does the best that is in him. If his victim was other than myself I'd praise him. But it rankles in my mind to be called proud names for qualities which I'd hate to possess ... or for acts of which I'm heartily ashamed. Would you like to be known only by your inferior work?

(iv)   Hogarth. A very kind, very wise, very lovable man, now in failing health. I'd put him high among the really estimable human beings. All my opportunities, all those I've wasted, came directly or indirectly, out of his trust in me.

(v)   Style. I make it a tin god, because I'm in need of the help of that god. People like Belloc and G.B.S. despise him, since they are endowed with the very utmost of his gifts.

(vi)   Contempt. Of course we don't really. A man gets carried away and says brave things ... but if you take him away into a quiet place and lend him your pocket mirror he will recant. Yet, if it were possible to man, it would be a lawful emotion. We can indulge it only of ourselves. Its counterfeiting holds much of envy. I'm sorry to have overstepped.

(vii)   The trial scene in *Joan*. Poor Joan, I was thinking of her as a person, not as a moral lesson. The pain meant more to her than the example. You instance my night in Deraa. Well, I'm always afraid of being hurt: and to me, while I live, the force of that night will lie in the agony which broke me, and made me surrender. It's the individual view. You can't share it.

About that night. I shouldn't tell you, because decent men don't talk about such things. I wanted to put it plain in the book, and wrestled for days with my self-respect ... which wouldn't, hasn't, let me. For fear of being hurt, or rather to earn five minutes respite from a pain which drove

1 i.e. Barrie, Bennett and Belloc.

me mad, I gave away the only possession we are born into the world with—our bodily integrity. It's an unforgivable matter, an irrecoverable position: and it's that which has made me forswear decent living, and the exercise of my not-contemptible wits and talents.

You may call this morbid: but think of the offence, and the intensity of my brooding over it for these years. It will hang about me while I live, and afterwards if our personality survives. Consider wandering among the decent ghosts hereafter, crying 'Unclean unclean!'[1]

The sting of the burning was very big in *Joan*: and G.B.S. would have made his play impossible by portraying it. Yet if the play was to be not a morality but life itself, he would have given the physical its place above the moral.

In Methuselah his human-kind ended in the supremacy of mind. The army has taught me that our race is running towards a supremacy of body. The criteria of camp, in sensation, in mind, in spirit, in conduct, are sensual, are sexual simply: and since I'm shut out from that I live among them as an oddity.

You speak of submissive admirers ... but that hurts them and me. I'll write you pictures of the two most concerned some day, and will try to show you how far from an object of admiration I must be to them. And the contrary? Do I admire them? There's not a clean human being into whose shape I would not willingly creep. They may not have been Colonel Lawrence ... but I know the reverse of that medal, and hate its false face so utterly that I struggle like a trapped rabbit to be it no longer.

What a mixed metaphor. Excess of emotion always ends in carelessness of style.

If you hadn't sent me the Brieux plays I couldn't have sent you this letter.[2] Probably I shouldn't have, anyhow. But it will a little explain my half-heartedness before my blessings. I dodge G.B.S. reading part of *Joan* to me, partly because he's great and I'm worthless: partly because it's my part to shun pleasures ... through lack of desert. There's expiation to be made: and the weak spirit is only too ready to lunch with you, or to enjoy a book, or to hide a quiet while in a cloud-defended cottage: any alleviation of the necessary penalty of living on ...

T.E.S.

You will perceive that my mixture of flu and malaria is over: all but the weariness after. Tonight you triumph. Congrats.

British Library

1 A. W. Lawrence has suggested to me that his brother very probably had in mind Leviticus 13, 45: 'And the leper in whom the plague is, his clothes shall be rent, and his head bare, and he shall put a covering upon his upper lip, and shall cry Unclean, unclean.'
2 Mrs Shaw had been much impressed by the contemporary French playwright Eugène Brieux and had translated two of his plays. It was doubtless their explicit sexual subject matter which prompted Lawrence's comment.

E. M. FORSTER
6.4.24   Clouds Hill

[...] Your coming here was a very great pleasure to myself: and a very great profit, I hope, to that difficult book I'm engaged in. You, being by nature a writer, won't realise how lost I feel in attempting to see whole, & improve what was more an experience than a creation of my seeking. The compulsion of circumstance upon me to write it removed it from the normal category of welten things.

Any other time you feel moved to come & see, not me but us, (for Palmer & Russell[1] gained from you as much or more than I did) please send word & come. You will be extremely welcome. Any stranger is, almost: but men who write or draw come nearer to my taste than others.

The prospect of reading your book in two months or so is a pleasant one. Time goes quickly here. I hope it will satisfy your standard when you see it in form.

I'd like, very much indeed, to see the unpublishable stuff: any of it you feel able to show me. It shall be safely kept, & returned quickly.

'Unpublishable' is a relative, even a passing qualification. *The Seven Pillars* earned it two or three years ago: and have lost it in that little time.
    [...]

Bodleian Reserve

E. M. FORSTER
9.V.24

Wonderful you should wish my book back again. Certainly it shall be sent when Doughty is finished with it. I'm glad you are reading the old man. To me, and to nearly all people who have had even a slight taste of the desert, that book brings a clear impression of it. It seems to me impossible but that you should enjoy it.

Your return to Clouds' Hill (which now has a bed in it, for hardy campers who like a solitary sleeping place) will be red-letter. Such interruptions to

---

1 Palmer and Russell were fellow privates of the Tank Corps who became Lawrence's special friends (see letters to R. A. M. Guy and Mrs Russell, Christmas Day 1923). Palmer — usually known as 'Posh' — worked with him in the Quartermaster's stores. Russell was eventually to be one of Lawrence's pall-bearers.

our ordinary smooth living are a joy. In camp there is so little daily change that we are like figures sitting deep in still water: so still, by reason of the clatter of senseless living about us, that often I fancy I hear time dragging slowly past me, like an endless snake. Do you remember how Sigurd lay in a pit in the way, while Fafnir crawled slowly down to water?[1] Something like that, is the feeling.

I don't seem to have put my remarks on your story[2] very well. That's good, because my mind has never cleared upon it. I agree with S.S.[3] as to its excellence: my memory is still concerned, not with its parts, but with its general impression: for anything to last with me three weeks is unusual: and this preoccupation is a daily one, almost. You have conveyed something, very powerfully: but it feels like a something quite foreign from the impression of the details, which I criticised. As though your two and two, put together, had made not four, but a prime number of some sort.

Technically, as writing, as a story, I don't think it quite so good as very much else of your writing: but what comes through is very strong. To try another metaphor . . . as if it were a fine stone, finer than most, but your cutting of it were not quite finished . . . or quite exact, anyway.

Why make it over-ripe? or cynical? That seems to me grievous; the thing is so healthy as it stands, in its meaning, that it seems a pity to taint any detail of it.

The writing which disgusts me is stuff aimed deliberately below the belt: Barrie: Belloc: much of Chesterton: they could write so well, & are too cheap in grain to wish to try. Your efforts are always so patent, that no one could ever be troubled by them. It isn't a subject which can give offence, but its treatment. Imagine the bawdiness if Kipling or Elinor Glyn or Aldous Huxley had tried to write *The Life to Come*!

Don't take my criticisms seriously. I have dabbled in writing, but have no vocation, & therefore no technical standard on which to base a judgement. Only I thought you might be interested to know that my absorption in the stream of your main idea was broken into sometimes by a detail, whose foreignness I took to be unessential to the story: but which quite probably you inserted deliberately. It's these conscious variations, flaws, in

---

1 Any reference to Sigurd by Lawrence is likely to be the product of his enthusiasm for William Morris, whose *Story of Sigurd the Volsung* was for him a book of seminal importance.

2 The story in question was *The Life to Come*, one of Forster's 'unpublishable' stories (because of its homosexual content) which did not appear in print until after Forster's death. See also Lawrence's comments on *Dr Woolacott* in his letter to Forster dated 21 December 1927 (p. 359).

3 Siegfried Sassoon.

the rhythm of ideas which mark the artist ... like the irregularities in Shakespeare's blank verse, I suppose.

Yournn
T.E.S.

Bodleian Reserve

HARLEY GRANVILLE-BARKER[1]

9.V.24   [Clouds Hill]

Many thanks for the page. I've decided to make it 14-point, after all, since that reads easier, to my eye, & to the eyes of four out of five of the men in Hut G. 25. Quaint, isn't it, to submit such an affair to such judgement? But it's seldom one can get such an approach to 'the man in the street'.

Netherton leaves me always with a feeling that camp is a horrible place, & that's a silly feeling, because I've chosen to make my living here, & to fuss about its inessentials is very near self-pity. The perfection of your surface strikes sharper, I expect, on a visitor than it does to the lord & mistress of the place: for one thing, we don't have to deal with a fire or two per week.

1 Harley Granville-Barker (1877–1946) — the hyphen was added half-way through his career — won distinction as an actor, a theatre director, a playwright and, from 1923 onwards, the author of the much admired *Prefaces to Shakespeare*. He and Lawrence had met at the Hardys' Dorchester home, Max Gate. Granville-Barker and his second wife — he had divorced and remarried — were living some thirty miles to the west of Dorchester at Netherton Hall in Devon, and were thus, thanks to Lawrence's Broughs, virtual neighbours. Until his divorce Granville-Barker had been very close to the Shaws (he had done much to establish G. B. S.'s reputation) and it has been suggested that Lawrence, as it were, took over the vacancy left by Granville-Barker's fall from favour (for more on this subject see particularly *Private Shaw and Public Shaw* by Stanley Weintraub, Cape, 1963). He and Lawrence never became intimate friends, but there was, writes his American biographer Eric Salmon, 'an immediate and spontaneous attraction between them which comes out very clearly in [their] letters' (*Granville Barker and His Correspondents*, Wayne State University Press, Detroit, 1987). Salmon's book prints their entire surviving correspondence, consisting of eight letters by Lawrence and two by Granville-Barker. Earlier the latter had published Lawrence's letters to him in 1939 in a privately printed edition, limited to fifty copies, entitled *Eight Letters from T. E. L.* One letter was printed in *DG*. I have included two in the present collection. The one printed here is valuable mainly for Lawrence's discussions of his variant initials; he was, however, wrong in stating that his birthday initials were T.E.C. His birth certificate gives both his and his parents' name as Lawrence.

    Lawrence and Granville-Barker had evidently been discussing the typeface to be used in the subscribers' edition of *Seven Pillars*. The decision recorded here held; the book was printed in Caslon Old Face, with the main text of the book set in 14 point.

Do tell me what your insurance people say. Their faces must be worth a good deal of smiling.

My genuine, birth-day, initials are T.E.C. The C. became L. when I was quite young: & as L. I went to Oxford & through the war. After the war it became a legend: & to dodge its load of legendary inaccuracy I changed it to R. In due course R. became too hot to hold. So now I'm Shaw: but to me there seems no virtue in one name more than another. Any one can be used by anyone, & I'll answer to it: while the postman delivers to my cottage anything with Clouds Hill on the envelope. He did say, once, quite early on, that my name seemed to be Legion, but that it wasn't his affair. As he's a Salvationist, the New Testament comes naturally to his lips.[1]

Consequently you may tell anyone anything you like about me & my book ... but please don't put yourself about. I don't want you to start working on my behalf ... but thought that perhaps you might some day meet a quaint rich person, one who would welcome a new curio for his gallery ... and one who would be grateful to you for the chance of picking up my confessions.

I see that in discussing Netherton, above, I forgot to add that therefore I wouldn't come down again for a while: not till I've ceased to be envious of your state. Many thanks, none the less, for your suggestion of an early return.

Yours sincerely
TES

Bodleian Reserve

D. G. HOGARTH
9.V.24

Yes, that was it. I took thought for a night, & then declined. The job[2] is a hazardous one (T. wants a 'literary' history, the C.I.D.[3] a 'technical') attractive, very, to me by reason of its subject. The terms (three years) compare unfavourably with the six which the Army offers: and the responsibility is one which I'd regret as soon as I had shouldered it. Also it's no use,

---

1 See Mark 5, 9, Jesus to the Gadarene demoniac: 'And he asked him, What is thy name? And he answered, saying, My name is Legion: for we are many.' Lawrence used the word 'Legion' to describe himself when writing to Liddell Hart in 1933 (*LHB*, p. 79).
2 Lawrence had been asked to write the official history of the Royal Flying Corps and Royal Air Force in the Great War.
3 Trenchard and the Committee of Imperial Defence.

having gone through the grind of climbing down to crowd-level, at once to give it up for three years decent living. It would leave me older, less strung up to make another effort at poor living. If I can complete my seven years in the Army I should be able to slip quietly into a job of some sort at the end. There is a garage near here which might take me on.

I hope you are fit again: much of the illness which you have had lately I put down to the plague of that ungrateful book. You must feel like a reprieved prisoner.

Here at Bovington I seem to sit still: so still that often I fancy the slow passing of time about me can be *heard*. Isn't it rare for a person, who has been as unsparing as myself, to be purged quite suddenly of all desire? Even the longing or regret for the R.A.F. sleeps now, except when I come suddenly at a turn in the road, on its uniform. *That* was another bar to the job: because I'd have had to visit aerodromes, & each time the home-sickness would have made itself felt afresh.

Writing to people I have known is becoming difficult for me. Where-fore ...

T.E.S.

DG

MRS CHARLOTTE SHAW
10.VI.24   Clouds Hill

I'm letter after letter behind, but have been nursing a broken rib, and awaiting a moment when I felt inclined. Bank Holiday was a camp orgy, and after it there is a little silence. I fear it will rain again this afternoon ... why do I always feel the weather so keenly in Clouds' Hill? ... The cottage is nearly closed in with mountains of rhododendron bloom, of the screaming blue-pink which I used to dislike: now that they are my plants I love them. Isn't it greedy to give such undue favour to one's own?

The important thing to answer is about *Cock Robin*[1] ... and I've been puzzling over it. You expected it to be difficult for me. That radiance thrown over the fact of birth ... it's at odds with my own mind and desire.

---

1 Mrs Shaw had sent Lawrence an article entitled *Who Killed Cock Robin?*, published in two parts in a quarterly review called *The Quest* (January and April 1924); the author was John Hancock, a poet and artist who had died in 1918, aged 22. In the July 1924 edition of the same review Hancock was described as a 'prophet-artist' and compared to William Blake.

It seems to me so sorry and squalid an accident — the beginning of a hazardous career fittingly closed by death: and of the two accidents death seems the greater, because it has causes and birth only has effects. I can't believe in that edifice he builds up, of pre-natal effort and consciousness on the part of the child-to-be. Nor that it could be so petty as to wish that its parents be deliberate in conceiving it. Why if fathers and mothers took thought before bringing children into this misery of a world, only the monsters among them would dare to go through with it. The motive which brings the sexes together is 99% sensual pleasure, and only 1% the desire of children, in men, so far as I can learn. As I told you, I haven't ever been carried away in that sense, so that I'm a bad subject to treat of it. Perhaps the possibility of a child relieves sometimes what otherwise must seem an unbearable humiliation to the woman: — for I presume it's unbearable. However here I'm trenching on dangerous ground, with my own ache coming to life again.

I hate and detest this animal side — and I can't find comfort in your compartmenting up our personalities. Mind, spirit, soul, body, sense and consciousness — angles of one identity, seen from different points of the compass.

Hancock is a very powerful fellow: his presentation of his case reeks with character: and with a rare wistfulness too. A man who could so sublimate birth, naturally hurried himself into death. For me there isn't such a course. It seems too serious a treatment. I think I'm sorry I was brought into the world. I think I'll be glad when I go: but meanwhile I can't associate myself with the process in any effort to end or mend it. It's like measles, or the broken rib I've been nursing the last fortnight: you wait, and it's a memory, and even some memories fade with time.

[...]

British Library

VYVYAN RICHARDS
26.VI.24   Clouds Hill

They bewilder me, rather, these very earnest men. Somehow in their survey the senses and sensual aspect of art seem forgotten: — and to me they are

the most important.[1] Perhaps that's because I live a beast-life among my
fellow-beasts; in the army inevitably life becomes physical, & we go about
only by feel, by the feels of things & persons. They stall us worse than oxen
or carriage-horses, feed us by rote, dress us by rule: and we respond as best
we can to their prompting & become more animal than savages, less
individual (because more fearful of opinion) than dogs.

Poof: —

I showed the aesthetics to Forster, a novelist of some standing & friend,
while at Cambridge, to this group. He liked their illustrations, but not their
attitude. It interested me, as it did him: but there seems to me no salvation
down this road.

My new feeling (a dreaded conviction is looming up in the near distance)
is that the basis of life, the *raison d'être* of us, the springs of our actions, our
ideals, ambitions, hopes are carnal as our lusts: & that the appositions of
mind & body, of flesh & spirit, are delusions of our timid selves.

Your lease enclosed: sorry for its delay. Life slips over me here, in a
quality of dull forgetfulness which endears the camp to me. Never before
have I lived so quickly & so barrenly.

[...]

Au revoir some day ... but why not come down here? A bed, tinned
food, bread butter & jam: a quiet cottage, very lovely. Any day after July
4. Wool station. Razor & tooth-brush & pyjamas not provided.

T.E.S.

Bodleian Reserve

1 Vyvyan Richards had presumably been engaging Lawrence in a discussion of the movement in the study of art and in literary criticism associated with his namesake I. A.
Richards, Fellow of Magdalene College, Cambridge, and an important figure in the
Cambridge English Faculty at this time. The book referred to in the third paragraph as
'the aesthetics' is probably *The Foundations of Aesthetics*, by Richards and C. K. Ogden,
with J. Wood, published in 1922. Richards and Ogden also collaborated in *The Meaning
of Meaning* (1923) while Richards published his influential *Principles of Literary Criticism*
in 1924. In his view irony and complexity in poetry were virtues, while vagueness and
sentimentality were not. For evidence that Forster seems to have largely shared Lawrence's
attitude see his letter (to an unidentified recipient) of 13 August 1930, in which, bracketing
Richards's work with his own *Aspects of the Novel* and Percy Lubbock's *The Craft of
Fiction*, he wrote: 'Books like mine or Mr Richards' or Mr Lubbock's are all very well
for students or examinees, but, seriously, I think they may do more harm than good to
those who are actually engaged in creative work.' (*Selected Letters of E. M. Forster*, Vol.
II, p. 94)

MRS CHARLOTTE SHAW
19.VII.24   Clouds Hill

[...] Kreutzer Sonata being played by Bruce (a Scotsman, inarticulate, excessively uncomfortable).[1] He comes up here often on Sundays, will enter only if I'm alone, glares and glowers at me till I put some Beethoven on the gramophone, and then sits solid, with a heroic aura of solidity about him: my room after four hours of Bruce feels like a block of granite, with myself a squashed door-mat of fossilised bones, between two layers. Good, perhaps, to feel like a prehistoric animal, extinct, and dead, and useless: but wounding also.

I can't write this afternoon. Can I ever?

                                                            TES.

British Library

ALAN DAWNAY
27.vii.24   Clouds Hill

Lord help us: did I write miserably?[2] Learn the unworthy reasons

  (a): being choked off by the Adjutant for impertinence — to wit, passing an officer at more than twice his speed, while motor-cycling.
  (b): having my face damaged and my lately-broken rib re-broken (I think) by four drunks after lights-out in the hut. An epidemic of drinking lately in A. Company.
  (c): my inability to help one of the few really decent fellows here, he having lately fallen into rather a bad mess, with much worse inevitably to follow.

Normally I preserve a decent balance, and try not to bother other people with my self-inflicted troubles. I'm not coming out of the Tank Corps (unless a sudden heat-wave melts Trenchard, whom I've annoyed lately by refusing to write the R.A.F. war-history). Nor am I going to be respectable ever any more. Why should you worry about my slow climbing down the social ladder?

1 One of the very few references in Lawrence's letters to John Bruce, the man he paid to inflict the numerous beatings which he suffered from 1923 onwards. See Introduction to this section.
2 In a letter to Dawnay of 11 July Lawrence had described himself as 'over-worked: tired; woollen- and wooden-headed' and stated that 'things have been a bit rough lately. (b— rough ... b— brutal ... b ... n^2)': i.e. bloody to the nth degree squared.

There comes a sudden impatience over me at times, when the ordinariness of ordinary people for one instant seems unbearable. If I were almighty, I'd blast them then: but instead I do something silly, which recoils on my own humble head: and being abnormally sensitive (*not* a raging terrible lion, as some people, including Trenchard, seem to think) I distress myself for days over a fault which may have been too slight for outward reproof. Then too I'm always, even now, trying to influence others beyond their capacity, and grieving when they return to type.

Lately the job of proof-correcting has made the war-memories very vivid to me, so that they have been coming back as night-terrors to shorten my already few hours regular sleep. When I'd woken up the other fellows five nights running they gave me a sort of barrack-court-martial, to keep me quiet. This was humiliating, and rather painful.

'Humiliating' . . . and just above I've called myself humble. There's a fine consistency, when one soldier resents being man-handled by other soldiers! However I am humble too, in spite of that.

Yes, Sales go well. The 100 will be up long before the book is ready. Cheers for everybody who has helped it.

Thanks for Barty's[1] address. I've written to him.

I'm old-fashioned enough to expect 75% of the world's lavatory basins and 30-guinea books not to coincide.

Shall run up to Oxford one Saturday or Sunday, if you are free ever.

T.E.S.

Bodleian Reserve

MRS CHARLOTTE SHAW
31.VIII.24

The proofs are not coming so soon. Pike, the printer, is taking a holiday in Cornwall, and meanwhile the work halts for our joint reflections.[2]

I want you to realise, even before you see his work, that Pike is an artist of great severity and carefulness, and that his pages are made as beautifully

---

1 i.e. General Sir William Henry Bartholomew, who as Allenby's Brigadier-General General Staff in 1918 had planned the operations for the advance from Jerusalem to Damascus.

2 Manning Pike was an American from Minnesota whose only experience in printing before taking on *Seven Pillars* had been in a small firm of commercial printers in his home town. Lawrence described him in a letter to the American book-designer Bruce Rogers in October 1927 as 'a difficult man, but a fine workman, and ingenious engineer and artist'. Pike worked on the book at two addresses in West London.

as he can compass them. To him the balances of lines and paragraphs and passages are vital: they are the elements of which the physical book is made up.

I have no share in this aspect of the book: my work has been only to write the hand-draft of it. The translation from manuscript to metal is his work, and is as difficult as mine. My paragraphs and prose have to be arranged as well, in metal, as they will go.

He is fortunate in having found a living author: for it makes his work much easier, often, to leave out a few words, or a few lines, to make a new paragraph begin here or there, to telescope two chapters:— and I've given him carte blanche to cut and change the text as he pleases (only refusing to let him *add* anything): this is fair, for words are as elastic as ideas, and type-metal isn't elastic at all. He has the harder job.

Neither Pike nor myself are proof-readers: we try to grasp paragraphs entire, and the mis-spelt word escapes us. Even sometimes we let words drop out, unknowing. So you will find many glaring errors in the pages.

And what form should your corrections take? Any you please. My pleasure is bounded only by your pains. Do as much, in each batch, as comes easy to you, avoiding laborious drudgery. In fact, read the thing as long as you can do so without boredom: without intolerable boredom. The wide margins make marking pretty easy.

As the hesitant nervous author I'll value most such corrections as affect the manner and matter of the expression of ideas: because they will tend to make the book better, and I dread strangers seeing the thing in its existing unworthy clumsy form. Surely I can't be so bad a writer as these pages seem to me to declare: and yet I've done almost my best at them. Their failure lies in my insufficiency, not in any sparing of effort.

My spelling is good, originally, and any errors in it, or in the grammar, will be frank misprints and therefore negligible or nearly so. However for other people's sake I'll be grateful for any corrected misprints: but the sense of the book is the thing. Do please try and knock out redundant paragraphs. My judgement has left me again, now it is a question of detail. I leave in the bad places, since I'm afraid that it's fear, not good taste, which prompts me to excise them.

What a pother about a trifle! G.B.S. has brought forth twenty books; and I'm in a mess over one. The first no doubt is hardest, but the difference must lie between us. Of course his genius makes him feel sure what is important, and what isn't, and my blundering imitation confounds essentials and inessentials. Also, you know, it's the only book I'll write, and it's an apology for my first thirty years, and the explanation of the renunciation which followed on them. . . .

I'm writing on a fine afternoon, after a broken morning. They gave me a pass, and I slept last night on the floor of the sitting room in Clouds' Hill, while one of the R.A.F. who shared Farnborough Camp with me slept in the bedroom. They have found me here, and come down for week-ends of books and music. We ran over to Corfe, in the rain, for breakfast (and a hot bath too: luxury) in the little Hotel: and you'd have laughed to hear me reconstruct the Castle there in all its periods. Once I wrote a book on 'Medieval Military Architecture in Europe, and its modifications in the light of the Crusades'.[1] Lord Curzon was pleased to commend it. Now ...

However that passed the fore-noon, and since then we have played a tinned version of the 7th Symphony, and all sorts of quartette snippets: and last night till 2 a.m. the Choral Symphony ground itself out in sections between tea-drinkings, to keep us awake. Whenever there was an interval Chambers (the R.A.F.) read *Methuselah*. What was Clouds' Hill? A sort of mixed grill, I fancy: but very good. Everybody is beginning to fall in love with it. The air of it is peaceful: and the fire burns so well. I'm the only fortunate in camp. The rest burn coal.

This is a silly hotch-potch letter: but the Air Force fellows are like Oxford undergraduates in their second term ... buds just opening after the restraint of school and home. Their first questioning, their first doubt of an established convention or law or practice, opens a flood-gate in their minds for if one thing is doubtful all things are doubtful: the world to them has been a concrete, founded, polished thing: and the first crack is portentous. So the Farnborough fellows used to come to me there, after 'lights out' and sit on the box by my bed, and ask questions about every rule of conduct and experience, and about mind and soul and body: and I, since I was lying on my back, could answer succinctly and with illumination. Those who seek me out down here are the keenest ones, and they have been following up the chase of the great Why themselves, since I disappeared: and the books they can get hold of are so mixed and dithering that they feel the question marks more than the progress.

Methuselah is a prime card to play in their case. It puts one side quite quintessentially. G.B.S. would laugh to see himself, the prime reaction against the carnality of barrack-life ... but that's the way it goes. You get a reinforced masculinity by herding men together and segregating them for 20 hours of the 24 ... and reinforced masculinity is a way of describing an animalism which is not the less bestial for being happy and deliberate.

There is no harm in colouring the other side to these fellows. They wouldn't come so far to live on tea and bully beef if they hadn't felt it already: and the best cure for feeling is to feel as quickly and as hard as possible. After all they go back to barracks tomorrow morning. So do I.

---

1 His university thesis. Lord Curzon was Chancellor of Oxford University when it was submitted.

A letter yesterday, and one today. What a spate of words! *Meistersinger* just starting. Help!

British Library

MRS CHARLOTTE SHAW
15.X.24

[...] You know, you talk about stinking fish, but when adventuring among you great planets I feel like a burned out cracked electric globe. Never more than 15 C.p. when new, requiring the current of cataclysmic events to chafe into me any sparkle of light, and now only fit for the outer darkness. That's why I can't say anything when G.B.S. works over my proof as if it was worth while. I know it isn't ... and it's such an overwhelming compliment. When a V.C. (a decoration given for a heedless act of physical valour) passes an army guard-room the guard turn out and salute: the poor shy soldier wearing it, isn't thereby puffed up to believe himself very brave. He convicts himself of fraudulence. It's like pricking the swelling frog.
    [...]
Ten million pities that G.B.S. didn't raise the Arab Revolt and write the history of it. There is a book of books gone to waste, because nobody made him a Brigadier-General! It's easy to be wise afterwards, I suppose. If I'm Prime Minister for the next war, all independent commands shall be given to the finest writers of the generation. We may lose the war ... but think of the glories to be published as the Peace rolls on!
                                                                    T.E.S.

[...]

British Library

LIEUTENANT-COLONEL W. F. STIRLING
15.X.24   Clouds Hill Moreton Dorset

Dear F.S.
    The book arrived a while ago. Very good of you to read it so quickly and to give me your notes upon it. I'm particularly glad you found few errors of magnitude. The thing is an effort of memory, and I have, after sad experience, a grave distrust of my accuracy after the event.

'The lack of climax'. Yes, I'm afraid that is partly intentional. The book was the record of me in the Arab movement: and before the end I was very weary, and moved in a haze, hardly knowing what I did. Up to Deraa, perhaps, I fought: after that clearly the crisis was solved in our favour, and the last advance and entry into Damascus were almost formalities. . . . things which had to be passed through, but which required no grip or preparation. Didn't you notice that I was three-parts vacant then?

The same with Nasir's pursuit-battle. I wasn't in it, and so I wrote not of it. That was the rule of the book. So far as it could be, it reproduced the sight of my eyes, and the evidence of my senses and feelings. If people read it as a history: — then they mistake it. I'll strengthen my warning against such a line: but to reboil the final crisis to get it hotter and fitter to the dramatic demands of the Revolt: — no, that I can't do, since day by day, as the years pass, I hate and despise myself more and more for the part I played in it. Today my wish is to strip off from the yarn all the little decorations and tricks and ornaments with which I have made it ever-so-little exciting: so that the core of it should stand out as a disenchanting, rather squalid, experience. That's today: and the book is being printed today for the final time. If I waited till tomorrow probably I'd give effect to this wish, and gut the whole yarn of its adventitiousness: and then all would cry out that I'd spoiled it. So the way of least resistance is to let it, generally, alone.

My memory of the entry into Damascus was of a quietness and emptiness of street, and of myself crying like a baby with eventual thankfulness, in the Blue Mist[1] by your side. It seemed to me that the frenzy of welcome came later, when we drove up and down in inspection. Am I right or wrong? I'll alter this, on receipt of your reply, for you had more leisure to remember than I had. In the book there are two welcomes set out, first a silent one, second a burst of popular excitement. It will be easy, if necessary, to make one only. Simplification is a virtue too.

'The falseness of Storrs'. . . . Oh yes, I saw it: but because I knew it, and he knew that I knew it, it had no share in our relations, which were between the real Storrs and the real me. Storrs could retort about the falseness of me . . . and there wasn't less or more in use. Each of us was a complete dramatic actor, as dressed in appropriate sentiments as in clothes.

The 'emollient' shall come out: but your gentleness and tact and the diversions by which you kept the peace between war-worn Young, Joyce and myself, and the professional competence of yourself which fed my whims and cured Young's wants . . . these shall be forcibly acknowledged, in a less ambiguous word or phrase. You were an astonishing comfort to

1 The 'Blue Mist' was Lawrence's Rolls-Royce tender.

the close of the adventure. What a foul job it was. I don't want readers to 'enjoy' the book.

In girding at discipline and servitudes I seek mainly to condemn myself. My life has been service, and I hate it ... service to an ideal of scholarship, to the nation-building demand of nationality, and now service in the ranks. As you say in such surrender there lies a happiness ... but this seems to me an immoral feeling, like an overdraft on our account of life. We shouldn't be happy: and I think I've dodged that sin successfully! The Tank Corps is a hefty penance for too rich and full a youth!

H. G.'s verdict is extraordinarily interesting:[1] I wish he would tell me what were the worst places, so that I could cut them out. The book is over long, and I don't like it, any part of it, much.

Do tell me about the Damascus business, so far as it hangs in your memory ... and at the same time check any other falsities which occur to you when thinking it over.

Yours ever
T.E.S.

British Library

SIR HUGH TRENCHARD
6.ii.25   Clouds Hill Moreton Dorset

Dear Sir Hugh

February is 'supplication month' ... so for the third time of asking — Have I no chance of re-enlistment in the R.A.F., or transfer? It remains my only hope & ambition, dreamed of every week, nearly every day. If I bother you only yearly it's because I hate pestering you on a private affair.

Last year I said all I could in my favour, & have no eloquence left. My history hasn't changed. Clean conduct sheet since then, which (in a depot) shows that I have been lucky as well as decent. I've kept my job as storeman in the recruits' clothing store, except for intervals of clerking (for the Q.M.), a Rolls-Royce Armoured Car Course, and a month in Company store. Official character (from the Q.M. who is good to me) 'Exceptionally intelligent, very reliable, and works well.' A descending scale, you will note: but I so loathe the Army that I might not work at all. Even in better days I was not laborious. 'Intelligent' was because I got 93% on my Rolls course: the highest marks ever given. 'Reliable' because when a company

1 H. G. Wells.

stores went wrong they borrowed me to enquire, check, make new ledgers, and wangle deficiencies.

I've lived carefully, & am in clean trim, mind & body. No worse value, as an Aircraft Hand, than I was. Last Sunday, I rode to Yorkshire & back, averaging 44 m.p.h. just for fun. The war-worry & middle-east are finished: and I'd be peaceful and moderately happy, if I weren't always seeing the R.A.F. just out of reach.

[...]

Please don't turn me down just because you did so last year and the year before. Time has changed us both, & the R.A.F., since then. I could easily get other people to help me appeal to you: only it doesn't seem fair, and I don't really believe that you will go on refusing me for ever. People who want a thing as long and as badly as I want the R.A.F. must get it some time. I only fear that my turn won't come till I'm too old to enjoy it. That's why I keep on writing.

Yours very apologetically
T E Shaw
Ex. TEL)
JHR)

R.A.F. Museum Hendon/HMH

MRS CHARLOTTE SHAW
26.3.25   [Clouds Hill]

[...] The Air Ministry are considering my transfer from the Army to the Royal Air Force. Such a thing would push me up into the seventh level of happiness. May is to be the month of decision. Perhaps a good thing may at last happen!

Yours
TES

British Library

DR C. HAGBERG WRIGHT[1]
12.IV.25   Clouds Hill Moreton Dorset

Dear Dr. Wright,

I saw General Wright yesterday and he told me that you still wanted a copy of my very expensive book. He has read it, & is naturally interested in the special subject. I doubt whether its appeal will be general enough to appeal to you: and I doubt whether it is to be advised as an investment. Thirty guineas is so high a first price, that I doubt there ever being any appreciation.[2] I hope to deliver the copies to subscribers towards the end of this year: but I am in the Army, & soldiers' lives are irregularly lived. So I promise nothing. There may be 130 copies, (if so many subscribers present themselves) since my aim is to sell enough (at 30 guineas each) to cover the total printing bills.

I don't want the book reviewed, or put in public libraries: none are going to B. M. Bodleian etc: nor should one go to the London Library. There will be an abridgement, in 1927, at a guinea, for public consumption. I suppose all this is agreeable to you?

Subscribers have to put a cheque for £15 15 0 to
                    Manager
              Bank of Liverpool & Martins'
                    68 Lombard St
                    E C 3
Cheque to be made out to T. E. Lawrence & marked 'Seven Pillars Acct'.

Will you let me know if you do finally decide to subscribe. I warn you that the book is long, detailed, discursive, technical: and that it contains no political disclosures whatever.

                                        Yours
                                        T E Shaw

London Library

1 Dr Charles Hagberg-Wright (1862–1940) was Secretary and Librarian of the London Library 1893–1940. He was knighted in 1934. His elder brother, the noted physician and pathologist Sir Almroth Wright (knighted in 1906), was the originator of anti-typhoid injections and other medical improvements. General Wright (see first sentence) was his younger brother, Major-General Henry Hagstromer Wright (1864–1948), who had been Engineer-in-Chief, Egyptian Expeditionary Force, from 1916–19.

2 In 1988 the going rate for a copy of the subscribers' edition was £18,000, according to the London bookseller, Henry Sotheran.

LIONEL CURTIS   CLOUD'S HILL
Undated[1]   MORETON
                                                          DORSET

This was Pike's first effort: please delete the apostrophe in your mind.

R.A.F. said — that the question of my transfer would be put up to Sir S. Hoare[2] on his return, which will be tomorrow. If any good comes my way I will write. So don't expect to hear from me!

Having you down here was a delight. The reason why I behaved so clumsily was because of the rarity of such occasions. George Lloyd (ex-Bombay)[3] has been here since.

                                                          T.E.S.

John Buchan: do you ever see him? Could I? Without seeming to wish to? Naturally, in other words.

All Souls College Oxford

MRS CHARLOTTE SHAW
16.V.25   [Clouds Hill]

I'm very sorry to hear that you and G.B.S. are ill. Influenza is becoming a perfect curse to everyone but myself whom it unaccountably misses. I called last Wednesday, on the chance that you might be in, but was unfortunate.

The R.A.F. after chopping and changing (nautical phrases which refer to a sailing wind) definitely turned me down. I have the feeling in my bones that this time the decision is final. Am I a pessimist? Not too quickly, anyway, for it has been nearly three years since my rejections began. Odd, to have tried so many ways of living, to have found only one of them thinkable as a permanency, to have endeavoured for seven years consistently to follow it, and to have achieved it for exactly six months in those seven years. Exactly what effect the disappearance of my last ambition will have upon my course I can't say yet, since for the rest of the year all my attention

1 Early May 1925. The address is printed on a correspondence card. Lawrence sometimes wrote Cloud's, sometimes Clouds' and sometimes Clouds: this letter suggests his own preference was 'Clouds Hill' — the version now universally used.
2 Cf. footnote 2 on p. 246. Sir Samuel Hoare was strongly opposed to the proposal that Lawrence should be readmitted to the Air Force and duly vetoed it on his return to Whitehall. The postscript suggests that Lawrence, already anticipating Hoare's refusal, was thinking of the 'chance' meeting with John Buchan to enlist his support which took place shortly afterwards — see next letter but one — and which began the process which would eventually get him what he wanted.
3 His former wartime colleague had been Governor of Bombay from 1918–23.

must be upon finishing the revise of the *Seven Pillars*. About Xmas I will have to make up this very veering and fickle mind, afresh.

[…]

T.E.S.

I will come up and see you as and when I can: but to make an appointment! No good. My mobility depends on Boanerges,[1] and the weather, and my energy: three variables.

British Library

JOHN BUCHAN[2]

19.V.25   Clouds Hill Moreton Dorset

Dear Buchan

I don't know by what right I made that appeal to you on Sunday.[3] It happened on the spur of the moment. You see, for seven years it's been my ambition to get into the Air Force, (and for six months in 1922 I realised the ambition), and I can't get the longing for it out of my mind for an hour. Consequently I talk of it to most of the people I meet.

They often ask 'Why the R.A.F.?' and I don't know. Only I have tried it, & I liked it as much after trying it as I did before. The difference between Army & Air is that between earth & air: no less. I only came into the army in the hope of earning my restoration to the R.A.F. and now the third year is running on, and I'm as far away as ever. It must be the ranks, for I'm afraid of being loose or independent. The rails, & rules & necessary subordination are so many comforts. Impossible is a long word in human dealings: but it feels to me impossible that I should ever assume responsibility or authority again. No doubt any great crisis would change my mind: but

---

1 i.e. his motor-cycle. Lawrence took the name from Mark 3, in which Jesus surnames his disciples James and John 'Boanerges, which is, The sons of Thunder'. The name was transferred from machine to machine.

2 John Buchan (1875–1940), 1st Baron Tweedsmuir, combined the career of a prolific novelist and biographer with a distinguished career in public life, which culminated with his appointment as Governor-General of Canada. During the war he had been with the Department of Information with responsibility for propaganda in the Empire and foreign countries and in this capacity had facilitated Lowell Thomas's trip to Arabia. For a fine account of Lawrence's character and achievements see Buchan's *Memory-Hold-The-Door* (1940), Ch. VIII.

3 Lawrence had, apparently, successfully contrived to meet Buchan in the street and had spoken of his desire to return to the R.A.F.

certainly the necessity of living won't. I'd rather be dead than hire out my wits to anyone importantly.

The Air Ministry have offered me jobs: a commission, & the writing of their history. These are refinements of cruelty: for my longing to be in the R.A.F. is a homesickness which attacks me at the most casual sight of their name in the papers, or their uniform in the street: & to spend years with them as officer or historian, knowing that I was debarring myself from ever being one of them, would be intolerable. Here in the Tank Corps I can at least cherish the hope that I may some day justify my return. Please understand (anyone here will confirm it) that the Battalion authorities are perfectly content with me. Nothing in my character or conduct makes me in any way unsuitable to the ranks: and I'm fitter & tougher than most people.

There, it's a shame to bother you with all this rant: but the business is vital to me: & if you can help to straighten it out, the profit to me will far outweigh, in my eyes, any inconvenience to which you put yourself!

I think this last sentence is the best one to end on, Yours sincerely
                                                    T E Shaw

DG

EDWARD GARNETT
13.VI.25

[...] Trenchard withdrew his objection to my rejoining the Air Force. I got seventh-heaven for two weeks: but then Sam Hoare came back from Mespot and refused to entertain the idea. That, and the closer acquaintance with *The Seven Pillars* (which I now know better than anyone ever will) have together convinced me that I'm no bloody good on earth. So I'm going to quit: but in my usual comic fashion I'm going to finish the reprint and square up with Cape before I hop it! There is nothing like deliberation, order and regularity in these things.

I shall bequeath you my notes on life in the recruits camp of the R.A.F. They will disappoint you.
                                                    Yours
                                                    T.E.S.

Post Office closed. So the stamps are put on at a venture.

DG

The hint of suicide in this letter so alarmed Garnett that he wrote at once to Bernard Shaw who promptly sent Garnett's letter to the Prime Minister, Stanley Baldwin, suggesting the possibility of an 'appalling scandal' unless something was done. Buchan also appealed forcefully on Lawrence's behalf. Baldwin decided to intervene and overrule the objections of Sir Samuel Hoare. How much the suicide threat was a real possibility or how much it was a dramatic gesture to force the issue it is impossible to say. Trenchard, for example, to whom Lawrence had made similar hints, did not take them seriously. (See *Trenchard* by Andrew Boyle, pp. 515–16) Lawrence's move was, however, undoubtedly an effective one.

E. M. FORSTER
17.VI.25   Clouds Hill Moreton Dorset

I'm very glad to see that you're in the land of the Angles, again. It seemed impossible to write to you abroad, though Arles and Avignon and St. Rémi, Aigues Mortes, St. Gilles and Beaucaire are symphonies of names. I hope you went to Les Baux, & Mont Majeur?

Clouds' Hill is proud, at this moment, with rhododendrons ... and the brake is full of birds' nests. Posh[1] asks me to tell you that the scarlet of your marsh-pimpernel is getting less. Perhaps its long season is ending.

The Isle of Wight? Don't like it: except a part, a muddy flat, called New Hampstead on the Newtown river, & that was many years ago.[2] An interesting woman (very E.M.F. character-like ... early novels) Mrs. Fontana, lives intensely at Brading, with two children.

Did I ever tell you how very much I liked *The Longest Journey*?[3] It struck me as more from the heart than any other of your work: and the characters were all three-dimensional, that rarest of (unintentional) creations. They keep on coming back to me, as people; not in virtue of any particular thing they say.

At this point the pen-nib was changed. I would not have you think the spluttering of the old one was rage. They are the mapping pens with which I correct proofs: and proofs are all about me as I write. The original text is finished correcting. What I am now doing is adjusting the elastic text to fit the inelastic type & page.

The Lowell Thomas review is an excellent idea, & should be great fun.[4] I resent him: but am disarmed by his good intentions. He is as vulgar as

1 Private Palmer.
2 Amongst other places the Lawrence family had lived briefly in the Isle of Wight before they settled in Oxford.
3 An early novel by Forster, published in 1907.
4 Forster had been asked to review Lowell Thomas's *With Lawrence in Arabia*, which had been published in 1924 in the United States, and was published in Britain in 1925.

they make them: believes he is doing me a great turn by bringing my virtue into the public air:

He came out to Allenby as an American official correspondent, saw a scoop in our side-show, & came to Akaba (1918) for ten days. I saw him there, for the second time, but went up country to do some other work. He bored the others, so they packed him off by Ford car to Petra, & thence back to Egypt by sea. His spare credulity they packed with stories about me. He was shown copies of my official reports, & made long extracts or summaries of them. Of course he was never in the Arab firing line, nor did he ever see an operation or ride with me. I met him occasionally afterwards in London in 1920.

So much for his basis. The rest of his book is either invention or gossip. Some of the invention is deliberate, though much that he put into his American magazine articles (red-hot lying it was) has been left out of the American edition of his book.[1] I've not seen the English edition. I thought the American version so disjointed & broken-backed as to be nearly unintelligible, as a history of me in Arabia or of the Arab Campaign above my head! However perhaps I am biassed.

His details are commonly wrong. My family isn't Irish from Galway (*we were an Elizabethan plantation from Leicestershire in Meath without a drop of Irish blood in us, ever) ... and they hadn't any ancestors called Lawrence (*which is a very recent assumption, no better based than Shaw or Ross or any other of my names.) His school & college yarns are rubbish: ditto his story that I was medically unfit, or a child when war began. I was employed in the Geographical Section of the General Staff in the War Office till December 1914.

I was never disguised as an Arab (though I once got off as a Circassian:[2] & nearly got on as a veiled woman!)

My height is 5' 5½"! Weight ten stone. Complexion scarlet. I have not been pursued by Italian Countesses.

You are at liberty to say, if you wish, that

    (a) I'm not going East again
    (b) Am not at All Souls
    (c) Am not breeding cows in Epping Forest
    (d) Am not writing books: and did not enlist to do so,
        but
    (a) Am still serving in the ranks, as was widely published in 1922 (this
        leaves it ambiguous whether R.A.F. or Army)

* Private information. It conceals a family mess.

1 Lawrence was doubtless referring to Lowell Thomas's articles in *Asia* of which he had written disparagingly to Fareedah el Akle in his letter of 3 January 1921 (see p. 183).
2 Possibly a reference to his escape from Deraa in November 1917: see *Seven Pillars of Wisdom*, Chapter LXXX.

(b) am distributing some private copies of my war book, which was
     written in 1919, & privately printed years ago, to my friends &
     their friends, with an undertaking not to reprint it in my lifetime
(c) am proposing to publish in U.K. and U.S.A. an abridgement of
     1/3 of the above, for public sale, in 1927
(d) and do please, above all, say that the Arab Revolt was a pretty
     scabious business, in which none of the principals can take any
     pride or satisfaction: and that my disgust with it expresses itself in
     my refusal to profit in any way by the spurious reputation I (most
     unjustly) won in it.

T.E.S.

In pp. 3 & 4 I write your review. Do please do something quite different.
Have I deserved a Lowell Thomas?

King's College Cambridge

ROBERT GRAVES
25.VI.25

Dear R.G.

You underestimate *Poetic Unreason*.[1] It isn't a bit over-worked: au con-
traire: one of the freshest things ever written on poetics. And the matter is
as good as the manner. The only place where I cavilled was the treatment
of *The Tempest*. God knows each of us have our own fancy pictures of
W.S. . . . and my fancy is to have no picture of him. There was a man who
hid behind his works, with great pains and consistency. Ergo he had
something to hide: some privy reason for hiding. He Being a most admirable
fellow, I hope he hides successfully.

[. . .]

The Viva must have been an appalling affair for your judges. If I'd been
there the door would have been locked (against rules, no doubt) and I'd
have produced a Thermos & some salted almonds, and said 'Mr Graves,
for appearance sake we have to pass 20 minutes in here. Can you do with
a cup of coffee?'

[. . .]

University of Harvard

---

1 Graves's *Poetic Unreason*, published in 1925, was an attempt to interpret poetry in terms
of the psychological process underlying its creation. It has been described as his 'most
overtly "Freudian" book'. Although it was already published, Graves was allowed to
submit it for a B. Litt degree at Oxford: hence the reference to the 'Viva' (i.e. viva voce
examination) in paragraph 2.

MRS CHARLOTTE SHAW
Saturday 4.VII.25 Clouds Hill

[...] About the R.A.F. John Buchan seems to have worked the oracle: anyway Trenchard and Hoare have agreed to let me back into the ranks, on any terms I please: and the matter will be put in hand straight away and completed — some time before October. I think Mr Baldwin said something to Hoare.

This has made the world feel very funny. The first effect was like a sunset — something very quiet and slow as if all the fuss and trouble of the day was over. Now I feel inclined to lie down and rest, as if there was never going to be any more voyaging. I suppose it is something like a ship getting into harbour at last.

The impulse to get that book finished by Christmas is over. I may be living on for years now, and so why hurry it? Also there isn't any longer any need for the book. I was consciously tidying up loose ends, and rounding the oddments off ... and now it seems there aren't any loose ends or oddments.

Don't get worried over this: a few days will see me square again, and I'll realise that it will be as well to finish all the consequences of the Arabian business before pushing off into the R.A.F. You see, if I can clean up the Arab mess, and get it away, behind my mind, then I can be like the other fellows in the crowd. Perhaps my mind can go to sleep: anyway I should be more ordinary than I have been of late. The relief it will be, to have the fretting ended.

In making this fresh start I'll be very careful to give people no grounds for thinking me in any way unlike, or in different circumstances to, the rest.

[...]

British Library

JOHN BUCHAN
5.VII.25   Clouds Hill Moreton Dorset

Dear Buchan

The oracle responded nobly. I was sent for by Trenchard on Wednesday last (horribly inconvenient, for my revolver course did not finish till Saturday, yesterday) and was told that I was acceptable as a recruit.

The immediate effect of this news was to put me lazily and smoothly asleep: and asleep I've been ever since. It's like a sudden port, after a voyage all out of reckoning.

I owe you the very deepest thanks. I've been hoping for this for so many years, and had my hopes turned down so regularly, that my patience was completely exhausted: and I'd begun wondering if it had ever been worth waiting and hoping for. Odd, that the Air Force should seem to me (after trial too!) as the only way of getting across middle age. I wish I could make you some sort of return.

Formalities will take some weeks: but I should change skins in September at latest.

Please inform your family that the bike (Boanerges is his name) did 108 miles an hour with me on Wednesday afternoon. I think the news of my transfer has gone to its heads: (cylinder heads, of course).

More thanks,

                                              Yours ever
                                              T E Shaw

DG

On 16 July 1925 Trenchard signed the order approving Lawrence's transfer back to the R.A.F. He was instructed to put in an application for transfer through his Commanding Officer at Bovington.

R. D. BLUMENFELD[1]
4.VIII.25   Clouds' Hill Moreton Dorset

Dear Blumenfeld

God forbid. I will never come up again, least of all now. Do you remember in 1922 'featuring' my Air Force stage? They gave me a night

1 Editor, *Daily Express.*

to clear out. Since then I've been wandering in the night of the Tank Corps, hoping to justify my return to the R.A.F. (the only life I covet) by decent conduct & obscurity. It seems to have worked: my application for transfer lies at this moment in the Air Ministry, & is being favourably, if slowly considered.

One word from you and I'm in outer darkness again. So for the Lord's sake keep calm.

Do you know I so hate that Arabian business that I'd give all the world (if it were mine) to wipe the record of it off my slate? The only consolation is that I've never made a half-penny out of it. Nor will I, rumours of profitable publication to the contrary.

So there you are: publicity (quorum pars magna estis)[1] has taken away

(i)   My pre-war job

(ii)   ,,   ,,   ,, name

(iii) My All Souls' Fellowship

(iv) All the poor opportunity I had of a fresh start to make a living and you suggest more of it!

Hoots!

Yours ever
T E Shaw

Not feeling at all miserable, because the R.A.F. is again opening its arms. Hoots again.

Bodleian Reserve

HIS MOTHER

18.VIII.25   Clouds Hill

It is so long since I wrote. Some day, you know, I will sit down & close everything: and never after write a letter or go to see a person or speak. Each day I find the satisfying of life's claims harder and harder. Existence is the heaviest burden we bear.[2]

Also your letters have stopped. Perhaps you feel it too. Or is it this Chinese nationality which has cut the road? I am delighted, of course, (except in so far as it may trouble you) to see such signs that the last, & politically the most degraded nation on earth is beginning to live. In time,

---

1 'Quorum pars magna estis': of which you are a substantial part.

2 This letter was not reproduced in *Home Letters*. Its despairing tone is all the more remarkable in that it was written (see paragraph four) on the day towards which he had been working ever since his ejection from the Air Force two and a half years earlier.

if the western powers go on long enough, China will realise her own character & throw off all presumption to control her.

My last letter was to suggest that you might find it necessary to retire out of your place southward or westward. Inevitably the awakening of China will be in the East, & will spread inland.

Today I leave Bovington, probably for Uxbridge, since I am again to join the R.A.F. That is a satisfaction to me.

Arnie & his wife are in Clouds Hill. They do not seem to me to understand the rarity & beauty of the place. They eat in it! In my day there was no cooking allowed. However they seem quiet & happy. I saw them only last week, when they were off to Weymouth for the day. I'll try & see them today before I go.

No other news.

Ned

Bodleian Reserve

Lawrence was sent first to R.A.F. West Drayton to be processed as a recruit, then after a brief spell back in Uxbridge, where he had begun his R.A.F. career just three years earlier, he was posted to the Cadet College at Cranwell, Lincolnshire, arriving there on 24 August. He was now and would remain for the rest of his service years 338171 Aircraftman Shaw.

MRS THOMAS HARDY
26.VIII.25   R.A.F. Cadets' College Cranwell Lincs.

Dear Mrs. Hardy

You see, it has happened! Quite suddenly at the end: so that I was spared a visit of farewell. It is best to go off abruptly, if at all.

I never expected the move to be so drastic. Cranwell is not really near anywhere (nor is it anything in itself): and the disorder of falling into a new station is yet upon me. The R.A.F. is a home to me: but it is puzzling to find the home all full of strangers who look upon me as strange. My known past always rouses curiosity in a new station. Probably in a few days things will be comfortable.

Alas for Clouds Hill, & the Heath, & the people I had learned in the two years of Dorset!

Please remember me to Mr. Hardy, who is no doubt wholly taken up now in *Tess*. You have a good actress.[1] I hope it will seem fitting both to you & the public. It is hard to please two masters.

You said to me that I might see that work of yours again, some time. Please don't forget that: though I can't seem either to read or to write in this noise!

Yours sincerely
T E Shaw

DG

COLONEL A. P. WAVELL
29.VIII.25   R.A.F. Cadets College Cranwell Lincs.

Dear Wavell

Your letter has followed me up here. I have changed my skin, & love the new one: though the job is less good, & the pay less, & the aspect of the countryside very bleak. However: if things were twenty times worse I would still do it with contentment, for the R.A.F. is a show of my own.

The book halts, staggers, for the moment. When I am settled, & can make leisure for myself, it will move on again.

Yours sincerely
T. E. Shaw

Bodleian Reserve

MRS CHARLOTTE SHAW
28.IX.25   R.A.F. Cranwell

Do you know what it is when you see, suddenly, that your life is all a ruin? Tonight it is cold, and the hut is dark and empty, with all the fellows out somewhere. Every day I haunt their company, because the noise stops me thinking. Thinking drives me mad, because of the invisible ties about me which limit my moving, my wishing, my imagining. All these bonds I have tied myself, deliberately, wishing to tie myself down beyond the hope or power of movement. And this deliberation, this intention, rests. It is stronger than anything else in me, than everything else put together. So long as there is breath in my body my strength will be exerted to keep my

---

1 Gwen Ffrangcon-Davies (b. 1891) was to play in a dramatised version of Hardy's *Tess of the D'Urbervilles*.

soul in prison, since nowhere else can it exist in safety. The terror of being run away with, in the liberty of power, lies at the back of these many renunciations of my later life. I am afraid of myself. Is this madness?

The trouble tonight is the reaction against yesterday, when I went mad:— rode down to London, spent a night in a solitary bed, in a furnished bedroom, with an old woman to look after the house about me: and called in the morning on Feisal, whom I found lively, happy to see me, friendly, curious. He was due for lunch at Winterton's (Winterton, with me during the war, is now U.S of S. for India).[1] We drove there together and had lunch in Winterton's lovely house, a place of which I'm splendidly fond, because it has been his for hundreds of years, and is so old, so carelessly cared for.[2] Winterton of course had to talk of old times, taking me for a companion of his again, as though we were once again advancing on Damascus. And I had to talk back, keeping my end up, as though the R.A.F. clothes were a skin that I could slough off at any while with a laugh.

But all the while I knew I couldn't. I've changed, and the Lawrence who used to go about and be friendly and familiar with that sort of people is dead. He's worse than dead. He is a stranger I once knew. From henceforward my way will lie with these fellows here, degrading myself (for in their eyes and your eyes and Winterton's eyes I see that it is degradation) in the hope that some day I will really feel degraded, be degraded to their level. I long for people to look down upon me and despise me, and I'm too shy to take the filthy steps which would publicly shame me, and put me into their contempt. I want to dirty myself outwardly, so that my person may properly reflect the dirtiness which it conceals . . . and I shrink from dirtying the outside, while I've eaten, avidly eaten, every filthy morsel which chance threw in my way.

I'm too shy to go looking for dirt. I'd be afraid of seeming a novice in it when I found it. That's why I can't go off stewing into the Lincoln or Navenby brothels with the fellows. They think it's because I'm superior: proud, or peculiar, or 'posh', as they say: and it's because I wouldn't know what to do, how to carry myself, where to stop. Fear again: fear everywhere.

Garnett said once that I was two people, in my book: one wanting to go on, the other wanting to go back. That is not right. Normally the very strong one, saying 'No', the Puritan, is in firm charge, and the other poor

1 Lord Winterton was Under-Secretary of State for India from 1922–4 and again from November 1924–9. In his autobiographical volume *Fifty Tumultuous Years*, published in 1955, he paid handsome tribute to Lawrence's genius and the range and fertility of his mind and also admitted to hero-worship of him.

2 Winterton's 'lovely house' was Shillinglee Park, Chiddingfold, Surrey. The venue was of special significance to all three of them in that it was at Shillinglee Park in 1921 that Lawrence and Winterton, together with Lord Harlech and Lord Moyne, had persuaded Feisal, in the course of a discussion lasting five hours and ending at 3 a.m., to put his disappointment at his ejection from Syria behind him and accept the kingship of Iraq.

little vicious fellow, can't get a word in, for fear of him. My reason tells me all the while, dins into me day and night, a sense of how I've crashed my life and self and gone hopelessly wrong: and hopelessly it is, for I'm never coming back, and I want to:

O dear O dear, what a coil.

Here come the rest: so here endeth this wail. No more thinking for a while.

I'm pitching it straight away to you as written, because in an hour I'll burn it, if I can get my hands on it.

British Library

HON. FRANCIS RODD[1]
6.XI.25   Cranwell

Dear F.R.

Your offer of the flat is uncommonly kind: & hits me close: but my affairs don't point to my being able to use it much. Week-ends at Cranwell are only alternate Saturday nights. Pleasant: but hardly justifies a flat in town. Christmas leave ... well, I ought to get a fortnight: but it was a privilege to be granted to 'airmen in their first year at a station only if their Commanding Officer signifies that they are of good character and satisfactory'. Do you think I will pass this test? I have grave doubts. They will not tell us till December 15. Christmas leave, if it comes, will be pleasant, like the week-ends. But it seems hardly to justify a flat in town.

So do try & find another tenant, of the shadow-loving sort. I'd have jumped at the chance, had I been free: had I had a decent certainty of using it for a month, even: but a fortnight, plus two potential week-ends. It wouldn't keep the place warm.

Concerning the book. The reprint differs, in many ways, from the 'Oxford' text, which is that which Childs had. I do not want to leave bibliophiles of the twenty-first century two variants, to spend useful hours comparing & cross-checking: so I propose to cause the six copies of the Oxford edition to disappear.

You shall have, since you want it, a copy of the new text: but it will be one of the plain texts, complete in every way as regards the letterpress, but

---

1 Hon. Francis Rodd (1895–1978: later 2nd Baron Rennell) had met Lawrence while serving in Intelligence in Egypt and Palestine and again following Lawrence's crash in Rome in 1919, when he had been staying with his father, James Rennell Rodd (later 1st Baron Rennell), at that time the British Ambassador to Italy. Rodd was himself a distinguished traveller and explorer.

short in the illustrations. Most people will regard them as no loss. It will be a handier book to move from one dwelling to another. The complete edition will be so very large & heavy.

These plain texts have been produced for the fellows who shared in the Arab business, and who are not rich enough to spend thirty guineas on a memento of [text unclear]. You come well under that category. They are paid for by the subscribers (the ultra-rich, the Haslamians[1] etc.) and so virtue is served: i.e. they are distributed gratis.

Do not expect it before March. (For how many Marches have I not said this to the subscribers! But each year the thing is never finished!)

Again many thanks for the flat notion. It was exceedingly kind of you.

Yours ever
T.E.S.

Bodleian Reserve

MRS THOMAS HARDY
9.XI.25

Dear Mrs. Hardy

[. . .] I'm in Lincolnshire now: very far off Dorset: very cold, very bare, the land all brown or green fields, with low dry walls of oolite dividing them. No hedges, no trees, no hills. It feels almost like a fen country, though Cranwell is high up. The churches are all spired, and very beautiful and large. That is fen-like, of course.

Once I got to Bovington, late on Saturday. They put me up in the camp, and I set off again at midday on the Sunday to return. It is a little too far for a winter ride, with the probability of wet roads under the wheels. When summer comes I'll hope to come more often, & will then call.

They tell me that *Tess* is very good, at Barnes. If it runs much longer I will be able to see it, for our cadets go home at Christmas, & that sets us, their slaves, free for long week-ends. I'm very glad it has gone so well. Are you and Mr. Hardy pleased? Or has it been modified to catch the many, & yourselves annoyed?

Don't bother answering these questions. *Tess* was out of your hands when the actors took hold, & you have no more liability than the composers whose jigs go on the barrel organs. It's only that I'm rather by myself, up here, & I had so nearly taken root in Bovington that I can't help thinking of it.

---

1 Haslam was a friend or associate of Rodd's: see letter to Rodd dated 28 January 1926 (p. 298).

Please give Mr. Hardy my very best regards. I've promised myself to call as soon as I have the chance. It's a solidity, to be sure that he will be in Max Gate whenever I can come.

Yours sincerely
T.E. Shaw

Bodleian Reserve

HON. FRANCIS RODD
21.XI.25   Cranwell

Excuse the pencil. It is being written in the hangar. Life has been a rush at Cranwell for the last week: & will be a rush till Dec 15, when the Cadets term ends.

I've got the keys. My very best of thanks. I'll do my best to use them— but you realise that I'm a man under authority. I've put in for the leave they will give me.

Good luck in U.S.A.

I must see your father's book.[1] Sounds interesting!

T.E.S.

A bell just ringing for me. Let it ring: till I've addressed this.

Bodleian Reserve

EDWARD MARSH[2]
21.XI.25   [R.A.F. Cranwell]

Dear E.M.

The red foot-note on page 257 is the only reference later than 1919, in

---

1 Rodd's father, James Rennell Rodd, wrote three volumes of autobiography under the title *Social and Diplomatic Memories* and was also a published poet. In his youth he had been for a time a close associate of Oscar Wilde.

2 Sir Edward Marsh (1872–1953) was a notable man of letters (editor of five volumes of *Georgian Poetry*, author of a memoir of Rupert Brooke and a translator of Horace and La Fontaine) and also private secretary to two great politicians: Asquith from 1915–16, and Churchill from 1917–22. Lawrence was writing to him in this last capacity: the 'him' in the opening paragraph is Churchill. The footnote referred to by Lawrence (to be found on p. 283 of modern popular editions of *Seven Pillars*) pays tribute to Churchill's settlement of the Middle East at the Cairo Conference.

my war-book. I haven't of intention said enough: because I feared that people might say that in praising him I was praising myself. And there is a limit to the disclaimers & protestations that a man can make.

Yet I don't think that he'll object to the briefness or the purport of the note. It's only going to you to make sure.

[…]

A miracle, (called Baldwin, I believe, in the directory, but surely a thing with wings & a white robe and golden harp)[1] put me back suddenly into the R.A.F., when I had completely lost hope. And now I'm a ludicrously contented airman: it's like the old ship Argo, on the beach after all her wanderings, happily dropping to pieces.

Let me have the proof back. S. v. p.

Yours ever
T.E.S.

Bodleian Reserve

LIONEL CURTIS
24.XI.25   R.A.F. Cadet College Cranwell

My lord

Your address was perhaps not the most exact possible: but it reached me. The above is better. I'm not a private now, but an Aircraftman, 2nd class. There is unfortunately no 3rd class, or I'd be that. I'm foolishly happy, and propose to stay 'put' till I'm ninety years old.

Yes. I will come & see you: but not for some while: three weeks perhaps: & then it will be a short quick visit.

Canada and the U.S. You deserve a little peace after such an ordeal. By good chance, Kidlington is peaceful: and Hales Croft very beautiful.[2] I like to know people with beautiful houses, for then I can go round the year touting for beautiful beds, & getting them. What a mercy it is to be small, & easily fitted in, whatever the crush.

The sweater is a great kindness. I hope you have not overdone it. A.C.II's are, as a class, almost immeasurably humble. They beg leave, each morning, of their flight sergeants, to live. I'm the juniorest A.C.II in Cranwell.

Yours
T.E.S.

All Souls College Oxford

---

1 Stanley Baldwin, Prime Minister. See Lawrence's letter to him dated 27 August 1931 (p. 457).
2 Hales Croft was Lionel Curtis's home at Kidlington, Oxford.

E.M. FORSTER
Sunday 29.XI.25   [R.A.F. Cranwell]

I have secured my pass for next week end: have been to church the last four Sundays, to make my claim to Dec 6. incontestable. Also I have read D'Indy's book, & the *Magic Flute*: and the *Prisoners of War*. So my conscience feels there is nothing left undone to prepare me for the occasion.[1] I'm looking forward to it immensely: and am at your disposal any part of the day from 11 a.m. onward. Only I hope it isn't cold. The snow & frost up here have been unbroken for days & days: and I am dying of it.

The D'Indy book is the best I've ever read on music.[2] Of course he must be a considerable musician himself. That is what makes the technical side of the book understanding & interesting even to a person who doesn't like me know the difference between Major & Minor.

I'm sending the D'Indy back so soon as the paper & string come conveniently to hand. This weather seems to close up every pore of activity. The writing this letter has been lying on my conscience as a hard lump since yesterday morning.

We have a gramophone here now, & I got the Polidor Fruhlings Sonata.[3] So that has nerved me. The rest of the hut play dance music: some of which is good fun.

The *Magic Flute* was intensely interesting, for its argument.[4] I suppose the somewhat irritating form has its uses, by conducting the ideas in smooth order before you? I don't like allegory unless it is opaque, so that it's only long afterwards that the slower brains begin to suspect that there was something behind the form. Have you read *They Went*, by Norman Douglas?[5]

Ackerley's play was first rate psychology. The people in it were our very selves. I liked it exceedingly. It is too purely real for literature ... or

1 The 'occasion' was a visit to Cambridge during which Lawrence would have the opportunity to meet some of Forster's literary friends.
2 The French composer Vincent D'Indy (1851–1931) was the author of a *Treatise on Composition*, based on his lessons at the Schola Cantorum in Paris, which he had founded in 1896.
3 The *Frühlingssonate* — *Spring Sonata* — is Beethoven's Sonata in F for piano and violin (Opus 24). The trade-name of the record company, misspelt by Lawrence, is Polydor.
4 *The Magic Flute* was a pacifist allegory by Goldsworthy Lowes Dickinson (1861–1932), Fellow of King's College, Cambridge. Forster, himself to be later a Fellow of King's, was to write Lowes Dickinson's biography (published 1934).
5 Norman Douglas (1868–1952), expatriate novelist and essayist, most famous for his travel books and his novel *South Wind*.
6 Ackerley's play: *Prisoners of War*, referred to in the opening paragraph, by Forster's friend J.R. Ackerley (1896–1967), had grown out of its author's experience as a junior officer in the First World War, in the course of which he had been wounded and taken prisoner, and had subsequently been interned in Switzerland. Written in 1919, it had

rather it is the sort of literature of which very gifted characters can produce one sample, for each life they live. Ackerley will not write anything more that's good. That's the way with human documents.

Lowes Dickinson, being Intelligence with a capital letter, should be more durably useful as a companion than the 'instinctive' people. Yet I can't help itching for the latter. There is always in my mind the thought that I'm perhaps going to meet a miracle at last. Which is why I've bothered you to know more about Lucas.[1] You can rule a line, as hard as this pen-stroke, between the people who are artists & the rest of the world.

About Sunday: send me a line to say where & when I'm to meet you: & fix up anything, anywhere you like, for the rest. Only, if possible, not too late. If the road is dirty it will take me two hours to get back: and 9.30 p.m. is the camp limit.

If the road is still snow-bound & ice-coated I'll come by train: which on Sundays will be even worse: slower, I mean.

Yours
T.E.S.

Your kindness is taken for granted, above; and my gratitude hides between the lines.

King's College Cambridge

MRS CHARLOTTE SHAW
26.xii.25

I haven't any ink in the hut, which is empty now, except for myself. So I'm writing, very languidly, since I have been working all day at my proofs. Book VI has been sent off in penultimate form to Pike: or rather, will go off on Monday morning, when the post-office opens. That is the 'bad' book, with the Deraa chapter. Working on it always makes me sick. The two impulses fight so upon it. Self-respect would close it: self-expression seeks to open it. It's a case in which you can't let yourself write as well as you could.

[...]

Christmas? I don't know what to say of it. The camp has come down to 40 men. They live in the wet bar, mostly. The hangars are locked up. I

---

at last been staged in 1925. Later Ackerley was to become well known as novelist, autobiographer, and Literary Editor of *The Listener*.

1 F. L. Lucas (1894–1967), poet and critic, also a Fellow of King's, was to become a friend and correspondent of Lawrence and a great admirer of him as a writer.

have been transferred as runner (i.e. orderly and charman), to the Accounting Section. A row of eight dirty offices, in a corridor. The old charman, (on leave) did not do them very well. So I've been going down there in the holidays, when the place is empty, and scrubbing or sweeping or window-cleaning. It passes the time, and I can lock myself in. The other fellows are all happy and friendly: but a drunk man is such a fool that he wears my patience to shreds in a few hours. It is only bad at night. Yes, I would call it a happy Christmas, on the whole. Mankind punishes himself with such festivals.

[...]

This book of mine is too ambitious — I wrote it too hard and big (G.B.S. will grit his teeth: — hardly and bigly — but that isn't modern enough). I've printed it too elaborately: illustrated it too richly. The final effect will be like a scrofulous peacock.

Don't worry that this letter is silly. You know what rot people talk of at night-time, round the fire. That's all it is: not a letter at all but yawny gossip. The world is dripping, outside: a thaw at last. The roads have been icebound, and Boanerges rusts in his stall. Did I tell you how I damaged him, and myself, three weeks ago, when the first snow fell? He is mended. My arm is cured. My knee nearly so. Till my leg can bend again I'll not ride him: and it is good to ride him. Chases off the broody feeling.

Falmouth. Did they give you a high seaward room, looking over the decayed green bones of the German submarines, like dead mackerel on the rocks? I hope not. The other side is rather jolly. Across the Fal you have St. Just, in Roseland, which is a good style for a new peer: and a beautiful place — or was. 1906, was it? I was a garrison gunner for a little in the old castle.[1] My mind was not so peaceful then, for I had not tried everything and made a final choice of the least ill.

Does my writing the word GUNTER[2] wake any guilty feeling in your mind? They disappeared like snow on the desert's face. My year (1917) was unlucky for snow. It lay for six weeks. The chocolates did not.[3]

British Library

1 This is an important reference to a much discussed episode of Lawrence's schooldays, namely his enlistment in the Artillery having left home 'at the urge of some private difficulty' (*LHB*, p. 81: the phrase occurs in Lawrence's rewriting of Liddell Hart's draft for the opening chapter of his '*T.E. Lawrence*' *in Arabia and After*). He was apparently bought out by his father. It has been argued that the story was invented but he was away from home for several months early in 1906 and this letter lends substance to his claim. The nature of the private difficulty has not been resolved.

2 Gunter's of Berkeley Square was a firm well known for the excellence of its confectionery and ices.

3 Letter annotated by Mrs Shaw at end: 'We were in Falmouth at Xmas and at Port Elliott after on a visit.'

HIS MOTHER
28.XII.25   [Cranwell]

[...] [Clouds Hill is very beautiful, & suits me. Though I will not live
there till I have been as long in the Air Force as pleases me. You know I
always wanted to be in the R.A.F.] [...]

I've sent you a *Blackwood* article, in which Candler, an Indian journalist,[1]
has written some butter & sugar stuff about me. Don't worry about that —
or me — or anything. People are solitary things (myself especially so) and
as long as it isn't true, I don't care what praise or blame I get. [You talk of
'sharing my life' in letters: but that I won't allow. It is only my own
business. Nor can anybody turn on or off the tap of 'love' so called. I
haven't any in me, for anything. Once I used to like things (not people)
and ideas. Now I don't care for anything at all.][2]

HL/Bodleian Reserve

HON. FRANCIS RODD
28.I.26

Dear F.R.

The 23rd, so Haslam said, was your day of return. I left my keys with
him: and he was going to leave them with his housekeeper, if he went to
Mexico. All this going is terrible.

I hope you are back, & over the first emptiness of return. I've got to
thank you for four exceedingly good nights in London. Four, you will say,
is too few to justify my holding those keys all the weeks: but consider the
quality of those nights. The place so quiet, so absolutely mine, and the door
locked downstairs, so that it was really mine. Why there isn't a lock in my
power at Cranwell, not even on the shit-house door! The happiness &
security of those nights were very keen.

---

1 Edmund Candler: official 'Eye Witness' with the Indian Expeditionary Force during the
  Mesopotamian campaign and author of *The Long Road to Baghdad*, published in 1919.
2 For a comment on his mother which sheds light on his determination to keep clear of
  her influence see his letter to Mrs Charlotte Shaw, 14 April 1927 (p. 322): 'I have a terror
  of [mother] knowing anything about my feelings, or convictions, or way of life. If she
  knew they would be damaged, violated, no longer mine.' In A. W. Lawrence's view he
  was emotionally damaged by her despite his best efforts to retain his own integrity.

I didn't read many books: but I worked the bath-machine over-time. The best of thanks possible.

Yours ever
T.E.S.

DG

COLONEL C.E. WILSON
19.2.26   R.A.F. Cadet College Cranwell

Dear Colonel Wilson

I held your letter up a while, hoping that the two present holders of my Oxford text would send them back to me. They haven't. You shall have whichever reaches me first. It will reach you in a week or so.

[...] I've shortened the new edition, shortened it considerably, by letting out wind, & making two words do for six. Where Archie Murray was described as 'jealous, spiteful, bad-tempered, vicious, clever, quick & narrow' he is now called 'feminine & feline'. Don't tell Mrs. Wilson of this improvement! They are improvements, though!

I apologise for the print of the Oxford text. It was not meant to circulate. The new one is decently done. It will follow in May perhaps. Proof-correcting is not a suitable activity for the barrack!

Yours ever
T.E.S.

Bodleian Reserve

MRS CHARLOTTE SHAW
22.2.26

I'm glad you are better. 'Flu is dangerous, for its possible consequences. The fellows here get chills on top of it and then become wholly sick. However, Ayot is a warm and comfortable home.

Mrs. Warren's Profession[1] is being welcomed in B. Flight. Three have already finished it and praise it. A fourth is dealing with it. *Stalky*[2] and *Mrs. Warren* at present dispute the field. I'm afraid G.B.S. will have a very difficult time dealing with Mrs. W.

1 *Mrs Warren's Profession*, Bernard Shaw's third play, had been written in 1893 but had long been banned and, though it had been performed privately, had only recently (28 September 1925) had its first public performance.
2 *Stalky & Co.*, by Rudyard Kipling.

Measles is a gift — though it has left me, personally, very tired and heavy-headed. Everybody in camp is getting it: so yesterday they cancelled Church parade. That obliterated the one real grudge an airman has against a weekend in Cranwell. I had ridden hard on the Saturday, to Barton on Humber: that road (from Lincoln) includes a stretch of seventeen miles: which I did in seventeen minutes, and felt better for. So on Sunday I sat about the morning in the hut, and played bits of gramophone records to myself. The others were skylarking, and playing rummy, a noisy card-game. So the Beethoven didn't disturb them. Nor did they disturb Beethoven.

The afternoon was fine — grey, heavy-clouded, windy: so I took Boanerges over to Nottingham, his birthplace, for a stroll. The roads were not fit for going fast, so we turned into by-roads and idled through Newark and Southwell. Nottingham is one of those 'Sunday' places — the market square deserted: dust and fog blowing unchecked along the empty streets. The crowds were going to a Wesleyan Mission in their Albert Hall (a hopeless name, Albert. It is ruined for a hundred years). I went instead to a Lyons shop, and ordered tea. The other people were amusing. They hadn't come from my planet, I think. The only friendly person was a black cat, who sat beside me and was exceedingly insistent upon the point of food. I bought an eclair and split it open down its length, like two little dug-out canoes. The cat flung itself upon them, and hollowed out all the pith with its grating tongue. When it got down to the brown shell, it sat back on its hind legs and licked its face lovingly. A Jew merchant-looking man on the opposite seat, also had cream on his cheek and tried horribly hard to lick it. Only his tongue was too short. Not really short, you know: only for that ... The cat was a very excellent animal. The human beings were gross, noisy, vulgar: they did the same things as the cat, but in a clumsy blatant way.

T.E.S.

Heaven knows why I've bothered to write you this nonsense. The moral spoils it. I should have put it into a preface.

British Library

LIONEL CURTIS
8.3.26

Dear Prophet
    I owe you — help! is it three letters, or four. I don't know where I am. Last night, at 10 p.m. I finished correcting the text of the *Seven Pillars*.

Gibbon at Lausanne: etc. etc.[1] Soft music off.

Lowell Thomas' book. Burn it please. No, don't: books are very hard to burn. Use it (them) to strengthen the embankment on the river front of Halescroft. No, don't. The swans haven't deserved that. Give it to Oman.[2]

Very sorry about your health. To be convalescent for months is a terrible business. I'm nearly over my measles, which have been pretty bad.

Major Marriott I've never heard of before. There are lots of these lunatics. In 1918 & 1919 Allenby got a library of gnostic pamphlets: & I've had a good many.

Your remark about ancestry, for which you apologised, I've entirely forgotten! So what can it have been? Bars sinister are rather jolly ornaments.[3] You feel so like a flea in the legitimate prince's bed!

All Souls College Oxford

F.L. LUCAS[4]

14.3.26   R.A.F. Cadet College Cranwell Lincs

Of course it has to be answered: but not easily. I told E.M.F., a week before that your opinion of my book would be important, since you were the best critic just now writing. Then your 'Authors' came along, & confirmed what, after all, was a hasty judgement, since I don't often see the weekly papers. I meant to write to you about your book, comparing your promising plantation of young trees with my builders'-yard of second-hand materials ... and the next step is your finding my thing good!

It puzzles me, and shakes my conviction that it is rotten: of course I'll come back to my own position, afterwards, when the shock of your judgement has died past. Surely you can see that the effective scenes in the book are made effective by writing 'tricks'? I always had the ambition to write something good & when the Revolt gave me a subject I tried to make up for what I felt to be my lack of instinct by taking immense pains: by studying how other people got their effects, & using their experience.

1 A reference to Edward Gibbon's eloquent description of the sense of freedom mixed with melancholy which he experienced when he finally completed his masterpiece *The Decline and Fall of the Roman Empire* and thus took 'an everlasting leave of an old and agreeable companion'.

2 Sir Charles Oman (1860–1946) was the mediaeval historian whose views Lawrence had vigorously attacked in *Crusader Castles*.

3 In heraldry a bar or bend sinister is an indication of illegitimacy.

4 Fellow of King's College, Cambridge, whom Lawrence had met during the visit to Cambridge arranged by E. M. Forster the previous November. See letter to E. M. Forster dated 29 November 1925 (p. 295).

So I built an enormous mass of second-hand ornaments into my skeleton
... and completely hid the skeleton under them. At least I think I spoiled
it, though I notice you detect a certain unity, where S.S. found a lack of
his 'architectonics'.[1]

It sounds very conceited, that I should go on believing the book rotten,
when you have written in the contrary sense. S.S. also called it epical
(though an epic hasn't yet been built on the feelings, as aside from the
actions, of men): and I've lived down his praise. So there isn't much hope
for your downing me. Yet I admit it is a knock, all the harder because I
was sure that your classical spirit would condemn me outright. It is also
awfully good of you to have written at such length.[2]

[...]

Bodleian Reserve

MRS CHARLOTTE SHAW
17.6.26

I have offended. I'm sorry. Things arise from differences in point-of-view.
'Dram-drinking', I said, thinking of the effect on me. A 'whisky bottle'
said you, looking at G.B.S. with new eyes. Yet if I had called him stimulating
no harm would have been done. I thought of 'drinking', you thought of
'dram'.

He is stimulating. He stimulates his household. That is why Ayot will
never be my good toast-and-water. I can only keep happy in the R.A.F.
by holding myself a little below par: if it's much below I mizzle: grow
sorry for myself. This happens if I get hurt, or am crazed overmuch by
some N.C.O. with a grievance to hand on. If I grow excited, then I chafe
at the tightness of uniformed life. When I'm at Ayot the serenity of the sky
overhead, and the keen air and the intellectual delight of fencing with a
real swordsman intoxicate me. Then I go back to Cranwell, and the
policeman in the guard room makes me stand to attention while he checks
my clothes and attitude. The contrasts are too great: G.B.S. talks to me as
if I were one of his crowd: the policeman as if I were one of his crowd:
and I get flustered and sorrowful. Hut 105 is balm to this: for there we are
all on the same footing: it is compulsory intimacy: not of mind, but of
existence. Everybody sees everybody in his shirt daily. Equality exists only
under compulsion, among the bullied.

1 S.S.: Siegfried Sassoon.
2 For a sample of Lucas's opinion of *Seven Pillars* see General Introduction, p. xxiii.

All this I've said before. I tried (All Souls and elsewhere) to live with decent people; and couldn't. There is too much liberty up aloft. I was able to avoid others all day long: and there is no goodness in being a recluse. So I wrote myself down a failure, socially: and I believed (I still believe) that I'd failed in my ambition to become an artist, at book-writing, by taking thought. Creative work isn't achieved by dint of pains. Consequently rather than be a half and half, a Cherry Garrard[1] or Stephens[2] or Stanley Baldwin, I backed out of the race and sat down among the people who were not racing. Racing, in these modern and specialised days, is a pursuit limited to thoroughbreds and detached observers sometimes wonder whether these over-tensioned, super-charged delicate creatures are bred really to improve the race, or just to give pleasure to men-fanciers.

However, that is another story altogether. I'm sorry I called it dram-drinking. What I wanted was a tipple the contrary, the converse of Lethe: the water (G.B.S. principles are sacred) of memory. My mythology breaks down. What are the waters of remembrance? Swinburne has a wonderful chorus of them in *Atalanta*. Is that squared up? When in the Tank Corps I so distrusted my fortitude that I would not take the leaves in my power. Now, at Cranwell, I am not afraid of the temptations to desert: but the equilibrium between conditions and expectations of life is so fine that I shun all disturbances. Happiness lies in maintaining this balance of opportunity and desire.

And also, like a cat, I love firesides, and rugs and quietude: and these things are outside the power of a serviceman. You and G.B.S. having them, will find a yearning for them contemptible. But it isn't really. People only feel little things (like me, the throb of my right wrist) when their bodies are at rest: and there is a world of importance in the little things.

Is this a sermon? It was meant to be an apology.

T.E.S.

British Library

1 Apsley Cherry Garrard: polar explorer and author of *The Worst Journey in the World* (Constable, 1922).
2 James Stephens, Irish poet and story-writer.

MRS CHARLOTTE SHAW
22.8.1926   George Hotel Edinburgh

The George Hotel—that's that—and outside it I walk down Bernard
Terrace, and feel as though I am about to be entertained at Ayot. Only
'Shaw' here still means a snuffy local lawyer-chap. The Scotch haven't yet,
the dear provincials, tumbled to the fact that G.B.S. has pre-empted his
name for the future, and assumed its past.

You know, as time passes, the number of names for a man ambitious to
write, is drawn in. Take my case. I wanted to make books. Lawrence was
impossible, since there is a very great but very strange man writing book
after book as D.H.L. I can smell the genius in him: excess of genius makes
his last book sickening: and perhaps some day the genius will burst through
the darkness of his prose and take the world by the throat. He is very
violent, is D.H.L.: violent and dark, with a darkness which only grows
deeper as he writes on. The revelation of his greatness, if it comes, will be
because the public grow able to see through his dark thinking ... because
the public begin to be dark-thoughted themselves. D.H.L. can't make
himself clear: he can't use the idiom of you and me. So often you find men
like that, and sometimes the world grows up to them and salutes them as
'kings-before-their-time' ... and sometimes nobody ever bothers about
them at all, afterwards.

However, I'm off the point: but nobody with any sporting sense of
D.H.L.'s fine struggle to say something would make it more difficult for
him by using the same name while his fate yet hung balanced: so I took
'Ross' as a yet unreserved name: and then I lost the hope of writing, and
here I am.

Not literally here. My purpose in Edinburgh is to see Bartholomew, the
map-making firm which is adapting a War Office map to the illumination
of the *Seven Pillars*. Tomorrow morning I will see them and tomorrow
afternoon I will be in Cranwell. It takes $7\frac{1}{2}$ hours, Boanerges, going respectably. The respectability is mine. Boanerges would go madly, if I would.
Alas, surely I grow old. Again and again, this morning, when we came to
a piece of road which invited ninety, I patted his tank and murmured
'Seventy only, old thing', and kept to it. The excuse I gave myself was that
Edinburgh was a long way and that there must be no full-open throttle on
a long journey. Indeed that was once my maxim: but today I kept the
maxim without being vexed thereby: and that is significant. Or is it only
that I have ridden too many hundreds of miles this last week. My time in
England draws short: and I'm not yet surfeited, but want to be. That
appetite of the well-fed for more food.

News? None. The colour printers are proving their last three prints. One
has 23 colours upon it. Lord save us! Kelman, a Constable partner, was

admiring some of the prints at Chiswick and said to the printer ... 'Now why shouldn't you give *us* some work of that quality?' 'We will', said Newberry, 'if you'll pay 10/- a print!' Exit K.

Bookbinding ... October. Distribution ... November. Deportation ... December.

I hope you and G.B.S. are well, fiercely active, hot and happy.

T.E.S.

British Library

MRS CHARLOTTE SHAW
24.8.1926   [London]

[...] At Cranwell I got your letter, doubting whether I liked your writing to me. I posted my Edinburgh note there, and came on here, wondering how I was to answer you: for therein lies the crux of the matter. It isn't any good my telling you that I look forward to your letters and enjoy them ... for you will not believe that unless I answer them in kind ... and I can't do that. It is easy when we are working together on a book: that gives me a peg to hang a letter on: but upon thin air! I can't. Candler said that I was essentially an unclubbable man: meaning one who took everything, and returned nothing. I like your letters: they are the only 'general' letters I ever get, for no one but yourself has persevered in writing to me: but though I like them as much as I do, I can't send the same sort of things back, any more than I can play any other game on earth. You know, I've never, since I was able to think, played any game through to the end. At school they used to stick me into football or cricket teams, and always I would trickle away from the field before the match ended.

The same apparently with letters. It isn't a Belfast-nonconformist-conscience: because I haven't any convictions or disbeliefs — except the one that there is no 'is'. You can go about the earth being interested in itself, for its own sake, because you believe in many things. Whereas I can't be interested in Durham, even, or in Boanerges, except I wish to interest another person in them.[1] Also I hate talking about the involutions and convolutions of my insanely-rational mind! By the way, you'll laugh at the in-keeping of my ride up to Edinburgh. I did a thirty-mile return-around, because my road came to a toll-bridge, and I never pay tolls! 'When a thing is inevitable, provoke it as instantly and fully as possible' said the *Seven Pillars*. My matter of fact ancestry compels me to carry my impulses

---

1 He had just ridden south from Edinburgh and explored Durham on the way.

into action. Imagine a person utterly lacking in common-sense, but with every other quality normal.

At Cranwell I greeted B. Flight, who came out and stroked Boanerges lovingly, and then fled again wildly down the Great North to London. It seemed harsh to roar through Codicote, though. When you come back I want to drop in, suddenly, again. A night is too long. One short sharp drink, and back, soberly, in the saddle.

It is altogether too late. Westminster has just struck a half-hour, which must be half-past one. It's only after midnight that I can write such rubbish.

T.E.S.

British Library

SIR HUGH TRENCHARD
20.11.26

Dear Sir Hugh

It is good of you to give me the option of going overseas or staying at home: but I volunteered to go, deliberately, for the reason that I am publishing a book (about myself in Arabia) on March 3, 1927: and experience taught me in Farnborough in 1922 that neither good-will on the part of those above me, nor correct behaviour on my part can prevent my being a nuisance in any camp where the daily press can get at me.

Overseas they will be harmless, & therefore I must go overseas for a while & dodge them. After a few years the bubble will be either burst or deflated, & I can serve again at home. England seems to me much the best place to be, anyway.

I'm sorry you should have been unnecessarily troubled. It had been my ambition that you shouldn't hear of or from me, after my readmission to the R.A.F. I'm perfectly happy in it on the ordinary terms: and if the other fellows knew that I used to know you, my character would be ruined.

Yours sincerely
T E Shaw

R.A.F. Museum Hendon/HMH

HON. FRANCIS RODD
3.XII.26   [R.A.F. Uxbridge]

I had an awful month: real hard labour upon my old-man-of-the-sea: final printings, plates, collection, collation, issue to binders, correction of subscribers' lists, allotment of copies. Yet though I sweated at it every possible hour of the day & night, seeing no-one and doing nothing else, even now it is not finished. About 20 copies have gone out, & most of the rest will go out about Christmas time: but the very special copies will hang on till the new year. I think my experience is almost a conclusive demonstration that publishing is not a suitable hobby for an airman.

I've crashed my bike & sold the bits, & am not good company for the world. They inspect us very often in the depot here, & on Tuesday morning we sail for Southampton. Karachi next stop, though only temporary. I'll write to you after I come to rest finally, and ask you how you like the massive volume. Amateur writers, & one-book-men always write at exhausting length.

[...]

I spent one week-end in a house with your Sahara book, & liked it,[1] though it is written to instruct, & my reading is for amusement. I'm awfully glad you took such care in the style & the arrangement. If every modern traveller ... however, enough said. A good book. My own is more ambitious, aimed, if I may say so, for a more remote star and falls proportionately shorter than yours. A case of over-vaulting.

Well, that's that. I'd have liked to have seen you, & did ring up three nights, when unexpectedly I found that my proper work had come to a temporary standstill ... but each time there was no reply. These things do not really matter, of course, but I should have liked it.

Yours
T.E.S.

Bodleian Reserve

1 Rodd had crossed the Sahara and published a book about his experiences and observations of the Touareg tribe under the title *People of the Veil* (Macmillan, 1926).

DICK KNOWLES[1]
3.XII.26

Dear Dick

I'm sitting in a very poor hut at Uxbridge, writing the same thing to dozens of people. On arriving in London for my 28 days leave I found the book not nearly ready for the binders. I put in a months hard work on it: have got all of it out to binders, and nearly half of its copies bound. Some 20 have been sent out already.

In doing this I spent the whole of my leave, seeing no one, & going to no concerts: not one single scrap of public music all that while: though by the goodness of my dentist,[2] I twice heard Harold Samuel play in his house.

I managed to squeeze out $\frac{1}{2}$ an hour in Clouds Hill: and $\frac{1}{2}$ an hour at the Hardys. I had meant to come to you last Sunday, & started about 7.30 a.m. but Islington streets were greasy (I had to see G.B.S. on my way) & I got into a trough in the wood paving, & fell heavily, doing in the off footrest, kickstart, brake levers, $\frac{1}{2}$ handlebar, & oil pump. Also my already experienced knee-cap learnt another little trick. Alb Bennett took the wreck for £100. I limp rather picturesquely.

So that is that. It's an explanation, for I've apologised too often today on paper to repeat it again.

I sent you a set of the largest possible proofs: the dirty old ' "B" Flight Manual' which circulated to so many people at Cranwell. Some squadron leader or other re-covered it!

The final book came out not so badly: the printing is lovely, some of the tail-pieces beautiful, some curious, some amusing: some otherwise: and the binding is being well done. Of course it is very large: too large but that I knew long ago, & was prepared to be shocked at. There were not quite enough copies, after all, so that I've not been able to give away many to the fellows who helped the Arab Show forward.

It is a strangely empty feeling to have finished with it, after all these nine years. Now comes the voyage east in the *Derbyshire*, a pause in being: and then will come a need to find enough interests in my reach to busy me henceforward. I'll write from India, when I've been posted somewhere permanently, and tell you how it feels like to be poor — and finished!

Yours
T.E.S.

DG/Bodleian Reserve[3]

1 Dick Knowles was one of the three sons of Sergeant W. A. Knowles, Lawrence's across-the-road neighbour at Clouds Hill. He followed Lawrence into the ranks of the R.A.F.
2 W. Warwick James, senior dental surgeon at the Middlesex Hospital and music enthusiast: he contributed an article on Lawrence's interest in music to *Lawrence by His Friends*.
3 First three paragraphs published in part in *DG*.

5 · The Years In India

1927–29

Lawrence went east without enthusiasm. 'I squat on deck with Smith, C.J.,' he wrote on 16 December 1926 from the S.S. *Derbyshire* to his R.A.F. friend Sergeant Pugh, 'lamenting Cranwell and England, and all good things.' When the long, unpleasant voyage was over he found himself in an R.A.F. camp at Drigh Road just outside Karachi. 'The Depot is dreary, to a degree,' he commented to Charlotte Shaw on 28 January, adding: 'its background makes me shiver. It is a desert very like Arabia: and all sorts of haunting likenesses [...] try to remind me of what I've been for eight years desperately fighting out of my mind.' To his American friend Colonel Ralph Isham (10 August 1927) he was even more outspoken: 'I hate the East. It holds bad memories for me.' However, to his old wartime comrade Lieutenant-Colonel F.G. Peake, now commanding the Arab Legion in Transjordan, he wrote wistfully (20 October 1927) of that 'delectable land. I am often hungry for another sight of its hills. Rum, too [i.e. Wadi Rumm]. If only... Drigh Road, this place, is dismal.' But this was written at a time when he had been stirred to think warmly of his wartime past by a letter from Mrs Shaw who had just met Feisal and had, apparently, aired the idea when writing to Lawrence that Feisal might not be averse to their working together again. Lawrence was taken with the possibility but swiftly rejected it. 'I don't think he wants me, really,' he told her on 18 October 1927. 'When with him I am an omnipotent adviser: and while that is very well in the field, it is derogatory to a monarch.' He was 'happy' that Mrs Shaw liked him. 'He has been king for six years, which is a deep experience. I wish you could have known him, as I did, when he was Feisal, just. One of the most attractive human beings I have ever met.'

He made no attempt to relieve the monotony by getting to know India; throughout his year and a half at Drigh Road he never once visited Karachi. Similarly at his second posting, Miranshah — in Waziristan, near the Afghan border — to which he transferred in June 1928, he never went beyond the confines of the camp. Though he found much to dislike about his exile from home and friends, he appreciated that it gave him, or at any rate appeared to give him, freedom from publicity. Writing to Mrs Shaw on 29 March 1927 he described himself as 'killing time there [i.e. at his R.A.F. depot] till my books are forgotten'. A distant Fleet Street seemed to offer little threat. 'The English Press [...] feels so old, after the three weeks and the journey.'

His work was undemanding and he had much free time, which he filled with reading, occasional writing for publication (see his letters to Evelyn Wrench and Francis Yeats-Brown) and with correspondence. At home there was the prospect of meeting his friends; as he wrote to Charlotte Shaw on 29 March 1927, 'In England there was a current of life round me, and I swam in it [...] and now my physical radius is cut down to a mile, my company to eleven airmen [...] all in the same uprooted state.' Without the prospect of seeing his peers letters offered the only method of contact. He received so many letters that he could answer only a small proportion of them, but to those to whom he wished to write he gave generous measure; his letters to Charlotte Shaw, E. M. Forster, Robert Graves, Sir Hugh Trenchard and Sergeant Pugh are sometimes many pages long. This is also the period of some of his most frank and revealing letters: to Charlotte Shaw about his family background and about his parents (particularly about his mother); to Graves and Forster about his sexuality; to his mother about the attitude of the West to China and about the missionary movement.

It was also at this period that he took the decision to change his name by deed poll to T. E. Shaw; see his letter to the Hon. Edward Eliot dated 16 June 1927.

Ironically, it was his chosen remoteness from civilisation which, in January 1929, abruptly brought his stay in India to an end. Some months after arriving in Karachi he had been offered a two-year plain-clothes engagement as a clerk to the British attaché in Kabul, and had turned it down because, among other reasons—as he told Mrs Shaw in a letter of 1 June 1927—'Probably the British military attaché in Cabul [sic] is only a glorified kind of spy. [...] Safety first, as they say in 'busses [i.e. aircraft]. Better the camp you know... and Drigh Road is as hidden a place as any in the world.' He had thought himself equally hidden in Miranshah, but now the news of a revolution in nearby Afghanistan combined with the fact that he was based only ten miles from the Afghan frontier led to sensational stories in the British press claiming that he was actively involved. In the *Daily Herald* report which broke the story (5 January 1929) he was referred to as 'the arch spy of the world'. At the time his most important extra-curricular activity was the task to which he had just been contracted by the American book-designer Bruce Rogers of producing a new prose translation of Homer's *Odyssey*. Moreover, this disturbance of his peace came only weeks after he had made a particular point of writing in gratitude to the daily paper of Lahore, the *Civil & Military Gazette*, which had taken the 'Home papers' of Britain to task for their obsession with Lawrence's whereabouts, stating, 'His station is known to us, but we see no reason for interfering with his desire for freedom from publicity.' Lawrence had told the Editor (29 October 1928): 'I have not done anything, for many years now, to deserve publicity: and I will do my best not to deserve publicity, in future.' All this was scarcely the stuff of sedition, but to Fleet Street the fact that a rebellion had happened so near to where Lawrence of Arabia was now based was enough; soon there were questions in the House of Commons while anti-imperialists burnt him in effigy on Tower Hill. The Air Ministry despite its own reservations acceded to the request of the Government of India that he should be removed from the sub-continent as soon as possible. Trenchard was prepared to offer him a posting in Aden or Somaliland but he also insisted that Lawrence himself should be consulted. Lawrence opted to come home.

SERGEANT A. PUGH[1]
16.XII.26   [On board the troopship *Derbyshire*]

Dear Sergt.
    Your letter to Uxbridge pleased me so that I repent the thinness of this reply to it: but we live on board in a clotted and organised misery which takes me out of the little inclination I ever had to write letters. Today is the tenth day at sea. Tomorrow is Port Said, where this letter can be posted. From the Canal is 21 days to Karachi, and land. Twenty-three times have I crossed this Mediterranean — twenty three times too many for my happiness. I squat on deck with Smith, C.J. lamenting Cranwell and England, and all good things. Smith asks you to distribute his best wishes among the Flight.
    [...] I don't start in fit order to smile at the discomfort of a trooper, because of the tangle of my affairs behind me, some private troubles, and my regret that I've got to go abroad again, when I'd been hoping to lie quietly in England for the duration. The combination of these things makes me drizzle softly about myself. Please remember me to Mrs. Pugh, & tell the fellows I'll send a decent scrawl, after they have fixed me somewhere in India for good.
                                        Yours ever
                                        T E S.

It's quite true about my being overseas. In London I saw Trenchard, who

1 A member of Lawrence's Flight at Cranwell. His reminiscences of Lawrence in the R.A.F., written for Robert Graves, are to be found in Chapter 31 of the latter's *Lawrence and the Arabs*.

very nicely gave me the choice of going or staying, on Winston's initiative. I had to choose to go, of course, damn it. I'm always hurting myself or my interests. T. says that he might let me sign on again, in 1930, if I was fit & wished it. If so I shall not be back till 1932, a whole age away.

Bodleian Library

MRS CHARLOTTE SHAW
11.1.27

This is one of a flock of letters which say to everyone,

	My address is
Room 2 out of a block of 8. The letters stand for Engine Repair Section — the mechanical shops — in which I'm a messenger clerk.	338171 AC2 Shaw Room 2. E.R.S. R.A.F. Depot Drigh Road Karachi India

I'd very much like that book of yours, for I have leisure, or shall have, to read it here, and the Indian atmosphere should be congenial to its philosophy.[1] Not that there is much of India about these stone built palaces in the sand. We are housed like hospital patients, sumptuously and barely.

The voyage out was better from Port Said to Basra (where I did not land), and overcrowded again from Basra to Karachi: so I am glad to stop here, only six miles from the port. Enough of travelling. Only one moment on the boat delighted me, as we steamed down the river from Basra for the sea, in early morning. The sun, not a third up its quadrant, was shining faintly against us through a mist. It cast our shadows on the deckhouse behind — a pale shadow only half our height; but across the shoulders of this shadow-body danced a blacker shadowed pair of legs: very strong and sharp these legs, with a curious shuttle-weaving play across their colour. I looked for the second illuminant, and saw that it was the projection of the sun from its image in the river: and the watering of the shadow-texture was a reproduction of the burnished ripples which sat firmly across the oiled water, dented into it, like hammer marks.

On the road out I read *War and Peace* (still good: very good: but not

1 See letter to Mrs Shaw dated 24 February 1927 (p. 317).

more-than-human, as I first thought) and all Pepys' Diary (Sub-human that! What a poor earth-bound lack lustre purblind worm). That, with Ecclesiastes and Synge's *Aran Islands*[1] represents all my recent food. Books are very dear here, owing to a duty which is charged on all imports. So please mark the value of the books you send me upon a modest scale. The *Seven Pillars* is not 'worth' 30 guineas to me!

I suppose I should tell you something of this place but I cannot. There is five years yet for talk upon paper between us.

By the way Synge said apropos of Aran Islanders,

'There is hardly an hour I am with them that I do not feel the shock of some inconceivable idea, and then again the shock of some vague emotion that is familiar to them and to me. On some days the island is my perfect home and resting place: on other days I am a waif among the people. I can feel more with them than they can feel with me, and while I wander among them they like me sometimes, and laugh at me sometimes, yet never know what I am doing'.

That is not very finely said (the first sentence being clumsy), but finely felt, I fancy. One feels it whenever one is again amongst strangers.

T. E. S.

British Library

ERIC KENNINGTON
11.1.27

[...] My opinion of Karachi? None, as yet. We are seven miles away from it, and on the way here saw only squalid back-yards from the carriage-windows. I'm going to mope about camp in my spare time, and avoid pleasuring in the town, so far as I can avoid it. Housed well, and fed well, in a blinding wilderness of sand.

It seems years ago since I sat to you. How did the bust please you after all? It seemed to me, on that last sitting, not to be quite finished, but to be magnificent. I hope the magnificence did not depart when the finish came.[2]

[...]

Bodleian Reserve

1 J. M. Synge's *The Aran Islands* (1907), an account of the way of life of the fishermen and peasants of the Aran Islands off the west coast of Ireland, was based on his experience of living among them.
2 Kennington had been working on the bust of Lawrence which is now in St Paul's Cathedral.

HIS MOTHER

11.1.27   R.A.F. Depot Drigh Road Karachi

I've only just got here, and cannot yet say what I think of the place. It is comfortable, almost magnificently-built, and cool. I am in room two, with fourteen fellows. It seems a quiet place, though the stone floors & high ceilings are noisy and distant, hospital-like, after the homeliness of Cranwell. [...]

Before leaving England I got my *Seven Pillars* finished, & sent out the early copies to specially privileged subscribers. You will laugh at me to hear that the first went to the King: but he wanted one, & I amused myself by treating him well! Arnie has your copy, to keep till you instruct him to the contrary. Its completion takes a load off my mind.

[Chinese politics do not improve much, though I'm glad to see their anti-foreign bias.[1] Salvation comes from within a nation, & China cannot be on the right road till, like Russia, she closes her eyes & ears to teaching & follows her own instincts to their logical and absurd limits. So long as she permits outsiders to teach or preach in her boundaries, so surely is she an inferior nation. You must see that. People can take from one another, but cannot give to one another.

It seems to me that the inevitable victory of the Canton party may be delayed yet a long while, & that the disorder is nearly bound to spread up the river till it reaches you. The journey is unwholesomely long, even in peaceful conditions. In war conditions it might be very hard, even if not dangerous to you — and I have noticed that there are no foreign casualties in all this unrest — and therefore I'd urge strongly that it's Bob's business to get you out before you are both compelled to go. There cannot be any conception of duty to urge him to stay. In olden days doctors & medicine were respectable mysteries: but science is rather out of fashion now: and it seems to me that the fate of everyone upon earth is only their own concern. It is no merit to prolong life, or alleviate suffering:— any more than it is a merit to shorten life or inflict suffering. These details are supremely unimportant.

Of course you will do as you like: remembering always that you are the

---

1 Lawrence was writing at a time of much upheaval in China, where a united front of Nationalists and Communists, strongly motivated by anti-imperialism and an opposition to Western ideas — hence his reference to 'anti-foreign bias' — and actively supported by Soviet Russia, was engaged in a military 'Northern Expedition' (so called because they were moving north from their original power base at Canton) to take over the country. Lawrence's concern at his mother's and brother's vulnerable, and in his view untenable, position in China was a regular theme in his 'home letters' from now onwards.

guests of China, & that guests should leave their hosts before the hosts are replete, so that their leaving shall be yet regretted.] [...]

N

Bodleian Reserve

MISS FAREEDAH EL AKLE
28.i.27   R.A.F. Depot Drigh Road Karachi

[...] This country, India, is not good. Its people seem to feel themselves mean. They walk about in a subdued, repressed way, also it is squalid, with much of the dirty industrialism of Europe, with all its native things decaying, or being forcibly adjusted to Western conditions. I shall be happy only when they send me home again, (which may not be till 1932). [...]

Bodleian Reserve

MRS CHARLOTTE SHAW
28.1.27   [R.A.F. Karachi]

Work here ends each day at 1 p.m., except on Thursdays and Sundays, when it never begins. We get up at 6. The hours from 1 p.m. till ten at night are for ourselves to fill. [...]

The Depot is dreary, to a degree, and its background makes me shiver. It is a desert very like Arabia: and all sorts of haunting likenesses (pack-donkeys, the colour and cut of men's clothes, an oleander bush in flower in the valley, camel-saddles, tamarisk) try to remind me of what I've been for eight years desperately fighting out of my mind. Even I began to doubt if the coming out here was wise. However there wasn't much chance, and it must be made to do. It will do, as a matter of fact, easily.

The home papers seem to be yapping about me, a little. I believe *The Times* started them off, though I have not seen its article. The troops blushingly lay before me snippets of *The People* or *Tit-Bits*, which represent me as a marvellous rifle-shot or a master of back-chat. Odd that my ordinary present should breed that type of story.

Two letters, this makes, in three weeks, while you haven't an address! Not fair; but it's my fear that later on our letters may peter out. Space and time are as real, or unreal, as us, and will affect us.

By the way, on that last walk in London (its quietude a very blessed memory) as we crossed Maiden Lane you betrayed that it was your hand which each Christmas deflected a share of Fortnum and Masons' wealth to the little crowd of us in camp. I'd narrowed the probability of it to three or four people but couldn't tax them, for fear of getting three or four helpings the next year. The goods were enjoyed as you would have wished. My curious taste delights in exotic things (exotic in the Services means food rarer than beef or potatoes): and the other fellows, who perhaps hadn't lived in the wider world, loved the luxurious 'adventures' of peach-fed ham or foie-gras. Dispensing the bounty made me feel quite the patron. If you had been more patient of thanks I'd have given you a picture of the surprised delight of Clouds Hill when the first case arrived. However, enough said.

The weather is smoothly fine, with a warm sun at mid-day; but the dark mornings are very cold, and the evenings too. I shall be glad when the winter ends, and real heat comes along. Dust-storms come, however, in spring, nearly every afternoon, they say: and as all this Sind desert is sand, dust-storms they will be! Still it's worth putting up with that for the sake of being warm.

T. E. S.

British Library

MRS CHARLOTTE SHAW
24.ii.27

[...] (vii) I've made a beginning on your little book.[1] A slow beginning, as throughout it will be slow progress, for my mind is inert, rather than curious or contemplative. Only abrupt contact with some flinty edge of actuality will strike a thought out of me. If I strive to dwell upon pure idea, my brain gets quickly moidered,[2] and wanders dreamily away down the broader problems of conduct. Conduct (doing) is really so much larger a subject than existence — not larger, perhaps, in the sense of feet and inches, but — well, you can explore Arabia, whereas we speculate vainly about Mars. To do a day's work, as I do, is only possible by taking for granted that we exist, a white lie which discourages us from being abstract-minded. Christianity has handicapped itself with a growing proportion of people since 1600 by apparently assuming (i) that we exist, (ii) that man is the centre of his universe, and (iii) that God is, more or less, analogous to man. When you say 'not proven' to (i), 'impossible' to (ii) and 'ridiculous' to

1 The 'little book' was a pamphlet entitled *Knowledge is the Door*, written by Charlotte Shaw and published in 1914. It was a study of the views on life, faith, spiritual healing etc. of the American writer and lecturer Dr James Porter Mills, whom she had met through the actress Lena Ashwell and by whose philosophy she had been deeply impressed.
2 i.e. bothered or fatigued.

(iii), then you lose patience with a crowd which fusses over details like transubstantiation. However your little book isn't so interested in super-structure as to neglect the foundations, so I have a better chance of liking it, than of liking S. Thomas Aquinas, who feels to me more like the founder of European dogmatic Christianity than its rather pitiful eponym. Also in this colourless place I have more time for speculation than ever before in my life. It's most severely colourless, except for the red roofs of the blocks, and the red lamp on the top of the wireless masts at night. I do not like it much. Karachi town is seven miles off, and most of it, they say, out of bounds to us. I have not yet been out of camp, and feel no urge to go out, specially.

T. E. S.

British Library

ROBIN BUXTON
4.iii.27   [Karachi]

Dear Robin
   It was good of you to send me that huge letter. This is a reply to it, seriatim.
   1) Karachi will do as a place of exile. The C.O. is light-headed, & gives us too much drill. The work hours are too few. The country round is without form or colour. The natives are poor gruel-feeding mean-bodied things. Our rooms are comfortable, & the atmosphere of the camp friendly. I'm reduced to reading Greek for some wanton employment of my spare time. The voyage out was worse than anything I expected ... and my standards of living aren't high.
   [...]
   4) Kennington's bust of me seemed to me very good. K. is a very fine artist, I fancy. He will want a lot of money for each copy of it, probably. The papers say the *S.P.* is up to £150: perhaps, in rare instances: but I doubt whether it stays there. The public imagine there are only 100 copies. Actually no one but myself knows how many there were: 128 were more or less subscribed for: and I gave away half as many, some complete & some incomplete. If I'd put a decent inscription into the copy you are selling I could have raised its value: but in the rush of that last week I left undone all the little things I might have done. I'm glad you like the second copy. Sell them both if you get bored with possession!
   [...]
   6) Anything you can reasonably do to keep Pike afloat is a good deed. I

respect the man, & am very sorry for him. I hope he has finished the distribution to subscribers. By my letters I judge he has nearly finished.

7) 'tempt you to divulge your feelings about your life'. Well: I feel that the writing complication is past: & with it the last vestige of responsibility for what I did in Arabia. Under Winston I put in order the actual situation in the Middle East, to my full content. In the *S.P.* I've put on record my 'why' and 'how'. So now that is all over, and I'm again a private person, and an insignificant one.

It remains for me to do something with the rest of my life. Having tried the big things & collapsed under them, I must manage something small. The R.A.F. in England suits me perfectly. If I could be always fit and at home and not grow old I'd stay in it for ever. India is exile, endured for a specific purpose, to let the book-fuss pass over. After India I may be still fit enough for a little more service in the R.A.F. at home. When my health drives me out of it (or Trenchard drives me out!) I'll try & get some quiet job, near London, which is the place I like. A night-watchman, door-porter, or else something like a chauffeur: though I will soon be too old for anything exposed. Perfection would be to do nothing: to have something like a pound a day from investments, & live on it, as I very well could. I've learnt a lot about living in the last five years: and have a curious confidence that I need not worry at all. Desires and ambitions & hopes and envy ... do you know I haven't any more of these things now in me, for as deep down as I can reach? I am happy when I'm sitting still, in complete emptiness of mind. This may sound to you very selfish ... but the other fellows find me human, & manage to live with me all right. I like so much the being left alone that I tend to leave other people alone, too.

Yours ever
T. E. S.

[...]

Bodleian Reserve

MRS CHARLOTTE SHAW
4.iii.27

[...] Allenby sent me a very pleasant letter: talking of our co-operation, and enclosing a message from Lady Allenby, who was always friendly. This relieves me, for it has been a fear of mine that his sense of proportion (a very sober and stern quality in him) somehow associated my person with the ridiculous reputation raised about it by the vulgar. You see, my campaign and fighting efforts were entirely negligible, in his eyes. All he required of us was a turn-over of native opinion from the Turk to the British: and I took advantage of that need of his, to make him the step-father of the Arab national movement: a movement which he did not understand, and for whose success his instinct had little sympathy. He is a very large, downright and splendid person, and the being publicly yoked with a counter-jumping opportunist like me must often gall him deeply. You and G. B. S. live so much with poets and politicians and artists that human oddness attracts you, almost as much as it repels. Whereas with the senior officers of the British army conduct is a very grave matter.

 [...]

British Library

ERIC KENNINGTON
25.iii.27

[...] So you feel old sometimes! Here in Karachi I not merely feel old, but am old. And you want to create: whereas I've bust all my head's blood vessels in an abortive effort to create, and am condemned not to exert myself in future. What would you do in such a case? Say ha ha and blow your brains out? Too messy.

 If only it were all over.

Yours
T. E. S.

Bodleian Reserve

MRS CHARLOTTE SHAW
29.3.27   Drigh Road Karachi India

Your expectation of a fat letter will be roused by the fat envelope: but it is not so much after all. I write a day early, because of the probability that I may be on guard in a day or two. Your last letter was written from bed, ill: and it was depressed: partly because you thought I resented the preface of G. B. S.: whereas it gave me several readings of pure joy — (after the first, I didn't trust him for that, and dashed through it heart in mouth, wondering what would happen. Only he was discretion itself, considering all he knew. I take it as the greatest compliment I'll ever be paid) — and I've sent it on to China reluctantly. This Chinese business is looking very bad. I try not to dwell on it. Mother is old, and not well: and adamant.

I hope it was only because you were yourself depressed. I sent you the Indian cutting to show you how G. B. S. reaches all over the world: and round it wrote a true account of All Souls, because I thought he had not done that well-meaning club justice. He does not like Oxford (Oxford is heaven from 18-21 years old, and spoils its natives for after life) but Oxford is a great love of mine, into which I only wish I could fit, and I don't want him to think that I have a grouse against it, or the British Government. Both have been generous to me.

Your mention of Richards' rushing into print amuses me. I hadn't heard of it. He is an unworldly sincere, ill-mannered Welsh philosopher, who makes a living out of candidates for Sandhurst or the Consular Service by coaching them in special subjects. We were at Jesus together and at Chingford for a few days. My books are at his house (3 Loudoun Road) in St. Johns Wood. An interesting man. I dug out this letter I wrote him in 1918 to send you: partly because I have nothing of my own to say this week, partly because it may interest you, despite its slightness and carelessness, as the only war-letter of mine which has survived, to my knowledge.[1] He kept it, oddly and I found it interesting enough, in 1925, to copy for myself at Clouds' Hill, where he brought it to show me. Indeed I suspect it has a value, as my only side light of the Arab period. I don't think Hogarth has any letters of that date: if indeed he keeps them. I've never yet begun to wonder about that question of letters. Of course somebody will want to write a life of me some day, and his only source will be such letters as chance has preserved. Had they been all kept, there would be a pretty complete history of events since 1910: volumes of stuff enough to discourage any historian: but chance will winnow his pile down. Lately I have, regretfully, destroyed many letters of yours: with a feeling that you would not like them shown to strangers: yet they are first class, as pictures of today, and historically valuable. It's vandalism to burn them, and yet, wouldn't you rather choose to be unknown, if you had the choice? There isn't any question either, of waste, or buried talents: for everything has existed and will exist everywhere and for ever, after all.

Now I should say something about your illness. Flu probably: and if so your second attack this winter. You will probably say more about it when you write next: and by today it will be over. Bother that three-weekly gap between your speech and my ear. However in a fortnight we will have a fortnightly air mail, which should bring down the 17 day journey to 10 days: that means a very great deal to me.

As you say, I'm not really in India. I'm careful not to be. I am at Karachi, in the R.A.F. Depot, killing time there, till my books are forgotten, and I return to England. The time killing is on a heroic scale. I wonder if peace

1 Letter to Richards dated 15 July 1918: see p. 149.

is really worth so many years of life. No doubt it is: but it is so complete a peace I can hardly realise that in England people must have talked quite a bit about myself and books. Not a whisper of it reaches here except in your letters, and in an occasional faded paragraph of the *Daily Sketch*, which is the reading-room paper. The English Press – in bulk, feels so old, after the three weeks and the journey. Whereas your cuttings do not date themselves. Odd, that is. It is good of you to send them: but I like them with a guilty conscience. You must spend too much of your very scanty leisure on them. Please do not over-do them, for my self respect's sake.

G. B. S. also sent me a letter last week. I wrote to him lately so we have crossed: and I won't write again yet. I have a feeling that letters to him must somehow be remarkable. It doesn't seem as though one could offer him any pearl less good than one's best: and when the pearl fishing is having a thin season there doesn't seem anything fit for him. I'd like to describe my oyster beds as exhausted. You cannot conceive how empty, uprooted, withering, I feel out here. It is really a case of having come to a stand. In England there was a current of life round me, and I swam in it: meeting people like you, reading many things, working at my book-printing, flying up and down the country on my Brough. And now my physical radius is cut down to a mile, my company to eleven airmen (two of my own draft from England, nine of previous drafts) all in the same uprooted state: with behind me the knowledge that I have finished the little show of activity which the revision of the *Seven Pillars* provided, and with a sense that this sense of having finished is really a conviction — a final certainty. There is not a germ of desire left inside my frame.

G. B. S. has tackled Baldwin again, apparently, on my behalf.[1] It is good of him, but he cannot play providence. Nor need he. The R.A.F. will not eject me again, at short notice. I give no one any offence out here: and in three years or five, when I come back, my books will have been forgotten, and will have taken all the sparkle out of my supposed romantic character, by having been forgotten. *Revolt in the Desert*, after the appetite excited by Lowell Thomas, comes as a dose of bromide, an anti-climax. Cape sent me a copy and I've looked through it and two of the fellows in the room have read it. They (spontaneously) confessed that it was a 'binder' (indigestible) through which only their knowledge of me had sustained them. You will find that the popular view, and all the people annoyed with my late reputation will now have their chance. So I calculate that I shall not be deprived of my living in the R.A.F. for at least the next seven years, by when I shall be 45, and approaching infirmity of body. Not really infirm, but too stiff and brittle to keep my place in the ranks: perhaps to want to

---

1 G. B. S. had been campaigning for Lawrence to be offered a pension for his services to the nation.

keep it. It is a hard life, even for a man with my history of privations. I'll leave with a good character, and that will enable such friends as Robin Buxton to recommend me for a London job. My aim is something like night-watchman in a bank or city office — a very quiet style of living, not physically arduous, nor much sought-after. To work at night and sleep by day is not the life for everybody: but it will suit me well enough, for I am solitary by nature, now, and will grow more so, in time, since my friends are nearly all much older than myself.

It is not like G. B. S.' programme for me, of £1000 a year, and a dispensary of patronage (Patronage! — and I'm like a squeezed orange, now being sun-dried) but it is likelier to be the real event. Do please suggest it to him, some day when he is in a smooth, receptive mood. It is hard for him, with all that inherent force and courage, to credit a man's being worn out at thirty-five. I feel as though the slow black oxen of the verse had been trampling their heavy way up and down my prostrate self, until there was not a whole bone or serviceable sinew left.

Apologies for so much introspection. But it represents no more than my life out here. [...]

British Library

MRS CHARLOTTE SHAW
14.IV.27   Drigh Road Karachi India

Two letters, really, last week. One, convalescent from the shelter on a fine day (all days here are fine, though the weather is still too cold, for my pleasure. Not once, since arrival have I felt that rich sticky hotness all over me. However it is mid April, now, and if they ever have any warmth in this ramshackle country, it must soon declare itself), all full of sunshine and spring winds. Very good. The second letter from London (obviously you are really better) discussing Winston and Plato, in that order.

And I am facing a blank. No sensations, feelings or desires since I wrote to you last. And even in books not much to say, for lately I've mooned about the camp or aerodrome in my spare time (which is now not as much as it was, because I have two jobs together) hardly opening a page. No Greek at all. I think the book reviews of *Revolt in the Desert* have worried me. You say you have seen some common notes in them. I've only been jarred by the improbabilities they spray out. 'Genius' comes once in each, ten times in some. Who are they to judge genius? I haven't the slightest awareness of any in myself. Talent, yes, a divinity of talent: but not the other quality which dispenses with talent and walks by its own light.

'Modesty' recurs: whereas I *meant* the abridgement to feel modest. Anything loud was excised, and little odd bits left in, as it were accidentally, to show the readers that, though not stressed, I was really in the middle of things. And if the modesty is deliberate or even conscious, then it's really a clever man's improvement upon pride. The reviewers have none of them given me credit for being a bag of tricks — too rich and full a bag for them to control. Nor have they seen (Col. Pope-Hennessy, whom I don't know, and haven't heard of before, least of all seen) that the Arabs were, as individuals, magnificent fighters. Used in single-man battles, as I used them, each was equal to three Turks: the issue of the campaign would have been the same, but quicker and easier for me, if the enemy had been British troops. We'd have gone through them like brown paper.

At the same time your Colonel has seen the intellectual basis of my lack of race feeling. It's because men are all puppets — but not, as he thinks, my puppets — God's, whatever every person means by the word God.

It's odd that I should pay attention to these cuttings, when I would not, probably, pay any attention to the reviewers' opinion if I met them in the flesh. I take it as a sign that perhaps my mind is not sound on the belief that my writing is no good at all. My appetite for action would be wild with delight if the rest of me could be brought to believe that its productions had an absolute value: but if you want to believe a thing very badly, it's a good reason for believing the contrary. Yet I like reading Mr. Robert Lynd and Mr. Ralph Straus and the rest of them 'Ita sunt avidae et capaces meae aures'[1] ... that was Cicero's confession, I remember. I don't think that Cicero had much to plume himself on. An eloquence which died with him, like an actor's art; a policy which was doomed before he had enunciated it; some unreadable speeches; some dressed-up letters. Nobody ever wrote a good letter in a fair copy. It's the first draft, or none. Believe me, who write the worst imaginable letters to everyone except yourself, and to yourself too! Only I'm so dazzled at our success in keeping the game going (three or four letters in the air at once) that I refuse to confess the total failure of my share. You know, to no one else can I, or do I, write anything at all. My mother hears from me about 4 times a year, and banalities only. I would like you, if you agreed (it is to take a risk) to see her if she comes to England now that China has closed itself to her. Mother is rather wonderful: but very exciting. She is so set, so assured in mind. I think she 'set' many years ago; perhaps before I was born. I have a terror of her knowing anything about my feelings, or convictions, or way of life. If she knew they would be damaged, violated, no longer mine. You see, she would not hesitate to understand them: and I do not understand them, and do not want to. Nor has she ever seen any of us growing, because I think

---

1 'So keen and receptive are my ears.'

she has not grown since we began. She was wholly wrapped up in my father, whom she had carried away jealously from his former life and country, against great odds, and whom she kept as her trophy of power. Also she was a fanatical housewife, who would rather do her own work than not, to the total neglect of herself.

And now two of my brothers are dead, and Arnie (the youngest) and I have left her, and avoid her as our first rule of existence: while my eldest brother is hardly her peer or natural companion. It is a dreadful position for her, and yet I see no alternative. While she remains herself, and I remain myself it must happen. In all her letters she tells me she is old and lonely, and loves only us; and she begs us to love her, back again, and points us to Christ, in whom, she says, is the only happiness and truth. Not that she finds happiness, herself.

Of course I shouldn't tell you all this, but she makes Arnie and me profoundly unhappy. We are so helpless; we feel we would never give any other human being the pain she gives us, by her impossible demands, and yet we give her the pain, because we cannot turn on love to her in our letters, like a water-tap; and Christ to us is not a symbol, but a personality spoiled by the accretions of such believers as herself. If you saw her, you whose mind has not grown a shell-case, perhaps you could show her the other sides and things of which she does not dream. If only she would be content to loose hold of us.

My father was on the large scale, tolerant, experienced, grand, rash, humoursome, skilled to speak, and naturally lord-like. He had been 35 years in the larger life, and a spend-thrift, a sportsman, and a hard rider and drinker. My mother, brought up as a child of sin in the Island of Skye by a bible-thinking Presbyterian, then a nurse-maid, then 'guilty' (in her own judgement) of taking my father from his wife.... To justify herself she remodelled my father, making him a teetotaller, a domestic man, a careful spender of pence. They had us five children, and never more than £400 a year: and such pride against gain, and such pride in saving, as you cannot imagine. Father had, to keep with mother, to drop all his old life, and all his friends. She by dint of will raised herself to be his companion: social things meant much to him: but they never went calling, or on visits, together. They thought always that they were living in sin, and that we would some day find it out. Whereas I knew it before I was ten, and they never told me; till after my father's death something I said showed Mother that I knew, and didn't care a straw.

One of the real reasons (there are three or four) why I am in the service is so that I may live by myself. She has given me a terror of families and inquisitions. And yet you'll understand she is my mother and an extraordinary person. Knowledge of her will prevent my ever making any woman a mother, and the cause of children. I think she suspects this: but she does not know that the inner conflict which makes me a standing civil war, is the inevitable issue of the discordant natures of herself and my father, and the inflammation of strength and weakness which followed the uprooting of their lives and principles. They should not have borne children.

There, that's too much I expect. You have the formative mind and will understand better than I do, or can. Or else you will not understand and will leave her alone. Don't let's, any way, discuss it again. It leads only to a general unhappiness.

T. E. S.

British Library

H. H. BANBURY[1]
20.4.27

[...] 'T. E. L.' Well, I'm 'T. E. S.' now, and may be T. E. anything shortly, for only the first two are authentic names. Original family began with 'C', but is not to be used, because the authentic family does not approve of me.
   [...]

Bodleian Reserve[2]

STEWART LAWRENCE NEWCOMBE[3]
27.IV.27

Dear Monster

Life rolls on. Soon you will be lucky, and will go to England. I will not.

Thank you ever so for the huge tin of caramels. The Post Office here nearly fell in love with me, out of greediness. It was very brilliant of you to choose a tin as large and as heavy as that monstrous book of mine. It's a good thing we are both monsters: otherwise books & tins like that would give us aches in the lower part of our chests. Life, as I said before, rolls on. I wish the blessed thing had a decent top gear.

Moascar is hot.[4] You lucky creature. India is a land of shivers and storms

1 Regimental Sergeant-Major, Royal Tank Corps; at this time also serving in India.
2 The remainder of this letter, mainly concerned with answering questions about the press reaction to *Revolt in the Desert*, is printed in *DG*. This revealing paragraph was omitted.
3 Son of Colonel Newcombe, named after Lawrence: born 1920.
4 Near Ismailia, Egypt.

of dust. I haven't been once decently warm since we landed.

I enclose you some grains of the Sind desert. We eat them here nearly every day.

Love and tickles
T. E. S.

Bodleian Reserve

EVELYN WRENCH[1]

5.V.27
Karachi

Dear Wrench

Your letter arrived duly, and has been thought over, but I can't imagine what sort of a reception you'd give to the only sort of stuff I'd consider writing. I'll never again use the name Lawrence, nor allow anything I write to be connected in any way with the reputation I have made as Lawrence. Nor will I ever write upon the Middle East, nor upon any political subject. Nor upon archaeology.

If you want poems reviewed, anonymously, or literature (biography, criticism, novels of the XXth Cent., sort of Forsters, Joyces, D. H. Lawrences, etc.) at an interval of three months from the fountain head:— but of course you don't. . . .

Probably you didn't think at the time that I was 5,000 miles off, and had finished with my Arabian incarnation.

Best of luck to the *Spectator*, in your hands.

Yours ever,

If despite time and space, you still feel charitable, why I'll be delighted! I'm not ambitious, financially (my pay, and sole resource is the R.A.F. 22/– a week), and not proud, critically, for I've never imagined that my writing was any good. So I'll do the very smallest stuff, gladly.

Bodleian Reserve

1 Evelyn Wrench (1882–1966) was founder of the English-Speaking Union and Editor of the *Spectator* from 1925–32. He was knighted in 1932. He and Lawrence had met through Lord Winterton shortly after the Armistice of 1918 and it was he who gave the theatrical producer Percy Burton permission to stage Lowell Thomas's illustrated travelogues in London under the auspices of the English-Speaking Union.

MRS CHARLOTTE SHAW
12.V.27   Drigh Road Karachi India

The languor deepens — not because of the climate, which remains, to my taste, on the cold side; with however, some beautiful warm nights, when it is a pleasure to lie still thinking:— but for some other mysterious reason. It may be old age, coming on: you know, I've had more sustained and fiercer physical ordeals than almost any man I've ever met: and always I watch myself for signs of a sudden breaking-down: one leg falling off, and white hair or baldness, and a mouthful of shed teeth as I wake at dawn. Well, it may be the approach of that which makes me so slowly contented now with leaving undone the things I ought to do: not my R.A.F. work: that I do punctiliously. Which reminds me of something I've forgotten this morning. . . .

Right, I have now swept out two rooms, which is my daily duty. I do that while the others go on parade, and thence to work. So most people call it 'a scrounge': that is, an expedient to avoid the parade. I'm delighted to miss the parade, of course: and in gratitude I sweep the rooms properly and conduct long careful hunts of mosquitoes, flies, ants, beetles, and bugs. The bugs are our chief trouble here. They live in the crevices of the iron beds and wooden fittings of the rooms, and plague us: but with creosote I've got them nearly extinct. Not quite because the sanitary section has now run out of creosote. However, with patience all things can be arranged. The room job also gets me off church on Sundays, a very great benefit. So in thankfulness for that I sweep and spray out my rooms on Sunday, which is considered extravagantly dutiful by my fellow-room-orderlies. There are five of us. We do it for the first hour every day. After that we go on to our proper jobs: in my case the keeping a record of all the little changes and defects and replacements of the engines as they pass through the shop on overhaul. [. . .]

Now, to your last letter from Malvern.

[. . .]

(ix) I do not want you to feel that in burning your letters I'm doing anything wanton. It's not that. They are personal documents, and I feel that they belong utterly to me, when they reach me: as though you wrote them only for me, and kept no share in them after you had posted them. They could not be shown to anybody else, without breach of intimacy between us. They change with time, like ourselves. I do not want to meet my past, round some future turn of the road. It does not do to live at all in memory. Nor can I keep them safely: what place have I where to keep anything? Service men have the privacy of gold-fish in their bowls. The other fellows read my books, and see my pictures, and use my mug and plates, and borrow my clothes, and spend my money, and overhear and oversee every act and word and expressed thought of mine from sunrise to sunrise. So what room have I for a private life? To be sociable we must live only on our surfaces, and keep underground any elements in us which would be strange or uncommon in the room. Every room of troops has its key, like a broken scrap of music, and we tune ourselves to it. My past, and my outside life (which I used to lead in England on week-ends when I went off from camp solitarily on Boanerges, the lonely ride before and after separating world and service) are now done with, except in so far as your letters and books draw them out: they are my week-ends: and I do not want the others to share in what I feel about them. So after I have read them I burn them: (not the books: they go round, all of them, except your note-book, and the *Seven Pillars*, which are hidden in my box, and looked at by stealth).

(x) 'No man liveth to himself, and no man dieth to himself.' No: that's right: but don't you see that in choosing the services for a way of life I chose the first part of your saying, in its extreme and bitterest degree? and that the second part is a mystery, if it means anything? I suspect it of being only a sounding mask of words, in apposition to the first part, to round off the rhythm of the phrase. Living is dying, really. You sometimes are in a room, with your door shut. I, never: and by making public everything that was in me (in the *Seven Pillars*) I have robbed the grave of the chance of holding secret anything which had been mine.

T. E. S.

British Library

DR A. E. COWLEY[1]
19.V.27   R.A.F. Depot Drigh Road Karachi India

Dear Dr. Cowley
   Someone has muddled the sending of the *Seven Pillars* to you. It should have been preceded by the same list of conditions as Kenyon's copy
   i) That for two years it was the personal property of the Librarian.
   ii) That it was to be returned to D. G. Hogarth if the Library received another copy from any other source in the two years.
   iii) That after the two years it might be transferred to the Library, but that it be made available only to [people *erased*] readers moved by some other motive than personal curiosity: and that this [condition

---

1 Bodley's Librarian, i.e. the head of the Bodleian Library, Oxford (see letter of 29 October 1914 (p. 66)). The original of this letter is pasted inside the Bodleian copy of the subscribers' edition of *Seven Pillars of Wisdom*.

erased] restriction remain in force till the book is republished after
    my death.
There, do you think I make an absurd fuss over a trifle? Perhaps; but a
fellow doesn't feel his own private feelings to be a trifle: and mine, I fancy,
is a book which would never have been written by anyone properly imbued
with the public school [feelings *erased*] spirit.

Also I justify myself in making conditions on the grounds that the book
is rare and valuable!

You'll have to index it under Shaw, that being my initials in it. God
help the catalogue with me, some day, for not even Lawrence is the correct
and authentic name which I will eventually have to resume. I've published
as Lawrence, as Shaw, as Ross: and will, probably eventually publish as C.[1]
What a life!

Your letter came to me four days ago, with the last mail, to Karachi,
where I languish for my sins in publishing a little bit of the *Seven Pillars*
called *Revolt in the Desert*. I'm due to stay here till Jan. 1932, worse luck.
I've put my address on the top of this scrawl: but Hogarth keeps in touch
with me, & will forward anything you want to send him.

I hope your fortunes, & Bodley's grow no less. Increase isn't a thing to
wish, blindly

Yours
T E Shaw

Bodleian Library

MRS CHARLOTTE SHAW
I. VI. 27

[...] My brother tells me that mother has suffered a lot by her stay in
China. I hope England will put her right again. She has been too long in
unwholesome surroundings and ways of thinking.
    [...]
A surprise last week: the adjutant sent for me (our first meeting) and
asked if I'd like myself recommended as clerk to the British Attaché in
Kabul: a two-year plain-clothes engagement. I was taken by surprise: but
explained that I wasn't a clerk, and couldn't undertake to make myself one
at short notice. It seems to me that I'd better stick as tight to Karachi as I
can: or to Drigh Road rather. Karachi remains seven miles away, so far as

---

1 One of several hints that he hoped ultimately to assume his father's name of Chapman
    (see General Introduction, pp. xxv–xxvi).

I'm concerned: and if it wants to see me, it must come up here: for voluntarily I will not pass the camp limits. I think that's a good rule. So I can be five years in India, and never see India or any part of India. Drigh Road is R.A.F. only, and might be any one of a hundred camps.

Please do not make public this offer of the adjutant's: the affair is to be confidential, I think. Probably the British military attaché in Cabul [sic] is only a glorified kind of spy. It would have been interesting to have seen the whole of the Khyber Pass: and I might have liked Afghanistan. However, it won't be. Safety first, as they say in 'busses [i.e. aircraft]. Better the camp you know … and Drigh Road is as hidden a place as any in the world. All Government land about it, and no residents or private houses or visitors. It's practically impossible for an outsider to meet me, against my wish.

T. E. S.

British Library

EUGEN MILLINGTON-DRAKE[1]

10.VI.27   Karachi

Dear Mr. Millington-Drake

I haven't, yet, signed any copy of *Revolt in the Desert*: and do not expect to. Whereas I signed every copy of the English edition of the *Seven Pillars*. This difference of treatment of the two books is evidence, I think, of the different regards I have for them. The little book is a mere pot-boiler, intended to pay for the big one: and will lose any temporary interest it may have when the big one is reprinted after my death. So I'd suggest that it isn't worth including in your collection?

Headlam, of Eton,[2] has a copy of the full text, which he probably makes available to the few people in his neighbourhood who may be interested in the side issues of the war. You will realise that the Arab revival is in no sense a consequence of the war. It merely took advantage of it.

Yours sincerely
T E Shaw

If I do change my mind and autograph copies, I'll let you know. Improbable, though.

Eton College

1 Eugen Millington-Drake (1889–1972) was educated at Eton and Magdalen College, Oxford, and became a distinguished career diplomat. He was present at the Paris Peace Conference, was knighted (K.C.M.G.) in 1938 and was Ambassador to Uruguay at the time of the famous *Graf Spee* affair in 1939.
2 G. W. Headlam was a housemaster at Eton College.

H. S. EDE[1]

16.VI.27   Drigh Road Karachi India

Dear Ede

I feel nervous. I'm an entirely ordinary person: nearly everybody is.
There are 14 fellows in this room with me, and we are all, at once, of a
muchness, and different. If you were here you would be 15th (and an
unlucky fifteenth, for there are only 14 beds!) and that's all there would be
to it.

When I wrote that book of mine I was trying very hard to do a thing
for which I am totally unfitted by nature:— to produce a work of creative
imagination — and all the strain of the unnatural effort came into the print,
and affects people. At least that's the only explanation I can give: for
the book, as writing, is entirely contemptible. A bag of tricks, quite
unconvincing.

And you are judging by a fragment only. The whole affair is quite unlike
Revolt in the Desert. May I suggest you develop your acquaintance with
Kennington (or with Augustus John) and borrow from one or other of
them the complete work? That gives the game away, and will destroy what
I feel sure is an illusion which some accident of an unrelated remark on
some page of mine has created in you. I couldn't have lived all these years
with myself and not have seen I was a remarkable person, if I was.★

                                        Yours ever
                                        T E Shaw

★ Perhaps you can see what I wanted to say. My syntax seems to have
collapsed. Will you remember me to Aitken,[2] some day you see him? I
used to plague him with offerings of small undesirable pictures.

Bodleian Reserve

---

1 Usually known as Jim Ede: at this time an assistant at the Tate Gallery, later the author
  of *Savage Messiah* (1931), a biography of the French sculptor Henri Gaudier-Brzeska, and
  the founder, in 1957, of Kettle's Yard, Cambridge, where twentieth-century objects and
  works of art are laid out in an environment which, in its deviser's words, is 'a refuge of
  peace and order, of the visual arts and of music'. He had visited the exhibition of *Seven
  Pillars* pictures at the Leicester Gallery in May 1927 thinking that Lawrence was 'just
  another War Lord' but had been much taken by the tone and style of Lawrence's
  Introduction to the catalogue; he then read *Revolt in the Desert*, and thereafter, even more
  impressed, began a correspondence which lasted till Lawrence's death and which he
  subsequently published in a limited edition under the title *Shaw–Ede: T. E. Lawrence's
  Letters to H. S. Ede 1927–35* (Golden Cockerel Press, 1942). All Ede letters in this book
  have, however, been credited to the Bodleian Reserve collection, which holds copies of
  them.
2 Also on the staff of the Tate Gallery.

HON. EDWARD ELIOT[1]

16.VI.27   Drigh Road Karachi India

Dear Eliot

Yes, I want to change my name formally. Will you try and do it as quietly and inexpensively as it can be done? I'd better be

Thomas Edward Shaw

in future. Of Pole Hill, Chingford, Essex, if they require an address.

I'm in some doubt as to my previous name, for I've never seen my birth certificate. I fancy I was registered as born on August 15, 1888 (which was not the real date, however!)[2] at Tremadoc, in Carnarvon County, N. Wales. My father and mother, who were not married: — or rather he was, but not to her — called themselves Lawrence, at least from 1892 onwards. I do not know whether they did so when I was born or not.[3] He died in 1919. She is still alive. I believe Lawrence was the name of her supposed father: but her mother (called Jenner) was not married to the original Lawrence. My father was a younger son of an Irish family called Chapman, of Killua, in Co. Meath. His own place was called Southhill, also in Meath. His widow, Lady Chapman, and her daughters still live there: but Killua has been sold. Debrett, I fancy, shows him as still alive: but actually, as I say, he lived with my mother elsewhere than in Ireland, from 1885 onwards, and died in Oxford in 1919 as T.R. Lawrence. Whether he changed his name formally or not I don't know. I suppose not, or his widow would have changed too, wouldn't she? They were not divorced: there isn't much divorce in Ireland.

I suppose we were an odd family, because it never struck me to ask him the facts of the name of Lawrence. His will might solve the question.

Perhaps, though, you won't require parents' names, for my deed-poll. Better not, if possible, for I don't want anyone to know about it, while my mother and step-mother are both alive. There are two or three skeletons, besides this, in the last generation's history.

Of course if Father registered me as Chapman, that will do, and there's no need to have the intermediate stage of Shaw, between Lawrence and it: for eventually, I suppose, Chapman it will have to be. There is a lot of land in that name knocking about: and I don't want to chuck it away, as Walter Raleigh, for whom I have a certain regard, gave it to my father's first Irish ancestor. I have a feeling that it should be kept in the line. My father's death wound up the baronetcy (a union title, of all the rubbish!) and one of my

1 Lawrence's solicitor and a trustee of the *Revolt in the Desert* fund.
2 He was actually born in the early hours of 16 August.
3 Both parents are named Lawrence in T.E.'s birth certificate.

brothers is breeding heirs. So the family looks like continuing, in the illegitimate branch![1]

I'm sorry to give you all this rigmarole: but my complete ignorance of deed-polls leaves me in the dark as to what facts you require. I've tried to give you

    (i)   my present name and address

    (ii) my since-birth name

    (iii) my father's name & address (he was a British, & not a Free-State subject: rather a hot unionist, too!)

    (iv) my mother's name

    (v) my date & place of birth.

I can't think of anything else they may want: except description or occupation. I'm an airman, now: and as 'Lawrence' was last employed in the Colonial Office as a temporary civil servant. I gave up the use of L. in August 1922.

                              Apologies again

                              Yours

                              T E Shaw

The Trustees of the Seven Pillars of Wisdom *Trust*

HIS MOTHER

16.vi.27   [Drigh Road Karachi India]

I was glad to get your letter at last. I'm sorry you tried to write to me before, but hope there was nothing in the letters which the man who got them shouldn't read. [Airmen, you know, dislike mention of love and God ... because they care about these things and people should never talk or write about what is important. Intercourse, and particularly social intercourse should be limited to trivial things.]

    [...]

I wonder what you and Bob will do. Low blood pressure is a good thing, in reason: but he is probably tired, and will want a rest. He has been away so long that England will have become strange to him; and that is a pity, for there will be of course no question of his going back to China. [The civil wars will last for a while yet, and after that a violently national Government will want to restore Manchuria and Korea. So for a long time

1 Arnold Lawrence had one daughter.

China will look after herself: indeed I think there will not be much missionary work done anywhere in future. The time has passed. We used to think foreigners were black beetles, and coloured races were heathen: whereas now we respect and admire and study their beliefs and manners. It's a revenge of the world upon the civilisation of Europe.]

N.

HL/Bodleian Reserve

JOHN BUCHAN
20.vi.27   Drigh Road Karachi India

Dear Buchan

(For I suppose you have dropped the Colonel. The label is a hindrance in politics, and a while ago I saw you in the Press, triumphing among the Scotch Universities.) Cape has just sent me a copy of the American edition of my *Revolt in the Desert*, and they tell me the introduction to it is by you. In which case I owe you many thanks. It is tactful, & interesting, and gives nothing away.[1] So it pleases me, and it must have pleased America, for they say 120 000 copies of the U.S.A. edition have been sold. Cape has sold 30 000 in England, too: so my debt is paid off in lordly fashion, and I have nothing burdensome on my mind. In a few weeks, I hope, the English edition will run out of print, and be let die. Then Things will be quiet, by the time I'm due for home: though that may not be till the winter of 1931, probably.

The reference to the Tank Corps makes me think you probably did write it: it is a most excellent red-herring. Probably some of the other statements are also herrings: — as the ascription of the abridgement to Edward Garnett (the friendly man of letters!). Cape would not lend me Garnett's text, to edit: so I had to make a new abridgement of my own, unaided except by two airmen from Cranwell. We did the whole thing in two evenings!

I wasn't rejected in 1914 for physical reasons. The W.O. were then glutted with men, and were only taking six-footers. As a fact I was then unusually strong. The *Seven Pillars* doesn't perhaps bring out clearly enough

1 Buchan replied immediately to Lawrence's letter: '... alas! you are thanking me for something I did not do. I would not have dared to write an introduction to a book of yours, and certainly not without your permission.' Buchan added in relation to *Seven Pillars*: 'When you do not get inundated with adjectives you are the best living writer of English prose.' (*Letters to T. E. Lawrence*, ed. A. W. Lawrence, 1962)

that I was wounded in nine different scraps (sometimes two or three damages at once: I have about 50 scars tallied on me) and had two attacks of dysentery, besides a touch of typhoid, blackwater, and much malaria: not to mention five broken bones. Also, I fancy I over-exerted myself during parts of the campaign, for I've never felt much good since. Yet in 1922, 1923, and 1925 the wreckage of my body was minutely gone over in recruiting offices, and each time I was passed fit for general service. So pre-war I must have been quite fit.

'Lawrence' like 'Shaw' was an assumption. My father's people were merchants in the Middle Ages: then squires in Leicestershire. In Tudor times they had promoted themselves to soldiering, and had married with a Devon family: by favour of one of these cousins (Sir Walter Raleigh) they got a huge grant of County Meath in Ireland, from Queen Elizabeth: and there they lived till the Irish Land Acts did away with most of the estate. My father had other troubles too, which made him change his name, & live abroad, in Wales and England, the latter half of his life. So there weren't any Lawrence ancestors or relations: but it's not my line to say so, since the fiction is less trouble than the truth.

My 'two-year expedition in native dress' is also fiction. All my walking tours in Syria were done in European clothes: and four months was the longest. I only wore Arab kit on one or two short treks after forbidden antiquities.

The three destroyed copies of my 'Oxford' proofs are accountable for: One was cut up to make Garnett's abridgement: and I needed two to make my own, more detailed, new text for Pike's printing. There are still the five bound copies in my hands: or rather, belonging to me, and stored with Hogarth, Kennington, Alan Dawnay, Mrs. Bernard Shaw, and E. M. Forster. I think of destroying them, eventually, so that only a single text shall survive to posterity! The *Seven Pillars*, as you know it, is a condensation, not an abridgement, of the Oxford text: and I think it is technically much better.

There, you probably know all this and more, & were throwing dust in the public's eyes. Serve them right, though I haven't the art to do it myself.

It will amuse you to know that my satisfaction with R.A.F. life keeps me contented in this dismal station and country. We spend much of our time playing infantry-games! However it is only for a term of years: and my appetite for England will grow & grow & grow, till, upon return, I'll lie down in the Strand and start eating the pavement in hungry delight. With any luck I'll have three years more to serve, after I get home. They will be great years.

Yours ever
T. E. Shaw

This letter is designed so as not to require an answer. It is written because I think you have again put me in your debt. I hope your copy of the *Seven Pillars* was a sumptuous one. I gave that order, but could not stay to see it done.

Bodleian Reserve

FRANCIS YEATS-BROWN[1]
23.VI.27   R.A.F. Drigh Road Karachi

Dear Yeats Brown
    [...] Did I say I'd review for you, or *try* to review? I'm not a writer by instinct, you know, & things come to me slowly with immense difficulty: and the quality of the things doesn't impress me, any more than the way I put them.
    However I'm going to have another try. My last two employers cast me away very firmly, after a trial. I'm expecting you to do the same.
    The books you mention in your letter of June 1 have not turned up. Book-post is quick; parcel post twice as long. Any way India is far off, so you must choose me subjects which, like Stilton, are the better for a little keeping.
    D. H. Lawrence I'll be delighted to have a try at. I've read all his stuff since *The White Peacock*.
    Hakluyt is only a name to me.[2] So on that you'll get the reflection of a fresh mind: if it does reflect anything.
    The Koran is barred. Nothing Arabian or related. Besides it's a proper mess of a book. A mixture of Bradshaw and major prophet and police news.
    Balzac: perhaps. I like him, like Shakespeare, at times.
    Guedalla I had the misfortune to meet at Oxford.[3]
    Disraeli's novels: no: I think not. I got through two of them. It was nearly as sad stuff as Chesterton's.

---

1 Major Francis Yeats-Brown (1886–1944), soldier and writer (notable particularly for his *Bengal Lancer*, published in 1930) was the Literary Editor of the *Spectator*. He had written to Lawrence following the latter's favourable response to the approach of his Editor, Evelyn Wrench, who was also his cousin.
2 Richard Hakluyt (1552–1616), geographer, historian and publicist of English explorations in the New World.
3 Philip Guedalla (1889–1944): Balliol-educated popular biographer and historian.

I'll do you the best I can: and will trust in you to turn it down at once if it doesn't reach *Spectator* level. Wrench suggests a pseudonym. Colindale was the last Tube Station I entered.[1] How's that? Split in halves? There's an American novelist called Dale Collins: but I can't think of anyone called Colin Dale.

Yours
T E Shaw

Bodleian Reserve

SERGEANT A. PUGH

30.VI.27   Karachi

Dear Sgt

Another letter! Really I'm getting a marvellous good writer. Do you remember how that tray on the table used to get blocked solid: and how then I'd stuff the new-coming letters into those pigeon holes on my left, till they too were tight: and then we'd light the stove, & I'd chuck the time-expired ones by armfulls into the fire, and groan over answering the rest?

Yet it was easy in 'B' Flight. *Here, I have to do all my letters in my own time*. Terrible: or it would be if we worked eight instead of five hours a day: and if I had the proofs of a book to correct in my evenings, and tarred roads and a Brough for my spare afternoons. But there aren't any of these things. I write no more: there is only one road (from Drigh Road to Karachi) and no motor-bike. Indeed, I keep clean my record of having not yet been outside camp bounds. Imagine an airman six months at Cranwell without going out!

We were all very sad here when Carr did not get here, the first time: and we all said 'Bad show' when he didn't get here the second time.[2] The first try was such a very good one, that the failure of the second machine came as a shock. I hope the R.A.F. will go on till they get the record, now,

---

1 Presumably because it is the nearest station to R.A.F. Hendon on the London Underground.
2 Flight Lieutenant (later Air Marshal) C. Roderick Carr had made two attempts, one in May, one in June, to fly non-stop from Britain — in fact from Cranwell — to India. On the first occasion he had ditched in the Persian Gulf; on the second he had had to return almost immediately. He had been accompanied by Flight Lieutenant Gilman on the first flight and by Flight Lieutenant Mackworth on the second.

if they lose every H.H.[1] in the service whilst trying.

Karachi Depot will not rival Cranwell in such efforts. The R.A.F. here is distinguished only when it turns out in infantry order for royal birthdays or Vice regal visits. On Nov. 3 I am going, in my person, to line a little bit of the street in honour of the second personage.[2] Usually on these occasions a group of six-foot people take station behind my back, and use me as a convenient low shelf for leaning on to view the procession. Street-liners should be as tall as lamp-posts and as wide as pillar-boxes.

Life here is definitely better. They pay me full-up now: so I have plenty of cash for stamps, and an occasional record (the Room gramophone is quite good, though harsher than I like them). If you came past our door you would hear Wagner & Mozart & Beethoven at all hours of the off-days. The other fellows prefer Layton & Johnson:[3] and some of them like Jazz. However it is a happy enough family, and we pull together fairly.

You wouldn't expect an ERS,[4] 190 strong, to be as decent a unit as a flight, anyhow, would you. The great point of B Flight was that we worked together, & slept together, & could live together, too, if we wanted. It put everybody keen to play up to the others.

I've had one piece of very good news: in the shape of a friendly letter from a very big noise.[5] He gives me to understand that I'm not to be five years in India. Probably not more than three. God be praised, though I don't know whether it's quite good form to want to scrounge out of part of my overseas tour. Only I've spent now nearly 15 years of my life away from England, in spite of a tremendous desire to get fixed into England so firmly that nothing but death would get me out of it. People always want to do what they aren't supposed to do.

My little book has sold 30,000 copies in England, and 120,000 in the States. So all my debts are most royally paid off, and my trustees will have a small balance to get rid of, in addition. I am taking steps to close down the sale of the English edition, which is a stage forward towards my return home. At the same time my American publisher has gone one step in the other direction, by deciding to commission a 'life' of me, for the autumn. Hard luck, for I haven't I fancy, finished my life yet. However there is no holding these wild Yanks. So my friends conspired to put the commission into the hands of Robert Graves, a very good modern poet, and recent friend of mine. He will write something quite good, and not at all cheap:

1 H.H.: Hawker Horsley, the aircraft used by Carr in his attempts.
2 The Viceroy of India at this time was Lord Irwin, better known by his later name, Lord Halifax.
3 Layton and Johnstone (not Johnson) were a black singing duo who were later to make a popular hit in Britain by their recording of 'Happy Days are Here Again'.
4 E.R.S.: Engine Repair Section.
5 The 'big noise' was doubtless Trenchard, who had recently written to Lawrence.

probably it won't suit the Yanks at all: but that will not grieve me. Graves will do his best to play the game by me. If he comes to Cranwell, be nice to him. He is absolutely to be trusted.

Give my regards to Mrs. Pugh, and to the flight, or rather so much of it as is still there!

Is Cranwell still decent? No trumpeters? no guards? no roll-calls? no general nonsense? Has the band stopped playing the Lincolnshire poacher? Does the hot water still work? Particularly I want to know if it's decently warm at reveille. Dusty will know. I used to bribe the stoker to do our fire first, in the mornings.

I heard last post that Nigger is the complete clerk. Does he carry an indelible behind one ear & a pen behind the other? Warn him that I'm keeping my hand in. I do as much logging of repairs & overhauls every week here as he does in six months: and we get 12 gross of split pins per week. Help. Help.

T.E.S.

Bodleian Library

FRANCIS YEATS-BROWN
8.VII.27   Karachi

Dear Y-B

There, I've got down to initials in which I feel more comfortable: because I don't know if you are man or woman. One never does these days — or any day really. Birth is such a toss-up. Till the child actually gets into the daylight it doesn't know its sex: and (except at tennis) there doesn't seem, later, much distinction in their performance.

This preliminary paragraph conveys the personal note. So your secretary (bound to be female, this one, at least) will lay this note before yourself. As I'm to write under a pseudonym I'd better be told how to address my contributions. The fewer people aware of C.D. in your team the better. For if talk began about that person I should cut his throat.

'If talk began'. I'm being more optimistic than I believe: but before starting a journey one should look where the road might eventually lead. I enclose you a note on D.H.L. Your books (taking 5 weeks by parcel post — book post is eighteen days) came to me on Wednesday (6/7/27). I read the three D.H.L.'s on Thursday, & have written this today. Too quickly, no doubt, but I did not want to keep you longer without a sample: besides I've been reading him since before the war, so that my mind was made up before this week.

As for the note, of course it's no good. By nature I wasn't meant to write. The job comes very hard to me. I can't do it without trying my very best: and if I've ever in my past written decently it was under the dire command of some mastering need to put on paper a case, or a relation, or an explanation, of something I cared about. I don't see that happening with literature and so I don't expect you to like what I write.[1]

I've signed it C.D. because it's the first, if you do print it, after all. I'd suggest the first five or six things worth signing be restrained to their initials. If the miracle continues after that (surely either your forbearance or my endeavour will break down) we might climb so far as Colin D., keeping the full truth about the D till it was certain that the fellow could write and had a character. In my heart I know he hasn't. People have been led away by his retinue of extraneous accidents.

Commend me to Wrench. Thank him for all your books. I'll try now to say something about Hakluyt, & Gerhardi, and some one new to me of the batch in hand.

TES.

Special apologies for the scruffy manuscript: but I have no typewriter.

Bodleian Reserve

EDWARD GARNETT
I.VIII.27

The slow months begin to total respectably. When I got here it was 7/1/27: and now I'm past the half year. Did ever free agent so long to be three years older?

This is a reply to your letter of June 27, which ended up with a well-introduced remark about my Uxbridge notes. I write this on the back of one, to show you that the not sending them as they are is only kindness to you. I wrote them pell-mell, as the spirit took me, on one piece of paper or another. Then I cut them into their sections, and shuffled them, as Joyce is supposed to have shuffled *Ulysses*, with the idea of curing you of any delusion you might be persuaded by the chorus of critical England to

1 Lawrence's review of the novels of D. H. Lawrence was published in the *Spectator* on 6 August 1927. It is reprinted in David Garnett's *The Essential T. E. Lawrence* (Cape, 1951) and in *Men in Print: Essays in Literary Criticism by T. E. Lawrence* (Golden Cockerel Press, 1940), edited by A. W. Lawrence, which also reprints a review by Lawrence of the short stories of H. G. Wells. In addition, he wrote two other pieces which were printed and a third, about the works of Walter Savage Landor, which was not — however, both Garnett and A. W. Lawrence included this in their respective publications.

entertain of me as a person of literary promise or capacity — where was I? — Ah yes: to disillusion you as to my literary ability — where was I? Ah yes: — to show you that I can't write for toffee, I decided to send them you. You would have thought them the raw material of a paper-chase. So I began at Clouds Hill to stick each class in some sort of order on to sheets of paper, meaning to have them stitched for you. But that did not work, for the sections were too intertwined.

So I am copying them seriatim into a notebook, as a Christmas (which Christmas?) gift for you. It is a posh manuscript, in my most copper-plated hand. It will be bound, and gilt-edged. Can I do more? (or less.) Please regard it as an expensive gift. Copying my old notes is like eating yesterday's vomit. I add nothing but take away repetitions, where vain. I 'did' three Church parades for example: and I believe they can be boiled to two: or even to one, which would be the quint-essence and exemplar of all my church parades.

Enough of this stuff. Do not expect it for ever so long. It is done against the grain. About a third of it is done. Am I making a fool of myself? Would you rather keep your illusion? There are sixty sheets like this. You understand they are not emotions remembered in tranquility: but the actual fighting stuff. Photographic, not artistic. All were in pencil. It's better than *The Seven Pillars*, in its class: as like as butter and cheese: that is, not like at all: but equally rotten. The *S.P.* showed that I could not ratiocinate: this that I can't observe.

[...]

DG

RALPH H. ISHAM[1]
10.viii.27   Drigh Road Karachi India

Dear Isham

Last week and this week your two very good letters came to me. It is most kind of you. I'll comment on the second:—

[...]

My de-luxe edition was financed by a banker friend of mine, to whom I gave security of its original pictures, its subscriptions, and the title deeds of some land I have in Essex. (Annual value of land £50 a year, which mostly goes in rates: capital value £3000 or more, as building land. I do

---

1 Lieutenant-Colonel Ralph H. Isham was an American who had served as a British officer in France and had been awarded the C.B.E. He had met Lawrence through Ronald Storrs in 1919. A contributor to *Lawrence by His Friends*.

not want it built over.) Total cost of the *Seven Pillars* was £13,500 of which £6,500 was covered as above. Balance of £7,000 has been met by the sale of *Revolt in the Desert* through Doran and Cape. The whole liability is now discharged, & I owe nobody anything.

Yes, I hate the East. It holds bad memories for me: and I am old enough to grudge my spending more years away from England, where only I feel at home. This is my fifteenth year abroad. Yet I had to ask the R.A.F. to put me on foreign draft, since the personal publicity unavoidable in connection with the sale of *Revolt in the Desert* would have rendered my life intolerable, and my presence a cursed nuisance to my C.O., in any camp in England. I am exiled, therefore, until the fuss of my books has died down in the Press. The R.A.F. will let me come in 1930: and it will not be safe for me to return before. So actually I'd be no better off as a free agent.

In England I found life in the R.A.F. not at all bad, after I got used to the rather bare conditions, and the excessive number of rules. When this foreign spell is ended, and I get home again I shall be quite happy.

Revolt in the Desert has sold enormously, and made a small fortune. I executed a deed by which its first receipts paid off my debts, and the balance is to go to a charity[1] in which I am interested. Did I tell you (I did not go about explaining myself) that I consider what I did in Arabia morally indefensible? So I refused pay & decorations while it lasted, and will not take any personal profit out of it: neither from a book about it; nor will I take any position which depends on my war-reputation. 'Arabia barred'.

Publishers would pay money for any article I wrote as 'Lawrence': but I have finished with that name, and printed all I mean to print about my war activity. I write occasionally under other names, but my stuff has no commercial value. I review books, and get myself free copies of books that way. There is no money in anonymous work. I can't write a novel, & if I did it would not be a good novel, probably. And I don't feel ambitious as a writer. I do not like the idea of struggling for 20 years, with a pen, potboiling, with the risk always of running dry. I can't, of course, write about Arabia. That is covered by the self-denying ordinance.

So you see the case is pretty hopeless. I have an excellent private intelligence, and have looked at myself and my prospects from every angle: and can see no way of bettering myself. I propose to stay in the R.A.F. as long as I can, it being the line of least resistance: and when it rejects me, to get a job as night-watchman at some Bank or block of offices in the City. You realise that I have no trade I can work at.

Lowell Thomas was 10 days in Arabia. He saw me for two of those, and again one day in Jerusalem: and afterwards I breakfasted with him once or

1 The R.A.F. Memorial Fund, re-named R.A.F. Benevolent Fund in 1933.

twice in London. His book is silly and inaccurate: sometimes deliberately inaccurate. He meant well.

No, I have written nothing else of any interest: a little archaeology, some translations from the French: some reviews of books.

My father's name (& therefore mine) was neither Shaw nor Lawrence. But the other day I adopted Shaw as my legal name. So it will be that till further notice. It is a short simple name, easily pronounced and spelt.

There, in answering your letter I have written mine. It is exceedingly good of you to want to help me so much, and I'd not hesitate to take advantage of it if my sense of fitness would allow me to profit by you. But experience has taught me that I will inevitably turn down every job I'm given the chance of getting — the truth being, I fancy, that the service has become a second nature to me, and that I'll feel lost if (or when) it chucks me out.

My regards to Mrs. Isham, the incognita. Please tell her that the odds against my visiting America are huge. But after 1930, if ever you come to London (and all good bankers do) then we will be able to see each other. Let's hope for that.

Yours very gratefully
T. E. Shaw.

Bodleian Reserve

MRS CHARLOTTE SHAW
18.VIII.27   Drigh Road Karachi India

[...] I've not written any letters of this sort to anyone else, since I was born. No trust ever existed between my mother and myself. Each of us jealously guarded his or her own individuality, whenever we came together. I always felt that she was laying siege to me, and would conquer, if I left a chink unguarded. So when Graves asked me about letters[1] I told him that only you (for the recent period) and Lionel Curtis (for the Tank Corps period) held anything illuminating. Curtis' letters are essays in misery, for I felt like Lucifer just after his forced landing, at that stage of my career. Yours are — well I don't know — you know more of them than I do, for they are thrown off quickly, and never dwell in my mind. But I never have to be conscious of an audience in writing to you. We misunderstand one another only over my book-writing, which I think is putrid rubbish, and you think

---

1 Robert Graves was writing, with Lawrence's help, a popular biography which was published later in 1927 by Cape under the title *Lawrence and the Arabs*.

is good. I'd like to go further, and say that we'd agree in the fundamental point that it fully represented the author's character and spirit! But do you think any man could sincerely write himself down as putrid rubbish? Even the clearest sighted person will cherish somewhere a reservation — that he cannot be so poor as the stuff he creates. I think my books do me an injustice. Therefore I wish I hadn't written anything. I wish I'd burned them, after I'd written them, when I saw their shortcoming: and whenever I come across an old letter, I wish the owner had burned that, too. We would be happiest if we left no trace behind. [...]

British Library

F. N. DOUBLEDAY
25.VIII.27   Karachi

[...] *Revolt in the Desert* now belongs entirely to a small Trust, of three decent people I know, who own all its present and future direct or derived rights, and have the obligation (after their expenses are paid) of applying all its profits to such charitable objects as meet with their approval. The not making any profit for myself out of what happened in Arabia (which I consider to have been a dirty show) has been a cardinal point with me since 1917. I've carried my scruple too far: to the point of having lost money over it. Today I'm much worse off than I was in 1916. But that is my own fault.

So you see the name 'Lawrence' bars itself. It is worth a lot of money, because of Arabia: whereas my father chose it for me because it meant nothing, to his family. The only authentic part of my name is the initials T.E. (they do not, I believe, translate into Thomas Edward ... but that's no matter) and most people who know me write to me as Dear T. E.! They feel safe at that. There aren't many things safe about what are beautifully called 'natural' children!
[...]

Bodleian Reserve

H. S. EDE
1.9.27

Dear Ede

I cannot write fluent letters: indeed letter-writing is very grievously hard in camp.

Your criticism of the *Seven Pillars* interests me very much. You are the first person to come to it, after *Revolt*. The people who have read the *S.P.* find *Revolt* unreadable.

Your criticism hits the mark most justly. In the *S.P.* I started out to write a history of the Arab Revolt: and the first third of the book is an elaborate building up of the atmosphere and personality of the Revolt. After the capture of Akaba things in the field changed so much that I was no longer a witness of the Revolt, but a protagonist in the Revolt. So the latter third of the *S.P.* is a narrative of my personal activity. If I were going to re-write the book tomorrow I could hardly do it differently. The interests of truth and form differ, there as generally.

In making *Revolt* out of the longer book I had no preoccupation with history or truth. It was necessary only to make a book, by the use of scissors. So I produced a thing which has some design and unity, and is by so much less honest and real than the *S.P.* for these 'selected' designs which rule Art today are not quite true, ever; though aesthetically they give greater contentment. Only, when it comes to a choice (as it may come to each man once or twice) you know aesthetic goes to the wall, always.

I've got fever on me, so will stop writing what my eyes are too staring to read.

                                        Yours
                                        T. E. S.

Bodleian Reserve

E. M. FORSTER
8.IX.27   Karachi

You get my first letter this week: anyway. Nearly I gave you my last letter of last week: but I had dysentery, and the flesh, being weak, suspected that the head was weak also. So I gave it a few days to settle down. All is very well now.

Your booklet (such a little one!) on *The Novel*[1] is superb. No other word

---

1 *Aspects of the Novel* (Arnold, 1927), the text of Forster's Clark Lectures at Cambridge.

fits it, because there's a complete lack of superbity about the manner & matter of it. So that the total effect is superb shows that the novel really belongs to you. It's like sitting at the feet of Adam, while he lectures to a University Extension Society about the growth and development of gardens. As soon as it came I rolled it out flat, and galloped through it: the names of some of the books & people I liked or disliked were in it, all right. Two days later I galloped across it again, seeing more of them: and this week, if my stretching and shrinking eyes will hold themselves to a page for an hour — this week I'm going to begin to digest it. There's a curious difference in tone, between you and Lubbock.[1] One treats the novel rather like the glazed unapproachable pictures in a public gallery. The other talks of novels as though they were things one writes. I expect you will find it one of the best-selling of your works.

[...]

By the way you called your novel-book 'a saucerful of last week's grapenuts'. And I called *The Seven Pillars* a 'builder's yard'. We do well in decrying our goods. Only you have the inestimable sauce of wit to make your seriousness tasty. The other day someone (disappointed) sent me a *Revolt in the Desert* to autograph. Before returning it I read some of it. Punk, of course: but better, so far as form & unity and speed and compactness went, than *The Seven Pillars*. Should I have mightily abridged *The Seven Pillars* before issuing it to subscribers? Say to a half? However I trust much to your collation. Robert Graves says he likes the Oxford text better. Its faults make it less chilly than the *S.P.*, to his diaphragm.

I'm sorry your short story isn't publishable. As you said, the other one wouldn't do for general circulation. Not that there was a wrong thing in it: but the wrong people would run about enlarging their mouths over you. It is a pity such creatures must exist. The *Royal Geographical Journal*, and *Journal of the Central Asian Society*, two learned societies, both found *Revolt in the Desert* indecent. It seems almost incredible.

I wanted to read your long novel,[2] & was afraid to. It was like your last keep, I felt: and if I read it I had you: and supposing I hadn't liked it? I'm so funnily made up, sexually.[3] At present you are in all respects right, in my eyes: that's because you reserve so very much, as I do. If you knew all about me (perhaps you do: your subtlety is very great: shall I put it 'if I knew that you knew ...'?) you'd think very little of me. And I wouldn't like to feel that I was on the way to being able to know about you. However perhaps the unpublished novel isn't all that. You may have kept ever so

1 *The Craft of Fiction*, by Percy Lubbock.
2 *Maurice*, Forster's overtly homosexual novel written in 1913–14 but not published until 1971, the year after Forster's death.
3 Mistranscribed as 'sensually' in *DG*.

much out of it. Everywhere else you write far within your strength.
    [...]

                                                        T. E. S.

DG/King's College, Cambridge

MRS CHARLOTTE SHAW
18.X.27

I'm writing in the Shop, in working hours, which is clean contrary to my
habit, and wish: for I give the R.A.F., usually, a very honest day's work.
But if they give me overtime, then I must fit my private affairs into their
hours. Not that there are really any hours, of course: we are paid for 24
hours a day for seven years: but trade union habit makes everyone regard
eight hours as a unit of working — so there we are!

    Which exordium, and this letter, is called forth by your letter of meeting
Feisal. Yes, that is a surprise. I'm awfully glad you liked him. For so long
he was only my duckling: and I crow secretly with delight when he gets
another inch forward on his road. When you think of the harrassed and
distant figure of Wadi Safra in 1916 — and then to the Hotel Regina Palace
in 1927: why it is very wonderful.

    After your letter came I lay awake all the Sunday night, arguing my
position (in Arabic: how much of it I have forgotten!) with an imaginary
Feisal. I made a distinct impression on him, and completely convinced
myself. I don't think he wants me, really. Not even the nicest man on earth
can feel wholly unembarrassed before a fellow to whom he owes too much.
Feisal owed me Damascus first of all, and Bagdad second: and between
those stages most of his education in kingcraft and affairs. When with him
I am an omnipotent adviser: and while that is very well in the field, it
is derogatory to a monarch: especially a monarch who is not entirely
constitutional. Feisal often has to lead his people: which is seldom the
conduct of G. R.[1]

    Also peoples are like people. They teach themselves to walk and to
balance, mainly by dint of trying and falling down. Irak did a good deal
of falling between 1916 and 1921: and since 1921, under Feisal's guidance
has done much good trying and no falling. But I don't think it yet walks
very well. Nor can any hand save it from making its messes: there is a point
where coddling becomes wicked. All my experience of the Arabs was in
the god-father role: and I think they have outgrown that. If they are to

---

1 George Rex, i.e. King George V.

make good as a modern state (how large an 'if') then it must be by virtue of their own desire and excellence.

So that I remain unrepentant. I was right to work for Arab self-government through 1919 and 1920: and my methods then, though not beyond criticism, were I think reasonably justifiable. The settlement which Winston put through in 1921 and 1922 (mainly because my advocacy supplied him with all the technical advice and arguments necessary) was, I think, the best possible settlement which Great Britain, alone, could achieve at the time. Had we waited for the French to come to their right mind and co-operate in a complete settlement, we would be waiting yet. And after June 1922 my job was done. I had repaired, so far as it lay in English power to repair it, the damage done to the Arab Movement by the signing of the Armistice in Nov. 1918.

The people who want me to go on keeping my hand on the plough are either unfair to the existing ploughmen, or unfair to the plough. The class of work I was doing is finished. Had I continued to be connected with Arab affairs I should have had to change my style and subject and status. I thought it easier — no I thought it imperative, to change roles altogether. Hence the clean break with my past which the R.A.F. represents.

It's because I've chosen the R.A.F. that people make a fuss of my abdication from Arab affairs. If I'd accepted a Governorship — of Cyprus, or Jamaica, or Borneo, they would have taken for granted my leaving the Arab sphere. And their sense of proportion seems to me all wrong. It's as good to serve in the R.A.F. as it is to govern Ceylon: I'd say that it was much better. You may condemn all service life, by holding a pacificist view: and if so you'll regard all soldiers and sailors and airmen as more or less brute beasts: but I have no such views — indeed few views of any sort: and no feeling that one sort or class or profession of man is better or worse than another.

So much for the side of it which affects myself. For what affects Feisal, I'm happy, indeed, that you liked him. He is one of the best people I know. Your remarks about his tenacity interested me. He is both tenacious and weak: perhaps these qualities always go together. It is easy to swing him off his point: and when released he tends to swing back to it. Therefore the French called him treacherous. He was (and perhaps is) still quite weak: but, I agree, tenacious. Very gentle, you know, and very kind, and very considerate, and outrageously generous to friends, and mild to his enemies, and cleanly and honest and intelligent: and full of wild freakish humour: though I suppose that is a little overlaid with kingliness, now. He has been king for six years, which is a deep experience. I wish you could have known him, as I did, when he was Feisal, just. One of the most attractive human beings I have ever met.

What you say about his looking young and happy and peaceful pleases me. Of course he has won great credit for himself: and that brings a man to flower. And in 1919 when John painted him he was up against very terrible conditions in Paris. No man could have looked other than broken with worry. Those five months in Paris were the worst I have lived through: and they were worse for Feisal. However, he learnt the whole art of politics, from them. Perhaps I did, too!

Feisal has been painted—
  (i) By Aug. John. At Manchester Art Gallery.
  (ii)   ,,   ,, In Kennington's house (TES. property)
 (iii) By Orpen
 (iv) By Laszlo
Sculpted—
  (v) By Mestrovic (Victoria and Albert)
 (vi) By Fudora Pleichen (in Bagdad)
There may be more. These I know. (ii) and (v) belong to me.

You know, without my telling you, how much I liked him. I talk of him always in the past tense, for it will be a long time before we meet again. Indeed I hope sometimes we never will, for it would mean that he was in trouble. I've promised myself to help him, if ever that happens.

As for Irak ... well, some day they will be fit for self-government, and then they will not want a king: but whether 7 or 70 or 700 years hence, God knows. Meanwhile Feisal is serving his race as no Arab has served it for many hundred years. He is my very great pride: and it's been my privilege to have helped him to his supremacy, out there, and to have made him a person, for the English-reading races. Gertrude has nobly supported him in this last effort. Her Bagdad letters give a splendid idea of him in action as a ruler.

Don't you think he looks the part, perfectly? Was there ever a more graceful walk than his? G. B. S. probably (being an emperor, himself) thinks poorly of kings: but he'd admit that I'd made a good one.

A very distinguished Person — to me in Nov. 1918,
'This is a bad time for Kings: seven new republics were proclaimed yesterday'.
me, cheerfully,
'Courage, Sir. I have made three new Kings in the East'.
Very distinguished Person 'I thought the remark was not in the best taste'.

Health absolutely as usual. Busy to death. A letter some day: post after next, probably.

British Library

LIEUTENANT-COLONEL F. G. PEAKE[1]

20.X.27   R.A.F. Depot Drigh Road Karachi India

Dear Peake

Apologies, should this reach you, for invading your peace. One of our 'lads' called De Pellette (yes, I know it sounds bad: but actually he is a Glasgow Scot) asked me yesterday did I know anyone military in Palestine? I thought at once of you, and provisionally said 'Yes'. He then disclosed that his idea of a life and profession when he left the R.A.F. was in the Palestine Special Police. Are these what we used to call the Gendarmerie? He says they are mostly in Trans Jordan, and that they go out, when they speak Arabic, as Sergeants in charge of districts.

I told him that, possibly, if I worried you, you'd give me a verdict of the excellence of the force, and the methods of its recruitment and its terms. He is about 28: and will not be free for over a year. By trade a fitter, and says he knows any make of car-engine. Used to be engineer on motor-yacht. Learnt some Arabic in Mesopotamia, and is learning more. A very solid, silent, not-sociable person: his drink is beer: but not extravagantly. Never even unsteady. Alas: he's married. A plague of women. By the way, do read Gertrude Bell's letters. They are splendid.

I wonder if you still ride up and down that delectable land. I am often hungry for another sight of its hills. Rum, too. If only... Drigh Road, this place, is dismal. But in 1930 I am due for home, and then I'll be very happy.

Give my regards to the Emir[2] : if he remembers me.

Yours ever
T. E. Shaw.

Imperial War Museum

E. M. FORSTER

27.X.27   Karachi

Now I have your short story.[3] It's the most powerful thing I ever read.

---

1 'Peake Pasha', commander of the Arab Legion in Transjordan, which he had founded in 1920 and would continue to command until his retirement in 1939. He had fought with Lawrence in the final stages of the Arab war. A professional soldier, he had a high regard for Lawrence's leadership and political vision.

2 i.e. Emir Abdulla of Transjordan.

3 The story — see paragraph 3 — was *Dr. Woolacott*, a homosexual ghost story first published in 1972, after Forster's death, in a collection entitled *The Life to Come*. For further comment on the story see Lawrence's letter to Forster of 21 December 1927 (p. 359).

Nearly made me ill: and I haven't yet summoned up the courage to read it again. Someday I'll write you properly about it. A great privilege, it is, to get a thing like that.

Virginia obviously hadn't seen it: or she wouldn't have put so much piffle in her note on you.[1] Which note also holds some very good stuff. I liked it: but she has only met the public side of you, apparently. Or else she doesn't know the difference between skin and bone.

I say, I hope you know what a wonderful thing *Dr. Woolacott* is. It is more charged with the real high explosive than anything I've ever met yet.

And the odd, extraordinary thing is that you go about talking quite carefully to us ordinary people. How on earth. . . .

However more later
T. E. S.

It is also very beautiful. I nearly cried, too.

King's College, Cambridge/Bodleian Reserve

SIR HUGH BELL[2]

4.xi.27   India

Dear Sir Hugh

You will probably remember me as Lawrence, my war-time name: we met several times in Cairo when Gertrude and myself were playing a tune on the political conference there in 1921. I've just been reading the 'Letters' which Mrs. Bernard Shaw sent me, and they have been so great a pleasure to me that I felt I must write to you and thank you for letting them come out. Until they were announced I hadn't realised that Gertrude was dead; after the Cairo business had finished my war-work so honourably and completely I left politics and enlisted in the R.A.F., with whom I am now near Karachi in India. I don't write much to people, and each service is a world of its own, which talks nothing, and reads little, of the worlds outside. So my not knowing that is usual.

1 In 1927 Virginia Woolf wrote an article on Forster, which was shown to him in draft and which did not please him. 'Part of the trouble', comments his biographer P. N. Furbank, 'though he didn't tell her so, was that he neither wanted to show her *Maurice* [his homosexual novel] nor to have his work summed up without it.' The article was later published in the *Saturday Review of Literature*, 17 December 1927.

2 The father of Gertrude Bell, who had died in Baghdad on 12 July 1926. A two-volume edition of her letters, selected and edited by her step-mother, Lady Bell, D.B.E, was published by Benn in 1927 (re-issued by Penguin, 1987).

I think she was very happy in her death, for her political work — one of the biggest things a woman has ever had to do — was as finished as mine. That Irak state is a fine monument; even if it only lasts a few more years, as I often fear and sometimes hope. It seems such a very doubtful benefit — government — to give a people who have long done without. Of course it is you who are unhappy, not having Gertrude any more; but there — she wasn't yours really, though she did give you so much.

Her letters are exactly herself — eager, interested, almost excited, always about her company and the day's events. She kept an everlasting freshness; or at least, however tired she was, she could always get up enough interest to match that of anyone who came to see her. I don't think I ever met anyone more entirely civilised, in the sense of her width of intellectual sympathy. And she was exciting too, for you never knew how far she would leap out in any direction, under the stimulus of some powerful expert who had engaged her mind in his direction. She and I used to have a private laugh over that:— because I kept two of her letters, one describing me as an angel, and the other accusing me of being possessed by the devil, — and I'd show her first one and then another, begging her to be charitable towards her present objects of dislike.

However, you won't want to know what I think; her loss must be nearly unbearable, but I'm so grateful to you for giving so much of her personality to the world. [...]

Yours sincerely,
T. E. Shaw.

Bodleian Reserve

MRS CHARLOTTE SHAW
10.XI.27

Yesterday Buxton wired me that Hogarth is dead: and that means that the background of my life before I enlisted has gone. Hogarth sponsored my first tramps in Syria — then put me on the staff for Carchemish, which was a golden place — then moved me to Sinai, which led to the War Office: which sent me to Cairo on the Staff: and there we worked together on the Arab business, until the War ended: and since then whenever I was in a dangerous position I used to make up my mind after coming away from his advice.[1] He was very wise for others, and very understanding, and

1 Lawrence's special relationship with Hogarth was known to his friends. On hearing of Hogarth's death Alan Dawnay wrote to Robert Graves: 'His will be a loss that I fear T. E. will feel tremendously. I always placed him an easy first in T. E.'s friendships and a good choice it was.'

comfortable, for he knew all the world's vices and tricks, and shifts and evasions and pretexts, and was kindly towards them all. If I might so put it, he had no knowledge of evil: because everything to him was fit to be looked at, or to touch. Yet he had his own position and principles, and was unmovable on them. Till I joined up he did everything for me. It was the first thing I did entirely on my own. So lately I have seen little of him: but I always felt that if ever I went back to living I'd be able to link up with him again.

Tomorrow the Viceroy, and this horrible celebration of an armistice of long ago.

T. E. S.

British Library

LIONEL CURTIS
17.XI.27   [Drigh Road Karachi India]

My Lord
Hogarth's death (not unexpected, from the tenor of his last letter to me) puts me out of action, temporarily. He always seemed to me the ripest man I'd met.

Call this not a letter but my answer to your note about Zimmern's *Who's Who*. Of course write anything you please: so long as you don't give away
    (i) my original family
    (ii) my present address.
I'd be grateful if you'd make it quite clear that in Winston's 1922 settlement of the Middle East the Arabs obtained all that in my opinion they had been promised by Great Britain, in any sphere in which we were free to act; and that my retirement from politics upon that, to me, happy event was necessarily final and absolute.

That is, if the biographies are such as to call for details. If it's only 'b. 1888 m. Eliza daughter of S. Dooly Esq. D.C.L. J.P. 2s. 3d. d. 1922' then so much the better. Do not give anything which could look like an address.

I believe D. G. H. wrote the Encyc. Brit. article. I have not seen it.

Who's Who pleased themselves over their note on me. They are a tiresome silly publication. Zimmern should have more sense.

Yours
T. E. S.

All Souls College Oxford

MRS CHARLOTTE SHAW
17.XI.27

[...] This week I send you a book. I've been trying to look at it with your eyes: realising its shabbiness and dirtiness, outside and inside, after seven years of keeping me company. I found that not even the *Oxford Book of English Verse* quite fitted my whim. So I took to copying, carelessly, in a little Morrell-bound notebook (a decent plain binding, once) the minor poems I wanted. Some are the small poems of big men: others the better poems of small men. One necessary qualification was that they should be in a minor key: another that they should sing a little bit. So you will find no sonnets here.

The worst is you do not like minor poetry: so that perhaps the weakness of spirit in this collection will only anger you: and then my notebook will not be a fair return for your notebook. In my eyes it is: for I'm not so intellectual as to put brain-work above feeling: indeed as you know, I don't like these subdivisions of that essential unity, man. It's like trying to pretend that our left hand and our right hand are hands as well as being ours. It's only our fancy to call them hands.

The book had only three or four empty pages when I sailed from Southampton and these I filled with a Wolfe poem and a scrap of Blake. In this last year I have slowly copied it into another book (with a few more blank pages) which will last me for another seven years.

You live always within touch of shelves, and can keep so many poets on tap that you won't feel how necessary a friend is such a notebook as this. Its poems have each of them had a day with me. That little hackneyed Clough, for instance, about light coming up in the west also: I read that at Umtaiye, when the Deraa expedition was panicking and in misery: and it closely fitted my trust in Allenby, out of sight beyond the hills. There's all that sort of thing, for me, behind the simple words.[1]

T. E. S.

---

1 The book affectionately described in these paragraphs, to which he gave the name *Minorities* and which contained 112 poems, was published by Cape in 1971, with an Introduction and notes by J. M. Wilson. The 'little hackneyed Clough' is the famous poem by Arthur Hugh Clough beginning 'Say not the struggle naught availeth'.

B. H. LIDDELL HART[1]

17.XI.27   Drigh Road

Dear Captain Liddell Hart

I'm putting this down to your innocent account: it must have been your letter to me which gave the perfectly damnable business side of the Encyclopedia my address. It's one of the world's worst firms: they used to send (indeed probably they still send) to me at All Souls, as to every fellow on its books, pages of frantic adjuration to buy something or other from them for 30/- as a final and unique chance! My prejudice against their method (they were clearing off the old stock before producing a new edition) became so strong that I feel a slight irritation at the mere sight of the Encyc. Brit.

Now, if they address me with two names, by the public post, they will do me a good deal of harm. Will you do me the favour of going to the business branch, and rooting out of their card catalogue every trace of my being, either as Shaw or Lawrence? It's a mockery to expect a fellow with a net income of below a pound a week to buy such a whale of information, as they sell. And if I had ten pounds a week I wouldn't buy it. Information isn't a thing I go hungry for.

I hope you'll manage this, reasonably soon: otherwise they'll sell my address to other advertising firms, and my already cumbrous mail will become impossible. Also perhaps they'd go on putting all the names and titles I'm doing my best to live down on the envelopes.

Yours sincerely
T. E. Shaw[2]

Liddell Hart Centre for Military Studies, King's College London

1 Captain Basil (later Sir Basil) Liddell Hart (1895–1970): military historian, friend and biographer of Lawrence.
2 Liddell Hart commented:
'He enclosed with the letter a printed post-card addressed to:

Col. Lawrence, 338171. A.C.2. Shaw,
Room 2, E.R.S., R.A.F. Depot,
Drigh Road,
Kaveehi. India.

If this address was a grotesque example of clerical error, obviously inconvenient, the card itself bore nothing more serious than a notification, sent out to all contributors, that the offices of the *Encyclopedia Britannica* were being moved to Regent Street.'

DAVID GARNETT[1]
30.11.27

Dear Garnett

That was a very pleasant letter to get: the *Seven Pillars* interests me so much, because I nearly burst myself trying to write it, and when I'd finished it, it seemed rotten to my judgement. It still does. I'd meant something so much more and different, while doing it.

[...] Your praise of certain (not named) paragraphs of the *Seven Pillars* is probably just. It is not difficult to write a good paragraph, I think. But it is enormously difficult to write a good book. The balance of parts, the movement of the whole frame along the ground, the architectonics, as SS[2] calls them: — those are the real things. An architect does not call his plan good till it suggests the elevation: nor the elevation good till it suggests the rooms behind. The decent paragraph is only the carving of an ornament on one stone of the house, & is as easy in a bad house as in a good one, so long as the workman likes it. Your saying that my tale moves, like us, on Damascus, is the best news I could have had. But it does not move as surely as we did; and the reality of the men who rode with me has somehow evaporated from my ink. I am not so sure I was lucky in my subject; it was recalcitrant to a degree, and I went over it 20 times to shape it somewhat. If only I could have invented! In the Irish Revolt Figgis had a similar subject, though, to my judgement, an easier one; yet it has defeated him, as signally as mine did me.[3] Indeed I'm not sure that my book isn't the better of the two.

[...]

You say it is odd as the only book by a man of action interested in motive; but surely it makes clear that I am not a man of action. I only filled the place of one, because none was available. I'm much better at writing

---

1 David Garnett (1892–1981), the son of Edward and Constance Garnett and grandson of Richard Garnett, was a novelist, critic, biographer (of Pocohontas), autobiographer (in three volumes, *The Golden Echo*, *The Flowers of the Forest* and *The Familiar Faces*), and an associate of the Bloomsbury group. He was a conscientious objector in the First World War but served in the R.A.F. in the Second. As well as editing the letters of Lawrence he edited the novels of Thomas Love Peacock and his own correspondence with T. H. White. He was sometimes referred to by Lawrence as Garnett iii. At this stage the two men had not met. Garnett began their correspondence; the above paragraphs are from the extremely long letter which Lawrence wrote in reply.

2 SS: Siegfried Sassoon.

3 Darrel Figgis, Irish writer and nationalist, who had been involved in 1914 with Erskine Childers in the gun-running to Howth and had been a prominent member of Sinn Fein throughout the Irish troubles, had recently (1927) published his *Recollections of the Irish War*.

than at soldiering and as I don't think my writing any good, you'll realise where I put my military capacity.

[. . .]

Bodleian Reserve

C. F. BELL

14.XII.27   Karachi

Dear C. F. B.

I sent you a wire (laconic, because I had only 5 rupees free to spend on it) last pay-day, withdrawing my trustees' offer of the John portrait of D. G. H. I hope it will be clear enough to enable you to take action. Will you return it to Colonel R. V. Buxton

c/o Martins' Bank
68 Lombard Street.

I'm sorry: because I liked the little drawing, as a portrait. I know I don't understand art enough to appraise it, that way: but two or three experts told me it was good. It was very like D. G. H., too. I knew he didn't like it: but I like none of my portraits, which are sixteen in number![1]

However, there it is. I shall be glad to have it, myself, if I ever have a place where I can put it. In barracks its life would be too uncertain. Also they do not encourage us to put up pictures!

The death of D. G. H. seems to have flattened me out, rather. He was

1 The portrait of Hogarth in question was drawn for, and was included in, the subscribers' edition of *Seven Pillars of Wisdom*; it was also included in *Revolt in the Desert* and the 1935 *Seven Pillars*. It was not, however, popular with its subject or his friends. Bell's explanatory note preserved with this letter gives the background: 'At Lawrence's request Hogarth spent a morning in [Augustus] John's studio. Hogarth described the artist's *modus operandi* with much humour. John made some five or six sketches in block chalk or charcoal and threw them on the floor as they were finished, and children and dogs ran about over them. At the end of the morning John picked out that which he thought best, or was least damaged, and said that was the portrait to be kept. Later on Lawrence suggested giving it to the Ashmolean and handed it over to Hogarth who brought it to me, asking what could be done with it as he couldn't bear it hanging in the Museum. I suggested that it should be removed from the frame and put away. This was done. I think everybody but Lawrence thought it a brutal libel, not even a caricature. After Hogarth's death Mrs. Hogarth particularly desired that it should not remain in Oxford as an acceptable likeness of her husband and asked me to withdraw it. I wrote to him [Lawrence] and a telegram) and this letter were his replies.' As it happens the final resolution of the problem caused by this portrait is the subject of Lawrence's last known letter; see p. 540.

like a reserve, always there behind me; if I got flustered or puzzled. And now I have no confidences.

I do hope that you & Leeds will be allowed to carry on the Museum as it should go: but I see the temptations before the Trustees: and archaeologists seldom love and admire one another. Leeds has done such selfless and splendid work that he should be unassailable: but he never dined often enough at high table. And you cannot help him, socially, because you never stood for much of that sort of thing yourself.[1]

I shall be afraid to come to Oxford now. Still, by 1930 all that may have changed.

Your letter gave me the impression that you were getting better. I hope so.[2] Ominously you gave no report of your own feelings.

I wish I'd been strong enough to stick to my resolution not to pass that book round. It has led by slow steps to *Revolt in the Desert*, and now to Robert Graves' life of me ... [with] God knows what more to follow: & myself made ridiculous by all this notice. A weary world, it is.

Yours
T. E. S.

British Library

E. M. FORSTER
21.12.27   [Karachi]

Do not regard this as a letter. I got your note about *Dr. Woolacott*, and am going to read it page by page, and send you my untouched commentary:[3]

---

1 Leeds duly became Hogarth's successor, remaining Keeper of the Museum until 1945.
2 Bell had been ill in hospital
3 This is the fuller comment on Forster's story *Dr. Woolacott* foreshadowed in Lawrence's letter of 27 October. Forster appreciated Lawrence's observations and adopted some of his recommendations. ('Replying to your note has excited me a good deal,' he wrote. 'There you were time after time on the spot, seeing me through.') But the note is less interesting for its views on Forster's story than for the light it casts on the much discussed subject of Lawrence's sexual nature, indicating clearly that what happened when Lawrence was captured by the Turks at Deraa in November 1917 (the experience in which, to quote *Seven Pillars*, 'the citadel of my integrity was irrecoverably lost') was enforced homosexual intercourse — male rape. It also suggests that Forster's story helped him to come to terms with his 'whimpering' reaction to that event. Moreover, it helped him to recognise that homosexuality could be presented in writing in terms that were — even if unpublishable — 'cleansing' and 'beautiful'. The note surely confirms that of his own volition he had not had, and did not contemplate having, any physical homosexual relations himself; just as his letter to Robert Graves of 6 November 1928 (see p. 387) confirms that he had had no heterosexual relations. See General Introduction, p. xxvi.

and as I've been firing my course of rifle-shooting this morning I am tired: and my head aches and I am very miserable. But the post goes tomorrow and last week also I did not write. I do not know what is the matter with me. I fancy it's the loss of Hogarth, for whom I had long cared very greatly.

I Par ii of page 1. 'Convalescence....' This would have been very good if 'Farm hands ...' had not begun the first paragraph. Your first par. is so good. It sets exactly the note, in 8 lines, of *all* you want to say. [...]¹

III 'Disease knows its harmonies'. You are wonderful in these phrases. They are like the notes of tenor bells. The conversation with disease is grandly true. [...]

The car lights are wonderful. I'd got frightened here, wondering how you would get out of it, and beginning to doubt you had skill to end what you had begun.

The rest is marvellous. There is no other word for it. It bruises my spirit. I did not know there could be such writing.

Is the mechanism of the ring necessary?

There is a strange cleansing beauty about the whole piece of writing. So passionate, of course; so indecent, some people might say: but I must confess that it has made me change my point of view. I had not before believed that such a thing could be so presented — and so credited. I suppose you will not print it? Not that it anywhere says too much: but it shows far more than it says: and these things are mysteries. The Turks, as you probably know (or have guessed, through the reticences of the *Seven Pillars*) did it to me, by force: and since then I have gone about whimpering to myself Unclean, unclean. Now I don't know. Perhaps there is another side, your side, to the story. I couldn't ever do it, I believe: the impulse strong enough to make me touch another creature has not yet been born in me: but perhaps in surrender to such a figure as your Death² there might be a greater realisation — and thereby a more final destruction — of the body than any loneliness can reach.

Meanwhile I am in your debt for an experience of such strength & sweetness and bitterness and hope as seldom comes to anyone. I wish my account of it were not so vaguely inadequate: and I cannot suggest 'more

---

1 [...]; over fifty lines of close textual comment have been omitted.
2 Death is virtually a persona in the story in that the central character, Clesant, a young, ailing country squire, dies following what purports to be an impulsive homosexual encounter with an attractive employee from his estate, who is really the ghost of a soldier fatally wounded in the Great War. The soldier had died refusing the ministrations of the same doctor— the Dr Woolacott of the title — who is notably failing to cure the doomed Clesant.

when we meet' for it will be hard to speak of these things without dragging our own conduct and bodies into the argument: and that's too late, in my case.

T. E. S.

King's College Cambridge

EDWARD GARNETT
23/12/27   Karachi

[...] Graves has indeed pulled the thing together since the typescript[1]. Yet I do not call it good. The truth is so much less flattering than the rumour. And he follows the old fault of regarding my war trouble as the biggest part of the show. Whereas my effort at construction with Winston after the War was a harder and better effort. And in the distant future, if the distant F. deigns to consider my insignificance, I shall be appraised rather as a man of letters than as a man of action. You know my opinion well enough to acquit of me conceit in saying this: you know I think myself a contemptible writer, a bag of tricks. Best-selling tricks, I grant: but tricks that no man with his one eye on the truth would have time for.

By the way I never heard how Cape regarded the stopping of *Revolt*. I hope he had realised from the first that if I had my way its sale would not pass the point of necessity. Had I been in London the stoppage would have come some three thousand pounds earlier. As it is I am most grateful to my Trustees for killing their golden goose. They showed a superb disregard for charity. I believe the R.A.F. Fund is £4,000 better off by me. Cape must see that this was a game which could not go on; each sold copy was so much more trouble for me ... and always there was the prospect of a cheap edition to make me desperate. How hard the lives of publishers would be, if their authors did not write for profit! I hope he regards rather the lump of money he did make out of *Revolt* than the little more he might have made out of it, in the duration. It is a common gag to call me unbusinesslike — and indeed there are things I care for more than money; but I do try to keep in mind that the people I have to do with are out for money, and I have tried my best to ensure their getting what they like. He has only to remember the percentage I insisted on getting for his firm on the contract with Doran, to be convinced of my attempt to deal fairly with him. I remain of course still mindful of my bond to offer him my second book, and I will set this right between us by sending him the text (for publication *in extenso*) of my R.A.F. notes; and then all will be as it ever was.★ [...]

★ This reads cryptic: I mean he will see they are not publishable, and will

1 *Lawrence and the Arabs.*

refuse them, thus acquitting me of any need to write anything else to get clear of promises.

Bodleian Reserve

RALPH ISHAM
2/1/28   Karachi

Dear Isham

Forgive the office typewriter, and my botching of its keys. It's in case I need a copy of what I say to answer your letter about Homer's *Odyssey*. It has knocked me out temporarily.[1] Why should you be so much better to me than I am to myself? The money suggested is wonderful,[2] but that only shows how well they expect it to be done: and I have no trust whatever in my writing. Agreed the reviewers spoke highly of it, when *Revolt* came out: but they speak as well of seventy percent of the books they notice, so one discounts that: and in my case they were astonished that a practical man could write at all. 'So clever of him, my dear, to be able to sit up' — as they'd say of a toy dog.

When your letter came I took the *Odyssey* down from the shelf (it goes with me, always, to every camp, for I love it), and tried to see myself translating it, freely, into English. Honestly, it would be most difficult to do. I have the rhythm of the Greek so in my mind that it would not come readily into straight English. Nor am I a scholar; I read it only for pleasure, and have to keep a dictionary within reach. I thought of the other translators, and agreed that there was not a first-rate one. Butcher & Lang — too antique. Samuel Butler — too little dignified, tho' better. Morris — too literary. That only shows the job it is. Why should my doing be any better than these efforts of the bigger men?

1 The background to this approach to Lawrence to translate the *Odyssey* is described in the introduction to the book from which this letter is taken: *Letters from T. E. Shaw to Bruce Rogers*, of which 200 copies were published in a private edition in 1933. Rogers, a distinguished American book-designer — whose reputation was well known to Lawrence — explained that it was while reading *Seven Pillars of Wisdom* in 1927 that it occurred to him that its author was 'the very man to translate the *Odyssey* anew.... Here at last was a man who could make Homer live again – a man of action who was also a scholar & could write swift and graphic English. But where was he? At that time he was to me a half-legendary person and I knew only that somewhere east of Suez was an air-craftsman who had legally changed his name to Shaw. I casually mentioned my project & my perplexity to Col. Ralph Isham, who startled me by exclaiming, "The very thing for Shaw to do! I'll write to him tomorrow — he's in Karachi".'

2 £800.

Bruce Rogers' dressing of the book will make it glorious, so that even an inferior version would pass muster. You are fortunate to be able to dine with him. I have for years admired him from ground level, and have even been able at intervals to buy books of his production; of course I've never met him: but you know, and he knows, that he's the ideal of all those who have tried to produce books. Or perhaps I should say, of all who have gone far enough in the direction of producing books to know what a job it is. It would be an awful thing if my share in the Homer did not justify its setting, in my own judgement.

So let me make stiff terms, in the hope of being refused an honour which I feel too great to carry off successfully. I can not refuse so profitable an offer bluntly.

1. I should need two years in which to complete the translation, after I began work on it.

2. I do not feel capable of doing it as well as Homer would have liked; and shall feel unhappy if it turns out botched.

3. I could not sign it with any one of my hitherto names. It must go out blank, or with a virgin name on it.

4. I would do the first book within six months of having concluded the agreement with the publishers; and if they were not satisfied with it I would agree to let the contract go, upon their paying me a fraction of the fee which the first book bears to the whole.

Notes on above:

1. Because it is long, and difficult. Probably I'd write it twice or three times before it felt right. Also I can't begin right off. I must get several of the older translations by me, to compare with.

3. And they would have to promise to respect this privacy. I hope never again to be the victim of the press.

4. Six months, because the writing of the first ten pages or so fixes the style of all the rest, and it is the hardest part. And I do not want to do it for nothing. Fifteen or twenty pounds would see me nicely through it.

My strongest advice to you is to get someone better, to do you a more certain performance: I am nothing like good enough for so great a work of art as the *Odyssey*. Nor, incidentally, to be printed by B. R.

Your kindness remains overwhelming. Do realise that I have no confidence in myself, and what I'd like is some little job, unquestionably within my strength and my leisure hours in the R.A.F.[1]

Yours ever
T. E. Shaw

Letters to Bruce Rogers

1 Despite his initial reluctance Lawrence finally agreed to Rogers' proposal, beginning his work on the translation in the spring of 1928.

HIS MOTHER
4.1.28   [Karachi]

That is much better: when we do not write so rapidly, our letters have time
to reach their destinations and answer their questions: so that we do not
need to repeat everything many times. It is not as though I had much to
say. Life with me is much the same, from week to week, or from year to
year: in camp at Farnborough, or at Bovington, or at Cranwell, or at Drigh
Road. One room is like another, in barracks, and one airman is like another
airman. We do not have changes or adventures. We stay still, and are
physically taken care of, like stock cattle.
      [...]
[Good thing you left China. Everything points to the slow development
of its internal politics ... in a century or so everyone there will have points
of view: and then foreigners will be able to learn things. The generation
which tried to teach them is finished. Bob must prepare for some other
walk in life than that. I hope very much it will be in England this time.
                                                                    N]

HL/Bodleian Reserve

MRS THOMAS HARDY
15.1.28   Karachi

Dear Mrs Hardy
    This is a Sunday, and an hour ago I was on my bed, listening to
Beethoven's last quartet: when one of the fellows came in and said that
T. H. is dead. We finished the quartet, because all at once it felt like him:
and now I am faced with writing something for you to receive three weeks
too late.
    I was waiting for it, almost. After your letter came at Christmas I wanted
to reply: but a paragraph in the papers said that he was ill. Then I held my
breath, knowing the tenuous balance of his life, which one cold wind would
finish. For years he has been transparent with frailty. You, living with him,
grew too used to it perhaps to notice it. It was only you who kept him
alive all these years: you to whom I, amongst so many others, owed the
privilege of having known him.
    And now, when I should grieve, for him and for you, almost it feels like

a triumph.[1] That day we reached Damascus, I cried, against all my control, for the triumphant thing achieved at last, fitly: and so the passing of T. H. touches me. He had finished and was so full a man. Each time I left Max Gate, having seen that, I used to blame myself for intruding upon a presence which had done with things like me and mine. I would half-determine not to trouble his peace again. But as you know I always came back the next chance I had. I think I'd have tried to come even if you had not been good to me: while you were very good: and T.H.

So, actually, in his death I find myself thinking more of you. I am well off, having known him: you have given up so much of your own life and richness to a service of self-sacrifice. I think it is good, for the general, that one should do for the others what you have done for us all: but it is hard for you, who cannot see as clearly as we can how gloriously you suceeded, and be sure how worth while it was. T.H. was infinitely bigger than the man who died three days back — and you were one of the architects. In the years since *The Dynasts* the Hardy of stress has faded, and T.H. took his unchallenged — unchallengeable — place. Though as once I told you, after a year of adulation the pack will run over where he stood, crying 'There is no T.H. and never was'. A generation will pass before the sky will be perfectly clear of clouds for his shining. However, what's a generation to a sun? He is secure. How little that word meant to him.

This is not the letter I'd like to write. You saw, though, how I looked on him, and guessed, perhaps, how I'd have tried to think of him, if my thinking had had the compass to contain his image.

Oh, you will be miserably troubled now, with jackal things that don't matter: You who have helped so many people, and whom therefore no one can help. I am so sorry.

                                                          T E Shaw

DG

1 Hardy had died on 11 January. Mrs Hardy replied (15.3.28): 'You say the news struck you as a triumph. When I saw him after he had been laid out I was spell bound [*sic*]. On his face was a radiant look of *triumph*. Never on any other face have I ever seen such a look, nor could I ever have believed it possible....' She also told Lawrence: 'He was devoted to you. Somehow I think he might have lived had you been here.... You seem nearer to him, somehow, than any one else, certainly more akin.'

ALAN DAWNAY
20.1.28   [R.A.F. Drigh Road Karachi]

I try now to answer letters on the flash — or not at all: and always on this paper, which rots in two years. So I'll cheat the fellow who tries to write 'my life and letters', out of some of his materials, anyway.

Graves' book is enough for a lifetime. I like it, because it puts paid, I think, to Lowell Thomas: who will now have to take his stuff from Graves' book or shut up. I like it because he has played the game most honourably with my likes and dislikes, and spared me all the unpleasantness he could. But it remains a horrid thing to happen to a fellow. My instinct told me it would be that: but I thought it worth going through with, because the effect of yet another book on me will be to surfeit the British Public. They will write me down, now, just as a person who wants to advertise himself, for some end which they can't see, and therefore will be all the more suspicious of. That should put me out of court as a public subject: and in the quietness which will follow I can come home and live unnoticed. When, depends a little on Cape, to whom I must write and ask intentions as to further editions, if any, of the Graves book.

Yes, Hogarth's going was a bad knock to me. I relied on him, always, to know where I was at, and why, without being told: and, for his existence there, I like Oxford. Now he has gone: and Hardy has gone since. If G. B. S. and Forster go, I'll have no writing friends left, anywhere. It's a misfortune, perhaps, to be so much older than one's generation.

I had Christmas in the Guardroom, where I took turns, with three others, in patrolling a verandah. Don't ask me why! All camps do it, and will do till some General asks 'Why'. When you are C. I. G. S. I shall hope for you to do it: and will remind you of this letter.

                                        Au revoir . . .? 1930.
                                        TES

Bodleian Reserve

DAVID GARNETT
16.2.28

Dear Garnett
    You are over-imagining the importance of my Uxbridge notes. I call them a book only in derision. They were written, as the basis for a projected book, night by night in August–November 1922. The book hasn't come off: and will never come off: for I now like the R.A.F. too well, despite its

faults, to put out a true account of it to a public which would not understand: which would read blame, where I'd written praise. They are artlessly photographic: interesting, perhaps, as documents.

Not to regard my conviction that I'm not a writer, and that my *Seven Pillars*, if it is any good, achieves it without any concurrence! [*sic*] Perhaps it was a very good subject, though I found it too large. However it was, the *Seven Pillars* is not going to have a successor: and my only motive in suggesting that you should read the R.A.F. notes was to cure you of the lingering suspicion that I could write, if I tried. I've tried once, very hard: and got these notes ready for another try, and that's all. You talk of my writing a story. Why I've never invented anything in my life!

To like Drigh Road: — now that would be an unhealthy sign. We agree there. I want to be in England, where there are clean blue roads, and people who think themselves as good as me in the streets. Of course I'm R.A.F. still, after I get home: till about 1935, probably. It is not as good as a monastery: because it turns you out when you get old or ill. Otherwise it would be my vocation, as you say. Too late!

There are no Holy Men, conscious or unconscious, real or pretendant, in the R.A.F. or the Army or the Navy. The ultimate intention of these three great institutions is non-Christian, which is anti-Christian: and every service man knows that his religion can't get any deeper than his lips. So few think it worth while to profess any. We get hot, instead, on football, or flying, or motor-biking.

Sorry you don't like Caesar's *Gallic War*. I call it a miracle of self-suppression: one of the most impressive things in print. My *Seven Pillars* is nearer Xenophon, a much less ambitious ancient.[1] Hats off to Caesar, though, for really pulling off the impersonal thing, and yet leaving his stuff palpitant with excitement.

Rough edges my preference? I like a rough texture, which is not the same thing. After correcting each paragraph of the *Seven Pillars* I used to forget what came before and after it: just see it for a moment as a single piece of writing: and watch through it for a high point: some idea or single phrase or single word which stung me awake. If it hadn't that, it was deleted, or improved. If it had that, O.K. If it had two or more, out came all but one, usually. [. . .]

I don't think, despite my patchy pleasure in French poetry since 1500, and French prose since 1890, I can be properly called Anti-French. A fellow must pick and choose in foreign literature. For instance I loathe Horace and love Virgil: a remark which would discredit a Roman's judgement: but is only a foible with an Englishman. These Aldingtons who have a spiritual

1 A reference to Xenophon's *Anabasis*, an account in seven books of the expedition of Cyrus against his brother Artaxerxes II, King of Persia, in 401 BC; Xenophon was a leading participant as well as chronicler.

home in France — they have only a physical home in England surely?
[...]

We seem to differ about E. M. F. and D. H. L.[1] I call the form of *The Plumed Serpent* very shapely and satisfying: and the architecture of most of his novels excellent. Of course his prose stammers often. Somebody said he was trying to make the solar plexus talk plain English.

E. M. F.'s crises are the crises of a super-sensitive mind: storms in tea-cups, I called 'em once: that is except the Pan solutions:[2] and Pan to him means physical excitement, I fancy. His best Pan-stuff is unwriteable, I fancy: but in his mind, very surely and succinctly. His social work (*The Longest Journey*, most significant of all) seems to me great ... just great, without qualification. It hangs permanently in my memory, as if it were stuck there: it's like rolling on a fly-paper, which I've seen a hairy lap-dog do. E. M. F.'s stuff clings.
[...]

Bodleian Reserve

SIR HUGH TRENCHARD
17.3.28   R.A.F. Drigh Road Karachi

Dear Sir Hugh
    I've been wondering, since the sea-mail left, if I'm forsworn. In 1922, when you let me enlist, I promised that the C.A.S. should see, first, any book I wrote on the R.A.F. I don't think it's a book:— but I posted something rather like one yesterday to Edward Garnett: and you'd better hear about it.[3]

    In those days I hoped to turn as much of me as had survived the war into a writer; and I thought the R.A.F. was a subject. So I made full and careful notes of Uxbridge. Afterwards, at Farnborough in 1923, I had a look at the printed *Seven Pillars* and realised I should never write well. So pop went that ambition; and the notes popped into my kit-box.

    In the midst of that misery I was kicked out of what had become my

---

1 E. M. Forster and D. H. Lawrence.
2 The Greek god Pan being associated with sudden fear (hence 'panic'), Lawrence is presumably referring to Forster's use of sudden dramatic twists of fortune in some of his novels.
3 Lawrence was writing two days after sending a fair copy of his 'R.A.F. notes' (i.e. *The Mint*) to Edward Garnett. In his accompanying letter (printed as *DG* 344) he wrote: 'I want it offered to Cape, for publication, in extenso, without one word excised or moderated [...] and I want him to refuse it, so as to free me from the clause in his contract of the *Revolt of the Desert*, tying me to offer him another book.'

profession: and so re-met Garnett, whose name you probably know as a critic of genius. Of course he's more than that; but that's only his reputation. I explained to him that the reason had fallen out of my existence — and so there wouldn't be another book. He remained curious. If not a book, what of the notes? I sort of grinned, and said 'I'll give 'em you, for keeps'. But they'd been left at S.O.P.[1] in one of the fellows' lockers; and they banged about the earth for years, occasionally coming into my hands. They felt unbearably vivid and meaningful to me, like a part of myself (for private reasons) and I didn't want to lose them: but at last you let me back again, and then I cared for them no more.

Garnett used to hint at his unfulfilled present, from time to time. So in Karachi I took them up, at last, to send him: but time had blurred their original pencil into unintelligibility, except for me. They'd been written nightly, in bed! So they had to be fair-copied; and I sweated on them for months, till they were all out straightly in a little note-book of 176 pages (70,000 Words) called *The Mint*. *The Mint*, because we were all being stamped after your image and superscription.

This note-book it was which I posted yesterday. Last night I made a lovely bonfire of the originals. Up came the orderly sergeant, and asked silly questions: wanted to know what I was burning. 'My past' said I. But suddenly I thought — perhaps they'll say I've written another book. Do you think so? If you care to see it you may. This letter will catch up, and I am sending Garnett a copy to show him it's your right to see it. That will explain the typing of an A.C.H.,[2] afraid to type well for fear they promote him into a soft-boiled clerk. It also shows devotion to duty, to send two Air-Mail letters in one week. Twelve annas gone west.

Garnett will not hawk the thing about; only his son will read it. After I'm dead someone may censor out of it an edition for publication. I shall not care, being dead; and the R.A.F. will be different and indifferent. Quite wrong of it: doesn't know its mercies: may be years before it has another A/C like me.

I don't advise even Garnett to read it; much less a man of action. 170 pages of my handwriting. It's a worm's eye view of the R.A.F. — a scrappy uncomfortable thing. I've been an uncomfortable thing while I wrote it. The ranks, even of your incomparable force, don't make for easy living or writing. Every word of this has been done in barracks. Any word used in barrack rooms has been judged good enough to go in; wherefore Scotland Yard would like to lock up the author. The general public might be puzzled, and think I didn't like the R.A.F. whereas I find it the only life worth living for its own sake. Though not the Depot. Uxbridge was bad, and I'd

1 S.O.P.: School of Photography, Farnborough.
2 Aircraft Hand.

have written and told you so, only that it seemed implicit, in your letting me join, that I should take my stuff quietly.

You'll please yourself, after all this. Garnett's address is No. 19 Pond Place, Chelsea, S.W.3.

T.E.S.

There's a laugh in the beast's tail. Gifts are lousy things, anyhow: and the sole copy of a second book by a best-selling author is about as seasonable a gift as a full-grown alligator. And I meant to please Garnett, who has been very good to me. He won't know whether to insure it, or burn it, or poke it in the British Museum.

Bodleian Reserve/HMH

MRS CHARLOTTE SHAW
20.3.28

[...] What you say about the Uxbridge notes, and their effect on you, delights me.[1] When you asked me for them I had to send them you. If you had not asked I should not have. Such intimate meats aren't meant to be hawked about. But if anyone of the qualified ones wants them: why then, upon their own head! I was not really very fearful of your head being bowed under them: though it is a test, rather. There never was, I fancy, such stuff put on paper before — or is this the vanity of every author? It's so hard to see that one's own intimacies may be other people's commonplaces of exchange. Parts of the notes shocked me: as much as the original experiences they try to mirror, though I tried very hard not to look shocked or sound shocked. But you take them exactly as I'd like everybody to (and as I fear hardly anybody would). I was very nervous after I'd posted them: and the second part is worse than the first. I think the third part, the Cranwell part, is sunny.

    [...]

I've told you in a letter crossing yours[2] (how can one explain across five

1 Lawrence had sent a rough copy of his 'Uxbridge notes' to Mrs Shaw some weeks earlier. He wrote on 2 January 1928: 'So soon as I found, at the end of your letter, your request for the Uxbridge notes (collected as *The Mint*) I unlocked my box, thrust the rough copy into an envelope, & took them to the post. It was a matter of minutes only, before I could think it over.' He had added the caution: 'Please regard yourself (in reading it) as being in an equivocal position, eavesdropping in a man's barrack.'

2 In 'the letter crossing yours' (dated 1.3.28) Lawrence had written: 'What you & G. B. S. think about the tightness & spareness of it pleases me more than pages of praise. Think of the tightness and spareness of our uniform: and for its bare severity look at the barrackroom. That is the scene, this the manner, those the figures. Service life is not freedom. It can be a contented slavery though.'

thousand miles, and six weeks?) that the hardness and bareness are the square and the barrack-room: and the tightness is our discipline and uniform. The service-man's life is cribbed, amazingly. We never get out of bonds. Only we see freedom about us in the trees and birds, and stars. That is why you'll sometimes find little landscape snatches — parts of the notes. The sight of nature sometimes reaches our notice, and tells us that we are not natural: — or rather, that our way of life is not. No more natural than a box-tree trimmed into a peacock: you don't call that a tree. The services are things of their own sort: a slavery of the spirit, I sometimes think.

I've tried not to remember back: not to introduce one idea or sentence or adjective which had not found place in my original notes. The temptation to write the book for which these were meant to provide the foundation, — that temptation died out years ago. The R.A.F. is now my very own service, and I learn to fit in, slowly: to give up my rights to personality.

[...]

T.E.S.

The permitted readers of them are:— (1) Mrs. Shaw. (2) Trenchard (if he wants) (3) Edward Garnett and David Garnett (if they want) (4) perhaps, I don't know: EMF. (5) D. G. H. if he had not died.[1]

British Library

HIS MOTHER
23.3.28   [Karachi]

There, I have sorted out, in the last three days, my recent letters. There are 132 business letters which I must answer: 26 letters from people I once used to feel with, & whose friendliness has gone on past our separation. I would like to drop them, but am too soft-hearted: and I have thrown away two boxes-full of stuff that did not matter.

My average mail is 20 letters a week: of which perhaps six or seven are of no importance. That just balances my maximum reply-capacity. I can afford two rupees (3/-) for stamps every week, & the little extra which envelopes & paper cost. So if everybody ceased writing to me from today I could be free of back-correspondence in ten weeks at 16 letters a week. Letters take on the average $\frac{3}{4}$ of an hour each, if you add in the getting pens & ink out of my box, & the job of getting them to the post office. So 12 hours a week (2 a day) for the next ten weeks would see me quit. Only

---

1 Written in the margin against the paragraph about his 'Uxbridge notes'.

each week there arrive more letters than I can answer. So the problem remains impossible. Also I refuse to waste all my leisure on letter-writing. The letters bore the people who get them as much as their letters bore me, I suppose. Who invented this curse?

I think I shall print a small card 'to announce cessation of correspondence' and send it to the 300 or 400 of my regular addresses. After that I shall write not more than one letter per week, & take a holiday once a quarter.

All of which nonsense has well filled these pages, & conceals the fact that nothing has happened here since I wrote to you last. All well. Hope Bob's better, & settling down.

N.

HL

SERGEANT A. PUGH
13.4.28

[...] I seem never to have answered your query re Miss Brown of Purley who wanted a photo of me. Let her cut one out of the *Daily Mail*. These flappers!

Hoots.

A publisher wrote & asked if I had any little poems I'd let him publish (a hen might as well lay cabbages as me write poetry) because if so he'd send me the latest Brough Superiors for the years 1928–29–30–31–32.

I told him a) That I had no poems
           b) That Karachi had no roads.

Hoots again.

TES

Bodleian Library

A. W. LAWRENCE[1]
2.5.28

Dear A

I am leaving Karachi soon, for some squadron up-country: and shall not

---

1 Arnold Walter Lawrence (b. 1900), T. E. L.'s youngest brother. Professor of Classical Archaeology, Cambridge University, 1944–51; Professor of Archaeology, University College of Ghana, and Director, National Museum of Ghana, 1951–57. Author of books on Greek sculpture and architecture, editor of Herodotus, etc. T. E. L.'s literary executor.

regret going, on the whole.[1] Will let you know my new address, when I have it.

They are nibbling again at the *Odyssey* idea. Hope it comes off.

Do you remember my telling you that you were my heir? There'll be about four pounds to inherit in cash, and £18 in the Bank, and some books, and Clouds Hill (perhaps). Not Pole Hill, which goes to Richards.

Also my copyrights which now no longer include *Revolt in the Desert*: but you will be O.C. the *Seven Pillars*, and the greater controls the less: so that should make up for the disappointment of the preceding paragraph.

I'm not consciously dying yet: I'm detailing these past facts to add a present fact to it. I have written out a clean copy of some notes I made in 1923 at Uxbridge, on a recruit's life in the R.A.F. of the time. They total some 80,000 words, and therefore amount, pretty well, to another book. Edward Garnett, of 19 Pond Place, Chelsea is the owner of the Manuscript, at present the sole copy. If he has it typed, which he may do, for security's sake, I'll have a copy sent to you. Garnett's son David will presumably inherit from his father, eventually.

The copyright of this M.S. of course remains mine, for life: and passes to my heirs, for the statutory period, which I believe is 40 years after death. I will not publish these notes (whose present name is *The Mint*) in my day. And I hope that you will not (without the permission of the Chief of Staff of the R.A.F. for the time being) publish them, if the option is yours, before 1950. They are very obscene.

Regard these things as possible windfalls for your child. They will not profit you much. What else? You know that John Snow, of Mallam's, the Solicitors, in St. Giles, Oxford, has my will: and that Eliot and Robin Buxton (R.B. c/o Martins Bank, 68 Lombard St. and the Hon. E. Eliot, c/o Kennedy, Ponsonby & Ryde, of Guildhall Chambers, Bishopsgate St.) are trustees and owners of *Revolt in the Desert*: and that Eliot has my Power of Attorney, to look after the *Seven Pillars*: and that Richards (V.W.) of 3 Loudoun Road, St. John's Wood, N.W.8 has my books, & can explain the situation of Pole Hill.

There, I think all those things are clear. As I say, I'm not conscious of dying: but while I'm informing you of the existence of *The Mint* I'd better put you again exactly informed of the other arrangements. Handy-like, to have it in a nut-shell.

TES.

Bodleian Reserve

1 The move from Karachi was at Lawrence's request. His immediate C.O. was content to have him among his team but, as he told Robin Buxton in a letter of 10 May 1928 (see *DG*, p. 607) 'higher up they panic, over my mere existence in the camp'. Miranshah, his second posting, was the smallest and most remote R.A.F. station in India. (N.B. Both Karachi and Miranshah are in what is now Pakistan.)

MRS CHARLOTTE SHAW
17.5.28

There we will forget *The Mint*. It is dead and buried. I am still tired: and in addition have a Nunc Dimittis feeling again. All the loose ends of my life have now been so tidied up. The Arab Campaign: fought, won, recorded, the political settlement, following on it, finished so far as my eyes can see. The things of Ibn Saud and the things of Irak go well. Palestine is not a country, but a religious museum or laboratory. Syria: that has been beyond man's wit for very long.

So there's the public part finished: and the private part is finished too. The causes that led me into the Air Force have come to their full consequence, and are dead, like the Arab business, probably: at least I have felt strong enough to put them out on paper. *The Mint* has been impossible to write all these years: for six years I have had its pieces in my bag, and it was not till England was away behind me that I could take it up and work on it. It is not easy, either, in this place and climate, and in service conditions, to write seriously. You'd have laughed, I think, if you'd seen me working away with a pencil, as I sprawled on my bed, afternoons and evenings, while the crowd chattered and wrangled over my head.

All this finishing and finishing for ten years without the faintest desire or stirring to begin anything anywhere again. I have no more notes for books in my bag: and no urge to join the boy scouts or the House of Commons. The R.A.F. seems natural somehow, as a way of living: and no other life seems natural: or is it that no energy to attempt any new life remains? Nunc dimittis ... if I had a Lord, and he were a decent fellow, he would tell his servant to go to sleep, in reward for having worked 'overtime', and very hard, for forty years: or I think he would. It is what his servant (if profitable) would ask as reward.

Of course G. B. S. at forty was just beginning to get in his stride, with plays: but between the power and courage of G. B. S., and my weariness, how great a gap! And when I think of lives for which I am very grateful: for poor Dowson, who wrote ten lovely poems, and died; for Rossetti, who wrote a few more, and died; for Coleridge, who wrote for two years, and then ran dry; why surely duration and bulk aren't the first considerations? It seems to me that the Arab Revolt, of activities of the body: and the *Seven Pillars* and *Mint*, of activities of the mind, may be all that my tissues can do. Certainly for the moment, it is all. I just labour, grudgingly, through the daily duty the R.A.F. compels from me: and lie restlessly on my bed (restlessly for the flies and prickings of external difficulty) during the other, very long, hours of this interminable day. It will be so good to be free of Drigh Road. On the 23rd, my move is: to

Peshawar,[1] to No. 20 Squadron R.A.F. But I will write from there (no letter next week: I shall be in the train, seeing half India) and tell you just what my address will be, and how the new conditions first strike me. Drigh Road has been dreary and even a little dangerous for me, lately: though now-a-days perhaps I grow too easily apprehensive of risk. I clutch my place in the R.A.F. like a life-buoy, because if it went from me I would sink, straight away. I hope *The Mint* will not make Trenchard hate me. He is so very kind and large: but it offends against his tradition of loyalty, and perhaps he will think me a scab for betraying my service. I wish you knew Trenchard. It would explain a good deal to you. Now D. G. H. has gone, he's the man whose opinion I shall be sorriest to lose. Of course he is not civilised, like D. G. H.; but he is larger.

A doleful letter, this, it seems to me, re-reading it in the dull light of early Thursday morning. My first daily job is to open the workshops, half an hour before the crowd come, so that the open doors and fans may air them. It gives me twenty minutes calm each day. You can safely ascribe the half of the above to the coming shadow of my move. I was meant for a stay-at-home, and the adventure of every new camp frightens me in advance.

[...]

You will be seeing my mother, perhaps, soon. [...] I wonder how you and she will get on. Well, I expect, for my mother is very unusual and remarkable. Remember that she was brought up as a charity child in the Island of Skye, and then had to fend for herself: and compare that with her present: and you'll be astonished.

Too many interruptions. I cannot do anything while people talk at and to me every minute. More, later, from Peshawar, about ten or 12 days hence, or whatever their mail-day is. It will be the usual scramble: sending off 20 letters to 20 people, saying where I now am.

T. E. S.

British Library

---

1 Capital of North West Frontier Province; Lawrence stayed there only briefly — by early June he was at Miranshah.

SERGEANT A. PUGH
9/6/28   R.A.F. Detachment Miranshah

Dear Sergt.

This is more like 'B' Flight, only as it happens their number is 'A'. Out on the drome they are just running up the engines (the same old Bifs[1]) for some practice flying: and I am sitting in the Office with lots to do, and not doing it. Instead I shall get busy on the typewriter, and knock you out a letter. A poor typewriter, for every now and then it stammers, and misses a few spaces. Cause unknown, but suspected to be old age and general debility. Poor devil, I feel for it, being near to that case myself . . . but we are lucky to have a typewriter of any kind here, in the ends of the earth; and if it stutters, why it's up to me to mend it, in my spare time.

Miranshah is an advanced station of the R.A.F., and lies ten miles from the Afghan border. In shape it is a mud and brick fort, about four hundred yards each way. The garrison are an irregular corps of Indian Scouts, who live in one compound, while we twenty five R.A.F. live in another compound. They are out of bounds to us, and we are out of bounds to them. A sociable arrangement, which makes for quietude. This Miranshah is almost the quietest place I have struck, in Stations.

The permanent Staff are three, a storekeeper, a wireless Corp. and a clerk, who will be me, I hope, if my filing and letter-writing and reliability of character and conduct earn me the privilege. At present I am lucky, for there is nobody else running for the job. The place is so remote that not many people have heard of it; I suppose that is why there is no rush to get the privilege of permanence here. It will be a scoop for the ACH class, if I carry it off.

No permanent Officer, but the three or four squadrons who are nearest detach a flight in rotation, to stay here for two months, and work from here up and down the tribal country which borders on the legal border. The Flight Lieutenant commanding this flight is the C.O. of the Station, during his spell of duty:— so I get a change of C.O. every few weeks. That is part profit, and part loss. At Cranwell, it would have been a dead loss. At Karachi it would have been gain. (I apologise, again, for somebody's typewriter; what sex is a typewriter? this is a dog of a one)

Being clerk is not so much fun as ACH in a flight, but in India there are coolies to do the washing down and donkey work, so the poor ACH loses most of his livelihood. Nearly all of us do paper work of some sort, here. And, to tell you the truth, it is rather messy, pulling busses[2] about, in this climate:— doesn't do you any harm, but you want a bath and change of

1 Bristol fighters.
2 i.e. aircraft.

clothes after half an hour of it: and the water is sure to be turned off, just then, and we can't afford new clothes weekly.

I have two years, or nearly, to do out here now, and if I am continually lucky, they will be done in Miranshah. You can hardly conceive the quiet of the tiny place. At night they shut it all up with barbed wire, and by day we are not allowed to go out beyond the edge of the aerodrome without an escort: not that the tribes are now unfriendly, but it is an old tradition that they ought to be, and so strict precautions are the rule in all these forts. Even by day, when the fort gates are open, there is an unbroken peace over us. We lie in a plain, some miles wide, and are ringed by a wall of mountains, sharp mountains, quite clear and clean in line; and these seem to keep off wind and access. I feel as though I had slipped over the edge of the world a little way, and landed on some ledge a few feet down the far side. We get few posts, and slow ones; have no shops or visitors or news; in fact it is like a little bit of Heaven; a perfect home from home. I have been looking for a place like this for years, with little hope that such a thing existed.

There is no luck about this letter, which has been four times on or off the machine already. Really, you know, the mornings are fairly busy. Of course we are not supposed to work in the afternoons; and as a fact there is then little to do; but I have a post to meet, or get off, and the arrear of the morning correspondence to finish up, so I make the job lengthen itself pretty well until the evening. Evenings are a bit dull, for I have no gramophone or records, yet, and no books, nor are my eyes quite up to reading in the half-light which is all the rooms allow us. But if I get the job for keeps, as I hope, then I will produce from some hat the price of a musical box; and records are waiting for me in Karachi to order up; and as Sergt. Williams used to discover, there are ways I have of bettering the lighting scheme laid down by the Works and Buildings Office. So soon after you get this letter there will be great changes in Miranshah. If Mrs Shaw and the others send me out, to here, as many books as they used to send to Cranwell, why then the local library will not hold them all, and I shall have to go round the departing Flights, saying 'Please do not go without helping yourself to at least two books'. It got like that at Karachi, where I received over 250 books, and mustered only 100 of them, when I left. That hundred were what the irks called the 'Binders', but which to my odd taste, included most of the attractive books to arrive. So I am pleased at the course of natural selection, and so (let's hope) were they. If they give me Miranshah for good, then I'll get those 100 sent up in a case by rail.

Anything else? Yes, of course, I should ask kindly after Mrs Pugh, and Miss Pugh, and Tug and Dusty (though Dusty will now have left you); but it does not seem any good thinking about home, here. We are too far off, and too cut off. It really feels as though things beyond those mountains did not exist. Perhaps that feeling will yield to time, and the arrival of letters from England:— but if it does not, then take fair notice that I am becoming an Afghan. I feel it, in the bones, this week.

Incidentally, we are 3000 feet up, and as cool as cool can be. Nearly midsummer, and the temperature probably not over 100. We do not know for certain as we have no thermometer. Happy Miranshah. But in winter we may be as cold as Cranwell. Heaven forbid. .... They say however that there is no snow, ever, on the ground: but rain in buckets, and the hills about all snow-tipped, and cold winds and other horrors.

[...]

Enough Rot
Au revoir.
T. E. S.

Bodleian Library

MRS CHARLOTTE SHAW
11.6.28   Miranshah

[...] This place I think is good: At least we are let alone, out of working hours, to do as we please. That inestimable boon was denied the Depot at Karachi. So I greatly hope that in a few weeks Miranshah will fit me like a suit that has been long worn. Long worn, indeed: it is only a fortnight since we came, and it feels like years. There has been the difficulty of learning the new job (I am really a clerk now, except in name and trade) which has meant overtime: of breaking myself tactfully to the new fellows: of getting used to high mud and brick walls as my view, with towers at intervals, and a frieze of the heads and shoulders of mountains, a few miles off, peeping over the wall-tops, very mistily. Weather thunderous: close, breathless, with occasional half-hearted showers of rain. Neither cold nor hot — just over the hundred, I think: but the fort has no thermometer. Afghanistan — did I tell you? — is about ten miles off. The people are friendly, but on guard: which represents our manner, too. An armed guard.
[...]
Your books here will be like water in the desert. The fellows are too few to play games, and so they go very short of amusement. Only tennis, I think. One of the officers has a little gramophone, which he has lent us twice. It did the Elgar Symphony for me, but only like a ghost of the

Karachi box, which was a good one. Still: this is Miranshah, and the *Odyssey* has been eating up *my* spare time.

[...]

British Library

HIS MOTHER

10.7.28   Miranshah Waziristan India

[...]

I'm glad you've met Mrs. Shaw. It's very hard to be a great man's wife. She succeeds with it. I like her. Hope you'll meet G. B. S. some time. He is like a tonic, and very kind. A most sensible, vigorous old man.

[...]

HL

SIR HERBERT BAKER[1]

17.7.28

Dear H. B.

This is most gorgeous news: do please accept my most relieved thanks. The shadow in front of everyone in the Services is always the day of discharge: and now I'll be happier about mine: though I expect all the same sorry to leave. The Bank of England: that does sound magnificently splendid. Apolaustic:[2]

I cannot tell when it is. If Trenchard is displeased with me, it will be in 1930 (March). If he is not displeased, he can let me alone till 1935 (March). I hope, of course, for the later date, but fear the earlier. He may have left

---

1 Sir Herbert Baker (1862–1946, knighted 1926) had provided, and would do so again, the garret sanctuary in Barton Street, Westminster, where Lawrence wrote much of *Seven Pillars* and many of his letters. He was an architect of considerable distinction — creator of many buildings in South Africa, the Rhodes Memorial on Table Mountain, Rhodes House, Oxford, India House and South Africa House, London, and the Indian and South African Memorials in northern France at Neuve Chapelle and Delville Wood respectively. He had also been associated with Sir Edwin Lutyens in the planning of New Delhi. At this time he was engaged in reconstructing the Bank of England and Glyn, Mills Bank in Lombard Street.

2 Baker had been lobbying at the Bank of England on Lawrence's behalf; the nature of the employment which might possibly be offered him is made clear in the following letter to Bernard Shaw.

before 1930, himself, in which case I may put up a fight for my extension. Fighting him is profitless, for I like and respect him so much that it's like having my hands tied behind my back.

Will you thank the Prophet, too? It is most good of you both. Please assure him and the Governor, if you see either of them while the matter is fresh in your (now very burdened) mind, that there are no seeds germinating in my bosom, to be brought out by jobs of any kind.[1] I'll do my bodily best in the job they give me, and be honest: that is all. To tell them that the volcano is not extinct is untrue, for one thing, and may well frighten them, on the other. There never was an orange drier squeezed than myself. Not a kick in the entire body. I will write nothing else, I'm sure, and do nothing else. Of course a sane man can never foretell his future: but it will be miraculous if any activity ever revives in me. No one can ever have felt so high and dry as myself, after 1922, since the ship Argo was drawn up by Jason after the Fleece quest, and excused further voyaging. I may look and sound cheerful, and I am cheerful: but that's a long way from growth. They used to tell me that it was just tiredness, and that time would make me dissatisfied with standing aside. How much time, I ask them, now? This is 1928, and I am 40; surely the rush is over. I have dug, and studied, fought a campaign, fought a political campaign, carried out a settlement, written two books — all by the time I was 34. Now I'm finished. If I forced myself to attempt more, against my conviction, it would be bad work I'd produce: & I am so tired.

Your difficulty in Lombard Street is a tiring one. Inform Buxton's neighbours that you are rebuilding Martins': and beg to enclose plans, specifications and estimates for the new premises which they will find necessary when their present buildings fall into *your* hole. Point out that their prompt acceptance of your scheme will save them cost and delay and disorganisation. With any luck you will rebuild half the street. It will be better than the Quadrant.

Miranshah is a fort, of the sort you saw: but its towers are square, with battlemented parapets, & machicolations for machine guns & search-lights: also iron gates, arched over, and all the rest of the mediaeval apparatus. To reach it from Peshawar we drove through Kohat and Bannu. I like it very much: but we are not allowed outside the barbed wire round the walls. So do not ask me about Waziristan, or Wazirs.

MORE THANKS
T. E. S.

Bodleian Reserve

---

1 The Prophet and the Governor (i.e. of the Bank of England): Lionel Curtis and Sir Montague Norman respectively.

BERNARD SHAW
19.7.28   Miranshah

[. . .] No, I am not adjutant, to this camp. Just typist, and i/c files, and duty rolls. I do what I am told to do, and rewrite the drafts given to me, meekly. The officers would need to be better than they feel themselves to be, for me to safely exceed the normal rank of R.A.F. clerk. Also, I'm not much good as a clerk; though I type a bit better than this, in the daylight.

You ask what is my expectation of life, when I'm discharged. I can tell you, without many 'ifs'. If Trenchard is displeased with me over *The Mint*, (those notes on the R.A.F. which you saw, and he has seen) he will make me leave the R.A.F. in February, 1930. If he does not bear me any grudge, he will leave me alone here, and at some camp in England, till 1935. Or Trenchard may himself leave the Air Force, and I find kinder treatment from his successor. However, in 1930 or in 1935, I will have to go out. My notion, if I have then a secured income of a pound a day, is to settle at Clouds Hill, in my cottage, and be quiet.

If I have to earn my bread and butter, I shall try for a job in London. The sort of job will depend on my health. My body has been knocked to pieces, now and then, and often overworked, in the past: so I do not feel sure of lasting very well. I have thought of a night-watchman job, in some City Bank or block of offices. The only qualification for these is Service experience; and honesty is the necessity which bars very many ex-service men from getting them. I can get good references, from people bankers will trust, so I have good hope of getting placed. Better than that, almost; for Sir Herbert Baker, the architect, who is building the new Bank of England, has spoken of me to the Council which runs it, and they have put a minute in their book that my application is to be considered as favourably as possible, if or when I apply.

You see, I have no trade to take up, and am old to learn, and tired of learning things. So I must look for an unskilled job; and I want an indoor job, if possible, in case I am not very fit. And I like London. And I'd like to work by myself. It is not easy to get on terms with people. On night work nobody would meet me, or hear of me, much.

I have been thinking hard for the last two or three years of what I should go for, if the R.A.F. came to a sudden end (you see, it is precarious: I depend on the favour of Hoare and Trenchard, and am the sort of fellow on whom people hang tales and believe anything, though I do my honest best to worm along inoffensively) and I have listened or joined myself to the other fellows whenever they have discussed civvy jobs:— and of everything I have heard, this night-watchman job sounds the most likely for me to be allowed to hold for good. You see, there is no more demanded of you than that the safe should be unbroken the next morning. You come on duty as the last clerk goes, and the door is locked. You come off duty when the first comer opens the door in the morning. No others ever hear of you, as an individual.

Thanks to Baker speaking to the Bank Committee, with whom he is in weekly touch, my way to the job seems to have been made suddenly easy. His letter telling me only reached me here, so you see it is recent news. I hope you will not tell anyone about it. The Bank Committee will not. The rest of the formalities would be done by their Staff-man. I will not have to see any of the big noises. The Bank of England is rather more than I had hoped for (or wanted) as it is really too good. Also the smaller Banks let their night men sleep in. Of course the new Bank building will have more room in it. A gorgeous place to live in, don't you think? But that is a trifle, anyhow. A single man can live anywhere, if his tastes are quite plain. Mine are getting plain. Up here I have begun to think with pleasure of the idea of eating ... once or twice.

Please do not laugh at this sketch of my intentions. What I have wanted and tried to do has always come off, more or less, except when it was trying to write; and then, despite all the good you have said of my books, I am assured of failure. Not complete failure, perhaps. I explain yours and my different judgements of my writing by my knowledge of the standard at which I was aiming, and your astonishment that 'a man of action' should be able to do it at all. A relative failure, let's call it. My aim may have been too high for anybody; it was too high for me. But I think one says just 'too high', not 'immodestly high'. I do not think aims are things modest or immodest, just possible and impossible.

Your ever
T. E. Shaw

I haven't answered your last line 'What is your game *really*?' Do you never do things because you know you must? Without wishing or daring to ask too deeply of yourself why you must? I just can't help it. You see, I'm all smash, inside: and I don't want to look prosperous or be prosperous, while I know that. And on the easy level of the other fellows in the R.A.F. I feel safe: and often I forget that I've ever been different. As time passes that war and post-war time grows less and less probable, in my judgment. If I'd been as accomplished as they say, surely I wouldn't be in the ranks now? Only please don't think it is a game, just because I laugh at myself and everybody else. That's Irish, or an attempt to keep sane. It would be so easy and so restful just to let sanity go and drop into the dark: but that can't happen while I work and meet simple-hearted people all day long. However, if you don't see it, I can't explain it. You could write a good play, over a room-full of Sydney Webbs and Cockerells asking me 'why'.

DG

E.M. FORSTER
28/8/28

[...] Of course *The Seven Pillars* is bigger than *The Mint*. I let myself go
in *The S.P.* and gave away all the entrails I had in me. It was an orgy of
exhibitionism. Never again. Yet for its restraint, & dignity, and form, &
craftsmanship, *The Mint* may well be better. By that I don't mean that *The
Mint* has *no* emotion, or *The Seven Pillars no* balance: only comparatively
it's so. E. Garnett, curiously enough, calls *The S.P.* reticent, and *The Mint*
a giving away of myself. Why, so far as myself is concerned, I wouldn't
hesitate to publish *The Mint* tomorrow!

In truth however, the publication isn't in my hands. Trenchard is not
the primary obstacle: though for him I have an admiration almost unlimited.
He's a very great man. I think he over-estimates the harm which *The Mint*
would do the R.A.F.: but what really holds me back is the horror the
fellows with me in the force would feel at my giving them away, at their
'off' moments, with both hands. To be photographed, they put on what
they call 'best' clothes, & brush their hair, & wash. To be portrayed, as in
my book, unadorned would break their hearts. You must remember that
The Mint is photographically exact: many of them have their real names!
No hut-full could trust itself to live openly together, if there was a risk of
their communion becoming public copy, in a few years time.

So *The Mint* shall not be circulated before 1950. By then the characters
will not matter. Poor old Stiffy is keeping a hotel in Essex now. He'll be
dead, & Trenchard, & perhaps myself: (dead or aged 62, the last item. What
a quaint performance *The Mint* will seem to a white-beard of 62!) [...]

DG

BRIGADIER-GENERAL SIR GILBERT CLAYTON
9.X.28   Miranshah

Dear Clayton

I wanted to put Sir Gilbert: but it became Clayton, irresistibly. We
always used to call you Clayton, amongst ourselves, in 15....

When the wireless fellow here brought me the notice about Irak which
he'd overheard in the air, the first thing I said was 'too late to do him
justice' — because you should have had it years ago: and the second thing
I thought was 'how very lucky for Irak, that he's been delayed until he's

really wanted.'[1] It's ever so good an appointment, from the point of view, and in the interests of, everyone but yourself. Bagdad requires the diplomatic, so much more than the administrative understanding. So I congratulate the whole show on their belated common-sense, and am sure that you'll take this view of it and smile at the past.

As I get further and further away from things the more completely do I feel that our efforts during the war have justified themselves, and are proving happier and better than I'd ever hoped. And some of this good progress is surely due to my keeping out of an area that I care too much for?

Give Feisal my regards, when you see him. Tell him that I thought a great deal of him during the war: and that I think far more of him now. He has lasted splendidly. He won't find this familiarity, from a person who stands right away from competition!

I laughed when I read of his instituting the Order of the Two Rivers. The Euphrates is my very old friend; and the Tigris isn't at all a bad river. I nearly wrote and asked him for one of his stars, to put on my hitherto empty coat. After all, I'm almost a foundation-member of his kingdom . . . if he can remember our talks of old days in Winterton's house, and in Mr. Churchill's house, and in the Suez Canal? Of course he has had so much to do, since all that, that perhaps he's forgotten with what difficulty against what prejudice *we* began. By 'we', I mean him & me. The Kingdom of Irak depended on such slender causes: & I'm so proud of it, now.

Anyway, give him my best regards, and guard your own head, against him & everybody. The only essential is that the show should go along its proper road, after all. So long as that happens the personalities it uses or breaks are trifles.

I'm awfully glad you've got up into the real saddle again.

Yours
T E Shaw

Bodleian Reserve

1 Clayton had just been appointed British High Commissioner and Commander-in-Chief for Iraq.

SIR HERBERT BAKER
29.X.28   Miranshah

Dear H. B.

I seem to trouble everybody I meet. Why should you and the Elizabethan magnate[1] be put to work, for my continued existence? or Trenchard 'waste' an hour of his time: though waste does not properly apply there, I fancy: meeting you is a pleasure, and meeting Trenchard a privilege, and the conjunction ought to have been ambrosial and nectary.

I burble: but didn't you like Trenchard? He is as simply built as Stonehenge, and serves equally as well for a temple, or a public meeting-place or monument. Altogether one of my admirations: though I fear he cannot follow the wimbling and wambling of my career. I puzzle Trenchard, and he misunderstands me, often. Not that any such tiny detail could distress him; or blot his greatness, in my eyes.

I have asked the R.A.F. to prolong my service to the limit of my engagement — till 1935, that is. We sign on for 7 years active, and 5 reserve: and a proportion of us are allowed to convert the reserve years into active. If the Air Ministry says Yes to my petition, they will please me, for I like the R.A.F. beyond measure.

It will seem to you improvident of me, to risk losing a permanency in the Bank for a transitory five years more of pleasure: but indeed I worked hard for this pleasure, and I want to have it while I am still fit enough to feel physical pleasure. My rackety life makes me expect an old age full of aches and ailments, so that I must enjoy myself while I can: and always there's a feeling that perhaps I'll miss old age by some happy accident.

So April 1930 will see me out of the R.A.F., if the Air Ministry refuse me: and April 1935 if they accept me. I shall not know till early next year. I think I have said this to you in a previous letter, and apologise for being no more definite. Will you present my respects to the Elizabethan,[1] and explain that he hasn't given me (or you) any promise to which anyone would wish to hold him: that when I'm out of the service I shall try and get a night-job, somewhere in the City: and that for what he has done, and you have done, I am deeply grateful? I hope I do not sound ungrateful, for clinging to the R.A.F. for as long as it will support me. I like it better than anything I have ever done: though it is England, and not India, wherein I dream myself, every night. I hope to come home early in 1930, anyhow.

[...]

Bodleian Reserve

1 Sir Montague Norman, Governor of the Bank of England: see Lawrence to Hon. Francis Rodd, 23 November 1934, where Norman is similarly described (p. 500).

EDITOR, CIVIL & MILITARY GAZETTE
29.X.28   338171 A/C Shaw R.A.F. Miranshah Fort Waziristan

Dear Sir

I have just been shown a very considerate paragraph in the *C. & M. Gazette*, dealing with my supposed whereabouts:[1] if I remember rightly, there was a similar instance some months ago, when I became the subject of other unfortunate rumours.

I send you this note, partly to thank you for promoting me to L.A.C. (a rank I will never reach, unless I can develop enough humour to work up square roots & vulgar fractions again, to pass an educational test which reminds me too unpleasantly of school-days for me to face it) and partly to assure you that I appreciate the different standpoint & manners of the *C&M* (and also *The Times*, of London, & other decent papers) as contrasted with the *Evening News* & the *Sunday Express* (also, unfortunately, of London).

A firm in England is making a film of *Revolt in the Desert*: much against my will, but I have no control or ownership or copyright of the Arab Revolt, as it happened to be an event, & not a fiction: and I fancy this desire to keep my name in the Press may be to boost their production. I have not done anything, for many years now, to deserve publicity: and I will do my best not to deserve publicity, in future. It displeases me.

So I hope if you read, next week, that I've gone to the South Pole, or to Jericho, or been made President of the United States, or written something sensationally unpublishable, that you'll go on believing me peaceably content in the R.A.F. It is a restful existence, though I prefer it to be in England, whither I hope to go in April 1930.

Believe me
Yours very gratefully
T E Shaw

University of Texas

---

1 The *Civil & Military Gazette* was the daily paper of Lahore, in what is now Pakistan. On 27 October 1928, in their regular feature 'By the Way', they had printed an item under the heading 'Lawrence of Arabia', of which the key sentences were as follows: 'The Home papers seem to be very intrigued over the whereabouts and activities of Colonel Lawrence, now in the R.A.F. as Leading Aircraftman Shaw. He has been variously reported in Afghanistan, Amritsar, the Gulf, Australia and Singapore.... We can only say that there is no particular mystery about the location of L.A.C. Shaw *alias* Lawrence of Arabia. His station is known to us, but we see no reason for interfering with his desire for freedom from publicity.' Small wonder the subject of the article was grateful and expressed himself accordingly; ironically it was only a few weeks later that the said 'Home papers', or some of them, found the sensational story they were hoping for.

ROBERT GRAVES
6.XI.28   Miranshah

Dear R. G.

This is two excellent letters you have given me about *The Mint*. The poor little thing interests me: because it's my only effort at really writing something about nothing. *Seven Pillars* was a historical necessity: I don't call it an option: but *The Mint* was a pure wantonness. I went to Uxbridge with the deliberate intention of writing something about service life: and I put down those notes evening after evening in the hut, with the blankets up to my chin, writing on the support of my drawn-up knees. They are the perfect exemplar of journalism, in its antique sense: & it interests me very much to find that you & Garnett & Forster (three very different people) all see something in them. It shows that the daily record needn't be as transient as, for example, the *Daily Mail*. A fellow can't read (even at Miranshah) a month-old *Daily Mail*.

About printing *The Mint* as you suggested:— thanks very much, but no. 'They' would hear of it, and say I'd written another book: and *The Mint* is 1922 and not a book. It's better left just as a manuscript diary. Diaries exist in thousands and are thought no harm of.

Your second (and unpublishable!) letter gave me a lot of keenly improper laughter. It was a good effort: though it would have shocked Squad IV.

Your remarks on Form & Style tickled me, particularly: also the instances. I wrote 'penis & scrotum' deliberately; not knowing in English any word for the latter. You call it 'bag of tricks': but I don't like periphrasis. 'Prick' is first rate: 'balls' is like calling the belly a stomach: putting the inside before the outside. Is there an English word, (still alive, I mean) for scrotum? Bothered if I know. The Latin alternatives appealed, just there, to my old fashioned sense of the incongruous. They still do!

'Resides not in drill'.[1] That, you say, is style. I like style, I fancy. The anticipation of an antithesis, which is not fulfilled is good. Old Asquith's speeches were intolerably boring because all the anticipations were bitterly fulfilled. 'All there is to be done is to write with ink on paper'. Alas, that is the last & easy stage. It's the balancing your subject before you begin on it: the scheming proportion for it, the adding wings and features to carry all your prepared ideas, fitly: and the spacing the few ornamental ideas each

---

1 In his commentary on this letter in *RGB* Graves wrote of *The Mint* that 'in the main I liked it very much, better than *Seven Pillars* because it had been written straight off, not brooded over', but that he believed it contained some examples of what its author evidently thought was 'style' which he saw as 'bad taste in language — pseudo-poetic ornament'; he had passed his views to Lawrence instancing such phrases as 'resides not in drill' and (see next page) 'pencillings of light'.

of us have, so as to relieve the monotony of the plain surfaces:— that's all got to be done before the easy ink on paper stage.

I know you didn't mean the remark to be taken so literally. You fell foul of my ornament, not because it is ornamental, but because it isn't: and you're sure right there. It comes in the wrong places, and it is clumsy. Yet the 'pencillings of light' were just as clear (are just as clear) to me as the sweat and swear-words. Only they are so much harder to put down. Anybody can catch the ugly to the life: but to make the smoothly beautiful at once beautiful and not sticky — aha, that's where the poet scores. Look at the *Memoirs of a Foxhunting Man*,[1] to see how magically simple things, like birds, come to life again, on paper, specially for Sassoon, without any twisting of words, or strange words. A man's a great writer when he can use plain words, without baldness. See how bald Theodore Powys[2] is, despite all his power to write ... It's because he's not big enough.

If a fellow isn't big enough he must do the other thing:— what you call style:— surface his work. It is a mode, too. The *War-and-Peace* plainness is better, perhaps: but one is fonder, often, of the rather less big work. It feels more homelike. That's the reward of secondary writers. They don't knock-out: but by their very smallness, or middle-size, they become good companions for ordinary people.

Lately I've been reading the *Odyssey* a great deal: & when I get tired of it I take up the *Aeneid*: and it is like stretching out in bed after a hard day: like stretching out in my bed is going to be, in half an hour, when I come off sentry: for it is half past two in the morning, and I'm sitting on a box under the pilot-light beside the arms-rack, scribbling away. We have to guard the beastly rifles, in memory of 1919 when the Mahouds used to try to steal them.

So I am quite unrepentant about 'resides not': 'resideth not' is Wardour Street: 'does not reside in' is too loose. 'There is no something-or-other-in' is too bald: had I used the last my statement would have been seen through. 'resides not' carried you on to expect more and you found a full stop, & forgot the argument. So So.

Drill may be beautiful:[3] but beauty is not perceptible when you are expecting a punishment every moment for not doing it well-enough. Dancing is beautiful: — because it's the same sort of thing, without the sergeant-major and the 'office'. Drill in the R.A.F is always punitive:— it is always practice-drill, never exercise-drill or performance-drill. Airmen haven't the time to learn combined rhythm. If they did learn it, their

1 Graves had just sent him (see end of letter) Siegfried Sassoon's *Memoirs of a Fox-Hunting Man*, the first part of his George Sherston trilogy, which had just been published.
2 T. F. Powys: allegorical novelist, one of the three Powys brothers, all of whom were well-known writers publishing regularly in the 20s and 30s.
3 Graves had objected to Lawrence's running down of arms-drill.

(necessarily) individual work with screwdrivers & spanners would suffer. Rhythm takes months to acquire, & years to lose.

No, I will never be an eminent literary man. Yet theirs are not the only hyaena-dens.[1] There is a hyaena coughing just outside the fort now: and in many barracks you get very near the den stage. I think literary men are probably not really different from you & me.

Thanks for Ar Hyd y Nos:[2] but I don't suppose I'll ever see the MS again: I gave it Garnett for keeps: and it probably won't ever be published.

Your last page, about fucking, defeats me wholly. As I wrote (with some courage, I think: few people admit the damaging ignorance) I haven't ever: and don't much want to. $1\frac{3}{4}$ minutes was the Bishop's remark.[3] Judging from the way people talk it's transient, if $2\frac{3}{4}$ or $3\frac{3}{4}$ or 3 hours & $\frac{3}{4}$s. So I don't feel I miss much: and it must leave a dirty feeling, too. However I don't want to convert you, or you to convert me: only in the circumstances your positive, comparative, superlative (we make it fucking good, bastard good, fucking bastard good) are meaningless to me. Wherefore I, instead, 'keep literature going', because I can understand these other adjectives, and not the airmen's one. Only you call the one lot inferior, & the others superior. That's because you have a standard, & it enables you to be censorious. I only see what's better than my *performance* (quite different to a mental standard, that) and so I admire & enjoy Wells, & Bennett, & Forster, & Sir Thomas Browne, & Rossetti, and Morris and everybody who deliberately tries to better his every-day speech (which is my definition of style). Not a bettering of speech, mind you: but an effort to better it. It's the trace of effort which warms my diaphragm:— beg pardon, cockles of my heart — whatever are cockles?

Ever so many thanks for the Foxhunter. It is a *book*.

TES

University of Harvard/RGB[4]

1 Graves had told Lawrence that writers who pursued style 'ended up as Eminent Literary Men, like old Saintsbury, whom I had recently visited (accidentally) in Bath, where he lived in a hyena-den filled with old books, medicine bottles and second-rate statuary'. Professor George Saintsbury had been an influential historian of literature around the turn of the century.
2 Graves had corrected Lawrence's Welsh.
3 See General Introduction, p. xxvi, and Lawrence's letter to F. L. Lucas, 26 March 1929 pp. 407–9.
4 The version of this letter in *RGB* is much edited.

MRS CHARLOTTE SHAW
20.XI.28

This will be a single line scrawl: you would not know my quiet little place, today. There are ninety of us, crammed into every hole and corner. I am the only typist. Senior officers rain on us out of the air like monsoons. The excuse for it all, is the destroying those poor few villages. I feel a disproportion of means: but no one has been hurt on either side, and the 'enemy' have yielded, and come in, and promised to be good: and so our bombs and house-breaking have saved a war, next spring. Therefore we can flatter ourselves with having saved some hundreds of tribal and military lives. So it has been worth while, probably.[1]

My sympathies, in such shows, are always with the weaker side. That's partly, perhaps, why I was able to help the Arabs whole-heartedly (Was it whole-hearted? Perhaps: but often I think that it's only in trying to write that my whole heart has ever been engaged: and then not for very long).

No more. Your D. G. H.-Doughty book came.[2] I have just caressed its pages. I wish D. G. H. could have lived for ever. You don't know how good he was to talk to, and to hear talk.

The 70 odd men will leave here in a day or two, and then I'll try and go easy for a few days. It has been difficult to lodge and feed them.

                                          T. E. S.

British Library

SIR HUGH TRENCHARD
21/XII/28   Miranshah

Dear Sir Hugh
    This morning I was in the cabin at broadcasting time, and the message came through that you had resigned. So it's all over, and I can't tell you how sorry I am.[3] Of course I know it's your wisest move, and you have

---

1 In an earlier letter Lawrence had told Mrs Shaw that a clan in the area had turned on its neighbours, the neighbours had asked for Government help, and 'Government had warned the offenders that air action would follow if they persist for 96 hours more.' He had added the comment: 'Each time we bomb, or soldiers shoot, it is a sign that the political officers have failed in their job.'
2 *The Life of C. M. Doughty* by D. G. Hogarth, published 1928.
3 Trenchard's resignation from the Air Force had been accepted but it was not to take effect until December 1929.

finished, and all that: but here I've just been able to take on for five more★,[1] as you go out. You'll feel it hard: for you have never really been in the R.A.F. at all. You've made it; and that means that you're not in it. People can't make things bigger than themselves: not bigger enough to get into. I'm sorry, because it feels nice, to be in it, like I am.

I think you have finished the job. A man would be slow, who couldn't exhaust all of himself into a thing in ten years. You were lucky to have the chance for ten years. No other man has been given a blank sheet, and told to make a Service, from the ground up. Neither the Army nor the Navy have a father, in the sense of the R.A.F. Now you'll see the child tumbling down and hurting its knees, and getting up again. Don't worry, more than you need. It's a very healthy, and tolerably happy child. A C.A.S. with leisure would make it happier: only your successor will be pretty hard-worked, I expect, like yourself. However your resignation means that the child is on its own, and sooner or later it'll make itself happier.

You'll feel exceedingly lonely and tired for a long time: and I wonder what you'll do: for you aren't old enough to settle down. Perhaps you'll go and govern somewhere. That will be only the shadow of power, after what you've had: but shadows are comfortable, after too fierce a light. So possibly you will be contented.

You'll be rather shocked to find that three weeks after you've gone (about the time you're reading this) your past services haven't any interest or value in the Government's eyes. It's what we can do, yet, which makes us regarded.

I've said to you, before, that in my eyes (very experienced eyes, and judgematical eyes) you have done the biggest and best thing of our generation: and I'd take off my hat to you, only that at Miranshah I do not wear one. There'll never be another King like you in the R.A.F., and I'll feel smaller under whoever it is takes your place. Allenby, Winston, and you: that's my gallery of chiefs, to date. Now there'll be a come down.

You know that I'm at your disposal (except in disposing of my body) at all times and circumstances.

Yours
T. E. Shaw

★ Salmond sent me on your message, yesterday. I needn't say I'm grateful. As for the people who want me elsewhere ... let 'em want. I know my own mind.

Bodleian Reserve

1 i.e. five more years.

MRS CHARLOTTE SHAW
31.XII.28 & 1.1.29

[...]

Your letter of 10th Dec. is, politically, all wrong. Waziristan is utterly peaceful. Some of our people the other day visited the clan we bombed (they have moved into the low-lands for the winter) and found them eager to talk over the ups and downs of life: laughing heartily at their well behaved neighbours, on one of whose bullocks a stray bomb fell! They say the war cost them £1200 in damages: and they won't do it again. They have paid for the people they murdered, and let their wretched prisoners go.

The Afghan business[1] is over the border, and behind high hills. While it remains civil war in Afghanistan it will hurt us no more than de Valera hurt Sussex. Only if the new king of Afghanistan (*if* there is a new king) declared war on India, to distract his subjects' minds from internal politics — then there would be a disturbance in N.W. India. Yet not much of N.W. India wants to become Afghan — as it would not go very far with good-will.

[...]

British Library

1 i.e. the rebellion against King Amanullah of Afghanistan which inspired some sections of the British press to absurd speculations as to Lawrence's involvement.

6 · LAST YEARS IN THE R.A.F.

1929–35

'The Afghan business is over the border, and behind high hills,' Lawrence had written to Mrs Shaw in his letter of 31 December 1928–1 January 1929. 'While it remains civil war in Afghanistan it will hurt us no more than de Valera hurt Sussex.' But thanks to the British press (see the Introduction to Part 5) he became a casualty of the war himself, and on 12 January 1929 he embarked at Bombay on the P. and O. liner S.S. *Rajputana*, bound for Tilbury in the Port of London. At Port Said he was not allowed ashore, not only to his annoyance but also to that of the British High Commissioner for Egypt, his old friend of wartime days, George, now Lord, Lloyd. The first letter in this section was written to Lloyd as his ship steamed westward across the Mediterranean. 'Your police', he wrote, [...] 'peeved me a little, for deportation from India (to curry the favour of Amanullah and the Soviets) has not made me, yet, feel criminal. Nor would my stepping ashore for an hour at Port Said have harmed Egypt.' However, if he was unable to see Lloyd the latter's son was on the ship going home to Eton and Lawrence went to talk to him in his cabin. 'I wish kids didn't have to grow up,' he told Lloyd. 'They are so beautiful, unfinished.' Lawrence was always benign to the children of his friends.

It was decided that he should be taken off the ship at her first landfall, Plymouth, but even there the press was lying in wait and the R.A.F. had to resort to evasive measures to enable him to escape to London. He was afraid (as it turned out, unnecessarily) that the Air Ministry might decide to be rid of him, because of the activities of the press and the questions raised about him in Parliament; and in order to grasp the latter difficulty he visited the House of Commons to argue his case with two Labour M.P.s who had challenged his serving in the forces under the 'false' name of Shaw. He managed to persuade them of his good intentions but his action did not endear him to the Air Ministry. His letter of 8 February 1929 in which he vigorously defended his actions to Trenchard — and then apologised in a much less aggressive postscript — must be virtually unique in exchanges between an ordinary serviceman and his chief. But these difficulties and the

394

disruption of his service life weighed heavily on him, as seems clear from a number of short staccato letters he wrote to various friends at this time. They include a repeated metaphor that he was to use again just before his death — in his last message to Lady Astor — some six years later. In several letters written on 28 February he used with minor variations the phrase 'Something's gone wrong with the works'; adding in Newcombe's case 'I can't wind myself up to meet people: instead I moon about, longing to get into Camp again', and concluding, 'I am sorry. Do you think my pipes are frozen?' Earlier on 22 February he had written to Trenchard's former private secretary T. B. Marson: 'For the moment I wander about London with my eyes on the pavement, like a man who's dropped sixpence, and can't remember in which street it was.' He continued: 'On March 8 I move to Cattewater (Plymouth) which is to be my next camp. I hope it will prove a homely place.'

R.A.F. Cattewater (the name was later changed, largely on his initiative, to Mount Batten) was to prove a homelier place than he could have imagined. Its commanding officer was Wing Commander (later Air Commodore) Sydney Smith, whom Lawrence had first met at the Cairo Conference and who had been in charge of the operation to spirit him off the *Rajputana*. C.O. and Aircraftman became close friends, and Lawrence was made especially welcome by Smith's family, which consisted of his wife, Clare (who was to become a great admirer and write a book about this period under the title — the phrase was Lawrence's — *The Golden Reign*), their daughter Maureen (known as 'Squeak') and several dogs. He was soon able to write to E. M. Forster (1 April 1929): 'I feel just like a plant taking root after a transplantation.' He was also to find satisfaction from this time forward in a style of work that appealed to him because it was as much a challenge to the hand as to the brain. Indeed there were numerous occasions throughout this period when he was content to let his intellect lie fallow. 'Books have not lain much in my way, lately,' he wrote to Sir William Rothenstein in April 1932; 'when dark comes I am tired, more inclined to read the *Happy Magazine* than Plato. So I compromise by reading neither, and am the better mechanic therefor.'

In his first year back in England he was one of the R.A.F. support team involved in the races for the Schneider Cup. Yet for most of his final Air Force years the work to which he applied his not inconsiderable talents as a mechanic (a talent about which he had cheerfully boasted to his family back in Carchemish days) was to do with boats — fast modern boats with air-sea rescue as their major role. They were to supersede the naval craft previously in use which had been found to be far too cumbersome and slow. As an increasingly valuable member of the research-team assigned by the R.A.F. to develop its own specialised vessels, Lawrence moved between a number of Air Force and marine establishments over the next few years —

Plymouth, Southampton, Cowes in the Isle of Wight, Felixstowe, Bridlington — spent much time in tests and trials, and even wrote an operational
text-book. When the first boats were finished and ready to show their paces
he invoked his friendship with the Editor of *The Times*, Geoffrey Dawson,
to get press-coverage of quality for an enterprise of which he was proud
to be part, the proviso being that his own connection with it was not
divulged; his letter to Dawson of 22 March 1932 describing what he and
his colleagues were about not only puts the whole matter in a nut-shell but
also has something of the vigour of his wartime despatches. Significantly,
he did not disparage his mechanical achievements as he did his literary
efforts. In September 1934, a few months before his discharge, he wrote to
Lord Lloyd: 'My boat work for the R.A.F. (now extending to the Army
and the Navy) has been successful, and lets me out of the Service with some
distinction, I think. After having dabbled in revolt and politics it is rather
nice to have been mechanically useful!' He was aware of an important
personal benefit in all this. 'I think many of us go wrong by being too
exclusively cerebral,' he wrote to Ezra Pound in December of the same
year. 'I've spent the last twelve years in the ranks of the Air Force. [...]
My own job has been producing motor boats: and I fancy that each concrete
thing I launched took away some of my bile.'

Apart from his time at Carchemish and to a lesser extent at Cranwell,
these were, on the whole, his happiest years. But he was never a man for
simple contentment across the board. His letters inevitably vary widely in
mood. 'If you are to go on knowing me', he wrote to H. S. Ede on 28
November 1929, 'you must allow for — expect — these sort of sulks.' In
that particular case he was riding his regular hobby-horse of the inadequacy
of letters as distinct from personal contact, but there were 'sulks' on other
subjects too. When in April 1929 *John Bull* divulged to its substantial
readership that 'your old friend "Lawrence of Arabia"' was planning to
publish a translation of the *Odyssey* anonymously in the United States, his
anger at yet another act of perfidy by the press spilled over into several
letters and he almost withdrew from his contract. The military historian
Major Archibald Becke, eager to discuss the 1918 Battle of Tafileh for the
purposes of the official history of the war, was told (28 December 1929):
'Your letter sits here on my table in the office, and I have been cursing it
at intervals. Why on earth should anybody bother about that old war any
longer?' T. C. Griffin of Montreal, claiming a tenuous acquaintance going
back to the war period, was told (17 April 1931): 'I hope you will pardon
my not remembering one of you more than another. It was — how long
ago? Nearly fifteen years, wasn't it? I am so old now, and it feels a lifetime
away.' He added: 'Nine years ago I enlisted, and have not thought about
the Middle East since. The Air Force life suits me, and I'm happy in it.'

He was also happy in extending the circle of his friends. One important new friend of this period was Lady Astor, to whom he wrote over forty letters between 1929 and 1935, many of them breezy and witty, others serious and frank. At times, indeed, he wrote to her almost with the intimate, confessional tone normally reserved for Mrs Shaw. Other new friends were the writers Henry Williamson and Frederic Manning, the playwright Noël Coward, and the politician Ernest Thurtle, one of the Labour M.P.s whom he met when he stormed the Houses of Parliament, with whose views on military reform and such subjects as the abolition of the death penalty for cowardice in war he had much sympathy. Meanwhile his friends of the barrack room, not discarded as he moved from station to station or even from service to service, were still regular recipients of his letters, written not out of duty but because of his genuine affection for them. If they were in trouble he was always prepared to take great pains to help them.

Throughout this period he worked when he could on the improvement of Clouds Hill. In a letter of 18 May 1934 he wrote to Mrs Shaw: 'My cottage is finished, inside and out, so far as alien hands can finish it — and I feel rooted now.' It was the same expression which he had used to Forster in 1929; but though he was happy at putting down roots at Clouds Hill, his roots in the R.A.F. were under threat and he knew that the day was rapidly approaching when he would have to leave the service which he had come to love. In a letter to E. H. R. Altounyan in April 1934 he wrote that he was looking forward to the 'unbounded leisure' that would soon be his, but this did not represent his general attitude; on the whole the prospect of his exit from the Air Force hung like a shadow over these years, growing ever more substantial as the months went by. In the letter to Lord Lloyd of September 1934 quoted opposite he wrote: 'In March I leave the R.A.F. and it feels like the end of living. [...] How does one pass the fag-end of life?' He expressed the same idea to Sir Ronald Storrs on the last day of January 1935, with under a month to go: 'After my discharge I have somehow to pick up a new life and occupy myself—but beforehand it looks and feels like an utterly blank wall.'

Part 6 concludes with Lawrence's own 'obituary' — written in reply to Robert Graves in February 1935.

LORD LLOYD[1]
22.1.29   [S.S. Rajputana]

Dear G.L.

I have, imaginatively, written you books and books of letters: but in our camps nothing happens big enough to engage the attention of a High Commissioner. It is only as now, when my past has intervened and spoilt my present, that there comes any cause of writing, really. You must be sure that always you have my best wishes and willingness.

As for telling you that I was coming! Well, your police knew that. They peeved me a little, for deportation from India (to curry the favour of Amanullah and the Soviets) has not made me, yet, feel criminal. Nor would my stepping ashore for an hour at Port Said have harmed Egypt.[2] However, as I'm English, more or less, they are almost bound to let me land there. It would please me to see the Government of India drowning in a ditch. Positively I would not cross the road to push them under.

For David, I have seen him: and, I hope, not spoilt his digestion.[3] A bit grim for the kid, to be inspected by his father's friends. I told him what you were really like, which was news to him, for there is a divinity which hedges heads of families. A nice kid, you have produced. He is more ornamental than ever you were, and less truculent. Of course he has a father to fight his battles. Perhaps his mouth will harden after he leaves home: do you think we should all fight our own courses? Since I changed ways, and learned to run and hide, life has been far happier. These days I am very meek and obedient. Indeed the officers begin to like me, here & there. A doormat.

However, back to David. He was very embarrassed by me. Have you been stuffing the poor child with Lowell-Thomas tales? The contrast between my person & my reputation is grotesque. I wonder if such shyness as his is one of your secret vices. It makes him very nice. The (apparent) lack of it does not injure your central goodness. It would have been a freak of nature if the child of you two had been nasty.

We compared you with Lord Curzon, and talked of Mussolini, and of Lenin, my preference. I tried to make him see the grandeur of Lenin. So you will see that our company in his little deck-cabin was mainly of your

---

1 Lawrence's former wartime colleague George Lloyd, now Lord Lloyd of Dolobran and High Commissioner for Egypt, a post he had held since 1925. He had previously (1918–23) been Governor of Bombay.
2 'At Port Said, last stop, they picketed the quay-side to prevent my going ashore. I'd like to say something with a B in it about the India Government': Lawrence to Aircraftman H. G. Hayter at Miranshah. See *DG*, pp. 639–40.
3 David Lloyd, Lord Lloyd's only son (1912–1985), was returning to England after a holiday with his parents in Egypt.

peers. (I apologise for dragging in poor Curzon).

On the way down from Lahore my pilot (who was sorry for my being so rudely deported) circled about Sukkur,[1] at my request, and explored the hundreds of miles of canals which begin to spin outwards from the unfinished dam.[2] You have written your name across a country as big as the south of England.

At Bombay I tried to see your dredger: but she was invisible. They told me that she (?he) had not been given a peerage when you went up. That's the sort of ungraciousness the Indian authorities are delighted in. [sic]

Up to Port Said I had been counting over the people I would see in England. One was to be your father-in-law, whose staunchness of mind made him a great experience.[2] At Port Said I picked up a Truth which told of his death. Please tell Lady Lloyd that I am, in my degree, very sorry. Half of the people I have liked in my time are now dead. Aubrey, you know: & Hogarth, & Thomas Hardy. Please go on living, for a while yet. David is only a sketch: beautifully begun, but shaped by others so far; we will see, later, how he shapes himself. I wish kids didn't have to grow up. They are so beautiful, unfinished.

Finished the paper: finished my letter. I hope for you three years more in Egypt, as prosperous as these: and then translation .... but after that there is nothing except an inner life in which to steep yourself.

T.E.S.

Churchill College Cambridge

SIR HUGH TRENCHARD
5/2/29   14 Barton Street Westminster

Dear Sir Hugh

May I have 36 days overseas leave? and leave the 28 extension of service leave★ till the difficulties pass by? I shall be glad to be safe in camp again.

Some anonymous people have bought and sent to me a motor-bike, the current model of the great things I used to ride. Its cost is three years of my pay: and I feel rather pauperised: but I will try to pay it back to them, in time.[3] I mention it only because it restores my liberty of action: and so I can report to Cattewater, easily, any time you like.

1 Lloyd as Governor of Bombay had been responsible for the launching of a vast irrigation scheme of which the central feature was a dam at Sukkur; he had also (see next paragraph) carried through a scheme for reclaiming land in Bombay harbour.
2 Lloyd's father-in-law was Commander the Hon. Frederick Lascelles R.N. Retd.
3 The donors were Mrs Shaw and a number of close friends.

I want to tell you, too, that I have explained to Mr Thurtle,[1] privately, the marriage tangles of my father (*you* probably know of them: *he* didn't, and is asking questions which might have dragged the whole story into the light) and I hope he will respect my confidence, and stop asking questions in the House. Probably an airman shouldn't discuss his family tree with an M.P.: but I can hardly ask the Secretary of State to intervene and save me from curiosity.

Yours ever
T. E. Shaw

*Which has no limit, before which it must be taken: we can have it anytime.

Bodleian Reserve

SIR HUGH TRENCHARD
8/2/29   14 Barton Street Westminster

Dear Sir Hugh

I will come in about Wednesday next, if you do not want me early, for any reason. Tomorrow I hope to go out into the country for four days, to stay with my mother. (Address: — T. E. Shaw, Holly Copse, Goring Heath, Oxon.)

As for the House of Commons raid, I think I was right. Mr. Thurtle was enquiring into what was very much my private business. In explaining this I explained practically the whole affair, and probably the Labour Group will ask you no more questions on my account. In that case, I shall expect you to feel sorry that I did not go sooner to the House!

As for Blumenfeld,[2] whom I tried to see, and for whom I left a message, he is a very old friend of mine, who never publishes any account of my vagaries. What advice he gave as to ending newspaper talk was therefore disinterested, and he knows more of Fleet Street than we do. He can hardly have told you that I was meaning to make any statement: I would not do so without your very specific order:—and perhaps not even then without an argument.

However I have finished Thurtle, and will not visit Blumenfeld (or any

---

1 Ernest Thurtle (see opposite page) had been asking questions in Parliament about Lawrence's alleged involvement in Afghanistan: Lawrence had 'explained' to him at the House of Commons — conduct considered unbecoming by the Air Ministry, hence the next letter to Trenchard.
2 Editor of the *Daily Express*.

other newspaper office) without your future leave.

Will you please shut up the *Daily News*? It goes on chattering, and a word from you to Sir Herbert Samuel, saying that it was my wish, would end the business. A silly rag of a paper.

Many thanks for the leave arrangements, and for the Cattewater posting. I shall breathe quieter when I get into camp again. Am still in uniform, and have not once been recognised in the street, though I walk about all day.

Yours sincerely
T. E. Shaw

I'm afraid the above reads too stiffly. That is the worst of type. I am very sorry to have annoyed you by my slight activity, and will be very patient henceforward. The trouble is that I know too much of Government Offices to have proper confidence in them. They are manned by people just the same as myself, or rather less so: and anything outside their files scares them! However you know them too.

Perhaps I should report that Sir P. Sassoon[1] has asked me to lunch on Thursday next; and that I'll go, unless you say no, meanwhile.

T.E.S.

Bodleian Reserve/HMH

ERNEST THURTLE[2]
9/2/29   14 Barton Street Westminster

Dear Mr Thurtle

I doubt whether you properly observed the street's name or the number of the house, the other night. Will you hand it on, please, to whoever will return my books — and please remind them to be uncommonly discreet over *The Mint*, the R.A.F. book; for I have been told by the Powers that my visit to the House was not approved: told very distinctly, I'm afraid.

It was very pleasant for me that you were so reasonable, that night. You

---

1 Sir Philip Sassoon (1888–1939) was Under-Secretary of State for Air.
2 Ernest Thurtle (1884–1954), Labour M.P. for Shoreditch, had served in the First World War first in the ranks and later as an officer and had been severely wounded at Cambrai in 1917. He had taken up a cause with which Lawrence was to be later associated when in 1924 he published a pamphlet titled *Shooting at Dawn. The Army Death Penalty at Work*, the purpose of which was to establish that executions during the war for cowardice and desertion were miscarriages of justice. He and Lawrence were regular correspondents between 1929 and 1935.

will realise that I can't spend an hour with everybody, explaining that there is no mystery: and I'm delighted to have had the chance, by lending you those two books, to give myself away to you completely. If Mr Maxton[1] will read some of them, he'll never be nervous about me, either, again.

Yours sincerely
T. E. Shaw

DG

T. B. MARSON[2]
22.2.29   14 Barton Street Westminster

Dear Marson

Indeed I am back: and not too quietly, as your letter remarked. Nearly got the sack again, I think. What a life.

There will be another crisis and spasm about August, when a film of my supposed adventures falls due. Hell.

What next?

For the moment I wander about London with my eyes on the pavement, like a man who's dropped sixpence, and can't remember in which street it was. Also it is more cold than I ever thought possible.

On March 8 I move to Cattewater (Plymouth) which is to be my next camp. I hope it will prove a homely place.

Thanks for the offer of hospitality. If it gets warmer, later on in the year, I'll ask if I may come then. I have got a month's re-engagement leave in reserve, to be taken when the film is released. Perhaps then?

Yours
T. E. Shaw.

I've put Wing Commander on the envelope. I hope that is so.

Bodleian Reserve

---

1 James Maxton (1885–1946) was Leader of the Independent Labour Party from 1926–46 and M.P. for Bridgeton, Glasgow. He had been a pacifist and a conscientious objector in the First World War. He had been with Thurtle during Lawrence's House of Commons visit.

2 T. B. Marson served in the ranks in the Boer War, joined up again in the First World War, lost a leg at Gallipoli and subsequently transferred to the Royal Flying Corps where he served under Trenchard. Until his retirement in 1926 he had been Trenchard's private secretary. Lawrence later helped him to get his autobiography, *Scarlet and Khaki*, published by Jonathan Cape.

HENRY WILLIAMSON[1]

22/2/29   14 Barton Street Westminster

Dear H.W.

They have posted me to Plymouth: so if ever the frost breaks (Brrrr . . . Ughhhh) a motor-bike will disturb Skirr Cottage.[2] A horrible bike: but so beautiful in its owner's eyes & heart!

It will be comic, our meeting: I am icy cold, & very English, & correct. Sober as judges used to be. However, all the more reason for meeting a wild man.

At least your reputation won't scare me off. A bas all the Hawthorndens. Hawthorn, forsooth! Den, forsooth!

It will not be for a while. A new camp takes learning: especially for me, who am always uneasy with a new crowd. But it will be 1929, & not 1930. Praise God!

                                               T E Shaw

Bodleian Reserve

COLONEL S.F. NEWCOMBE

22/2/29

Dear S.F.

I am in London, rather distractedly & jerkily, with one suit of plain clothes, & two suits of uniform, & a motor-bike: I see hardly anyone, & don't know what to say to them, when I do see them.

On March 10 R.A.F. life begins again — at Cattewater, which is Plymouth. It will be a blessed relief. Now, it's like being lost.

1 Henry Williamson (1895–1977) had recently won popular and critical acclaim as the writer of the classic work *Tarka the Otter*, published in 1927, for which (see paragraph 3) he was awarded the Hawthornden Prize in 1928. He and Lawrence had become acquainted through Edward Garnett, to whom Lawrence had sent an immensely long and detailed critique of *Tarka* which Garnett had forwarded to Williamson. They subsequently opened correspondence. Williamson later wrote a warm appreciation of their relationship in *Genius of Friendship 'T. E. Lawrence'*, (Faber and Faber 1941). In addition to writing novels based on observations of nature, he also wrote a series of fifteen novels of contemporary life called *Chronicle of Ancient Sunlight*. His fascination with Fascism was to lead to his internment for a time in the Second World War and to some clouding of his reputation as a writer. All letters to Williamson in this selection are printed in whole or in part in *Genius of Friendship*.

2 At Georgeham in North Devon, where Williamson had moved after some years in Fleet Street to live a modest country life. Tarka's river, the Taw, flows into the sea at nearby Barnstaple.

My regards to N. the Second: and to Mrs. Newcombe, whom I shall hope to see, some time.

Yours
T.E.S.

Bodleian Reserve

ALAN DAWNAY
28.2.29   14 Barton Street Westminster

I am frozen in London. The bike is in Nottingham,[1] and the roads all ice and snow: so she cannot travel them. The first day of melting I will go up there, by train, and ride her down. But will it ever melt?

If God is good, I'll try and call in Aldershot on my way down to Plymouth: — about March 8. If only it were tomorrow! I do not think I shall ever go on leave, for pleasure: only to dodge publicity is the misery justified. Something's gone wrong with the works, and I find myself breaking every engagement, and avoiding everyone.

They tell me your child is ill. I am so sorry.

TES

Bodleian Reserve

DAVID GARNETT
28.2.29   14 Barton Street Westminster

Something seems to have gone wrong with my works: and I find myself breaking every engagement, and seeing nobody.

This warns you, therefore, not to be frantic if I perjure myself next Wednesday.

Do I call at the Nonesuch about 7.30?[2] I shall,★ unless you say 'no'.

Yours
T. E. Shaw.

★ Subject to reservation in 2nd paragraph.

Bodleian Reserve

1 The Brough motor-cycle factory was in Nottingham.
2 David Garnett was editing Shakespeare for the Nonesuch Press.

COLONEL S. F. NEWCOMBE
28/2/29   [14 Barton Street Westminster]

Dear S.F.

Please apologise humbly for me to Mrs. S. F. Something has gone wrong with the works: and I can't wind myself up to meet people: instead I moon about, longing to get into Camp again — on March 8, thank goodness.

Please remember me to Jimmy,[1] when next you see him or write to him. I am sorry. Do you think my pipes are frozen?

                                                    T.E.S.

Bodleian Reserve

MRS CHARLOTTE SHAW
12/3/29

This is only to report progress. My address is

> 338171 A/c Shaw
> R.A.F. Cattewater
> Plymouth.

It is a tiny station, on a rocky peninsula, projecting into the Sound. From my bed the sea lies 30 yards to the South (at high tide: — beach all rock) and 60 yards to the North. The whole peninsula, with its quays and breakwaters, is R.A.F. There are about 100 of us living on the rock, in six huts. Today I had a hot bath. The airmen all praise the camp and its conditions, but complain that it is hard and slow to reach the town of Plymouth, from it. This will not distress me.

My job? Not settled. For a fortnight I 'mark time' in the Headquarters Office: and then they give me to the Workshop's Officer, to employ clerically or on his motor boats. It seems to me that there are very few disagreeables here. The food is excellent: the place is comfortable: restrictions very slight, and those sensible. The Commanding Officer, of course, I know and like.

In the hut are two gramophones, and a wireless set with *very* loud speakers. It will not be easy to work, here, at first: but probably after a week my ears will be as deaf to hut noises, as to the wash of the sea (which

---

1 Newcombe's son Stewart was usually known as Jimmy.

now transports me!) and the mooing, like strained cows, of the liners groping for the Sound's entrance in the foggy mornings.

The beauty of the camp's setting is quite beyond my eyes to see, wholly. The weather is misted sunshine, and there is a subdued sparkle everywhere. In summer it will be blazing-bright. The promontory is like a fossil lizard stretched out into the Sound, with its head towards Plymouth, and its root in golf-links, which are a cascade of green lawns falling towards the sea.

The Air Ministry had notified the camp a month ago that I was coming to it: and so no one took any interest in my actual arrival. It was old news.

As for the reading:[1] — I write tonight to Lady Astor saying that I will do my best to come: but I shall not know, till the Friday night, whether they will let me go or not. The usual week end is only 'after duty Saturday' (1 p.m.) till midnight Sunday. I cannot get up and down on that: but I am owed four days' leave, and shall try to get two of them for the 23rd and 24th.

The bicycle is a heavenly machine. My ride down here was a golden occasion.

So you must understand that all is very well. After I've written these 20 or so letters, I shall try Homer again!

T.E.S.

Oh, I'm sorry. On the way down I saw John Buchan, who said he had heard (? from Trenchard) of *The Mint*, and wanted to read it.

Now it's been lent to F. L. Lucas: and John Buchan is a busy man, a great benefactor to me. It would not be right to put him to the pain of reading that illegible little MS. Its handwriting is shocking. Of course there is a decent explanation: but I cannot tell that to anyone I meet.

So I told him that you had a typed copy. If he bothers you for it, you'll probably have to lend it him, and then will hate me! Blame, partly, the R.A.F. manner, which holds all property as common.

T.E.S.

British Library

1 See next letter.

LADY ASTOR[1]

12/3/29   R.A.F. Cattewater Plymouth

Dear Lady Astor

I'd immensely appreciate hearing that G.B.S. reading, and if I can possibly wangle leave for Saturday and Sunday I will attend (probably in uniform, but I shan't mind your being differently dressed!) on the 23rd.

If I do not turn up, then please blame the R.A.F. rather than my expectant self.

                                              Your sincerely
                                              T E Shaw.

Bodleian Reserve

F. L. LUCAS

26.3.29   R.A.F. Cattewater Plymouth

I don't want to write tonight, but I must. I'm on Fire Pickets all this week (i.e. distracted & oppressed) and can't settle down to read or write. However, if I don't write you'll wonder what's the matter.

Your letter about *The Mint* delights me because it is really useful. Detailed criticism is the only useful kind. Ever so many thanks. Now I'll run through it & see if there are notes to reply.

About my writing more — No: if ever I had to write again, by such necessity as made me write the *Seven Pillars*, of course I'd do it: but it's not a thing to be undertaken wantonly. I have nothing now to tell anyone: nothing to preach: nothing believed. Wherefore I cannot go on writing, can I?

Of course *The Mint* is a cherrystone compared to the *S.P.* but I think it is a better piece of work: smaller in its faults (and in its virtues) but more like a work of art, as a whole. The *S.P.* was an afterthought, after the Revolt had ended. *The Mint* was meant to be written — and these are the notes which were to guide my writing, some day. I really think, too, that

---

1 Viscountess Astor (1879–1964), born Nancy Witcher Langhorne in Virginia, U.S.A., was the wife of Waldorf, 2nd Viscount Astor of Cliveden. When her husband, who had been Unionist M.P. for Plymouth from 1910–19, went to the House of Lords on his father's death in 1919, Lady Astor succeeded to his constituency, holding it until 1945. She had previously married Robert Gould Shaw II (married 1897, divorced 1903). Lady Astor was the first woman M.P. to take her seat in the House of Commons (but not the first to be elected; Countess Markiewicz had been elected in 1918, but as a Sinn Feiner had refused to sit). This letter was apparently the first in their long and lively correspondence.

the *book* would have been written if my R.A.F. career had not been suddenly interrupted.

It interests me that you should feel the R.A.F. less 'big' than the Arab Revolt. Of course it isn't: Damascus and Cranwell are different, but if Cranwell feels less, then that's because it is less well conceived and written down.

I thought Cummings had made a very good thing of *The Enormous Room.*[1]

Others besides yourself have been troubled by the gap between Depot and Cadet College. I was very unhappy at Farnborough, & decided not to put it on record. A mean C.O.: and a bad show, Farnborough was. After it I had $2\frac{1}{2}$ years Tank Corps, which is a different subject, & would I think only confuse the R.A.F. picture. From the Tanks I returned for three days to Uxbridge, the R.A.F. Depot, & *went thence to Cranwell*, as I describe. That gave me the chance to carry the story straight through. Do you think I ought to expand the 'explanation' into greater length, & detail the Farnborough & Tank Corps digressions? I have some raw notes: but they are pretty grim reading.

My bowels have twice or thrice destroyed my poise of stoical indifference, which is proper to a man of action! A bit of a handicap, is funk: to people of the V.C. class, in which reputation would put me! Of course I know, in myself, that I'm not a brave person: and am not sorry. Most brave people aren't attractive.

In 'Last Post' the all clear signal I handed down the hut was that Corporal Abbinett was again in Bed! Sorry. Too much compression there, apparently.

I do think that conscious, deliberate exercise is an evil thing: but I didn't class 'prostitution' as important. There are so many prostitutions that one can't take them tragically.

The period of enjoyment, in sex, seems to me a very doubtful one. I've asked the fellows in this hut (three or four go with women regularly). They are not sure: but they say it's all over in ten minutes: and the preliminaries — which I discounted — take up most of the ten minutes. For myself, I haven't tried it, & hope not to. I doubt if any man could time his excitement without a stop-watch: and that's a cold-blooded sort of notion.[2]

I would like to say more about Trenchard some day. A very noble and unusual person.

We do regard flying as a sort of ritual: more an art than a science, it is. Unreasonable to expect other people to feel like that, of course: but it is not an unpresentable Crusade: compared with the Lord's Sepulchre.

You don't like my saying that the old Depot is reformed away: and wish

1 See p. 434, footnote 2.
2 See General Introduction p. xxvi and letter to Graves of 6 November 1928 (p. 387).

for a moral. But I tried not to moralise or condemn more than the instruments through whom the system worked. As a victim I have hardly the right to condemn.

I am glad you feel the difference between Cadet College & Depot. E.M.F. said that Cadet College didn't 'come through' as a happy place. I re-read the MS, before it went to you, & was inclined to disagree with him.

It seemed to me to contain better 'bits' than the first two parts. No doubt they are too 'bitty': a whole Cadet College would be longer than Depot.

[...]

Of course one is always apart & intact: but to see another airman in the street is (for me) like one ship sighting another at sea. The sea becomes not lonely, all at once.

Yes, I would like the dedication of your novel:[1] everybody would. You are a very good writer. Your poems (of which I'll write to you when I feel less unworthy of them) prove it. They are a delight.

Yours
T.E.S.

DG/Bodleian Reserve

HERBERT READ[2]
26.3.29   R.A.F. Cattewater Plymouth

Dear Read

Excuse pencil. I have no ink for the moment. *All Quiet* is a most interesting work. Your judgment 'distilled bitterness of the generation shot to pieces by the war' is exactly fitting. Incidentally it would have been a bigger book without that bias. The railing against our elders of p. 19 is not worthy of a man. Our elders are only ourselves: there is no difference between one generation & another — nor, in war (or in that war) between class & class. The war-fever in England rose from bottom to top, & forced our unwilling government's hand. It was the young (youth) & the ignorant (age) who, as usual, made the war. Wars are made in hot blood, not in cold blood. Of course Cramer[3] suffered so much that one must excuse him.

---

1 Lucas dedicated his novel *Cécile*, published in 1930, to Lawrence.
2 Herbert, later Sir Herbert Read (1893–1968), poet, critic and former wartime soldier; he had sent Lawrence a copy of *All Quiet on the Western Front*, by the German writer Erich Maria Remarque, which had just been published in English.
3 As written: Lawrence had apparently mis-remembered the writer's name.

Lots of people lose their balance when they have suffered painfully. Yet the war was all our faults.

It's surely well written — and I expect the goodness is in the German, as well as in the translation. The dying man's voice 'like ashes': lots of phrases like that. It is over-written sometimes, the killing of Duval in the crater — that should have been short: so should the shelling in the graveyard. He squeezed his orange too dry there.

He does his pathos wonderfully — the death of Kemmerich: the wounded horses (one of the highlights of the book): the chapter of going home on leave (the highest light of all, I think). Only the pathetic stop is like the organ's vox humana. It's too easy. That point also makes me think Cramer not so much strong as sensitive. [...] He revolts too much, usually, against his horrors: but he was only a lad, & it's quite likely he has some Jew in him. The point of view is hardly that of a German amongst Germans. The care with which he inserts the daily coarseness & carnality of army life feels foreign too. I suspect him of not being pure German. Not that it matters what he is. The book is international.

I've seen nothing in English war novels so good as this, and I have read very many of them. [...]

University of Victoria, British Columbia

F. W. EASTON[1]

1/4/29   R.A.F. Cattewater Plymouth

Dear Corporal

You'll envy me, here. There is a H.Q. Flight (Office & motor-boat & transport personnel, & W/T) and a Squadron: under W/Cmdr. Smith. About 150 in all. They are going to add a second Squadron, later. This one has no flying-boats yet, but hopes for them, this month. It is a quiet decent station, not windy, but all new as yet. We'll see, in 6 months, how it shapes. I'm typing D.R.O's[2] for a living. 'What a change' you'll say: that's about all I do, too: but I'm to go to the Marine Section, & do something on a motor boat, this month.

I went over to Plymouth once, & saw Mrs. Easton. It is about two minutes walk from the ferry. She looked washed out, but well: by that I mean she had obviously been ill, but was over it, & the fine weather coming should make her fit again. The two kids were great sport: one of them

1 Corporal, R.A.F.
2 Daily Routine Orders.

your exact image. So decent & clean, & quiet. The whole show pleased me. I only stayed a few minutes, as I had just come down from London by bike, & it was getting late in the evening. That was a week ago. Since I have been C.C.[1] doing fire picquet. It lasts a week, & is binding, for I've wasted four fine holiday days on it. Just my luck. Fire Picquet is the camp's only snag.

Very sorry poor little Miranshah went west. It was a good place. I shall remember it with great pleasure. [...]

Imperial War Museum

ERNEST THURTLE
1.4.29   Cattewater Plymouth

Dear Thurtle (This sounds very familiar)

I have read your little bomb. It would modify all subsequent wars.[2] I do not see it coming off: but I think the death penalty will cease pretty soon. The debates on it in the House make my blood boil. I wish I could talk to some of the old stagers for a few minutes, about funk & courage. They are the same quality, you know. A man who can run away is a potential V.C.

A possible modification of the enlistment regulations *might* be brought in by some progressive government: to allow service men to give notice (a month, 3 months, six months: even a year: plus such money penalty as seems equitable) & leave the service in peace time. At present to buy yourself out is difficult. The application is usually refused. Anyway the permission is an act of grace: whereas it should be a right. I think the knowledge that their men could leave the service would effect a revolution in the attitude of officers & N.C.Os towards us. It would modify discipline profoundly, for the good, by making it voluntary: something we could help, if we wished. We would become responsible, then, for our behaviour. At present we are like parcels in the post. It is the peace-army & navy & air force which is the concern of parliament. War is a madness, for which no legislation will suffice. If you damage the efficiency of war, by act of Parliament, then when the madness comes Parliament will first of all repeal its damaging acts. Wars, in England, well up from below: from the ignorant: till they carry away the (reluctant) Cabinet.

Graves' book isn't apocrypha: but it is not to be taken seriously. I eat

1 Confined to Camp.
2 Probably a reference to Thurtle's *Military Discipline and Democracy*, published 1920.

anything except oysters & parsnips. I live in barracks (i.e. we dog-fight promiscuously). What is handshaking? The reason I had no overcoat was financial. It seemed a wicked waste of 3 or 4 pounds, for a mere month.★ When I felt cold I changed into uniform. G.B.S. lent me his second overcoat: but it was too gigantic a cloak for my normal wear. If it rained: yes: or late at night. Our evening was not too chilly. I'm very susceptible to cold: in England I'm always getting into hot baths, whenever they are available: because then only I am warm enough. Yet I never get what they call 'a chill'. Odd: because usually I get all the infections going!

Please don't get the public feeling that I'm different from the crowd. By experience in many camps I have assured myself (so certainly that all the print in the world won't shake my conviction) that I'm a very normal sort of Anglo-Irishman.

Women? I like some women. I don't like their sex: any more than I like the monstrous regiment of men. Some men. There is no difference that I can feel between a woman & a man. They look different, granted: but if you work with them there doesn't seem any difference at all. I can't understand all the fuss about sex. It's as obvious as red hair: and as little fundamental, I fancy. I will try & call at Temple Fortune Hill, & pay my respects: but I will make no promise. London's centre holds so many pleasures for one who has wasted 20 years abroad: and I'm selfish enough to go walking by myself usually. A sense of social duty does sometimes overcome me, & while it lasts I pay calls, & try to recall my manners. Only so often (especially in new houses) I feel like a Zoo beast without bars to defend me. There are all these absurd stories, with, in my fancy, people watching to confirm them, or make new ones. I know that is absurd: but you can write it down as a nervous affliction. The wearing a false reputation is as itchy a job as a false beard. Mine drives me crazy.

Yes, I get a huge correspondence: and the answering the justifiable percentage (20%) makes an inroad on my time. Also there is a Yankee dealer who pays £20 for my letters. Would you write, *ever*, if that happened to you?

If ever you come to the far west, by all means let me know, & if I can we'll meet somewhere: but my bike has no pillion: so you are safe not to break the speed law on my tail. Airmen are not allowed to carry pillion riders, or ride pillion. Another injustice! Poor troops. Yet I wouldn't change with any civilian.

Yours
T E Shaw.

Cattewater is shaping well. I shall like it, in the warm weather (if any).

★ I daren't spend my little reserve of cash. Any moment press chatter may extrude me from the R.A.F. & I've got to live while trying to find a rumour-proof job.

DG/Bodleian Reserve

E. M. FORSTER
1.4.29   R.A.F. Cattewater Plymouth

Dear E.M.F.

There we are! It is a decent little camp, quiet & easy. Very beautifully placed in Plymouth Sound. A spine of rocks & grass, like a fossil lizard, swimming out from the Devon shore towards the Hoe. Our hut is just above sea level, & has the open Sound 30 yrds to the S: and the Cattewater (harbour) to the N. about 70 yards away. In summer it should be a heaven, when the sun shines. Now it is chillish: not bad.

There are 150 of us in the station, of whom 50 live in Plymouth.

They are not generous about week-ends: after duty Saturday till midnight Sunday: so I will not be able to come up to see people except rarely. Perhaps when summer time comes.

I have not settled in, properly, so have not done any of my *Odyssey* job, bar the three days of this Easter holiday, when I have stuck tight to it, & done the 9th book, in rough draft.

Nowt else to say, alas. I feel just like a plant taking root after a transplantation.

                                                                    TES.

Called in at Clouds Hill on my way down. It looked so beautiful.

Bodleian Reserve

W.M.M. HURLEY[1]
1.4.29   R.A.F. Cattewater Plymouth

[...]

It is quaint your being in Amman. Difficult flying; the hardest, I think there is. That Jordan valley is a terror in summer and the Palestine 'dromes are not too good.

Peake is a very good fellow. He has stuck splendidly to three or four

---

1 Flight Lieutenant R.A.F.

thankless jobs, and made a deal out of them. A hot, impatient, soul, too.[1]

I enclose you some sample pages of Joyce's latest (not yet ready for publication in book form) and remarks by A.E. on Joyce and his poetry.[2] There is this colony of dispossessed English and American and Irish writers living rather intensely in one another's cheap lodgings in Paris and writing desperately hard. I fancy, for myself, that they are rather out of touch with reality; by reality I mean shops like Selfridges, and motor busses, and the *Daily Express*. At least there is a hot-house flavour about their work, which makes me wonder if it's a wholesome day-to-day food. Remarkable, certainly, but a bit funny. However people who do not practise writing aren't really qualified to judge of it.

Yours sincerely
T. E. Shaw

DG

MRS CHARLOTTE SHAW
Monday 8/4/29

I am sorry for you:[3] which is the only language that English provides for any occasion of loss: and so I suppose we are not built by the nature of our race to do or think more than that. Yet it feels inadequate.★

She being now beyond your care, it remains to think about yourself and G.B.S. and I am very glad that you hope to leave next Sunday. The effect of death, in my experience, is gradual and cumulative. You will find yourself more miserable a month after it (if your sister has counted in your life's background) than a day after it. So I'd like you to be away, and in a strange climate, which makes other demands on your mind and body. Also G.B.S. is tired. Probably it is much harder to write plays at 70 than at 40: and he has been ill, which perhaps was not (like the play) his fault. Anyway, he should be taken beyond reach of Miss Patch[4] and the papers.

[. . .]

T.E.S.

★ If our feelings could speak, they wouldn't speak English, would they?

British Library

1 See p. 351.
2 Joyce: James Joyce. 'A.E.': the pseudonym of George William Russell.
3 Mrs Shaw's sister had just died.
4 Blanche Patch was G.B.S.'s secretary.

SIR HUGH TRENCHARD
16.IV.29   R.A.F. Cattewater Plymouth

Dear Sir Hugh

I hope you realised that my not writing meant that all was well. Cattewater is in a lovely place, and will be perfection if the weather and water get hot. The camp is a good one: comfortably laid-out, compact and small, and we are a happy family: or two families: one of H.Q. the other of 204 Squadron. Mine is H.Q.: we are *quite* happy. The Squadron will be happier when it has machines, as you remark. It is hard for its technical people to sit here without jobs or tools. For the H.Q. people this lull before work is a god-send: it means that routine can be got running before the strain begins. Routine matters quite a lot in sections like Stores and Transport and Workshops. Now I am workshops. They put me into a bare room, in an empty shop (no machinery or benches!) and said 'Start a workshop routine'. I *did* reply that I was an A.C.H.[1]

There are other things to do, also. Too much paper work, and too few clerks. So for a while I typed D.R.Os.[2] Then someone (everyone, almost) felt that there must be Station Standing Orders. So I was put on to compile the 'general' parts of those. God be praised that the technical orders didn't come my way!

John Bull (a weekly paper) has just announced that I do no duties.[3] Hard: very hard. Nine of my first twenty days here I was on fire-picquet.

The bike is magnificent. It has taken me twice to London (fastest time 4 hrs. 44 minutes. The *Cornish Riviera* train is 13 minutes better than that: but it does not start at Hyde Park Corner and finish at Cattewater).[4]

I heard about your lecture. My officer, who is of the sporting type, a fine pilot, and lover of fast cars, liked what you said. He called it the most *severely* practical speech he ever heard. So if you'd tried to be Winstonianly eloquent, you didn't succeed! Winston's speaking is never severe. To collect all the officers was a great idea. Twice, I think, you've done that. Uxbridge must have been blue from end to end. I wish everybody could meet you.

---

1 Aircraft Hand.
2 Daily Routine Orders.
3 The popular magazine *John Bull* had published on 13 April an editorial paragraph titled 'Still in the Air', in which it was stated that 'Aircraftsman [*sic*] T. E. Shaw — your old friend "Lawrence of Arabia" ' had signed on for a further five years in the R.A.F., where he was 'not much troubled with duties' and divided his time between ' "leave of absence" in London, tinkering with a "super-sports" motor-bicycle, and literary work. The last takes the form of translating Homer's "Odyssey" into English. His version will be published anonymously in America in the autumn book-season this year.'
4 The *Cornish Riviera Express* started at Paddington and finished, travelling via Plymouth, at Penzance.

The R.A.F. would be happier as it knew your aims better. It is supremely hard, in a big show, to get through to the rank and file a clear knowledge of where they are going. You've got a lot through: but not enough to satisfy me, your very particular subordinate.

I enclose a separate sheet, of pure pearls.[1] If you find them too pure and pearly for your Deportment Department, then put them in the fire. They are trifles. It is the trifles that irritate and do most harm.

I hope you will come down. The more abruptly the better, for then our agony of preparing for you will be short. Sharp it must be, but make it short. Choose a fine day. Today the world is weeping, and Cattewater feels as dismal as the sky and sea.

Wing Commander Smith is a trump.*

Yours,
T. E. Shaw.

* This, as you said, is 'only for you'! A/Cs shouldn't have opinions upon Wing Commanders.

Bodleian Reserve/HMH

H. A. FORD[2]
18.iv.29   Cattewater Plymouth

Dear Flight

Here we are: and as for choking off the Press — he will be my friend for life who finds how to do that. I do nothing — and they talk. I do something — and they talk. Now I am trying to accustom myself to the truth that probably I'll be talked over for the rest of my life: and after my life, too. There will be a volume of 'letters' after I die & probably some witty fellow will write another life of me. In fact there is a Frenchman trying to write a 'critical study' of me, now. They make me retch — and that's neither comfortable nor wholesome. I have thought of everything, I think: to join a newspaper (they do not eat each other, the dogs) — but what a remedy

---

1 A list of irritating service practices which Lawrence thought should be abolished, such as the wearing of bayonets, particularly at church parades, or the carrying of 'the silly little stick we have to carry when we walk out', etc. In the event all his proposed reforms were put into effect. See also letter to Liddell Hart pp. 425–6.
2 Flight Sergeant, R.A.F.

for the disease: to emigrate — but those colonies are as raw as wood alcohol: to commit some disgraceful crime & be put away: — but I have some people whose respect I struggle to keep. I don't know.

Meanwhile here we are. Cattewater treats me very kindly, & I have work enough to keep me pre-occupied: and in the evening a musical box to discourse Beethoven & Elgar; Oh, a super-box, like a W/T[1] set inside, with an exquisite smoothness and fullness of tone. I assure you, it is good.

I read your 9th Symphony score very often, trying to keep pace with the records. Music, alas, is very difficult. So are all the decencies of life.

In August I may be in Malvern. They are doing G.B.S.' new play[2] there on Aug 19th.21.27. & 31. and *Heartbreak House*, a marvellous work of art, on 23. & 28. and I'd like to hear them. It is not sure, for the Schneider Cup may make me very busy about that time. But if possible I'll be there. Any chance of you? It is near Shrewsbury: perhaps I might come over one night?

Yours
T. E. Shaw

That snobbery 'He does not associate with the other airmen, except a few of the more intellectual' — God, it's poisonous. If I could get that reporter by the neck he would want a new one in 5 minutes.

DG

B. E. LEESON[3]

18.4.29   R.A.F. Cattewater Plymouth

Dear Leeson

We'll have to meet in London probably, unless I ever get to Nottingham again. That is as near as I am likely to get to Manchester. And when? God knows: not till after the Schneider Cup race, for which I'm a cross between clerk and deck-hand on a R.A.F. Motor Boat.

You do well to distrust the newspaper stories of me. Gods, what a foul imagination they do conjure up! Because I don't drink or smoke or dance, all things can be invented. Please believe that I don't either love or hate the

---

1 Wireless Telegraph.
2 *The Apple Cart.*
3 Leeson was a former Royal Flying Corps officer who had served briefly with Lawrence in 1917.

entire sex of women. There are good ones and bad ones, I find: much the same as men and dogs and motor bicycles.

It will be after September, as I said.

Yours

T.E.S.

Bodleian Reserve

MRS CHARLOTTE SHAW
27.IV.29

This cannot be more than a line, for there is little to say. In fact my only news is of a meeting — here — with Lady Astor. I was in Plymouth, paying a reluctant call, when a pea-hen voice screamed 'Aircraftman' from a car: and it was her. Next day she rang up the Wing Commander, and was allowed all over the station. We sparred verbally at each other. She got on my motor cycle: I drove with her and Michael[1] to her housing estate, to her house (supper), a children's club she runs in Plymouth. It has since been in the papers. Serves me right for walking about with a talkie sky-sign.

She was very nice: at her swiftest and kindest: one of the most naturally impulsive and impulsively natural people. Like G.B.S., more a cocktail than a wholesome diet.

There: you see that that's that. (Hooray: 3 thats in a row). Life is fairly good. The flaw is that *John Bull* has announced that I do no work in camp, but tinker with my motor-bike and translate the *Odyssey*, and since that note appeared I've not been able to touch the *Odyssey*. I must think out what to do about it now. The sensible thing would be to give it up: the next-best thing to sign it T E Shaw. Either move is difficult. I will ask Bruce Rogers, and see what he thinks.

Nancy's seat at Plymouth should be pretty safe.[2] She seems to hold the town in her fingers — they are all friends and enemies, and none neutral. The R.A.F. is wholly hers, of course.

This is written under difficulties, and is no more than a note. I owe G.B.S. a letter, for the proof-preface of *Immaturity*[3] came, and is wonderful reading. If this collected edition is going to be illuminated by such historical notes, it will be very valuable.

1 Lady Astor's son, born 1916.
2 i.e. in the General Election, which took place on 30 May. It *was* safe, though nationally the Labour Party won 288 seats to the Conservatives' 260.
3 Shaw's early novel, written in 1879, rejected by numerous publishers, finally published in 1930.

Only I won't start on that now, while I'm in a trough of the waves. Up and down it is, always.

Weather here dry, mostly, and cold always. I am glad you get some sunlight: but beware of the bora. I have had them. They kill people who are taken unawares.

TES.

British Library

A. E. (JOCK) CHAMBERS
27.IV.29   Cattewater Plymouth

Dear Jock

So there you are. One said dead, one deserted, one signed on: and all the while you sort letters in the Post Office. Such a nice job, sorter. If you send the Glasgow letters to Costa Rica nobody can trace it to you: and the *Daily Mirror* makes a snappy paragraph & *Punch* ditto.

I am now at Cattewater, & very seldom stir out of camp: so we can't hope to meet till my leave comes, if come it does. I hoard that month, against the dread day that a film about me may be released. *If* it comes I take the month, & hide somewhere.

Clouds Hill is still there. I saw it for an hour in February. It is lovely as ever: only chimney-pots are added as a monument of the new tenants' taste. Jock, the old tenants were 'some' people. You & me, & Guy, of the R.A.F. and the brothers Salmond, (Marshals of sorts) Hardy, Graves, Siegfried Sassoon, poets: Forster, Tomlinson, Garnett, prose-writers. Spencer & John, artists. It was a good place while it lasted. I wish there was a Clouds Hill in every camp, assigned for the use of aircraft hands.

[...]

Jock, I'm very weary of being stared at and discussed and praised. What can one do to be forgotten? After I'm dead they'll rattle my bones about, in their curiosity.

Au revoir
T. E. S.

[...]

DG

BRUCE ROGERS
1/5/29   R.A.F. Plymouth

Dear B.R.

Today I had meant to send you Book VII & VIII: instead of which I must tell you of my worries. It's been published (in *John Bull*, of all the world's press!) that I'm doing an *Odyssey*: and since that day I haven't done a stroke. Up till then I'd been trying to get on with it. Seven is complete, all but the last look-over. Eight is having its third revise. Nine is started: but that was all March work: and since, as I say, there has been nothing.

I'm wondering all the time what to do. (i) If I were free to do so, I'd like to return you your payment and cancel the whole business: but I am aware that this cannot be done without your consent. It would be the best solution, in my own interests. Other alternatives are

(ii) To acknowledge the work: which I will not do.

(iii) To find a ghost who will put his or her name to it, and accept the public responsibility for it.

I had not expected this trouble, before publication: *After*, yes: but somehow that didn't matter. You'll realize, I hope, that I can't carry on as it is.

Will you see Walker and Merton,[1] and present them the difficulties, as they stand? I want to be as reasonable and helpful as possible, and only hope that their more sober experiences may find a road out of what seems, to me, rather a deep hole.

I return Book I & II. W. (whom I do not know personally) has been very light with them. This is a relief. I seem to have made no howlers. Comments are attached to the sheets, where necessary.

Please believe that I'm very sorry about this. I've been racking my head for a way out for about three weeks, now, and cannot achieve anything.[2]

Yours
T E Shaw

I'm glad you doubted the Dorsetshire rumours. I have not been out of camp (except to Plymouth on business) for a month.

Letters to Bruce Rogers

1 Sir Emery Walker, the eminent printer and process engraver, who had helped William Morris to establish his Kelmscott Press, was contracted to publish the limited British edition of Lawrence's *Odyssey*; Wilfred Merton was his associate.

2 As will be seen from later letters, Lawrence overcame his doubts and continued his work of translation.

MRS CHARLOTTE SHAW
1.5.29   338171 A/c Shaw R.A.F. Cattewater Plymouth

[...]
   I had a nice word, quite accidentally, from F. L. Lucas, an exquisite
Cambridge don: he said (apropos of nothing, or of *The Mint*, rather) that
reading the *Seven Pillars* had been one of the experiences of his life. And
he has read everything. I wonder if there's something in it, after all. Only
I can't believe that there's anything in me rare enough to make my work
rare. You see, I'm so exactly like the other fellows in the hut.
   [...]

British Library

MRS CHARLOTTE SHAW
22.V.29   [R.A.F. Cattewater Plymouth]

Today came your telegram saying Venice: so here goes, though there is
little yet to say, and I'm yet unfixed in feeling.
   Whitsun gave me an unexpected holiday: so I went to Granville Barker.
He looked older and softer. She seemed less tragic. In fact, I liked them
both better than before. Much good talk about books. He is a high-brow,
but very intelligent: and has read enormously. They have been in Arizona,
and the Indians there have caught their fancy. Justly so, too.
   Thence to Max Gate. Mrs. Hardy was troubled, because the locals want
a T.H. memorial, and want her to put up most of the funds for it, without
having her will as to its form. Cockerell isn't behaving well.
   Thence to Cambridge, where I saw Lucas (F.L.) and Forster. We talked
rather like Aldous Huxley characters: froth: thence to London, where I saw
Laura Riding. She has broken her pelvis, and three bones of her spine, but
will recover, they say, in six months. For love of an Irishman, Geoffrey
Phibbs (who did not love her any more) she had thrown herself down four
stories into Graves' area at Chiswick. R.G. jumped after her, but was not
hurt.[1] Nancy, Robert's wife, has now gone to live with Phibbs. Phibbs'

---

1 Laura Riding, née Reichenthal, American writer and divorcee (b. 1901), had been living
  with Robert Graves and his wife Nancy Nicholson in a *ménage à trois*, which she described
  as a 'wonderful Trinity'. Their flat at 35A St Peter's Square, Hammersmith, was known,
  according to Graves, as 'Free Love Corner'. Geoffrey Phibbs was a Norfolk-born Anglo-
  Irish poet (author of a collection of poems called *The Withering of the Figleaf*, published
  in 1928), who had fallen in love with Laura Riding, changed the 'Trinity' briefly into
  a foursome, and had then quarrelled and departed, following which, as indicated in
  Lawrence's letter, Laura Riding had tried to commit suicide by jumping from the fourth

wife lives every six months or so with David Garnett (*Lady into Fox*).[1] They are mad-house minds: no, not so much minds as appetites. I think the mess has mainly solved the difficulties of Robert. He has now been delivered from Nancy, and is confirmed towards Laura, whom he will have the job of supporting (with Nancy's four children) on next-to-no-money. Poor R.G. He is a most excellent and truthful person, drowning in a quagmire.

[...] The election is hotly on, I believe. They say there have been rowdy meetings at Plymouth. Nancy[2] provokes them, and then does not secretly like the row: though outwardly she revels. I got another letter from her, which I must answer somehow. I'm afraid, a little, of her impulses.

TES.

British Library

LADY ASTOR
6.vi.29   338171 A/c Shaw R.A.F. Cattewater Plymouth

Dear Lady Astor

How often we write to one another! It is an affecting spectacle.

So there you are, M.P. for again a while. Not so long a while as usual, I fancy. However you'll have more fun while it lasts. My chief regret at the passing of the Government is that Sir Philip Sassoon loses the US. of S. for Air! Winston will be happier in opposition, & may make friends with his party now. For the rest, I'd do the lot up in a bundle (the very splendid Prime Minister of course not included)[3] and sell them for 2d. if 2d. was bid. Winterton & Ormsby Gore excluded from the sale catalogue, because I like them.

I apologise for keeping the G.B.S. letter for so long. I wanted to offer it to Gabriel Wells (a book-seller) who would have given me the price of a Rolls Royce for it. The R.R. I should have driven to Cliveden & handed over to you, or to Michael, if you refused the bargain. It is a gem of a letter.

Alas, I can't come to Cliveden. Nor will I see Elliot Turner. Thank you all the same. The best way to be content in the service is to stick close to

---

floor of no. 35A, with Robert Graves following suit by jumping from the third floor. Graves was not badly hurt but Laura Riding was rushed to hospital, where expert medical help saved her from being permanently crippled.

1 *Lady into Fox*: a novel by David Garnett which Lawrence much admired.
2 Lady Astor.
3 Stanley Baldwin.

it, taking only such reliefs as one's own pocket affords. The helplessness of money: that's a very often forgotten point.

Some day, if you revisit Plymouth quietly, ring up 1634, and we'll brighten the life of the Exchange girls, again.

Yours sincerely
T. E. Shaw

University of Reading

DICK KNOWLES   [R.A.F. Cattewater Plymouth]
5.7.29

[. . .] Today we flew to Calshot, and went on to Portsmouth, for a Schneider Cup Committee. I'm a spare-part clerk, in that business. Nearly got to Lee, only the wind and sea were too S.W. I'd hoped to see you.

The wish of people to see Clouds Hill will soon fade: if only the press will leave me alone now, then all the trouble will be forgotten. The papers feel sore at having made fools of themselves over me and Afghanistan: and will not readily invent another yarn. That film project is dead, too, I think. In fact, all's looking well for my peaceful old age.

The new Brough is good: but this is June and she has done only 3500 miles. Something very wrong. However I have to go to London on Saturday, and on Saturday week. So if those days are fine, it will be 4500 miles. Brough will disown me, if I ride so little.

Congs. on your L.A.C. Not the honour: but the cash![1]

Yours,
T.E.S.

Bodleian Reserve

MRS CHARLOTTE SHAW   [R.A.F. Cattewater Plymouth]
10.vii.29

This immense letter of yours shames me. You have so much to do. So have I: and I neglect writing because of it. Today I asked the Wing Commander to find me an understudy. That's the first time, I think, that I've ever asked for help in the R.A.F.: or in anything else, possibly.

Lady Astor was very nice, and almost quiet, at moments, when I saw her a week ago. I think she will be very nice when her legs get tired of

---

1 Knowles had been promoted to the rank of Leading Aircraftman.

running. She leaves me breathless. I told her she was a cocktail of a woman, and about as companionable as a typhoon. That shocked her: so I explained that G.B.S. was a cocktail too, and that you were not. You were habitable: but you are rather like the Semitic God, of whom it is easy to say what isn't, but impossible what is. I have never tried to describe you in words. Did I tell her that the blend of you and G.B.S. was a symphony of smooth and sharp, like bacon and eggs? Possibly. Conjoined you would be complete humanity. Whereas poor Nancy is only a whirling atom.

If they give me an assistant soon I will try and do some *Odyssey*: today I am just exhausted.

Malvern:[1] the fog of doubt hangs as thick as ever over August, and will hang till at least July 24, when a meeting at the Air Ministry may throw us all out of our jobs, as incompetents. So I'll cast a shot at a venture: book me for August 27th night please. I will try and stick to that. If I fail I'll arrange to sleep in some haystack.

As for feeling 'at home' with you: that is not the word. I do not wish to feel at home. You are more completely restful than anyone I know, and that is surely better? Homes are ties, and with you I am quite free, somehow.

Yours
T.E.S.

British Library

LADY ASTOR
12.7.29   R.A.F. Cattewater Plymouth

Dear Lady Astor

That was a beautiful letter you sent me: — but you & I ought to be too busy to write beautiful letters. The Wing Commander sends for me and says — 'Shaw, just write a nice letter for me to this' & back comes a thing like this. That is that. We are lavish with thisses and thattes tonight.

I do like the woods of Cliveden; and if ever I get good enough to play pilot to that Moth, it'll come to rest there or at Sandwich, some day. By all other sorts of transports you are too far. As for the merit of work, study the ant's contribution to animal happiness and then be lazy, like me. I have time to hear & see & smell the unlikenesses of every-day things. So I am

---

1 Lawrence had promised to go to the Malvern Festival (started by Sir Barry Jackson mainly as a festival for plays by Bernard Shaw) where *The Apple Cart* was to be performed. The Shaws went there every year unless on one of their frequent journeys abroad.

never short of attentions. And I cling to camp because there I feel I belong. Belonging is a good feeling.

Yours ever
SHAW.

There I beat the W/C. He cannot type his own name.

University of Reading

B.H. LIDDELL HART[1]
14.VII.29   Corfe

I'm here, temporarily settling some problems concerning my Dorsetshire cottage. Going back this afternoon. I hope this letter will arrive in time. Your wire was sent on to me.

1. Directly, the C.A.S. might abolish, by a word, bayonets and walking-out canes. Bayonets because they are costly (16/- each), take long to maintain (about 1 hr. per month, except where a buffing-wheel is available), ugly, and useless. I'd call them dangerous, for there was an idiot Squadron Leader who used to practice open-order attack, in France: waving a sword himself. A fool like that might easily throw away a squadron. Aircraft are a long-distance weapon, and bayonets are out of place in them.

2. The walking-out cane I can leave to common sense. You saw mine: and saw that it's a silly bodkin of a thing, no use as stick or weapon, and no ornament. It was designed, I believe, to keep troops hands out of their pockets: but R.A.F. tunics and breeches have inaccessible pockets, in which no man can keep his hands. Whereas hands and stick both go into our overcoat pockets.

The C.A.S. (Trenchard) has already done two or three of the reforms I urged on him, and repeated to you. So the job is lightened.

3. Kit inspection is another bore. It's supposed to be held monthly, and troops have to show all their kit. This is ridiculous. Our working dress is inspected daily, our walking-out dress weekly, in the normal course of duty. All that is required (besides these two suits, in case of active service which is the justification of kit inspection) is spare socks, spare shirts, pants. Instead of laying everything, which confuses the eye of the Inspecting Officer, and involves everything being very tightly folded, to be got on the bed, troops should (once a quarter) leave out on their beds their spare

---

1 Letter written following a discussion with Liddell Hart about certain practices current in the R.A.F. which Lawrence feared might inhibit recruitment. Liddell Hart offered to bring them to notice in official quarters privately. See also p. 416.

underclothing, and go off to work. And the inspection should be done by the Flight Officer and his N.C.O., at leisure. It shouldn't be a parade, or a beauty-show: but an inspection to make sure that our normally-invisible kit was serviceable and complete. There is no need for us standing by. That makes us hot and ashamed, and the decent officers feel like nosey-Parkers, and avoid looking at us.

4. The last thing is a very small point. In the navy, an officer or N.C.O. entering the men's mess takes his hat off, whether on duty or not. The airmen would like this to become the general rule in the R.A.F. It is in some stations, where the C.O. is ex-navy.

There were many other things I'd like to talk about: marriage-establishment rosters, overseas-rosters, posting of airmen in England to the stations most convenient to them (a Scotchman in Plymouth: home fare — £5: an Englishman in Leuchars: ditto). Pillion-riding on motor cycles (airmen are the only people in England forbidden it: not soldiers, not sailors. It's rather an insult to what we fondly hope is the most dangerous service). The week-end pass (I'd make after duty Saturday till Reveille Monday free for all men not warned for duty. Every station keeps a duty crew). I'd make an Air Ministry regulation about plain clothes. At present one C.O. allows them, and another restricts them. Chaos and irritation. It is a very valued privilege, I'm sorry to say. Church parade. This is the most annoying parade of the week. Couldn't it be made voluntary? I think I could get the consent of the two archbishops to that, if the Air Ministry is shy of the C. of E.

DG/LHB

T. B. MARSON
23.VIII.29   R.A.F. Cattewater Plymouth

Dear Marson

I saw Boom today:[1] he inspected Cattewater, and spoke to me: gently telling me off as usual!

Do you know, he is looking old? His moustache is going white, and he looks nearly his real age. I am sorry. You know he is finally resigning at the end of this year, and John Salmond[2] comes in. It's the end of an epoch, in my life and judgement. I shan't feel as I do about the R.A.F. after he has gone. One takes a pride in being under Boom.

1 'Boom' was Trenchard's nickname.
2 Sir John Salmond was Trenchard's successor as Chief of Air Staff.

You've been very nice in asking me to see you, at your place, this autumn. I'm of the Schneider Cup party, and tomorrow we move to Calshot, for three weeks at that worst of stations. Alas.

After the Cup (the Italians are asking tonight to have it postponed: alas again!) perhaps they will give me leave: and then I shall try to persuade my bike of bikes into Gloucestershire. Time is so short: people I want to see, would like to see, so many. Alas again. Life just fizzes past, and after it perhaps things do not greatly matter. I should have written to you before. Desperate venture, farming now-a-days. I hope you show up all the others at it. The big men make money, I'm told: but you aren't rich, yet, probably.

Yours
T.E.S

Bodleian Reserve

HENRY WILLIAMSON
23.VIII.29

Dear H.W.

I have orders to move to Calshot tomorrow–& the Italians are asking to have the race postponed! Such is life.

The last three weeks have been one great rush. I hope the Race isn't postponed, & that all the rush will be over by Sept 12. I want some peace: badly.

It was very pleasant to see you, & Mrs Williamson: & the kid; I'm always a bit sorry for children.[1] We've had a hell of a bad time: so'll they, I suppose.

Among my 100 leave plans is a night or two with you in the new place:[2] don't be alarmed. I can sleep on the doorstep, & your food is luxury itself, after the R.A.F. In 48 hours we could tear to pieces all contemporary books, & begin English literature with a new clean sheet!

In this camp one is always on duty: and I want to be able to look at and

---

1 Lawrence's visit to Williamson had taken place some weeks earlier in late July. For an account of this visit and Williamson's reaction to meeting Lawrence in the flesh, see *Genius of Friendship*, p. 29: e.g. 'He knew what I was going to say before I said it ... His reflexes were extraordinarily quick and sensitive: quicksilver.... I felt ... for the first time in my life, I was becoming real and strong.' Williamson also described Lawrence's remarkable impact on him and his family in his contribution to *T. E. Lawrence by His Friends*: 'We felt like otters, or Arabs,' etc.

2 The Williamsons had moved to another house in Georgeham.

listen to trees & running water, at my leisure, with no whistles or parades to keep on interrupting.

There's an interesting book coming out next year: a life of Gaudier Brzeska: the French sculptor: by Jim Ede, of the Tate Gallery.[1] <u>Good.</u>
Yours
T.E.S.

Bodleian Reserve

ROBERT GRAVES
3.IX.29   Calshot

Dear R.G.

There should, I feel, have been more to say about this section: but there is not.[2] Except for the epilogue (which is good, appetising, rather curiosity-exciting stuff, and with a falling-close about its paragraphs that makes its genial effect a little sorrowful) the writing is not distinguished, like the first part. I have missed the middle, I fear. They must have kept it at Cattewater. I have written to the Post Corporal, and asked him to trace it and send on. This Calshot is the hell of a place for mails. We get nothing through.

I've toned my letter down, in the first sentences: and suggested slight cuts later.[3] Is it moral to cut out parts of letters already written & sent? Or should they appear whole. I do not know: but if you can modify this one as I suggest, then it will be kinder to Egypt. One says more to a man's back than to his face.

Nowt els. A good book, this one of yours will be, I think: and you were quite right to cut short the events of 1929. You have had a bad year of it. I hope the weather will be calmer for you now. Please congratulate L.[4] on walking round the table. Not enough, but much. I'll hope to see you, if

---

1 *Savage Messiah*, by H. S. Ede, published 1931. (Reprinted by the Gordon Fraser Gallery, 1979, 1987)
2 Lawrence had been reading part of Graves's classic work *Goodbye to All That*, which was shortly to be published.
3 Some paragraphs of a letter by Lawrence to Graves about Egypt appear in chapter 31 of Graves's book. The letter is printed in full in *RGB* (21 October 1925).
4 Laura Riding.

you are still in England when I am free:— if I am ever free. We work from seven in the morning till eleven at night here. I hope it will end soon.[1]

T.E.S.

University of Harvard

ROBERT GRAVES   Cattewater
13/IX/29

Dear R.G.

A rush to read this today & to get it off to you. Ouf! I'm glad that Schneider Cup is over. Too much like work.

This is very good.[2] The war is the best part (terrible idea: is the war always going to be the thing we do best?) and completely carries on & up the excitement of the opening chapters. Most excellent. Your pictures of wounds & nerves are exactly as they should be: sane, decent, *right*.

S.S.[3] comes out very well. I'm glad of that, for I like him: homosex and all. He's a fighting man, & generous. Hates his family millionaires.[4]

I'm glad, too, that there is so much humour, so little unalloyed spleen, in the book. You have had enough lately to embitter a saint — and the saint laughs, a little wryly.

No corrections or changes to make, on the point of taste or prose. It's very good writing, and the characters are so alive. A very good book. The rise & fall is noticeably planned, & excellent.

T E S

University of Harvard

B. E. LEESON   14 Barton Street S.W.1
11.X.29.

Dear Leeson

Your maid guessed correctly. I was trying a new thing for George Brough, and its engine had run so remarkably that I was half an hour in advance of schedule. So I said 'Manchester, Ha: Victoria Park' (I knew V.P. in the B.C. period) and swirled off there to pass the time of day with you,

1 Lawrence drew a long arrow down the page from the first sentence to the last two sentences and wrote in the margin: 'This is why'.
2 This: *Goodbye to All That*: see previous letter.
3 S.S.: Siegfried Sassoon. For a comment on Lawrence's statement 'I like him; homosex and all', see General Introduction, p. xxvi.
4 Sassoon had become a Socialist following his experiences during the war; in the 1918 election he had campaigned for Philip Snowden and had inveighed against the idle rich — a category in which he included his own millionaire cousins.

if you had happened to be lunching at home. Only, of course, you were not. It is often like that in a grey world. Put it to the credit of Manchester that (despite appearance and temptation) it was not raining on that day.

Life otherwise is rather accidented. I have met many hard looks and bad words from the great men of the R.A.F. lately. My head is bowed and not bloody.

Commend me to the maid. You are a plutocrat. I have no maid: nor even a wife: whereas you have two women to look after you. Mohammedan!

Yours
T.E.S.

Bodleian Reserve

MRS CHARLOTTE SHAW
26.X.29   Saturday night, later

The sun shone, frostily I admit, but *shone*. So I could not throw in my present liberty. In fine weather tramps have an ideal life. Therefore I hope to go off a.m. on Sunday into Wales, or Norfolk, or Yorkshire (probably it will be Kent, after all) and eat more smooth miles of road.

Today I went to Chingford, and said good-bye to Pole Hill. It was marvellously beautiful. Our oak 'cloister' has settled into the hill-side, and grown moss, and dignity. My poor trees have added three feet to their stature since a year ago, all except the cypresses, which were to have been an avenue, for my walking when I felt sad; but the drought has browned three of them to death. However they are not wanted: I will not be there when they (and myself) become old: and for the sadness, it was very present with me this afternoon, in the knowledge that I had lost these fields. I wonder why we get so fond of fields? Commonplace fields, you might call these, only that no common place could afford so proud a view. Today it was perfection, for the mist and the cold air held all the smoke of all the chimneys, so that every ridge was sharpened at the top by the waves of grey vapour rising from the next valley. All the sky-lines were remote, and lovely, and it would have been enough for the rest of my day's thinking just to have sat there till dark and watched everything blur into one blackness, starred with lamps. Only of course I couldn't stop, for the place won't be mine next month: and all the tenants came to me, so sorry for themselves, but telling me not to care, as the forest was the proper owner of the hill. In process of years the tenants have weeded themselves of the unfit, until today there is not one who doesn't often sit still in enjoyment of the view. The police sergeant who has reared his family there in six years says that he's trying to persuade himself that he can be happy in a semi-detached street-house, without four acres of wild garden: but that it'll be like a cell after liberty. He took me down to the bottom field, to see the peep over the lake that he thinks the most beautiful of all the vistas. 'There isn't a house or man-made stick in view' he said: and it was just that which I found lacking to the perfection. It is selfish, isn't it, to take delight in not seeing neighbours? Pole Hill seemed to come nearer to me today than ever before: always, then, I was going to hold it, or held it: and today I had agreed to let it go. Epping Forest will be very good to it, of course: a better master than I have been. Only no corporation can like a place quite as much as the owner who'd saved to buy it, yard by yard, for years.[1]

Enough of all that sob-stuff. I'm off early tomorrow, if it is bright: and I'll stay every night with some ex-fellow of the Tanks or R.A.F.; and after the weather breaks, or I'm broke, or the leave is ended, I'll make for Plymouth, trying to call at Whitehall or Ayot on the way.

O'Casey was *good*.[2]

TES.

British Library

ALAN DAWNAY
31.X.29   Union Jack Club 91 Waterloo Road London

Dear A C D

Lady Clayton's income will be made up to about £1000 by Government.[3] This seems to me (and I hope to you) satisfactory. Do not yet give the news any *extended* currency, as people dislike having their good deeds anticipated: but please see that MacEwen, or other person in touch with her, warns you for me if there is any later hitch in the business.

And don't whisper my name, anyhow, please. The Air Ministry would

---

1 Lawrence's selling of Pole Hill marks the end of his long-held ambition to found a private printing press. His intended partner, Vyvyan Richards, had meanwhile helped Robert Graves and Laura Riding to set up the Seizin Press in their flat in St Peter's Square, Hammersmith.
2 Lawrence had seen O'Casey's anti-war play *The Silver Tassie* at the Apollo Theatre, London.
3 Sir Gilbert Clayton had died on 11 September. It was characteristic that Lawrence should have interested himself in the financial welfare of his former chief's widow; he showed a similar concern for the dependants of deceased fellow servicemen.

chalk a new black mark against me, if they heard I'd been interested. One has to be so cursed careful.

Yours
T.E.S.

Bodleian Reserve

JOHN BROPHY[1]

19.XI.29   R.A.F. Mount Batten Plymouth.

Dear Brophy

Don't let's 'Mr' each other. My past reputation can balance your present social superiority, and make us quits!

I'm sorry about the essay. I have decided — in 1922 I decided — not to try to go on writing. Agreed that with my name on, it sells like tripe: but I've posted it anonymously to this editor & that, and got it all back again. Perhaps the emotion (in solution) in it made the *Seven Pillars* much better than the rest of my writing. Anyway they would not buy it, and I have had seven years without trying to write, and am all the easier for being spared the labour. I think I did write better than the average retired military man: but between that and 'writing' there is a gulf. I have talked to many whom I think great writers. All of them have a likeness, in that they get some pleasure out of the phrases as they are born. Not the finished work, perhaps. Few look back with pleasure: but there is joy in the creation, and I had never anything but weariness and dissatisfaction. This I put down to my works being an imitation, made with great care and pains and judgement, of the real thing.

So I gave it up, I hope finally. Not without having tried it well, you know. 1st book burned:[3] 2nd (*Seven Pillars*) published privately: 3.rd still in manuscript. God forbid there being a fourth. It is true that I do translations. My style is easy and correct, and the publishers pay me well for unsigned or pseudonymous versions of French books, and an occasional Greek, such as I am at now. The proceeds very usefully supplement my R.A.F. pay, which isn't enough for my motor bike's costs, and they involve no publicity at all.

[...]

Bodleian Reserve

---

1 Writer, co-editor with Eric Partridge of *Songs and Slang of the British Soldier, 1914-1918*; contributor to *Lawrence by His Friends*.
2 R.A.F. Cattewater had been renamed R.A.F. Mount Batten as from 1 October 1929.
3 The first *Seven Pillars of Wisdom*, written but not completed before the war.

H. S. EDE
28.xi.29   338171 A/c Shaw R.A.F. Mount Batten Plymouth

Dear Ede

Peccavi: and still I go on sinning: this is not a letter, but an apology for not writing: and why I don't write I can't say. To meet you, now, would be a delight: I'd ride two hundred miles, with you at the end of it, if I might: only I must not: and if I can't meet, I won't have the paper-business which is so second-best. If you are to go on knowing me you must allow for — expect — these sort of sulks.

I had a leave while you did — and wandered twice or thrice round the Tate, seeing nothing so exciting as your fish. I did see Aitken, who told me of your coming 'board'. I hope you defeated it. I laughed and laughed over your sun-bath letter: you sound well: you look well: so don't blame the poor board which has more ears and eyes than heads.

I'm glad Heinemann are taken with *G-B*.[1]

I assure you that it's a really good book: of course de luxe is best: but it wouldn't fall dead in paper covers, broché, at 6d! I hope it comes out soon and sells like — *Revolt in the Desert*!!!

Yours
T.E.S.

Bodleian Reserve

MAJOR ARCHIBALD BECKE[2]
28.XII.29   R.A.F. Mount Batten Plymouth

Your letter sits here on my table in the office, and I have been cursing it at intervals. Why on earth should anybody bother about that old war any longer? One does not learn hints for the next one from details of engagements: after a fight starts the rest is common sense and ingenuity. Strategy, the great lines of approach, may be learned from books and maps — not

---

1 Ede's biography of Gaudier-Brzeska, *Savage Messiah*.
2 Major A. F. Becke, R.A. (Retd), was a military historian employed by the Historical Section of the Committee of Imperial Defence. He was engaged in compiling the maps for the volume of the History of the Great War dealing with military operations in Egypt and Palestine from June 1917 to the end of the war, of which the author was Captain Cyril Falls. It was published in 1930.

tactics. That silly book of Henderson's did our staff such harm.[1]

As for the scrap at Seil el Hesa, wasn't it rather an indecent show?[2] I haven't copies of either of my books here, but I meant to make it plain in them that the fight was an exception to my practice, undertaken in bad temper as a sardonic jest — whose poor taste I saw later, when the casualties came home. Throughout it I was quoting to myself absurd tags of Foch and the other blood-fighters, and in every movement I was parodying the sort of thing they recommended, but exaggerating just enough to make it ridiculous. The account I wrote of the fight afterwards was in the same vein: a parody of a proper dispatch. The Palestine Staff took it seriously: I hope your section is not going to follow their mistake.

You want me to check the affair now, on my twelve-year-old memories, against air photos of the ground. Isn't that overdoing what was originally meant (as I told you) to be a joke? You've only got to put yourself in my place as I then was to see how hopelessly out of key Seil el Hesa was with all my other conduct. Tafila wasn't worth the men to us: killing Turks was no part of our business. The whole thing's absurd.

So I hope you'll give up the idea of presenting any 'study' of this so-called battle. Battles are usually the last refuge of fools in open war: and I'm very sorry I ever fought this one.

Yours sincerely
T E Shaw

(If you go on with the grisly dissection of my trifle, I suggest that this note be printed as its postscript. It would restore the thing to scale!)

University of Texas

1 'That silly book of Henderson's': a reference to *The Science of War* by Colonel G. F. R. Henderson (1854–1903), edited by Neill Malcolm and published in 1906. Its intention, in its author's words, was to provide 'a clear insight into the innumerable problems connected with the organisation and command of an armed force'; it was also the author's hope that his book would help to 'train the judgement of young officers so that when left to themselves they may do the right thing'.
2 Seil el Hesa: also known, as Lawrence implies later in the letter, as the Battle of Tafila, or Tafileh, 25 January 1918. Lawrence's attitude to the action as given here is much in line with his account in Chapters LXXXV and LXXXVI of *Seven Pillars of Wisdom*.

MAJOR ARCHIBALD BECKE
31.XII.29

Dear Major Becke

I've cut about the larger print a bit: substantially your map appears to square with my memories, but the main Turkish effort was along the ridge afterwards cleared by the men of Aisna.

Perhaps your conventions do not distinguish between machine guns & automatics. Our party had at least one Vickers (I remember putting up its sights eventually to 3000 and spraying the retreat) but mostly Hotchkiss automatics: the Turkish captured guns were mainly that little air-cooled thing they fitted into their two-seater aircraft: I can't recall if they had any Maxims or not. I rather think they had: — sledge-guns, probably.

There were present Emir Zeid, G.O.C.[1] the Arabs, and Jaafar Pasha (then a Major Gen. Arab Army, & Brig. Gen. Turkish Army) his adviser. So I do not quite know on what rule you go, in putting my Majority on the ridge!

Sorry I can't help about the Crusader Castles. The thesis was not for publication, & I have no idea what happened to it; I lent it to Lord Curzon about 1919: and don't remember it since:* a typescript, it was, with plans & photos.[2]

The Syrian castles are very interesting. The first Crusaders put up their standard square keeps: later they divided into two schools: what I call the 'Hospital' took their inspiration from France, & kept on building Frenchified castles all over the hills: and the 'Temple' school put up colourable Byzantine buildings. At least so I concluded after examining about 50 of the ruins out there. Of course features of machicolation etc. developed better out East, because there was no timber for hourds.[3] My general conclusion was that Europe affected Syria rather than Syria Europe.

The entrance to Krak is 'a long way after' Rum Kalaat (Hromgl of Walther von der Vogelweide) near Samsat on the upper Euphrates — a most interesting fort.

Yours
T E Shaw

* Except for a half-notion that he gave it me back & I bound it: but I don't remember this well enough to swear to it. It was only a thesis — a first study. Not worth printing.

University of Texas

1 G.O.C.: General Officer Commanding.
2 This copy of the thesis is in the possession of Jesus College, Oxford.
3 Machicolations: openings for dropping missiles. Hourds: screens.

MRS CHARLOTTE SHAW
Sunday 19/1/30   Mount Batten

I have been Homering all morning and afternoon, and must not delay for
long: only there is so much I should say to you: first of all thanks for reading
that XIth Book. I am afraid it is very difficult. I have been over it three or
four times since it came back, and have managed about 100 minor alter-
ations. That is for the good. I changed, so far as I could, all the places you
had marked. It is very difficult.

What you say about it is about what I feel: a sense of effort, of hard
work: of course there must be this. I never wrote (for printing) an easy line
in my life. All my stuff is tenth-thoughts or twentieth-thoughts, before it
gets out. Nice phrases in letters to you? Perhaps: only the difference between
nice phrases in a letter (where one nice phrase will carry the thing) and an
Odyssey where one phrase not-nice will spoil it all, is too great to carry a
comparison.

How like a book all the above sentences! Perhaps I am not writing to
you, but for my some-day 'Life and Letters'. If you think so, then burn the
thing, and prevent (as Homer would say) the day of its returning.

    [. . .]

British Library

MRS CHARLOTTE SHAW
6.2.30

I hope it will be all right, a fortnight hence, when they break the plaster
corselet: Laura Riding (Graves' No. ii) is recovering. She did the same hurt
to herself. So there is hope. If only the bones have set straight.

My work did not end on Friday. So I got another day from W/Cmdr.
Smith, and finished on Saturday at noon, just in time to see Wilson in the
shop before it shut.[1] I said to him 'who wrote *Her Privates We* — (that
being a superb lovable book, what *The Mint* ought to have been) — for I
know his touch?'. He said 'I think it begins with M . . .' and rang up Peter

1 J. G. Wilson of Bumpus the booksellers.

Davies.[1] That let a flood of light in: So to P.D. I said 'You haven't heard of me, my name is Shaw: but perhaps you've read a thing called *Revolt in the Desert* which I published as Lawrence. Did the author of *Scenes & Portraits* write *Her Privates We?*'[2] He was flabbergasted, having promised not to give it away. In the sequel Peter Davies, Wilson and your servant lunched at Barrie's and talked much shop. (Barrie in excellent wit: likened George Moore to a decayed gold-fish!).

Scenes & Portraits, which John Murray probably published, has been one of my friends since undergraduate days, so of course *Her Privates We* is bound to make me happy. I wonder if you will like it. It is a war book, of course, but with a difference. There is so much laughter and happiness in it: and it is beautiful. The troops in it are real, at last. Manning is a very exquisite person. So queer. A great friend of Galton, while Galton lived.

It was a very good holiday, and has finally demoralised me. Not a word of Greek this week!

T.E.S.

British Library

FREDERIC MANNING
25/2/30   Mount Batten Plymouth

Dear Manning

No, it wasn't Rothenstein[3]: and I cannot get up to London this week. Now-a-days I'm lucky to fetch London once in three months, and it is only a month since I was there. As for the authorship of the book — the preface gives it away. It is pure *Scenes & Portraits*. How long, I wonder, before everybody knows? You need not worry at their knowing. It is a book everyone would have been proud and happy to have written.

Of course I'm ridiculously partial to it, for since 1922 my home has been

1 Peter Davies was a distinguished London publisher. He was one of the five Llewellyn Davies brothers who were befriended by J. M. Barrie and for whom Barrie wrote *Peter Pan*. Davies committed suicide in 1960, aged 63.

2 *Scenes and Portraits*, published in 1909, was by the Australian-born writer Frederic Manning (1882–1935), poet, short-story writer, and reviewer before the war for the *Spectator* (see next letter). He had served with a British regiment as a private in the war, taking part in the Battle of the Somme. *Her Privates We* (1930) was his fictionalised acount of this experience, published under the name 'Private 19022'.

3 Manning had written (11 February 1930): 'Was it some uncanny *flair*, that led you to me; or did Will Rothenstein tell you that he has some letters from me with my regimental number on them, 19022?' (*Letters to T. E. Lawrence*, which includes twelve letters by Manning).

in the ranks, and Bourne[1] says and thinks lots of the things I wanted to have said. But don't imagine that I'm anything like so much of a lad as he was. The R.A.F. is as gentle as a girls' school, and none of us drink.

I have read too many war books. They are like drams, and I cannot leave them alone, though I think I really hate them. Yours, however, and Cummings' *Enormous Room* and *War Birds*[2] seem to me worth while. *War Birds* is not literature but a raw sharp life. You and Cummings have produced love-poems of a sort, and yours is the most wonderful, because there is no strain anywhere in the writing. Just sometimes you seem to mix up the 'one's' and 'his's': but for that, it is classically perfect stuff. The picture about $\frac{2}{3}$ through of the fellows sliding down the bank and falling in preparatory to going up for the attack, with the C.O.'s voice and the mist — that is the best of writing.

I have read *Her Privates We* twice, and *The Middle Parts of Fortune*[3] once, and am now deliberately leaving them alone for a while, before reading them again. The airmen are reading the *Privates*, avidly: and E. M. Forster (who sent me a paean about the *Privates*) has *The Middle Parts*. Everyone to whom I write is loudly delighted with the *Privates*. I hope the sales will do you good.

Peter Davies is trying to use my dregs of reputation as one more lever in the sales. Do not let that worry you. Adventitious sales and adventitious advertisements are very soon forgotten: the cash will remain with you, and your book be famous for as long as the war is cared for — and perhaps longer, for there is more than soldiering in it. You have been exactly fair to everyone, of all ranks: and all your people are alive.

This is not a very sensible letter. I am very tired, and this weather gets me down: only I owed it to you to thank you for the best book I have read for a very long time. I shall hope to meet you some day and say more — and bore you by saying it — for what is so dead as a book one has written?

Yours
T. E. Shaw

DG

1 Private Bourne was the hero of *Her Privates We*.

2 *The Enormous Room*, by E. E. Cummings, was a brilliantly written acount of a three-month detention in France in 1917; *War Birds* was written by Elliott Springs, an American who had served as an officer with the Royal Flying Corps and Royal Air Force in 1917-18.

3 The original unexpurgated version of *Her Privates We*, published in a limited edition in 1929.

MRS CHARLOTTE SHAW
25/2/30   RAF Mount Batten Plymouth

I am a little sad that you do not like *Her Privates We*. In that is the reality of the common Englishman: and Bourne, the educated little cock-sparrow, is the commonest and most human-like of them all. I think it more of a love-book than a war-book, and have read it three times, without satisfying myself.

I agree with your weariness against all ordinary war books: but for those who fought they are like dram-drinking, and cannot be refused, however one may hate them. Books about ourselves, you know. I cannot help scanning (even if it is always in disgust) anything that appears in print about myself. There is a fascination—a longing to get it over and *know*. *Her Privates We*, however, did not disgust me. I liked it.

[...]

Poor Boanerges has rusted all over, and I only rub more grease over him, instead of going out for a long fast run. How can I, with the long-suffering Odysseus sitting on my neck all the while? It will be all better, when this cold passes, and things get happy again.
                                                              .S.

British Library

ROBIN BUXTON
25/2/30   R.A.F. Mount Batten Plymouth

Dear Robin

Have you got my bawdy book—*The Mint*, I mean? Somehow I fancy that Herbert Baker lent it you: because I have need of a copy of it—or shall have need of it in 3 weeks time, to lend an interested person.

I apologise for inflicting such a thing on you: or no: I didn't inflict it on you. I created the horrid thing, & you have brought it on yourself. It is Vol II of my life, all the same. A bit of a come down after the *Seven Pillars*.
                                                        T.E.S.

Bodleian Reserve

MRS CHARLOTTE SHAW
27.3.30

[...]

My St. Andrews-degree trouble is easily over: Barrie & Buchan[1] played up and freed me from it. I think the public occasion would have been unbearable. A reaction from publicity, which began in me about 1919 has grown stronger since year by year. I like to see my name in the papers — no: when I see it I get a snatch of horrified interest — and I hate anybody telling me they have seen it.

[...]

British Library

HENRY WILLIAMSON
3.V.30

It has been behind my eyes, in my head, for weeks to answer: but it seemed necessary to send some *Odyssey* too: and now you are ill: or are you just back, & feeling convalescent?

The *Village Book*[2] sounds good: and I'll look forward to reading it. Your prose is a very conscious & beautiful thing.

These *Odyssey* pages aren't sent for criticism: but to show you that no one can help in them. Translations aren't books, for in them there is no inevitable word: the whole is approximation, a feeling towards what the author would have said: and as Homer wasn't like me the version goes wrong whenever I let myself into it. Consequently the thing is a pot-boiler only, a second-best: and I do not have page-proofs. Bruce Rogers does all the printing part. I send him a typed copy of my stuff, and that is the end of it. These are actual printed sheets, and the few pencil corrections on them are my reading comments.

The work is not meant to interest you: the Homer who wrote the *Odyssey* was an antiquarian, a tame-cat, a book-worm: not a great poet, but a most charming novelist. A Thornton Wilder of his time.[3] My version, and every version, is inevitably small.

---

1 Lawrence had been invited to accept the degree of Doctor of Laws at St Andrews University, and had written to John Buchan, who had been behind the offer, begging him to get it withdrawn.
2 A book of stories of village life, first published in 1930.
3 American writer, particularly well known for his novel *The Bridge of San Luis Rey*, and for his play *Our Town*.

Will I ever get to your place again? This Greek eats and drinks all my leisure hours. However I have bought my Dorset cottage out of its profits, as provision for my years when the RAF will not have me any more: so probably it is worth while.

I hope W. III is a successful & howlingly successful infant.

TES

Bodleian Reserve

MRS CHARLOTTE SHAW
15.VIII.30

[...] On Wednesday I lunched with Philip Sassoon, with whom came Nöel Coward. He is not deep but remarkable. A hasty kind of genius. I wonder what his origin is? His prose is quick, balanced, alive: like Congreve, probably, in its day. He dignifies slang when he admits it. I liked him: and suspected that you probably do not. Both of us are right.

Thence here, all last night in the train. Head like a boiled apple. Tomorrow I am to fly across into Kent and back on Monday. Meanwhile *The People* has discovered me at Filton, near Bristol, and the German Press is confident I am in Kurdistan.

[...]

S.

British Library

NOËL COWARD[1]
15.VIII.30   338171 A/c Shaw R.A.F. Mount Batten Plymouth

Dear N.C.

Here are your R.A.F. notes. After looking at them you will agree with me that such tense and twisted prose cannot be admirable. It lacks health. Obscenity is vieux jeu, too: but in 1922 I was not copying the fashion!

Don't be too hard on them, though. They were meant, not for reading, but to afford me raw material for an introductory chapter to my mag. op.

---

1 The eminent actor, dramatist and composer (1899–1973, knighted 1970), famous for a string of successes on both stage and screen. 1930 was the year of his play *Private Lives*, to a rehearsal of which (see fourth paragraph) Lawrence had been invited. He was later present at its second performance.

on an airman's life. Unluckily I survived the Depot only to be sacked when on the point of being posted to a Squadron, the real flying unit. There followed a long spell of army life, wasting the novelty of barracks, till I broadened out into the present common-place and lasting contentment.

Obviously these notes libel our general R.A.F. life by being too violently true to an odd & insignificant part of it. So out of my head & with no formal notes I attempted a Part III to show the happiness that came after the bullying. Only happiness is such a beast to put on paper.

Meeting you was such a surprise and pleasure to me. I had often (and quite inadequately) wondered what you were like. Now I'll try to work the rehearsal you suggested into some later raid upon London. The going-round of wheels fascinates me. So I found Wednesday wholly delightful.

Yours
T E Shaw

Please do not keep them longer than you can help — or I shall forget where they are, and be troubled!

Bodleian Reserve

HENRY WILLIAMSON
6.IX.30   R.A.F. Mount Batten Plymouth

Dear H W

It is even as you say: autumnal weather. I wish I knew what was the matter with me. Some unformed impulse keeps me in camp. I am always putting in passes, and saying 'I will go out this week-end': and when the time comes I cannot get into breeches & puttees, so the bike rusts in the garage and I moon about the water's edge in camp, dreaming or dipping inconsequentially into books.

It has come to this, that I feel afraid and hesitant outside. The camp itself is like a defence to me, and I can't leave it. I think I have only been outside three times this summer. [...] I am like a clock whose spring has run down.

I hope you will not hate the U.S.A.[1] So many people do, whereas it all sounds to me so strong and good. Canada less so, but then I like towns because only by contrast with cities do trees feel homelike, or seas look happy.

Will they send this rot on? Probably not. Have patience with me, when

---

1 Williamson had written to say that he was going to America on an extended visit.

you come back, and sooner or later we will meet and talk, without the bike waiting on the kerb outside.

[...]

Yours
T.E.S.

Bodleian Reserve

NOËL COWARD
6.IX.30   Mount Batten Plymouth

Dear N.C.

It is very good to laugh: and I laughed so much, and made so many people laugh over your 'may I call you 338'[1] that I became too busy and happy to acknowledge your letter.

I hope Liverpool went off well. Edinburgh — so the press said, but how they lie — went into fits over your mixed grill. I fancied you were coming thence direct to London, but clearly not. It must be very hard and uphill work winning province after province before attacking the headquarters: and London is likely to be your easiest conquest, too. The bits I saw[2] went so swingingly.

Your praise of my R.A.F. notes pleases me, of course, more than it puzzles me. I'm damned if I can see any good in them. Some artifice — yes: some skill — yes: they even come off, here and there: but the general impression on me is dry bones. Your work is like sword-play; as quick as light. Mine a slow painful mosaic of hard words stiffly cemented together. However it is usually opposites that fall in love. At any rate I propose to go on looking forward, keenly, to seeing more of your works and work, and perhaps of yourself, if a kind fate lets me run into you when you are not better engaged.

I'm hoping to get to London some time in October, for a week-end perhaps.

Yours
T E Shaw

DG

---

1 Noël Coward had begun a letter to Lawrence written on 25 August 1930, 'Dear 338171 (May I call you 338?), I am tremendously grateful to you for letting me read your R.A.F. notes ...'
2 Of *Private Lives*.

F. N. DOUBLEDAY[1]

18.IX.30   [Collieston near Aberdeen Scotland]

Effendim

Rotten pen and foul paper, but here on the North East edge of Scotland I've just heard that you are 'out of the wood'. So much to be thankful for, yet no more than is fitting. Understand, that yourself and illness do not go together! I think of you always as part pirate, like Kidd, part buccaneer like Morgan, with moments of legitimacy like Farragut. It is unthinkable to think of an Effendi incapable of bearing arms. So please recover quickly that we may laugh again. Meanwhile come on leave with me for ten days!

Come northward many miles above Aberdeen, and then strike towards the sea across the links, which are sand-tussocked desolations of charred heather and wiry reeds, harbouring grouse to whirr up alarmingly sideways from under-foot, and rabbits so lazy that they will hardly scuttle their snow-white little tail-flags from the path. Add a choir of larks and a thin high wind piping over the dunes or thrumming down the harsh stems of heather.

They are three miles wide, these links, and ever so desolate, till they end abruptly in a rough field whose far side is set on edge with a broken line of cottages. Behind their roofs seems to be pure sky, but when you near them it becomes sea — for the cottages have [been] built round all the crest of the grassy sea-cliff and down it too, cunningly wedging their places into its face wherever there was a flat of land as wide as two rooms. Almost to the beach the cottages fall. Beach, did I say? It is a creek of sand, cemented along one side in a grey quay-wall from which and from the opposing rocks up run the grass-grown cliffs in heart-comforting bastions to the houses fringed against the sky. The creek's a fishing port. You could find room to play a game of tennis in it, perhaps, if the tide went dry. So there are no bigger boats than dinghies and no room for any: nor heart for any with the jaws of greycold reefs champing white seas outside, all day and night.

Imagine whole systems of slate-like slabby rocks, flung flat-wise and acres square, thrusting out into the maddened North Sea which heaves and foams over them in deafening surges. The North-Easter, full of rain and so misted

---

1 Of this letter to Doubleday (frequently addressed as Effendi or Effendim because of his initials) John Buchan wrote: 'he [Lawrence] never wrote better prose than his description of the bleak sea coast of Buchan' (*Memory Hold-The-Door* p. 217). From Knightley and Simpson's *The Secret Lives of Lawrence of Arabia* (pp. 199–200) it appears that the holiday was arranged mainly so that he could submit himself to a harsh physical regime which included not only horse riding and swimming in cold seas but also birching by John Bruce. Bruce later commented (ibid, p. 200); 'Here is a man subjecting himself almost beyond human endeavour, willingly, and in the midst of it all he writes a four-page letter in the gayest possible manner.'

that our smarting eyes can peer only two or three hunched yards into it, is lifting the waves bodily into the air and smashing them upon the rocks. There is such sound and movement out there in the haze that our eyes keep staring into its blindness to see the white walls rolling in. The concealed sun makes all white things half-luminous, so that the gulls become silvered whenever they dip suddenly to turn a knife-edged cartwheel in the spray: and the thunder of the seas enforces a deafened silence on all other things, so that we feel as much as see the energy let loose. Each big wave makes the air quiver and sends a shading reverberation across the shore about our bodies.

That is the fighting of the sea against the land: and the sea's casualties have filled the port, around the elbow that the jetty makes. There the water is stifled and heaves sickly under a mat of sea-suds one foot thick. You know the creamed and bubbly foam that blows up a beach when the wind rises and the sea, together? Well, that flocculent stuff is all impounded in our bay, filling it so full that black water and jetty and steps and rocks and beach are all invisible, buried under it like a corpse in a blanket.

'Curse the fellow and his seascape,' you are saying. 'Am I paid to read his manuscript?' Peace, Mrs. Doubleday will take it away and burn it, so soon as you roar in anger.

What are we doing here? Nothing, practically. There are 3 of us — Jimmy who used to work in Canada but came home in 1914 and was a gunner for four years in France: now he jobs horses in Aberdeen: — Jock, the roughest diamond of our Tank Corps hut in 1923; — and me. We have Mrs. Ross' cottage lent to us and reluctantly in turn sweep its floor and fetch the water and coal. For meals thrice a day we spread our coats to the wind and fly to the cliff-top, where the Mrs. Baker-and-Butcher feeds us in her parlour. Then heavy inside, we slide down hill to the cottage again in the cove: for ours is the nearest hovel to the high-tide mark. That is good in fair weather and exciting today. Great flocks of surf beat tattoos on the roof till the tide turned.

But what do we do? Why nothing, as I said. Jimmy has his horses to groom and feed and exercise. Sometimes we do the last for him. Jock fishes: boys bring him mussels and he waves a pole from the quay at the wild wild waves. Once up came a codling from the yeasty deep, the poor orphan taking pity on him. He brought it us in silent manly pride, and we made him clean it. Scrape scrape his knife went, like a man cleaning a flower-pot. We helped him eat it, too.

Most of our food is fish, I remember. There is a local industry, called sperling. Cut open a round fish, flatten it, dry him bone-white for days on a rock of wire netting, smoke him, boil him in milk. Not bad, tasting like dull veal. The local people are lovers of sperling, though, and taste more in them than I do. Then there are baby soles, four-inch things too small for sale in the city with the adult soles. They are fried and delicious. Down with great soles henceforward.

The cottage has 3 rooms. Jock took the middle one with big bed and fire-place. Ours open from it and are cold. So we make his our sitting room, and have pushed the bed into the corner, farthest from the fire where I sit and think all day, while turning over the swimming suits to dry. Also I eat pounds of peppermints (pan-drops they call them: Aberdeen and excellent) or read H. G. Wells' *History* in a dollar edition lately produced, as you may have heard, by a young and pushing publisher in the States. I wish I had a dozen copies to give away: but only one ran the customs gauntlet to do Cassells out of his English rights. Believe me, it's a good book. 8/6d in England and a dollar in the almighty-dear States.

I tried to get Heinemann's elephant book *Novels Today* in Aberdeen but they had it not. Distribution faulty, for Lady Eleanor Smith and Strong are both first-class. The book-shop lady tried to work off on me a thing called *Angel Pavement,*[1] also by Heinemann. She said everybody was buying it. 'Not quite everybody', I protested politely. 'This very man' she said 'wrote *Good Companions*'. 'Dreary artificial sob-stuffed thing' I snorted, having luckily read *Good Companions*. 'You *are* hard to please' she grumbled, offering me *The Boy's Book of Colonel Lawrence*[2] at a reduction, seeing I was in uniform and he now in the R.A.F. I told her I knew the fellow, and he was a wash-out: then I bought a *Daily Express* and escaped the shop. Alas, for I wanted to read *Dewar Rides*[3] again.

Effendi, what folly makes me want to talk rot to you when I hear you are ill? The whole man is a gladiator: who demands tall talk? Why babble when he is (temporarily) hurt? God knows. Ask Mrs. Doubleday to take the nasty thing away again.

Our tea-time now. The winds have stopped, but the waves increase. They are so big that only two roll in to the minute now. I wish you could hear the constancy and fresh repetition of their thunder, and the sharpness and loneliness of the gulls questing through the spume. The poor gulls are hungry from the storm and beset our roof for the food-scraps we throw away. They have the saddest, most cold, disembodied voices in the world.

Evening now. I must go up the shop for oil for the lamp. The shop is the post office and I'll then send this off, before its length frightens me and makes me burn it.

Au revoir, Effendim, soon, let's hope.

T. E. S.

1 By J. B. Priestley.
2 By Lowell Thomas.
3 By L. A. G. Strong.

P.S. for Mrs. D-D—Make it London next summer too! and we *will* get to Kipling this time.[1]

DG

MRS CHARLOTTE SHAW
5.XII.30   [Plymouth]

I am working on Book XX now mostly, with an occasional glance at 18 or 19 to try and better them in detail, before fair-copying. One grinds again and again over each passage till the corrections begin to restore former readings. Then it is finished.

As you say 1930 has been a bad year for you. And for me? No. I have nearly finished the Greek and it has been a quiet year, of no publicity at all. This has been the first year for ten years to leave me quite at peace. I think that is very good. One or two more, and my existence will be taken for granted.

So that is to my credit: and so is the *Odyssey*: and so is the speed-boat. And I have read several books which delighted me. In music I have been less fortunate, having got to hear no new thing of great moment to me. Only I hear so little music that perhaps I should not expect it. A Delius cello sonata, an Elgar Symphony, a Brahms Double Concerto: one cannot go on hoping for wonders indefinitely. These were my three years' joys.

I am sensibly older, with more aches and pains, and a lesser inclination to extend myself. That perhaps is the worst sign. Only a strong man can live heedlessly, as I wish to do. A single man who is poor has difficulty when he is old. Only I am not old yet: just older.

I have not met, this year, people I much wish to meet again. Noël Coward perhaps. But I have seen Manning after some years, and Siegfried Sassoon. You remain the solitary woman who lets me feel at ease with her, in spite of all the benefits you heap on me. Usually I am a very grudging taker, too.

I have flown only once this year, against 100 times last year. That was Lord Thomson's doing, and he seems to have frightened me off flying, for I have not been up since he died.

Tell me, before next Thursday, please, what your plans are for December 20. I have to come up for Lady Astor, and I thought perhaps I might push on to Ayot or Whitehall, for an hour or two, if you would be seen at either. I must spend Saturday night at Cliveden, and be here on Sunday

---

1 Lawrence and the Doubledays had planned to visit Rudyard Kipling at his country home, Batemans, in Sussex.

night, so there is not much time: only the morning of Saturday. We have not met since your hurt.

Manning has republished *Scenes & Portraits*, with a very touching little note to me. I like the graces of that book. Also the Gregynog has printed the *Stealing of the Mare*,[1] which I am liking to read again. It is not good, nor authentic desert: but true something-or-other.

Cakes & Ale, that Somerset Maugham, made my flesh creep: It was wrong to do that. Those who did not know him will see Hardy there.[2]

Bed-time — long ago.
T.E.S.

British Library

LADY ASTOR

31.XII.30   R.A.F. Mount Batten

[...] I feel inclined to send a postcard to Sandwich, explaining how much I enjoyed that night at Cliveden, and what an excellent ride back I had (including a race across the Plain with a sports Bentley: well, not so much a race as a procession for the Bent. which did only 88. I wished I had had a peeress or two on my flapper bracket!)

[...]

University of Reading

1 The Gregynog Press was a publishing firm specialising in rare and finely printed books. *The Stealing of the Mare* was by Wilfred Scawen Blunt, originally published in 1892.

2 *Cakes and Ale*, published 1930, portrayed the widow of a recently deceased Grand Old Man of Letters, Edward Driffield, whom many people took to be based on Thomas Hardy. In character Rosie Driffield was quite unlike Mrs Hardy, but, according to *The Second Mrs Hardy*, by Robert Gittings and Jo Manton, 'the *outward* circumstances of her life as Hardy's wife and widow were satirized with such uncanny insight that she herself saw the likenesses, and shrank from doing anything that might "give colour" to them, after she had read the book.' (Chapter 15, p. 131) Gittings and Manton also state that though in many ways Driffield was unlike Hardy, the book contained 'biting parodies which could only apply to the novels of Hardy, and to those of no other writer'. Hence Lawrence's strong reaction.

MRS CHARLOTTE SHAW
6.2.31

You will have seen the news of our crash here, in the papers. It was due to bad piloting, on the part of a man who (as we all know) should never have flown with passengers. He would not be convinced of that. Fortunately he died with the rest.[1]

It was horrible to see a huge Flying Boat so cast away by incompetence. I happened to be standing by the sea watching it come in to alight. So that is going to involve me in Enquiries and Inquests. At the Enquiry (which is an R.A.F. affair, not open to the Press) I propose to say just what I saw, and what it meant, in the endeavour to bring the responsibility home upon an Air Marshal Webb-Bowen at the Air Ministry, who refused to listen to reports made him on 3 separate occasions regarding this officer's unfitness to fly. I shall try to do it without getting myself into trouble if I can. If not — well, I think such a case had better not happen again, and I have facts enough to prevent its happening again, if I publish them.

You will not expect me to write again till this is over — a week at least. [...]

                                                        T.E.S.

British Library

MRS CHARLOTTE SHAW
16.2.31

Not a letter
    The talks still go on. Perhaps the inquest will end on Wednesday and that will be all.

    I was made clerk for the Air Ministry Court of Inquiry, and was able to approve and agree with its findings. G.B.S. will laugh at that.

    Please thank him for his letter. When all is over I shall be so relieved.

    I think all goes well with what I wanted. Saw Nancy lately. She told me of your new chill. Do you think you should get out of England for two months? With G.B.S.? Only don't ask me where. I think the people of Palm Beach would welcome him, and he could go via Bermuda and so

1 The crash, of an Iris III seaplane, had taken place on 4 February within sight of R.A.F. Mount Batten and with Lawrence and Clare Sydney Smith as spectators. For a full account of the occasion and of Lawrence's organising of the subsequent attempts at rescue (even though his Commanding Officer was present) see Clare Sydney Smith's *The Golden Reign* (Cassell, 1940), Ch. XXII.

miss the States: or there is Cape-Town: or the Dutch East Indies. Java is lovely they say.

I should suggest going or returning via Plymouth, selfishly!

T.E.S.

British Library

HENRY T. RUSSELL[1]

16.ii.31   R.A.F. Mount Batten Plymouth

Dear Mr Russell

Savage[2] has sent me on your letter, and I'm writing to say that my so-called 'seclusion' is a myth. I live in barracks, which is about as public a life as any human being can live. If I do not give interviews or write to the papers every week, it is only because I have nothing I want said. You are up against a contented being, who is perfectly willing to see you or anyone else — but will not put himself to the expense & toil of coming up to London except when absolutely compelled.

As for the Arab business: I had a hateful war: and after it $2\frac{1}{2}$ years of a dog-fight with the British Cabinet to secure the fulfilment of the promises to which they had made me an unwilling and post-facto accessory. When Winston Churchill fulfilled all that was humanly attainable of those promises I was free to quit events and return to the class & mode of life that I belong to & feel happy in.

Revolt in the Desert is now withdrawn from circulation, and the whole business of my work & myself is over and done with. No value or significance can lie in unrelated episodes. My reputation which still persists in the cheaper newspapers is only founded on what I didn't do or am not, and so long as no truth comes out I am not harmed by it. The last thing I desire is to be 'put across' correctly. Truth hurts!

So while, as I said, I haven't the smallest objection to seeing you, the result, on your side, will be nil. There are no wrongs to put right, no remorse or agony. Only a very ordinary and pleased creature whose position in the R.A.F. forbids him to give interviews for publication.

Forgive this long egotistical letter: but you asked for it —

Yours ever
T. E. Shaw

University of Texas

1 Henry T. Russell was a United Press correspondent.
2 Raymond Savage: Lawrence's literary agent.

EDWARD MARSH
10th March 1931   Mount Batten Plymouth

Dear E.M.

This letter, typed more or less ill, is for your owner,[1] please. May your polish and style support its bluntness, in his eyes!

A namesake of his, Bertram Thomas, our Agent at Muscat, has just crossed the Empty Quarter, that great desert of southern Arabia. It remained the only unknown corner of the world, and it is the end of the history of exploration. Thomas did it by camel, at his own expense. Every explorer for generations has dreamed of it. Its difficulty can best be put by my saying that no Arab, so far as we know, has ever crossed it.

Now something good must be done for this most quiet and decent fellow, in the Birthday Honours, if not sooner. It may be all arranged; but if not I beg you see to it. Do not let the swag be all carried off by the Rositas[2] and Lawrences of the vulgar Press. Here is one of your own men doing a marvel.

Give him a K.[3] will you? Well, it's a mouldy sort of thing, but as a civil servant he cannot refuse. So it would do: but your sense of fitness, which o-emmed Henry J.[4] (now I address E.M. & not J.H.T.) might prefer a C.H.,[5] or some other honour of which I know nothing.

Properly he should be India Office; but his success decorates England. K.C.S. eyes or ees would be unfitting. Better a Michael & George.

I trust the imagination of J.H.T. to understand your enthusiasm & mine for what is the finest geographical feat since Shackleton and to persuade his colleagues into action and unanimity. It will be a welcome change for them all.[6]

Will you also say that his *Seven Pillars* is not forgotten? This is not bribery of a Cabinet Minister, but the paying of a forgotten debt. The only available copies are of the U.S.A. edition, and it may be weeks yet before I have the chance to get it brought safely through our Customs. Yours constantly (but not too often!)

T. E. Shaw.

DG

1 J. H. Thomas, then Secretary of State for the Colonies. Marsh was his private secretary.
2 A reference to Rosita Forbes (1893–1967), the well-known traveller and travel-writer.
3 i.e. a knighthood.
4 Henry James had been given an O.M. (Order of Merit).
5 Companion of Honour.
6 Thomas was not honoured as Lawrence had suggested but he received the Founder's Medal of the Royal Geographical Society, the Burton Memorial Medal of the Royal Asiatic Society and Gold Medals from the Geographical Societies of Antwerp and America.

T. C. GRIFFIN[1]

17.IV.31   R.A.F. Mount Batten Plymouth

Dear Griffin

The *Hardinge* was very good to us — and to me — but she was also a great ship, crowded with people, and I was preoccupied with cares & weariness in those two war-years. So I hope you will pardon my not remembering one of you more than another. It was — how long ago? Nearly fifteen years, wasn't it? I am so old now, and it feels a lifetime away. Nine years ago I enlisted, and have not thought about the Middle East since. The Air Force life suits me and I'm happy in it.

So I cannot tell you anything about what happens now in the Red Sea. I don't write there, nor do they write to me. It wasn't a good time, and I like to forget it.

Seven Pillars, that book of mine? One copy did go to Canada, I think. Was it to a Colonel Leonard, at Montreal? I have no copy of my own, and have not seen the book for years. It's rather long, and I fancy dull. All the story part went into a popular version called *Revolt in the Desert*: but that's had its day, too!

I hope your affairs aren't bad. Most people's are, alas.

Yours

T E Shaw

Bodleian Reserve

ROBERT GRAVES

21.IV.31

Dear R.G.

I have been trying to write to you for months, but couldn't. All manner of jobs have descended on me, for the Air Ministry (after we had been campaigning for two years) suddenly decided to have a try at new types of marine craft for the R.A.F.: and with poetic justice pitched on me to conduct the trials. So imagine me as mainly a mechanic and tester, oilskin-covered, urging speed-boats up & down Southampton water through the rain & wind at noisy rates. In your sunshiny warmth a pleasant picture: here it is wintry-weather, and I am frozen and soaked, but interested. A job quite worth doing. Very difficult, engrossing, and very exhausting.

---

1 A correspondent writing from Montreal who claimed to have met Lawrence when he was a temporary naval officer on board H.M.S. *Hardinge*, during the Hejaz campaign. This letter was printed in facsimile in the *Montreal Daily Star* on 20 May 1935.

It paralyses all my hope of finishing that beastly *Odyssey* to time, nor can I read anything. By evening my eyes are raw with salt-water and rheumy with wind, & I go to bed. So I can only acknowledge receipt of your Heinemann & other poems, Laura's: and Len Lye's.[1] I have looked at them: skimmed them even, unworthily, and descended to *Tit-bits* and the *Happy Magazine*, which seem to go with speed-testing and water-sports.

All that you have promised me has come: and many letters from you both. I am an ingrate: yet I cannot help. Only in sheer necessity can I put pen to paper, except to report engine-performance, consumption, and hull design modifications.

Fortunately your last night's letter (I am in lodgings at Hythe, near Southampton, and shall be here till some time in May) provided such a necessity. On the back are notes for a Jules Verne aircraft of about 1980 A.D.[2] Too long for your need: rather technical perhaps. Only a rag, of course. Your letter did not give the date of your hero. If he is to be alive tomorrow, then perhaps his aircraft is a bit too advanced for him. If so make the motors petrol-electric. Cut up blade protrusion to .5 mm., double the landing speeds: reduce ceiling to 12000 m. make his speed what you think fit (I aim at sound: about 800 feet a second say 900 k.p.m.). This machine would have to be oxygenated at full speed & height, of course. The designer should be a Spanish lady, I think; the aircraft trade being by 2000 A.D. entirely in the hands of the modistes: or is your hero a strong silent man?

If the skit is too Verney, then cut out the technical terms till the paragraphs run: and delete the antennae like cat's whiskers and the rotor propulsion.

In great haste: just going down to try an entirely new *British* marine motor: something designed to challenge the U.S.A. predominance.

Yours
T.E.S.

What should I call you on an envelope? Señor?

University of Harvard/RGB

1 Graves and Laura Riding, now living together in Majorca (hence Lawrence's postscript), had transported their press with them and had produced several books of their own writings and also a collection of letters by their friend Len Lye, a New Zealander of lively and original mind whom they had come to know in London.
2 Graves and Riding were attempting to write together a novel devised specifically to catch the attention of Hollywood in the hope that it would be made into a successful — and lucrative — film, and Graves had written to Lawrence asking him to supply 'an autogyro of the future'. Lawrence obliged, as indicated here, providing the machine with, *inter alia*, 'beam-antennae' which would signal the presence of anybody within 300 metres — virtually an anticipation of radar. The book was published in 1932 under the title *No Decency Left* and with the distinguished authors disguised under the pseudonym 'Barbara Rich'. It was, however, a commercial failure and was not published in America.

S. C. ROLLS[1]

10.VI.31   Plymouth

Dear Rolls

I've been away for two months more, testing and tuning speed-boats for the R.A.F. We are getting a type of our own, with twin 'Invicta' engines: does 30 m.p.h. and is a good sea-boat.

Because of this work, I've been on day and night, pretty well, and haven't had letters sent after me: so your letter turned up on Saturday, when I came 'home' for a few days.

Your Northampton offer sounds good: only I have so little free time. I shall try and blow into you all the same somehow, this autumn, if only I get a month off, and the weather is possible. Last year I spent the whole month working on a foreign book-translation, money making: because it rained every day, and so I never got past London.

So prepare Mrs Rolls not to bang the door on an undersized object in scruffy blue uniform, if it arrives some odd autumn day, suddenly.

Yours

T. E. Shaw

Bodleian Reserve

LADY ASTOR

10.vi.31   Plymouth

Dear Peeress

Indeed and I was asleep & abed. How good of the Corporal to tell you! We had a hard $7\frac{1}{2}$ hours run down from Southampton here in our motor-boat, got in before 7 p.m., ate, made down our beds, & slept nobly till Sunday morning.

Now I hope to be at Mount Batten for a month. Ring me up (before 10 p.m., if possible) and we will meet.

No pillion. The new Traffic Act puts pillion-affording beyond modest means, and forces the love-sick to screw nasty iron-spring-things to their back mudguards.

1 S. C. Rolls had been Lawrence's driver in the last year of the Arabian campaign; he later described his experiences in *Steel Chariots in the Desert* (Cape, 1937), which includes a highly favourable account of Lawrence, whom he much admired. At the time of this letter he was Governing Director of the Imperial Autocar Company, Northampton, and Proprietor of the Rolls Motor Company, Northampton.

No speed-boat either, now. I have much testing of the R.A.F. boat still to do, and cannot put my own pet in the water till that is all done.

So you will have to make do with my undistinguished person, unaided except by an anglo-irish tongue.

Au revoir
T.E.S.

University of Reading

MR & MRS ERIC KENNINGTON
10.VI.31   Plymouth

Dear Celandine and K.

I've been away for months, testing and tuning speed-boats in South-ampton Water: but got back on Sunday to find the Hardy photographs waiting on my bed.[1]

It is superb: and better than that, *fine*. It holds somehow that strange effect of living within himself that always Hardy gave me. In bronze, when the over-statement of those excavated eyeballs will be corrected, the figure will be beautiful as well as a memorial.

I am so glad, for I liked old T.H. beyond reason, and the commission came to E.H.K. partly by my fault, and it was a terrible grind for him, and I felt sad about it: but now all ends for the best, with everybody.[2]

Excellent: excellent: excellent.

T.E.S.

Bodleian Reserve

---

1 i.e. photographs of Kennington's statue of Thomas Hardy which stands — or more correctly sits — at the top of the town in Dorchester, Dorset. It was unveiled by Sir James Barrie on 2 September 1931.
2 Kennington wrote at the side of the letter: 'No need for grief. I enjoyed the work enormously. E.H.K.'

MRS CHARLOTTE SHAW
26/VI/31

A point about Pte. Meek occurred to me last night, driving back from
Torquay as guide to an R.A.F. car: (or is it Meake?).[1] He wouldn't have
told the Colonel that he was his Intelligence Officer. He might have said 'I
do the Intelligence work' or more likely 'I am also your Intelligence Staff,
Sir' ... to which the Colonel would have responded by dwelling on the
Staff, probably, and forgetting the Intelligence. The Meeks of the world
are shy of describing themselves as officers.

It is so hard to judge by just one act of a play. Who could deduce *The
Apple Cart* from its 2nd Act? But I liked this new thing. It should get home.

Rifles at the ready: stand by·with the maroons: sights up to 2000, over
their heads, no hitting: contact. Charge your magazines (or cut-outs open,
if magazines were already charged). Ten rounds rapid fire ... something
like that.

Meek wouldn't have said illiterate ... at least he doesn't. His difficulty is
having not passed the educational exam. for promotion. He would probably
have said that he hadn't got his educational certificate. 'Not educationally
qualified' is written on my half-yearly return for promotion!

These squalid accuracies should not affect G.B.S. He must write so that
the audiences will comprehend.

Yesterday I launched my own boat and went off to Polperro, in Cornwall,
a 25 mile run. It was pleasant, sparkling sun and sea, out: and soft rain with
a choppy sea, home. The poor boat's first run for months. The other thing
has been smashed in two places (not irreparably) by her barbarian new
owners. A pity: she was such a good boat. Photo herewith.

I've had to promise the *Odyssey* in August, if possible. So that means a
month of leave upon it. If it goes well we shall be able to meet several
times. If not — then I shan't deserve privileges.

It was so good to see you restored: for that was what I felt. I had been
fearing that all this illness might have sapped you.

The Cadet College at Cranwell wanted G.B.S. to lecture to them! How
reputations change. Imagine him before a Service audience twenty years
ago. I laughed![2]

                                                            T.E.S.

British Library

1 Bernard Shaw had included a caricature figure in the Lawrence mould in his most recent
  play *Too True To Be Good*, under the name of Private Napoleon Alexander Trotsky
  Meek. Lawrence happily acted as adviser to G.B.S. in order to ensure the correct use of
  military vocabulary.
2 G.B.S. had been a vigorous opponent of the First World War and had incurred much
  unpopularity at the time, to the extent that his plays were no longer performed and he
  lost numerous friends.

MRS CHARLOTTE SHAW
15.VII.31

[...]
I have promised Lady Astor to take her for a trip in my motor boat this afternoon, if weather and sea permit. It looks showery, but is momently fine. I wonder if she will come and like it. You would, because water is so mobile, various and virginal. She will want only to go fast, I fear.

British Library

STANLEY BALDWIN[1]
27.VIII.31

Dear Mr. Baldwin
    I am not quick at saying the right thing on staircases — and yesterday I was thinking instead of how well Ronald Storrs would run Egypt. So I fear I let you imagine that the giving to you of a paltry book counterbalanced the years of pleasure you have given me. Six years to date, and nearly four more to run, I hope, before my time expires. The mouse is very much indebted to his lion, and feels it.
    No acknowledgement please....

Yoursincerely
T E Shaw

Cambridge University Library

1 Rt Hon. Stanley Baldwin (later Earl Baldwin of Bewdley) (1867–1947) had already been Prime Minister twice (1923, 1924–29) and would be Prime Minister again (1935–37). In 1925 he had personally sanctioned Lawrence's return to the Air Force (see pp. 281–2); hence the latter's profound gratitude to him, in recognition of which Lawrence had forwarded a copy of *Seven Pillars* to him through John Buchan in December 1926. The place and occasion of their apparently chance meeting on the day before this letter was written is difficult to establish, but by date it happened just two days after the formation of the 1931 National Government under Ramsay MacDonald in which Baldwin took the post of Lord President of the Council. If Lawrence sought to procure the appointment of Sir Ronald Storrs as High Commissioner for Egypt he did not succeed; Storrs, at this time Governor of Cyprus, was appointed Governor of Northern Rhodesia in 1932.

MRS CHARLOTTE SHAW
14.X.31   Mount Batten

Oh, I've got so many letters to do, all in a hurry. It seems a shame to begin with you, but unless I do, perhaps I won't reach the end and leisure for days yet: and you have waited a long time for a reply. I didn't have letters sent on to me, in doubt as to my movements, and hoping to get back soon.

I think it is going to be all right. The routine has stiffened, with the going of Group Captain Smith, and I, at least, feel less secure: but the present C.O. (Wing Commander Burling) shapes well. He will do, I fancy. I'm going to keep more to myself this time, as with the last C.O. I had too much to do.

Now I have nothing: nothing at all, except a very occasional proof from Emery Walker's (Sir E. is improving: gets into the garden!) and the typescript of Bertram Thomas' story of his trip across the Ruba el Khali of Arabia, which I am reading for him, trying to make marginal hints like yours in the *Seven Pillars.* So I hope to be able to read a lot this winter, and hear some gramophone music, and ride the bike, and drive the boat: it is rather fine to be owner of all one's 24 hours daily again.

About Hugo Wolf: you cannot have heard the right songs, or there must be some flaw in your singer. Schubert and water! Wolf seems to me far finer and rarer as a song-writer than anyone else I have ever heard. He has good poems to set, and sets them marvellously. I should very much like to hear all the records that H.M.V. do of him: and your subscription will be a great joy: but do please perfect it by yourself hearing these records, and enjoying them. I am sure Wolf is good, and you are bound to like him.

I'm hoping to get up to my cottage for this week-end. There are many good records, and I intend to hear some Handel. There was a good *Judas* on the wireless last night, from the Continent somewhere: and it reminded me of the *Messiah* at Miranshah.

Do you remember F/Lt. Smetham, our queer kindly officer at Miranshah? On Friday in London I met him. He is at the Air Ministry. He told me he has many of the Miranshah records with him, still. He bought them from the irks there, by exchanging for them such tunes as 'Do shrimps make good mothers?' which the irks preferred.

It is going to be so good, being on my own this winter. I hope there will be good books published. Are the G.B.S. musical and book-review volumes out yet? I am going to ask you for the loan of them, when possible. I can keep them in the office only, and therefore clean.

Last summer feels years ago: how is G.B.S.? And is there any news of *Too True To Be Good*?

(On Friday I was on the embankment near the Temple, just after seeing F/Lt. Smetham. A little bare-headed man rushed up and said 'Colonel

Lawrence?' 'Used to be', I replied. 'I want to photograph you'. 'But who are you?' I asked. 'My name is Howard Coster'.[1] 'A professional?' I asked. 'Yes, but this is for myself. I don't want to sell it or show it. You and Gandhi are the two people I want to take'. So I went along, for the joke of it, and he put me on a little chair, made me take my tunic off, and photographed me about a dozen times. A little shop in Essex Street. Rather a nice little stammering man, I thought. Works for *Vogue!* Had chased me for 5 minutes, afraid to speak!).

T.E.

British Library

BERTRAM THOMAS[2]
7.XII.31   Hythe

Dear Thomas

I got your doubled letter, via Plymouth and direct, and wired back that I'd get something done by the end of last week: and did. I hope you have had it.

A poor, lame thing: but the only reaction stirred in me by your book was a sense of thankfulness that it was alright. Misery, anger, indignation, discomfort — those conditions produce literature. Contentment — never. So there you are.

It will need your censorship: and the proper spelling of all the people's names: and anyhow it is a poor thing. But it will save Jonathan's face, at least.

I am sorry: but what writing ambitions and faculties I did possess have flickered out. Yet they told me yesterday, from London, that my last report on the 8/28 dinghy engine we are testing was altogether the goods. So I am consoled. The bow still has a string.

Yours sincerely
T.E.S.

We probably stay here another week — but everything is very uncertain

Bodleian Reserve

1 Howard Coster was a leading photographer; he had opened a studio in London in 1926, specialising in men's portraiture. He had served in the First World War in the photographic section of the R.A.F.
2 See letter to Edward Marsh of 10 March 1931, p. 451. Lawrence had written a Foreword to Thomas's book *Arabia Felix*, which was published by Jonathan Cape.

HON. EDWARD ELIOT
7.xii.31   Hythe Southampton

Dear Eliot

I have been meaning for months to write to you, but some ghost stood between us. Probably it was fear of a talk to your girls' school. How would I dare not refuse that? To one person I can talk honestly. To two with some circumspection. To three only from behind a mask. To four hesitatingly. To five in words of one syllable. To six only yes or no. Seven means silence.

How many are the daughters? If it is less than seven may I, in apology, come along one afternoon and tell them that I cannot talk, have never tried to talk, will not, I hope, ever try to talk? Hang it all, I am a contented being, wanting nothing for myself or anybody else, & contentment is uncreative. It is a little folding of the hands for sleep.

As I wrote that paragraph I grew aware that I do want something. One F/Sgt. Hutchinson of Mount Batten fell overboard one night between us & Plymouth and was drowned. As the accident was in his own time, not on duty, the R.A.F. disclaimed responsibility: which is all very well, but did not un-widow him, or get rid of Mrs H's two, young daughters. We subscribed about £30, which has helped. We appealed to the R.A.F. Memorial Fund, which sent her £5 in two helpings. She has a widow's pension of 18/– a week from the Free State Government. (She lives in Dublin): but that is great penury, in Dublin. A decent woman.

We want her to get about £20 a year for the next ten years, by when her children will be grown. I saw Col. Birch, who is secretary to the R.A.F. Memorial Fund: and he says he can't make a regular grant: but would, if his Dublin branch would apply regularly, & if we would find him £20 a year, subscribed to his general fund.

Would it inconvenience the Trust to pay £20 each year into the general fund? I do not know how it would square with your discretion and the deed. Will you let me know? Mount Batten have squared the matter for 1931, all right: but it is a small station, and we cannot go on much longer finding funds.

I am sorry to trouble you. I had expected old Birch to agree, but he says his income is overdrawn: and was shocked when I said that all the best people and countries were drawing on capital, now-a-days.

                                                    Yours
                                                    T.E.S.

This letter goes to Robin,[1] as I cannot remember more than the 2nd. & 3rd. names of your firm as it used to be before you moved. I am in Hythe

1 Robin Buxton.

for a while yet, testing a new R.A.F. motor boat & engine, but shall be back at Plymouth before Christmas.

Bodleian Reserve

GEOFFREY DAWSON
22nd March 1932   Myrtle Cottage Hythe Southampton

Dear G.D.

Are you still editing the national newspaper? [1] I think so, from a copy I saw some weeks ago. It felt correct.

Today it struck me that as editor you might be interested in the new type of motor boat that we have been producing lately for the R.A.F. I'm partly the guilty cause of them — after a big crash a year ago in Plymouth Sound, which showed me convincingly that we had nothing in the Service fit to help marine aircraft in difficulties. Nor could the Navy supply even an idea of the type of craft we needed. The Navy is rather Nelsonic in its motor-boats. I suppose it knows something about steam. I don't, anyway, so I give them credit for it. In petrol engines they are a wash-out: and they are not yet aware of what the States and Italy have done to improve the breed of fast motor-boat-hulls.

So the R.A.F. (partly, as I confessed above, at my prompting) went into the science of it, and have had produced for them, by the Power Boat works of Hythe, here, an entirely new type of seaplane tender. They are 37 ft. boats, twin engined, doing 30 m.p.h. in all weathers, handy, safe and very cheap. Many of their features are unique. They cost less than any boats we have ever bought before.

All this has been done through the admiralty, in the teeth of its protests and traditions. Now the boats are finished, the sailors are beginning to take notice, & wonder if there isn't something in it.

Why don't you send your marine man down to see them? On Tuesday and Wednesday next (29 & 30) we have ten to a dozen of them cavorting about Southampton water all day. If he rang me up at the British Power Boat Works (Hythe 102) I would have him picked up at Southampton, and given a show. My name, of course, not to be mentioned. Robertson, the publicity king of the Air Ministry, is prepared for the publication of details. The ordinary press is only looking for stunts: but these boats are

1 i.e. *The Times.*

novel, and really interesting. Their performance is extraordinary. What about it? It deserves notice and serious criticism.[1]

It's short notice: but on Thursday 31st March we distribute the fleet to all our coastal stations. I hope to take the furthest of them, to Scotland, myself. A four-day cruise: which is my reward for a year's hard work.

Yours ...
T E Shaw

Bodleian Library

ARTHUR HALL[2]

15.IV.32   Myrtle Cottage Hythe Southampton

Dear Brum

It is too late, now, for your kid's christening. The poor little creature will be fixed and named. Poor little beast.

I have been away for many weeks. These boats were finished and had to go out to Coastal stations, and I went with one and another of them, showing the new crews how they worked. In the end I got as far as Donibristle in Scotland, near the Firth of Forth bridge. 700 miles of a journey, it was, and very rough weather. They are good boats. At Donibristle they kept me another fortnight, explaining things, and then I came back by train. There are two more sorts of boats to get built.

How is the kid? and Mrs. Hall? I hope all well. I couldn't have been a god father [sic] anyhow, for I'm no child-maker. Life isn't very gay, I fancy, and I shouldn't like to feel that I'd brought anyone else into the world to have such times as I've had, and still have. You are happier, perhaps: I have found nothing to justify my staying on, and yet one can't go. It's a sad state — but a fellow ought to keep his troubles to himself, I suppose.

Best of luck
Yours Shaw

Bodleian Reserve

---

1 Dawson accepted Lawrence's suggestion and sent down not his Marine but his Aeronautical Correspondent to cover the trials. See Lawrence's letter of thanks to Dawson opposite.

2 Former Aircraftman, R.A.F.: from Birmingham, hence 'Brum'.

GEOFFREY DAWSON
21.IV.32   Hythe Southampton

Dear G.D.

Your aeronautical expert, Shepherd, wrote for us two quite admirable articles — or at least I thought them quite admirable. I hope they have not got you into trouble with anyone. The boats are good and deserved notices. They have had them, good measure and good stuff, and that's over. I am most grateful to you for your interest.

I wonder just how S. did his writing, because he seemed to take no notes, just looked calmly at them & listened easily — yet all the stuff came out in print, admirably expressed and arranged. It struck me as a little better than most reporting I've met.

You said 'pay a visit if in London': and I did: but the chair was empty, and *The Times* being commanded from one of its flanks. I'm a seldom visitor but will try again.

                                    Yours
                                    T E Shaw

Bodleian Library

SIR WILLIAM ROTHENSTEIN
22.4.32   Myrtle Cottage Hythe Southampton.

Dear Sir William? (a)[1]
Dear Rothenstein? (b)
(a) Too stiff, surely.
(b) Too familiar, from an airman to a Civil Servant.

I'm very sorry that your letter got no answer. I never got it, either.* I've been in Hythe now for nearly a year, testing motor boats or watching over their being built. A difficult, occupying job; that I am glad to do, for it needed doing and no-one else in the R.A.F. had my experience to do it. But I should prefer less of it.

As for letters, by all means use them as you wish, tempering your freedom with discretion. One doesn't write letters for publication, and so uses more licence in speech than is polite. If I call poor Orpen a squirt of a painter, for instance, then forgive it and suppress it. I can rely on you for anything of the sort. It is good of you to write and ask. Most people do not bother! I'm sure your writing will have style.

1 Rothenstein had been knighted in 1931.

Books have not lain much in my way, lately. We work in the boat-yard all the daylight hours, and when dark comes I am tired, more inclined to read the *Happy Magazine* than Plato. So I compromise by reading neither, and am the better mechanic therefor.

Homer? a pot boiler, long ago done with. When, or if, it will be published is not my concern. The Greek isn't very good, I fancy: and my version is frankly poor. Thin, arty, self-conscious stuff, the *Odyssey*. I believe the *Iliad* to be a great poem — or to have fragments of a great poem embedded in it, rather. But the *Odyssey* is pastiche and face powder.

Yours,
T. E. Shaw.

★ I suspect there being a packing case of letters awaiting me in Plymouth, to which I may return in July.

Bodleian Reserve

K. W. MARSHALL[1]

6.IX.32   Mount Batten Plymouth

[...] I had no letters sent on to me. So when I got back there was a mound of them on the table waiting. Into that I have dug a little. I hope there are no more of yours to find: for already I have 30 to answer — and God knows when I'll finish, if ever.

Don't worry about the fate of an odd letter or two. My letters ceased being personal seven years ago, when an American magazine advertised a batch as 'characteristic products of a remarkable adventurer.' That cured me of writing sense.

I have not read anything except the *Happy Magazine* for months: but in Plymouth I may have time, again. That will be noble.

[...]

Bodleian Reserve

---

1 A bookseller whom Lawrence befriended and who occasionally stayed at Clouds Hill. Later a member of the publishing house of Boriswood Ltd.

HENRY WILLIAMSON
6.IX.32   Myrtle Cottage Hythe Southampton

Dear H.W.

Another year gone, and us still wide apart, despite
one perfectly good Silver Eagle Alvis, and one
        „   „   Brough.

I spend my days & nights working on motor boats, still, and chase all
round the English coast after them or in them. Web-footed now, and quack
before meal times.

I have not written to anyone till tonight for months. Now I have written
sixteen letters. That is not correspondence but massacre, and I am ashamed.

Likewise I have read almost nothing: and only by the pile of letters
awaiting reply can I gauge how far I lag behind human decency. As for
books, there stand two shelves of them. How can I ever get a free mind
again.

As for writing books, myself: I have done one. 'Handbook to the Class
of 37 ft 6 ins. RAF. Motor Boat', 30,000 words of the packiest stodge. It
will not be included in my collected works.

I hope you are not more penniless than the rest of us: nor unhappy.

Yours
                                                        T E Shaw

Bodleian Reserve

MRS CHARLOTTE SHAW
16.IX.32   Plymouth

There: I am 'home' again — but for the moment only. Tomorrow I go on
leave and shall get to London in a few days: and then call on you. *Very*
tired again.

About W. B. Yeats' letter. You know, it staggers me that I should
seriously be considered in such company.[1] All the best Irish, except AE, I
fancy: and many of the not-so-good, too. I don't think any other country
of the size would produce such a list.

I would like it, because it is a gesture on my part, that I am Irish: and I
would like to think that. My work from the *Seven Pillars* onward, probably

1 The leading Irish poet and playwright W. B. Yeats (1865–1939) had written to Lawrence
to inform him that he had been nominated to the new Irish Academy of Letters, by virtue
of being the son of an Irishman.

does not justify my joining that company. My reputation probably does. So on the whole I ought to say Yes to W.B. and to thank him for an unexpected and extraordinary compliment. Will you write for me?[1] I should be troubled in writing to him: for I have regarded him always as an exquisite and unattainable poet. He passes the test of the bigger people that his later work is more interesting, if less melodious, than his early work. Those *Tower* poems were splendid.[2]

It feels so odd that he should think of me as a writer. Disturbing: for I felt so sure, as time passed without any impulse to write: that I was right in thinking those books more or less accident. I know, of course, that I have the art of stringing words, and all the tricks of writing: but there is nothing to say. And while there is so much to do, it seems stupid to shut one's hands to that, and go on staring about to find something to write.

I am good at doing, too: despite their sending me away from Hythe. Merit did not enter into the question. Today I put right a boat here.

It will be good to see you in London again. Let us do another *Too good* .... and take the *Odyssey* Ms. to Wilson.

                                                            T.E.S.

British Library

GEOFFREY CUMBERLEGE[3]

12.X.32   R.A.F. Mount Batten Plymouth

Dear Mr. Cumberledge [*sic*]

Since your letter came I have seen Bruce Rogers — seen him twice in his last days here, for he has sailed for the States — and we have discussed generally the American edition of the *Odyssey*. Incidentally he showed me a suggested page of it.

I am aware of the importance of the money side of it to B.R. and will allow anything to be done to favour it — short of having an English public edition. Books are miseries, and if I could, there would be no more of

---

1 Mrs Shaw duly wrote for him, and Lawrence shortly afterwards received the following reply: 'Your acceptance of our nomination has given me great pleasure, for you are among my chief of men, being one of the few charming and gallant figures of our time, & as considerable in intellect as in gallantry & charm. I thank you/Yours/W. B. Yeats.' (*Letters to T. E. Lawrence*, p. 213)

2 *The Tower* was a collection of poems published in 1928.

3 Geoffrey Cumberlege (1891–1979) was then Managing Director of the New York branch of the Oxford University Press, which published an unlimited edition of the *Odyssey* in the United States.

them. I hope never to put out anything in England again. The States don't matter to me: I do not care what they do or say. Nor will there be any blow-back on this side. English booksellers are stiff-necked. They do not import American books: and if they do, the public refuse them. So unless someone actually advertises the thing over here, there will be no demand: and imports can be checked by Walker's, as an infringement of his copyright!

I have dealt with the royalty question direct with B.R. as you suggested. He bought out Colonel Isham's interest, which was a good act: but not immediately profitable to me, for had the burden been Isham's there would have been no name of translator on your edition! In my contract for doing the english version I secured myself expressly against all association with any edition of the book.

So I want you to realise that in accepting the use of my name upon your edition I am sacrificing what I regard as very important. I do not want you or anyone to imagine that I have let B.R. down. He understood from the beginning that I was opposed to any mention of myself. Had the version been done in my two years in India, and promptly printed, no curiosity about it would ever have arisen.

I shall be much more careful and exacting upon any future occasion — unless this experience teaches me to prevent future occasions!

Yours
T E Shaw

Worcester College Oxford

SIR EDWARD ELGAR
12.X.32   Mount Batten Plymouth

Dear Sir Edward

In the one week I have had letters from you and from W. B. Yeats — and it is a little difficult for an ordinary mortal to say the happy things when public monuments around him come suddenly to speech. I have liked most of your music — or most that I have heard — for many years: and your 2nd Symphony hits me between wind and water. It is exactly the mode that I most desire, and so it moves me more than anything else — of music — that I have heard. But thousands of people share my liking for your music, and with better reason for they know more about it than I do: so this doesn't justify the kindness of the Shaws in bringing me with them that afternoon.[1] The chance of meeting you is just another of the benefits that have accrued to me from knowing G.B.S., who is a great adventure.

There are fleas of all grades; and so I have felt the awkward feeling of having smaller creatures than myself admiring me. I was so sorry to put you to that awkwardness: but it was inevitable. You have had a lifetime of achievement, and I was a flash in the pan. However I'm a very happy flash, and I am continually winning moments of great enjoyment. That Menuhin-Concerto is going to be a pleasure to me for years: and the news of your 3rd Symphony was like a week's sunlight. I do hope you will have enough enthusiasm left to finish it. There are crowds of us waiting to hear it again and again.

Probably it feels quaint to you to hear that the mere setting eyes upon you is a privilege: but by that standard I want to show you how good an afternoon it was for me, in your house.

Yours sincerely
T. E. Shaw

DG

E. M. FORSTER

22.X.32   Plymouth

Dear E.M.F.

I am sorry about this. I cannot send you a copy of the Emery-Walker printed *Odyssey*[2] that I translated. I know it is only a pot boiler, and the *Odyssey* is not much good, anyhow: but it felt right to give it you.

And now I can't. The things cost twelve guineas, and I got only a handful of them: and the people to disappoint are those who know enough to forgive a slight.

If it had had anything of mine in it, you would have had it necessarily: but this second-hand English is no more personal than the filling in of an income-tax form.

I hope you are afloat and engaged. Lately my hull has been not too fortunate. A dose of fever and cold: and a sense of exhaustion. Give me a few weeks and I will be well again.

---

1 On 2 September 1932 Lawrence had gone with the Shaws to Elgar's home in Worcester to hear the test pressings of the recording of Elgar's Violin Concerto, with the 15-year-old Yehudi Menuhin as soloist.

2 Lawrence was referring to the English limited edition of the *Odyssey* of 530 copies.

Lately I was sent the D.H.L. letters.[1] His ungenerousness astonishes me. I can hardly believe that any 800 pages of my writing would fail to include at least a half-word of satisfaction at something someone had written or done.

[...]

I am so sorry about that *Odyssey*: but I just can't put down so much money, now.

Yours
T.E.S.

Bodleian Reserve

GEOFFREY CUMBERLEGE

14.XI.32[2]   Plymouth

Dear Cumberlege

Thank you for your letter of Nov. 2. I am glad you and B.R. are happy concerning the U.S.A. editions of the *Odyssey*. They tell me the Emery Walker edition is going off fairly well — at least it has paid expenses.

So far as I am concerned there is no objection to the U.S.A. edition being sold in India — or in any other British possession or dominion; I live in England, and the ban applies only to the U.K. & Free State of Ireland. If your press will do its best to restrict the British sales (and imports) it may do its worst in the rest of the earth![3]

Yours
T E Shaw.

Worcester College Oxford

MRS THOMAS HARDY

3.xii.32   Mount Batten Plymouth

Dear Mrs. Hardy

I am sorry that your copy[4] should have got muddled, somehow. One

---

1 *The Letters of D. H. Lawrence*, edited by Aldous Huxley, published 1932.
2 Lawrence dated this letter 16.XI.32, but the postmark on its envelope — Plymouth Devon Nov 14 1.30 PM — justifies the date as printed.
3 The English edition was not only limited but also anonymous.
4 Of the *Odyssey*.

has now gone direct to Max Gate, and you should find it there as soon as you return.

It is not in any way a remarkable work. As translation it is faithful, within the limits I lay down in a little postscript to the book. The English is very schoolmastery — by which I mean that relative clauses, prepositions and particles are correctly placed. There is too much inversion — twisting of sentences to compress the English into little more space than the much more concise Greek. There are some colloquialisms: no slang, I hope; if we call slang those colloquialisms which not everybody yet understands and uses.

As production the book is a fine example of its kind: and you will like it, if you like the kind. I am rather neutral towards the whole effort. Everybody dislikes his last book, of course: but this is only a pot-boiler, and little intensity went to it. I did it as well as I could, of course, but did not feel like signing it. So I have not marked your copy. I will, if you particularly wish it, of course.

The money is being useful. There were wood-beetles eating the roof of Clouds Hill: and it is now being doctored and sprayed. That is the first object. Then the kitchen downstairs is to be cemented and turned into a book-room, with shelves. I may ask your Parsons expert (I have lost his name & address!) to do the shelving. The third object, if the money lasts, will be a bath and hot-water boiler. How tickled old Homer would have been! He used to enjoy his hot baths, anyway.

I am sorry they went to China: but it was inevitable. They are best there, while they feel it is a duty. I wish they could grow out of that: for my mother, at least, is not fitted for overseas living. Also they were happy in the cottage. Perhaps they will come back?

Yours sincerely
T E Shaw

University of Texas

HARLEY GRANVILLE-BARKER
23.XII.32   Plymouth

Paris is pleasant, you say. My longest experience of it was in 1919, during the Peace Conference. So I shall not ever think of it as pleasant.

And I can't come to your *Place* and place there,[1] because the Air Force prevents, and the last time (1921) I wanted to cross France they refused me

---

1 A pun on the Granville-Barkers' Paris address — the *Place des Etats-Unis*.

a visa. It is unfortunate to have the name of a spy!

[...]

Don't read the *Odyssey* aloud to Mrs. G.B., please. She would die of it, and both of us suffer a sense of loss, as Homer would say. It must have been nice to live in a literary period when even a platitude was a discovery, and clichés were waiting to be made. He was very successful in both these ways, I think.

The *Odyssey* to me represents — a bath, a hot-water plant and bookshelves in my cottage. So I have no regrets: but it is not one of my collected works. You were unwise to buy it.

I'm glad to hear that Shakespeare approaches vol. iii[1] and finality. What will you do afterwards? After having had a period of acting, one of production, one of play-writing, one of criticism ... what next?

And me? Oh, I'm going to retire to Dorsetshire, to my cottage, and neglect its garden.

Yours
T. E. Shaw

Bodleian Reserve[2]

E. H. R. ALTOUNYAN[3]
9.1.33   Mount Batten

Dear E.A.,

Your letter (I'm glad you are still in England: to save me reproaches for keeping your article too long) is the sort that the most gratified writer alive would yet thank you for: and I don't feel very proud of my writing. So you can imagine how it pleased me. By all means keep the fat book so long as it suits you. That copy is a collection of spoiled sheets, cut and pressed into smallness, and usually it belongs to Mrs. Bernard Shaw — but she is away on a world cruise with G.B.S.

What the muezzin said was, I fancy — and after fifteen years it is probably fancy — 'wa el besharra[4] ... No English word or phrase even would

---

1 i.e. Volume III of Granville-Barker's *Prefaces to Shakespeare*.
2 Also published in Granville-Barker's *Eight Letters from T.E.L.* (1939) and in *Granville-Barker and his Correspondents* (1987).
3 Ernest Altounyan, who had first met Lawrence in his Carchemish days, was a doctor in Aleppo where his father had founded the Altounyan Hospital which was famous throughout the Levant. He was a great admirer of Lawence and later wrote a poetic work *Ornament of Honour* in his memory.
4 See *Seven Pillars of Wisdom*, Chap. CXX.

translate it, so I paraphrased in his spirit rather than his letter. I only wish that 'ya ahl el Sham' had been better rendered than by 'people of Damascus'. The Arabic 'ahl' is a fine word. The worst of being a habitual translator is that one gets in the way of trying to squeeze every sponge dry — and so few authors really *intend* all the contents of their sponges. Words get richer every time they are deliberately used ... but only when deliberately used: and it is hard to be conscious of each single word, and yet not at the same time self-conscious.

I mustn't slip again into the technique of writing. Writing has been my inmost self all my life, and I can never put my full strength into anything else. Yet the same force, I know, put into action upon material things would move them, make me famous and effective. The everlasting effort to write is like trying to fight a feather-bed. In letters there is no room for strength.

Am I morbid? Only with people inclined to it, I fancy. By myself I do not brood at all, having so much to do. That vision of the wholeness of life is not a visitor to me, but always there, like a background to the diggings and the war and the R.A.F. Wherefore I get a sense of the sameness and smallness of everything, including us: and so I would not voluntarily put another into my place. Too much glory or none? Why I think the nones, who eat and drink and chase their appetites, are wholesomer. And I like cats and camels, therefore.

This is a silly letter. So was yours. I liked it, too. English people don't write about the verities as a rule, for the good reason that such subjects exceed us, and we look foolish in their shadow.

The two studies of the Euphrates valley are exactly in place in my cottage, and perfect there. I cannot choose between them, or consider sending one back. Call them lost to you, both! I am most glad to have them, for Carchemish was a happy place, and they form a link.

Would you be so interested in me as a writer — not a visioner of life. but just a penman — as to wade through my next-after-the-*Seven-Pillars* book? It has remained in typescript, and is a study of the R.A.F. recruiting depot. Not much glory, but life, in its way. It is short, rather mannered also but better, as writing, than the earlier book, I think.

Yours

T.E.S.

DG

B. H. LIDDELL HART
Whitmonday '33[1]

Dear L-H

I have read this twice, once to get its idea, and once with a pencil in hand.[2] It has been a queer experience — like going back, in memory, to school — for by myself (though with far less knowledge, and hesitatingly) I had trodden all this road before the war. It is a very good little book: modest, witty and convincing. You realise, of course, that you are swinging the pendulum, and that by 1960 it will have swung too far!

So far as I can see strategy is eternal, & the same and true: but tactics is the ever-changing language through which it speaks. A general can learn as much from Belisarius as from Haig — but not a soldier.[3] Soldiers have to know their means.

I can't write an introduction: none is necessary. Your sub-title should be 'a tract for the times.'

Yours
T E S

Fitzwilliam Museum Cambridge

ALAN DAWNAY[4]

16.VI.33   119 Clarence Road East Cowes I. of W.

Extravagant person. Your letter tore across the Solent in a speed-boat from Hythe, and I was 'phoned to meet and collect. Fortunately the Post Office is next the landing stage, so you had a quick answer.

Only one thing tempted me. 'They will require the manuscript ...' I saw myself approach the mike and mellifluously say 'The B.B.C. caused me to deposit with them the text of my possible delivery upon Feisal

1 Whit Monday was 5 June in 1933.
2 Lawrence was referring to Liddell Hart's book *The Ghost of Napoleon*.
3 Belisarius was a Byzantine general who had achieved success by employing hit-and-run tactics involving small units at small cost; Sir Douglas Haig (later Earl Haig of Bemersyde), British Commander-in-Chief in the First World War from December 1915, had won (eventual) success by the use of massed forces at high cost.
4 The background to this letter is that King Feisal of Iraq was about to pay an official visit to Britain and that Alan Dawnay had just been appointed Controller of Programmes at the BBC, though he had not yet taken up his post. The BBC archives have no record of any formal approach being made to Lawrence at this time, so it is very possible that Dawnay himself decided to sound out whether Lawrence would be prepared to commemorate the event with a radio talk.

tonight. I have forgotten that stupidity. Here goes for what I really think
...' And then the red light would pop out and the announcer would say
'Now we will have a short programme of gramophone records ...'

That would have been worth fifteen guineas, but not the sack from the
R.A.F. Remember that I am *not* (yet) a private person: but when I am, my
hat, I'll be private.

Upon withdrawal to Clouds Hill I will go through my address book and
to each name send a printed card 'To announce cessation of correspondence'.
That will also be worth fifteen guineas.

I hope you do the Feisal touch. If you see the dear man remember me
very kindly to him. Say I am very proud of having helped his beginning.

Yours
T.E.S

Bodleian Reserve

ALAN DAWNAY

30.VI.33   119 Clarence Road East Cowes Isle of Wight

How did Feisal-broadcast go? Did you do it? I hope so. They say he is
clean-shaven now: that must make a difference.[1]

Reason for writing 'Do you recall anyone named B. Ley Roberts on
our staff in Arabia?' I don't. I have asked Goslett, too. Gent is now in
business in Cairo and boasts his connection as a reference.

Daily Mail states that I have left the R.A.F. Improbable!

Yours
T.E.S.

Sorry for bothering you: a card saying 'Never heard of him' would be
sufficient answer, if true.

Bodleian Reserve

---

1 Apparently there was no broadcast about Feisal at this time. There was, however, a
broadcast later that year on 8 September, a brief obituary of him by Lord Allenby, Feisal
having died in Switzerland at the age of 50.

MRS CHARLOTTE SHAW
23.VIII.33   13 Birmingham St Southampton

There, I have worked here and watched August slipping away, often saying to myself 'It will be easier soon' — and instead the work piles up. We are in arrears now, and by the end of September we are to finish the first twelve boats.

Of course the work is good, and I lose myself in it, for the while: but not always. If I had a magic carpet and could instantly move myself — but even when time permits it, the twin enemy, space, contains my gross body. They sent me to Kent the first week-end, to talk boats with Sir Philip Sassoon — half an hour of business in two days of a visit — and I must go to him again this week-end. Once I went to London. Five days in Bridlington. One at Farnham . . . so it lengthens out.

It is, perhaps, a little excuse that there is no real play: nothing that wants any of the audience to do anything after they go out. But the plays never mattered at Malvern: it was the hills, and the quiet light across that great plain towards the river, and something uplifted in the spirits of yourself and G.B.S. Also this year you talked of Elgar, and the newspapers said that he was ill.

If you see him will you present my constant pleasure in his music, whether human rendered or from my box? Nobody who makes sounds gets so inside my defences as he does, with his 2nd Symphony and Violin Concerto. Say that if the 3rd Symphony has gone forward from those, it will be a thrill to ever so many of us. He was inclined to grumble that the rewards of making music were not big, in the bank-book sense: but by now he should be seeing that bank-books will not interest him much longer. I feel more and more, as I grow older, the inclination to throw everything away and live on air. We all allow ourselves to need too much.

[. . .]

Liddell Hart has (in haste) finished his book on me.[1] Cape spoilt it, by asking for less military consideration and more life. So he only tells again the three-times-told story, and I am sick of my divagations. When one acts, one has a reason, or instinct, and is privately satisfied. But the past gets all snailed over when these others try to explain it.

I hope Malvern has been good. This has been the best summer weather of my memory: an abiding marvel, the way the sun has shone and the wind blown warm. I have loved all the background of my days, and swum often, and worked hard. Is G.B.S. still at work revising that playlet and play? Will he play them, or just print them and let the stage go hang? It is a problem, to be an elder dramatist.

1 Published by Cape in 1934 as '*T. E. Lawrence' in Arabia and After.*

I met H. G. Wells in the train three weeks ago. 'You' I said rashly 'probably want to write no more stories now'. He replied 'I dare not: my reputation is too great to risk a failure: and one writes a good story only by writing three or four bad ones, and till the public has read them the good does not appear from the bad. So I can only afford to write histories and things'. There is something behind that: probably an excuse for having grown up.

I hope you are well and happy.

T.E.S.

British Library

MRS CHARLOTTE SHAW
31.VIII.33　　　　　　　　　　　　　　　13 Birmingham St Southampton

Yesterday was a DAY. At 1.45 p.m. water, driven by the smallest ram ever installed anywhere, began to flow into my cottage at Clouds Hill. The pipes are a hundred yards long: the ram was turned on at 10 a.m. without public ceremony: it worked steadily for hour after hour: and at 1.45, as I have said the water arrived at its destination. The single, oldest and only inhabitant of Clouds Hill took off his R.A.F. cap with a simple gesture (to avoid knocking it against the roof-beam) and collected the first pint in a pint mug. It arrived in four minutes, and the S.O. and O. inhabitant then drank it. The taste was of red lead and galvanised iron: but the quality was wet, indubitably: and they say that in four weeks the taste will be unalloyed water. I hope so: for otherwise my drinking water will come from the spring by bucket![1]

If a pint in four minutes seems to you little, reflect that it works all day and all night at that rate. It is copious; excessive. Indeed I have laid down a spill-pipe, which will feed the kitchen of my neighbour, Mrs. Knowles, with my surplus. Both of us are henceforward endowed with running water. We feel so rich and happy.

Now for the bath.[2] It has arrived, but must wait for fixing till its boiler, cistern and burner are in order. Some date in October, I hope, there will be the sound of a hot bath at Clouds Hill. I shall feel like telegraphing you the news. Imagine that a mere translation of the *Odyssey* does me all this good!

1 David Garnett described the ram as 'one of the most admirable of the ingenuities of Clouds Hill'.
2 The manufacturer of the bath was the former supply and ordnance officer at Akaba, Raymond Goslett.

News of my mother, after a long interval. Well, and gently busy with her house and living. My brother better in health and not overworked. The country round about not peaceful enough for anybody's liking. I hope they are not put to anxiety or hardship.

Please tell G.B.S. of my house-wetting. It is an achievement, to have made so small a ram. The parent spring only gives half a gallon a minute: so a quarter of pint per minute is an excellent product. Nice things, rams.

T.E.S.

British Library

HIS MOTHER
27.IX.33   Southampton

[Poor Arnie. You are inclined to persecute him, you know. People brought up together, when full grown, rather resent their relatives. I think Arnie does not want to see too much of us, and the best treatment for that is to see too little. When he feels safe — sure that we are not trying to 'get at' him — he will lose that nervousness. If any of us really needed anything, we would help each other. Till then, do let each manage his own affairs!

I saw Mrs Fontana[1] a few times during this summer. She was made unhappy by Guido's death,[2] for it was a hidden consumption, that she had never suspected. Her daughter Tacita still exists, and has gone to London to study art. Guido was married and had lately lived in S. America. Mrs Fontana has just enough to live on, but is not employing herself well, and feels aimless. A nervous, shrinking person, not easy to help. She sent messages to you, remembering you distinctly.]

Bodleian Reserve

MRS CHARLOTTE SHAW
9.XII.33   13 Birmingham St Southampton

I wish it were not so cold: I can only hold the pen sideways in my fingers, and that makes sprawly writing. Also the Indian Ink is frozen. I hope you are still warm in London. This goes there, on the chance.

Nancy says you are better: not much, I fancy, in this weather. The

1 Widow of the former British Consul in Aleppo, R. A. Fontana. (See p. 505.)
2 Guido: her son.

English are a tough people, but England kills them off. By the way, what are people to do if the Free State cuts away from England? If only de Valera was an admirable man; but that underhung jaw and the fishy eyes repel me.

I hope *On the Rocks*[1] still marches strongly. Next week, about Thursday night, I am half-promised a visit to London. This week was half-promised, too, but failed. Is there any difficulty of getting a seat? You know that I like to provide for myself.

The real motive of this letter, however, isn't altruism: something happened to me last night when I lay awake till 5. You know I have been moody or broody for years, wondering what I was at in the R.A.F., but unable to let go — well last night I suddenly understood that it was to write a book called 'Confession of Faith', beginning in the cloaca at Covent Garden, and embodying *The Mint* and much that has happened to me before and since as regards the air. Not the conquest of the air, but our entry into the reserved element, 'as lords that are expected, yet with a silent joy in our arrival'. It would include a word on Miranshah and Karachi, and the meaning of speed, on land and water and air. I see the plan of it. It will take long to do. Clouds Hill, I think. In this next and last R.A.F. year I can collect feelings for it. The thread of the book will only come because it spins through my head: there cannot be any objective continuity — but I think I can make it whole enough to do. *The Mint*, you know, was meant as notes for something (smaller) of the sort. I wonder if it will come off. The purpose of my generation, that's really it.

Anyway I shall tell no one else: so Liddell Hart will not get after it! Three years hence we'll know.

                                                        T.E.S.

British Library

LADY ASTOR
11.xii.33   13 Birmingham Street Southampton

Mi Vykowntess
    Let me qualify the 'any retired Colonel'.[2] I should have said 'any Colonel who has retired into the R.A.F.'
    I cannot answer your letters because I cannot read them all! They are monologues, too, like conversations with our dear good Queen. Only by

1 G.B.S.'s latest play.
2 In a letter to Lady Astor dated 1 June 1933. Lawrence had described himself as pottering about Clouds Hill 'like any other retired Colonel'.

grace of the headed notepaper do I know whence they come. I cannot answer your wires, because often I have not a shilling to spare. Your wires are gloriously legible.

'A very tall dark woman'. Let me think over my recent past. I have never met Lady Londonderry. He is very tall, but not dark, I think. Mrs. Gubbay (met at Lympne) is dark and a woman: but not very tall, judged by myself: and you are little smaller than me. Mrs. Lionel Curtis is tall, but always makes a brown impression on me. Mrs. Scott-Paine (wife of the boat-builder with whom I work here) is tall: but I don't know what colour she would wash to. The present outward decoration is magenta and cream. Who else was there? Ah! a Lady Juliet Duff, relic of a generation before your own. She is very tall, but white: and there is the Mrs. Siegfried Sassoon-to-be.[1] I think she was dark, but, I seldom photograph women: nor do I know her name. Probably it's her you are after. She lives near Christchurch with her mother, in an Edwardian-Gothic house. Do not suspect us of an affair. Siegfried is a better man than me, and she was honestly in love with him, and in terror of her life of proving inadequate. I tried to cheer her up, without being foolishly optimistic. I liked the foolhardy creature. Fancy taking on S.S.

Overleaf you talk of the tall dark woman with her shiny broad mouth, and hope that she will make me happy. I hope so, too, if it has to be — but only a walrus has such a mouth, I think. May I postpone the swimming lessons till next summer? Warn me when she comes! And warm me!

I saw Mrs. Shaw a fortnight ago. She has since been ill. So be glad I did not call and find you in.

I hope the play will go well. They were hurt by *Too True*'s short run. Odd how men like repeating their successes — and women their failures!

Your last page contains the word Plymouth — but I never get there now. Southampton always. I also see the word 'Bobbie' twice.[2] Him I have yet to meet. I hope he is well and open again.

Your last ominous sentence is 'How <u>much</u> do you see of this tall d— woman?' That might be more happily expressed, perhaps. Awful thought. Does 'd—' mean what it usually does? Is she Lady Portarlington?[3] Help!

T.E.S.

University of Reading

1 Siegfried Sassoon married Hester, daughter of Sir Stephen Herbert Gatty, a week after this letter was written on 18 December 1933. Lawrence was one of the guests.
2 'Bobbie': Robert Gould Shaw III, Lady Astor's son by her first marriage, to Robert Gould Shaw II.
3 Lady Portarlington: the mother of Lawrence's friend Lord Carlow.

ALEC DIXON[1]

21.XII.33   13 Birmingham Street Southampton

Ahoy! Still there? Perhaps. Indeed I am a hot correspondent.

Boats, boats, boats: that is my life. And yours? Not so regular, I hope.

Permanent address Clouds Hill, Moreton, Dorset. In 14 months they give me my lounge suit, and there I am, fixed. The cottage has now water, a bath, bookshelves. No bed. One sleeps where one can. No kitchen. One feeds in Bovington. No drains. One — under any bush, beyond sight of the windows!

No good writing more elaborately, till I hear if you are in the South Seas or where not.

By the way. I have never seen any of your books. What about it?

Yours
T. E. Shaw

I flew over Maidstone (at 2000 feet) last summer!

Bodleian Reserve

SIR EDWARD ELGAR

22.XII.33   Clouds Hill Moreton Dorset

Dear Sir Edward,

This is from my cottage and we have just been playing your 2nd Symphony. Three of us, a sailor,[2] a Tank Corps soldier, and myself. So there are all the Services present: and we agreed that you must be written to and told (if you are well enough to be bothered) that this Symphony gets further under our skins than anything else in the record library at Clouds Hill. We have the Violin Concerto, too; so that says quite a lot. Generally we play the Symphony last of all, towards the middle of the night, because nothing comes off very well after it. One seems to stop there.

You would laugh at my cottage, which has one room upstairs (gramophone and records) and one room downstairs (books): but there is also a bath, and we sleep anywhere we feel inclined. So it suits me. A one-man house, I think.

The three of us assemble here nearly every week-end I can get to the

---

1 Dixon had been a Tank Corps Corporal at Bovington. He subsequently served (1926–31) as a Detective-Inspector in the Straits Settlements Police. He was the author of two books, *Extreme Occasion* and *Singapore Patrol*.

2 Jock Chambers, who had served in the Navy before joining the Air Force.

cottage, and we wanted to say 'thank you' for the Symphony ever so long ago; but we were lazy, first: and then you were desperately ill, and even now we are afraid you are too ill, probably, to be thinking of anything except yourself: but we are hoping that you are really getting stronger and will soon be able to deal with people again.[1]

There is a selfish side to our concern: we want your Symphony III: if it is wiser and wider and deeper than II we shall very sadly dethrone our present friend, and play it last of the evening. Until it comes, we shall always stand in doubt if the best has really yet happened.

Imagine yourself girt about by a mob of young pelicans, asking for III: and please be generous to us, again!

Yours sincerely
T. E. Shaw

DG

LADY ASTOR
31.XII.33   13 Birmingham Street Southampton

[...]
One day last week (Wednesday I think it must have been) I came to London and registered my motor-bike for 1934. Also I asked after Sir Herbert Baker, who is going on well, regaining himself: and then a memory of a half-deciphered sentence in your last letter caused me to ring up St. James' Square. You were reported absent. I felt glad that you had better things to do.

I am sorry about the dark lady, and rather frightened. Where is safety, if I am rumoured to have lost my heart to a lady of sixty, upon once visiting her after lunch to apologise for not lunching? A lady whom I had met for the first time at Lympne in the summer? It is rather hard, I think. Probably it would be wholesome for me to lose my heart — if that monstrous piece of machinery is capable of losing itself: for till now it has never cared for anyone, though much for places and things. Indeed I doubt these words of 'hearts'. People seem to my judgement to lose their heads rather than their hearts. Over the Christmas season two men and four women have sent me fervent messages of love. Love carnal, not love rarefied, you know: and I am uncomfortable towards six more of the people I meet, therefore. It's a form of lunacy, I believe, to fancy that all comers are one's lovers: but what

---

1 Elgar was suffering from inoperable cancer; he died on 23 February 1934.

am I to make of it when they write it in black on white? If only one might never come nearer to people than in the street. Miss Garbo[1] sounds a really sympathetic woman! The poor soul. I feel for her.

I would now like to turn to happier things, and be brisk for a last paragraph: but no use. Those two in China have been silent for a month, which means lost letters or uncivil unrest across their line of communications. They were wrong to court martyrdom thus inaccessibly.

[...]

DG

LIONEL CURTIS
19.3.34   Union Jack Club London S.E.1

My Lord Prophet
Your letter and Philip's wire met me on Sunday in Southampton, as I got back from Birmingham.[2] So this morning I wired to him that I was sympathetic but sorry — and tonight (ordered to London suddenly for an inspection tomorrow at Brentford of a searchlight) I failed to find him in his lordly burrow of St. James.

The defence question is full of snags and is being ineptly handled by Lords Rothermere & Beaverbrook. I agree that the balance of expenditure on Navy, Army and R.A.F. is wrong: but I do not want R.A.F. expenditure increased. Our present squadrons could deal very summarily with France. When Germany wings herself — ah; that will be another matter, and our signal to reinforce: for the German kites will be new and formidable, not like that sorry French junk.

All we now need is to keep in ourselves the *capacity* to expand the R.A.F. usefully, when the times make it necessary. For this we must have:—
(1) Aerodromes enough, sited in the useful places.
(2) Aircraft firms well equipped, with up-to-date designers, designs, and plant.
(3) Brains enough inside our brass hats to employ 1 and 2.

1 Greta Garbo (b. 1905), legendary Swedish film actress, famous for her remark 'I want to be alone', originally spoken in the film *Grand Hotel* in 1932. She ultimately solved the problem of being the focus of much publicity by retiring into private life in her mid-thirties; her last film, *Ninotchka*, was made in 1939.
2 Curtis had written to tell him that the *Round Table* was to publish an article arguing that a large part of the money currently being spent on the Navy should be spent on the Air Force; Philip Kerr, Lord Lothian, had wired him to ask for a meeting to discuss the subject.

(1) Easy — but means another 15 aerodromes, each costing £20,000: they take about three years to bring into being.
(2) In hand; excellent; but hampered by
(3) The direction of R.A.F. and Air Ministry. Our air-marshals are rather wooden headed, and some of the civilian A.I.D.[1] inspectors and technicians who handle design are hopeless. Consequently our military aircraft are like christmas trees, all hung with protruding gadgets, our flying boats are a bad joke, our civil aircraft are (almost) the world's slowest; and air tactics and strategy are infantile.

More money should be spent at once on (1) above: and research made into flying boat development (after sacking the present authorities) and wireless-controlled aircraft. Also to develop the art of sound-ranging, and anti-aircraft gunnery. If I had my way, I would constitute a new Flying Boat department of Air Ministry, and have in a dozen good naval men to give it a start.

Upon the Navy I have views also. Our air bombs are not going to sink capital ships; but will render them useless as fighting platforms, and probably uninhabitable. This in only three or four years time. The defence of surface craft against aircraft will be found in manoeuvre:— in being able to turn quicker on the water than the plane can in the air — not difficult, with small ships, as water gives you a firmer rudder. So I expect to see the surface ships of navies, in future, limited to small, high-speed, manouvrable mosquito craft, none larger than the destroyers of today.

There are controversial points in the above, and to argue them one must consider smoke-screens, the one-pounder pom-pom, trajectories, dive-arcs, b-bombs; all sorts of technical things. But I am prepared to maintain my thesis in most company. Do not, however, take this exposition of it as exhaustive or even fair. To deal with imponderables, layer upon layer of imponderables, more resembles faith than argument.

I wish I could have run through your Round Table argument and talked it over with you.

Accordingly
T.E.S.

Off to Southampton tomorrow p.m. after a meeting in Air Ministry

DG

---

1 Air Inspection Department.

E.H.R. ALTOUNYAN
7 April 34

[. . .] I have another 12 months of the R.A.F. and after that the prospect of unbounded leisure. I wait for this to happen, with great longing. Work no longer excites me; for more than a short spasm. Tired, I think: and probably getting old, without having physically adjusted myself to the restrictions of age.

[. . .] Your poem — essentially it is one, a poetic history — is so long, so interwoven, so exhausting, that it demands full attention.[1] Don't be hurt by the word exhausting. I do not mean wearisome but wearying. It is a strenuous exercise to reach much of it. Like boxing, which is a severe art, whereas golf is easy. You are a muscular poet, and few readers will ever grapple with you competently.

This tax upon your readers is physical. It is possible that intellectually you may make an equal demand. Your metaphysic, your physiology, your philosophy may be as articulated and articulate as [the] forcefulness of your writing. My mind slides over what it fails to understand, and is not troubled at having such depths under its keel. So I do not weary my brain as I read your poems. If your subsequent readers do, why then more of them will fall by the wayside. Be merciful to the reading public! It is not a merit to write, like Blake in his prophetic books, for the very few. The very few are not so useful as the very many. To imagine ourselves — because we are freaks — to be therefore rare and admirable creations is to deceive ourselves. Two-headed chickens and Siamese twins are rare — and unfortunate. Generally they are bottled young.

[. . .]

I have 1800 other letters to answer, and have spent all this time, and wasted all this ink, on addressing a being 2000 miles away from me in space, and three weeks in time. Long before you get this note you will be a different creature, and out of reach of all my thoughts. That is the murrain upon correspondence. Five minutes of a meeting, once a blue moon, was worth all the letters that Lord Chesterfield addressed to his son.

[. . .]

DG/Bodleian Reserve

1 Altounyan had asked Lawrence to read his poetic writings — he had set down his thoughts in a flood of poems of wide variety both in subject and quality. He regarded Lawrence as 'the only person who understands me'.

B. H. LIDDELL HART
Sunday 7 April '34   13 Birmingham Street Southampton

Yes, we blew and rolled about the sea, and made Devonport after some interesting days. Thence I returned to the old job. 'Here' is getting precarious, I fancy: a gent, describing himself as the French Consul, rang the bell this morning and then produced a *News Chronicle* card. If it develops I shall have to move.

I am dead against any further publication of the Arab Revolt, and would refuse to permit any of my photographs to be reproduced for the purpose — either here or in the States. So that hamstrings Dodd, Mead, I fancy![1] There has been far too much said already about the affair, which I devoutly wish had never happened: or do I wish that Newcombe, Joyce and Vickery had pushed it to a successful conclusion?

Anyway, I shall not move another turn towards ventilating it again.

[...]

LHB

GEORGE BROUGH
3 May 1934   13 Birmingham Street Southampton

Dear G.B.

I was in Wolverhampton for a while, looking at some engines of Henry Meadows — and at Lincoln before that. So I took the chance of passing near Nottingham to look in (during a beastly wet day, of course) and see the new marvel being born.

It looks most promising — and most expensive. I shall be broke but happy. Please take your time over it. The old hack has done only 20,000 miles, and is running splendidly. My breaking the speedometer drive has had the curious effect of putting up my average nearly six miles an hour! My last two long rides have been at 49 and 51 m.p.h. respectively. It looks as though I might yet break my neck on a B.S.[2] [...]
                                                    Yours ever
                                                    T.E.S.

Bodleian Reserve

---

1 Liddell Hart had had a letter from the American publishers Dodd, Mead and Co., stating that the examples of Lawrence's photographs published in his biography had suggested to them the idea of a pictorial history of the Arab Revolt, with photographs and accompanying text by Lawrence. Liddell Hart had passed on the idea in the 'faint hope', as he put it, that Lawrence might relax his rule of taking no profit from his part in the Revolt.

1 B. S.: Brough Superior.

LINCOLN KIRSTEIN[1]
11 May 1934   13 Birmingham Street Southampton

[...] Your review of Liddell-Hart's book does, as you said, succinctly convey your position. I'm rather regretting L-H's surrender to my 'charm'. Had he maintained his critical distance and examined my war-time strategy and tactics with a cool head, the results would have been interesting — to me, at any rate! He is a good military thinker. But instead there comes only Panegyric III, and I'm rather sick of my virtues. The worst of being oneself is that one knows all one's vices, too! And honestly it isn't fair to keep on harping on the credit side.

I suggested a meeting out of sheer altruism. If we ever come together you will see that I am human. There ain't any such super-creatures as you would fain see: or if there are, I haven't been lucky enough to meet one.

Your favourable judgment of *The Mint* would give me unqualified delight, had you flavoured your remarks upon me with some salt. I took a lot of trouble, in writing *The Mint*, to ram it full of all the feeling I could muster. The R.A.F. was a huge and gorgeous subject. Oh, I meant to make a whale of a book. What came into being was hardly its introduction — and now I don't feel that I'll ever write anything again. It is hard to have learnt so hard how to write — and then to have nothing to write about.

Don't forget to let me know if you do ever get across. Ede or Garnett will know my address. A meeting will be good for you.

Yours
T. E. Shaw

Bodleian Reserve

LADY ASTOR
11 May 1934   13 Birmingham St Southampton

Mi Ladi

Useless for me to promise to come to Cliveden for a week-end or a night, or a visit. I should only break tryst. One does not come: or go: anywhere, now a days: The rare exceptions are to the two or three people

---

1 Dancer, writer and promoter of the School of American Ballet. He had conceived an enormous admiration for Lawrence and had written a favourable review of Liddell Hart's biography. An earlier letter to Kirstein is included in *DG*.

who would be hurt by my refusal. You are more or less a man of my own size, and above courtesy.

My mother and brother are still in their C.M.S. Hospital at Mienchu in Szechuan, a rich province far up the Yangtse in China. They are running it, while the staff doctor has a year's home leave. After that year — well, who knows? They are well, they say — but the place is so remote that news is months old, and my mother is old, and her letters are exactly those she would write from anywhere she was. So I cannot visualise them there.

It always seems to me that contact, to be real, must be physical. We can only pretend to understand and keep company with those far off. Minds change nearly as quickly as bodies, and these scrappy, old and inadequate letters convey nothing from one to the other. Sometimes the sham seems hardly worth the keeping up — but my mother will never feel that. She writes often and at length, and cries out for letters as when at home she cries out for our love ... as if it could be turned on in a tap. Don't play the mother too long to your kids, please! If you are interesting enough they will keep in touch. If not — why don't wish it!

Yours
T.E.S.

An airman for very little longer, alas!

University of Reading

HENRY WILLIAMSON
14.V.34   13 Birmingham Street Southampton

This is a splendid surprise. I had somehow imagined you settled in America for months. The letter, the cotton-bale, the excellent nuts (I eat one per week, ritually, as I visit my cottage where they are stored) had all confirmed me in that feeling of your being gone.

I dislike people going very far away. They seem to lose their actuality, their roots. I fancy that contact with plain men, one's equals, is a necessity for mental health. They 'place' us.

Sorry about the book — or, rather, about the U.S.A. verdict upon its prospects. I expect the *Falcon*[2] has frightened the publishers over there. You handled them too freely, perhaps.

If you can become objective again, for a spell, it will give us something deeper

1 Williamson had sent Lawrence a bag of pecan nuts from Augusta, Georgia.
2 *The Gold Falcon*, which Williamson had published, anonymously, in 1933.

and more exciting than what you have written before, I hope. The subjective stuff is wonderful exercise, but temporary in its value: or temporal, rather, for its significance seems to ebb and flow with the times. Good for now, rotten in 20 years, interesting again after sixty years. Whereas the objective stuff does not date.

However you have the gift of twisting surprises out of ordinary words and situations and happenings: so none of your writing can fail to give at least technical pleasure. Sometimes I would wish you one skin more, for daily wear, however. Your writing costs you too much.

I should like to come to your valley-country: but there are five target boats to put through their paces now in close succession: and after them six dinghies: and in any hours that I can snatch between the boats I must visit my cottage, for that half-ruin and wholly unfinished place must be cleaned up enough, by this winter, to act 'home' to me in the spring. March next; exit of T.E.S. from the Air Force: very sad, I think, this freedom will be at first: but then it should be a safe feeling, to have the house to live in, without rule, (I have never had any sort of house of my own before) and there are so many things I have not yet done, that I can hardly be lonely or bored.

I'm not, I think, a lonely person; though often and generally alone. There is a distinction. I like your hypothesis to explain my character,[2] by the way. It has experience behind it, I fancy. For myself, I do not know. I measure myself against the fellows I meet and work with, and find myself ordinary company, but bright and sensible. Almost I would say popular!

We will find ourselves together soon!

T.E.S.

Bodleian Reserve

MRS CHARLOTTE SHAW
18.v.34   13 Birmingham St Southampton

You will think it queer, but I have been looking and longing for this news to appear in the Papers. Your return makes England seem furnished, somehow. I so seldom call: yet my two visits to London while you were

---

1 Having read Liddell Hart's biography of Lawrence in the U.S.A. Williamson had used this pretext to offer him a lengthy analysis of his character.

away found the place barren: and I came back here sooner than was necessary, just because there seemed no point in wandering about.

So apparently you are a focus.

I hope the trip has left you satisfied and well. You were so ill when you went that I was afraid for you: and New Zealand may have been too like England for a change.

G.B.S. of course flourishes. I do hope you are.

Boats, boats, boats since you left, and yet more to do. But my cottage is finished, inside and out, so far as alien hands can finish it — and I feel rooted now, whenever I pass its door. Such a lovely little place, and so plain. It is ingenious, comfortable, bare and restful: and cheap to maintain. I do hope you'll be able to see it with me some time soon.

I'm ever so glad you are here.

T.E.S.

We were too late for that Third Symphony after all. He sent me a note about it, just before he died.

British Library

HON. EDWARD ELIOT

24 May 1934   13 Birmingham St Southampton

Dear Eliot

Two events lately. A splurge in the *Daily Mail*, talking of a film to be made around my squalid past. I wonder how much it is true? The article talked glibly of the *Seven Pillars*; so I imagine it is mostly the perfervid imagining of one of the horde of publicity men who afflict the film world.

The second happening was an alarm by Liddell Hart, offering me proofs that I was being personated in London.[2] I took it coldly, and declined his proofs, for never a week passes without my receiving a letter from some poor woman or other, distraught with the fancy that the airman she walked

---

1 The impresario behind this latest attempt to make a film out of Lawrence's wartime exploits was the famous Sir Alexander Korda.

2 Lawrence was being impersonated by one George Henry Rogers, who had emigrated to Canada in 1924, returned penniless and had conned a number of business-men into accepting his advice and supporting him financially on the strength of his being Colonel Lawrence of Arabia. He had apparently shown considerable knowledge both of Arabian affairs and of mechanics.

out with in 1920 or 1930 something was me. Clearly personation is a common event — but as a sop to L-H, who is sincere and serious, I suggested he should try to interest you in his tale. Please take it very calmly. If I don't call myself TELawrence, I see no reason why others shouldn't.

Life is all motor-boats still — so far as the Daily Press permit me to be active. In March begins the leisure of leisures. After March how we shall sleep.

Tell your film negotiators that I'll be a very awkward pebble in the rock of their progress!

Yours
T E Shaw

Bodleian Reserve

ROBIN BUXTON
7.vi.34   13 Birmingham St Southampton

Dear Robin
    [. . .]
I saw Alan D. ten days back . . . persuaded him and E.[1] to drive me over to my cottage between them: and we talked all the way there and back. He takes the B.B.C. as seriously as a profession, and worries over it. I, alas, never worry over anything. Alan D. worries over the cost of children, and what-not. Very bad for him. I do not think he is really ill, or badly broken down: they have got him in time. Only nerves take so long to cure.

Savage is a nuisance with his film-greediness; but I suspect that Korda will not play. I am too recent to make a good subject — too much alive, in fact. I warned Eliot that the Film Company might be ceded his and your rights in *Revolt in the Desert* . . . but that I doubted if that would give them the power to put a lot of living people on the stage. They might be able to reproduce me . . . but you and Alan D. and Joyce and Feisal and all the Arabs . . . to each man his own right, I fancy. Better wait till we are all dead. Tell the Inland Revenue that too. You have given them already more than they deserve, morally.

We have done our best to safeguard the cottage from heath fires, by open spaces. Two sides (E and S) are safe; but I wish there was rain. My

---

1 Hon. Edward Eliot.

pool holds only 2000 gallons at the moment, but slowly increases. Seven thousand is its capacity. Let's hope for rain, all together!

Yours
T.E. Shaw

Bodleian Reserve

HON. EDWARD ELIOT
8.vi.34   13 Birmingham St Southampton

Dear Eliot

I suppose there is no help for it, but coming up.[1] When isn't so easy. We are in the midst of a batch of target boats, and busy from morning to night.

However: any day this coming week, except Saturday, can be made free. Send me a wire to this address, or write well beforehand. The Post Office in Southampton is quaint. It hands out letters only about 9 a.m. and I go to work at 8.30. So I never get my mail till 7 p.m. when I get back once more.

I quite see that it ought to be stopped. If this next week won't do, then I can come up any day after June 24 ... but from June 16 to June 24 I am provisionally booked for a coast trip round the S and E coasts, with this batch of boats.

This is kind of you. I hope it has not been a care and trouble. Do not take it too seriously. If only the poor wretch *could* take my war name and all that it connotes!

Yours
T E Shaw

Bodleian Reserve

HON. EDWARD ELIOT[2]
26.vi.34   13 Birmingham St Southampton

Dear Eliot

I have been away cruising in some of our boats ... hence the delay. Back last night.

---

1 i.e. to confront his impersonator.

2 Lawrence and Eliot had met the impostor George Henry Rogers in Eliot's office and Rogers had signed an undertaking that he would never use Lawrence's name again; he had also apologised for any trouble or inconvenience caused. Mr Jenny (third paragraph) was one of the businessmen taken in by Rogers' imposture.

First of all, I have to thank you for so admirably handling that business in London. It was one of my queerest experiences. I feel that I took advantage of your kindness most unwarrantably. That you should be the King Pin of the City Solicitors makes it all the worse. However we could hardly leave the little man alone.

I am returning Mr. Jenny his 'horoscope' with thanks ... and being entirely non-committal about his inventions. The poor child.

As for telling Rogers' father ... I agree, but suggest that it ought to be done as it were in confidence. I gathered that his father was not very fond of him: and it would do the thing no good to get Rogers chucked out of his home. If the father could keep a careful eye on him, as a result of a tactful warning, without going to extremities? I feel that in bothering Rogers Père we extend the circle of unhappiness.

Your letter dissuading Jenny from publicity is admirable, and will properly scare him off it.

Remains the Directorship. Do you know, that sounds almost exactly right? I have a good deal of book-trade practical experience, and would probably (even on such occasional terms) be able to pull my weight. As for writing of my own — I couldn't promise anything. It is very unlikely that I will ever (after this long interval) write anything again.

But it must wait. Robin holds the key to the future. If by manipulating my investments he can produce me the full £100 a year, then I am quit of any need for a job. By so much as he fails, do I need a supplement. Our accounting will be in the middle of March, 1935. After that, may I try you again — it being understood meanwhile that nobody is bound, and no offers held open?

There, I think everything is cleared up, and I hope you will see it as I do. 'Imitation', so the proverb says 'is the sincerest form of flattery.' Decidedly I dislike flattery. The poor little worm. What a hole he finds himself in, now. I wish he hadn't done it. I'll encounter repercussions of it, probably, years hence.

If only it would rain: for six days, so they write me, the heath has been blazing round my cottage, and some of my bushes have been burnt. I wish I could get there to see how hurt it is. If that little place goes I'll be properly up against it.

Yours
T E Shaw

Bodleian Reserve

ROBIN BUXTON
14.vii.34   13 Birmingham St Southampton

Dear Robin

Well, if they want to film the rotten book, they must. Will you please try and arrange for the scenario to be shown you ... and for me to see it, before it is used? And then for the film (before any showing to Press or Trade) to be shown to you? I am so desirous of keeping the flesh they cut to its exact poundage ... and to give as little offence as possible.

Stirling — yes, I suppose he would be the best of our party: more savoir commerce! The poor little man will delight in a job.

As for the actor to play me ... well, Walter Hudd was magnificent ... but perhaps Leslie Howard might be more unlike, which would be an advantage![1]

Our Grocery speculation fell a bit flat, didn't it? Or are we on the right side? I couldn't quite see from the published account!

This thing came.... will you bestow it on the correct individual amongst the multitude that stand behind grills?

                                              Yours
                                              T. E. Shaw

Bodleian Reserve

LADY ASTOR
27.vii.34   13 Birmingham St Southampton

Peeress

You accuse me, with superficial reason — but a dry orange cannot be expected to utter juice. My fault is to myself in going dry, and the causes for that are innate. One can be poised, busy and content while engrossed in some loved toy: but when a man lifts his head and looks round him, he grows terrified instanter. How can one even try to rationalise the life outside one's skin?

Mrs. Shaw told me, in no more words than this, that you were troubled

---

1 Walter Hudd had played Private Meek in *Too True To Be Good*. Leslie Howard, an actor with a considerable reputation on both stage and screen, had just starred with Bette Davis in the film adaptation of John Steinbeck's novel, *Of Human Bondage*. He was later to appear with much acclaim in such films as *The Scarlet Pimpernel*, which was screened in 1941, just two years before he died in a wartime air crash (shot down by the Germans) in 1943. Arguably Howard was a more apposite casting for Lawrence than his ultimate screen impersonator, Peter O'Toole.

but bearing your troubles. Well, that's (I suspect) almost the universal experience. When we are young we hope, when we are old we have given up hoping: but the between-times are hard. If you ever feel you must talk to somebody, will you send for the collected Poems of Cecil Day Lewis[1] and read them? It is not much (only four or five slim volumettes) but sincere, intelligent, grimly-good and of today. The *Observer's* fatuous literary gent said last Sunday that he had never heard of Day Lewis. I wrote an indignant protest to Garvin. Day Lewis does me good, you see; and in our way we are not unlike, so you might gain from him too. *Beechen Vigil*,[2] his first poems, are his most musical. He is a famous poet, of some five years ago, and probably not yet exhausted. A schoolmaster, I believe.

I fear that this return to China has not been a great pleasure to my Mother. She writes already, as it were, longingly, of 'coming home in eighteen months'. Eighteen months must seem a long time to give away, at 70: and my brother is 50. I only hope they will have the courage to come home, instead of persisting in an outworn 'call'. I feel that the spirit of the day is against the missionary profession. We do not feel confident enough in our selves to preach or inculcate.

Their coming home will be a problem, too, of course. My brother must do some altruistic work, in doctoring, to content his conscience. If he can do it in a decent place, where my mother can live with him? He is capable of slumming, or fever-hospitalling, or other impossibility. Mother needs a little garden, for flowers, and somewhere to walk in; and a house (not too big) which she can polish with her own hands. 'How unlike Cliveden', you say! Well, well. But my mother has never learned our lesson of giving in, and of doubting our own competence universally. She is fitted only to dictate in a *small* world. That trusting the other fellow (which is laziness on the debit side, and sunshine on the credit side) is beyond her grasp. It is also the secret of bigness, I believe.

In a recent letter she told me how useful your parting gift to her of rugs had been. They have great cold winter journeys. I am sure she would be hurt if I did not take a chance which offers and repeat her gratitude to you. My mother does not encourage kindness, in her brisk utility: but when she receives it, she is touched. No wonder all her children are queer. With such a father (you did not know him, I expect ... before your time) and such a mother, we have no chance of being useful citizens of this great country. If only they sold single tickets to the Moon, now! I think they would elect me President, there.

1 Cecil Day-Lewis (1904–72), the well-known Irish-born Oxford-educated poet and writer; associate of W. H. Auden and Stephen Spender. Poet Laureate 1968–72. He wrote as C. Day Lewis, and also, in a second career as a detective novelist, under the pseudonym Nicholas Blake.
2 Published in 1925.

And talking of those who favour the Moon, how is James Stephens,[1] whom I met, twice and only, at your house or houses? Do you still see him? A small and rare artist, who has written about five good books. I re-read him ever so often. Yes, a moon-dweller, assuredly. But I suppose your days and rooms are full now of American tennis champions. Five and a half times better than cricket, is tennis, for only two need join together to play it. Indeed, I'm not sure that 22 are not necessary for cricket. No wonder the noise of cricket rolls across the land like a battle.

Milady, I am tired. I lie on my back at noon, in my hired bed-room in Southampton. They have given me the day off, and I take it recumbently. I do not really want to write to anyone: but if I put it off for a day, the post of tomorrow will cover the past letters with its new leaves ... and then tomorrow and tomorrow and tomorrow, till in despair I slide the heap into a box and post it to my cottage, where it awaits March 1935.

In March 1935 the R.A.F. takes away from me the right to serve it longer, and I relapse into self-supporting life. My cottage, 35/– a week, 24 hours a day. I am so tired that it feels like heaven drawing near: only there are people who whisper that heaven will bore me. When they tell me that I almost wish I were dead for I have done everything in life except rest, and if rest is to prove no refuge, then what is left?

So, you see, the issue of it all is, that I do better not to write and trouble people with my ideas till I can blow a confident tune again and hearten them. Some tune like the Purcell *Trumpet Voluntary* on the Columbia Record. Next day a lot of pessimists obscure your great hall at Cliveden with their 'crisis-talk', just you put the *Trumpet Voluntary* on the gramophone, and blow their cobwebs back to Hades. Bless you.

T.E.S.

University of Reading

ERIC KENNINGTON
6.VIII.34.   13 Birmingham St Southampton

Oh yes, I take my time; indeed I take time to answer any letter. Why? Well, I think it is mainly laziness. There is my R.A.F. work which has to be done to schedule, willy nilly: so what is not compulsory is told to wait on the mood. And letter-writing, being difficult, is seldom the mood.

For it is very difficult to write a good letter. Mine don't pretend to be good ... but they do actually try very hard to be good. I write them in

---

1 The Irish poet and story-writer.

great batches, on the days when at length (after months, often) the impulse towards them eventually comes. Each tries to direct itself as directly as it can towards my picture of the person I am writing to: and if it does not seem to me (as I write it) that it makes contact — why then I write no more that night.

Yet, as you would say if I was there to hear you, the letters as they actually depart from me are not worthy of this strained feeling. At the far end they appear ordinary. Yes, that is because I'm not writer enough to put enough of myself into any work. Or better, because there is not enough of myself to share out and go round. There has been, upon occasion. Both the *Seven Pillars* and *The Mint* (but *The Mint* especially) stink of personality. Where has it gone? Don't know. I'm always tired now, and I fritter myself away month after month on pursuits that I know to be petty, and yet must pursue, faute de mieux.

'What the hell's the matter with the chap' you'll be asking. You send me a sensible working-man of a letter, reporting progress — or at least continuity — and I burble back in this unconscionable way. I think it is in part because I am sorry to be dropping out. One of the sorest things in life is to come to realise that one is just not good enough. Better perhaps than some, than many, almost — but I do not care for relatives, for matching myself against my kind. There is an ideal standard somewhere and only that matters: and I cannot find it. Hence this aimlessness.

It is a pity, rather, that I took so many years teaching myself this and that and everything: for now that I'm full enough to weigh a lot, I've nowhere in which I want to use that weight. If I'd cared less about learning and more about doing things, the story would have been different. It's a common way in the world. The fuller the cask, the less active the damned thing seems to be.

Let's come down to earth. You still carve. I still build R.A.F. boats. On March 11th next that office comes to an end. Out I go. Clouds Hill awaits me, as home (address will be Shaw, Clouds Hill, Moreton, Dorset) and I have nearly £2 a week of an income. So I mean to digest all the leisure I can enjoy: and if I find that doing nothing is not worse than this present futile being busy about what doesn't matter — why then, I shall go on doing nothing. But if doing nothing is not good — why then, I shall cast loose again and see where I bring up.

Is C. well? And Xto?[1] Say that I hope to come and see you some day ... please.

Yours
T.E.S.

DG

1 Celandine Kennington and her son Christopher.

LORD LLOYD
26 Sept 1934   13 Birmingham Street Southampton

Dear G.L.

Yes, I know: for once your strictures upon my failure to answer letters have a basis. Your Vol. II came to me months ago.[1] I read it at once, admiringly; it being so much more vivid than No I. Now it sits beside its brother on the 'history' shelf of my cottage, with inside its back cover (I hope, still) the half-page of notes which I scribbled there as I read it, so that when I thanked you for the gift I might have something more (or less, perhaps) than mere gratitude to say.

I may be able to get to my cottage this week-end: it is 45 miles from here, and I go when I can, but rarely, all the same. If I do, I will pull out that slip and repeat it to you.

I haven't any valid reason for not writing: just the works are running down. In March I leave the R.A.F. and it feels like the end of living — so close that nothing between now and then can count. Afterwards — well, I don't know. How does one pass the fag-end of life? If there was any thing which I wanted to do, or thought worth doing, or seeing, or trying, or preventing even ... but I'm facing a vacancy. Indeed, yes, the machine is run down. Time's revenge.[2]

It was a lively decent book: but I will not anticipate my tiny collection of notes. Next week, if I'm lucky to be free this Saturday afternoon — but I very much fear our new Diesel craft will want testing again. My boat work for the R.A.F. (now extending to the Army and the Navy) has been successful, and lets me out of the Service with some distinction, I think. After having dabbled in revolt and politics it is rather nice to have been mechanically useful!

Yours with apology and remorse
T.E.S.

Churchill College Cambridge/Bodleian Reserve

1 Lord Lloyd had sent Lawrence the two volumes of his book *Egypt since Cromer.*
2 Lloyd's and Lawrence's lives took vastly different courses, but their mutual respect and affection remained strong. When shortly after Lawrence's death Lloyd bought a house in the country for his wife, at Offley, near Hitchin, he named it Clouds Hill in Lawrence's memory.

MRS CHARLOTTE SHAW
16.xi.34   Ozone Hotel Bridlington Yorks

Long-overdue, indeed, my visit to you; and this heading will show why it
will add to its length. Only, set against that the twice lately that I have
drawn Whitehall Court and found — no, I must abandon my metaphor.
G.B.S. is as un-foxed as you are vixenless.

'Ozone Hotel'. It was named, I think, for summer time. The R.A.F.
occupy it each season, but the last of them went yesterday. I felt him go
with a pang, like foretasting myself on February 28th next. I wish the world
did not change. This blue protective coating has meant so much to me. I
go back to the self of 1920 and 1921, a crazy pelican feeding not its young
but its spirit-creations upon its bodily strength. I had hoped, all these years,
that I was not going to be alone again.

[. . .]

My history is uneventful. That film is going to fall through, I think: a
relief, for the film world only lives by publicity. Somebody called Bray,
they say, has lately published a book which proves that I was a dud, in the
war.[1] Do you know, I'd be almost glad to think so: but he has very rudely
not sent me a copy of his book, and I don't feel that it would be decent of
me to buy one. I wonder who he is, and what he is trying to do, so late in
the day? It is too late to bury John Brown.

[. . .]

China — all well. They are looking forward to return here twelve months
hence. For good, I hope.

                                                          T.E.S.

British Library

FREDERIC MANNING
16.XI.34   Ozone Hotel Bridlington

Alas, you see, it never came off.[2] My visits to Cranwell and Nottingham
were postponed — and then came a sudden transfer to the unfashionable
winter resort. I wander about a large garage and watch ten R.A.F. boats
being reconditioned. A tricky unsatisfying job, for however done, they
could be done better.

My motor bike remains in far-off Dorsetshire, as Homer would say.

1 See further comment in letter to Mrs Shaw dated 'Monday night late' (p. 507) and
  accompanying footnote.
2 Lawrence had hoped to visit Manning at his home at Bourne, Lincolnshire.

Peter Davies wrote to me that you were still consumed with a longing to write that old book which has so often refused to come to you. I beg of you, don't. Copy the poise and equal mind of E. M. Forster, whose every book is acclaimed by the highbrowed as a masterpiece, and who yet refrains successfully from ever deliberately achieving another. There are so many books, and you have written two of the best of them. To covet a third is greedy. Don't be a book-hog. Read something instead, and (if you find anything good to read) please benefit me by sending me its name: this person is always hungry to read.

March approaches. In March I put on flannel trousers (after taking off blue breeches and puttees) and retire to my cottage in Dorsetshire, where I shall own the whole twenty-four hours of my day, even as you do, and have the responsibility, even as you have, of filling them. Candidly, the prospect of unalloyed leisure terrifies me, for I shall not have enough money to kill time with travel and motor cars and calls and meals. There will be only about 25/– a week, for all purposes.

I wish you could see my cottage. It pleases and tickles me. No kitchen, no food, no cooking equipment, no bed, no drains, no sanitation. No water even, while this drought-in-the-deep-springs persists. There are two rooms, one book-lined the other slenderly furnished with a gramophone and records. Upstairs is one chair, downstairs one chair. A bath and boiler, in cupboards: two sleeping bags, zipp-fastened and labelled in embroidery MEUM and TUUM. When night falls the cottager takes up his bag, unfolds it on the piece of floor he momently prefers, and sleeps. No good for your infirmity, but I've hitherto been always uncouthly well. The village, a mile off, provides meals. I forgot to describe the large garage and swimming tank in the garden, if an untended wilderness of brushwood can be called garden. A bas gardens, I cry, if one has to care for them oneself.

Enough rubbish for one time: but please don't do violence to yourself for some fancied reader's sake. You have your spacious and upholstered niche in our literature. Rest in it.

Yours
T.E.S.

Michell Library, Sydney, N.S.W.

HON. FRANCIS RODD
23.XI.34   Ozone Hotel Bridlington Yorkshire

Dear F.R.

By the accident that a friend of mine was passing my old lodgings in Southampton as my older landlady was handing your letter back to the postman, it reaches me here, only ten days late. I expect to work in Bridlington (on the ten Air Force boats that are refitting for next season) till the end of February when the R.A.F. goes on its way without me.

I shall feel unutterably lost without my blue covering. Twelve years it has been, of engrossing work with a very happy companionship for the off-duty hours. Few war-relics have been so fortunate as I in the aftermath.

I've even saved money and Robin Buxton has invested it for me until it brings in more than 25/- a week. So if you bogeymen[1] (I read the *New English Weekly*!) don't crash the solar system shortly I should be able to live at peace in my cottage, with all the twenty four hours of the day to myself. Forty-six I am, and never yet had a whole week of leisure. What will 'for ever' feel like, and can I use it all?

Please note its address from March onwards — Clouds Hill, Moreton, Dorset — and visit it, sometime, if you still stravage the roads of England in a great car. The cottage has two rooms; one, upstairs, for music (a gramophone and records) and one downstairs for books. There is a bath, in a demi-cupboard. For food one goes a mile, to Bovington (near the Tank Corps Depot) and at sleep-time I take my great sleeping bag, embroidered MEUM, and spread it on what seems the nicest bit of floor. There is a second bag, embroidered TUUM, for guests.

The cottage looks simple, outside, and does no hurt to its setting which is twenty miles of broken heath and a river valley filled with rhododendrons run wild. I think everything, inside and outside my place, approaches perfection.

Now to business. That enclosed message ought to have been instantly dealt with, by a plain Yes or No. Will you please say No, for me, but not a plain No. Make it a coloured No, for the Elizabethan of Herbert Baker's naming has given me a moment of very rare pleasure which I shall not tell to anyone, nor forget.[2]

---

1 For 'bogeymen' read 'bankers', a profession to which both Rodd and Buxton belonged.
2 The 'Elizabethan of Herbert Baker's naming' was the Governor of the Bank of England, Sir Montague Norman, and the message to which Lawrence was saying no was the offer of the Secretaryship of the Bank of England, transmitted to Lawrence through Francis Rodd, who had been a foreign adviser to Norman before joining the bankers Morgan Grenfell. See General Introduction, page xxviii, where this offer is discussed; evidence to confirm that it took place was made public in a Sotheby's Catalogue for 18 December 1986 in which Lawrence's letter appeared as lot 163, together with Rodd's explanation

Please explain how by accident it only came to me tonight, when I got back after work, too late to catch the evening mail from this petty seaboard town.

These newspaper praises lead a fellow to write himself down as a proper fraud — and then along comes a real man to stake himself on the contrary opinion. It is heartening and I am more than grateful.

There — please work all that into your 'NO': explain that I have a chance (if only I have the guts to take it) of next year possessing all my time.

Yours ever
T E Shaw.

DG/Sotheby's

LADY ASTOR
26.xi.34   Ozone Hotel Bridlington Yorks

Bad of you, Viscountess, thoroughly bad. I had written you my 1934 letter ... and you'll admit it was a beauty. Black ink, white paper, firm if crabby handwriting: well punctuated (*lavishly* punctuated) neatly paragraphed: signed even. That's a letter for which at the Anderson Galleries in New York you could have got several dollars.

In return, instead of the gracious silence, or the 'Rest Harrow' single-sheet of arabesques ending in a lightning sketch of the Hampton Court maze, I get a six pages of legibility, in which I cannot even pretend to misunderstand a word: with an 'Astor' in *Roman* characters on the last page (only proof of femininity a couple of postscripts) ... and, cruellest stroke of all, an enclosed letter from a Queen (you know what I think of even English Queens, and this one is Balkan 'to be returned'.

Serpent. You knew my sense of duty would compel me to return it: and my punctilious sense of the proper and kindly would not let me return it in silence.

---

of the circumstances in which the proposal was made. As Sotheby's catalogue writers put it, 'Although, of course, Lawrence lacked business experience, he was believed to have had sufficient qualities and stature to fill the post of Secretary, who was not only keeper of the records of the Court of Governors, but their legal *persona* representing the Bank.' The letter is reprinted here from Garnett, with the difference that Herbert Baker's name is given where Garnett omitted it, thus leaving out the vital clue to the nature of the offer made, in that Baker, who had apparently sponsored Lawrence for the post, was the Bank of England's architect. Garnett evidently considered the matter as being still one of confidence, referring to Lawrence's refusal of 'an extremely important position in the City of London'.

Hence I must spoil the 1934 letter with a sequel!

You are universal when you say of Day Lewis 'I couldn't understand all of it or him — or you'. We all say that, except when we are treating of half-wits. I read the *Observer* again yesterday, but forgot to read the leader. I hope it wasn't Philip (Lothian) again. That old man writes too much. (Tell him I said this: it strikes me as one of the most improbable statements even I have ever made.)

I'm very romantic, they say: I often think of it over my evening fish and chips. As for Miss Cohen,[1] she is apparently romantic too. I heard long ago that she wanted to marry me: but Harriet is not one of my pet names, and there is no piano at my cottage, and I like her gramophone records. Yet I cannot imagine playing one's wife to oneself on the gramophone. Can you? Would you like a Waldorf speech on a record for Christmas? Would he like one of yours?

December 18th.? Now you know that in my R.A.F. embodiment I never decide 24 hours ahead. Probably I shall be at Bridlington still. If not, I would like to reach my Dorset cottage, for my neighbour and tenant, Mrs. Knowles who was a great friend, dropped dead suddenly last week — or rather she was found dead on the floor, having apparently fainted and hurt herself falling. That strands me, rather. I have very much I should see to. So please forget me, for this year. After March I have too much time, alas.

Yes, we cannot help trying to do something, again and again. We are fools, but there it is. Might as well try to stop sleeping.

Mrs. ——[2] wrote to me ever so often at first. I have sent two notes back. Am I a beast? But she wants something which I want to keep, and she ought to understand it. There are Untouchables, thank Heaven, still, despite the Ghandi's of this world. Or is it Gandhi? Philip (either) will know.

Neat introduction of my next subject, again. Philip (Lothian) has a plan for me? Why, I have a plan for myself, which is to cease from all plans. People absurdly over-estimate my capacity. I get offered job after job, in which I should make a colossal fool of myself. Fortunately I know better. Only last week I received a shocking offer, which I'd blush to repeat. The bigger they are, the less I'm tempted.

That room idea . . . do you know I almost dally with it? Only tubs should stand on their own bottoms. I shall leave the RAF with 25/– a week, which is all right for my cottage, but will not keep me for long in London. Yet to live on you would be either charity or a confession of failure to keep

---

1 Harriet Cohen (1895–1967), the internationally famous concert pianist.
2 Name omitted: the wife of an R.A.F. officer.

myself. I think I won't. I hope I won't. It would be a hole in my armour. Of course I lose the Union Jack Club when I leave the Service.

No, I don't know Sir K. Wood. A Postmaster, I think.[1] I want all the telegraph and telephone poles taken away and their wires put below ground, just to add spaciousness to our roads: and beauty, too. At night the wires look lovely in approaching headlights—but it is too high a price to pay for their daylight ugliness.

My Mother and Brother were together again (she had spent 2 months on holiday in the hills, against the heat: and I read harm into that. I think she must have been ill to agree to live away from him) and in their Hospital Compound. They talk already (looking forward—again a disquieting sign) to coming home next winter, when their replacement comes. I hope that is return for good. I cannot see her wandering again: and I am going to ask everybody who is charitable to try to find some do-good medical job in England which might ensnare him. He is incurably other-seeking, you know. Like some Peeresses.

My poor bike. It is laid up in my cottage, and when I next ride it, it is only to the maker's, to hand it back. Here I go about, less splendidly, on a push-bike.

I do hope O'Casey will make enough out of New York to establish him finally. It was a fine play: though that 2nd Act of the Silver Tassie sticks in my memory as the best stage thing I ever saw. I saw it and saw it and saw it, too!

G.B.S. and 'Charlotte' have both been ill. The Yank Admirals cannot have agreed with them. I suggest you ask the Yanks and the Japs to meet. . . . if you are insured

Yourrrrrrs
T.E.S.

[. . .]

University of Reading

MLLE SCHNEEGANS[2]
26.xi.34   R.A.F. Felixstowe

Dear M. Schnéegans

I hope you will pardon my replying in English. Though I can read French easily, I never gained the power of speaking or writing it.

1 Sir Kingsley Wood (1881–1943) was Postmaster-General. Later Chancellor of the Exchequer in Churchill's wartime Government.
2 'Schneeganz' means 'snow-goose' in German. Mlle Schnéegans (not Monsieur as above) was anxious to discover the origin of her name and had been inspired to write to Lawrence

Those who have allowed themselves to produce lives of me (amongst them my friend Mr Graves) have availed themselves, I fear, of much artistic licence, in giving me abundance of qualities and accomplishments which actually I possess only in very small degree, if at all. Thus my knowledge of history and social manners was never great and is twenty years in desuetude.

The point you raise about the Schnéeganz is curious. I think it improbable that any family name of the Rhineland can go back even into the early Middle Ages, much less to the epoch of St. Columba, who was a Celt, and a religious, as were his companions. I do not think they are likely to have had acknowledged descendants, and I do not remember that their mission was accompanied by any movement of families from Celtic Ireland to Middle-Europe.

Would you not be content to establish a claim to descent from one of those famous later 'Wild geese' as Europe called them, the Irish legitimists and loyalists who left this country by edict of our King William of Orange, and fought for their exiled King James II under the banner of your Louis XIV? Some few were Protestants, most Catholics; and their military prowess was one of the main obstacles that faced the Duke of Marlborough in his campaigns. They were very famous as Wild Geese, in five languages, and I can conceive nothing more likely than that one of them, settling in Strasbourg, should have lost some difficult Irish name and been known by the title of his Legion.

I am sorry to give you only a hypothesis: and to give it after six months. It was rather astonishing that your letter to that address should have found me at all!

I envy you a residence in Cahors. It is so long since I followed the Lot from its hills down almost to Bordeaux, but I vividly recall the beauty of its swift reaches: and your bridge is superb. The town was full of interest to me as an archaeologist. It is unfortunate that I cannot come back. The best part of France, to my mind, is from Limoges to Albi: and the most historical.

It would have pleased me to have been of service to you: but alas, you need a real cyclopaedia — and I am out of date.

Yours sincerely
T E Shaw

Jesus College Oxford

---

by admiring references by his biographers to his vast historical knowledge. His reply is of particular interest in that it was the one letter from Lawrence's later life included by E. M. Forster in his unfinished selection, which only covered the pre-war archaeological phase: it appealed to Forster as an echo of those long-lost days.

MRS WINIFRED FONTANA[1]
28.XI.34   Ozone Hotel Bridlington Yorks

You see, I am no longer in the Temperate Zone. Here are ten R.A.F. boats in dire need of overhaul and here am I watching (on behalf of Air Ministry) a contractor do the work. Bridlington in winter is a silent place, where cats and landladies' husbands walk gently down the middles of the streets. I prefer it to the bustle of summer, because my February-looming discharge from the Air Force makes me low-toned. It is like a hermit-crab losing his twelve-year-old shell, and I hate the pleasure that my service has been, coming thus to an arbitrary end.

Probably I shall be here till the end, and then my plan is to move to Clouds Hill, Moreton, Dorset (the cottage) and stay there till I feel I can stay there no more: there being a hope behind my heart that perhaps I shall like it and not wish to come away. My savings come out poorly, I fear, amounting to just 25/– a week. I had hoped for more, so as to live easily. However . . .

[. . .]

E.A.[2] is depressed. He says he faces bankruptcy (I fear his fevers may have put the patients to fright: they may feel that he cannot succeed his father) and the flush has gone from his writings. Poor E. I wish he could be helped. I read in the great poem-sequence often: it is and it isn't. How tell him?

Vale atque salve . . . . when I'm free, I hope.

                                                       Yours
                                                       T.E.S.

[. . .]

Bodleian Reserve

EZRA POUND
7.XII.34   Ozone Hotel Bridlington Yorkshire (Eng.)

Dear E.P.

Indeed, indeed I've written to you: three times or more, and with hard-earned postage stamps. However at long last . . .

---

1 The widow of the former British Consul at Aleppo; cf. letter to Lawrence's mother on
  p. 477.
2 Ernest Altounyan. The 'great poem-sequence' is referred to on p. 484.

I laughed over your letter. You were so hot about something. Now in England (good) the most telling style is understatement. To say that 'you fear some of your adversary's premises may be not well founded' is damaging. To call him a canting nit-wit only provokes a smile. You'd say 'cunting', I fear; there are six shits in your letter. If that happens to me more than once a day, I know that some recent meal is disagreeing with me. More peace to your stomach!

I'm sorry, as I said, about Orage.[1] He is a real loss. For another to continue the *New Age* would not console me any more than if Henry Newbolt (after your premature demise) should in pious memory utter a Canto.[2] It is Orage who mattered: not what he believed or bit. We admire the spirit of the bull-terrier, without endorsing its action in biting the postman's trousers. To my mind both Guild Socialism and Social Credit were levities to engross the mind of Orage.

Your sheet of questions — they don't matter, either. I don't care a hoot for economics, or our money system, or the organisation of society. Such growths are like our stature; what time I have for thinking (not enough, I agree) goes, or tries to go, upon themes within my governance. A fig for financiers.

Of course I know that economics is the fashionable theme, today. A fad almost. Everybody talks and writes about production and exchange and distribution and consumption. Twenty years ago science was *the* subject that we all let off hot air about. It was going to do what the lads fancy political economy will do now. Ah well; I'm 46, and if I live another 20 years there may be a prevalent fashion less dull than economics, and perhaps I'll join in that.

I fancy much of this superior sort of sniffing at today is a result of bad education. By that I don't mean lack of Oxford.... I left a fellowship at Oxford to join the Air Force, so I've stated in very clear implication what I think of Oxford for grown-ups. It's a worse ignorance than that. A lovely example is quoted by you in the current *N.E.* where some American sneers that Wilson lost his better in sacking Lansing. Lansing was a fourth-grade clerk. The fellow who wrote that had never met the two men — except with a prejudice: and from things you yourself have said I deduced that you'd never met Montague Norman. 'Bogeymen', in my travels in Arabia, were always the tribe beyond the next. You have to be ignorant of a thing to fear it or hate it, if it's a man-made thing.

---

1 A. R. Orage, who had just died, had been editor of the influential periodical *The New Age* from 1907-22, and after nine years away from London — spent partly in Fontainebleau and partly in New York — had edited the *New English Weekly* (referred to as *N.E.* in this letter) from 1931 to his death.

2 Pound had been writing his masterwork the *Cantos* since 1917; he was to continue doing so until 1970.

I think many of us go wrong by being too exclusively cerebral. I've spent the last twelve years in the ranks of the Air Force; and nobody so in daily contact with people who work at crafts could get so heated as the *N.E.* does about the regimentation of the world. My own job has been producing motor boats: and I fancy that each concrete thing I launched took away some of my bile. Whereas the uttering of a poem only increases it. Old Gandhi would prescribe for you a daily wrestle with the spinning wheel, to grow contentment. The English working men are another creation from us. Abstract ideas are another name for maggots of the brain. Heads are happy when they employ hands, not when they earn idleness for them.

Dear me, how sententious I get! Only some instinct tells me that the people who fuss about the money of the world are on the wrong tack. Money only serves to keep us alive: and people like you and me wouldn't impair the usefulness of the world if we went down. I incline to resent our presuming to tell our physical betters what ought to be done. Disposing other people's minds is an infectious activity.

Let's get down to ground. I'm time-expired, almost, and in two months must return to civil life. My address will be Clouds Hill, Moreton, Dorset, a tiny cottage in four acres of heath land. I've put by enough to bring me in 25/– a week, and have faith enough in the stability of the City to risk retiring on it. Leisure is the only thing I've never had, and always liked the look of. I think I can use spare time with gladness, ad infinitum: or rather for 24 years, which is my 'expectation.'

Will you never come back? The States, England, even Paris? Time-lag forsooth! Rapallo is years away from Texas, as Texas from Rapallo.[1] Who dare put one before the other? Not dunne, O E.P.!

yours
T.E.S.

Bodleian Reserve

MRS CHARLOTTE SHAW
Monday night, late[2]

[...] Your chill troubles me, rather. Annually you have them, now (before going round the world) and again, soon after you get back. As G.B.S. has gone to Ayot, he presumably thinks it 'only a cold'. But it sounds uncomfortable.

1 Pound had lived in Rapallo, Italy, since 1925.
2 Mid-December 1934.

Casement. Yes, I still hanker after the thought of writing a short book on him. As I see it, his was a heroic nature. I should like to write upon him subtly, so that his enemies would think I was with them till they finished my book and rose from reading it to call him a hero. He had the appeal of a broken archangel. But unless the P.M. will release the 'diary' material, nobody can write of him. Do you know who the next Labour P.M. might be? In advance he might pledge himself, and I am only 46, able, probably, to wait for years: and very determined to make England ashamed of itself, if I can.

Shifting Sands[1] came and I have read it, not perhaps too well. Akaba beach could have been taken by ship's gunfire, like the beach of Gallipoli. What I wanted was the 50 miles of mountain defiles behind the beach, which could (I still think) only have been taken by us from inland. The Arabs are *not* good at military attack, and Bray's instances are all made in ignorance. His warfare knowledge is very poor, apparently.

As for Damascus, I did wait till Allenby's troops came up: but what Bray means is that his 'two Divisions of Arab Legion' should have been formed, and made into a common front with the British Army: with a civilised Arab Army, the French would have had poorer grounds of complaint. This is true: but the Arab Legion never exceeded 600 men. It could never have been made into even a Battalion: not even one battalion could have been fed and moved along our line of march. He could as reasonably have maintained that a great Arab fleet in the Mediterranean might have made France pause! One of my minor qualities is always to accept (in lieu of the whole loaf) just so many ounces of bread as providence makes possible.

I remember Bray now. He suffered from persecution-delusions and was a very honourable Indian Army Captain, who threw up his job under the Arab Bureau on some point of principle. I was not concerned (it was early on, before I joined the great) and don't know what it was. This book isn't of any critical value: I'm sorry, for there is a real book to write, some day, on the difference between the politics of the Desert and the Sown. That was my problem, and none of these sharpshooters will face it. Bray hasn't enough head, of course.

His picture of Leachman[2] chimes with what I saw: but it rather astonishes me that Bray forgives our tearing down all that organised colony-govern-

---

1 *Shifting Sands* by Major N. N. E. Bray (Unicorn Press, 1934). Bray accused Lawrence of frittering away 'material, money, time and lives' on secondary objects such as attacks on the Hejaz Railway when all efforts should have been directed to achieving a major Arab military success. Bray was an Indian Army officer who was attached to the Hejaz operation in its early months only.

2 Lieutenant-Colonel Gerard Leachman was an Indian Army officer well known for his pre-war travels and his work as a political officer during the Mesopotamian campaign and after. He was murdered by an Iraqi tribal chief in 1920. Bray was a great admirer and wrote his biography, *Paladin of Arabia* (1936).

ment that A. T. Wilson[1] built in Irak. I expected him to criticise that, the biggest decision I ever took. Instead he appears to approve, though without mentioning my part in the change.

I don't suppose anybody will ever trouble to dig out the Foreign Office Archives about Rabegh and Hussein's claims upon us, and Ibn Saud's part during the war. Better for Bray if they don't!

As soon as you are better, please tell me by a postcard, at least.

[. . .]

T.E.S.

British Library

B. H. LIDDELL HART
[31 December 1934]   Ozone Hotel Bridlington

Returned to find your note, upon which warmest congratulations. . . . I am sure that you will be able to correlate the three Defences and Offences to the general benefit.[2]

So I can only wind up by hoping that you are as pleased as myself. I implore you . . . to use your new enlargement for some unprofitable but worthy book. Give us some reflections upon the relations of density to type of war: working out the influences of much or little land-room upon tactics. . . .

For myself, I am going to taste the flavour of true leisure. For 46 years have I worked and been worked. Remaineth 23 years (of expectancy). May they be like Flecker's

'a great Sunday that goes on and on'.[3]

If I like this leisure when it comes, do me the favour of hoping that I may be able to afford its prolongation for ever and ever.

So these are our joint and separate wishes for 1935 and all that.

LHB

1 Sir Arnold Wilson (1884–1940) had been Acting Civil Commissioner in the Persian Gulf 1918–20. Lawrence had been highly critical of the policies with which he was associated.
2 Liddell Hart had just been appointed Military Correspondent of *The Times*.
3 Lawrence was recalling the Prologue to *The Golden Journey to Samarkand* by James Elroy Flecker:

> When the great markets by the sea shut fast
>   All that calm Sunday that goes on and on:
> When even lovers find their peace at last,
>   And Earth is but a star, that once had shone.'

My last letter for this year. Next year I am going to draw in my ink-horns: for this year I have tried — vainly! — not to spend more than 2/– a week on post. After February my total means will be 25/– a week, and I shall not spend more than three pence weekly upon post; After the first week, when I have to warn people that I am ceasing to write.

These reflections continue my mood of last Friday night. It was pouring with rain as I left London and rode up the Great North Road. At the crest of that rise towards Welwyn I had to pull my front forks back into the main road: they had turned off towards Ayot. If it had been finer, then I might have indulged my appetite: but as old age comes forward my strength of purpose goes. Had I called at Ayot that night and found you both there, no power but yourselves would have set me again into the night and the rain northward: and I felt that you might press me to stop. Such a dog's night, it was.

Instead the Brough purred smoothly, to Royston and Biggleswade and Stamford and Grantham and Bawtry and Goole and Bridlington. Even the rain ceased after a while, and I got in warm and dry. Today I have cleaned the good servant till it shines again. All the last two months it has been stored at Clouds Hill, until I felt that it almost shared my unhappiness in our separation.

Your news of health makes me feel a little unquiet. A young man overstrains in some race or game and falls exhausted. Half an hour later he is happily eating a meal. So was I, till I got to Uxbridge and tried to keep pace with the other fellows in the Hut. Then I found that I was fagged out for hours after their recoveries. As for G.B.S. he is as old again as I was; the strain of that collapse will hang behind his eyes for weeks. Beg him to be careful: or perhaps better not, for he is wilful enough to react against advice. Better, I suppose, to break than to rust away: but how I hate both choices.

I hope you get securely and well on to your *Reina del Pacifico*, and I hope the cruise is a success. I have always had a picture of Magellan in my mind, and would like to see his Straits. They were dangerous for sail, but today all such narrows are easy water. I saw your ship once. She was good to look at.

When you come back my great change will have happened. I wonder ... I wonder how it will be with me. Twelve years ago I thought that the question of an 'after' to the Service would never happen: the twelve years felt as though they would be enough for me. Yet here I am still strong and trenchant-minded, but with nothing in my hand. I have learned only the word NO in 46 years, it seems. However, I suppose myself is my own business and I should not trouble others with it. At least you will find me very different, after this.

I spent Christmas at my cottage. Mrs. Knowles, my tenant across the road, had suddenly died a few days before, and it was necessary to talk leases and arrangements. Fortunately her eldest son, who I like, is hovering on the edge of marriage and wishes to settle there after it. So the peace of Clouds Hill continues. Mrs. Knowles and I were friends.

Between paragraphs I have eaten one of your chocolates. That is why there are so many short paragraphs. Thank you. I wish I could have seen you last Friday, and yet got here to time. They kept me till afternoon at Air Ministry.

I do hope that voyage is excellent. When you come back, Time will mean nothing to me: Then we can meet and not write.

                                                                    T.E.S.

British Library

H. S. EDE
3.i.35   Ozone Hotel Bridlington Yorks

No: the address is not spoof. I have been here for some months doing my last R.A.F. job, overseeing the refit of ten of our boats in a great garage in the (empty) town. A summer seaside resort is an uncanny place in mid-winter.

The refit is due to be completed by the end of February; and early in March I 'get my ticket'. It's like a blank wall beyond which I cannot even imagine. Exactly what leisure is like, whether it will madden me or suit me, what it means to wake up every day and know there is no compulsion to get out of bed ... it's no good. When it comes, I shall try to deal with it; but now, beforehand, I can only say that I wish it had not to be.

The assets are my cottage in Dorsetshire (Clouds Hill, Moreton, Dorset ... you have the address just right) 25/– a week, a bike. If to that I find myself in possession of a quiet mind, then I shall be fortunate. I think I have to 'draw' this mind when I draw my discharge; and dare only hope to find it full and quiet. I do not often confess it to people, but I am always aware that madness lies very near me, always. The R.A.F's solidity and routine have been anchors holding me to life and the world. I wish they had not to be cut.

    [...]

Bodleian Reserve

ARTHUR RUSSELL
3.1.35   Ozone Hotel Bridlington Yorks

Dear Russ

I spent three nights at Clouds Hill, liking the place, but not easy in mind, for Mrs Knowles died suddenly a few weeks ago, and her son, Pat, wants to take on her place and is puzzled how to do it. So we camped there, he in her house and I in mine, and ate a chicken for Christmas and wondered how we were going to work out.

How are you? Do you still drive your bus and swim every morning and think about things? My time in the R.A.F. ends two months from now, and I have not a plan or a notion in my head, for the future. I often think of you as a person to whom I could perhaps come for a while, until I can see better what I want. I am old now, and there seems to be nothing that I care to do. I have a little money (enough to bring me in about 25/– a week) and a Brough (which has to go back to George next month) and a push-bike. Do you think, if I came to Coventry, that you could find me some quiet place in which to settle for a little time, to make up my mind? Nothing definite to be fixed yet: perhaps when March comes I won't need it: but I may want to get away from myself, somewhere where I will not be talked about or known. I think you are the only Coventry chap I know, so it might be a good place. I thought of getting a room, or a bed, anyway, with some working family; till I can pull myself together. I hate leaving the R.A.F. and feel like a snail whose shell is being pulled off him!

Don't let this worry you; and don't fix anything up: but as you go round, just keep one eye open for a backwater in which I could be quiet (and cheap) for a spell. I don't want to do anything: just to moon about and think!

Clouds Hill is charming, now, I think. I hope to live there, after the change has happened and been forgotten: but I don't want to go there till then. I might get to dislike it, you see.

Do send a line here (I am overseeing the refit of ten Air Force boats at Brid. and shall be here till the end of Feb.) and tell me if you are prosperous or not.

Yours
T E Shaw

University of Texas

A. S. FRERE-REEVES[1]

7.1.35   Ozone Hotel Bridlington Yorks

Dear F.-R.

What good books Heinemann's (sometimes) publish! I have just been reading Ford Madox Ford's *It was the nightingale,* and it seems to me that at last he has risen to his full height.[2] He was always a figure — if you remember his *English Review* you remember the most heartening uprush of English Literature in our generation — and he has written now delicately and now greatly ... greatly is it; I wonder. I was thinking of the war tetralogy. That uncomfortably-named Tietjens, that flux and flourish of characters all devoid of charm, that refusal of each paragraph of every volume to be set on fire. Yes, I think it is probably a great book, though how it can be, without charm, Heaven only knows. Why doesn't your firm collect its bits from Duckworth (wasn't it Duckworth) and re-set it in one fat volume?

However there's been a shelf of Hueffers and Fords ... and at the last he mellows and produces a book of enchantment. The ichor[3] lies in his having now drawn himself at full length. Nobody he meets keeps an aura; but he makes himself more charming, because more full and human, as the pages go on. I like the humour, the pride, the fastidiousness, the folly (even the prejudices of ignorance, where he tries to blacken Lloyd George and Hitler — far be it from me to defend those two great ones.[4] They can forget people like him and me); and most of all I enjoy the superb technical competence. He laughs so well at himself, and never overdraws a mood.

Never? Well, I'm not sure. About six times he tells us how adeptly he handles the time-switch, and about 500 times he does handle it adeptly. I could have done either without the praise, or without the example. By insisting on both we are led too much to see the wheels going round. And he didn't correct the last draft enough after it got into type. At least five

1 Publisher; a director of Messrs Heinemann, London.
2 Ford Madox Ford, formerly Ford Hermann Hueffer (1873–1939); his autobiographical volume *It was the nightingale* — one of several — had been published in 1933. He had founded the *English Review* in 1908 and edited it for fifteen months. The 'war tetralogy' referred to by Lawrence was a sequence of novels published between 1924 and 1928 now known as *Parade's End*; Christopher Tietjens was its central character.
3 In Greek mythology ichor was the ethereal fluid supposed to flow in the veins of the gods.
4 That Lawrence saw Hitler as 'great' does not imply approval of his regime or its policies. Cf. Winston Churchill: 'Although no subsequent political action can condone wrong deeds, history is replete with examples of men who have risen to power by employing stern, grim, and even frightful methods, but who, nevertheless, when their life is revealed as a whole, have been regarded as great figures whose lives have enriched the story of mankind. So may it be with Hitler.' (*Great Contemporaries*, 1937)

sentences fail to parse correctly (five? what's that to the five thousand in *Eimi*, which also Heinemann's should publish in England. Sell 500 copies, I think, and lose £50, but what a credit to your taste. *Eimi*, by E. E. Cummings.[1] The U.S.A. publishers are called Covia and Friede: 'und' I suppose) and not five sentences but nearly the 500 this time are disfigured by a plethora of 'thats', thats conjunctive, relative, demonstrative. In one nasty sentence there lay four of them.

I suppose I'm hypercritical of prepositions and link-words; they trip my ear but not my eye nor my mind. The book as a whole and in all its parts is ravishing. It also told us the proper story of the review and of Pound, and of Quinn. Lately I've had a letter or two from Pound who (misled perhaps by his name into thinking himself a born economist) seems to have run off on a new hobby-horse of financial theory. I think perhaps my art of boat-building is now the only one the silly ass has not tried and done fairly well. It wouldn't matter, but that all the time we are missing a full-sized poet, thereby. Still, he might have died young, and that would have come to the same thing, except to himself. Always angry, is Ezra P.

I hope F.M.F. feels, now he has done it, that he has done it, for good? It seems to me almost perfect as writing, quite perfect in taste, and lovely in matter. He has twice before tried to draw himself: or perhaps I have only come across two of several tries; but this time he has succeeded and made his success seem effortlessly easy. It *is* a good book. I am writing to you in the hope that perhaps you have not read it word for word. I began by tossing through its first pages, but soon stopped and went back and digested them one by one. The thing is beautifully fine-knit, and has not a spare word in it — except that swarm of nasty thats, of course!

Do give yourself a day off-duty and bribe her Reeveship to keep your door against callers and read it end for end. There is no youth or promise to excite you — but fulfilment, fulfilment. Ever so good.

Yours
T. E. Shaw

University of Texas

1 *Eimi* (1933) has been described as 'a typographically difficult but enthralling journal of a trip to Russia'.

ARTHUR RUSSELL
18.1.35   Ozone Hotel Bridlington Yorks

Dear R.

That is kind of you. I shall come, either for a look-see, or for a stay-put-for-a-while. The losing of the R.A.F. is going to hit me quite hard.

I'm glad it's a coach, and not a bus. A bus is dull. In the coach you ought to get variety. I shall volunteer to punch your tickets, if any.

My Brough still goes like unholy smoke, when I turn its taps on. But I have a feeling that it will have to go soon. Did you ever see my little motor boat? It was a gem. They have it now at Felixstowe (Officers Mess toy) and I only hope they get from it a tenth of the fun I had.[1]

Yes, you must see Clouds Hill this year, if things permit. I have all my books and records there, and love it.

Don't come to Bridlington. I work all day at the boat-shed, and have to visit York, Sheffield and London frequently, at irregular times. Even if I had promised to be here, I mightn't be able to keep it. Patience. March is very near, alas!

Regards to No 96.

                                                    Yours
                                                    T.E.S.

University of Texas

MRS CHARLOTTE SHAW
26.1.35   Ozone Hotel Bridlington

Miss Patch will send it on. I hope you are right out of the path of this storm, which is starring all the black windows with wild hail at the moment. It is westerly, an off-shore wind for Bridlington and a great gale which beats the sea down to flatness, and puckers and purfles the running gutters and pavements of the town. Indeed I hope you are not in a ship near it.

This is not a letter, but to report that last Monday Eliot and I lunched with Alexander Korda, the film king. He was quite unexpectedly sensitive, for a king; seemed to understand at once when I put to him the incon-veniences his proposed film of *Revolt* would set in my path ... and ended

---

1 The 'little motor boat' was the *Biscuit*, a small speedboat which had been given to him and which he had restored to working order during his posting to R.A.F. Cattewater/Mount Batten; he had had many outings in it, with, among others, Mrs Sydney Smith and Lady Astor.

the discussion by agreeing that it should not be attempted without my consent. He will not announce its abandonment, because while he has it on his list other producers will avoid thought of it. But it will not be done. You can imagine how this gladdens me. Eliot took it like a dear.

Thereafter I sat to John for two days, twice each day; and he painted with great ease and surety (a new John, this) a little head-and-shoulders of me in oil, R.A.F. uniform, with cap on head. I think it much the best thing of me he has ever done. It sparkles with life, is gay-coloured and probably not unlike my real face when thinking. So lively and clean. He himself agreed that it had come off and was comforted, as lately he has found it hard to finish anything. In his pleasure he went on to do two charcoal drawings of me, three-quarter lengths, standing — and then gave me the better of them. I have put it with Merton, who took over the business from Emery Walker, and have asked him to copy it, for safety. A fine swagger drawing: small head, thin body and big knees!

That's a good budget of news. May you and G.B.S. be prospering, wherever your ship is. Voyaging is like flying: whatever the drawbacks, everybody who is not at sea or in the air wishes he was! But what a night! A harbour-night, for sure.

                                                                    T.E.S.

British Library

BERNARD SHAW
31.1.35   Ozone Hotel Bridlington Yorks

Dear G.B.S.

This is very bad news. I had been imagining you both off safely for South America, acquiring your winter dose of sunlight. I am so sorry.[1]

You say she is making ground, which is so far good; but that return of blood poison may be very severe on the heart. How Arthurian it sounds, to have an old wound re-open! Please, when she is better, say how very much I'd like to come and see her, though this job is now beginning to accelerate towards its finish (on March 1) and I am likely to be rushed off my feet as the weeks pass. March 1 is my sad date, when I go: and it is also the date for the completion of these ten boats' refitting.

Too True made an awful lot of talk. Bridlington in winter is a large village only, and I'm a known character. So I funked going to see the play.

---

1 The Shaws went on their travels later in the year and were in South Africa at the time of Lawrence's fatal accident in May.

They would have cheered or jeered, probably: cheered, I'm afraid; so I funked it. Sorry. They also did it at Oxford! In London people don't worry, having full-sized affairs daily; but here in these provinces any reputation is rare: and *Too True* surprised them with its immediacy. 'It isn't really entertainment at all' said one foreman. 'It means something'.

I won't write, because you'll have worry enough as it is: but do take care of yourself. You aren't used to the English winter, either ... not of late, anyhow.

Yours
T.E. Shaw

British Library

T. W. BEAUMONT[1]   Ozone Hotel Bridlington
31.i.35

Dear Beaumont

I vary between my cottage (Clouds Hill, Moreton, Dorset: my only permanent address) and this place, where I'm watching ten boats under repair for the R.A.F. Very fully engaged, and always dodging about, like a flea with a bad conscience.

My time runs out a month hence, and I shall be very sorry. The work passes my time, and the last twelve years would have been long, without it. Yes, I shall be really sorry.

Someone (Mrs Bernard Shaw, I think it was) sent me a copy of Major Bray's book. It wasn't as silly as the Sunday Papers tried to make out: but there wasn't anything to it. Bray is a quite honest but not very wise fellow, who was in Jeddah for a while right at the beginning of the Arab business, and then went to Mesopotamia. I have not heard from him for years, but there was nothing in the book to which one could object.

No, Clouds Hill wouldn't look right with a valet! It is a cottage in the middle of a great heath, of bracken and heather. Two rooms; no bed and no kitchen, and no drains, but a spring in the garden, and a feeling of utter peace. I may go there for a while after my discharge.

Yours
T E Shaw

You ask me for my foot size ... it's six, usually!

---

1 T. W. (Tom) Beaumont served with Lawrence in 1918: his name is listed in Appendix I of *Seven Pillars of Wisdom* as a member of the Hejaz Armoured Car Company.

But don't go and bust your firm, pinching slippers off them. I hope it prospers, and yourself.

I'd meant to try and see you, but am so busy when here, and so often in the South, that I can't either find time to get to you, or security to make an engagement. Let us leave it till after March 1.

Bodleian Reserve

SIR RONALD STORRS

31.1.35   Ozone Hotel Bridlington

Dear R.S.

No; alas, Hythe will know me no more. I have only a month to do in the R.A.F. and will spend it up here, overseeing the refit of ten R.A.F. boats in a local garage. The name of the Hotel is real.[1] So, I think, is the ozone, or is it the fishmarket that smells? It is empty, cold, and rather nice. [...]

I hope you are restoring yourself to the former trim, now that that has become your primary duty. Your best excuse for retiring is to benefit thereby in health. Your handwriting retains its vigour.

Alas, I have nothing to say at the moment. After my discharge I have somehow to pick up a new life and occupy myself—but beforehand it looks and feels like an utterly blank wall. Old age coming, I suppose; at any rate I can admit to being quite a bit afraid for myself, which is a new feeling. Up till now I've never come to the end of anything.

Ah well. We shall see after the Kalends of March. Indeed, I venture to hope we shall see each other, but I don't know where I shall live, or what do, or how call myself.[2]

Postal address? Here till Feb. 28 and thereafter the only suggestion is to write to T. E. Shaw, at Clouds Hill, Moreton, Dorset, which is my tiny cottage. If I don't stay there, I shall at least visit it sometimes.

Please regard me to Lady Storrs: and please make yourself again into fighting trim: or, perhaps you are now. Good.

                                                    Yours
                                                    TES

Bodleian Reserve

1 Storrs had suggested that 'Ozone Hotel' was an alibi.
2 See General Introduction, pp. xxv–xxvi.

ROBERT GRAVES[1]

4.2.35   Ozone Hotel Bridlington Yorks

Dear R.G.

I have been — by lack of thought — guilty of a great fault in taste, and I am so sorry about it.[2] Please believe it was neither conscious nor sub-conscious. When I told you that I might be short of money at Clouds Hill I had completely forgotten — as for years I have forgotten it — how long ago I was able to help you when you were in difficulties. I was stupidly thinking aloud. Long ago I found out what income I needed for retirement and set it aside, invested. The rest — what I had and what I made — I spent on friends and books and pictures and motor-bikes and joys of sorts. Five years ago I found I needed more, to spend on improving my cottage; so I did that *Odyssey* translation, and put in bath and heater of my own choosing or designing, always secure in the knowledge that the income was safe and intact ... and then down goes the rate of interest and the income shrinks. It is enough to make a saint swear, for had I foreseen it, I would have reserved more. Now when I wanted to be at ease (I have a deep sense that my life, in the real sense, my Life, is over) I have to make about £700 more.

It is very good of you to offer to share the job with me ... but needless. I can easily make that. Easier still could I make ten times that; it's the stopping short that is skilful. I blame not circumstances but my own bad calculating. I pride myself on being knowing and did not foresee the Treasury-induced spell of cheap money. Another eight or nine years and the rates will bound up. Meanwhile my peace must be mixed with effort. Damn.

I had guessed that you would be running short, and had wanted to tell you how my time of spending was over and so I couldn't help you any more. Then the *Claudius* big noise came along and I saw that you were safe. Safe, I think, now for quite a while. Your next book will be bought

1 Graves had been invited by a London daily newspaper to write an obituary of Lawrence to be filed away in its 'morgue', whereupon he had written to Lawrence enquiring 'rather jokingly' what he was to do about the request, and asking 'whether he [Lawrence] would like to take on the job himself and, like the Aztecs, leave nothing to chance' (*RGB*, p. 179). This was Lawrence's reply. An abridged and adapted version of the letter was published as the lead story (headlined MYSELF — BY LAWRENCE) in the *Evening Standard* on 20 May 1935 — the day before Lawrence's funeral — with an introductory article by Graves. Subsequently it was published in *DG* — apart from the opening section — and *RGB*. The text in both these books shows evidence of substantial rewriting, particularly in the final paragraphs.

2 In a letter not printed here (*RGB*: 13 January 1935) Lawrence had written about the modest financial prospects facing him on retirement, whereupon Graves had offered 'to help him with his cottage troubles' (*RGB*, p. 179).

on the merits of your last, always supposing it is not poetry! That is a comfortable state ... but less comfortable than mine, for I am safe now, and only need another slight effort to be comfortable for all time. You may not ever look to cease work, wholly: though I am glad to hear that the Balearics are cheap for living. I had feared their prices would rise with their popularity. If you hear that I have done something else, you will be able to put the motive to it. I shall be rounding off my capital. You will be a reserve, only if ever I get meshed (like you at Boar's Hill) and unable to help myself; which will be bad management, with my notoriety to help me!

New page, new subject. I saw Alexander Korda last month. I had not taken seriously the rumours that he meant to make a film of me, but they were persistent, so at last I asked for a meeting and explained that I was inflexibly opposed to the whole notion. He was most decent and understanding and has agreed to put it off till I die or welcome it. Is it age coming on, or what? But I loathe the notion of being celluloided. My rare visits to cinemas always deepen in me a sense of their superficial falsity ... vulgarity, I would have said, only I like the vulgarity that means common man, and the badness of films seems to me like an edited and below-the-belt speciousness. Yet the news-theatres, as they call them (little cinemas here and there that present fact, photographed and current fact only), delight me. The camera seems wholly in place as journalism: but when it tries to re-create it boobs and sets my teeth on edge. So there won't be a film of me. Korda is like an oil-company which has drilled often and found two or three gushers, and has prudently invested some of its proceeds in buying options over more sites. Some he may develop and others not. Oil is a transient business.

Money explained, films considered. Let us now pass to the epitaph. Yes, Hogarth did the morgue-men a first sketch of me in 1920, and they are right to overhaul their stocks. Rather you than Liddell Hart, who seems to have no critical sense in my regard. I won't touch it myself, but if you do, don't give too much importance to what I did in Arabia during the war. I feel that the Middle Eastern settlement put through by Winston Churchill and Young and me in 1921 (which stands in every particular ... if only the other Peace Treaties did!) should weigh more than fighting. And I feel too that this settlement should weigh less than my life since 1922, for the conquest of the last element, the air, seems to me the only major task of our generation; and I have convinced myself that progress to-day is made not by the single genius, but by the common effort. To me it is the multitude of rough transport drivers filling all the roads of England every night, who make this the mechanical age. And it is the airmen, the mechanics, who are overcoming the air, not the Mollisons and Orlebars. The genius raids, but the common people occupy and possess. Wherefore I stayed in the ranks and served to the best of my ability, much influencing my fellow airmen towards a pride in themselves and their inarticulate duty. I tried to make them see — with some success.

That for eight years, and now for the last four I have been so curiously fortunate as to share in a little revolution we have made in boat design. People have thought we were at finality there, for since 1850 ships have merely got bigger. When I went into R.A.F. boats in 1929, every type was an Admiralty design. All were round-bottomed, derived from the first hollow tree, with only a fin, called a keel, to delay their rolling about and over. They progressed by pushing their own bulk of water aside. Now (1935) not one type of R.A.F. boat in production is naval.... We have found, chosen, selected or derived our own sorts: they have (power for power) three times the speed of their predecessors, less weight, less cost, more room, more safety, more seaworthiness. As their speed increases, they rise out of the water and run over its face. They cannot roll, nor pitch, having no pendulum nor period, but a subtly modelled planing bottom and sharp edges.

Now I do not claim to have made these boats. They have grown out of the joint experience, skill and imaginations of many men. But I can (secretly) feel that they owe to me their opportunity and their acceptance. The pundits met them with a fierce hostility: all the R.A.F. sailors, and all the Navy, said that they would break, sink, wear out, be unmanageable. To-day we are advising the War Office in refitting the coast defences entirely with boats of our model, and the Admiralty has specified them for the modernised battleships: while the German, Chinese, Spanish and Portuguese Governments have adopted them! In inventing them we have had to make new engines, new auxiliaries, use new timbers, new metals, new materials. It has been five years of intense and co-ordinated progress. Nothing now hinders the application of our design to big ships — except the conservatism of man, of course. Patience. It cannot be stopped now.

All this boasting is not to glorify myself, but to explain; and here enters my last subject for this letter, your strictures upon the changes I have made in myself since the time we felt so much together at Oxford. You're quite right about the change. I was then trying to write; to be perhaps an artist (for the *Seven Pillars* had pretensions towards design, and was written with great pains as prose) or to be at least cerebral. My head was aiming to create intangible things. That's not well put: all creation is tangible. What I was trying to do, I suppose, was to carry a superstructure of ideas upon or above anything I made.

Well, I failed in that. By measuring myself against such people as yourself and Augustus John, I could feel that I was not made out of the same stuff. Artists excite me and attract me; seduce me. Almost I could be an artist, but there is a core that puts on the brake. If I knew what it was I would tell you, or become one of you. Only I can't.

So I changed direction, right, and went into the R.A.F. after straightening out that Eastern tangle with Winston, a duty that fell to me, I having been partly the cause of the tangle. How well the Middle East has done: it, more than any part of the world, has gained from that war.

However, as I said, I went into the R.A.F. to serve a mechanical purpose, not as leader but as a cog of the machine. The key-word, I think, is machine. I have been mechanical since, and a good mechanic, for my self-training to become an artist has greatly widened my field of view. I leave it to others to say whether I chose well or not: one of the benefits of being part of the machine is that one learns that one doesn't matter!

If you remember the history you will see that Laura and I never met. Nancy and I met, definitely, at Oxford. Laura saw me too late, after I had changed my direction. She is, was, absolutely right to avoid communication with me. There is no woman in the machines, in any machines. You are different. I do not pretend to classify or rank; but you can understand a mechanic serving his bits-and-pieces, whereas she could not. I do not know or care if you are better, or she: it is merely that I like your work, and you could (mutatis mutandis) have done as I have done. Whereas she and I could never have changed places. The bar between us was not her artistry, but her self and mine: and quite likely her sex and mine.

All this reads like a paragraph of D.H.L., my step-namesake. I do not think for a moment that I have got it right, but I hope from it your sense of character will show you that there are no faults on either side, but common sense, the recognition of a difficulty too arduous to be worth the effort of surmounting, when there are so many other more rewarding activities within reach. Don't worry or regret or desire me to change the face of nature. We are lucky to have proportion and toleration to pad our bones.

Yours

T.E.S.

What a whale of a letter! I apologise. Five minutes talk would have been so much more fun! Let's hope he does do *Claudius* and you have to help. I told him *No Decency*[1] was a pretty good film-subject, too!

DG/RGB/Sotheby's[2]

1 i.e. *No Decency Left*, written by Robert Graves and Laura Riding under the pseudonym 'Barbara Rich'. See letter to Graves dated 21 April 1931 (p. 452).
2 The letter was given by Graves to Sir Alec Guinness (who had played Lawrence on the stage in Terence Rattigan's *Ross* and Feisal in the Sam Spiegel/David Lean film *Lawrence of Arabia*). Guinness sold it in December 1987 at Sotheby's on behalf of Brompton Oratory. It is now in the United States.

7 · THE FINAL WEEKS

February–May 1935

On 26 February 1935 Lawrence bicycled south from Bridlington, an airman no longer, on his way home to Clouds Hill. His arrival was delayed by the knowledge that journalists were besieging the cottage, and even after he reached it, their presence drove him away. Eventually, having appealed for help to Churchill and arranged a truce with senior members of the press, he was left alone.

'Next year', he had written to Charlotte Shaw on New Year's Eve 1934, 'I am going to draw in my ink-horns [. . .] and I shall not spend more than three pence weekly upon post.' The principal weapon in this attempt to reduce the volume of his correspondence was a specially printed card bearing the message: 'To tell you that in future I shall write very few letters' — the realisation of the idea which had first occurred to him in India. By including a copy of this card with every letter he sent he hoped to discourage replies and at last stem the tidal flow.

Nevertheless during these last weeks between his leaving the Air Force and his premature death he wrote numerous letters, though some were little more than brief notes on the back of the specially printed card. At times he wrote almost in protest; 'What ails me', he complained to Robin Buxton on 13 April, 'is this odd sense of being laid aside before being worn out'. However, many, perhaps the majority, of his notes and letters from this period have a world-weary tone, suggesting a reversion to his 1929 mood of 'something broken in the works' — a phrase which he used in his last communication with Lady Astor, written on 8 May. A note to her three days earlier implies that the passage of time had brought no sense of improvement in his general psychological condition: 'something is finished with my leaving the R.A.F. It gets worse instead of healing over.' 'There's such a blank, afterwards,' he told two R.A.F. officer friends that same day, 5 May, while on the following day he wrote to Bruce Rogers, 'I'm "out" now, of the R.A.F. and sitting in my cottage rather puzzled to find out what has happened to me, is happening and will happen. At present the feeling is mere bewilderment. I imagine leaves must feel like this after they have fallen from their tree and until they die.' The 'fallen leaf' metaphor also occurs in a letter written on 6 May, to Eric Kennington, a letter which ends with what almost has the ring of a valediction: 'Peace to everybody.'

Yet on other occasions he wrote eloquently and at length, showing that his statement to Mrs Shaw in his letter of New Year's Eve 1934 that he was still 'strong and trenchant-minded' was no empty claim. Indeed, several of the letters of the last few days before his accident are most vigorously written—that to Ralph Isham on 10 May, in anger at hearing that an American university had published a letter of his without seeking permission, being particularly forthright. The letter to 'Posh' Palmer of the same date shows him offering lively encouragement to an old friend who, apparently, was in a state of near-suicidal depression, telling him that the gas-oven offered no solution and inviting, indeed virtually commanding, him to visit Clouds Hill. The last letter of all, to Karl Parker, the newly appointed Keeper of the Fine Art Department of the Ashmolean Museum, Oxford, dated 12 May, is generally brisk and business-like, though it contains the sentence: 'At present I'm sitting in my cottage and getting used to an empty life.' He looks forward, however, to the time when this 'spell' is over and 'I begin to go about again'.

PETER DAVIES
Thursday, 28 Feb 35

Dear P.D.

On Tuesday I took my discharge from the R.A.F. and started southward by road, meaning to call at Bourne and see Manning: but to-day I turned eastward, instead, hearing that he was dead.[1]

It seems queer news, for the books★ are so much more intense than ever he was, and his dying doesn't, cannot, affect them. Therefore what has died really? Our hopes of having more from him—but that is greed. The writing them was such pain—and pains—to him. Of late I had devoutly wished him to cease trying to write. He had done enough; two wonderful works,★[2] full-sized: four lesser things. A man who can produce one decent book is a fortunate man, surely?

Some friends of mine, in dying, have robbed me; Hogarth and Aubrey Herbert are two empty places which no one and nothing can ever fill. Whereas Doughty and Hardy and Manning had earned their release. Yet

1 Manning had been one of Peter Davies's authors.
2 The asterisks are Lawrence's: the 'two wonderful works' were *Her Privates We* and *Scenes and Portraits*.

his going takes away a person of great kindness, exquisite and pathetic. It means one rare thing the less in our setting. You will be very sad.

My losing the R.A.F. numbs me, so that I haven't much feeling to spare for the while. In fact I find myself wishing all the time that my own curtain would fall. It seems as if I had finished, now. Strange to think how Manning, sick, poor, fastidious, worked like a slave for year after year, not on the concrete and palpable boats or engines of my ambition, but on stringing words together to shape his ideas and reasonings. That's what being a born writer means, I suppose. And to-day it is all over and nobody ever heard of him. If he had been famous in his day he would have liked it, I think; liked it deprecatingly. As for fame-after-death, it's a thing to spit at; the only minds worth winning are the warm ones about us. If we miss those we are failures. I suppose his being not really English, and so generally ill, barred him from his fellows.[1] Only not in *Her Privates We* which is hot-blooded and familiar. It is puzzling. How I wish, for my own sake, that he hadn't slipped away in this fashion; but how like him. He was too shy to let anyone tell him how good he was.

Yours ever
T.E.Shaw

DG/Mitchell Library, Sydney, N.S.W.

ARTHUR RUSSELL
6.iii.35   [London]

Dear Russ

Thank you: you are a comfort. When I come, I'll suggest my doubling up with you, and so I'll be able to pay my shot to your people more easily.

It will not be just yet. The newspaper men are besieging Clouds Hill, and till they ease off I'm going to keep gently on the move. First I have business in London, with my Bank to find out what my means will be after I straighten everything up. Then I have a long call to make in Scotland, before the summer visitors get there. But I promise myself a rest at Coventry, with a nice sort of safe feeling. You shall have fair warning, too. I don't want to come till this restless 'lost' feeling I now have has gone dull. The R.A.F. meant a lot to me.

Yours
S.

University of Texas

---

1 Manning had been born in Sydney and was a chronic asthmatic.

HON. FRANCIS RODD
6.iii.35

Thank you very much. I feel lost, now, but everything passes.

Don't look for me in Dorset till the summer is passing: the Press lay siege to my cottage and I must keep away. Going to the Midlands, I think: but we shall certainly meet somehow soon.

TES

Bodleian Reserve

ALEC DIXON
6.iii.35

It is a feeling of aimless unrest: and of course I am sorry, while knowing it had to be.

Clouds Hill is beset by pressmen, and because of them I stay momently in London, with an idea of wandering in the Midlands, perhaps, for a while. After they tire, the cottage should be a peaceful place. Pat Knowles, the Sergeant's eldest son, hopes to marry and settle on that side of the road. He and I get on easily,

I hope the book goes. What an ache of a profession writing is! Yet there must be at least a craving in it, for here you are at *Tinned Soldier* before the other is accepted. I shall not object to anything you may say: but I prefer sauce to butter, if one has to choose between overdoses of condiment!

I wish I wasn't too old to carry on!

Yours
T.E.S.

I'm sending out dozens of the enclosed.[1] Good idea?

Bodleian Reserve

1 i.e. his specially printed card.

WINSTON CHURCHILL[1]

19 March 1935   c/o Sir Herbert Baker 2 Smith Square Westminster

Dear Winston,

I wonder if you can help me? My RAF discharge happened about three weeks ago, and I've since had to run three times from my cottage in Dorset (where I want to live) through pressure from newspaper men. Each time I've taken refuge in London, but life here is expensive, and I cannot go on moving about indefinitely.

My plan is to try and persuade the press people, the big noises, to leave me alone. If they agree to that the free-lancers find no market for their activities.

What I am hoping from you is a means of approach to Esmond Harmsworth, who is the new Chairman of the Newspaper Proprietors Association. He used to know me in Paris, 16 years ago, but will have forgotten. If you could tell him I exist, and very much want to see him, I could put my case before him in ten minutes and get a Yes or No.

I am writing to you because I fancy, from something you once said, that you are (or were) on good terms with Esmond — who anyway used to be a decent person. If you can get in touch with him, without embarrassing yourself, I would be most grateful.

I'll see Sir Herbert Baker tomorrow and get him to keep for me any message that may arrive during this week. I believe his Smith Square house is on the telephone, if that simplifies things: though it usually is more trouble than it is worth.

I'm sorry to appeal in this way; but they have got me properly on the run. I blacked the eye of one photographer last Sunday and had to escape over the back of the hedge!

Yours
T. E. Shaw

Churchill Papers[2]

---

1 Churchill, who retained a great admiration for Lawrence despite his 'hiding his talent in a napkin while the Empire needed its best' (*T.E. Lawrence by His Friends* p. 201), invited him to visit Chartwell on the following Sunday. Lawrence arrived on his push-bike for what was to prove their last meeting.

2 Printed in *Winston S. Churchill* by Martin Gilbert, Companion Part 2 to Volume V (Heinemann, 1981).

EDWARD W. DAVIES[1]
27/3/35   Clouds Hill

Dear Mr. Davies

I hurl another autograph recklessly towards you, in thanks for your letter of the 21st which I found waiting for me here last night. Will you please, when you find a good chance, thank Mr. Gleave for his good offices? By degrees peace will become ensured!

Since I saw you I have seen several Directors and Owners of Agencies (can one own an agency?) and made working arrangements with most of them. I also saw Mr. Esmond Harmsworth, and have at his request written him a letter to lay before the N.P.A.[2] If they do not rear up and fall over backwards with rage at it, then I am likely to be ignored by the entire London Press hereafter.

If you have opportunity in the future, please do your best always to suppress me. I am most grateful for what you have already done.[3]

Yours sincerely
T.E. Shaw

Bodleian Reserve

SIR EVELYN WRENCH
1 April 1935   Clouds Hill Moreton Dorset

Dear E.W.

Yes, Mrs. Hardy knew my H.Q. and here your note waited till I came. I have been owing you a letter for so long — ever since I read *Uphill*,[4] which had a poignant directness of impact that I found somehow very gracious.

1 Of the Newspaper Society, to which Lawrence had turned for help because of press harassment.
2 Newspaper Proprietors Association; see previous letter. A draft of Lawrence's letter to Harmsworth is printed as *DG* 569.
3 Davies was plainly delighted to have come to the aid of so distinguished a figure as Lawrence and wrote back by return: 'Thank you for your letter of yesterday. I suppose Liddell Hart could write an admirable chapter on my strategy in extracting a further sample of your writing, but he would be wrong again, as my letter was prompted by the vanity of wanting to let you know that I had done something. Even in fable, I believe the mouse doesn't help the lion more than once in a lifetime; still, if the chance should ever arise again, it will be my pleasure no less than my duty.'
4 *Uphill*, published in 1934, was the first volume of Wrench's autobiography; he had written to Lawrence asking for permission to write about him in the second volume, *Struggle*, which appeared later in 1935.

Need I be in the new one? Often I wish I had known at the beginning the weary lag that any sudden reputation brings. I should have refrained from doing even the little that I did; and now I would be left alone and able to live as I chose. To have news value is to have a tin can tied to one's tail. However what you say will not be vulgar: and therefore it may serve to correct (at least in my own esteem) some of what others have said.

I cannot say about London: my income is a 'country' one and therefore my town visits will not be frequent. I was there a fortnight ago, to see Esmond Harmsworth and enlist his aid with the Press to leave me alone. Now I am hoping to stay here quite a while, finishing off my cottage after my own liking. There is pleasure (and engrossment) in arranging and fixing one's surroundings. I find I spend nearly the whole day, beginning job after job and laying them aside, part-done. The sense of infinite time, all my own, is so new.

I've thought out the enclosed card idea, to ease the labour of answering letters. Good, don't you think?

Will it do if I come up in the summer? Or do you ever travel (not that I can put anybody up: I camp out amidst the ruins!) or can we do it on paper? I would like to be useful to you, any way I can...

Yours
T. E. Shaw

Bodleian Reserve

GEORGE BROUGH
5.IV.35   Clouds Hill Moreton Dorset

[...] I've only ridden the ancient-of-days twice this year. It goes like a shell, and seems as good as new.[1] The push-bike is a reality, though. I came down here from Yorkshire on it and have toured much of the S. of England on it in the last three weeks. It is dull hard work when the wind is against: but in lanes, and sheltered places and in calms or before winds, wholly delightful. So quiet: one hears all the country noises. Cheap — very! not tiring, up to 60 or 70 miles a day, which is all that I achieve, with sightseeing: and very clean on a wet road.

The loss of my R.A.F. job halves my income, so that my motor cycling would have been much reduced for the future, even without this 30 m.p.h. limit idea. I had half-thoughts of a touring sidecar, for long jaunts, with the push-bike for leisured local trips, but we shall see. The old bike goes so

---

1 Lawrence had just re-licensed his motor-cycle.

well that I do not greatly long for its successor. If only I had not given up my stainless tank and panier bags and seen that rolling stand! But for those gadgets my old 'un would still be the best bike in the S. of England. Good luck with your fan!

Yours
T E Shaw

DG

LADY ASTOR
Friday 10.IV.35   Clouds Hill

The pressmen came here again. There was a brawl, and one of them got hurt. I applied to the Newspaper Proprietors Association against the nuisance: and life has since been easier.

The place is natural, somehow: and I feel as if I might stay in it always: if only they will go on forgetting me. There are enough pottering-about jobs to fill a whole working day. I still wish it was the R.A.F. ... but that is wasting my time. I am sorry not to have used the room. . . .[1]

T.E.S.

University of Reading

ROBIN BUXTON
13.IV.35   Clouds Hill Moreton Dorset

Dear Robin
    The Press have not troubled me for two weeks: nor in that time have I looked at a newspaper. So we are quits, I think.

    Life here is pottery;[2] I think in time I will get used to the feeling that nobody wants me to do anything today. For the moment it is a lost sort of life. [. . .]

    I do not like civil life, nor leisure.

    Thank you for sending the Hogarth portrait so swift to Oxford. I hope they will like it, this time. Things point that way, I think, but I shall hear for certain in ten days or a fortnight.

---

1 Lady Astor had given him a key to her house in Plymouth and offered him the use of a room whenever he wished it.
2 i.e. pottering: cf. previous letter.

My little cottage is charming, I think, for what it is. What ails me is this odd sense of being laid aside before being worn out. However I mustn't bore you with that, and Time is on my side.

Yours
T.E.S.

Here is a cheque for my mother: which please fling into the overdraft!

Bodleian Reserve

ROBIN WHITE[1]

13.IV.35   Clouds Hill Moreton Dorset

You will think this is a voice from the dead: and that is almost what it is. I left the RAF (time expired) a month ago, and feel like a lost dog.

Actually that hasn't driven me to letter writing: I find it a worse task than ever. When one has nothing to do, the idea of writing becomes wholly repellent. But for two years I have been carrying about with me a letter on *Antelope*-headed notepaper, meaning to answer it, and the blunted conscience was at last rasped into life by meeting four days ago a little man (name unknown: certainly a naval officer: probably Fleet Air Arm: doing a course at the RAF School of Photography at Farnborough, now; and destined for the *Leander* soon. Can you place him from that?) who told me you were still on or in the *Antelope*. Two years in one ship sounds so incredibly persistent that I feel I must snatch the moment and communicate with you. I hope it is true. The *Antelope*, as a folder from Messrs. Turner and Newall on my table tells me, has their asbestos lagging on her steam pipes. She looks like a destroyer, otherwise: but the photograph is mostly bow-wave and smoke.

You will have forgotten your letter. It was mostly about the Bruce Rogers *Odyssey*, then a recent acquisition. I have my grave doubts about that book. The translation is too unfaithful: too deliberately unfaithful. The print too delicate. The roundels neither true Greek nor new. Bruce Rogers got the ideas from books of drawings from Greek Vases, and adapted freely. However there it is. The cheap edition has sold well in the States: and the dear edition (for England) is nearly all sold. The crash in the U.S.A. meant that none of the expensive copies went there at all, though 250 had been so earmarked. Consequently poor England was asked to absorb the lot.

---

1 A Lieutenant in the Royal Navy. There is an earlier letter to him, dated 10 June 1931, in *DG*.

There are about 50 still unsold, I believe; but they are going.

It *was* a pot-boiler, almost literally. The heater of my bath, and the bath itself, depended on it. All works well.

[…]

You mention my R.A.F. boats. The Navy Controller, an Admiral called Henderson, is ordering them by the dozen for all ships. *Warspite*[1] is to have her complete equipment hard-chined: and every destroyer is to have a 16-foot 18-knot dinghy. The War Office are equipping themselves with them too. I have great development plans, which I have left to my successors — and there is no successor yet. Our latest boat does 48 m.p.h. 'Our' I say: poor fool. It's all over.

This is permanent (and only) address.

Yours ever
T.E. Shaw

Why is a destroyer a bad design? — because it has too much length for its beam. Beyond four beams to the length one loses speed — in planing boats: and destroyers to be clean and fast should plane. By fast I mean 70 knots with the present machinery — or h.p.

Bodleian Reserve

G.W.M. DUNN[2]
5.V.35　　　　　　　　　　　　　　　　　　　　　　Clouds Hill

I hope your signing on came off. Alas, If I were only 10 years less old. Something has gone dead inside me, now.

John[3] likes Gore[4], Cézanne and Epstein. Is rather deaf and quite formidable. He usually gets £50 for a drawing. If I see him before you do, I shall prepare him for canteen prices, instead. He is a great figure. Poor John.

If you come as far as that, come a little further[5]　and sleep on my settee for a night (or more, if your poor bones allow).

T.E.S.

Bodleian Reserve

1 H.M.S. *Warspite* was one of the Navy's leading battleships. Completed in 1915, she took part in the Battle of Jutland, was reconstructed 1934–7 and served throughout the Second World War.

2 G.W.M. Dunn had been in the R.A.F. with Lawrence as an Aircraftman. He was also, thanks largely to Lawrence, a published poet; his *Poems — Group One* was published by Cape in 1934.

3 Augustus John.

4 Transcribed as 'Grew' in Bodleian copy, but almost certainly Spencer Frederick Gore (1878–1914), an artist whom John greatly admired and who had been a fellow member of the Camden Town Group.

5 John's home at Fordingbridge, Hampshire, was only some twenty-five miles from Clouds Hill.

FLIGHT LIEUTENANTS W.E.G. BEAUFORTE-GREENWOOD
AND H. NORRINGTON
5.V.35   Clouds Hill

Dear BG-and-N

They look lovely ... in exact keeping with their upper room.[1] By day
they sit on a brown oak mantel shelf above a S.S. fender. By night they
move to my writing table (as at present) or to my reading chair. They clean
easily; stand solidly and feel good. I only wish that they had not been
possible — in other words that our association had not ended. I try to cure
myself of the habit of saying 'we' when I mean the air.

Life here is quiet and good enough, but a very second best. I advise you
all to hang on as long as you feel the job is in your power. There's such a
blank, afterwards.

Very many thanks for a very comforting action.

Yours
Shaw

University of Texas [2]

ERNEST RHYS[3]
5.V.35   Clouds Hill

Dear Sir Ernest,

I hope it is Sir Ernest ... these Kings are sometimes so remiss in doing
their duty ... or would it go against the grain to decorate an editor who
had swallowed up a poet and celtic scholar?

Anyhow, about *Revolt in the Desert*. I ought not to speak for it, as I

---

1 Beauforte-Greenwood and Norrington, with whom Lawrence had worked on the
development of R.A.F. speed boats, had lunched with him at Hythe in late April and
presented him with two hand-made stainless steel candlesticks as a personal memento of
their association. The candlesticks are still at Clouds Hill.
2 This letter is included in Beauforte-Greenwood's contribution to *T.E. Lawrence by His
Friends*.
3 Ernest (not Sir Ernest) Rhys (1859–1946), founding editor of J. M. Dent's famous Everyman's Library, launched in 1906 with the intention of providing a comprehensive library
of representative works of all time. Rhys had written to Lawrence asking for permission
to add *Revolt in the Desert* to his title list.

parted with all rights in it before publication. It was a financial expedient, rather than a book, and of it I am heartily ashamed. Its present owner is a lawyer, the Hon. Edward Eliot, of Ingram House, Fenchurch Street. You may write to him, if you please: but I think it will be vain, for I own the master-copyrights of the *Seven Pillars* (from which text the *Revolt* was extracted) and am inflexibly opposed to any reprint. If I could have my way and live for ever, neither of them would ever again appear; but mortmain is not a pretty custom, so in my will I am not making any disposition of the *Seven Pillars* rights, other than letting them pass with what other property I may die in possession of, to my heirs.

The heirs may republish if they will: but I am in hopes that it will not be in your time.

We needn't regret this, artistically, for it would do your Everyman no good to descend to such popular lines. Advertisement sells a poor thing as easily as a good one, I'm afraid . . . and better

Yours
T.E. Shaw

Bodleian Reserve

LADY ASTOR
5 May 1935

It is quiet here now, and I feel as though I were fixed in my cottage for good. It is as I thought . . . something is finished with my leaving the R.A.F. It gets worse instead of healing over.

When I see the little latch-key in my pocket I get sorry for having troubled you without cause. Am I to send it back? I am most sorry.

T.E.S.

Bodleian Reserve

BRUCE ROGERS
6.v.35   Clouds Hill

Dear B.R.

Very welcome back! *Back* you will notice, with a smile. You seem right, somehow, on this side.

I'm 'out' now, of the R.A.F. and sitting in my cottage rather puzzled to find out what has happened to me, is happening and will happen. At present the feeling is mere bewilderment. I imagine leaves must feel like this after they have fallen from their tree and until they die. Let's hope that will not be my continuing state.

Money is very short, and this is the only spot, apparently, where I can afford to live: but it is too soon to judge of that. In a few months time I will know for sure if my savings are enough, or not. Meanwhile I am practising a not un-amusing penury — or parsimony, rather. Also I work enough at wood-cutting and gathering, pipe-laying and building to tire me out thoroughly by each early afternoon ... and then follows a heavenly laze, in the sun, if available, or by my fires if not.

But on the whole I think I prefer engrossment to comfort. Perhaps comfort is an acquired taste which grows with its indulgence?

We must meet: and I cannot put you up. My activities have reduced the cottage to chaos and almost forbid me to sleep in it! So tell me where and when you will be somewhere (London and Oxford are equi-distant from here) and I shall do my best to arrive.

Your Melville book might be of great value. Clarel was not wholly good. His notes for it (which these must be, I think) will afford a very valuable check on how he wrote. As for the Bible ... if you find a spoiled sheet, may I have it? Those I had at Plymouth got too soiled to be fair. Dirty places, R.A.F. workshops.

Yours
T.E.S.

More Letters to Bruce Rogers

ERIC KENNINGTON
6.v.35   Clouds Hill Moreton Dorset

Dear K.

All over bonfires, the beautiful Dorset, to-night. Twenty six, I think, so far, from my window. Ah well, poor George![1]

1 The bonfires were in celebration of the Silver Jubilee of King George V.

Don't bother about those drawings. Leave it a little while till I revive my humanities and come up to see you. I plan a raid on Holly Copse, to stay with you for a night or two ... possible? At your discretion, absolutely: but I do not want to interfere with your development as a nurse. What is the illness? I do hope (by your light hearted reference to it) that it's either over or safe.

The tympanum sounds good. I wonder what it is in. Stone goes out of date slowly, I think.

'You wonder what I am doing'? Well, so do I, in truth. Days seem to dawn, suns to shine, evenings to follow, and then I sleep. What I have done, what I am doing, what I am going to do, puzzle me and bewilder me. Have you ever been a leaf and fallen from your tree in autumn and been really puzzled about it? That's the feeling.

The cottage is all right for me ... but how on earth I'll ever be able to put anyone up baffles me. There cannot ever be a bed, a cooking vessel, or a drain in it—and I ask you ... are not such things essential to life ... necessities? Peace to everybody.

T.E.S.

DG

LADY ASTOR[1]
8.V.35   [Clouds Hill]

No: wild mares would not at present take me away from Clouds Hill. It is an earthly paradise and I am staying here till I feel qualified for it. Also there is something broken in the works, as I told you: my will, I think. In this mood I would not take on any job at all. So do not commit yourself to advocating me, lest I prove a non-starter.

Am well, well-fed, full of company, laborious and innocent-customed. News from China—NIL. Their area now a centre of disturbance.

TES

DG/Reading University Library

1 See General Introduction, p. xxix. Lady Astor had written: 'I believe when the Government reorganizes you will be asked to help reorganize the Defence Forces. If you will come to Cliveden Saturday, the last Saturday in May ... you will never regret it.'

10.V.35   Clouds Hill Moreton Dorset

Dear Dunn

Not yet, please: everything here is ready for you, and the country beautiful but E. M. Forster (novelist, humanist and critic) has written to suggest himself for some time 'about the 20th'. I cannot do two people together . . . and it is as well so, for it would be to waste one of them. There are the physical limitations of the house . . . the tiny cottage of two rooms . . . to consider.

I will write to you again as soon as E.M.F.'s plans have precised themselves.

For coming . . . Wool at 4 miles is the nearest station, Dorchester is 12. Train service to Wool is poor, but I have no time table. Apply Waterloo perhaps. If time presses, use the good service to Bournemouth, and send me word (not by telegram, for that takes 2 days and comes eventually by post) by letter a little while beforehand. Letters come every morning early by sidecar from Dorchester. So even that takes time. But if you notify me in time I can meet you in Bournemouth by Brough and bring you the wretched journey here (22 miles) on the carrier. Bournemouth has many more trains than Wool, and it might just make the difference between possibility and impossibility.

E.M.F. will not probably stay more than four or five days, but once he endured a fortnight. The cottage was more comfortable then, however. He is a dear and delightful person.

Nothing more till I can give you a sure date.

                                            Yours
                                            Shaw

Bodleian Reserve

10.V.35   Clouds Hill

Dear Isham

Merton, like the wholly gentle and decent man that he is, was delighted to hear that I had repaired in his name the Firm's involuntary omission to send you one of the Limited *Odysseys*. He has written to confirm you in my forecast. Excellent ending to a malentendu.

New subject. The enclosed. Who or what is this self-styled 'University' and where are its manners? They have apparently bought somewhere a letter from me to someone, and have published it without even attempting to ask my permission first.[1] As you know, I greatly dislike the publication of private letters (except after very full consideration) and therefore the insult is greater than the injury. Yet the injury is not negligible. My writing does command a certain market price, and they have stolen it.

As soon as I was sent the column, my mind turned to you. You must be learned in U.S.A. law: you may know a really good hard bad-tempered blackmailing lawyer. When the Anderson galleries published that letter which accompanied your proof of the *Seven Pillars*, I wrote to Nelson Doubleday and suggested that as my American publisher he might be able to twist their tails. He didn't, or couldn't. I do not know how copyright stands in the States: but the bad manners of this effort, at least, seems to me so flagrant that if the University has my refutation, it could be made to squirm.

A caution, though. My total income is now less than 30/- a week, and all of it must go on necessaries. So please don't involve me in any expense greater than the income of one week ... say seven dollars the limit. But if your lawman can squeeze anything from the purse of the pirates, then he will be welcome to it for himself. I want to hear a squeal from them, to teach them manners (or if that is too much, prudence) in the hereafter.

Yours
T E Shaw

Bodleian Reserve

E. 'POSH' PALMER
10.V.35   Clouds Hill

Many people oh excellent P, would like to make a complete break with the past — but pasts are unavoidable facts. You can (by the aid of a gas oven) make a complete break with your future ... but that's all![2]

And at Clouds Hill there are no gas ovens, so I shall look forward to seeing you this summer as soon as all the plants have been watered. Pat Knowles and I are the sole inhabitants — two funny little creatures each on his side of the roadway, but meeting often and friendlily.

---

1 The note 'Leland Stanford', not in Lawrence's hand, in the margin of the Bodleian Library's photostat copy of this letter suggests Stanford University, California (founded in 1885 by Leland Stanford, Governor of California), as the offending institution. However a search kindly undertaken at my request by the Stanford University Library failed to locate the letter in question.

2 'Posh' Palmer had apparently been suffering from both financial and marital troubles.

And ten days hence we expect E.M.[1] for a short stay. The place is not very comfortable, I fear (and the wish for comfort is not yet strong in me. Frankly I do not aim at it!) and so he cannot dare stay long.

You will be a marvellously welcome person as and when you please to come. You will be an abused and conscience haunted major if you fail to come soon.

Beethoven's Violin Concerto in D Major (Op 61) we had and have, it is 'it'.

HHB[2] was here two days before your letter and has returned to Perham Down. He leaves the Army in January next, is jerky but not much altered in face or mind.

Eddington and Jeans are only pen pushers out to make their public atone. Be at complete peace and forget them.[3] But DON'T MISS CLOUDS HILL.

TES

I put an S on the envelope to show how seriously I intend you to visit the Hill this summer. Bring your worst clothes and few of them, I'm as scruffy as ever.[4]

Christopher Matheson

K.T. PARKER[5]

12.V.35   Clouds Hill Moreton Dorset

Dear Parker

I am delighted that your expert scrutiny has passed the John. To me it has always seemed a powerful and characteristic drawing: but ownership blinds the judgment, and then I liked both Hogarth and John as people. So I couldn't trust myself. However if it is a decent drawing, there is only one fit home for it, and that's in your place. Hogarth was so much the Ashmolean, for his last years.

In my letter to Leeds I asked that it should be classed as a drawing, not

1 E. M. Forster.

2 Regimental Sergeant-Major H.H. Banbury.

3 Sir Arthur Eddington and Sir James Jeans were well-known scientists with a talent for writing hugely popular — and at times philosophically contentious — books about contemporary science and astronomy.

4 The envelope was addressed to E. S. Palmer — perhaps a more formal style than usual?

5 Keeper of the Department of Fine Art, Ashmolean Museum, and of the Hope Collection of Engraved Portraits from 1934–62 and Keeper of the Museum from 1945–62. He was knighted in 1960.

hung on the back-stairs among the former Keepers. This is in accordance with a wish of Mrs. Hogarth's. She dislikes it as a portrait — which is the side that most pleased me! I will also ask you to see that its label does not carry either my current or my obsolete name! That's a habit we had long ago, when Woolley and I were adding a hundred objects a year to the Collection. It looks all wrong to star oneself all over the cases and screens!

At present I'm sitting in my cottage and getting used to an empty life. When that spell is over and I begin to go about again, I shall see what John thinks of the Ashmolean as a home for some really joyful drawings ... things done out of delight for himself.

Yours
T E Shaw[1]

Bodleian Reserve/The Essential T. E. Lawrence

On 13 May Lawrence received a letter from Henry Williamson proposing a visit to Clouds Hill, so he rode down to Bovington Post Office on his motor-cycle and sent Williamson a telegram with the message: 'Lunch Tuesday wet fine cottage one mile north Bovington Camp SHAW.' On his way back he came upon two errand boys on bicycles riding towards Clouds Hill and in attempting to avoid them clipped the wheel of the rear bicycle. He crashed, flying over the handlebars and suffering severe head injuries as he hit the road. He died on 19 May in the Bovington Military Hospital without having recovered consciousness. He was aged 46.

His funeral took place two days later at the nearby parish church of Moreton. Among the mourners were Mr and Mrs Winston Churchill, Lord Lloyd, Lady Astor, General Wavell, Augustus John and Siegfried Sassoon; the pall-bearers were Sir Ronald Storrs, Eric Kennington, Colonel Newcombe, Corporal Bradbury, Private Russell and Pat Knowles. A. W. Lawrence was the only close relation present as his mother and elder brother were still in China. The body was not buried in the churchyard proper but in a small graveyard a few hundred yards down the road.

A bust by Eric Kennington was subsequently placed in St Paul's Cathedral, London, where other famous Britons such as Nelson, Wellington

---

1 This was probably Lawrence's last letter. He had given the original of Augustus John's drawing of Hogarth (see p. 358 on this subject) to the Ashmolean, but it was not liked either by Hogarth or Hogarth's wife or by C. F. Bell. Following Hogarth's death he had cabled from Karachi to the effect that the drawing should be withdrawn. His proposal to Leeds, referred to here, that it should be held as a work of art worthy of retention rather than as a portrait of a former Keeper for public display, together with Parker's favourable response to it, seems to have resolved a long-standing difficulty.

and Gordon of Khartoum are commemorated. Perhaps the most striking memorial, however, also by Kennington, is a sculpture in Portland stone depicting Lawrence recumbent in Arab clothes, in the tiny church of St Martin in Wareham, a few miles across the heath from Clouds Hill.

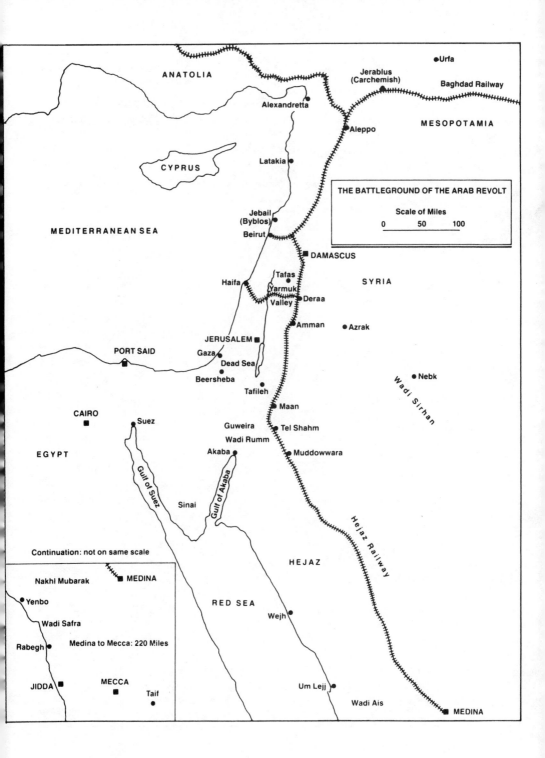

ANATOLIA

Urfa

Jerablus
(Carchemish)

Baghdad Railway

Alexandretta

Aleppo

MESOPOTAMIA

Latakia

CYPRUS

MEDITERRANEAN SEA

Jebail
(Byblos)

Beirut

DAMASCUS

Tafas

Haifa

Yarmuk

SYRIA

Valley

Deraa

Amman

Azrak

JERUSALEM

Gaza

Dead Sea

Beersheba

Nebk

Wadi Sirhan

Tafileh

Maan

CAIRO

Suez

Guweira

Tel Shahm

Wadi Rumm

EGYPT

Akaba

Muddowwara

Gulf of Suez

Gulf of Akaba

Sinai

Hejaz Railway

THE BATTLEGROUND OF THE ARAB REVOLT

Scale of Miles

0   50   100

HEJAZ

Continuation: not on same scale

Nakhl Mubarak

MEDINA

Yenbo

RED SEA

Wadi Safra

Wejh

Rabegh

Medina to Mecca: 220 Miles

JIDDA

MECCA

Taif

Um Lejj

Wadi Ais

MEDINA

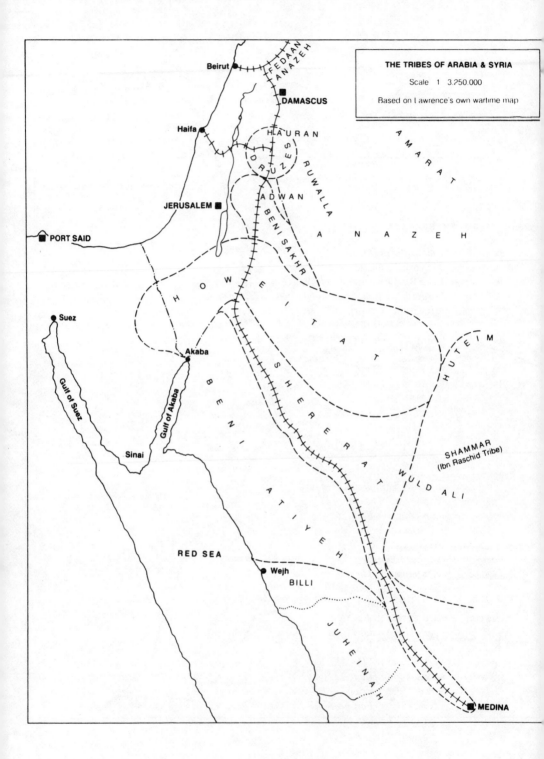

Select Bibliography

Abdullah: *Memoirs* (Cape, 1950)

Aldington, Richard: *Lawrence of Arabia—a biographical enquiry* (Collins, 1955)

Altounyan, E. H. R.: *Ornament of Honour* (Cambridge University Press, 1937)

Antonius, George: *The Arab Awakening* (Hamish Hamilton, 1938)

Arab Bulletin (fascimile reprint): Archive Editions, Gerrards Cross, 1986

Boyle, Andrew: *Trenchard* (Collins, 1962)

Brown, Malcolm & Cave, Julia: *A Touch of Genius, The Life of T. E. Lawrence* (Dent, 1988)

Bray, N. N. E.: *Shifting Sands* (Unicorn Press, 1934)

Buchan, John: *Memory Hold-The-Door* (Hodder & Stoughton, 1940; Dent paperback, 1984)

Charmley, John: *Lord Lloyd and the Decline of the British Empire* (Weidenfeld & Nicolson, 1987)

Churchill, Winston: *Great Contemporaries* (Butterworth, 1937)

Dunbar, Janet: *Mrs G. B. S. A Portrait* (Harrap, 1963; Harper & Rowe, 1963)

Farson, Daniel: *Henry, An Appreciation of Henry Williamson* (Michael Joseph, 1982); reprinted as *Henry Williamson, A Portrait* (Robinson Publishing, London, 1986)

Fitzherbert, Margaret: *The Man Who Was Greenmantle*: A Biography of Aubrey Herbert (John Murray, 1983; Oxford University Press, 1985)

Forster, E. M.: *Selected Letters* (Volume II), edited by Mary Lago and P. N. Furbank (Collins, 1985)

Furbank, P. N.: *E. M. Forster, A Life* (Volume II) (Secker & Warburg, 1978)

Garnett, David (editor): *The Letters of T. E. Lawrence* (Cape, 1938; Spring Books, London, 1964); *Selected Letters of T. E. Lawrence* (Cape, 1938; Reprint Society, 1941; Cape 1952); *The Essential T. E. Lawrence* (Cape, 1951)

Graves, Richard Perceval: *Lawrence of Arabia and his world* (Thames & Hudson, 1976); *Robert Graves, The Assault Heroic 1895–1926*: (Weidenfeld & Nicolson, 1986; Papermac, 1987)

Graves, Robert: *Goodbye To All That* (Cape, 1929; revised edition, Cassell, 1957; Penguin Books, 1960); *Lawrence and the Arabs* (Cape, 1927; Doubleday, Doran, 1928)

Graves, Robert & Hart, Liddell: *T. E. Lawrence to his Biographers* (Cassell, 1963)

Grigg, John: *Nancy Astor, Portrait of a Pioneer* (Sidgwick & Jackson, 1980)

Grosvenor, Charles: *The Portraits of T. E. Lawrence* (The Otterden Press, N. J., U.S.A. 1975, new edition 1988)

Hart, Liddell: 'T. E. Lawrence' in Arabia and After (Cape, 1934)

Hyde, H. Montgomery: Solitary in the Ranks (Constable, 1977)

Kirkbride, Sir Alec: A Crackle of Thorns (John Murray, 1956); An Awakening (University Press of Arabia, 1971)

Knightley, Philip & Simpson, Colin: The Secret Lives of Lawrence of Arabia (Nelson, 1969)

Lawrence, A. W. (editor): T. E. Lawrence by his Friends (Cape, 1937; abridged version 1954); Letters to T. E. Lawrence (Cape, 1962)

Lawrence, M. R. (editor): The Home Letters of T. E. Lawrence and his Brothers (Blackwell, 1954)

Lawrence, T. E.: Crusader Castles (Golden Cockerel Press, 1936; Michael Haag, 1986; new edition by Denys Pringle, Clarendon Press, Oxford, 1988); Fifty Letters; 1920–35 (Humanities Research Center, University of Texas, 1962); Letters from T. E. Shaw to Bruce Rogers, privately printed, 1933; More Letters from T. E. Shaw to Bruce Rogers, privately printed, 1936; Men in Print (edited by A. W. Lawrence, Golden Cockerel Press, 1940); The Mint (Cape, 1955; unexpurgated text, Cape 1973, Penguin, 1978); The Odyssey of Homer (translation; Oxford University Press, U.S.A., 1932; Oxford University Press, Great Britain, 1935); Oriental Assembly (edited by A. W. Lawrence, Williams & Norgate, 1939); Revolt in the Desert (Cape, 1927; Doran, 1927); Secret Despatches from Arabia (edited by A. W. Lawrence, Golden Cockerel Press, 1939); Seven Pillars of Wisdom (Cape, 1935; Doubleday, 1935; Penguin, 1962); Shaw-Ede, T. E. Lawrence's Letters to H. S. Ede 1927–1935 (Golden Cockerel Press, 1942); T. E. Lawrence: Letters to E. T. Leeds (edited by J. M. Wilson, The Whittington Press, 1988). See also under David Garnett and M. R. Lawrence

Mack, John E.: A Prince of Disorder (Little, Brown, 1976; Weidenfeld & Nicolson, 1976)

Marriott, Paul J.: The Young Lawrence of Arabia 1888–1910 (published by the author, c. 1978)

Monroe, Elizabeth: Britain's Moment in the Middle East, 1914–1956 (Chatto & Windus, 1963)

Mousa, Suleiman: T. E. Lawrence—an Arab View (Oxford University Press, 1966)

Ocampo, Victoria: 338171 T. E. Lawrence of Arabia (translated by David Garnett, Gollancz 1963)

Philby, H. St John: Forty Years in the Wilderness (Robert Hale, 1957)

Richards, Vyvyan: Portrait of T. E. Lawrence (Cape, 1936)

Rolls, S. C.: Steel Chariots in the Desert (Cape, 1937)

Salmon, Eric: Granville-Barker and His Correspondents (Wayne State University Press, Detroit, 1987)

Seymour-Smith, Martin: Robert Graves, His Life and Work (Hutchinson, 1982; Holt, Reinhart & Winston, 1982)

Smith, Clare Sydney: The Golden Reign (Cassell, 1940)

Stewart, Desmond: T. E. Lawrence (Hamish Hamilton, 1977)

Stirling, W. F.: Safety Last (Hollis and Carter, 1953)

Storrs, Ronald: Orientations (Ivor Nicholson & Watson, 1937; definitive edition, 1943)

Thomas, Lowell: With Lawrence in Arabia (Century, 1924; Hutchinson, 1925)

Thompson, V. M.: 'Not a Suitable Hobby for an Airman'—T. E. Lawrence as Publisher (Orchard Books, 1986)

Villars, Jean Beraud: *T. E. Lawrence or The Search for the Absolute* (Sidgwick & Jackson, 1958)

Wavell, Colonel A. P.: *The Palestine Campaigns* (Constable, 1928)

Weintraub, Stanley: *Private Shaw and Public Shaw* (Cape, 1963)

Weintraub, Stanley and Rodelle (editors): *Evolution of a Revolt* (Pennsylvania State University Press, 1968)

Williamson, Henry: *Genius of Friendship 'T.E. Lawrence'* (Faber & Faber, 1941)

Wilson, J. M.: (editor): *Minorities* (Cape, 1971); *Lawrence of Arabia* (Heinemann, 1988)

Yardley, Michael: *Backing into the Limelight* (Harrap, 1985)

For a comprehensive bibliography of works by or about Lawrence see Philip M. O'Brien, *T. E. Lawrence: A Bibliography*, St Paul's Bibliographies, 1988.

Index of Recipients

General Index